e-Book and Digital Course Materials for

MW00997350

rials

Sociology of Sport

TWELFTH EDITION

George H. Sage, D. Stanley Eitzen,
Becky Beal, Matthew Atencio

**This code can be used only
once and cannot be shared!**

If the code has been scratched off when

Carefully scratch off the silver coating to
see your personal redemption code.

you receive it, the code may not be valid.
Once the code has been scratched off,
this access card cannot be returned to
the publisher. You may buy access at
**www.oup.com/he/
sage-eitzen-beal-atencio-12e**.

The code on this card is valid for 2
years from the date of first purchase.
Complete terms and conditions are
available at **learninglink.oup.com.**

Access length: 6 months from redemption
of the code.

VIA **OXFORD learning link**

Visit **www.oup.com/he/
sage-eitzen-beal-atencio-12e**

Select the edition you are using and
the student resources for that edition.

Click the link to upgrade your access
to the student resources.

Follow the on-screen instructions.

Enter your personal
redemption code when prompted.

VIA YOUR SCHOOL'S LEARNING MANAGEMENT SYSTEM

Log in to your instructor's course.

When you click a link to a protected resource,
you will be prompted to register for access.

Follow the on-screen instructions.

Enter your personal
redemption code when prompted.

For assistance with code redemption or registration,
please contact customer support at
learninglink.support@oup.com.

OXFORD

SOCIOLOGY OF SPORT

SOCIOLOGY OF SPORT

TWELFTH EDITION

George H. Sage

D. Stanley Eitzen

Becky Beal

Matthew Atencio

OXFORD
UNIVERSITY PRESS

Oxford University Press is a department of the University of Oxford.
It furthers the University's objective of excellence in research, scholarship,
and education by publishing worldwide. Oxford is a registered trade mark
of Oxford University Press in the UK and in certain other countries.

Published in the United States of America by Oxford University Press
198 Madison Avenue, New York, NY 10016, United States of America

Library of Congress Cataloging-in-Publication Data

Names: Sage, George Harvey author. | Eitzen, D. Stanley, author. | Beal,
Becky, author. | Atencio, Matthew, 1975- author. | Sage, George Harvey.
Sociology of North American sport.
Title: Sociology of sport / George H. Sage, D. Stanley Eitzen, Becky Beal,
Matthew Atencio.
Other titles: Sociology of North American sport
Description: Twelfth Edition. | New York ; Oxford: Oxford University Press,
[2023] | Eleventh edition: 2019. | Includes bibliographical references
and index. | Summary: "Now in its twelfth edition, Sociology of Sport
offers a compact yet comprehensive and integrated perspective on sport
in North American society. Bringing a unique viewpoint to the subject,
George H. Sage, D. Stanley Eitzen, Becky Beal, and Matthew Atencio
analyze and, in turn, demythologize sport. This method promotes an
understanding of how a sociological perspective differs from commonsense
perceptions about sport and society, helping students to understand
sport in a new way"—Provided by publisher.
Identifiers: LCCN 2022032758 (print) | LCCN 2022032759 (ebook) | ISBN
9780197622711 (Paperback) | ISBN 9780197622735 (epub)
Subjects: LCSH: Sports—Social aspects—United States. | Sports—Social
aspects—Canada | Sports—United States—Sociological aspects. |
Sports—Canada—Sociological aspects.
Classification: LCC GV706.5 .E57 2023 (print) | LCC GV706.5 (ebook) | DDC
306.4/83097—dc23/eng/20220727
LC record available at https://lccn.loc.gov/2022032758
LC ebook record available at https://lccn.loc.gov/2022032759

Printing number: 9 8 7 6 5 4 3 2 1

Printed by Lakeside Book Company, United States of America

Dedicated to our families.

Becky would like to acknowledge her deceased parents, David Beal and Judith Beal, who worked hard to provide opportunities for her growth and encouraged her to use her voice. Becky also dedicates this to her spouse, Jennifer Sexton, for all her love and support throughout the years. Matthew would like to thank his own family, Lyndsey, Eilidh, and Sylvie, for their support during the writing process.

Thank you.

We'd like to thank several people who provided insights and information for this edition. Included are Carina Reyes, Samantha Rossi, Susan Ortwein, Rita Liberti, Duke Austin, Jeff E. Stein, Josh Atencio, Jackson Atencio, Andres Atencio, Julien Puech, Mike Geddes, Michael Lee, Paul Carpenter, Anne Schmitt, Matt Bell, MaKenna Duda, Christina Rodriguez, and Pierrick Desfontaine.

CONTENTS

PREFACE

It is with great sorrow that we share with readers that both of the original authors of this textbook have passed away. George Sage died on February 11, 2019, and D. Stanley Eitzen died on July 3, 2017. They coauthored *Sociology of North American Sport* through ten editions. George coauthored through the eleventh edition.

Stan and George were good friends and they were foundational to the field of the sociology of sport. Throughout their careers they published widely and they served in leadership roles in the North American Society for the Sociology of Sport. They were highly respected for their mentorship, their genuine concern for others, and their commitment to social justice. Becky Beal knew George Sage for over thirty years. George was her doctoral advisor and was a continual source of personal and professional support. Becky was deeply touched by George and Stan's invitation to join their team on the eleventh edition.

To ensure the continued commitment to writing an up-to-date quality textbook, Matthew Atencio was invited to join as a coauthor for the twelfth edition. Matthew and Becky have collaborated for nearly twenty years on research studies and publications that address contemporary sociological issues emerging in sports. Matthew is a renowned scholar in the field and he serves as Co-Director of the Center for Sport and Social Justice at California State University, East Bay.

THE PURPOSE OF THIS TEXT

Sport is sometimes trivialized as a playground separate from the real world. This is certainly not an accurate representation of sport's role in society. More accurately, sport is a microcosm of society as well as a site of constant cultural shifting. Indeed, as a microcosm and as a phenomenon for social and cultural changes, sport in the United States and, in fact, throughout the world, has a profound influence on the lives of large numbers of people of all ages.

Three goals have continued to guide our endeavors in writing this book. Our first goal is to analyze sport sociologically and, in so doing, to demythologize sport. This method promotes an understanding of how a sociological perspective contrasts with common-sense or taken-for-granted perceptions about sport and society. For most readers, this will result in understanding the activities, processes, and impacts of sport more systematically and critically. We identify various social theoretical perspectives and explore the ways in which they contribute to an understanding of contemporary sport. Our experience is that this approach helps readers to incorporate implicitly the sociological perspective in their repertoire for understanding other parts of the social world.

Our second goal is to highlight to our readers in sociology—as well as readers in sports management, physical education, kinesiology, and other related fields—the importance of including the sociology of sport as a legitimate subfield in each of these disciplines. Our message to all of our readers is that sport is a social activity worthy of serious inquiry. It is a substantive topic as deserving of sociologists' attention as the standard specialties: family, religion, and politics. Not only is sport a microcosm of the larger society, but also sports phenomena offer a rich context in which to test sociological theories. Indeed, although the mechanical and physiological factors of sport are important, the social milieu in which participation is embedded is crucial. A sociological view of sport serves as a lens to examine who participates, how, when, and where, and the consequences of such participation. Sport involvement is more than just making use of the body and leveraging strength, endurance, and fitness to achieve competitive objectives.

Our final goal is to make readers aware of the positive and negative consequences of the way sport is organized in the United States and elsewhere in the world. We are concerned about some of the trends in contemporary sport, especially the movement away from athlete-oriented activities and toward a more impersonal and profit-driven vision of "corporate sport." We are committed to advancing sport and society in a more humane, sustainable, and socially just direction. This requires, as a first step, a thorough understanding of the principles that underlie the social structures and processes that create, sustain, and transform the social organizations within the institution of sport.

Our aim is to excite readers about current sociological issues, problems, and trends in sport. Accordingly, the order of the chapters has been arranged to fit logically with a sociological analysis. Furthermore, all of the chapters have been thoroughly revised, and the content has been updated. We have tried to incorporate the salient research and compelling events that have occurred since the publication of the previous edition of this book.

The title of the last eleven editions of the book included "North America," wherein the focus was primarily on the United States with selected Canadian examples. Although we appreciate some of the shared sporting histories of the United States and Canada, we believe that the title may have implied that more of the twenty-three countries that make up North America would be included. Additionally, given the cultural variation and diverse sociological phenomena found among the twenty-three nations constituting North America, we decided to focus on the United States while at the same time making relevant connections with international sporting contexts.

ORGANIZATION

In Chapter 1, we describe the unique focus of sociology as a discipline and identify the different analytic levels employed by sociologists. We identify the major sociological theories that provide different and important ways to understand sport. Next, we show how sport provides an ideal environment for utilizing certain sociological instruments and methodologies and affords a setting for the testing of sociological theories. We then introduce the concept of sustainability as it pertains to economic, social justice, and environmental issues facing the sporting world.

Sport represents one of the most pervasive social institutions in the United States. In Chapter 2, we discuss the relationships among technological, industrial, and urban developments and the rise of organized sport.

The major theme of this book is that sport is a microcosm of society. Salient social values are concomitantly identified in Chapter 3, and we discuss how sport reflects and reinforces the core values, beliefs, and ideologies of American society. In this edition, we include discussion on how these values impact our views of the sporting body.

Chapter 4 analyzes two major social problems in sport: (1) violence, including participant and fan violence, athletes' abuse of women, and violence against athletes, and (2) substance abuse and doping by athletes. A discussion of athletes and their mental health is also provided in this chapter.

Sport is typically assumed to be an egalitarian and meritocratic institution. In Chapter 5, we examine these two assumptions as they relate to social class and social mobility. The analysis shows that these beliefs are largely myths that reflect broader societal ideals.

Systematic and pervasive discrimination against racial and ethnic minorities has been a historical feature of American society, but many Americans believe that sport has been racially neutral and is free of racism. Chapter 6 documents the historical and contemporary facts illustrating that sport has had and still has many of the same racial problems as larger society. The chapter identifies experiences and issues pertaining to people of color in the United States, including African Americans as well as Latino/as, Asian Americans, and Native Americans. A discussion of racial discrimination in sport is also provided as this relates to the ways in which athletes of color are often unable to obtain positions of power within major sports.

The theme of Chapter 7 is that the world of sport has largely been the domain of males and that sociocultural forces have combined to marginalize female sport involvement. In fact, masculinity has long been the standard of how "real" athletes have been identified. Thus, we discuss how these traditional masculine standards impact those who have nonnormative gender identities or sexualities. We discuss gender inequities that persist despite changes in opportunity structures.

For many people in the United States, involvement in sport begins in both public and privatized youth sports programs. In Chapter 8, we describe how children and their families are socialized into various sporting programs, and we discuss some of the social and personal consequences of these youth sports experiences.

Sport and high school education are inexorably intertwined in the United States. Chapter 9 examines interscholastic sport, focusing on the social sources responsible for the organization and promotion of sports programs, the consequences of school sports programs, and the problems surrounding the extensive provision of school sport in the United States.

Chapter 10 is devoted primarily to the realm of high-profile intercollegiate sports. This form of sport is extremely popular and can provide multiple benefits to student-athletes who participate. Yet, we also focus here on the numerous problems that compromise the integrity of the higher education mission.

Economic factors play an overriding role in much of contemporary sport in the United States. The emergence of unprecedented affluence in certain sectors, along with the increasing public interest and investment in sport, has led to certain economic impacts. Chapter 11 describes the multidimensional aspects of economic considerations in sport, involving actual participants as well as owners and corporate sponsors.

In Chapter 12, we introduce the social purposes of the mass media and their relation to sport and, in so doing, reveal the symbiotic relationship that exists between media entities and sporting members. We also outline the ways in which the Internet and social media, in addition to television, have become essential forms of mass communication within contemporary sport.

Although the sport establishment has historically disavowed any relationship between politics and sport, they are integrally connected. In Chapter 13 then, we discuss the close ties between the two and show that there are several characteristics inherent in both institutions that serve to guarantee this strong yet sometimes controversial relationship.

In Chapter 14, we explore the relationship between one of the oldest universal social institutions—religion—and one of the newest, in terms of a highly organized leisure activity—sport. We trace the changing relations between the two institutions and illustrate how contemporary sport has many of the characteristics of a religion. We also describe how religious agents and agencies use sport to promote religion and how athletes employ magico-religious rituals, taboos, and fetishes in the hope of enhancing their performances.

The final chapter speculates on the future of sport in the United States. The prevailing idea here is that since sport reflects society, sport will undoubtedly undergo some transformation as society and technologies change. We describe several current trends and possible future changes in society and discuss how each is likely to influence the evolution of sports in the United States and elsewhere. The chapter then reveals various trends in sport sustainability that are both social and institutional in nature. A final discussion pertains to the socially inclusive and environmental aspects of contemporary sports; we suggest that these elements will greatly influence sport provision and participation by people in the foreseeable future.

Each chapter in this edition has a "Notes" section that provides readers with relevant references to the various topics found in the chapter. These, along with the contemporary audio and visual resources that are now integrated within each chapter, can be quite useful to students, instructors, and researchers who seek additional information on a given topic.

NEW TO THIS EDITION

A lot has happened in the world of sport since the eleventh edition of this text appeared. The revisions for this twelfth edition have therefore been extensive, and we hope students, instructors, and practitioners will appreciate the additions and updates.

EXPANDED EXPLANATION OF SOCIOLOGICAL THEORIES AND THEIR RELEVANCE TO SPORT

Sociological theories provide contrasting ways of understanding social life. In this edition, we have written a more extensive explanation of sociological theories and their relevance to sports. After providing a detailed description of the various sociological theories in the first chapter of the book, we explain and elaborate on how those theories are relevant to understanding the sports topics that are the focus of the following chapters.

UPDATED CONTENT AND REFERENCES

This edition focuses on current issues that are coming to the fore in the sport world. The activity of youth sport, for instance, is becoming increasingly privatized, which has severe implications in terms of enhancing existing social inequities. While youth sport was once generally accessible in a public sense, increased privatization has created barriers that are now faced by many youths and their families who would like to become involved. Moreover, this book engages with significant developments in high school and intercollegiate sports as these activities have become increasingly contoured by commercialism, which subsequently increases pressure and stress on

institutions, coaches, and their athletes. In this vein, we likewise discuss new legislation that allows student-athletes to profit from their name, image, or likeness. Altogether, the expanding realms of youth, high school, and intercollegiate sport compel us to contemplate how they can evolve in ways that remain true to their original intentions. Recent trends in the social problems of sport—violence, substance abuse, doping, and mental health—are highlighted in this edition.

The sociological topics of sport change rapidly, so we have updated, described, and analyzed these transformations. For instance, social media plays an increasingly vital role in sport, so we identify the new social media forms and their relevance in contemporary sport. Then, new technologies have also led to the prominence of Esports that are now considered important to the modern sporting landscape with increased participation and sponsorship. Further, advancing technology is greatly influencing the nature of collegiate and professional sports in terms of athlete performance, venues, and fan experience. This edition additionally reports on how environmental considerations that are in the mainstream worldview are also impacting our current sporting experiences; individuals and institutions must now grapple with issues such as climate change. Moreover, the recent COVID-19 pandemic has impacted the trajectory of modern sport in several ways that are identified throughout the book's chapters. With each new trend and development in the sociology of sport we have provided the most up-to-date analysis, along with key recommendations emanating from the field, and the book has numerous references and supplemental materials that support this new content.

EXPANDED FOCUS ON DIVERSITY AND SOCIAL JUSTICE

This text has always recognized the importance of diversity in sport and society, and previous editions have provided information on specific racial and ethnic minority groups in relation to sport. In this edition, new demographic trends in the United States are also highlighted in terms of sporting affiliations and preferences. Furthermore, in this edition there is enhanced discussion regarding contemporary social movements, such as Black Lives Matter, which are also explained in their relationship to politics as well as the racial and ethnic dynamics of sport. Also, the chapter on religion (Chapter 14) now includes more discussion of issues facing Muslim athletes. In terms of social inclusion, this edition highlights opportunities for and achievements of minority and female athletes and coaches. This version of the book also describes innovative sport development programs that directly seek to promote inclusivity. Then, the influence of globalization is discussed in terms of how it can inspire more diverse participation, although it can simultaneously lead to a monocultural perspective of sports.

NEW TABLES AND FIGURES

Tables and figures from the previous edition have been updated to account for changes in the subject from the previous edition. There are also new tables and figures to illustrate subject matter that is new to this edition. Youth sport participation levels in team sports, the salaries of professional athletes and coaches, the wealth of the owners of professional sports team franchises, and the value of these franchises are a few examples of subjects addressed in the updated tables and figures.

NEW "THINKING ABOUT SPORT" BOXES

There are more than twenty-five boxes in this edition, several of which are new. These boxes feature thought-provoking essays on sport topics that expand on and supplement the regular textual content in each of the chapters in which they appear. For example, in Chapter 7 there is a new box entitled "Trans and Nonbinary Athletes Challenging the Binary Structure of Sport." The box describes how modern sport has been based on an incorrect assumption that human sex is a binary and, in turn, sport has been used to structure and regulate "appropriate" gender behaviors. Another example of a new box is found in Chapter 2, entitled "Technology and Social Values: The Rise of Disability Sports," where the sociohistorical conditions that gave impetus for the creation of disability sports are discussed. A new box is also

provided in Chapter 6, which reveals how young Japanese American men such as Bob Hayashida once participated in baseball in the internment camps of World War II; this sport was an important activity in their camp experience and helped them to maintain a sense of community.

NEW PHOTOS

Many of the photos in this edition are new, and they provide a pictorial supplement to the historical and contemporary sports topics discussed in the text. We have selected photos illustrating the diversity of participants in American sports representing all levels.

WEB RESOURCES

All web resources have been updated to highlight current sports organizations and resources. Web resources are available at www.oup.com/he/sage-eitzen-beal-atencio-12e.

AUDIOVISUALS EMBEDDED IN THE CHAPTERS

New to this edition are audio and visual clips embedded directly in the chapters in alignment with topics in the written text, with additional resources for each chapter available on the website. These sources include podcasts and video clips that highlight some of the key points of each chapter.

ACKNOWLEDGMENTS

We thank the following reviewers commissioned by Oxford University Press:

> Steven Aicinena, University of Texas Permian Basin
> Kimberly Fox, Bridgewater State University
> Phil Lewis, University at Albany
> Scott M. Myers, Montana State University
> Krystion Obie Nelson, University of North Carolina, Charlotte
> Alicia Richards, University of Illinois
> Rebecca Rodriguez Carey, Emporia State University

Many thanks to our contributor for this edition: E. Missy Wright, Associate Professor at California State University East Bay.

TOWARD AN UNDERSTANDING OF SPORT

CHAPTER 1

THE SOCIOLOGICAL ANALYSIS OF SPORT IN AMERICAN SOCIETY

What sports can do for everyone, no matter the shape or size or race or ethnicity or religion. . . . People find teams, people find players, people find colors because of sport . . . and it brings people together like none other.

—LEBRON JAMES, *NBA SUPERSTAR*[1]

Rupp Arena is located in downtown Lexington, Kentucky. It serves as home court to the University of Kentucky men's basketball program and is named after legendary former Kentucky coach Adolph Rupp. With an official capacity of 23,500, it is currently one of the largest arenas in the United States designed specifically for basketball. (Photo: Andy Lyons/Getty Images)

Sport is a ubiquitous word and activity, and people in the United States relish playing it, watching it, and reading about it. During the recent COVID-19 pandemic lockdowns, sport was indeed a major facet of life that was greatly missed by participants and spectators of all ages. However, when people hear there is a field of academic study called sociology of sport, they typically ask, "What has sociology got to do with sport?" The short answer is that sociologists study social behavior of all kinds, from interpersonal social relations to group formations to formal social organizations. Sport is fundamentally a social phenomenon that encompasses all of these social forms of human activity. For this reason, sport is viewed as an appropriate and relevant topic for study by sociologists.

Sociologists also realize that sport is an extraordinarily popular and pervasive worldwide social endeavor and therefore a suitable subject for study and analysis. Indeed, we are inundated daily by sports, in part because of the massive expansion of youth, high school, and intercollegiate sports; the enormous growth of professional sports; and the expanded mass media coverage of sports events, especially on television and the Internet, during the past twenty-five years.

It occurred to us that since so few people seem to realize that there is a field of academic inquiry called sociology of sport, it would be appropriate to begin with a definition of the word that is the subject of this book—*sport*. This will be followed by a brief discussion of the sociology of sport as a field of study. We then describe the pervasiveness of sport in the United States.

What is sport? There is no universal definition of sport, mainly because such a variety of games and physical activities are conventionally called sports. Generally, we define sport as any competitive physical activity that is guided by established rules. John Loy, one of the first generation of sport sociologists, defined sport "as any form of playful competition whose outcome is determined by physical skill, strategy or chance employed singly or in combination."[2] Interestingly, this traditional characterization of sport must now account for emerging popular activities such as Esports and action/lifestyle activities, as we discuss later in this book.

Looking ahead at the context of this book's inquiry, we note that several components and categories of sport exist and require further elaboration. We shall outline these differentiated aspects of sport in the following paragraphs.

The object of study in this book, sport, encapsulates several attributes including competition, physical activity, and rules in varying degrees. Competition, the first of the three characteristics of sport, involves the attempt to defeat an opponent. This opponent may be a mountain, a record, an individual, or a team. The second characteristic involves physical activity. One attempts to defeat an opponent through physical abilities such as strength, speed, stamina, and accuracy. The outcome is also determined by the employment of strategy and tactics, not to mention chance. Rules, the final characteristic of sport, distinguish it from more playful and spontaneous activities. The scope, rigidity, and enforcement of the rules, however, vary by type and level of sport, as we shall see.

We recognize that our definition of sport and its inherent attributes is too broad to be entirely adequate, especially given the dynamic and complex nature of these activities. A pickup game of basketball and a game in the National Basketball Association are examples of two related but at the same time very different activities that fall under our definition.[3] In the same way, an improvised game of football is sport; so is professional football—although it has been argued that professional football is not sport because of its big-business aspects or because it is more like work than play for the participants. Clearly, there is a need to differentiate several levels—even as some sports overlap across them. We do that by labeling them informal sport, organized sport, and corporate sport. These distinctions have been made by other sport analysts, and many of the ideas that follow stem from their insights.

Informal sport involves playful physical activity engaged in primarily for the enjoyment of the participants. A touch football game, a skate park gathering, a neighborhood "street" basketball game, and a playground game of baseball or soccer are examples of this type of sport. In each of these examples, some rules guide the competition, but these rules are determined by the participants and not by a regulatory body. Furthermore, there are no formalized teams or leagues in informal sport.

The sport of basketball crosses all levels of sports participation, from the informal neighborhood pickup game to street tournament games to organized high school games to the corporate levels of the National Basketball Association and the Olympics. (Photos: Courtesy of Norma Ibarra; Paul Topp | Dreamstime.com)

The presence of a rudimentary organization distinguishes *organized sport* from informal sport. There are formal teams, leagues, codified rules, and related organizations. These exist primarily for the benefit of the players by working for fair competition, providing equipment and officials, scheduling, ruling in disputed cases, and offering opportunities for persons to participate. Public recreation department sport leagues, civic-sponsored sport leagues, Little League programs, interscholastic teams and leagues, and low-pressure college team leagues are examples of organized sport that have not lost the original purposes of the activity.[4]

A strong case can be made, however, that many youth sport programs have become too organized to maintain the goal of fun through the participation of young athletes. If so, they belong in the corporate category, as we shall see in Chapter 8. The same is true for high school sport in some situations, as illustrated in Chapter 9.

Corporate sport has elements of informal sport and organized sport, but it has been modified by economics, politics, and the mass media. According to observers of sports trends, corporate sport is a profit-oriented, institutionalized version of sport. It is sport as spectacle, sport as big business, sport as an extension of power politics. Thus, while athletes may intrinsically experience pleasure in these activities, they also seek to gain extrinsic rewards from them

(e.g., large salaries and high status), provide entertainment for fans and alumni, and garner potential profits and publicity for team owners, universities, and other business interests.

Whereas sports organizations at the organized sport level devote their energies to preserving the activities for the participants' interests, organizations that operate at the corporate sport level have enormous power (often a monopoly). With that power, they often become more interested in perpetuating the organization through public relations, making profits, monopolizing the media, beating out opposing organizations, or merging leagues to limit opposition and to control player salaries. Professional sports leagues, big-time college athletics governed by the National Collegiate Athletic Association (NCAA), and mega-events governed by the Fédération Internationale de Football Association and the International Olympic Committee are examples of the sophisticated bureaucracies that characterize corporate sport and sometimes subvert the pleasure of participating for the sake of the activity itself.

The three levels of sport can be placed on a continuum from play to work. As one moves from informal to corporate sport, the activities become more systematic, with a subsequent loss of autonomy and intrinsic pleasure for athletes. Although informal sporting activities are gaining popularity, corporate sport continues to dominate the sporting landscape in the United States; therefore, we will give considerable attention to corporate sport in this book. That level is but an extension of the organized sport level, however, so we will also direct our attention toward organized sport participation.

AN OVERVIEW OF SOCIOLOGY OF SPORT AS A FIELD OF STUDY

Sociology of sport as an organized field of study is just over sixty years old. It began at about the same time that sport psychology, sport history, and sport philosophy were emerging as academic disciplines with a sport focus.

Most current sport sociologists were attracted to this field of study through their own involvement in sport, first as youth sport athletes, then as high school athletes; a few were college athletes, and several were professional athletes. As college students, these future sport sociologists—seeking to find a career to meet their needs and interests—took courses in the sport sciences. In addition, while enrolled in college courses in traditional disciplines, such as psychology or sociology, they found ways to integrate those subjects into their interest in sports. Many who ultimately became sport sociologists were able to enroll in a sociology of sport course.

Sociology of sport has advanced to the point where it is taught in most colleges and universities, and it has attracted a group of dedicated scholars with interests in research and publication (see Box 1.1). There are currently about 1,200 faculty members teaching courses in the sociology of sport in Canadian and American colleges and universities. This is not a large number as academic and scholarly societies go, but the quantity of such courses has been increasing steadily throughout higher education, and the future looks good for the development of the sociology of sport.

Sociology of sport scholars are often utilized as consultants and experts by various media outlets when they are doing a story with sociological relevance. Moreover, sport sociologists frequently publish their research in a variety of mainstream sociology journals as well as other journals in the humanities and social sciences genres beyond the three identified in Box 1.1.

Sport sociologists who teach, research, and publish were attracted to this discipline for many reasons. Some were inclined toward a career involving sport because of their personal experiences in sport during their childhood and adolescence. Others were interested in pursuing an understanding of the connections between sports and the family, education, economy, politics, mass media, religion, and cultural identities such as race, gender, or disability. Like academic scholars in other disciplines seeking to advance knowledge in their discipline, sport sociologists aspire to learn about and understand the complex

---

BOX 1.1 *THINKING ABOUT SPORT:* SCHOLARLY ORGANIZATIONS AND PUBLICATIONS IN THE SOCIOLOGY OF SPORT

Virtually every academic discipline (also called field of study) has formed associations or societies and created journals with the purpose of providing an outlet for advancing knowledge in the discipline through exchanging research findings and social networking as well as promoting its assets, visibility, and diversity.

In North America, the sociology of sport has a scholarly organization named the North American Society for the Sociology of Sport (NASSS). At present, there are about 400 NASSS members. The official scholarly publication of NASSS is the *Sociology of Sport Journal*, which is published quarterly by Human Kinetics Publishers. A second publication, the *Journal of Sport & Social Issues*, is published by Sage Publications (no relation to the coauthor of this text). Annual NASSS conferences are held in cities throughout the United States and Canada.

Internationally, the sociology of sport is represented by the International Sociology of Sport Association (ISSA), which was founded in 1965. The ISSA sponsors a scholarly publication titled the *International Review for the Sociology of Sport*, published by Sage Publications. ISSA is also a research committee of the International Sociological Association. At present, ISSA has some 250 members from countries throughout the world. ISSA holds annual conferences, including congresses in conjunction with the World Congress of Sociology and the Pre-Olympic Scientific Congress.

sociological meanings of and connections between general social practices and sport in the hope that they can make positive contributions to both sport and society. We hope this overview of sociology of sport is helpful to readers for developing an understanding of what this field of study is about. The remaining sections of this chapter deal with general topics and issues that will form a foundation for the specific subjects described and analyzed in the chapters that follow.

THE PERVASIVENESS OF SPORT

We begin with a brief description of the importance of sport in society, followed by an introduction to the discipline of sociology and a discussion of how the sociological approach aids in our understanding of sport.

Although seemingly a trivial facet of life, sport is important, particularly as our social lives become increasingly leisure oriented. Sport constitutes much of our everyday conversation, reading material, recreational activities, and discretionary spending. According to the Physical Activity Council, nearly 75 percent of Americans are involved in some type of sport activity, recreational endeavor, team sport, or fitness

Skateboarding, like other sports that originated as informal activities, began with friends skating together. Skateboarding has recently become more corporate, which has increased the mainstream popularity of the sport. There is more diversity in participants and styles of skateboarding than ever before. (Photo: svetikd/Getty)

programs in 2020.[5] One event, the annual New York City Marathon, often attracts more than 50,000 participants.

With the amount of interest in sport, it is not surprising that sport is big business. Here are a few examples:

- According to *Forbes* magazine, the Dallas Cowboys were worth $5.7 billion in 2021.[6]
- Dak Prescott, the Dallas Cowboys quarterback, made $107.5 million in 2021, making him the highest paid athlete in the United States.[7]
- LeBron James earns $95.4 million, which includes approximately $64 million from endorsements, memorabilia, and media and he has an annual salary of $31.4 million.[8]
- Alabama's Nick Saban was the highest paid coach in college football in 2020, earning a total of $9.3 million in salary and bonuses.[9]
- In 2017, the Texas A&M University athletic department reported $212 million in operating revenue.[10]
- A thirty-second advertisement during the 2020 Super Bowl cost $5.5 million.[11]
- NCAA men's basketball saw an overall attendance of 30,267,725 fans for the 2020 season across all divisions (Divisions I, II, and III).[12]
- The NCAA women's basketball overall attendance during the 2018–2019 season was 23,009,964 spectators.[13]

Online and print news outlets devote more space to sports than to a variety of other topics, including business news, which would seem to be of more importance in a capitalist economy. *USA Today*, known as the nation's newspaper, devotes one of its four major news sections to sport; in recent years articles about sports have increasingly been appearing in the other sections as well. For many readers, sports sections are the most closely examined part of their daily read.

Evidence of sportsmania is also seen in the amount of television time dedicated to sport: almost one-fifth of major TV network time is devoted to sport, and some cable and satellite networks provide twenty-four-hour sports coverage. Most professional sport organizations now have their own subscriber TV networks (e.g., NFL Network, MLB Network, NHL

Network, NCAA Network). Television networks bid billions of dollars for multiyear rights to televise college basketball tournaments, professional sports, and the Olympic Games. Approximately $10 billion annually is bet illegally on the Super Bowl outcome. Recently, the U.S. has made sports gambling legal which will increase this domain.

Table 1.1 shows the extraordinarily large scale of sports spectatorship in the United States. When these numbers are multiplied by the average cost of tickets, parking, and refreshments, the amount generated by sports attendance is huge. Similarly, with about half of the U.S. population regularly participating in sports, the amount spent on sports-related goods is enormous (about $50 billion in 2020 just in retail sports sales).

Clothing and fashion are significant parts of every culture. Sport and physical activity have impacted broader fashion trends. For example, sneakers are prevalent footwear, hoodies are common in the tech culture, activewear is now worn in nearly every setting, and skateboarding brands have crossed-over into the broader youth fashion market.

Language is another fundamental feature in every culture, and the language of sports idioms pops up constantly in Americans' speech and writing. Idioms are common phrases or terms whose meanings are not real but can be understood by their popular use. Take, for example, these terms from baseball: ballpark figure, bush league, cover all the bases, heavy hitter, pinch hit, screwball; or these from boxing: pull your punches, saved by the bell, throw in the towel, down for the count. Undoubtedly, readers can think of other commonly expressed phrases from their favorite sport.

THE DISCIPLINE OF SOCIOLOGY

In this section we turn to an examination of the substantive topics that currently form the discipline of sociology. As we have noted, sociology is the systematic study of social behavior interpersonally, in groups, and in organizations. Sociologists are especially interested

TABLE 1.1   NUMBER OF SPECTATORS AT MAJOR SPORTS EVENTS IN 2019

Sport	Number of spectators
Major League Baseball	68,500,000
National Hockey League	22,186,851
National Basketball Association	22,124,559
National Football League	17,061,787
Major League Soccer	8,694,584
Women's National Basketball Association	1,331,632
NCAA Div. 1 Football	36,707,511
NCAA Div. 1 Men's basketball	27,001,383
NCAA Div. 1 Women's basketball	8,240,648

Note: We chose to use 2018-2019 statistics to illustrate attendance trends before the Coronavirus pandemic. In 2020 live attendance at sport events dropped significantly, although attendance has rebounded since then.

Sources: MLB: https://frontofficesports.com/mlb-attendance-2019-2/; NFL: https://www.sportsbusinessjournal.com/Daily/Closing-Bell/2022/01/11/NFL-Attendance.aspx; NHL:https://records.nhl.com/history/attendance; MLS: https://soccerstadiumdi-gest.com/2019-mls-attendance/; NBA: https://www.si.com/nba/2018/04/12/nba-sets-all-time-attendance-record-fourth-straight-year; WNBA: https://www.acrossthetimeline.com/wnba/attendance.html#aggregate=Total&season=2019; NCAA Div. 1 College Football: http://fs.ncaa.org/Docs/stats/m_basketball_RB/2020/Attendance.pdf; NCAA Div. 1 Men's Basketball: http://fs.ncaa.org/Docs/stats/m_basketball_RB/2020/Attendance.pdf; NCAA Div. 1 Women's Basketball: http://fs.ncaa.org/Docs/stats/w_basketball_RB/2021/Attend.pdf

in the social patterns that emerge whenever people interact over periods of time. They also study human groups and organizations, the size of which can range from a couple to a church, from a family business to a corporation, from a community to a nation. Regardless of size and purpose, similarities exist in group structures and in the processes that create, sustain, and transform them. In other words, a group that forms to make quilts for charity will be similar in important ways to a group that forms with the goal of winning football games. We know, for example, that through recurrent interaction certain characteristics emerge: (1) a division of labor; (2) a hierarchical structure of ranks (i.e., differences in power, prestige, and rewards);

(3) rules; (4) punishment for the violation of rules; (5) criteria for the evaluation of things, people, ideas, and behavior; (6) a shared understanding of symbols with special meanings (gestures, objects, or specialized language such as nicknames); and (7) member cooperation to achieve group goals.

Sociologists are interested not only in the underlying order of social life but also in the principles that explain human social behavior. Sociology is joined in this quest by other social science disciplines—namely, psychology, political science, economics, history, and anthropology. Each of the social sciences has a unique orientation. Psychological explanations of human behavior focus on personality, mental processes, and human behavioral characteristics. Political scientists are concerned with governmental organization and the forms and uses of power and authority. Study of the production of goods and services is the domain of economists. Historians concentrate on individuals (mostly leaders), events, and trends of the past. Origins, development, and characteristic patterns of cultures, past and present, are the interests of anthropologists.

Each of the various social sciences is useful to sociologists because they all have humans as their central subject. Indeed, the literature of sociology is rich with information drawn from other social sciences in the pursuit of studying sociological questions. These might be the social conditions in the community or society such as varying degrees of unemployment, inflation, leisure time, urban blight, or restricted opportunities for minority groups.

An extremely important external influence on human behavior has to do with the meanings that the members of a social organization share. These shared meanings constitute culture. Under the rubric of culture are the standards used to evaluate behavior, ideology, customs, and expectations for persons occupying various positions—all of which limit the choices of individuals, regardless of their biological heritage or psychological proclivities.

Each individual in society is, because of his or her wealth, occupation, education, religion, racial and ethnic heritage, gender, and family background, ranked by others and by himself or herself. Placement

in this complex hierarchy exerts pressures, both subtle and blatant, on people to behave in prescribed ways. As sociologists have accumulated knowledge about all of these topics, they have integrated information from other social sciences to supplement their sociological findings.

The goal of this book is to provide a comprehensive sociological analysis and explanation of sport in the United States. Such an inquiry, we hope, not only will be interesting and meaningful but also will introduce readers to a new way of understanding the social world in general and the phenomenon of sport in particular.

ASSUMPTIONS OF THE SOCIOLOGICAL PERSPECTIVE

We have seen that human behavior is examined through different disciplinary lenses and that each field of inquiry makes important contributions to knowledge. Of the disciplines focusing on human behavior, sociology is commonly the least understood, so we plan to introduce readers to the sociological ways of perceiving and interpreting the role of sport in society. We begin by enumerating the assumptions of the sociological approach that provide the foundation for this unique way of viewing the world.[14]

Individuals Are, by Their Nature, Social Beings

There are two fundamental reasons for the assumption that humans are naturally social beings. First, children enter the world totally dependent on others for their survival. This initial period of dependence means, in effect, that each individual is immersed in social groups from birth. Second, throughout history individuals have found it advantageous to cooperate with others for defense, for material comforts, to overcome the perils of nature, and to improve technology.

Individuals Are, for the Most Part, Socially Determined

The assumption that individuals are socially determined stems from the first assumption of the sociological approach—that people are social beings. Individuals are products of their social environments for several reasons. During infancy, children are at the mercy of others, especially parents. These persons can shape the potential behaviors of infants in an infinite variety of ways, depending on their proclivities and those of the society.

Parents have a profound impact on their children's ways of thinking about themselves and about others; they transmit religious views, attitudes, and prejudices about how other groups are to be rated. Children are punished for certain behaviors and rewarded for others. Whether children become bigots or integrationists, traditionalists or innovators, saints or sinners, athletes or nonathletes depends in large measure on parents, siblings, peers, and others with whom they interact.

Parents act as cultural agents, transferring the ways of the society to their children. As a consequence, a child is born not only into a family but also into a society, both of which shape the personality characteristics and perceptions of each individual. Society shapes our identity, our thoughts, and our emotions. Thus, the structures of society become the structures of our own consciousness; they do not stop at the surface of our skin but, rather, penetrate and envelop us. One's identity is socially bestowed and shaped by the way he or she is accepted, rejected, and defined by others. Whether an individual is considered attractive or plain, witty or dull, worthy or unworthy depends on the values of the society and the groups in which the individual is immersed. One's interactions within a specific social environment thus determine how certain characteristics will be evaluated.

Suggesting that we are socially determined is another way of saying that we are, in many ways, dependent on and manipulated by social forces. A major function of sociology is to identify the social forces that affect us so greatly. Accordingly, one task of sociology is to learn about issues such as racism, sexism, and homophobia in an effort to understand how they work. This sociological undertaking has never been more critical, given our current social divisions and civil unrest. This is often difficult, however, because we typically do not recognize the existence and extent of these issues. Social forces may have

prompted us to believe and to behave in racist, sexist, and homophobic ways.

Saying that people are dependent on and manipulated by social forces does not imply a total social determinism. Such words are merely used to convey the idea that much of who we are and what we do is a product of our social environment. However, society is not a rigid, static entity composed of robots; there are nonconformists, deviants, and innovators as well. Although the members of society are shaped by their social environment, they also change that environment. Human beings are the shapers of society; in other words, they possess *human agency*, meaning that they have the capacity to make choices and to impose those choices on the world. This is the third assumption of the sociological approach.

Individuals Create, Sustain, and Change the Social Forms within Which They Conduct Their Lives

An old but still popular saying—that "we are captains of our fate"—contains a core insight of sociology. In brief, the argument is that individual persons within social groups of all sizes and types (families, peer groups, work groups, athletic teams, corporations, communities, and societies) form, and are formed by, their members. The groups and organizations that interacting persons create become a source of control over them (i.e., they become puppets of their own creation), but the continuous interaction of individuals within groups and organizations also changes, influences, and helps construct and maintain these social entities.

Two important implications stem from this assumption that groups are created and sustained by persons through interaction. The first is that through collective action, individuals are capable of changing the structure of society and even the course of history. Individuals are not passive. Rather, they actively shape social life by adapting to, negotiating with, and changing social structures. This process, too, illustrates human agency.

Second, these social forms that are created and changed by people have a certain momentum of their own that restricts change. Although human-made, the group's expectations and structures also take on a sacred quality—a sanctity of tradition—that constrains behavior in socially prescribed ways. By extension, we can infer that social arrangements, because they are a result of socially constructed activity, are imperfect. Slavery benefited some segments of society by systematically taking advantage of others. A competitive free enterprise system creates winners and losers. The wonders of technology make worldwide transportation and communication easy and relatively inexpensive, but they also create pollution and waste natural resources. These examples show that both positive and negative consequences emanate from human social actions and organizations.

THINKING AS A SOCIOLOGIST: SOCIOLOGICAL IMAGINATION

Sociologist C. Wright Mills, in his classic *The Sociological Imagination*, articulated an unusual form of creative thinking that has been a benchmark for sociologists for more than half a century. He referred to this style of thinking as a *sociological imagination*, which requires an awareness of the relationships between the individual and the broader society inasmuch as individual circumstances are inextricably linked to the structure of society. A sociological imagination, according to Mills, enables sociologists (actually, all of us) to realize the connections between our immediate, personal lives and the detached, impersonal social world that surrounds and shapes us. The sociological imagination involves several related components:[15]

- The sociological imagination is inspired by a willingness to view the social world from the perspective of others.
- It involves moving away from thinking in terms of the individual and her or his problems, focusing rather on the social, economic, and historical circumstances that produce the problems. Put another way, the sociological imagination is the ability to see and understand the societal patterns that influence individuals, families, groups, and organizations.
- Possessing a sociological imagination, one can move from examining a single unemployed person to analyzing the societal change from manufacturing to a service/knowledge economy, from a homeless family to the lack of affordable housing, and from a racist coach to institutional racism.

- Applying a sociological imagination requires renouncing the taken-for-granted assumptions about social life and establishing a critical distance. In other words, one must be willing to question the traditional explanations for the structural arrangements that shape social behavior.
- When employing this imagination, one begins to see the solutions to social problems not in terms of changing individuals but in terms of changing the structure of society.

UNITS OF SOCIOLOGICAL ANALYSIS

We have seen that sociologists are interested in social organizations and in how social forces operate to channel human behavior. Sociologists working at the macro level are concerned with the structural components of society, including race and gender, that are often reflected in key institutions. These institutions may be educational, economic, political, religious, or media oriented. In addition, micro-level sociological studies are being conducted to ascertain how individuals and groups engage in sporting contexts by attaching meaning to certain rituals and symbols.

The pervasiveness of sport throughout the United States is evident at the micro level with informal localized play. It exists also at the macro level, which is structured by teams, leagues, and large sport organizations. At both levels a great deal of learning occurs that socializes participants into the larger culture. (Photo: Press Association via AP Images)

The Micro Level

The micro-level approach to sociology is concerned with the interpretation of social interactions found in everyday, localized sporting practices that are found "in the field." There is thus a specific focus here on the dynamic and diverse processes by which participants construct and reproduce their social worlds.[16] The important sociological insight here is that meaning is not inherent in an object; instead, people actively come to define their sporting realities and shape their experiences and meanings through interactions with others. In essence, participants socially construct codes and norms within their regular sport cultures.

At the micro level, the emphasis is on the structure and processes of relatively small groups. Sociologists of sport interested in micro-level perspectives and interactions have conducted various kinds of research by interviewing, watching, and listening to subjects. This type of research therefore often involves qualitative and ethnographic "field research" to understand the dynamic nature of social interactions that occur on a frequent basis. Micro-level research into sport practice has greatly increased since the 1990s, and in this time frame the integration of various sociological theories to analyze research phenomena has grown (we will discuss some of these theories later in the chapter). Recent research encompasses field-based investigations delving into a wide variety of sporting contexts where regular or "everyday" sporting activities occur. Studies here range from investigations into weekend "surfing mom" groups to the behaviors of competitive street basketball players.[17]

In some cases, sociologists of sport have researched sports teams, for example, to understand how certain organizational characteristics and practices may lead to success or failure. This could involve studying how certain leadership principles and organizational structures influence how participants (athletes, coaches, and administrators) understand and navigate their various team activities.

Sport sociologists have also researched sports teams to examine the important social processes of competition and cooperation. Sport provides innumerable instances in which competition and cooperation occur separately and simultaneously. On the one hand, sports contests are instances of institutionalized conflict. Therefore, they may serve to control undesirable aggression and violence in socially acceptable channels. On the other hand, sports teams require positive interpersonal dynamics such as cohesion and cooperation to be effective.

Further ideas that are frequently investigated at the micro-level of practice include the processes of identity formation for participants undertaking regular sporting interactions. A key question here is, How do participants understand their place in a social network, and gain a sense of self, by engaging with those around them? Another line of inquiry involves unpacking social dynamics that occur during regular participation in small-group activities. Power differences are often examined here, to see how certain sport contexts may privilege some participants over others for various reasons and in different ways. This type of research, for example, has been used to understand how many women and girls have become discriminated against in certain activities based on belief systems and codes of practice found in these sports.[18]

The Macro Level

Social behavior exists in a larger social setting—a context that is also structured—with its own norms, values, statuses, roles, and social institutions. These components of social structure constrain social groups and the attitudes and behaviors of individuals, regardless of their group memberships.

Societal norms are societal prescriptions for how one should act and dress in given situations—for example, at a restaurant, church, school, concert, or football game. In other words, norms are situational. Why is the national anthem played at sports events but not at concerts? Clearly, behavior considered appropriate for spectators at a football game (e.g., spontaneous screams of exuberance or despair, the open criticism of authority figures, and even the ritual destruction of goalposts) would be inexcusable behavior at a poetry reading. We know what is expected of us in these different situations. We also know how to act with family members, with teachers, with elders, and with children. Thus, behavior in society is patterned and norm structured. We know how to behave, and we can anticipate how others will behave. This allows social interaction to occur smoothly.

Values are also part of society's culture. They are the criteria we use in assessing the relative desirability, merit, or correctness of objects, ideas, acts, feelings, or events. This is the topic of Chapter 3, so we will only state here that members of society are taught explicitly and implicitly how to judge whether someone or something is good or bad, moral or immoral, appropriate or inappropriate. People in the United States, for example, overwhelmingly believe that winning—in school, in sports, in business, and in life—is a legitimate goal. They not only value success but also know precisely how to evaluate others and themselves by this critical dimension.

Statuses and roles are social positions (statuses) and behavioral expectations (roles) for individuals. There are family statuses (daughter, son, sibling, parent, husband, wife); age statuses (child, adolescent, adult, elder); gender statuses (male, female, nonbinary); racial statuses (African American, Asian, Native American, White); and socioeconomic statuses (poor, middle class, wealthy). For each status, there are societal constraints on behavior. To be a male or a female in American society, for example, is to be constrained in a relatively rigid set of expectations. Similarly, African Americans and others of minority status have been expected to "know their place," as recent events and protests have illuminated. Historically, their place in sport was also segregated, and they were denied equal access to sports participation with Whites. Even with civil rights laws requiring equality, the place of racial minorities often remains unequal—in sport at certain playing positions, head coaching, and administration.

Societal institutions are universally characteristic of societies, but popular usages of this term are imprecise and sometimes even incorrect. Sociologists use the term to mean social arrangements that channel behavior in prescribed ways in the important areas of social life. Social institutions are devised by the persons making up a society and passed on to succeeding generations to provide "permanent" solutions for crucial societal problems.

In sociology, a social institution is not merely something established and traditional (e.g., a teacher who has worked at the same school for forty-five years), nor is the term limited to a specific organization such as a school, a prison, or a hospital. An institution is much broader in scope and in importance than a person, a custom, or a single social organization.

Another way to characterize social institutions is to say they are cultural imperatives. They serve as regulatory agencies that channel behavior in culturally prescribed ways. All societies face problems in common, and their members are continually seeking solutions. Although the variety of solutions is almost infinite, there is a similarity in the outcomes sought—namely, stability and maintenance of the system.

Social institutions for family, education, polity, education, mass media, and religion thrive as part of all contemporary societies. For example, human societies instill in their members predetermined channels for marriage. Instead of being allowed a host of options (e.g., polygamy, polyandry, or group marriage), in a given society sexual partners are expected to marry and to set up a conjugal household. The actual options across human societies are many, but most partners tend to choose what their society deems appropriate. The result is a patterned arrangement that regulates sexual behavior and ensures a stable environment for the care of dependent children. See Table 1.2 for a list of common societal tasks and the resulting institutions.

Unity and stability are crucial for the survival of society, and social institutions tend to provide these. By definition, then, social institutions are conservative. They provide the answers of custom and tradition to questions of societal survival. For this reason, any attack on a social institution is often met by aggressive, even violent, opposition.

Over the course of the past two centuries—with industrialization, modernization, globalization, and advanced technology—sport has become a social institution in nations throughout the world. Several societal needs are popularly believed to be served by sport:

- Sport serves as a safety valve for both spectators and participants, dissipating excess energies,

TABLE 1.2 COMMON SOCIETAL TASKS AND RESULTING SOCIAL INSTITUTIONS

Societal problems	Social institution
Sexual regulation; maintenance of stable units that ensure continued births and care of dependent children	Family
Socialization of newcomers to the society	Education
Maintenance of order; distribution of power	Polity
Production and distribution of goods and services; ownership of property	Economy
Understanding the transcendental; searching for the meaning of life and death and humankind's place in the world	Religion
Understanding the physical and social realms of nature	Science
Providing for physical and emotional health care	Medicine

tensions, and hostile feelings in a socially acceptable way.

- Athletes serve as role models, possessing the proper mental and physical traits to be emulated by other members of society.
- Sport is a secular, quasi-religious institution that uses ritual and ceremony to reinforce the values of society, thereby restricting behavior to the channels approved by custom.
- Sport serves as a source for learning the skills and strategies of some of the most popular cultural physical activities, while also promoting health and physical fitness.

Micro and Macro Levels and This Book

The primary focus of this book will be at the macro level. We will describe how sport reinforces societal values. We will analyze the reciprocal linkages of sport with other institutions—sport and education, sport and religion, sport and politics, sport and the economy, sport and the mass media—and we will ask who benefits, and who does not, from the way sport is organized. Although the level of analysis is macro, the research findings from micro level studies will be included whenever appropriate to illustrate the social function of sport.

SOCIOLOGICAL THEORIES: CONTRASTING WAYS TO SEE AND UNDERSTAND SOCIAL LIFE

The previous sections about the discipline of sociology and units of sociological analysis set the stage for a description of social theories. Like other academic disciplines, sociology has theories that are generalized explanations of how, in this case, the social world explains the social order. Some social theories explain aspects of the social world and enable prediction about future events, but sociology theories are better understood as models that work in a limited range of settings; as such, they are always tentative, subject to new research findings and changing social conditions.

On reading the word *theory*, many readers roll their eyes and say, "Oh, no, not theory again." But because theory is so fundamentally a part of every knowledge domain, learning about it is essential if one hopes to become knowledgeable about a field of study. And in any case, theory is not all that complicated. It is merely an explanation or a set of statements that attempt to explain observed phenomena and can be used to test predictions or hypotheses.

We all use theories, albeit informally, every day of our lives. We are constantly processing thoughts like, "Given the experiences that I have had, if I take this action, I believe that will happen." We create and revise personal frameworks that enable us to make sense of the world that we see around us; our unique "lens" is used to regularly question widely held assumptions and practices. All of us undergo dozens of these mental machinations and activities each day. We are developing and using theory when we do so.

A fundamental feature of a scientific discipline (field of study) is that it is grounded in theoretical formulations; it is theory driven. A sociological theory offers an explanation of social life by making assumptions about the general patterns found. It is a way of making sense of the complex social world.

Those who prepare for a career in sociology must spend many hours of study learning about the theories of the leading social theorists of the past and present time. As a result, most sociologists come to be guided by one particular theoretical perspective. They do not necessarily reject other theoretical formulations, but the focus of attention, the questions they ask, the relationships sought, the interpretations rendered, and the insights unraveled by one of the theoretical perspectives appear more persuasive than alternatives.

Several social theoretical perspectives provide vantage points from which to view social life. Each of these guides our thinking, narrows our perceptions to certain relevant phenomena, and, in doing so, helps us understand our social life. In the pages that follow, we discuss several major theoretical perspectives that are used to understand the social world and, for our purposes in this book, the world of sport. Each of these perspectives is useful because it focuses on a different feature of social life, providing insights missing from the others.

FUNCTIONALISM

The functionalist perspective views a society as analogous to a living organism, with each part—brain, heart, lungs—contributing functionally to the organism's survival. Thus, a human society is viewed as composed of various interdependent parts, primarily the social institutions—the economy, education, religion, government, and so forth—as the structured components that maintain the social system as a whole, contributing and promoting social value consensus and stability. The parts of the system are basically in harmony with each other, exhibiting the characteristics of cohesion, consensus, cooperation, reciprocity, stability, and persistence.[19] The high degree of social system cooperation—and societal integration—is accomplished because there is a high degree of consensus on societal goals and on cultural values.

Consensus in a social system, according to the functionalist perspective, is achieved through the interdependence of the different parts of the system. Although there are obvious differences in resources among the various groups and organizations in society, countervailing pressures are expected to prevent abuse, exploitation, and domination by one group. Functionalists view activists' efforts to bring about social change as undesirable; all social change is expected to be gradual, adjustive, and reforming because the primary social process of

functionalism emphasizes cooperation and basic social stability. Even the poor and powerless are not expected to rebel because they have internalized the values of the society and they believe the system is intrinsically just. Societies, then, are basically stable entities.

Functionalist advocates acknowledge that dynamic persuasive social change efforts can lead to disruptions and that instability can lead to social system disorder, even volatility. However, self-correcting mechanisms of the social system are expected to reverse societal dysfunctions and restore the system's status quo.

Sport in the United States from a Functionalist Perspective

Functionalists examining any facet of society emphasize the contributions that various parts make to the stability of society. Sport, from this perspective, unifies and preserves the existing social order in several ways. For instance, sport is viewed as symbolizing the American way of life—competition, individualism, achievement, and fair play. Not only is sport compatible with basic American values, but also it is a powerful mechanism for socializing youth to adopt desirable character traits, such as accepting authority and striving for good health and physical fitness, both of which are useful for promoting and maintaining a nation's strength.

For functionalists, American sport supports the status quo by promoting the unity of citizens through patriotism—the national anthem, militaristic displays, and Christian religious rituals that accompany sports events. Can you imagine, for example, a team that espouses antiestablishment values in its name, logo, mascot, and pageantry? Would we tolerate a professional sport team called the Atlanta Atheists, the Boston Nazis, the Pasadena Pacifists, or the Sacramento Socialists? Functionalists view sport as inspiring us through the achievements of athletes, and the feelings of unity in purpose and loyalty of fans are displayed.

Functionalist theorists focus on the integrating benefits of youth, high school, and intercollegiate sport for students, faculty, alumni, and community members. They also look for positive consequences for participants such as grades, self-esteem, career aspirations, and the career mobility patterns of former athletes.

Clearly, then, sport from the functional perspective is seen as good: sport socializes citizens into proper social behavior, sport unites, and sport inspires. Conversely, questioning or criticizing sport, or American nationalism in any way, is viewed by functionalist theorists as challenging a foundation of America's social order. A recent example of this can be seen in the public outrage when some professional athletes began either sitting or kneeling during the playing of the U.S. national anthem.[20]

CONFLICT THEORY

The social theorist who articulated the fundamental tenets of conflict theory, Karl Marx, never called his theoretical formulations "conflict theory," but despite the demonization of Marx, especially in the United States, his ideas about capitalist society have been historically adopted and modified and enunciated as conflict theory.

The assumptions of conflict theorists are quite different from those of functionalist theorists. Instead of the social harmony that functionalism conceives, the conflict theory perspective posits conflict as endemic to capitalist societies, especially because of the social class differences that emerge in capitalist society resulting from the ways people are organized for production, distribution, and consumption of material goods. The conflict perspective views things that people desire, such as property, prestige, and power, as largely possessed by the socially elite, resulting in a fundamental cleavage between the wealthy and powerful and the disadvantaged—namely, the working class. Moreover, the wealthy and powerful class uses its resources to maintain its power and advantages.

The emphasis of the conflict perspective, then, is on the social, political, and material inequalities in society and on the ways in which societal power and wealth are intertwined and dominate the rest of society, frequently leading to disharmony, disruption, instability, and conflict. Of course, conflict can take many forms, not necessarily outright violence; disagreement, tension, and hostility surrounding needs, interests, values, and goals are likely to be more prevalent.

Functionalism's vision of social harmony, stability, and consensus is seen as unrealistic and illusionary by conflict theorists. They argue that what happens in society is that the wealthy and powerful, through their control of the decision-making apparatus, maintain their advantages by fostering ideological conformity—although it is sometimes achieved by coercion—through the government, economic system, schools, churches, and other social institutions. This is seen as an effective means of maintaining social order because it can be sustained through popular compliance, resulting in the underclass of individuals defining conditions that are actually hostile to their interests as being legitimate—a condition that Karl Marx called *false consciousness*.[21]

Sport in the United States from a Conflict Theory Perspective

The conflict perspective contends that society reflects the interests of the powerful and advantaged and that sport at every level—youth, high school, college, and professional—is organized to exploit athletes and achieve the goals of the elite (e.g., profits, recognition, public relations, prestige). Moreover, any critical questioning or instigation for reform in sports is repressed in several ways.

First, the prevailing myths of capitalism, especially the notion that anyone can succeed if he or she works hard enough, are promoted and reinforced in sport. Popular locker room slogans reinforce this: "Outwork the Competition," "Don't Just Dream, Work Hard," and "Play as Hard as You Can for as Long as You Can." The highest praise a coach can give to an athlete is to say that she or he is "a hard worker." Second, sport diverts the attention of the large mass of people away from the difficulties of poverty, job insecurity, rising debt, and limited life chances that many of them experience.

Third, sport gives false hope to oppressed people of color. Many are led to believe that sport is a realistic avenue of upward social mobility; indeed, the high visibility of the few professional athletes seems to provide "proof" that sports ability readily translates into monetary success. The reality, however, is that only an extremely small percentage of athletes ever achieve professional status. For example, only one high school basketball player of one hundred (1 percent) becomes an NCAA Division I player, and only one NCAA Division I player of one hundred (1 percent) becomes an NBA player. These figures are similar for other sports (more discussion of this last point is found in Chapter 5).[22]

One sport sociology research tradition from a conflict perspective has focused on intercollegiate athletics. This research illuminates the power that the NCAA has over athletes, the cozy relationship between the NCAA and television networks, the resistance of the NCAA and university administrators to implementing Title IX (which requires equal treatment for women), the big-business aspect of big-time college sport, illegal tactics by coaches in recruiting athletes, and the exploitation of athletes.

CONFLICT/CULTURAL SOCIAL THEORIES

Several variants of the conflict perspective have gained popularity. We shall not attempt to identify or describe all of them because that would take us far afield from our main interests in this book. However, we do think it is useful to briefly identify and discuss those variants that have had the most influence in sociology of sport: hegemony theory, feminist theory, and racial theory. As a general category, they are often referred to as critical theories or cultural theories.

Hegemony theory, feminist theory, and racial theory—like conflict theory—seek to understand the sources of power, how power works, and how individuals and groups exert human agency—meaning the capacity of individuals to act independently and make their own free choices—as they cope with, adapt to, and change existing power relationships. Instead of seeing society as dominating individuals completely, these theories view human agency as an omnipresent option.

Hegemony Theory

In sociology, hegemony refers to the social, cultural, and ideological sites of power and domination and the political and economic influence exerted by dominant individuals or groups. Beyond that, hegemony theorists critique the social forces that prevent people from seeing and understanding the forms of power and domination that exist in society and affect their lives,

especially those forms that privilege men over women, rich over poor, and Whites over people of color.[23]

Hegemony theory stems from conflict theory, but it adds ideology and culture to the importance of the economy, politics, and other sites of dominance and influence in society. This theory is often originally attributed to Antonio Gramsci, who believed that ideas could serve to influence people just like physical power; his ideas were expanded on by others, including 20th century intellectuals from the Frankfurt School in Germany who critically examined how various media forms including art, music, and film impacted human society. Hegemony theory thus highlights the ways in which dominant groups reproduce their values and interests via government, economic, media, education and sporting contexts. By dominant groups we mean the powerful and wealthy who control most of the land, capital, media, and technology. It is they who have the capacity and mechanisms to manipulate the social, political, and economic values of society. It is thus often the case that their views become taken up and reproduced as the dominant worldviews.

Sport in the United States from a Hegemony Perspective

Applying hegemony theory to sport requires that we step back from thinking about sport merely as a place of personal achievement and entertainment and study sport as a cultural practice embedded in political, economic, and ideological formations. Of particular relevance is the question of how sport is related to the concepts of social class, race, and gender, as well as the control, production, and distribution of economic and cultural power in the commodified sport industry.[24] Moreover, it is important to understand here that identities and practices reflecting social class, race, and gender intersect, as we will demonstrate throughout this book.

Hegemony theorists agree with functionalists on many features of society but differ significantly in interpretation. Both sets of theorists agree that sport socializes youth, for example, but hegemony theorists view this process critically because they see sport as a mechanism to socialize youth into obediently following orders, working hard, and fitting into a system that is not necessarily beneficial to them. Both agree that sport reinforces the status quo. Instead of interpreting this as good, as functionalists maintain, a hegemony theorist views this as bad because it reflects and strengthens the unequal distribution of power and resources in society.

While recognizing that sport is a microcosm of society, hegemony theorists also emphasize that the conditions of sport can change from the top down (from power structures) or from the bottom up (from the human agency of the participants themselves). Whereas functionalism and conflict theories explain social life as deriving from a single source (value consensus for functionalists and the economy for conflict theorists), hegemony theorists emphasize the diversity of social life, stressing that understanding hegemonic practices requires looking at a number of forces (e.g., historical, cultural, economic, and political forces and the media).

Feminist Theory

Feminist struggles for political, social, economic, and educational equality of women have roots extending back in history for centuries. Feminist theories began as critiques of the dominant social theories that did not include women or did not take women's issues seriously. According to feminist theorists, inequalities faced by women are related to differential access, different treatment and exploitation, patriarchy, and male dominance. While critiquing these social and political relations, a great deal of feminist theory focuses on the promotion of women's rights and interests.

During the past hundred years, feminist issues have included social injustices as well as access to employment and equality in the workplace, equal political representation, equality of educational opportunity, redress for sexual harassment in all social institutions, and legal access to contraception and abortion. Feminist theory rests on two fundamental assumptions: first, that human experiences are gendered, and second, that women are oppressed within patriarchy and have a commitment to change those conditions. Three of the most prominent themes addressed in feminist theory are patriarchy, stereotyping discrimination, and oppression.[25]

Sport in the United States from a Feminist Perspective

Sport from a feminist theoretical perspective is seen as a gendered activity in which males have the power. Some examples of feminist research topics focusing on sport are the ideological control of women through the underrepresentation of women athletes in media images, the trivialization of women athlete's accomplishments, the hidden discourse of homophobia, and "the construction of women as unnatural athletes and of female athletes as unnatural women."[26] Chapter 7 is devoted to a discussion of gender in American sport. In that chapter, we describe and analyze a variety of feminist theoretical topics as they play out in sport.

Race Theory

Race theory integrates specific frameworks including racial formation theory and critical race theory (CRT), which can both be used to systematically examine the social construction of the racial concept, in accordance with institutional, political, and historical perspectives.

Racial formation theory draws on the notion that racial meanings and identities are socially created and thus remain unstable and politically contested. Furthermore, in this framework, racial constructs that underpin daily life are viewed as being formulated through social institutions and structures that directly align with dominant racial ideologies and representations. Under this perspective, there is the notion that prevailing societal constructions and practices of race are subject to change, at individual, organizational, local, and global levels.[27]

CRT, is "a framework from which to explore and examine the racism in society that privileges whiteness as it disadvantages others because of their 'blackness.'"[28] Its main concern is with the inescapable and inherent racism that is an everyday occurrence for people of color, a racism that is thoroughly rooted in the social fabric of American society (and other societies as well), permeating its social structures and practices. Because racism is entrenched, it permeates all of the social institutions in which the White majority has profited, and continues to profit, from the persistence of such social practices;

consequently, it tends to become a covert mechanism for maintaining racial prejudice and discrimination.

Overall, race theory's primary mission is to analyze, deconstruct, and socially transform society to improve relationships among race, racism, and power. This theoretical perspective has been applied in a variety of contexts where institutionalized oppression based on race occurs, especially in legal–judicial and political contexts as well as in the educational realm, where educational opportunity and experiences form the basis for the future acquisition of income, wealth, health, and longevity.

Sport in the United States from a Race Theory Perspective

According to sports studies scholar Kevin Hylton, for CRT analysts "the question is not do we live in a racist society? Rather it is a conclusion: we do live in a racist society and we need to do something about it. Therefore, anti-racism should be mainstreamed into the core business of sport."[29] Racial formation theory also reminds us of the ways that Whiteness has been constructed as normative and privileged within our sporting histories, reflecting public policies that have viewed and treated people of color as those to be exploited and objectified in negative ways. It thus behooves us to understand, from a racial formation point of view, how socially constructed race identities and racial relations in diverse sporting contexts mirror racist ideologies that are manifest in dominant structural systems and policies. A sociological lens can be used here to investigate the role that prevailing sporting institutions and their stakeholders play in this process of racial formation.[30]

Major concerns about racial relations and racism remain in our society, and these concerns filter into the domain of sport. It can be said that the history of sport in the United States reveals that sport has simultaneously been a powerful reinforcer of racist institutions and ideologies as well as serving as a potential instrument of opportunity for African Americans and other people of color. We can see from recent events that athletes and leaders of color are illuminating the major role that race plays in sport, reminding us that much progress needs to be made

here, with an eye toward re-envisioning sport to be more racially tolerant and inclusive. With African Americans and other people of color playing such prominent historical and political roles in U.S. sports, sociological researchers are incorporating race theory into their research arsenal. In Chapter 6, the roles and experiences of racial-ethnic minorities in sport are examined along these lines in more detail.

SOCIOLOGICAL THEORIES AND SOCIOLOGY OF SPORT: OUR POSITION

Thus far we have identified and described several social theoretical perspectives, stressed that each has its unique view of the social world and how it works, and acknowledged that each provides valuable insights for understanding society. Each has its strengths and weaknesses, but none is endorsed by all sociologists. In the course of the following chapters, we will provide additional information about the relevance of these theories to the various chapter topics. As we do so, we will refer to the functionalist perspective using that term. However, in the interest of brevity we shall conceptually collapse conflict, critical/cultural, hegemony, feminist, and race theories into a single concept, which we will call the conflict/cultural perspective because they are all underpinned by critiques of domination and oppression.

As for social theories and our positions regarding the social world of the United States, we draw certain insights from each of the social theories. However, our perspective assumes a basic critical stance about contemporary social practices and organizations for three reasons.

First, we are critical of existing power arrangements because they are, by definition, oppressive toward the powerless segments of the population. This perspective has gained currency, as we can observe from recent sporting social movements that challenge the unequal power structures found in many sports. We therefore question the functionalist perspective because it fosters the status quo. Conversely, the conflict/cultural perspective of social structure demystifies, demythologizes, and, sometimes, emancipates.

This, we feel, is the appropriate core of a sociological perspective.

In concordance with the general field of sociology, our underlying assumption is that things are not as they seem in sports. For example, do school sports serve educational goals? Are athletes in big-time collegiate programs exploited? Does participation in sport actually build character? Are sports free of racism? Are school sports sexist? Is sport a realistic mechanism of upward mobility for lower-class youth? Is success, or failure, the most common experience of athletes? In making such queries, we question existing myths, stereotypes, and official dogma. This type of critical examination of sport tends to sensitize us to the inconsistencies present in American sport.

Second, our perspective directs attention toward social problems emanating from current structural arrangements. We ask, under contemporary social arrangements, who gets what and why? Who benefits from and bears the social costs of change and stability? Sport, much like the core institutions of the economy, religion, and family, is an area where these kinds of questions typically are not asked.

Third, our perspective seeks to determine how social arrangements might be changed to enhance the human condition. This leads us to the two goals we have had in writing this book:

1. To report what is known about sport and society from social science research.[31]
2. To make the case for reform. As social scientists, we are obliged to be as scientific as possible (using rigorous techniques and reporting all relevant findings, whether or not they support our values). At the same time, however, we are committed to moving sport and society in a more humane direction. We therefore speculate about the future of sport from social and environmental sustainability perspectives.

To accomplish these goals, we combine a scientific stance with a muckraking role. The latter is important because it compels us to examine such social problems as drug use in sports, the prevalence of racism and sexism in sports, illegal recruiting, inhumane treatment of players by bureaucratic organizations and authoritarian coaches, and the perversion of the original goal of sport. Only by thoroughly examining such problems, along with the traditional areas of attention, will we realistically understand the world of sport and its reciprocal relationship with the larger society.

Sociology is not a comfortable discipline; looking behind the "closed doors" of social life can be unsettling, even troubling. A critical/cultural analyst of society must ask lines of questioning such as these: How does society really work? Who really has the power? Who benefits under the existing social arrangements, and who does not? Asking such questions means that the inquirer is interested in looking beyond the commonly accepted explanations, in seeing through the facades of social structures. The sociological assumption providing the basis for this critical stance is that the social world, its political system, its economic system, its educational system, its laws, its ideology, its distribution of power, and its sports institutions are all created and sustained by people. And, as a consequence, they can be changed by people. If we wish to improve imperfections in our society, then we must attempt to understand how social phenomena work and learn what changes will help achieve our goals.

The sociological perspective is discomforting to people who are invested in the traditions of the status quo. However, using a sociological lens to understand our social world, we can become liberated from the ideologies and practices of domination, oppression, injustice, discrimination, and so forth that exist in the United States.

KEY TOPICS IN THE STUDY OF SPORT AND SOCIETY

An analyst of society is inundated with data. They are faced with the problems of sorting out the important from the less important and discerning social patterns of behavior and their meanings. Consequently, they need shortcuts to ease the task. A focus on sport is just such a technique for understanding the complexities that exist in the larger society.

Sport is an institution that provides scientific observers with a convenient laboratory within which to examine values, socialization, stratification, and bureaucracy, to name a few structures and processes that also exist at the societal level. The types of games people choose to play, the degree of competitiveness, the types of rules, the constraints on the participants, the groups that do and do not benefit under the existing arrangements, the rate and type of change, and the reward system in sport provide us with a microcosm of the society in which sport is embedded.

Suppose an astute sociologist from another country were to visit the United States with the intent of understanding dominant values, the system of social control, the division of labor, and the system of stratification. Although they could find the answers by careful study and observation of any single institution, such as religion, education, polity, economy, or family, an attention to sport would also provide answers. It would not take that sociologist long to discern the following example qualities in sport that can also be found in present broader American society.

THE HIGH DEGREE OF COMPETITIVENESS

Competition is ubiquitous in the United States. Americans demand winners. In sports (for children and adults), winning—not pleasure in the activity—is the ultimate goal. The adulation given winners is prodigious, whereas losers are maligned. Consider, for example, such popular locker room slogans as "Show Me a Good Loser and I'll Show You a Loser" and "Lose Is a Four-Letter Word" or the different ways in which the winner and the loser of the Super Bowl or NBA championship are evaluated. Clearly, to be second best is not good enough. "Nobody remembers who came in second" is the conventional wisdom. The goal of victory is so important for many that it is considered laudable even when attained by questionable methods. "Whatever you can get away with" is another conventional insight.

THE EMPHASIS ON MATERIALISM

Examples of the value Americans place on materialism are blatant in sport (e.g., players signing multimillion-dollar contracts, golfers playing weekly for first-place awards of more than a million dollars, professional teams being moved to more economically fertile climates, athletes generating revenue streams through lucrative sponsorships, and stadiums being built at public expense for hundreds of millions of dollars).

SPORT PARTICIPATION DETERMINED BY SOCIAL CLASS

The types of sports that Americans participate in often depend on one's social class background. Certain sports are used by some members of society to reinforce their upper-class privilege, and specific mechanisms are used to maintain the high status of these sports and their participants. Those coming from lower social class backgrounds often face tremendous barriers to regularly participate in many American sports. This difference between social classes and their participation patterns occurs within the free market provision of sports found in the United States.

THE PERVASIVENESS OF RACISM

Although conditions have improved greatly over the past forty years, racist attitudes and actions still strongly impact the participation experiences of minority group members in American sport. Just as in the larger society, racial minorities in sport are rarely found in positions of authority and often fail to benefit appropriately from their participation.

THE PERVASIVENESS OF MALE DOMINANCE

Men generally control sport. Almost every major professional, amateur, and educational sport organization in the United States is under the management and control of men. The proportion of women in leadership and decision-making positions in American sport, those with power and influence, is quite small—far smaller, certainly, than would be expected based on the number of female sport participants. Shifts in the balance of gender dominance in sports have occurred slowly.

Sport continues to contribute to the perpetuation of male dominance through four minimalizing processes:

1. Defining—by defining sport as a male activity;
2. Directly controlling—men control sport, even women's sport;
3. Ignoring—by giving most attention to male sports in the media and through community and school budgets, facilities, and the like; and
4. Trivializing—women's sports and women athletes continue to be considered secondary, especially in the mass media.[32]

THE DOMINATION OF INDIVIDUALS BY BUREAUCRACIES

Conservative bureaucratic organizations, through their desire to perpetuate themselves, curtail innovations and deflect activities away from the wishes of individuals and often from the original intent of these organizations. Many sport organizations—the NCAA, intercollegiate athletic conferences, professional sport leagues—pride themselves on having adopted bureaucratic business practices.

THE UNEQUAL DISTRIBUTION OF POWER IN ORGANIZATIONS

Autocratic and hierarchical organization characterizes American economic enterprises. The structure of sport in the United States is such that power is in the hands of the wealthy (e.g., boards of regents, corporate boards of directors, the media, wealthy entrepreneurs, professional sports ownership groups, and the NCAA). Evidence of the power of these individuals and organizations is seen in the exemptions allowed them by provincial and state governments, as well as by the U.S. national governments, in dealing with athletes, in tax breaks, and in the concessions that communities make to entice professional sports franchises to relocate or to remain and, incidentally, to benefit the wealthy of that community.

THE USE OF CONFLICT TO CHANGE UNEQUAL POWER RELATIONSHIPS

Conflict, in the form of lawsuits, strikes, boycotts, and demonstrations, historically and in more recent times has been used by labor groups, minorities, and the poor to rectify grievances. It is used by the less powerful (e.g., people of color, women, and athletes) in sport and in society for similar reasons. Recent events in the American sporting landscape reflect this type of challenge to dominant power structures. For instance, a plethora of athletes of color have recently been protesting against collegiate and professional sport organizations/leagues and their prevailing rules and practices. Furthermore, the U.S. women's soccer team recently filed a major lawsuit against their governing body to eventually obtain fair compensation for their international achievements. These are just a few key examples that represent challenges to unequal power relationships found in sport.

SPORT IS NOT A SANCTUARY: DEVIANCE IS FOUND THROUGHOUT SPORT

Corruption, law-breaking, unethical behavior, delinquency, and so forth are endemic to human societies. Because sport reflects society, bad actors and bad actions will be found in sport just as they are in other American social institutions. Both fairness and unfairness are found. There are ethical and unethical athletes, coaches, and athletic administrators. Cheating is often accepted, drugs are common, fans fight one another; coaches abuse their athletes; nothing is beyond belief. On a daily basis, we can find examples of these deviant sporting practices as they are reported in various types of media.

SUMMARY

Sociology of sport as an organized field of study is less than sixty years old. Although it is not a rapidly growing field of study, it has advanced to the point where it is taught in most colleges and universities, and it has attracted a group of dedicated scholars with interests in research and publication as well as in teaching the subject.

The perspectives, concepts, and procedures of sociology are used in this book to describe and explain the institution of sport in the United States. The subject matter of sociology is social behavior and social organization. Although there have been some descriptions, there is no universal definition of sport, primarily because there is such a variety of evolving games and physical activities that are conventionally called sports. Sport involves different types of social organizations, such as teams and leagues. These, in turn, are part of larger social organizations, such as schools, communities, international associations, and society. The task of this book is to assist readers in understanding the principles that underlie the structures and processes that create, sustain, and transform these social organizations. Most important, from our standpoint, this undertaking requires that readers examine the social arrangements of sport from a critical stance.

Some sample questions that must direct curious readers are these: How does the social organization really work? Who really has the power? Who benefits, and who does not? What criteria or valuations serve to benefit certain people and groups in sport over others?

Several social theoretical perspectives provide vantage points from which to view social life. Each of these guides our thinking, narrows our perceptions to certain relevant phenomena, and, in doing so, helps us understand our social life. We present several major theoretical perspectives that are used to understand the social world and—for the purposes of this book—the world of sport.

The two fundamental themes of this book are introduced in this chapter. The first is that sport is a microcosm of society and its values and structures. Perceiving the way sport is organized, the types of games people play, the degree of emphasis on competition, the compensation of the participants, and the enforcement of the rules is a shorthand way of understanding the complexities of the larger society in which sport is embedded. The converse is also true. The understanding of the values of society, of its types of economy, and of its treatment of minority groups, to name a few elements, provides important foundations for the perception or understanding of the organization of sport in society.

The second theme is that the prevailing form of sport—the corporate level—has indelibly altered the original forms of sport, some would say for better while others contend it is for worse. Some would even suggest that instead of player-oriented physical competition, sport has become a spectacle, a big business, and an extension of power politics. In essence, this view holds that play has become work while spontaneity has been superseded by bureaucracy. This would signal that the goal of pleasure in our physical activity has been replaced by extrinsic rewards, especially money. But sport, like all social phenomena, can be understood in multifaceted ways reflecting both positive and negative processes and outcomes. Indeed, sport is constantly changing in accordance with broader technological, economic, and demographic shifting, and thus the possibilities for evolution and

perhaps reorientation in sport are endless. Thus, as you go through the chapters of this book, it is crucial to contemplate, from a sociological perspective, how the various contexts of sport can become a sustainable part of future lives. We will return to the notion of sustainability at the conclusion of this book, because this perspective fundamentally implies creating relations of respect and inclusion toward other people, as well as our natural world, through sporting practice.

Learn more with this chapter's digital tools, including web resources, video links, and chapter self-assessment quizzes at www.oup.com/he/sage-eitzen-beal-atencio-12e.

NOTES

1. Frank Isola, "LeBron James Says President Trump 'Trying to Divide Us through Sport,'" *New York Daily News*, September 26, 2017, np.

2. John W. Loy, "The Nature of Sport: A Definitional Effort," in *Sport, Culture and Society: A Reader on the Sociology of Sport*, 2nd ed. (Philadelphia: Lea & Febiger, 1981), 23–32. Also see John W. Loy and Jay Coakley, "Sport," in *The Blackwell Encyclopedia of Sociology*, Vol. 9, ed. George Ritzer (Oxford: Blackwell, 2007), 4643–4653.

3. For a thorough discussion on the differences between play, game, and sport, see John W. Loy and Jay Coakley, "Sport," in *The Blackwell Encyclopedia of Sociology*, Vol. 9, ed. George Ritzer (Oxford: Blackwell, 2007), 4643–4653.

4. For examples of people who compete for the sheer joy of the competition, see Robin Chotzinoff, *People Who Sweat: Ordinary People, Extraordinary Pursuits* (New York: Harcourt Brace, 1999).

5. 2021 Physical Activity Council Report, the Physical Activity Council's Annual Study Tracking Sports, Fitness, and Recreation Participation in the US, http://www.physicalactivitycouncil.com/.

6. Mike Ozanian, "World's Most Valuable Sports Teams 2021," *Forbes Magazine*, May 14, 2021, https://www.forbes.com/sites/mikeozanian/2021/05/07/worlds-most-valuable-sports-teams-2021/?sh=106cdd363e9e.

7. Brett Knight and Justin Birnbaum, "2021, Highest-Paid Athletes," Forbes, https://www.forbes.com/athletes/.

8. Kurt Badenhausen, "NBA Highest-Paid Players: LeBron James' Career Earnings Will Hit $1 Billion in 2021," *Forbes Magazine*, February 12, 2021, https://www.forbes.com/sites/kurtbadenhausen/2021/01/29/the-nbas-highest-paid-players-2021-lebron-curry-durant-score-combined-235-million/?sh=458b64f86ea2.

9. Adam Andrzejewski, "Head Football Coaches at Alabama, Clemson, Ohio State & Notre Dame Collectively Made $25.9 Million," *Forbes Magazine*, December 30, 2020, https://www.forbes.com/sites/adamandrzejewski/2021/12/30/top-four-football-coaches-in-ncaa-national-playoff-collectively-made-259-million/?sh=2e1d7e2331d8.

10. Steve Berkowitz, "Texas A&M Athletics Department Joins Texas in $200 Million Operating Revenue Club," *USA Today*, January 30, 2018, https://www.usatoday.com/story/sports/college/2018/01/29/texas-am-operating-revenue/1077373001/.

11. Brian Steinberg, "NBC Seeks Record $6 Million for Super Bowl Commercials (EXCLUSIVE)," *Variety*, June 16, 2021, https://variety.com/2021/tv/news/super-bowl-commercials-price-record-1234998593/.

12. Pbrock, "NCAA Men's Basketball Attendance," NCAA, August 17, 2020, https://www.ncaa.org/championships/statistics/ncaa-mens-basketball-attendance.

13. Pbrock, "Women's Basketball Attendance." NCAA, August 7, 2020, https://www.ncaa.org/championships/statistics/womens-basketball-attendance.

14. D. Stanley Eitzen, Maxine Zinn, and Kelly Eitzen Smith, *In Conflict and Order: Understanding Society*, 14th ed. (Boston: Pearson, 2016), chs. 1–2; Kerry Ferris and Jill Stein, *The Real World: An Introduction to Sociology*, 5th ed. (New York: W. W. Norton, 2016), chs. 1–3.

15. This is the original publication in which "the sociological imagination" was articulated. See C. Wright Mills, *The Sociological Imagination* (New York: Oxford University Press, 1959); see also D. Stanley Eitzen and Kelly Eitzen Smith, *Experiencing Poverty: Voices from the Bottom*, 2nd ed. (Boston: Allyn & Bacon, 2008).

16. Peter Donnelly, "Interpretive Approaches to the Sociology of Sport," in *Handbook of Sport Studies*, ed. Jay Coakley and Eric Dunning (London: Sage, 2000), 77–92. For an insightful example of interpretative sociology, see Joseph R Gusfield, "Sport as Story: Form and Content in Athletics," *Society* 37 (May/June 2000): 63–70.

17. Lucy Spowart, Lisette Burrows, and Sally Shaw, " 'I Just Eat, Sleep and Dream of Surfing': When Surfing Meets Motherhood," *Sport in Society* 13, no. 7 (2010):1186–1203, DOI:10.1080/17430431003780179; Matthew Atencio and Jan Wright, ""We Be Killin' Them": Hierarchies of Black Masculinity in Urban Basketball Spaces," *Sociology of Sport Journal* 25, no. 2 (2008): 263–280.

18. For example, see Matthew Atencio, Becky Beal, and Charlene Wilson, "The Distinction of Risk: Urban Skateboarding, Street Habitus and the Construction of Hierarchical Gender Relations," *Qualitative Research in Sport and Exercise* 1, no. 1 (2009): 3–20.

19. George Ritzer and Steven Seidman, *Contested Knowledge: Social Theory Today*, 6th ed. (New York: Wiley–Blackwell, 2016).

20. Lorenzo Reyes, "Kaepernick Supporters Show Solidarity," *USA Today*, May 25, 2017, 6C; Jarrett Bell, "Kaepernick Earns Place in History," *USA Today*, May 18, 2017, 3C. For a full description of functionalism and its relationship to sport, see John W. Loy and Douglas Booth, "Functionalism, Sport and Society," in Coakley and Dunning, *Handbook of Sport Studies*, 8–27; see also Wesley Longhofer and Daniel Winchester, eds., *Social Theory Re-Wired New Connections to Classical Contemporary Perspectives*, 2nd ed. (New York: Routledge, 2016), 68.

21. George Ritzer and Jeffrey N. Stepnisky, *Classical Sociological Theory*, 7th ed. (Thousand Oaks, CA: Sage, 2017), 154–185; see also Ben Agger, *Critical Social Theories*, 3rd ed. (New York: Oxford University Press, 2013).

22. For a discussion of the conflict perspective and its relationship to sport, see Bero Rigauer, "Marxist Theories," in Coakley and Dunning, *Handbook of Sport Studies*, 34–47; see also "Probability of Competing beyond High School," NCAA, http://www.

ncaa.org/about/resources/research/probability-competing-beyond-high-school.

23. The theory of hegemony in class societies is fully presented in Antonio Gramsci and Quintin Hoare, *Selections from the Prison Notebooks*, ed. Geoffrey Nowell Smith (New York: International Publishers, 1971); see also Adam Morton, *Unravelling Gramsci: Hegemony and Passive Revolution in the Global Economy* (London: Pluto Press, 2007); David Forgacs, *Antonio Gramsci: Selections from Cultural Writings* (New Delhi: Aakar Books, 2015).

24. George H. Sage, *Power and Ideology in American Sport: A Critical Perspective*, 2nd ed. (Champaign, IL: Human Kinetics, 1998).

25. See bell hooks, *Feminist Theory: From Margin to Center* (Boston: South End Press, 2000); see also Wendy Kolmar and Frances Bartkowski, *Feminist Theory: A Reader* (New York: McGraw-Hill, 2013).

26. Susan Birrell, "Feminist Theories for Sport," in Coakley and Dunning, *Handbook of Sport Studies*, 68.

27. Howard Winant, "Race and Race Theory," *Annual Review of Sociology* 26 (2000): 169–185.

28. Jean Stefancic and Richard Delgado, *Critical Race Theory: The Cutting Edge*, 3rd ed. (Philadelphia: Temple University Press, 2013); see also Kevin Hylton, *"Race" and Sport: Critical Race Theory* (New York: Routledge, 2009), 22; Billy J. Hawkins, Akilah R. Carter-Francique, and Joseph N. Cooper, eds., *Critical Race Theory: Black Athletic Sporting Experiences in the United States* (New York: Palgrave MacMillan, 2017).

29. Kevin Hylton, "How a Turn to Critical Race Theory Can Contribute to Our Understanding of 'Race': Racism and Anti-Racism in Sport," *International Review for the Sociology of Sport* 45, no. 3 (2010): 338; see also Kevin Hylton, "Talk the Talk, Walk the Walk: Defining Critical Race Theory in Research," *Race Ethnicity and Education* 15, no. 1 (2012): 23–41.

30. For example, see Susan Birrell, "Racial Relations Theories and Sport: Suggestions for a More Critical Analysis," *Sociology of Sport Journal* 6, no. 3 (1989): 212–227; see also Michael Omi and Howard Winant, *Racial Formation in the United States*, 3rd ed. (London: Routledge Press, 2014); see also Stanley Thangaraj, "Playing through Differences: Black–White Racial Logic and Interrogating South Asian American Identity," *Ethnic and Racial Studies* 35 (2012): 988–1006.

31. For an excellent anthology of sociology of sport research and essay literature, see D. Stanley Eitzen, *Sport in Contemporary Society: An Anthology*, 10th ed. (Boulder, CO: Paradigm, 2014); see also D. Stanley Eitzen, *Fair and Foul: Beyond the Myths and Paradoxes of Sport*, 6th ed. (Lanham, MD: Rowman & Littlefield, 2016).

32. Adrienne N. Milner and Jomills Henry Braddock II, *Sex Segregation in Sports: Why Separate Is Not Equal* (New York: Praeger, 2016).

CHAPTER 2

SOCIAL AND CULTURAL TRANSFORMATIONS AND THE RISE OF SPORT IN THE UNITED STATES

Throughout American history the form and purpose of sporting events have been closely connected to the larger society from which they arose.

—RICHARD O. DAVIES[1]

College basketball teams in the first years of the twentieth century were becoming popular. Shown here is the basketball team of the former Colorado Normal School—also called the Colorado Teachers College—now the University of Northern Colorado. Basketball was a new sport, having been invented by James Naismith in 1891, a Canadian American physical educator and innovator, while he was a physical education instructor at what is now Springfield College. After students in his class showed enthusiasm for playing basketball, Naismith wrote the original rule book. Naismith lived to see basketball adopted as an Olympic demonstration sport in 1904 and as an official event at the 1936 Summer Olympics in Berlin. (Photo: Courtesy of the University of Northern Colorado Archives)

History helps us understand change and how a social institution, in this case sport, came to have the features it currently has. Whenever we try to know why something is as it presently is, we have to look for activities and events that occurred earlier. The forms, functions, and practices of sport in any given society are rooted in historical, social, and cultural traditions, and it is our contention that a study of sport based solely on the present will result in an incomplete picture of sport as a social and cultural practice. Thus, one who studies the sociology of sport in the United States without learning about sport's history on this continent will never truly understand the social and cultural forces that underpin contemporary sport. In this chapter, we examine the changing sociocultural conditions of American society over the past 400 years and attempt to demonstrate how these conditions have affected and influenced the rise and current state of American sport.

The United States has had different stages of historical development: colonization and control by the British, war for independence from the British, a period of westward expansion including further colonization of indigenous lands and people, reliance on slave labor, a massive influx of immigrants from Europe, and urbanization and industrialization during the late nineteenth century. Through much of the twentieth century there were waves of immigration and the United States became globally powerful politically and economically.

Fostered by a variety of historical, political, social, and economic conditions, sports have become a major national pastime for the people of both countries. From agrarian societies whose inhabitants had little time for games and sports except on special occasions, Americans currently watch hours and hours of sports weekly and consider it almost a duty to participate in some form of exercise or sport for recreation.

PRE-COLUMBIAN AND COLONIAL TRADITIONS IN THE UNITED STATES

For many centuries before European colonization began in what is now the United States, Native American settlements were scattered throughout North America. It is estimated that some 6 to 8 million native peoples were dispersed across the continent at the time of Columbus's voyages. What is clear is that although there was great diversity among the cultures of Native Americans, they all enjoyed a variety of physical play and game activities. In his book *American Indian Sports Heritage*, Joseph Oxendine—himself a member of the Lumbee tribe who grew up in a segregated Native American community in North Carolina—asserts that "games among traditional American Indians ranged from the seemingly trivial activities primarily for the amusement of children to major sporting events of significance for persons of all ages."[2] Typically, there was a close linkage between the games and sports and the world of spiritual belief and magic.

Among the various sports engaged in by Native Americans long before European settlement in the New World lacrosse seems to have been one of the most popular; thus, lacrosse is often recognized as the oldest American sport, with roots running deep in Native American history. It is perhaps the best known Native American game because it is currently played in clubs, secondary schools, and universities throughout the United States.[3]

THE COLONISTS RESTRICT PHYSICAL ACTIVITIES

During the two centuries following Columbus—the sixteenth and seventeenth centuries—Spain, France, and England explored and colonized most of North America. But by the late eighteenth century, Great Britain had triumphed over the other two countries and controlled the entire eastern half of what is now the United States and the eastern two-thirds of what is now Canada (except for two small fishing islands off the coast of Newfoundland, which remained under the control of France).

We are accustomed to thinking that the wide array of formalized participant and spectator sport that we currently enjoy has always existed. But, unimaginable as it seems, there were no formally organized participant or spectator sports during the colonial period in North America. In the first place, people had little leisure time or opportunity to engage in games and sports. The harsh circumstances of wresting a living from the environment necessitated arduous daily work. Colonists had to devote most of their efforts to basic survival tasks.

A second factor restricting sports involvement was the church. Religion was the most powerful social institution in the American colonies. Puritanism was prominent in the New England colonies, and other Christian religions dominated social life in the middle and southern colonies. (The subject of sport and religion is examined more fully in Chapter 14.)

All of these religious groups placed severe restrictions on play and games, with the Puritans being the most extreme. They directed attacks at almost every form of amusement: dancing for its carnality, boxing for its violence, maypoles for their paganism, and play and games in general because they were often performed on the Sabbath. Moreover, religious sanctions were closely bound to the dislike of playful activities of any kind. Honest labor was the greatest service to God and a moral duty. Any form of play or amusement signaled time wasting and idleness and was therefore defined as wicked. That everyone has a calling to work hard was a first premise of Puritanism. Followers believed that it was not leisure and amusement but diligent work that symbolized the glorification of God.[4]

Laws prohibiting a form of social behavior and the actual social customs and actions of a people rarely coincide. In the case of the colonies, religious and legal strictures failed to eliminate the urge to play among the early settlers. Although frequently done in defiance of local laws, sports such as horse racing, shooting matches, cockfights, foot races, and wrestling matches were engaged in throughout the colonies to break the monotony of life.

The most popular sports of the gentry were cockfighting, hunting, dancing, and—most popular of all—horse racing. Other recreational activities were popular among those who frequented the taverns. The tavern was a social center, primarily for drinking but also for all manner of popular pastimes, such as cards, billiards, bowling, and rifle and pistol target shooting.[5]

As colonial settlement moved westward in the eighteenth century, religious restrictions against sport became less and less effective. Men and women in the backcountry enjoyed a variety of competitive events when they met at barbecues and camp meetings. They gambled on these contests, especially horse races, cockfights, and bearbaiting.

The physical activities that marked these infrequent social gatherings were typically rough and brutal. Two popular activities were fistfights, which ended when one man could not continue, and wrestling, in which eye gouging and bone-breaking holds were permitted.[6] Horse racing was the universal sport on the frontier because every owner of a horse was confident of its prowess and eager to match it against others. Both men and women were skillful riders. The other constant companion of the frontiersman—the rifle—engendered a pride in marksmanship, and shooting matches were a common form of competition.[7]

Life in the colonies was quite different for African slaves, who numbered approximately 200,000 in the mid-eighteenth century, just before the American Revolution. The majority lived in what is now the southeastern United States, where plantations had developed. Most plantation slaves worked in the fields, but some were craftworkers, messengers, and servants.

Slaves were often given the responsibility for the care and maintenance of the horses owned by plantation owners for the purpose of entering them in the popular horse-racing events throughout the South. Because Black slaves were often adept at handling horses, many plantation owners used them as jockeys for the horses they entered in races. Boxing was also popular; some plantation owners pitted their slaves against slaves of other plantation owners, with owners gambling on the outcome an integral part of the bouts.[8]

When not working at their assigned jobs, games and sporting activities were commonly played in slave quarters by children and adults. Most plantation owners actively promoted these physical activities as a way to foster social harmony, relaxation, and fun. We will have more to say about African Americans in sport in Chapter 6.

EARLY NINETEENTH CENTURY: TAKEOFF OF INDUSTRIALIZATION, TECHNOLOGY, AND ORGANIZED SPORT

Play, games, and sports in every society are always closely tied to the political, economic, religious, and social institutions as well as the cultural traditions and customs. The major catalyst for the transformation of American sport was a series of inventions in England in the late eighteenth century that completely changed the means by which goods were produced. These inventions made possible technological advances that ushered in two of the most important developments in human history—the industrial revolution and the technological revolution.

The major characteristic and social consequence of the industrial revolution was the factory system. The initial impact was seen in the textile industry. The spinning of thread and the weaving of cloth had traditionally been done at home on spinning wheels and handlooms, but new methods for performing these tasks enabled them to be done in factories by power-driven machinery.

Other industries emerged. The successful smelting of iron with the aid of anthracite coal was perfected around 1830. By 1850 improved methods of making steel had been developed. Steel production was the backbone of industrial development because the machinery for factories was primarily made from steel. Artisans and craftspersons were transformed into an industrial workforce.

As Figure 2.1 shows, the proportion of workers engaged in agriculture has steadily decreased—from approximately 60 percent in 1850, to 40 percent in 1900, to less than 10 percent in 2016. Industry needed a plentiful supply of labor located near plants and factories, so population shifts from rural to urban areas began to change population characteristics and needs. Urbanization created a need for new forms of recreational activities, and industrialization gradually supplied the standard of living and the leisure time necessary to support broad-based forms of recreation and organized sport.[9]

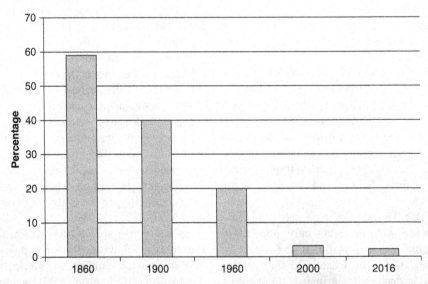

FIGURE 2.1   Percentage of Labor Force in Agriculture Source: U.S. Bureau of Labor Statistics, Labor Force Statistics from the Current Population Survey, "Employed persons by detailed industry, sex, race, and Hispanic or Latino ethnicity," February 2016, and earlier releases, http://www.bls.gov/cps/tables.htm Washington, D.C., 2012.

BUILDING A FRAMEWORK FOR ORGANIZED SPORT

In the first few decades of the nineteenth century, Americans enjoyed essentially the same recreation and sports as they had during the colonial period. As conditions gradually changed from a rural to an increasingly urban population and from home trades and individualized occupations to large-scale industrial production, a growing interest in spectator sports emerged. Rowing, prizefighting, foot racing (the runners were called pedestrians), and similar activities were especially popular, but the sport that excited the most interest was horse racing, with its traditions going back to early colonial days.

In May 1823, a horse race between Eclipse and Sir Henry—the superstar horses of that era—attracted one of the largest crowds ever to witness a nineteenth-century sporting event in America. A crowd estimated at 75,000 overwhelmed the racecourse. But thoroughbred racing was not the only popular form of horse racing. Harness racing had an enthusiastic following, and it has even been claimed that harness racing was the first modern sport in the U.S.[10]

Native American games of lacrosse, snowshoeing, and canoe activities were adopted by the settlers in the regions that currently exist as northern United States and Canada. British and French settlers also took enthusiastically to physical activities that could be played in the cold northern climate, so sleighing, ice skating, and curling were popular in the winter, whereas hunting, fishing, fox hunting, and horse racing were popular in the short summers.[11]

The transformation from occasional and informal sport to highly organized commercial spectator sport began during the period before the American Civil War. Thus, the framework of modern sport was established during the first half of the nineteenth century, setting the stage for the remarkable expansion of mass popular sport and professional sport that followed in the second half of the nineteenth century.

THE TECHNOLOGICAL REVOLUTION AND SPORT

Technological advances have been a dominant force for social change, for adaptations in social relationships, and for the transformation of business and governmental organizations over the past 200 years. Beginning in the early nineteenth century, technological advances made possible the large-scale manufacturing that is characteristic of industrialization. Through technology, which is the practical application of science to industry, many kinds of machines, labor-saving devices, and scientific processes were invented or perfected. Technological development was one of the most significant forces transforming sport from informal village festivals to highly organized sports. Of course, the technological revolution was only one of the factors contributing to the rise of modern sport, but ignoring its influence would result in an incomplete understanding of contemporary sport forms.

New Forms of Transportation Broaden Sport Opportunities

One area of technological innovation that had an enormous impact on the rise of sport was transportation. Travel of any kind was difficult and slow in the pre-1800 period. A distance that today takes hours to travel took more than the same number of days in those times. Modes of transportation were limited to foot, horse, and boat. Roads, when they existed, were primitive, dangerous, and often blocked by almost impassable rivers.

The first notable technological breakthrough in transportation came in the early nineteenth century with the development of the steam engine. This invention and its use on boats made it possible to fully develop river traffic. The first successful steamboat in the United States, the *Clermont*, was built by Robert Fulton, and in 1807 it chugged 150 miles up the Hudson River from New York to Albany in about thirty hours. In time, steamboats stimulated the building of canals and the enlarging of rivers, thus opening new areas that had previously been isolated and cut off from commerce and trade.[12]

The steamboat did not solve all the transportation problems; river travel was of no help to people who did not happen to live near large rivers. Furthermore, it was not a particularly fast mode of transportation because the large steamers sometimes had to thread their way carefully through narrow or shallow water.

A new form of transportation began to compete with river transportation around the time that canal building reached its peak. This was the railroad. A fourteen-mile stretch of the Baltimore and Ohio Railroad was opened in 1830. Railroad construction expanded rapidly—mostly short lines connecting principal cities—and by 1840 nearly 3,000 miles of track were in use in the United States.

It was the steamboats and railroads of the first half of the nineteenth century that had the first significant impact on sport. As one of the first products of the age of steam, steamboats served as carriers of thoroughbred horses to such horse-racing centers as Vicksburg, Natchez, and New Orleans, all located along the Mississippi River. Crowds attending horse races or prizefights were frequently conveyed to the site of the event via steamboats. The riverboats on the Mississippi and the St. Lawrence also served as carriers of racing or prizefight news up and down the river valleys.

More important to the development of organized sport was the railroad. In the years preceding the American Civil War, the widespread interest in thoroughbred and harness races was in great part nurtured by railroad expansion, as horses and crowds were transported from one locality to another. Similarly, participants and spectators for prizefights and foot races were commonly carried to the sites of competition by rail. Scheduling the fights where they would not be disrupted by the authorities frequently became necessary because prizefighting was outlawed in many cities. This meant that spectators often had to use the railroad to get to the site of the bout.

New Forms of Communication Enable Dissemination of Sport Information

As important as transportation was to the rise of sport in the United States, the new forms of communication over the past century and a half have been equally significant. The invention and development of the telegraph was the most important advance in communication during the first half of the nineteenth century. Samuel F. B. Morse perfected an electrical instrument by which combinations of dots and dashes could be transmitted along a wire, and the first telegraph line was built between Baltimore and Washington, D.C., in 1844. Soon telegraph lines stretched between all the principal cities, and by 1860 some 50,000 miles of line existed east of the Rockies. Meanwhile, Western Union was extending its lines to the Pacific Coast, putting the Pony Express out of business a little more than a year after it was founded.

From its invention in 1844, the telegraph rapidly assumed a significant role in the dissemination of sport news because newspapers and periodicals installed telegraphic apparatuses in their offices. Only two years after its invention, the *New York Herald* and the *New York Tribune* had telegraphic equipment. By 1850, horse races, prizefights, and yachting events were regularly reported over the wires.

Simultaneous with the development of the telegraph, a revolution in the dissemination of news occurred with improvements in printing presses and in other processes of newspaper and journal production. The telegraph and the improved press opened the gates to a rising tide of sports journalism, but the journalistic exploitation of sports did not actually take off until the last two decades of the nineteenth century.

Whereas advances in electrical forms of communication were instrumental in the rise of sport, other communications media supplemented and extended sport publicity. In the early years of the nineteenth century, sports were more directly aided by magazine and book publishers than they were by newspapers. However, the rise of sports journalism was closely tied to new inventions in printing processes as well as to the telegraph network that spanned the continent in the mid-1800s.

As early as the 1830s, several of the largest newspapers were giving extensive coverage to prizefights, foot races, horse races, and other sports. What was perhaps the most notable newspaper concerned with sports in the United States—*The Spirit of the Times*—appeared in 1831 and survived until 1901.[13]

LATTER NINETEENTH CENTURY: THE BEGINNINGS OF MODERN SPORT

Entering the second half of the nineteenth century, the United States was predominantly a land of small farms, small towns, and small business enterprises.

But over the next fifty years economic, technological, and social changes transformed the lives of Americans. The country evolved from rural and traditional society into a modern, industrialized nation. By the beginning of the twentieth century, citizens and immigrants were laboring in factories owned by large corporations.

Before 1850, U.S. industry had been largely concentrated in New England and the mid-Atlantic states, but by 1900 industrialization and manufacturing spread out to all parts of the country. As the factory system took root, however, a capitalistic class began to emerge, and a new form of business ownership, the corporation, became the dominant form of organization.

By the 1890s, corporations produced nearly three-fourths of the total value of manufactured products in the United States. The large corporations developed mass-production methods and mass sales, the bases of big business, because of the huge amounts of money they controlled. To accommodate corporations, cities passed ordinances—ugly laws, they were called—which were laws that protected corporations while discriminating against workers with disabilities (see Box 2.1).

As technology increased the means of industrial production in the United States, more and more people gave up farming and came to the cities to work in factories and offices. They were joined by a seemingly endless stream of immigrants who sought a better life. Factories multiplied, and towns and cities grew rapidly. The first U.S. Census, completed in 1790, recorded a population of nearly 4 million, about 6 percent of whom were classified as urban; by 1900 the population had risen to 76 million, with some 40 percent living in urban areas. Figure 2.2 shows the general pattern of growth in urban population. From 1860 to 1910 the number of U.S. cities with populations greater than 100,000 increased from nine to fifty.

URBANIZATION AND THE RISE OF MODERN SPORT FORMS

Urban influences in the United States had made their marks by the mid-nineteenth century, and the increasing concentration of city populations and the monotonous and wearisome repetition of industrial work created a demand for more recreational outlets. Urbanization created favorable conditions for commercialized spectator sports, whereas industrialization gradually provided the leisure time and standard of living so crucial to the growth and development of all forms of recreation and sport (see Figure 2.2).

Towns and cities were natural centers for organizing sports. The popular sport of horse racing centered in New York, Boston, Charleston, Louisville, and New Orleans, and the first organized baseball clubs were founded in such communities as New York, Boston, Chicago, St. Louis, and Toronto. Yachting and rowing regattas, foot races, boxing events, billiard matches, and even the main agricultural fairs were held in or near the larger cities.

BOX 2.1 *THINKING ABOUT SPORT:* THE CHANGING SOCIAL STATUS OF "DISABILITY"

In 1881, the city of Chicago passed an ordinance (often referred to as "ugly law") that read, "Any person who is diseased, maimed, mutilated, or in any way deformed, so as to be an unsightly or disgusting object, or an improper person to be allowed in or on the streets, highways, thoroughfares, or public places in the city, shall not therein or thereon expose himself to public view, under a penalty of a fine for 1 dollar." Additionally, some people with disabilities or physical abnormalities were used as entertainment in the nineteenth and early twentieth centuries, in what were called *freak shows*. In short, people would pay money to see these "exotic" and "strange" examples of humanity. Ableism, similar to sexism or racism, is the ideology that some bodies/people are better than others. The aforementioned law and entertainment spectacle reproduced ableism as they reinforced the social definitions of "normal" and "good" bodies and, thus, constructed a hierarchy of human diversity. The historical disdain of disability was also expressed through derogatory terms including cripple, feebleminded, or imbecile.

Sources: Ron Berger, *Introducing Disability Studies* (Boulder, CO: Lynne Rienner, 2013), 7–8; Brett Smith, ed., *Paralympics and Disability Sport* (New York: Routledge, 2014).

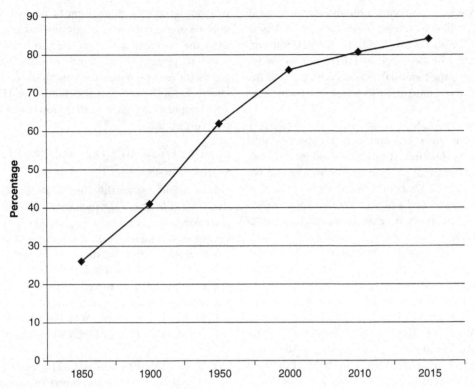

FIGURE 2.2   Percentage of U.S. Population in Urban Areas Source: U.S. Census Bureau, 2000 Census of Population and Housing, *Population and Housing Unit Counts PHC-3*; 2010 Census of Population and Housing, *Population and Housing Unit Counts, CPH-2-1, United States Summary*; and "Percent Urban and Rural in 2010 by State," https://www.census.gov/geo/reference/ua/urban-rural-2010.html, accessed March 2013.

Diffusion of Sport from the Upper to the Lower Classes

Nothing in the recreational and sport scene was more startling than the sudden spread of sporting activities from the wealthy class into the upper middle, the middle, and even the working class. Millionaires pursued horse racing, yachting, lawn tennis, and golf. Working women and young ladies of the middle class turned to rowing and cycling, and working-class men played pool, fished, hunted, backed their favorite boxers, and gradually tried their hands at the sports of the affluent classes.

During the second half of the nineteenth century, people tried to adapt to the new urban-industrial society by forming subcommunities based on status. One type of status community was the athletic club, formed by younger, wealthy men who shared a common interest in sports. The private clubs were a major stimulus to the growth of yachting, baseball, lawn tennis, golf, track and field, and country clubs. Thus, members of the social elite deserve much credit for early sporting promotion and patronage.[14]

New sports introduced by the wealthy were often adopted by the working class. Baseball is a classic example of this pattern. From an informal children's game played throughout the eighteenth century, baseball developed codified rules in the 1840s, and groups of upper-social-class men organized clubs, taking care to keep out lower-social-class persons.

Portraits of the original Cincinnati Red Stockings team members, ca 1869. This was the first professional baseball team in the United States. The Red Stockings played games from coast to coast and chalked up a fabulous winning streak of sixty-five games without a defeat. (Photo: Library of Congress)

The first Stanley Cup Champions. The Stanley Cup was first awarded to the Montreal Hockey Club in 1893 when the team won the 1893 American Hockey Association of Canada season. The team then had to defend its champion title through both league championships and challenge games organized by the Stanley Cup trustees. Until 1912, these challenges could take place before or during a league season. After 1912, the trustees ordered that challenges only take place after all league games were completed. Professional hockey was among the sporting pursuits fostered by railroad development. (Photo: Hockey Hall of Fame/Library and Archives Canada/PA-049464)

The first of these baseball clubs, the Knickerbockers of New York, was primarily a social club with a distinctly upper-class flavor; it was similar to the country clubs of the 1920s and 1930s before they became popular with the middle class. A baseball game for members of the Knickerbockers was a genteel amateur recreational pursuit, with an emphasis on polite social interactions rather than an all-out quest for victory.[15]

In the United States, the Civil War wiped out this upper-class patronage of the game, and a broad base of popularity existed in 1869 when the first professional baseball team, the Cincinnati Red Stockings, was formed. This was followed in 1876 by the organization of the first major league, and baseball became firmly entrenched as the American national pastime by the end of the century.

At about the same time, ice hockey, which was to become Canada's national pastime, was making its own early history. It seems to have been played in its earliest unorganized form in the mid-1850s, but the first public showing of the game took place in 1875. Ice hockey quickly became a favorite sport of Canadians and Americans.

As cities grew, an element of the population that journalists referred to as "rabble" and "rowdies" stimulated interest in organized sports. Wherever sports events were held, members of this group could be found gambling on the outcome and generally raising the emotional atmosphere of the event by wildly cheering their favorites and booing or attempting to disconcert those whom they had bet against. Although sports organizers publicly condemned the actions of this unruly element, they secretly spurred them on because this group often helped ensure the financial success of sporting events.

The Role of African Americans in Sports during the Nineteenth Century

Despite living under conditions of slavery in the southern colonies, African Americans engaged in a wide variety of games and sport. Some were even trained by their plantation owners as boxers and jockeys. Emancipation in the mid-1860s gave African Americans hopes of participating in sports along with Whites, but the post–Civil War years saw a mass social disenfranchisement of African Americans. Although a few African Americans played on professional baseball teams in the second half of the nineteenth century, many White players refused to play with the Black players, so team owners stopped hiring Blacks. As other professional and amateur sports developed during the latter nineteenth century, African Americans were barred from participation in most of the White-owned teams and leagues. This led to African Americans forming their own teams and ultimately the Negro Baseball league was founded in 1920. During the latter nineteenth century, horse race jockeying was an exception to the common practice of segregation (see Box 2.2).

This issue is also discussed in more detail in Chapter 6.

The Role of Immigrants in Sports during the Nineteenth Century

Between 1870 and 1900, some 12 million persons immigrated to the United States. At the beginning of this period, one-third of all U.S. industrial workers were immigrants; by 1900, more than half were foreign born.

Immigrants contributed to the rise of sport in a variety of ways. First, many immigrants settled in the cities and became a part of that urban population that sought excitement through sport and recreation as an antidote to the typically dull and monotonous jobs they held. Second, because a great many of these nineteenth-century immigrants did not possess the strict religious attitudes toward play and sport of the fundamental Protestant sects, they freely enjoyed and participated in sports of all kinds. Third, the immigrants brought their games and sports with them. Cricket, horse racing, and rowing were widely popular with the British immigrants. The Germans brought their

---

BOX 2.2 *THINKING ABOUT SPORT:* HORSE RACING AND THE GREAT AFRICAN AMERICAN JOCKEYS

Baseball was not America's first "national pastime." Before the Civil War it was horse racing that captured the sporting interest and enthusiasm of Americans. One hundred fifty years before Jackie Robinson broke into Major League Baseball, African American jockeys competed alongside Whites in horse races throughout the country. Despite the slavery system, racehorse owners and trainers recognized the skill, courage, and determination of African American jockeys and did not hesitate to use them to win horse races. But most Americans are unaware of the excellence of the African American jockeys during this period because, as one historian put it, "The black jockeys were ridden out of history." The status of Black jockeys remained high in the years immediately following the Civil War. Indeed, in the first Kentucky Derby, held in 1875, the jockey on the winning horse was an African American, Oliver Lewis. More impressive, of the fifteen jockeys in that race, thirteen were African Americans. This was not unusual: until Jim Crow laws set in, segregating Blacks and Whites near the end of the nineteenth century, African Americans dominated the sport of horse racing—much as they do NBA basketball today. Most

horse-racing historians regard Isaac Murphy as the greatest jockey in the country in the decade and a half between 1884 and 1900. Murphy won his first Kentucky Derby in 1884. He became the first jockey to win two consecutive Kentucky Derbys, and his record of riding three Kentucky Derby winners was not equaled until 1930.

By the end of the 1890s, African American jockeys were the subjects of virulent racism sweeping the country in the form of a landmark U.S. Supreme Court decision, *Plessy v. Ferguson*, which upheld the constitutionality of racial segregation in public venues under the doctrine of "separate but equal." In his book *The Great Black Jockeys*, historian Edward Hotaling laments, "By the early 1900s, the great black jockeys had gone from winning the Kentucky Derby to not being able to get a mount. . . . For all intents and purposes, they had vanished from the American racetrack." And their records of excellence, courage, and achievements have all but vanished from sports history, along with the admiration that should be theirs.

Sources: Edward Hotaling, *The Great Black Jockeys* (Rocklin, CA: Forum, 1999); Katherine C. Mooney, *Race Horse Men: How Slavery and Freedom Were Made at the Racetrack* (Cambridge, MA: Harvard University Press, 2014).

love for lawn bowling and gymnastics. German *turnverein* (gymnastic clubs) opened wherever Germans settled; by the time of the Civil War, there were approximately 150 American *turnverein* with some 10,000 members.[16] The Irish seemed to have a particular affinity for the prize ring, and some of the most famous nineteenth-century boxers in North America were immigrants from Ireland. Two Irish American boxing champions, John L. Sullivan and James J. Corbett, were among the most popular sports heroes of the century.

The Beginnings of Intercollegiate Athletics

The entire focus of Chapter 10 is on intercollegiate sports, so we forgo detailing the history of intercollegiate sports until that chapter.

The first American colleges were established during the colonial period. They were small, widely scattered, and religiously oriented, and in what became the United States, most were less than thirty years old when the colonial period ended. During the latter half of the nineteenth century, colleges became the source of one of the most popular forms of sport: intercollegiate athletics.

Intercollegiate athletics began in the United States in 1852 with a rowing match between Harvard and Yale. But it was not until the 1870s and 1880s that intercollegiate sports became an established part of higher education and contributed to the enthusiasm for athletic and sporting diversions. Football became an extremely popular spectator sport during this era. It was a sport for the affluent classes rather

The playground in a tenement alley, a substandard multifamily poor neighborhood in the urban core, usually in Boston or New York, in the latter nineteenth and early twentieth centuries, often occupied by newly arrived immigrants. This is a typical tenement image of kids playing games and sports in the street while multiple lines of laundry flap merrily in the breeze. While some neighborhoods were composed of a heavy percentage of a given ethnic group, most tenements contained a wide variety of nationalities. (Photo: Playground in Tenement Alley, Boston, 1909 (b/w photo), Hine, Lewis Wickes (1874–1940)/ Private Collection/J. T. Vintage/Bridgeman Images)

than for the masses because it largely reflected the interests of the college students and alumni; the pigskin game (an early nickname for the sport) nevertheless did develop into a national sport by 1900.

After students organized teams, collegiate sports revolutionized campus life, serving as a major source of physical activity for many students and a significant source of entertainment for other students, alumni, and the general public. In the United States, intercollegiate athletics gradually became more than merely a demonstration of physical skills between rival institutions. Students, alumni, and the public began to regard victory as the measure of a college's prestige. Campus and commercial editors increased their coverage, and sports events became featured items in newspapers and magazines. As a result, this increased coverage focused attention on winning and made contest results appear to be an index of an institution's merit.

Thus, a belief emerged throughout American colleges that winning teams favorably advertised the school, attracted prospective students, enhanced alumni contributions, and—in the case of state-supported universities—increased appropriations from the state legislature. The notion that successful teams brought renown to the college (and to its president) must surely have been in the mind of University of Chicago president William Rainey Harper when he hired Yale All-American Amos Alonzo Stagg in 1890. He asked Stagg to "develop teams which we can send around the country and knock out all the colleges. We will give them a palace car and a vacation too."[17]

One of the oldest notions about female participation in sport was the idea that vigorous physical activity tended to "masculinize" the physique and behavior of girls and women. Nevertheless, even though females maintained a "ladylike" appearance into the first decades of the twentieth century, they played a variety of games and sports. The college women in the photo are participating in sports, adopting the appropriate clothing they were expected to maintain while playing. The athletes even attracted a rather large group of spectators to watch the activity. (Photo: Library and Archives Canada)

TECHNOLOGICAL INNOVATION AND SPORT: TRANSPORTATION

Technological innovation continued to serve as a dominant force for shaping social change throughout the second half of the nineteenth century. Transportation was one of the most prominent areas of its influence, as the growth of the railroad industry continued throughout the latter nineteenth century. Shortly after the Civil War, the Central Pacific and Union Pacific workers laid the final rail to complete the first transcontinental line in North America. Other lines followed in the last three decades of the 1800s.[18]

The railroad played an instrumental role in staging the first intercollegiate athletic event, a rowing race between Harvard and Yale. According to sport historian Ronald A. Smith, "the offer by a railroad superintendent to transport and house the crews of the two most prestigious colleges [Harvard and Yale] at a vacation spot over a hundred miles from the Cambridge campus and nearly twice that distance from New Haven was the beginning of . . . college sport in America."[19] The offer was accepted, and the Boston, Concord, and Montreal Railroad transported the participants and fans to New Hampshire's Lake Winnipesaukee for the event.

The first intercollegiate football game, between Rutgers and Princeton, was attended by students riding a train pulled by a jerky little locomotive engine that chugged out of Princeton, New Jersey, on the morning of November 6, 1869. The historic McGill–Harvard football match of 1870, which pitted a Canadian university against an American university, would not have been played without the convenience of railway transportation. Throughout the final decades of the nineteenth century, intercollegiate athletic teams depended on the railroad to transport teams and supporters to football, baseball, and rowing events as well as to other collegiate athletic contests.

Fledgling professional baseball clubs made use of the rapidly expanding railroad network in the 1870s, and the organization of the National League in 1876 became possible primarily because of the continued development of connecting lines. As major league baseball developed, the formation of teams followed the network of rail lines, a pattern that remained basically undisturbed until the late 1950s, when teams began to travel by air.

Many other sporting pursuits were fostered by railroad development after 1865. Widespread interest in thoroughbred and trotting racing was in large part sustained by the expansion of the railway system. Interregional races became possible, and horses and spectators were carried from all over the country to track races. The rail lines capitalized on public interest in prizefighting, too, despite its illegality, and frequently scheduled excursion trains for important bouts. America's first heavyweight champion, John L. Sullivan, acquired his popularity largely through his train tours to various parts of the country.

TECHNOLOGICAL INNOVATION AND SPORT: COMMUNICATION

The Atlantic cable, successfully laid in 1866 by Cyrus Field, did for intercontinental news what the telegraph had done for national communication. The cable reduced the time necessary to send a message between Europe and North America from ten days (by steamship) to a moment or so. This advance in communication was a boon to sports enthusiasts because it overcame the frustration of having to wait two or three weeks to get sports results from England and the rest of Europe.

In 1869, when the Harvard crew traveled to England to row against Oxford on the Thames River, enormous national interest centered on the match. Along the sidewalks in New York, the Harvard–Oxford race was the main topic of conversation. According to a New York newspaper reporting on the event, the results of the race were "flashed through the Atlantic cable as to reach New York about a quarter past one, while the news reached the Pacific Coast about nine o'clock, enabling many of the San Franciscans to discuss the subject at their breakfast tables, and swallow the defeat with their coffee."[20] All this was the culmination of a campaign in transatlantic news coverage that had begun months earlier and served as the first real test of the Atlantic cable. The combination of telegraph and Atlantic cable aroused great interest in international sport.

The major communications breakthrough in the latter part of the nineteenth century was the telephone, which was first exhibited at the Centennial

Exposition in Philadelphia in 1876. There, Alexander Graham Bell demonstrated that an electrical instrument could transmit the human voice. Although at first most people thought of the telephone as a plaything, business and industrial leaders saw its possibilities for maintaining communication with their far-flung interests.

Newspapers were one of the first businesses to make extensive use of telephone service, and the sports departments founded by many of the newspapers in the last two decades of the nineteenth century depended on the telephone to obtain the results of sports events. By the end of the century, the telephone was an indispensable part of sports journalism.

The expansion of sports journalism in the latter three decades of the nineteenth century related not only to the universal use of telegraphy by publishers, which made possible instantaneous reporting of sports events, but also to the realization by editors of the popular interest in sports. Indeed, sport emerged as such a standard topic of conversation that newspapers and magazines extended their coverage of it in the 1880s and 1890s.

At the same time, the number of newspapers in the United States increased sixfold between 1870 and 1900 (from 387 to 2,326), and their combined circulation rose from 3.5 million to 15 million. Publishers and editors recognized the growing interest in sport and began to cater to it to win large circulations. New York papers such as the *Herald*, the *Sun*, and the *World* devoted enough attention to sports that a new form of reporter, the sports journalist, emerged. It remained, however, for William Randolph Hearst to develop the first sports section for his paper, the *New York Journal*.[21]

The publication of various kinds of books about sports increased in the mid-nineteenth century, too. Athletic almanacs and dime novels extolling the exploits of athletes and sportsmen grew in popularity. Two books by Thomas Hughes, *Tom Brown at Rugby* and *Tom Brown at Oxford*, were responsible for a rising desire for sports fiction. In 1896 Gilbert Patten began pouring out a story a week of the heroic achievements of a fictional athlete by the name of Frank Merriwell to meet the demand for boys' sports stories. At the height of Frank Merriwell's popularity, circulation reached an estimated 200,000 copies per week. Before he was through, Patten had produced 208 titles, which sold an estimated 25 million copies.[22]

TECHNOLOGICAL INNOVATION AND EQUIPMENT TO PLAY MODERN SPORTS

Modern sports are dependent on inexpensive and dependable equipment for their popularity. Corporate organization and basic production of goods developed in sport just as they did in other industries. Although the manufacturing and merchandising of sporting goods were still in the pioneer stage of development in the late nineteenth century, much of the growing popularity of sport and outdoor recreation was the result of technological advances that made possible the standardized manufacture of bicycles, billiard tables, baseball equipment, sporting rifles, fishing rods, and numerous other items.

The first major sporting goods corporation was formed in 1876 by Albert G. Spalding, a former pitcher for the Boston and Chicago baseball clubs. Beginning with baseball equipment, he branched out into various other sports. By the end of the century, A. G. Spalding and Brothers Company had a virtual monopoly in athletic goods. Department stores, led by Macy's of New York City, began carrying sporting goods on a large scale around the early 1880s. Sears, Roebuck devoted eighty pages of its 1895 catalog to sporting equipment.[23]

With the rising popularity of numerous sports in the twentieth century, advances in technology that have made possible the introduction of newer and better equipment, and improved manufacturing and distribution methods, the sporting goods industry has become a multimillion-dollar-a-year industry. Several large corporations control a major portion of the business, but with the proliferation of sports, many small companies also produce a variety of sports equipment.

OTHER TECHNOLOGICAL BREAKTHROUGHS AND SPORT

Other technological advances had a marked, although perhaps less obvious, influence on the transformation of sport. Improvements in photography developed rapidly in the years following the Civil War, as cumbersome equipment was replaced by the more mobile Eastman Kodak, which also produced clearer pictures. Indeed, sport played an important role in the early development and popularization of the camera. In 1872 professional photographer Eadweard Muybridge, known for his pioneering work on animal locomotion, made the first successful attempt to record the illusion of motion by photography. He was interested in discovering whether a trotting horse leaves the ground entirely at some point in its gait (it does). By setting up a battery of cameras that went off sequentially, he successfully photographed the movements of the horse. The clarity of these pictures led Muybridge to realize that his technique could be extended to analyze the movements of all kinds of species. He subsequently photographed a host of walking and running animals. His monumental eleven-volume study, titled *Animal Locomotion* (1887), included thousands of pictures of horses, birds, and even human athletes. Other experimenters gradually perfected the techniques that gave birth to the true motion picture.

We have already described how advances in the use of electricity led to important developments in communication, but the use of electricity to produce light had an equally significant impact on sport. When Thomas A. Edison invented the incandescent bulb in 1879, he inaugurated a new era in the social life of North Americans. With the invention of the light bulb, sports events for the first time could be held at night. Within a few years, electric lighting and more comfortable accommodations helped lure athletes and spectators into school and college gymnasiums and into public arenas and stadiums.

Prizefights, walking contests, horse shows, wrestling matches, basketball games, ice hockey games, curling matches, and other sports began to be held indoors in lighted facilities. Madison Square Garden in New York City had electric lights by the mid-1880s (the current Madison Square Garden is its fourth incarnation), where they were used for a variety of sports events. Much of the appeal of indoor sporting events was directly attributed to the transformation that electric lighting made in the night-life of the cities.

One final example of the part an invention has played in sport is the vulcanization of rubber by Charles Goodyear in the 1830s. It eventually influenced equipment and apparel in every sport. Elastic and resilient rubber balls changed the nature of every sport in which they were used; equipment made with rubber altered many tactics and techniques. The pneumatic tire developed in the 1880s revolutionized cycling and harness racing in the following decade, and it played a vital role in the rise and spectacular appeal of auto racing.

THE CULT OF MANLINESS AND SPORT

The technological, social, and occupational changes of the nineteenth century prompted concern about the impact of modernization on traditional cultural male roles and behavior. There was mounting evidence that modernization was indeed altering institutions of socialization and drastically changing traditional male roles and responsibilities. Writers, educators, and influential national leaders expressed fear that men were losing "masculine" traits—such as toughness, courage, ruggedness, and hardiness—to effeminacy. There were even worries about the future of the United States if men lost their masculine traits. Various organizations—the Boy Scouts, the YMCA, and athletic clubs—arose to promote a broadly based devotion to manly ideals to toughen up boys for life's challenges.

Within this perceived threat to masculinity, sport, with its demands for individual competition and physical challenge, was advocated as an important preparation for manhood. In towns and cities throughout the United States, sport rose as a counterforce to what many men saw as the "feminization" of American civilization. Sport was seen as a sanctuary from the world of female gentility; it catered to men who felt a need to demonstrate their manhood. Organized sport participation had become a prominent source for male identity and a primary basis for gender division.

The cult of manliness became pervasive in the upper and middle classes and rapidly trickled down to working-class social life. One sport historian declared, "The frequency with which writers began to assert that sport could serve as a means of promoting manliness was in direct response to both the impact of modernization on urban society and the role of modernization in redefining the masculine role and creating a new middle-class view of proper sexual behavior."[24]

Defining sport as an inculcator of manliness had the effect of discouraging women from all but a few sports—and women could participate in those only in moderation. Indeed, women who wished to participate in competitive sports and remain "feminine" faced almost certain social isolation and censure.

Of course, it was not just the cult of manliness that discouraged female involvement in sport. Responsibility for domestic labor and childrearing weighed heavily against women's engagement in sport as either participants or spectators. Victorian attitudes and religious moral codes also militated against sport for women. Despite these obstacles, many upper-class and college women were ardent participants in croquet, archery, lawn tennis, rowing, and bicycling (see Box 2.3).

MUSCULAR CHRISTIANITY AND INTELLECTUALS

In parallel with the cult of manliness, another cultural trend was gaining attention. The grasp of religion on the early-nineteenth-century mind was so strong and conservative that sport could penetrate only the periphery of social life. But reaction to the Puritan belief that pleasure was the companion of sin emerged when liberal and humanitarian reform became a major concern. One aspect of the social reform that became known as the "Muscular Christianity Movement" was

the effort to improve the physical health of the population. The crusaders noted that a great deal of human misery was the result of poor health, and they believed that people would be happier and more productive if they engaged in sport to promote physical fitness and enhance leisure.

Muscular spirituality leaders were highly respected persons, willing to risk their positions and reputations on behalf of exercise and sport. The Beecher families, famous for their Christian reform positions, were among the first active crusaders for exercise and sport. Catharine Beecher wrote a book in 1832 entitled *Course of Calisthenics for Young Ladies*, but her most influential book was *A Manual of Physiology and Calisthenics for Schools and Families*, published in 1856. This book not only advocated physical exercise for girls as well as for boys but also promoted the introduction of physical education into American schools.

Throughout the second half of the nineteenth century, physical activity continued to be supported by many respected persons. Noted author Oliver Wendell Holmes claimed that more participation in sport would improve everything in American life, from sermons of the clergy to the physical well-being of individuals. Equally vigorous in his advocacy of sport was the renowned Ralph Waldo Emerson, whose status in the intellectual community served to increase the impact of his support. The combined attention of the clergy, social reformers, and intellectuals to the need for physical fitness and wholesome leisure had a favorable effect on public attitudes because sport suddenly became important to many people, especially the young, who had previously shunned it.[25]

BOX 2.3   *THINKING ABOUT SPORT:* WOMEN ON BICYCLES

For women of the latter nineteenth century the first struggle was for the right to ride a bicycle, because there was a segment of society that staunchly believed that physical activity should remain a man's world and that women should refrain from active pursuits. Susan B. Anthony, a prominent American civil rights activist who played a pivotal role in the nineteenth-century women's rights movement, described the socially

significant role the bicycle had in advancing women's status: "Let me tell you what I think of bicycling. I think it has done more to emancipate women than anything else in the world. It gives women a feeling of freedom and self-reliance. I stand and rejoice every time I see a woman ride by on a wheel . . . the picture of free, untrammeled womanhood."

Source: Quoted in Sue Macy, "The Devil's Advance Agent," *American History* 46, no. 4 (October 2011): 45.

SOCIAL PHILOSOPHY AND ORGANIZED SPORT

The profound changes in interpersonal relations created by the technological and industrial revolutions required that moral and social justifications be sought for the role of capitalism, the economic system in which trade and industry are controlled by private owners for profit. Leading capitalists found their chief justification in two related ideas: the gospel of wealth and social Darwinism. According to the gospel of wealth, great rewards awaited those who applied themselves and followed the rules. Money and success are the just rewards for hard work, thrift, and sobriety; the mass of humanity remains poor because of their own laziness and natural inferiority. Government, according to this notion, should merely preserve order and protect property; it should leave control over the economy to the natural aristocracy, who have won and hold their leadership in the competitive struggle of the marketplace.

Social Darwinism, probably the most important social philosophy in the latter third of the nineteenth century, supplied a biological explanation for the gospel of wealth. As an integrated philosophy, it was largely the product of the fertile mind of the British political theorist and sociologist Herbert Spencer. Spencer was profoundly impressed by Charles Darwin's findings in the field of biology, and he constructed his system on Darwin's principles of the survival of the fittest. Darwin had reported that in the animal world an ongoing, fierce struggle for survival destroys the weak, rewards the strong, and produces evolutionary change. Struggle, destruction, and the survival of the fit, Spencer argued, are essential to progress in human societies as well. The weak threaten the road to progress and deserve to perish. The strong survive because they are superior.

Spencer's theories had great popularity and markedly penetrated American thought. American historian Richard Hofstadter claimed that "American society saw its own image in the tooth-and-claw version of natural selection and . . . its dominant groups were therefore able to dramatize this vision of competition as a thing good in itself."[26] This was the case for several reasons but perhaps chiefly because social Darwinism clearly suited the needs of the ruling business interests. It justified the "success ethic" in the name of progress; it justified economic warfare, poverty, exploitation, and suffering as the survival of the fittest.

The chief American expositor of social Darwinism was William Graham Sumner, who in 1875 at Yale taught one of the first sociology courses in the United States. Sumner based his sociology on the notion that human life encounters formidable obstacles and threats to its survival. There is a fundamental struggle to "win" (a favorite word of Sumner's) under the conditions imposed by nature. In this process humans always compete with others. Sumner argued, "Every man who stands on the earth's surface excludes every one else from so much of it as he covers; everyone who eats a loaf of bread appropriates to himself for the time being the exclusive use and enjoyment of so many square feet of the earth's surface as were required to raise the wheat."[27]

Sumner linked competition to the emergence of virtues, such as those of perseverance and hard work, which were presumed to be answers to the struggle against nature. Winning was seen as the just reward of the superior individual; losing was viewed as the overt manifestation of inferiority.

A number of observers have noted that the rise of highly organized sport coincided with the emergent popularity of social Darwinism and that the high degree of emphasis on winning games demonstrated in American sport is an orientation congruent with this social philosophy. American football players often remark that success in their sport is like "the law of the jungle" or "the survival of the fittest."

TWENTIETH AND TWENTY-FIRST CENTURIES: THE MODERN WORLD AND SPORT

The United States witnessed a population explosion in the twentieth century; it began the century with 76 million and ended it with a population in excess of 281 million and an urban population of around 85 percent of the total. The concentration of large groups of people in towns that soon would become thriving cities made it possible for sport to be transformed from informal and spontaneous events to organized, highly competitive activities. In other words, industrialization and urbanization were major contributors to the rise of sport, greatly enhanced, of course, by the revolutionary transformations in communication, transportation, and other technological advances.

THE MATURING OF MODERN SPORT

The final three decades of the nineteenth century saw the rising tide of sports begin to take a place in the lives of Americans, but it was in the first half of the twentieth century that the sporting spirit became a prominent part of the social life of large numbers of people. Between 1900 and World War II, sport became the most pervasive popular cultural practice in the United States. See Box 2.4 for the rise of disability sport.

Urban areas fostered sport through better transportation facilities, a growing affluent class, a higher standard of living, more discretionary funds for purchasing sporting equipment, and the ease with which leagues and teams could be organized. The wealthy were no longer the only people with the leisure and the means to enjoy recreational pursuits. Working-class persons gradually won shorter working hours and higher wages, enabling them to spend larger sums of discretionary money on entertainment, one form of which was sport.

Thus, sport discarded its aristocratic trappings and rapidly emerged as a popular form of entertainment and recreation. James Bryce, a British observer of American life in 1905, wrote, "[Sport] occupies the minds not only of the youth at the universities, but also of their parents and of the general public. Baseball matches and football matches excite an interest greater than any other public events except the Presidential election, and that comes only once

---

BOX 2.4 *THINKING ABOUT SPORT*: TECHNOLOGY AND SOCIAL VALUES: THE RISE OF DISABILITY SPORTS

Two major factors have impacted the rise of organized disability sport. First is technology. Similar to able-bodied sports, technology has given rise to different sports including wheelchair sports, implements used for skiing, and the technology of prostheses. Another major factor is social values embedded in democracy: the right for all people to participate in society. The other major social value is the benefits of participating in sport, including physical, psychological, and social health. But the main catalyst for disability sport was World War II. So many people were permanently injured from the war that a rehab and sport industry grew to address these folks' physical activity needs. The Olympics involved some disability sport events in tandem with their games in the summer of 1960 and for winter sports in 1976. Many organizations for people with specific disabilities worked together and over the years evolved into the International Paralympic Committee (1989). In the United States, the governing body for Olympic and Paralympic sport is called the United States Olympic Committee.

With regard to the United States, one of the oldest and most effective organizations supporting and promoting sports for people with disabilities is the nonprofit National Sports Center for the Disabled (NSCD), which began in 1970 with children with amputations from Children's Hospital in Denver, Colorado. Currently, participants come to the NSCD from all fifty states and from countries all over the world. They can choose from among twenty winter and summer sports, from skiing and snowshoeing to river rafting and rock climbing. More than 23,000 lessons are provided annually. The NSCD Competition Program is the largest of its kind in North America. The program has been successful at attracting and training some of the best ski racers with disabilities and placing them on the U.S. Disabled Ski Team. Twelve of the NSCD-sponsored thirty-four athletes who competed in the Winter Paralympic Games in Sochi brought home fifteen medals in their respective sport.

Another national organization serving the needs of the disabled is Disabled Sports USA, which was founded in 1967 by disabled Vietnam veterans. It was first called the National Amputee Skiers Association, but after going through a series of names, it settled on its present one. Activities include winter skiing, water sports, summer and winter competitions, and fitness and special sports events. Participants include those with visual impairments, amputations, spinal cord injury, dwarfism, multiple sclerosis, head injury, cerebral palsy, and other neuromuscular and orthopedic conditions. Recently, Disabled Sports USA and Adaptive Sports USA merged under the umbrella of Move United. This organization is aligned with the U.S. Olympic and Paralympic Committee.

Sources: For a thorough description of the programs of the NSCD, go to its website at http://www.nscd.org/; see also Nigel Thomas and Andy Smith, *Disability, Sport and Society: An Introduction* (New York: Routledge, 2009); Dikaia Chatziefstathiou, Borja García, and Benoit Séguin, eds., *Routledge Handbook of the Olympic and Paralympic Games* (London: Routledge, 2021); Brett Smith, ed., *Paralympics and Disability Sport* (London: Routledge, 2014).

in four years. . . . The American love of excitement and love of competition has seized upon these games."[28]

No single event heralded the beginning of what has been designated the era of modern sports, but the Roaring Twenties acted as a bridge connecting the old pastimes to twentieth-century sport. Sport seemed to be the most engrossing of all social interests in the 1920s; it became a bandwagon around which students and alumni, business and transportation interests, advertising and amusement industries, cartoonists and artists, novelists and sports columnists rallied. Indeed, the 1920s are still looked upon by some sport historians as sport's golden age. Some of America's most famous athletes rose to prominence during those years: Babe Ruth, the "Sultan of Swat"; Knute Rockne and the "Four Horsemen of Notre Dame"; Jack Dempsey, heavyweight boxing champion; Bill Tilden and Helen Wills Moody in tennis; and Bobby Jones and Glenna Collett in golf. In

Canada, Howie Morenz, James Ball, Ethel Catherwood, Bobbie Rosenfeld, and Myrtle Cook thrilled the masses with their sports achievements. These are only a few of the coaches and athletes who contributed to the growing popularity of sports.[29] See Box 2.5 for the story of Jim Thorpe, perhaps the greatest athlete of that era.

From the 1920s onward, sport increasingly became a pervasive part of American life, penetrating every level of the educational systems and the programs of social agencies and private clubs. This became especially true of the business world; sport affected such areas of the economic system as finance, fashion, mass media, transportation, communication, advertising, the sporting goods industry, and a variety of marginal enterprises that profit from sport.

United States business and labor organizations contributed to the rise of sport through organized industrial recreation programs for millions of workers. During the nineteenth century, most industrial leaders

---

BOX 2.5 *THINKING ABOUT SPORT:* JIM THORPE, THE ORIGINAL ALL-AMERICAN

Despite the sports achievements of the athletes most frequently identified as the greatest of their era, a persuasive case can be made that Jim Thorpe's achievements surpassed all others of the twentieth century. Thorpe excelled in not one but several sports at the highest level. Accordingly, in 1950 the Associated Press named Thorpe the greatest athlete of the first half of the twentieth century. In 1999, he was ranked third on the Associated Press list of top athletes of the twentieth century. And from 1996 to 2001, he was repeatedly awarded ABC's Wide World of Sports Athlete of the Century award.

Jim Thorpe was a Native American born and raised on the Sauk and Fox Nation reservation in Oklahoma. In 1904, as a teenager, Thorpe enrolled at the Carlisle Indian School in Carlisle, Pennsylvania. Following a hiatus of several years, he returned to Carlisle, and his athletic career took off under the coaching of "Pop" Warner, one of the most renowned American college football coaches at that time. The little-known and little-respected Carlisle football team nevertheless played against the best college teams in the country. In 1911 and 1912, Jim Thorpe played both offense and defense and was also the team's kicker and leading tackler. In 1911, he scored all of Carlisle's points in an 18–15 upset of Harvard while leading Carlisle to an 11–1 season. In 1912, he made 25 touchdowns and 198 total points and led Carlisle to the national collegiate championship. Thorpe was chosen as an All-American in both 1911 and 1912.

Thorpe's sports achievements were not limited to football. He was one of the most versatile athletes in modern sports. In 1912 he won a place on the U.S. Olympic track-and-field team, and at the Olympic Games in Stockholm, Sweden, he won Olympic gold medals in the pentathlon and decathlon. However, when it was discovered that he had played two seasons of semiprofessional baseball before competing in the Olympics, thus violating the Olympic amateur rules, his Olympic titles and medals were revoked. However, in 1983, thirty years after Thorpe's death, the International Olympic Committee restored Thorpe's status as an amateur, and duplicated Olympic medals in his name were given to the Thorpe family.

Between 1913 and 1919 Thorpe played major league baseball for the New York Giants, the Cincinnati Reds, and the Boston Braves. While playing major league baseball, Thorpe continued to play football. In all, Thorpe played with six different teams during his career as a professional football player, ending with a stint with the Chicago Cardinals in 1929, when he retired at the age of forty-one.

Perhaps the most impressive manifestation of Jim Thorpe's athletic stature is that he was inducted into the College Football Hall of Fame, the Pro Football Hall of Fame, and the Track & Field Hall of Fame. No other athlete of the twentieth century comes near that accomplishment.

Sources: Kate Buford, *Native American Son: The Life and Sporting Legend of Jim Thorpe* (New York: Random House, 2012); William A. Cook, *Jim Thorpe: A Biography* (Jefferson, NC: McFarland, 2011).

showed little interest in the health and welfare of their employees; by the beginning of the twentieth century, however, voices inside and outside industry were pleading for consideration of the worker as a human being, with special focus on the worker's physical and mental health. Business and labor leaders began to realize that perhaps opportunities for diversion, whether in intellectual or recreational directions, might enhance employee health and morale and increase productivity.

The idea of providing company-sponsored recreation as a phase of business management caught on, and programs of all sorts came into existence. By the 1950s thousands of companies were sponsoring various forms of industrial recreation with more than 20 million employees participating. From the 1930s to the 1950s, the best amateur teams in basketball, baseball, and softball were company-sponsored teams. The National Industrial Basketball League included the Phillips 66ers, the Goodyear Wingfoots, and the Peoria Caterpillars. Championships in the National Baseball Congress and Amateur Softball Association were dominated by company-sponsored teams.

Industrial employee recreation programs have grown enormously over the past fifty years, and today industry spends more on sports equipment than all schools and colleges combined. Three-fourths of all firms employing more than a thousand people have some form of exercise and sports program, and more than 10,000 companies now have full- or part-time recreation managers.

Labor unions, originally formed to acquire better pay and working conditions for industrial employees, gradually broadened their interests to include the health and mental welfare of their members. The United Automobile Workers established a recreation department in 1937 based on a strong policy of organized recreation for all ages. Other unions have programs that include almost everything in the way of leisure-time activities. Among these are team and individual sports, social functions, dancing instruction, handicrafts, orchestras, and hobby clubs.

Two major developments in sport characterize the past thirty years: the colossal expansion of amateur and professional sports and the boom in participant sports. Amateur sports, from youth to intercollegiate athletic programs, have multiplied at a bewildering pace. Baseball and football in the United States were once about the only sports sponsored for youth, but now there are organized youth programs in more than twenty-five sports—from swimming to motor bicycling—and it is possible for children as young as six years of age to win a national championship. High school and collegiate programs, which used to be limited to three or four sports for males, have now been expanded to include fifteen to twenty sports for both males and females.

Professional sports teams are corporate organizations that function similarly in many respects to corporations of any other kind, albeit with certain tax and monopolistic advantages not given to other businesses. In 1922 the U.S. Supreme Court exempted baseball from antitrust legislation. Since that time owners of baseball and other professional sports teams have used that decision, and more recent ones, to define their special legal and economic position. (The legal and economic position of corporate sport is more fully discussed in Chapter 11.)

The first professional baseball team was player owned and player controlled, but major league teams were organized into business corporations in the latter part of the nineteenth century and continue as business enterprises made up of separate corporations under a cartel form of organization. The National Football League (NFL) began in 1920, and industry had a hand in its development. The Acme Packing Company in Green Bay, Wisconsin, sponsored a local team, which was fittingly called the Packers; and in Decatur, Illinois, the A. E. Staley Manufacturing Company started the team that became known as the Chicago Bears. From these humble beginnings, professional football is now a multibillion-dollar-a-year business, and most of the franchises in the NFL are worth more than $1 billion each.[30]

Ice hockey is another team sport that first became popular in the late 1800s, but its early development took place in Canada rather than in the United States. The first professional hockey team was formed in 1903, and the first professional league was established a year later. In 1917 the National Hockey League (NHL) was organized.

The first rules for basketball were composed in 1891 by James Naismith, a physical training instructor at what is now Springfield College. Basketball quickly became popular in secondary schools and colleges, especially women's colleges; by the 1920s, teams of paid players were touring the United States. But it was not until after World War II that a stable professional league was established: in 1949 the National Basketball Association (NBA) was organized.

Over the course of the twentieth century more than a dozen professional team sport leagues were formed, but the Big Five—consisting of baseball, ice hockey, football, soccer, and basketball—have retained an enduring dominance in spectator attendance and general popularity. Table 2.1 outlines the origins of America's leading professional sports.

On-site spectator sports in the United States have gross paid admissions of an estimated $33.1 billion per year. Some 45 million admissions are paid to horse racing, 73 million to professional baseball, 22 million to professional basketball, 22 million to the NHL, 49 million to college football, 44 million to college basketball (men's and women's), and about 18 million to professional football.[31] These figures are, of course, dwarfed by the number of people who watch televised sports events.

TABLE 2.1 ORIGINS OF THE MAJOR PROFESSIONAL TEAM SPORTS LEAGUES

League	Founding year
Baseball	
National League	1876
American League	1901
Soccer	
MLS	1996
Hockey	
National Hockey League	1917
Football	
National Football League	1920
Basketball	
National Basketball Association	1949

Participant sports, the second main development of the past generation, have been products of increased leisure and income. The construction of facilities and the manufacture of equipment inexpensive enough for the large mass of working-class people have had an important impact on participant sports. Moreover, a concerned awareness of the increasingly sedentary lifestyle of persons in all socioeconomic strata and of the rise in diseases related to this lifestyle has stimulated mass participation in sport and exercise.

Perhaps most remarkable is the running boom that has swept the United States, where there are more than 25 million runners/joggers. Virtually every major city has a marathon that draws thousands of runners (e.g., Boston, New York, Portland, Atlanta). Even allowing for a considerable margin of error in the participation reports, sport involves an enormous number of people. Increased leisure and income are undoubtedly the main causes for the extraordinary development of participant sport in the current generation.

TWENTIETH-CENTURY TECHNOLOGY AND SPORT: TRANSPORTATION

By the beginning of the twentieth century, almost every realm of American social life, including sport, shared in the powerful impact of the railroad, and in the years leading up to World War II this influence continued unabated. Perhaps one of the most significant contributions of the railroad to sport in the twentieth century was the opening of new areas for recreation. For example, the initial stimulus for the popularization of skiing was the "snow train."

The first snow train left Boston's North Station in 1931. Four years later such trains were leaving New York's Grand Central Station; on board were thousands of ski enthusiasts intent on spending a weekend on the slopes of New England. Railroads were responsible for the development and promotion of a number of America's most popular winter sports resorts in the western states and provinces.

As important as the railroads were to improving transportation and stimulating industrialization, their impact on the social life and transportation habits of Americans was minuscule compared to that of the development of the automobile. This invention and subsequently that of the airplane resulted in two modes of transportation that revolutionized travel and numerous other aspects of life.

In addition to their contributions to transportation, the automobile and airplane created new industries involving billions of dollars in capital and employing millions of workers. They stimulated the construction of millions of miles of highways, and they spawned many industries and occupations related to auto and aircraft production and use. The growth of metropolitan areas, especially suburban and satellite towns outside large cities, was also stimulated by the automobile.

Inventors in Europe and the United States had successfully developed an internal combustion engine powered by gasoline by the last decade of the nineteenth century. Initially, however, there was little general interest in the converted bicycles that were the first automobiles because they were used either for racing or as a toy for the rich. Then a young man by the name of Henry Ford saw the potential of the automobile as a means of popular transportation. Realizing that he would have to gain financial backing for the auto through racing, he built a huge-engine racing car, the "999," and hired a professional bicycle rider by the name of Barney Oldfield to race it. After the 999 easily won against its challengers, the 999 did what it was intended to do: it advertised the fact that Henry Ford could build a fast motorcar. A week after the race he formed the Ford Motor Company.[32]

Racing was the first and foremost attraction of the automobile in the days when its usefulness for any other purpose was questioned. In 1895 H. H. Kohlsaat, publisher of the *Chicago Times–Herald*, sponsored the first automobile race in America; automobile races had already become a fad in Europe. Early automobile manufacturers recognized the commercial value of races and used them as a major marketing technique to win public interest. This aspect of automobile racing continues. Throughout the twentieth century, automobile racing grew in popularity and included a bewildering array of

forms—midget autos, stock cars, hot rods, drag racing, NASCAR, and so forth. Annual NASCAR revenue is significant and has been estimated at $100 million.

The automobile contributed to the rise of sport in many ways beyond racing. It was a significant instrument for cultural change to the modern lifestyle. For countless millions, it progressively opened broader horizons of spectator and participant sport. It provided an easy means of transportation from city to city and from the country to the town or city. Thus, large stadiums and other sports facilities could be conveniently reached by large groups of people. Also, for the first time, golf courses, ski resorts, tennis courts, bathing beaches, and areas for such field sports as fishing, camping, and hunting were within practical reach of large masses of the population. All this would have been impossible without the transportation provided by the automobile.

In 1903 Orville and Wilbur Wright successfully flew an airplane, but it was not until World War I that airplanes were used on a large scale, first for scouting enemy movements and later in actual combat. During the 1920–1940 era, aircraft design was improved, airports were constructed, and regular passenger, mail, and express lines were established. World War II provided for further development, and soon airplanes became the prominent mode of long-distance public transportation. Airplanes have in effect shrunk the continent—actually, the world—by reducing traveling time.

Until about the mid-1950s, most professional and collegiate athletic teams traveled by rail. With improvements in all phases of air transportation, the airplane became the common carrier of teams. The expansion of professional sports franchises from the East and Midwest into the West and the South and the increased number of pro sports teams could only have been achieved with air travel. Interregional collegiate football and basketball games were rare until air travel made it possible to take long trips in a short period of time. Interregional contests then became a part of the weekly schedule of collegiate sports.

Auto racing traces its roots to the creation of the first gas-fueled autos in the late nineteenth century. The Indianapolis 500 is a U.S. automobile race held annually since 1911 (except for the war years 1917–1918 and 1942–1945). The race always takes place at the Indianapolis Motor Speedway in Indianapolis, Indiana It draws crowds of several hundred thousand people and is among the world's best-attended single-day sporting events. It is held on the weekend of the U.S. Memorial Day holiday. (Photo: Heritage Image Partnership Ltd/Alamy Stock Photo)

THE TECHNOLOGICAL REVOLUTION AND SPORT: COMMUNICATION

Mass communication is the glue that serves to integrate people into their society, and it has helped shape and mold the development and popularity of the sport culture. In 1896 an Italian scientist, Marchese Guglielmo Marconi, patented the wireless technology and showed the possibility of telegraphy without the use of wires. Within a few years, wireless telegraphy was carrying messages to all parts of the world.

One of the first stories to be covered by wireless was a sports event. Marconi was hired by the Associated Press in 1899 to report on the international yacht race involving Scotland's Sir Thomas Lipton's *Shamrock* and America's *Columbia*. Thus, wireless communication took its place along with the telegraph and the telephone in intensifying public interest in sport and stimulating the rise of sport.

The next important step in electrical communication was the radio, which until 1920 was mainly a toy for amateur scientists. However, in 1920 a radio station in Pittsburgh began broadcasting, and a new communication medium and industry was under way. Radio broadcasting of sports events actually preceded the beginning of public broadcasting. On August 20, 1920, the radio station of the *Detroit News* went on the air to announce the results of the World Series baseball games. This was before the first public radio station in Pittsburgh made its initial broadcast in November of that year. Also in 1920, the first college football game was broadcast from a station in Texas.[33]

Radio came of age in the hectic 1920s, and although music and news broadcasts were the standard programs, sports events were rapidly absorbed into the entertainment schedule. One sports history analyst declared, "Broadcast radio . . . joined the roiling swirl of sports ballyhoo. . . . Radio not only gave distant fans their first real-time play-by-play accounts, the medium also created the first true national audience. Radio was one of the last components in creating the period's mass culture."[34] Radio and sports were indeed natural partners. Radio dominated broadcasting during the 1930s and 1940s; it was not until the early 1950s that television began to overshadow radio in providing information and home entertainment. Persons under the age of forty have grown up watching television; it is just taken for granted. Indeed, most American homes currently have at least one television set, with these sets being used for several hours each day. Some media experts claim that college students today spend more waking hours watching television than doing any other single thing.

Although television had been experimentally developed prior to World War II, it was not until the late 1940s that technology and marketing combined to produce models for home use. The major television boom occurred in the early 1950s; by 1957 television was a fixture in most households and no longer a novelty. As television sets became available to the public and the broadcasting of programs expanded, it quickly became evident that televised sports events would be immensely popular, and television continually expanded its coverage of sports. More will be said about the television–sport nexus in Chapter 12.

Broadcasting of sports started with descriptions of play sent via telegraph in the 1890s. The first radio broadcast of a baseball game occurred in August 1921 over KDKA from Pittsburgh's Forbes Field. The game was between the Pittsburgh Pirates and the Philadelphia Phillies. The first play-by-play radio broadcast of the MLB World Series was in 1922. In Canada, the first radio broadcast of an ice hockey game took place in 1923 with the broadcast of the third period of a game between Midland and North Toronto of the Ontario Hockey Association. (Photo: Associated Press)

During the first half of the twentieth century, as the United States' population grew and urbanization expanded, newspapers flourished and the sports page became an indispensable part of every newspaper. The same sport history analyst we quoted previously noted, "Better information distribution helped foster increased sports coverage. News syndicates, newspaper chains, and wire services facilitated widespread dissemination of event reporting. Individual papers didn't have to send a reporter to the game any longer, because they could just buy the Associated Press (AP) write-up."[35] From a concentration on a few sports, such as baseball, college football, horse racing, and boxing, attention was gradually given to an enormously wide range of sports. Currently, many newspaper publishers believe that the sports section is the most important factor in a newspaper's circulation.

Along with the newspaper, magazines and books have done much to attract attention to sports in the past century and a half. Even before the American Civil War, a host of turf journals appeared; many periodicals were also devoted to field sports and outdoor life. Sports journals proliferated in the late nineteenth century, so that almost every sport had at least one periodical devoted to it. This trend has continued, and a substantial portion of shelf space in newsstands is occupied by magazines about sports. (More will be said about this in Chapter 12.)

In its early years the motion picture industry concentrated primarily on boxing. The first commercial motion picture was a six-round bout between Young Griffo and Battling Barnett in 1895. Motion pictures of boxing championships were one of the most popular forms of spectator sport in the first three decades of the twentieth century and served to stimulate the public appetite for organized sports. In recent years videotapes, computers, high-speed cameras, and an array of photo communication instruments have become indispensable to coaches for scouting opponents and for reviewing the performances of their own athletes. Collegiate and professional coaches of some sports spend as much time electronically viewing as they spend on almost any other coaching task.

The impact of the still camera cannot be overlooked either. Beginning in the early years of the twentieth century, newspapers and magazines made extensive use of pictures to show the performance of athletes in the heat of competition or to illustrate the correct (or incorrect) method of performing a skill. The popularity of sports magazines, especially *Sports Illustrated*, is largely a result of the superb photographs that are part of each issue. This has had the effect of further nurturing sports by keeping them in the public eye.

OTHER TECHNOLOGICAL INNOVATIONS AND SPORT

Although indoor sports were greatly stimulated by electric lighting, baseball, America's national pastime, did not discover the value of this invention until the 1930s. Social historians record 1930 as the year of the emergence of night baseball. The first such ventures took place in Des Moines and Wichita in the summer of 1930. Several minor leagues quickly adopted night baseball, but it was not until 1935 that Cincinnati played the first night major league game. Only in the 1940s did night baseball gain general acceptance in the major leagues; the first World Series night game was not played until 1975. The owner of the Chicago Cubs for many years, Philip K. Wrigley, never accepted night baseball, and lights were not installed at Wrigley Field until the summer of 1988.

SPORT IN EDUCATION

The system of intercollegiate sport is unique to the United States, and it has been one of the most significant forces in the development of American organized sports. High school sports are modeled on this system, and many nonschool youth sports programs have been organized as feeder systems to the high school and college programs. Finally, the intercollegiate programs serve as a farm system for many of the professional sports.[36] (In Chapters 9 and 10 we discuss the topic of sport in education in depth.)

SUMMARY

In this chapter we have reviewed the rise of sport in the United States. Contemporary sports are grounded in political, economic, technological, and social conditions and events of the past. Sports today are possible only because of what has happened in the past, and sports of the future will depend on what happens in today's societies.

Despite overwhelming natural and social barriers that made involvement in games and sporting activities difficult for European colonists in North America, colonists still engaged in a wide variety of playful physical activities. But it was not until the beginning of the nineteenth century that conditions became favorable for organized sports to become a popular cultural practice for large numbers of citizens. Technological innovations and the accompanying industrial revolution were instrumental in stimulating a transformation in social conditions that gave rise to modern sport. Urbanization was also a significant factor because the evolution of modern sports in the United States became possible only with large urban populations scattered across the continent. During the nineteenth century, influential persons among the clergy and the intelligentsia, as well as social reformers, helped develop the attitudes, values, and beliefs that are the foundation of modern sport in both countries.

During the first half of the twentieth century, sport became a pervasive part of American life, penetrating every level of the educational systems and the economic and cultural systems in the form of professional sports. The two major trends in sport that characterize the past thirty years are the enormous expansion of amateur and professional sports and the burst of growth in participant sports.

Learn more with this chapter's digital tools, including web resources, video links, and chapter self-assessment quizzes at www.oup.com/he/sage-eitzen-beal-atencio-12e.

NOTES

1. Richard O. Davies, *Sports in American Life: A History*, 3rd ed. (New York: Wiley and Blackwell, 2017), 2.

2. Joseph B. Oxendine, *American Indian Sports Heritage* (Lincoln: University of Nebraska Press, 1995), 3; see also Roxanne Dunbar-Ortiz, *An Indigenous Peoples' History of the United States* (Boston: Beacon Press, 2014); Frank A Salamone, ed., *The Native American Identity in Sports: Creating and Preserving a Culture* (Lanham, MD: Scarecrow Press, 2012).

3. Donald M. Fisher, *Lacrosse: A History of the Game*, reprint ed. (Baltimore: Johns Hopkins University Press, 2011); see also Janice Forsyth and Audrey R Giles, *Aboriginal Peoples and Sport in Canada* (Vancouver: UBC Press, 2013).

4. Bruce C. Daniels, "Sober Mirth and Pleasant Poisons: Puritan Ambivalence toward Leisure and Recreation in Colonial New England," in *Sport in America: From Colonial Leisure to Celebrity Figures and Globalization*, Vol. 2, ed. David K Wiggins (Champaign, IL: Human Kinetics, 2010), 5–21.

5. David K Wiggins, ed. *Sport in America*, Vol. 2, *From Colonial Leisure to Celebrity Figures and Globalization*, 2nd ed. (Champaign, IL: Human Kinetics, 2010); see also Benjamin G. Rader and Pamela Charlene Grady, *American Sports from the Age of Folk Games to the Age of Televised Sports*, 7th ed. (New York: Routledge, 2016).

6. Elliott J. Gorn, "'Gouge and Bite, Pull Hair and Scratch': The Social Significance of Fighting in the Southern Backcountry," in *Sport in America*, Vol. 2, ed. David K Wiggins (Champaign, IL: Human Kinetics, 1995), 35–50.

7. Steven A. Riess, *Sports in America from Colonial Times to the Twenty-First Century: An Encyclopedia*, 3 vols. (New York: Routledge, 2011). For an excellent discussion of Canadian sports and other physical activity during this period, see Don Morrow and Kevin B. Wamsley, *Sport in Canada: A History*, 3rd ed. (New York: Oxford University Press, 2013).

8. Katherine C. Mooney, *Race Horse Men: How Slavery and Freedom Were Made at the Racetrack* (Cambridge, MA: Harvard University Press, 2014); T. H. Breen, "Horses and Gentlemen: The Cultural Significance of Gambling among the Gentry of Virginia," in Wiggins, *Sport in America*, Vol. 2, 23–39. For a good discussion of the swimming feats of slaves during the colonial period, see Kevin Dawson, "Enslaved Swimmers and Divers in the Atlantic World," *Journal of American History* 92 (March 2006): 1327–1355.

9. Michael Zakim and Gary J. Kornblith, eds., *Capitalism Takes Command: The Social Transformation of Nineteenth-Century America* (Chicago: University of Chicago Press, 2012).

10. Maryjean Wall, *How Kentucky Became Southern: A Tale of Outlaws, Horse Thieves, Gamblers, and Breeders* (Lexington: University Press of Kentucky, 2012); Melvin L Adelman, "The First Modern Sport in America: Harness Racing in New York City, 1825–1870," in Wiggins, *Sport in America*, Vol. 2, 5–32.

11. For an extended discussion of this topic, see Morrow and Wamsley, *Sport in Canada: A History*.

12. For an excellent discussion of the *Clermont* steamboat on the Hudson River, see John H.

Hamilton, *Hudson River Pilot: From Steamboats to Super Tankers* (Hensonville, NY: Black Dome Press, 2001), ch. 2.

13. William David Sloan, *The Media in America: A History*, 9th ed. (San Ramon, CA: Vision Press, 2014); Richard C. Crepeau, "Sport, Television and the Media," in *The Routledge History of American Sport*, ed. David K. Wiggins and Gerald R. Gems (New York: Routledge, 2017), 225–267.

14. Rader and Grady, *American Sports*; in 1897 one of these clubs, the Boston Athletic Association, sponsored the first Boston Marathon, now one of the world's premier sports events.

15. There are many histories of baseball, but two of the best are George Vecsey, *Baseball: A History of America's Favorite Game* (New York: Modern Library, 2008), and John Feinstein, *Where Nobody Knows Your Name: Life in the Minor Leagues of Baseball* (New York: Anchor, 2015).

16. Dann Woellert, *Cincinnati Turner Societies: The Cradle of an American Movement* (Charleston, SC: History Press, 2012); see also Annette R. Hofmann, "Lady *Turners* in the United States: German American Identity, Gender Concerns, and *Turnerism*," *Journal of Sport History* 27 (Fall 2000): 383–404.

17. Amos Alonzo Stagg, quoting William Rainey Harper, in a letter to his family dated January 20, 1891, quoted in Richard J. Storr, *Harper's University: The Beginnings* (Chicago: University of Chicago Press, 1966), 179.

18. There is a large literature on the history of railroading in North America, but these two books stand out: Claude Wiatrowski, *Railroads across North America: An Illustrated History* (Minneapolis: Voyageur Press, 2007); and Kevin EuDaly, Mike Schafer, Steve Jessup, Jim Boyd, Steve Glischinski, and Andrew McBride, *The Complete Book of North American Railroading* (Minneapolis: Voyageur Press, 2009).

19. Ronald A. Smith, *Sports and Freedom: The Rise of Big-Time College Athletics* (New York: Oxford University Press, 1990), 27–28.

20. *Frank Leslie's Illustrated Newspaper*, Vol. 29 (New York), September 28, 1869, 2.

21. Sloan, *The Media in America: A History.*

22. Rader and Grady, *American Sports*, 100–101.

23. George H. Sage, "The Sporting Goods Industry: From Struggling Entrepreneurs to National Businesses to Transnational Corporations," in *The Commercialization of Sport*, ed. Trevor Slack (New York: Routledge, 2004), 29–51.

24. Michael Kimmel, *Manhood in America: A Cultural History*, 3rd ed. (New York: Oxford University Press, 2011); see also Clifford Putney, *Muscular Christianity: Manhood and Sports in Protestant America, 1880–1920* (Cambridge, MA: Harvard University Press, 2003).

25. Shirl J. Hoffman, *Good Game: Christianity and the Culture of Sports* (Waco, TX: Baylor University Press, 2010).

26. Richard Hofstadter was a professor of American history at Columbia University. He became an iconic historian whom twenty-first-century scholars continue to cite because his publications remain relevant in illuminating Herbert Spencer's social Darwinism. See Richard Hofstadter, *Social Darwinism in American Thought*, reprint ed. (Boston: Beacon Press, 1992), 201; see also Alexander Rosenberg, *Darwinism in Philosophy, Social Science, and Policy* (New York: Cambridge University Press, 2000).

27. Although this reference is quite dated, the quote we have used provides the best articulation we have seen of Sumner's position on social Darwinism. See Albert Galloway Keller, ed., *Essays of William Graham Sumner*, Vol. 1 (New Haven, CT: Yale University Press, 1934), 386.

28. James Bryce, "America Revisited: The Changes of a Quarter-Century," *Outlook* 25 (March 1905): 738–739.

29. For interesting biographical accounts of some of the luminaries of sports in the 1920s, see Michael K. Bohn, *Heroes & Ballyhoo: How the Golden Age of the 1920s Transformed American Sports* (Dulles, VA: Potomac Books, 2009).

30. Rader and Grady, *American Sports*; see also Frank P. Jozsa Jr., *National Football League Franchises: Team Performances, Financial Consequences* (Lanham, MD: Lexington Books, 2016); Mike Ozanian, "The NFL's Most Valuable Teams 2016," *Forbes*, September 2016, 41–41.

31. A variety of sources were needed to compile these figures, but the single best source is Plunkett Research, Ltd., 2016, http://www.plunkettresearch.com/sports-recreation-leisure-market-research/industry-and-business-data

32. Henry Ford, *My Life and Work: An Autobiography of Henry Ford* (New York: CreateSpace Independent Publishing Platform, 2015); Richard Snow, *I Invented the Modern Age: The Rise of Henry Ford* (New York: Scribner; 2014).

33. Sloan, *The Media in America: A History.*

34. Michael K Bohn, *Heroes and Ballyhoo: How the Golden Age of the 1920s Transformed American Sports* (Lincoln, NB: Potomac Books, 2010), 7.

35. Kohn, *Heroes and Ballyhoo*, 5.

36. Jeffrey Montez de Oca, *Discipline and Indulgence: College Football, Media, and the American Way of Life during the Cold War* (New Brunswick, NJ: Rutgers University Press, 2013). The author goes beyond a traditional sports history to analyze the relationships, social structures, and meanings among sport, militarism, and American nationalism during the Cold War era

CHAPTER 3

SPORT AND AMERICAN CULTURE AND VALUES

The lessons learned by participating in sport transcend the playing field and contribute to shaping the character and culture of America's citizens.

—THE U.S. ANTI-DOPING AGENCY, *"What Sport Means in America: A Survey of Sport's Role in Society"*

The Los Angeles Sparks' Candace Parker heads to the bench for a time out with seconds left as Minnesota Lynx players celebrate winning the championship game of the 2017 WNBA Finals. (Photo: AP Photo/Jim Mone)

Many concepts and terms that sociologists use are mystifying to the average person. *Social organization* is one such term. Yet its meaning is straightforward: Social organization is the process by which human behavior becomes organized to deal with the social situations in which people find themselves. People belong to many social organizations because each addresses specific social tasks, such as education, religion, and work. These organizations can vary in size from small, such as a sports team, to huge, such as a corporation (e.g., Microsoft or Amazon).

One facet of social organizations is *culture*, which refers to the knowledge and values that members of a social organization share and that unite them and guide their behavior; it consists of the language, religious beliefs, food, clothing, material objects, and other common artifacts and characteristics of members of that particular social organization. It is through culture that people and groups define themselves, adapt to shared expectations, and become part of a community or society. Social values are a central element of culture (also called cultural values); they are collective conceptions for evaluating and judging what behavior is considered appropriate, desirable, moral, proper, and important. We discuss the meaning of values in more detail in the following paragraphs.

CULTURE, VALUES, AND SOCIAL THEORIES

Culture and values are typically enduring and are sustained and reproduced from one generation to the next. Without the intergenerational social transmission of culture and values, each generation would have to re-create their own customs, beliefs, language, rituals, and so forth. However, culture and values are not fixed and unchanging. Change is ongoing—sometimes slowly, other times quickly—depending on particular conditions. See Figure 3.1 for examples of how some values of American college first-year students have changed considerably, whereas others have basically endured. Every social organization has members who do not internalize and adopt the cultural values. There is even a derogatory word for such individuals—deviant.

All of the social theories that we identified and summarized in Chapter 1 concur that culture and values are essential to social organization, although their perspectives on this issue vary. For adherents of functionalist theory, collective values solve the fundamental problem of social integration. They are symbolic representations of existing society and therefore promote unity and consensus in a society, and they must be preserved because social stability requires a consensus and the support of group members. For functionalists, social cultural customs, rituals, traditions, and myths build strong common values that provide support, consensus, and stability while strengthening the social order.

Conflict/cultural theorists acknowledge the crucial role of culture and values in creating and maintaining stability and consensus in society, but in capitalist society—the main focus of conflict/cultural theorizing—the most powerful members are a dominant capitalist social class who form and shape cultural values that preserve their powerful economic, political, and social interests. This ruling capitalist class constructs and controls not only the means of economic production but also the apparatus for shaping cultural values through the social institutions of education, economy, religion, politics, and media in ways that benefit capitalist interests within that society to the detriment of the less powerful and less influential citizens at large.

In Chapter 1 we identified various social theoretical variants that are classified as conflict/cultural theories. Although they have compelling differences, all of these theories consider culture and values central concepts in social analyses. Yet each has its own unique point of view. We shall only briefly examine culture and values as they relate to hegemony, feminist, and racial theories.

As we also noted in Chapter 1, one of the features of hegemony theory is its focus on cultural patterns of dominance and the role that dominant, powerful groups play in shaping culture and values. These dominant groups translate their enormous economic resources into social and political ideologies about cultural values that are disseminated through all of the social institutions. Such ideologies thus come to be seen as norms that legitimate social beliefs and

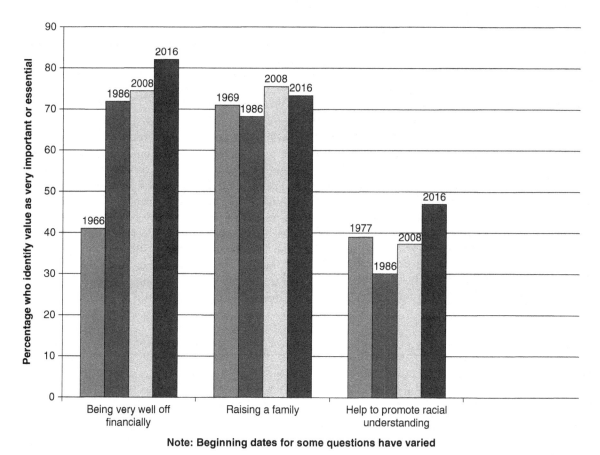

Note: Beginning dates for some questions have varied

FIGURE 3.1 Freshman Trends in Students Values Source: Kevin Eagan, Ellen Bara Stolzenberg, Hilary B. Zimmerman, Melissa C. Aragon, Hannah Whang Sayson, and Cecilia Rios-Aguilar, *The American Freshman: National Norms Fall 2016* (Los Angeles: Higher Education Research Institute, UCLA, 2016).

practices; they seem right and natural—a simple matter of common sense or of human nature—but the reality is that these ideologies overwhelmingly benefit the dominant class. In this way, according to the hegemonic perspective, a dominant class penetrates all levels of the society with its version of cultural reality. Domination is contoured primarily through an "active consent" of the mass of members, but it is a consent that has been molded by a domineering leadership.

Various feminist and racial theorists share hegemony theorists' interpretation of the social production and reproduction of cultural values. They maintain that dominant groups form and shape culture and values through the various social institutions that keep women and minority racial and ethnic groups subordinate and subservient to the dominant class.

One of the most often-heard statements about sport is that it is "a microcosm of society." If indeed sport is a microcosm of society, then the types of sports, the way in which sport is organized, and who participates as well as who does not all offer clues about the nature of a society. The study of sport, like the study of any social institution, should provide important indicators about (1) a society's culture, (2) a society's values, (3) a society's social structure (social stratification and social organization), and (4) a society's problems.

SPORT AS A MICROCOSM OF CULTURAL VALUES

In Chapter 1, we stated that the relationship between sport, on the one hand, and society, culture, and values, on the other, is interdependent. This is because cultural values affect the kinds of sports that are played, the way they are organized, the way they are played, and the motivations for participation in them. However, the converse is also true in that sport affects the culture and values in a society. To illustrate the interdependence of American cultural values and the popularity of sports, in Box 3.1 we share experiences we had with students at the beginning of a sociology of sport course.

To briefly illustrate, sport, like all social institutions, is conservative primarily because it reinforces cultural values, thus fulfilling a social function that functional theorists view as essential for social order, whereas conflict/cultural theorists tend to view sport as reinforcing the inequities of the status quo.

THE AMERICAN VALUE SYSTEM

Humans are a valuing species.[1] That is, human beings live in an affectively charged world where some things are preferred over others. Some objects, people, or ideas are considered wrong, bad, or immoral; others are believed to be correct, good, or moral. Some goals are deemed worthy; others are not.

Values are the culturally prescribed criteria by which individuals evaluate persons, behaviors, objects, and ideas as to their relative morality, desirability, merit, or correctness. Thus, values are the basis for making decisions. The phrase *culturally prescribed* is an important qualifier in this definition because it

---

BOX 3.1 *THINKING ABOUT SPORT:* CULTURAL VALUES, SPORT, AND THE PRIVILEGING OF DIFFERENT BODIES

At the beginning of our sociology of sport course we ask the students to identify sports that are considered both legitimate and illegitimate by mainstream American culture. Invariably, American football, basketball, baseball, ice hockey, and soccer make the "most legitimate" list. On the other hand, table tennis, cheerleading, bowling, and video game sports often come to the forefront of the "less legitimate" sports. Sports for people with disabilities are left out altogether.

This exercise prompts a lively debate about what constitutes "real" sport. As the conversation unfolds, the students soon realize that they are weighing which American cultural norms and values are privileged and which are marginalized. As noted in this chapter, mainstream sport represents the dominant value systems in American culture, such as competition, success, and materialism. Those do permeate many sports, but, importantly, the most "legitimate" or privileged sports such as those just noted also accentuate particular body types. Most students typically identify sports where large, muscularly strong, young, and able bodies are dominant. Significantly, these sports often involve using bodily force to overcome opponents.

These are the sports and bodies that get most media coverage and are celebrated as the living representation of the best in our society. Not only are these sports promoted through media, but also the state has been involved in publicly funding and thus sponsoring them through school systems and parks and recreation departments. The privileging of these sports has the impact of devaluing smaller, older, or differently abled bodies, essentially labeling them as less athletic and even as unhealthy. This has been the case historically with women's bodies (e.g., "throwing like a girl") and other bodies that are considered fragile or weak. When these assumptions are made, then it is often inferred that these "less-than" bodies are inappropriate for mainstream sport, making it more difficult to argue for equal opportunities. This dynamic has been expressed in the struggles over gender inclusion (see Chapter 7) and with inclusion of people with disabilities in sport.

Additionally, the win-at-all-cost behaviors expected of athletes include extreme competitiveness, violence to others and self, and willingness to bend the rules. The promotion of other behaviors such as cooperation or a self-expressive/aesthetic orientation is commonly met with derision. And those alternative, less competitive behaviors are then labeled as appropriate for "weaker" bodies. In this case, men who are strong, big, and able-bodied are often discouraged from doing sports such as gymnastics or figure skating because it would be a sign of accepting a weaker social position. Overall, assessing sport's place in mainstream culture gives one insight into not only the norms and values that we tend to celebrate, but also the types of bodies that are deemed most legitimate and, thus, privileged.

implies that human beings are *socialized*—that is, taught the criteria by which to make such judgments. Children learn from their parents, peers, places of worship, schools, and the media what is right or wrong, moral or immoral, correct or incorrect.

Before we begin an examination of values widely held in the United States, several caveats should be mentioned. First, diversity precludes any universal holding of values. Some individuals and groups reject the dominant values, and members of certain ethnic and religious groups have very different values. Moreover, differences in emphasis of the dominant values exist because of region, social class, age, and size of community.

Second, cultural values are not always consistent with individual behavior. For example, hard work is valued as the means to success, yet rich persons who may have inherited their wealth are still highly esteemed. Moreover, the value of equality of opportunity Americans verbally embrace is inconsistent with the injustices suffered by people on the margins, most notably the poor and minority groups.

Third, the values themselves are not always consistent. How does one reconcile the coexistence of individualism with conformity or of competition with cooperation? To minimize the problem of inconsistencies, we will present only the most dominant values of the United States and illustrate how they are expressed in sport.[2]

INDIVIDUAL STRIVING FOR SUCCESS AND COMPETITION IN SPORT

The highly valued individual in the United States is the self-made person—the person who has achieved status and become wealthy through his or her own efforts in a highly competitive system. Cultural heroes are Americans like Bill Gates, Oprah Winfrey, Ralph Lauren, and Steve Jobs, each of whom rose from humble origins to the top of her or his profession.

Success is typically narrowly defined as individual achievement—winning first place, winning a championship, outdoing all others. In the occupational world economic success (income, personal wealth, and possessions) is the most commonly used measurement of success. Economic success, moreover, is often used to

measure personal worth. Indeed, it has often been observed that the striking feature of U.S. culture is to identify standards of personal excellence with occupational achievement. This cultural narrative featuring an individual striving for success is often expressed in popular cultural representations of sport. For example, many films that highlight sports, such as the *Rocky* series, showcase the ideals of the underdogs striving hard for success and heroically overcoming obstacles to be better athletes and people. Additionally, Netflix had a recent a series called *Last Chance U*, a drama that documented how athletes with troubled pasts use community college sport to turn their lives around. Stories of real-life athletes who have come from impoverished backgrounds to reach the pinnacle of their sport, such as LeBron James and Serena Williams, also resonate with American audiences because they provide "proof" that in the United States any individual can make it if they work hard, have grit, and have talent. As noted in the following, it is believed that striving for success through competition brings out the best in people.

Competition is highly valued. In fact, it is often contended that competition has made the United States the dominant nation in the world. It is not just competition, however, but winning in competitive situations that is so highly valued. Permeating U.S. life is an almost religious belief in the power of competition to achieve success. Being victorious in competition is so highly valued that extraordinary rewards are heaped on victors. Thus, the United States has been characterized as a "winner-takes-all" society by some social analysts.[3]

Motivated by the hope of being victorious in competition or by fear of failure, many citizens believe that the United States must be first in war, the arms race, the Olympics, or the race to place humans on Mars. This competitive zeal was behind the United States' race to be the first nation to land its citizens on the moon.

Competition pervades all of the social institutions of the United States. The prominence of competition in schools is seen in the selection process for athletic teams, cheerleading squads, debate teams, choruses, bands, and play casts. In each case, competition among classmates is the criterion for selection.

Even the grading system is often based on comparisons of classmates with one another.

The foundation of the capitalist economic system is competition: businesses compete against each other for customers for their products and services, and workers compete against each other for the best-paying and highest-status jobs. American governments are composed of officials who have competed against others in elections to secure their positions.

Even youth social–recreational programs are based on competition. The Cub Scouts program, because of its reliance on competition, is considered an all-American organization. In the first place, individual status in the den or pack is determined by the level one has achieved through the attainment of merit badges. Although all boys can theoretically attain all merit badges, the boys are pitted against one another to see who can obtain the most. Why is such a practice accepted, indeed, publicized? The answer, simply, is that this type of competitive youth activity is symbolic of the way things are done in virtually all aspects of American life.

An important ethical consequence of this extreme emphasis on competition is that some people take advantage of their competitors to compete successfully. This is done rather routinely in political campaigns with "dirty tricks," misleading advertising, and illegal contributions to win elections. In the business world, we find some people who use theft, fraud, interlocking directorates, and price fixing to get ahead dishonestly. Following are some examples of how this zeal to win has caused people to cheat.

Organized sports start at a very young age—as young as five years old. The players quickly learn that competition is highly valued and success is often narrowly defined as winning. (Photo: © barbsimages/Shutterstock.com)

- About sixty major corporations have had to restate their earnings after overstating them to boost their stock value.
- The Internal Revenue Service has found consistently that three of ten people cheat on their income taxes.
- Employees embezzle or pilfer an estimated $10 billion from their employers annually.
- The Center for Academic Integrity has found that the percentage of students who approve of plagiarism is rising, and it estimates that 75 percent of all students have been involved in some form of cheating.[4]

There is a growing belief that hypercompetitive social values are having an adverse effect on the traditional moral values that are often considered fundamental to American societies. Moral values are the communal and shared cultural principles and standards that govern day-to-day living in societies. They are important for maintaining unity, harmony, and honor among people.[5] For example, the Golden Rule is a moral code that urges us to treat others as you would like others to treat you.

National surveys seem to support this belief. According to the 2021 annual Gallup Values and Beliefs Poll, 67 percent of Americans say the U.S. morals are in decline, and 47 percent describe the state of morals as "poor."[6]

We now turn to discuss how competition and success values are held in sport. The functionalist perspective views sports as an almost sacred activity that socializes participants about competition values. As in the larger society, there is a tremendous emphasis in the United States on competitive success in sport. Winning is glorified by all who participate.

Soccer players carrying out the traditional postgame hand-slap with opponents. A great deal of social learning of cultural values occurs in youth sports: sportsmanship, competition, self-discipline, sacrifice, authority. (Photo: USAG-Humphreys)

Coaching statements such as the following exemplify this emphasis on winning.

In our society, in my profession, there is only one measure of success, and that is winning. Not just any game, not just the big game, but the last one.

(Former head coach of the Oakland Raiders)

Our expectations are to play for and win the national championship every year. . . . Second, third, fourth, and fifth don't do you any good in this business.

(Former head football coach at the University of Miami)

Whether in school or in business or in politics or in sports, Americans demand winners. Coaches are fired if they are not successful; teams are booed if they play for ties or when they go on losing streaks. A recent story in *USA Today* indeed notes that professional sport teams with poor records will often lose their fan base.[7]

Inevitably, coaches faced with the option of taking a tie or gambling on winning (with a high probability of losing) will go for the win with the comment, "We're not here to play for a tie." The thirty-one teams in the NFL who do not win the Super Bowl in a given year are considered losers. Not even the members of the runner-up team consider themselves successful: for them, they did not win the only game that really counts. Indeed, a popular mantra in American sports is that "Nobody remembers who took second place." Interestingly, this American sporting mentality seems to be manifesting elsewhere; it was recently observed that athletes who placed second in a tournament immediately removed their second-place medals during an award ceremony in Europe.[8]

It is a fact that coaches do all they can to socialize their athletes with the value orientation that winning is the most admired achievement in sport. They reinforce winners with praise, honor, and status, meanwhile giving them certain extra privileges or leeway. Numerous reinforcers are used to illustrate that the primary goal of sports competition is to succeed (to win). Coaches also do all they can to instill in their athletes the character traits that they believe will produce winning teams (e.g., loyalty, enthusiasm, initiative, self-control, confidence, poise, hard work, and ambition).

High-profile athletes and teams are often afraid to fail because of the pressures hoisted on them by the American culture that values only winning as a success. A recent example of this pressure to win comes from the Tokyo 2020 Summer Olympic Games, where gymnast Simone Biles gave the following comment after the U.S. women's team got the silver medal: "We hope America still loves us."[9]

The demand for winners is found at all levels of sport. Beginning with many youth sports, winning is everything, as evidenced by the pressures commonly found in adult-sponsored children's sports programs. Parents can get caught up in the desire for their children to be winners. For example, it has become common for wealthier parents to hire private individual coaches for their children and place them in private club sports at early ages, giving them a competitive advantage. In addition, parent behavior toward young athletes and to each other during competitive events can also reflect overcompetitiveness, as we discuss in Chapter 8 on youth sports.

An example of the emphasis on winning among youngsters can be seen in the contests sponsored by businesses and corporations. For example, the NFL used to sponsor a Punt, Pass, and Kick contest for youngsters six through fifteen years of age. Iterations of this contest took place from 1961 to 2017. Aquafina and the MLB continue to sponsor a Pitch, Hit, and Run contest for baseball skills. In each case, winners are selected at the local level and proceed through the various state and regional tournaments until a national winner is found for each age category. In one year, there were 1,112,702 entrants in the Punt, Pass, and Kick contest and only 6 winners. Why would an organization sponsor an event that produced 6 winners and 1,112,696 losers? Perhaps the reason is that this, too, is a microcosm of the larger society.

The obsession with winning has led to scandals throughout the sports world, as we shall note throughout this book. Most visible is the illegal recruiting of athletes by colleges, universities, and even some public high schools.[10] For instance, in the quest to succeed (i.e., win), several coaches have violated NCAA regulations by arranging to have transcripts altered to ensure athletes' eligibility; by enrolling athletes in classes and obtaining academic credits for them for coursework never taken; by allowing substitutes to take admissions tests for athletes of marginal educational ability; by paying athletes for nonexistent jobs; by illegally using government work-study funds for athletes; and by offering money, cars, and clothing to entice athletes to their universities.[11]

When "winning is everything," players and coaches may turn to other forms of cheating. Many athletes take drugs to enhance their performance artificially. This practice is so commonplace, even expected, in some sports that we might call steroids that increase bulk and strength *vocational drugs*.

At perhaps the most competitive extreme, sport technologists might turn to "genetic engineering." With the advances in the genetics behind sports performances and genetic manipulation, it has been suggested that athletes by design may become possible whereby from conception athletes are genetically optimized. Indeed, the World Anti-Doping Agency has already asked scientists to help find ways to prevent gene therapy from becoming the newest means of doping. But eventually, preventing athletes from gaining access to gene therapy may become impossible.[12]

In team sports, players may try to gain an unfair advantage by such practices as "doctoring" a pitch or "corking" a bat in baseball, curving the blades of the stick beyond the legal limits in hockey, or pretending to be fouled in soccer and basketball. In automobile racing, fuel tampering and "boosting" the manifold pressure to gain a horsepower advantage has been done by the sport's leading stars. While many rule-breaking practices have been around sports for decades, they continue to occur with frequency and with increasing sophistication.

In a recent national survey of nearly 9,000 Americans representing the general population, coaches, athletes, and parents of athletes involved in sports, two-thirds agreed that sport overemphasizes the importance of winning.[13] One of the problems with the hyperemphasis on winning is that it tends to warp sport. Sport, in its pristine form, emphasizes the playing of the contest with thrills achieved from strategy, luck, finesse, cunning, practice, and skill. When winning is everything, however, the playing of the game becomes secondary. In effect, the destination becomes more important than the journey. When this occurs, sport is diminished. Today, at all levels of sports, the most important thing is not merely to take part but to win; the most important thing is not the struggle but the triumph; the essential thing is not to have played well but to have won.

Sport is thus based heavily on the social value of competition. Competition can be a productive element of society as well as in sports. It has been said that the best games or contests occur when all participants give their best efforts. The processes that go toward winning a competition, such as intensive training, strategic preparation, and determined performances, are indeed laudable. However, many people in society, including sporting participants, believe that competition is equated with winning only. Therefore, when it comes to competition, the phrase that is often invoked is "Not everyone should get a trophy."

Research has shown that there are many benefits for all ages and abilities to be involved in sport (including camaraderie, sense of community, health, and self-efficacy). Perhaps, then, new visions and types of sports programming emphasizing more cooperative and inclusive values are needed to achieve these outcomes. These emerging forms of sport could help balance the "winner-takes-all" mentality that currently dominates our sporting landscape. High-profile exceptions to this traditional belief system also occasionally occur (see Box 3.2).

Such a heavy emphasis on winning is not a natural phenomenon but rather a cultural one. Games in many societies have no competitive element but reflect a different emphasis because of their cultural values. For contrast, let us examine a game from another society that would never capture the enthusiasm of Americans.

The Tangu people of New Guinea play a popular game known as *taketak*, which involves throwing a spinning top into massed lots of stakes driven into the ground. There are two teams. Players of each team try to touch as many stakes with their tops as possible. In the end, however, the participants play not to win but to draw. The game must go on until an exact draw is reached. This requires great skill,

BOX 3.2   *THINKING ABOUT SPORT: TWO ATH-LETES AT THE RIO OLYMPIC GAMES*

All who participate in organized sports in North America are socialized with the value that winning is what sports are about and that winning is the most admired value in sports. But sometimes the most inspirational sports activities do not involve winning or achieving medals at all. Actions at the 2016 Rio Summer Olympics by two track-and-field athletes—one from the United States and one from New Zealand—are a good example.

It all started when New Zealand's Nikki Hamblin fell on the track during a semifinal heat of the women's 5,000-meter race. Unable to avoid Hamblin, Abbey D'Agostino tripped over her, stumbling to the ground herself. Rather than getting up and trying to win the race, leaving Hamblin on the track, D'Agostino stopped and helped her off the ground. As

D'Agostino then continued on, pain in her ankle from her fall began to settle in, and she collapsed to the ground. This time it was Hamblin who assisted D'Agostino. Hamblin remained with D'Agostino for some several meters before leaving her to complete the race. Limping badly, D'Agostino, too, eventually finished the race.

After the race, Hamblin said, "I'm so grateful for Abbey for doing that for me. I've never met her before. Isn't that so amazing?" Although Hamblin and D'Agostino failed to meet the qualifying time for the heat, both were included in the 5,000-meter final.

Sources: Associated Press, "Runners Help Each Other after Fall: 'Get Up. We Have to Finish This.'" *New York Times*, August 16, 2016; Chris Chavez, "Abbey D'Agostino, Nikki Hamblin Exemplify Olympic Spirit after Falling in 5,000 Meters," *Sports Illustrated*, August 16, 2016.

---

since players sometimes must throw their tops into the massed stakes without touching a single one. *Taketak* expresses a prime value in Tangu culture, that is, the concept of moral equivalence, which is reflected in the precise sharing of foodstuffs among the people.

This example underscores our contention that a society's sports mirror its basic values. Cooperative societies have sports that minimize competition, and aggressive societies have highly competitive games.

During the 2016 Rio Olympic Games, New Zealand distance runner Nikki Hamblin and U.S. runner Abbey D'Agostino were four laps from the end of their heat in the 5,000-meter race when they collided. Hamblin stopped to assist D'Agostino of the United States after the collision. (Photo: Ian Walton/Getty Images)

THE SOCIALLY VALUED MEANS TO ACHIEVE IN SPORT

There are three related, highly valued ways to succeed in the United States. The first is through *hard work.* Americans, from the early Puritans to the present day, have admired persons who are industrious and denigrated those who are not. Many, therefore, assume that poor people deserve to be poor because they are allegedly unwilling to work as hard as persons in the middle and upper classes. This meritocracy explanation places the blame on the victim rather than on a social system that systematically thwarts efforts by the poor. Their hopelessness, brought on by a lack of education, by their skin color or gender, or by a lack of experience, is interpreted as their fault and not as a function of the inequalities in power and politics embedded in the economic system.[14]

This typical interpretation, moreover, is underpinned by the success of some individuals who grew up in poverty—the rags-to-riches example that we discussed previously. These individuals are presented as dramatic evidence that a meteoric rise in fame and fortune is possible through the blending of hard work and talent. However, some persons succeed not because of the openness of the system but because they managed in some way or another to overcome its roadblocks.

The two remaining valued means to success are *continual striving* and *deferred gratification.* Continual striving has meaning for both the successful and the not so successful. For the former, it means that a person should never be content with what she or he has; there will always be more property to own, more money to make, or more games to win. For the latter, continual striving means a never-give-up attitude, a belief that economic success is always possible, although it may be improbable.

Deferred gratification refers to the willingness to deny immediate pleasure for the sake of later rewards. The hallmark of the successful person in America is a willingness—to stay in school or to work at two jobs or to go to night school regardless of the obstacles, in the hopes that the delay will result in achieving a goal. It is also important to note here that social class differences impact whether individuals can be future- or present-time oriented. For instance, youth with lesser means are focused on day-to-day situations resulting from socio-economic structural constraints, whereas the children of the affluent have more time and energy to plan for future endeavors. We will discuss how social class backgrounds orient people in different ways in Chapter 5.

Turning to sport specifically, we can see that in organized and corporate sport, as in society overall, the goal of individual achievement must be accomplished through continuous hard work and sacrifice. The work ethic is also the sports ethic. Someone wins with enough work and sacrifice or, conversely, someone loses without enough work. This is institutionalized by the slogans that coaches use to inspire hard work in their athletes:

The will to win is the will to work.
Practice makes perfect.
Success is 99 percent perspiration and 1 percent inspiration.
There is no substitute for hard work.

Especially in the United States, as we have noted, there is a distinctive abhorrence in sports for athletes and teams who lose more often than they win despite their dedication and sustained best efforts to achieve victories. Athletes and coaches who lose are variously accused of not trying hard enough, not sacrificing enough, and not wanting to win badly enough; some are even called quitters. Conflict/cultural theorists

regard this as sport's adaptation of a common belief found in our general society: that everyone can be successful if they want to be, and conversely, those who fail do so because they did not work hard or "want it" enough. When this view is applied to sport, it becomes the false idea that winning can be achieved simply by hard work and that losing can be blamed on individual lack of effort.

PROGRESS OVERCOMES THE STATUS QUO IN SPORT

Societies differ in their emphasis on the past, on the present, and on the future. Americans, although giving some attention to each time dimension, stress the future. They neither make the past sacred nor remain content with the present. They place a central value on progress—on a brighter tomorrow, a better job, a bigger home, a move to the suburbs, a college education for their children, and self-improvement.

Americans are generally not satisfied with the status quo; they want growth (bigger homes, better cars, larger shopping malls, more businesses moving into the community, increased profits, and more sport championships). Many want to change and conquer nature (dam rivers, clear forests, rechannel rivers, seed clouds, spray parks and residential areas with insecticides, and replace grass with artificial turf), although the ecological crises are leading more and more people to question this value.

Although belief in progress in the United States implies that change is good, some things are not easily changed because they are considered to have a sacred quality: social institutions, cultural values, and the nation-state. Thus, although they value technological and economic progress, Americans resist fundamental social changes in their society.

Within the context of sport, coaches, athletes, and fans often place a central value on progress. Continued improvement (in mastering new techniques, in winning more games, or in setting new records) is the aim of all athletes and teams. This mindset is reflected on a banner placed on Stanford University's practice football field. It reads, "You are getting better or you are getting worse, you never stay the same." This push for continual progress impacts track-and-field stars, swimmers, and athletes in other sports where performances can be precisely quantified; they undergo great pressures to set new records each time they compete. Indeed, athletes in team sports are always under pressure to achieve outstanding win–loss records. These demands come from the fans, from the press, from promoters, from parents, and often from the athletes themselves.

MATERIALISM: ACQUISITIONS AND CONSUMPTION IN SPORT

"Hard work pays off" is a basic belief in American culture. The payoff is success, not only in one's profession, but also in economic standing, in income, and in the acquisition and consumption of goods and services that go beyond adequate nutrition, medical care, shelter, and transportation. The superfluous things that we accumulate or strive to accumulate, such as country club memberships, jewelry, stylish clothes, lavish houses in prestigious neighborhoods, boats, second homes, swimming pools, and season tickets to the games of our favorite teams, are symbols of success in the competitive struggle. The acquisition of material attributes reflects the "good life." Simultaneously, material wealth provides symbolic cultural value because it is seen as evidence of adherence to the American value system.

The American emphasis on materialism is reflected in the motives of college students. As Figure 3.1 illustrates, surveys of first-year college students find that "being very well-off financially" has become of much greater value to college students over the past forty years. This materialism is also seen indirectly in the most commonly chosen major: business.

The emphasis on having things has long been a feature of citizens because the United States has always been a land of opportunity and abundance. Although many persons are unable to fully participate in this abundance, the goal for most persons is to accumulate those things that bring status and that provide for a better way of life by saving labor or enhancing pleasure in their leisure time.

Within the highly competitive American societal context discussed previously, materialism has become an important value consideration in sport. As we will discuss throughout this book, big-time college and

professional teams in particular are driven by maximizing material profit. High schools, the NCAA, professional team owners, and various conferences/leagues make lucrative arrangements with television networks that have a dramatic effect on sports (e.g., scheduling, game timing, and number of time outs). The capacity to obtain sponsorship deals from multinational corporations is a major consideration for sport teams. This aspect of sports directly influences organizational vision and day-to-day internal and external operations.

Furthermore, professional teams that do not show a high enough profit may be moved to another city in the search for more money because team owners typically have no loyalty to the cities that subsidize them. They move their teams to places where more money can be generated, or they threaten to move to receive greater benefits from their host cities.

Athletes, too, are plainly motivated by material concerns, and rightfully so given high risks of injury and intensive stress to perform in the public eye. They often have short careers when compared to coaches, managers/directors, and owners. Several athletes in high-profile sports have rich salaries, but they also use their name and resources to reinvest in other ventures. The trend toward creating a brand, monetizing that brand by being a social media influencer, and diversifying one's portfolio is becoming standard. For example, LeBron James, a basketball player, made $96.5 million in 2021. Tom Brady, a football player, made $76 million. Naomi Osaka, an elite women's tennis player, made $60 million, of which $5 million came from playing tennis.[15] In Chapter 1 we reported that Dak Prescott, the Dallas Cowboys quarterback, was paid $107.5 million in 2021, making him the highest paid athlete in the United States. Today, even lower-division athletes can make significant incomes that supplement and even exceed their professional contract salaries by providing online and on-ground coaching as well as healthy lifestyle tips. Athletes will also use free agency; team sport athletes move from team to team, securing ever-larger contracts and potential sponsorship and marketing deals. Some question whether many athletes only want to get huge salaries and create lucrative brands, rather than playing for the love of the game and being loyal to teammates and fans.

Olympic athletes parlay their sports accomplishments into millions for endorsements, personal appearances, and the like. College football and basketball coaches frequently break their contracts to coach at another school for more money. Free agents in professional sports commonly sign with the highest bidder and often try to renegotiate contracts before they expire. In such instances, team and fan loyalty is secondary.

Athletes hire agents and lawyers to negotiate for the highest possible bonuses and salary arrangements. They hold out individually and even strike collectively, on occasion, for better material comforts (see Chapter 11). Furthermore, athletes often engage in activities calculated to increase attendance at contests. Team rivalries and individual matchups are hyped up by participating athletes in the media domain before big games. Fighters and their promoters are especially known for creating a spectacle before events to increase hype. Star athletes also devote much of their energy to making money by endorsing products and projects, making personal appearances, and giving inspirational talks.

Sports fans, too, are influenced by material considerations. They like plush stadiums and arenas with expensive scoreboards and other amenities. They are excited by athletes playing for large stakes (e.g., the difference between first and second place in a golf tournament may be as much as a million dollars). Fans also closely follow high-earning celebrity athletes on various social media platforms.

Conflict/cultural theorists have been critical of the "big business" that permeates all levels of contemporary sport, where profitability has become more important than the health and safety of athletes. They are also critical of the coercion and exploitation employed by teams and leagues to push athletes to harmful physical and psychological extremes.

SOCIAL CONFORMITY IN SPORT

Social organizations do not tolerate total freedom by individual members. As we noted in Chapter 1, for functionalism to avoid disorder and lawlessness,

social organizations/nations must socialize its members into accepting the beliefs, values, and practices of the social organization/nation and even believing the system is intrinsically just. Without a minimum of cooperation and of conformity to laws and customs, there is anarchy. To avoid disorder and lawlessness, societies socialize individuals into acceptable beliefs, values, and practices. For their part, individuals actually seek to be socialized. We seek the approval of our family, peers, and colleagues and therefore try to be successful by some shared standards of achievement or of conformity. Conformity, then, is a characteristic of all social organizations. The degree of conformity required, however, varies greatly from one social organization to another.

Analytically, we can separate conformity in American society into two levels. At one level are the official expectations of behavior by the community, the state, and the nation: the customs and the laws individuals are expected to obey. Deviations from these expectations are punished by fines, imprisonment, gossip, or other negative sanctions. The threat of these sanctions is usually enough to ensure conformity. More than this, however, we are socialized to accept a great deal of conformity.

At another, more personal, level, individuals tend to conform to the expectations of groups with which they closely identify: families, peers, ethnic groups, religious groups, and work groups. Within the context of society-wide expectations for behavior, there is greater diversity: suburbanites conform to other suburbanites, as do inner-city residents, teenagers, celebrity culture, union members, and businesspersons with their peers. Some social analysts have characterized U.S. citizens as being *other-directed*. By this they mean that Americans are oversensitive to the opinions of others. They continually have their antennas out, picking up signals from those important to them. Other analysts point to the same phenomenon in the organizational context of social life. They argue that the proliferation of bureaucratic organizations in every social institution over the past two generations forces many persons to conform. Rules must be followed, boats must not be rocked, if individuals are to get ahead in bureaucracies.

Bureaucratic organizations are authoritarian and hierarchical. They are also rational. That is, they are based entirely on certain understood and accepted rules designed to efficiently serve the organizations' goals. The interests of organizations are paramount in the development of these rules (as opposed to the interests of individuals), and the formal aspects of bureaucracies manifest these interests and rules.

The influence of bureaucracies is a source of norms regulating a large number of activities both within and beyond large-scale organization boundaries. So powerful and so pervasive are the organizations that employ bureaucratic methods that the value orientations engendered by this form of organization, especially efficiency and productivity, attained the status of core values for the United States. They so permeate the fabric of every social institution that the socialization process is largely devoted to conditioning youth to this orientation.

As we have highlighted, conformity is highly valued in all of the social institutions of America, and this valued attitude and behavior are replicated in sport. Sport teams and other organizations generally demand that their athletes conform to the societal norms in terms of public presentation and performance. For instance, at the Tokyo 2020 Summer Olympic Games, the International Olympic Committee and event organizers banned social media teams from posting pictures of athletes kneeling during events.[16] The demand of conformity in sporting practice probably relates to two factors: first, teams and organizations feel that their cultural and economic status may be jeopardized if they permit athletes to act outside societal standards; second, these types of institutions tend to be conservative themselves and believe it is important to reproduce conservative values through their athletes.

Coaches of team sports also place a high value on team unity, emphasizing subordination of self to team success. Athletes are expected to subordinate their wills to achieve team success, as numerous coaching clichés indicate, including popular ones such as "There is no 'I' in team" and "Teamwork makes the dream work."

Another aspect of external conformity found both in sport and in the larger society is the acceptance of authority. Coaches typically structure coach–athlete relationships along authoritarian lines, and their system, the rules, and the structure of power are not usually challenged. They analyze and structure team positions for the precise specialization of the athletes, and they endeavor to monitor and control player behavior throughout practice and contest periods.

This trend has been enhanced by technology. For example, MLB launched a new era in analytics in 2016. Using a tracking technology called Statcast, MLB can now gather game data and statistics in ways it never has before. Under this form of management, the athletes are the instruments for achieving organizational goals. In most cases they are not consulted about team membership, practice methods, strategy, team rules, or any of the other dynamic functions of a team. Thus, athletes learn the structure of contemporary corporate society by living the hierarchy of power within modern sport.[17] Under the pretext of a game that is supposed to develop the character of the participants, sport in fact reproduces the world of work. Thus, play is transformed into work. The playfulness, fun, and creativity of sport are muted by the absolute control of coaches over their teams and players; if players wish to participate, they must conform to the coach's system. Indeed, many coaches tell their athletes, "It's my way or the highway." Indeed, it has been suggested by one sports educator that individual identity and expression are not really celebrated in the competitive sports world. Under the team-based mentality, she argues, athletes are expected to depart from being complex and unique individuals and become lost in the team. This sports educator thus speculates how sports coaches can better appreciate individual contributions to collective sports activity.[18]

SPORT, CHARACTER, AND ATHLETIC BODIES

Sport has been seen as a means to build character, and that character represents the values of particular groups or cultures. In this volume we focus on American cultural identities. One reason parents want their children to participate in sport, beyond having fun and socializing, is so they learn the prevalent cultural values. It is assumed that through sport one can learn how to succeed in the United States: through hard work, continual striving, and competition one can increase their chances of winning and attaining material success. In fact, many organizations value those who have done sport because they are assumed to have learned how to be team players as well as being committed to continual striving, progress, competition, and desire to be successful. The Enterprise rental car company, for example, often hires college graduates with athletic backgrounds because they perceive that these individuals have the aforementioned attributes.[19] This view that being a sport participant is good for workforce success is widely accepted and promoted.[20]

Interestingly, many people correlate a person's physical body to these same values. If one appears to be "fit" or "athletic" looking, then people assume they practice (and embody) these American values, which translates into more status.[21] The shape of one's body thus confers status, since it seemingly signifies whether one is a successful athlete or not.[22] It is important to note that the ideal athletic body takes slightly different forms for men and women. Young men often feel pressure to do sport or regular physical activity to ensure they are perceived as normatively masculine.[23] Currently, this is an emphasis on muscularity with lean and well-defined muscle mass, especially the "six-pack" stomach. It is common for men to take pictures of their muscles during or after a workout and post them on social media. This pressure to meet these masculine standards of strong and muscular, as fit or athletic, is prevalent among males. For women, fit and athletic bodies are given status, but simultaneously appearances of femininity and sexiness are also a primary form of status for women. Then, normative expectations of femininity involve limits on the size and strength of women's bodies. For all genders, the current expectation is that to be "good' and "healthy" one needs to engage in sport or physical activity while also eating in a manner that seemingly aligns with such activities. Although this is a common understanding and practice, many researchers have noted that, in fact, there are many body types can

actually be considered healthy.[24] Nonetheless, girls and women are expected to conform to standards and work to construct a body that appears to be "fit" and thus suited to sporting practice.[25]

These normative expectations of "good" bodies impact people with disabilities in more complicated ways because they are often regarded as ungendered and not capable of elite performances. Researchers from the University of Ottawa found that male athletes with disabilities used sport participation to develop their masculine identity. Women athletes with disabilities face traditional gender norms and, thus, had to balance being strong and athletic with maintaining a feminine appearance.[26]

SPORT AND TECHNOLOGY

Technology has been thoroughly infused in our culture. The world of sports has made tremendous use of technology, and much in current sport is the product of technological innovation. We, therefore, want to end this chapter by highlighting the growing reliance on technology as a means to achieve success. In this way, the use of technology amplifies the values we already noted in the chapter, including competition, progress, materialism, and social conformity. This has impacted how we practice sport, how sport organizations train their athletes, how sport organizations sell products, and how fans experience sport.

The collection of data through various technologies is common practice in high-level sports. Organizations are using technology to more quickly collect and assess data on their athletes and teams, as well as others. This trend is referred to as *big data*, which has been applied in several ways. One type of implementation is using data to assess the training of individual athletes. For example, professional sport teams use numerous technologies to monitor players by recording physiological responses that, in turn, are used to assess players' limits and capacities. The data are used, for instance, to individualize each player's training, competition, and recovery schedules. Another example is how sport organizations use data analysis to choose which athletes (at the lowest cost possible) can contribute to their teams. The use of big data was made popular in the novel and subsequent movie, *Moneyball*. This story features the Oakland A's

MLB team, which did not have a big budget to buy the best talent, and how they were consequently able to use analytics to uncover trends in less expensive players' abilities. Thus, they could build a very good team more cheaply by assessing massive amounts of data on individual players. Another data-based approach involves sport organizations using technology to monitor their consumers to develop more targeted marketing strategies.[27]

The use of technology and data assessment can also be seen in recreational as well as elite athletes who wear self-tracking devices to measure physiology, sleep, and food intake. These metrics then can be downloaded and used to plan workouts. Many of these devices include a GPS, such as Strava, that can track one's biking or running routes. In turn, these apps have a social network associated with them, allowing folks to compete with others digitally (even those they have never met).[28] Similar forms of technology have been applied to surfing, including watches that monitor tides, weather conditions, and moon phases. Surfers, too, have apps that record speed, count the waves ridden, and provide access to a larger social network. Having the latest technological gear also reflects one's material possessions and demonstrates that one is committed to their individual progress, two fundamental values in the United States.

Another technological trend pertains to the actual materials used. Technology has always greatly influenced the way sports are played and observed. Scientific advances in materials have revolutionized sporting goods and equipment and transformed training and coaching methods. The high-tech synthetic materials now used in athletes' apparel and equipment have been major contributors to the improvement of athletes' performances in almost every sport. Technological innovations are transforming many sports—from NASCAR (aerodynamic cars) to the NFL (helmet radio)—modifying strategy, playing styles, and even game rules.

As for training, conditioning, and coaching, to a great extent the emergence of superior athletic performance is a consequence of a pool of specialized experts who are knowledgeable about the newest biotechnologies. These are sport scientists—biomechanists, exercise physiologists, biochemists, nutritionists, and orthopedists—whose expertise is being widely used by trainers and coaches.

We generally applaud the use of technology in creating better living conditions for people, whether that be medicine, transportation, or food and water security. Nonetheless, it is important to critically reflect on some of the ethical implications of its use, particularly within various spheres of sport. One ethical discussion reflects a healthy debate about how and what types of technology allow for fair play and which ones may give an unfair advantage. For example, there are hypoxic chambers that mimic training at altitude, which increases red blood cells that allow one to carry and use more oxygen. Yet, blood doping (taking out your own blood, storing it, and then injecting it back into your system), which has the same effect, is seen as cheating. Why is there a distinction made? Who is more likely to have access to these new technologies?

Additionally, there have been questions about the integrity of particular sports with the use of new technologies. This was illustrated in swimming during the first decade of the twenty-first century. Speedo, along with NASA, designed a competition swimsuit that would reduce drag: the full-body LZR Racer released in 2008. Yet, within a short period of time, so many world records were broken that the international swimming governing body, FINA, banned the technology in 2010.

As we have noted, technology is at the heart of much of our new economy, especially as different organizations try to quickly and nimbly analyze data sets to create predictive models to identify target markets in more nuanced ways. Another ethical question arises from this type of big data's use in regard to the privacy of recreational athletes: To what extent are personal GPS devices tracking information about you that can be sold back to other corporations? How have the new in-home fitness programs (Peloton, Mirror, etc.) used your personal data? These are some of the ethical questions that are important to consider and debate as we reflect on what uses of technology can be beneficial for the well-being of all those involved in sport.

SUMMARY

Stakeholders in sport—owners, administrators, coaches, athletes, and fans—interact and integrate with broad national, social, cultural values and practices. These social processes are the foundation for what we—and numerous others as well—noted with the generalization that sport mirrors a society's basic social values, that is, that there is an association—an elective affinity—between society and its sports.

It is thus clear that American values are strongly reinforced and reproduced in sports. Just as important is the insight that sport in society, through its organization and the demands and the emphases of those in power, reinforces dominant societal as well as economic values. This reciprocity places sport squarely in the middle of society's "way of life." Both social theories that we identified and summarized in Chapter 1 agree that culture and values are essential to social organization, although their beliefs on this issue vary. Functionalists stress that socio-cultural customs, rituals, traditions, and myths build strong common values that provide support, consensus, and stability while strengthening the social order. Conflict/cultural theorists acknowledge the crucial role of culture and values in creating and preserving stability and consensus in society, but in capitalist society—the main focus of conflict/cultural theorizing—the most powerful members are a dominant capitalist social class who form and shape cultural values that sustain their powerful economic, political, and social welfare.

We should keep these theoretical discussions in mind in subsequent chapters as we examine the positive and negative consequences of sport in society and ultimately look at the sustainable future of our sporting endeavors. It is precisely because sport is so intertwined with the fundamental values of society that any critique on traditional sporting values and institutions is usually challenged or ignored. Criticisms of our leading sport values, and the institutions and figures that are beholden to them, have even been characterized as unpatriotic. However, given the outline of values provided in this chapter, including competition, materialism, and individual and team conformity, all buttressed by the incorporation of technology, it behooves us to consider how people in society might navigate such prominent values and attributes. Given that many of us are immersed in sport and its accompanying set of values, how might we come to understand and even

critique this value system to find more enjoyment and meaning? How might we benefit from sport in terms of how we develop certain values and character traits, while remaining aware of potentially negative impacts on our bodies, sense of self, and communities?

Learn more with this chapter's digital tools, including web resources, video links, and chapter self-assessment quizzes at www.oup.com/he/sage-eitzen-beal-atencio-12e.

NOTES

1. Much of this discussion on values can be found in D. Stanley Eitzen, Maxine Baca Zinn, and Kelly Eitzen Smith, *In Conflict and Order: Understanding Society*, 14th ed. (Boston: Pearson, 2016), ch. 3.
2. Erik Olin Wright and Joel Rogers, *American Society: How It Really Works*, 2nd ed. (New York: Norton, 2015). There is a substantial literature on U.S. values, much of it having a particular political viewpoint. The following publication focuses more on the topic of values than on that of politics: David M. Haugen, *American Values* (San Diego, CA: Greenhaven Press, 2014).
3. Stephen J. McNamee and Robert K. Miller Jr., *The Meritocracy Myth*, 3rd ed. (Lanham, MD: Rowman & Littlefield, 2013); Michael J. Sandel, *Tyranny of Merit: What's Become of the Common Good?* (New York: Farrar, Straus and Giroux, 2020).
4. Stephen J. Anderson, *The Culture of Success* (Oakland, CA: Yes Press, 2015); see also J. R. Slosar, *The Culture of Excess: How America Lost Self-Control and Why We Need to Redefine Success* (New York: Praeger, 2009).
5. Sandel, *Tyranny of Merit*.
6. Lydia Saad, "Stable U.S. Moral Ratings Obscure Big Partisan Shifts," Gallup, June 15, 2021, https://news.gallup.com/poll/351140/stable-moral-ratings-obscure-big-partisan-shifts.aspx.
7. Grant Suneson, "These Pro Sports Teams Are Running Out of Fans," *USA Today*, July 20, 2019, https://www.usatoday.com/story/money/2019/07/15/nfl-nba-nhl-mlb-sports-teams-running-out-of-fans/39667999/.
8. Chris Davie, "England Players Take Off Runners-Up Medals after Euro 2020 Final Defeat to Italy," *Metro*,

July 11, 2021, https://metro.co.uk/2021/07/11/england-players-take-off-runners-up-medals-after-euro-2020-final-defeat-to-italy-14911940/.

9. Nancy Armour, "US Women's Gymnastics Team Claims Silver in Team Final after Simone Biles Withdraws at Tokyo Olympics," *USA Today*, July 27, 2021, https://www.usatoday.com/story/sports/olympics/2021/07/27/us-womens-gymnastics-silver-tokyo-olympics-simone-biles/5383082001/.

10. Mike Baker, "Bellevue Football Report: Coaches Violated Rules for Years, District Obstructed Investigation," *The Seattle Times*, May 26, 2016, https://www.seattletimes.com/sports/high-school/bellevue-football-report-finds-coaches-violated-rules-for-years-district-obstructed-investigation/.

11. George Dohrmann and Thayer Evans, "How You Go from Very Bad to Very Good Very Fast," *Sports Illustrated*, September 16, 2013, 30–41; Glenn Harlan Reynolds, "Higher Ed Sports Lower Standards," *USA Today*, January 15, 2014, 10A

12. Lisa M. Guth and Stephen M. Roth, "Genetic Influence on Athletic Performance," *Current Opinion in Pediatrics* 25, no. 6 (2013): 653–658; see also Dov Greenbaum and Mark B. Gerstein, "The Age of Genetically Optimized Sports," *The Wall Street Journal*, July 24, 2012, A13.

13. U.S. Anti-Doping Agency, *Executive Summary: What Sport Means in America* (Colorado Springs, CO: U.S. Anti-Doping Agency, 2011); see also D. Stanley Eitzen, *Fair and Foul: Beyond the Myths and Paradoxes of Sport*, 6th ed. (Lanham, MD: Rowman & Littlefield, 2016), ch. 4.

14. Michael B. Katz, *The Undeserving Poor: America's Enduring Confrontation with Poverty*, 2nd ed. (New York: Oxford University Press, 2013); see also Edward Royce, *Poverty and Power: The Problem of Structural Inequality*, 3rd ed. (Lanham, MD: Rowman & Littlefield, 2019). Christopher B. Doob, *Poverty, Racism, and Sexism: The Reality of Oppression in America* (New York: Routledge, 2021).

15. Brett Knight and Justin Birnbaum, "The World's Highest-Paid Athletes 2021," *Forbes Magazine*, accessed July 27, 2021, https://www.forbes.com/athletes/.

16. Sean Ingle, "Tokyo 2020 Social Media Teams Banned from Showing Athletes Taking the Knee," *The Guardian*, July 21, 2021, https://www.theguardian.com/sport/2021/jul/21/tokyo-2020-olympics-social-media-teams-banned-from-showing-athletes-taking-the-knee.

17. Albert Chen, "The Metrics System," *Sports Illustrated*, August 22, 2016, 45–48.

18. Jeff Kassouf, "Dania Cabello Q+A: On Futbolistas 4 Life, Sports Liberation Education and Allowing Free-Play among Youth," *The Equalizer*, July 25, 2018, https://equalizersoccer.com/2018/07/25/dania-cabello-futbolistas-4-life-film-sports-liberation-education-free-play/.

19. Enterprise Holdings, "Enterprise Teaming Up with Athlete Network for Fifth Straight Year," Press Release, July 13, 2017, https://www.enterpriseholdings.com/en/press-archive/2017/07/enterprise-teaming-up-with-athlete-network-for-fifth-straight-year.html.

20. For example, see "Seven Key Career Skills You Pick Up Playing," Bright Network, https://www.brightnetwork.co.uk/graduate-career-advice/key-career-skills/five-things-every-young-person-needs-know-about-getting-ahead-your-career/seven-key-career-skills-you-pick-playing-sport/; see also Amy Lindgren, "Working Strategies: The Benefits of Sports for Your Career," *Twin Cities Pioneer Press*, August 18, 2018, https://www.twincities.com/2018/08/18/working-strategies-the-benefits-of-sports-for-your-career/. Accessed July 10, 2021

21. For example, see Jürgen Martschukat, *The Age of Fitness: How the Body Came to Symbolize Success and Achievement*, trans. Alex Skinner (Medford, MA: Polity: 2021).

22. James Brighton, Ian Wellard, and Amy Clark, *Gym Bodies: Exploring Fitness Cultures* (London: Taylor & Francis, 2020).

23. Maya Lefkowich, John L Oliffe, Laura Hurd Clarke, and Madeline Hannan-Leith, "Male Body Practices: Pitches, Purchases, and Performativities," *American Journal of Men's Health* 11, no. 2 (2017): 454–463.

24. For example, see "Size Diversity & Health at Every Size," NEDA, https://www.nationaleatingdisorders.org/size-diversity-health-every-size, accessed July 22, 2021; or Autumn Rauchwerk, Anne Vipperman-Cohen, Sridevi Padmanabhan, Woheema Parasram, and Kate G. Burt, "The Case for a Health at Every

Size Approach for Chronic Disease Risk Reduction in Women of Color," *Journal of Nutrition Education and Behavior* 52, no. 11 (2020): 1066–1072.

25. For example, see Kristin Walseth and Thea Tidslevold, "Young Women's Constructions of Valued Bodies: Healthy, Athletic, Beautiful and Dieting Bodies," *International Review for the Sociology of Sport* 55, no. 6 (2020): 703–725.

26. Diane Culver and Majidullah Shaikh, *Gender Equity in Disability Sport: A Rapid Scoping Review of Literature* (Ontario, Canada: University of Ottawa, 2020).

27. Brad Millington and Rob Millington, "'The Datafication of Everything': Toward a Sociology of Sport and Big Data," *Sociology of Sport Journal* 32, no. 2 (2015): 140–160, http://dx.doi.org/10.1123/ssj.2014-0069.

28. Stephen Poulson, *Why Would Anyone Do That? Lifestyle Sport in the Twenty-First Century* (New Brunswick, NJ: Rutgers University Press, 2016).

CHAPTER 4

SOCIAL PROBLEMS AND U.S. SPORT

Violence, Substance Abuse, and Mental Health

> Even though I'm excited for the start of the year, we need to be honest about the fact that football is a violent sport, and many things that people like about it, including me, is the violence. It's not just violence in the abstract, it's people's lives who are tremendously impacted by this.
>
> —CHARLIE CAMOSY, *professor of Christian ethics at Fordham University*[1]

Oklahoma State's J. D. King (28) stiff-arms Texas Tech's DaMarcus Fields (23) during an NCAA college football game in Lubbock, Texas. (Photo: Brad Tollefson/Lubbock Avalanche-Journal via AP)

In Chapter 1, while describing what sociology of sport is about, we emphasized the close relationship between sports and the broader American society; in our survey of the history of sport in the United States in Chapter 2, we stressed the same point; and in Chapter 3, while explaining American values, we accentuated the close sport–society relationship. In the remaining chapters of this book, we examine a variety of topics that have been studied by sport sociologists with the goals of understanding and explaining the social characteristics of U.S. sport in the twenty-first century.

There is perhaps no topic that illustrates the sport–society association better than the prevailing social problems in those societies. It is not an exaggeration to say that the United States is plagued by a number of common major social problems—poverty, racism, sexism, health care, environmental destruction, and crime, to name just a few. *Sports Illustrated* columnist Steve Rushin astutely noted, "No other area of human endeavor offers the opportunity to confront social issues as consistently as sports."

OVERVIEW OF SOCIAL PROBLEMS IN SPORT

SOCIAL THEORIES AND SOCIAL PROBLEMS

As a preliminary to focusing on the social problems in sport, we briefly explain how the social theories we identified in Chapter 1 account for social problems. As we have noted before, functionalism views the social system as interdependent parts linked together into a stable, cohesive, cooperative entity. Social problems occur when members of society have not been adequately socialized toward adopting the prescribed norms and values that underlie the social cohesion and stability of that social system. Just as biological systems become ill when organs and cells do not function normally, society becomes "ill" when its parts—its citizens and culture—do not behave appropriately. Preventing or solving social problems requires strengthening social norms through proper socialization and moral education, much of which may be accomplished in the family, schools, religion, and workplace.

The conflict/cultural perspective views social problems as arising from competition among various groups and interests for power and resources, and it contends that particular components of society exercise power and control arising from particular unequal social arrangements. Social problems result when the mass of the population is denied access to many of the political, economic, and social resources available to the powerful and wealthy. Solutions to social problems lie in eliminating inequality, injustice, and discrimination among social classes. Stronger controls are necessary to restrain the powerful and wealthy and to ensure that decisions and practices are based on promotion of the common good rather than on increased power and profit for the privileged.

EXAMPLES OF SIGNIFICANT SOCIAL PROBLEMS IN SPORT

In the past decade, there have been a variety of social problems at every level of the sports world. On almost everyone's list, violence and substance abuse have a prominent place. More recently, there has been growing concern for the mental health of athletes. An outcry about violence in sports has been triggered by the upsurge in the frequency of concussions among players in several sports—especially football, soccer, and ice hockey. Numerous suggestions for changing the rules, modifying the equipment, and providing better medical attention at all events have been advanced. Literally hundreds of violent sports incidents occur each year involving groups of athletes, as in bench-clearing brawls; other incidents occur in athletes' private lives, between spectators and athletes, and just among spectators.

Substance abuse is also a prevalent problem in sports. Steroids have been a staple among male athletes for decades, but researchers have recently found that steroid use has increased at an alarming rate among females. When the widespread use of Sudafed (a medication with pseudoephedrine) was revealed, it was referred to as the "NHL's dirty little secret" because of the on-ice "boost" it gave the players. MLB's Barry Bonds was subject to an ongoing federal investigation into his alleged use of steroids. Internationally, the Tour de France has been laced with positive drug tests and doping charges, and

Lance Armstrong, winner of a record seven consecutive Tours de France between 1999 and 2005 before he was disqualified from all those races and banned from competitive cycling for life for using illicit performance-enhancing drugs, is the best known. The U.S. Anti-Doping Agency labeled him a "serial" cheat who led "the most sophisticated, professionalised and successful doping program that sport has ever seen."

In the recent Summer Olympics in Tokyo, one of the top gymnasts of all time, Simone Biles, pulled out of much of the competition because of mental health issues. She explained, "I have to do what's right for me and focus on my mental health, and not jeopardize my health and well-being." Earlier in 2021, top tennis player Naomi Osaka withdrew from the French Open, also for mental health issues.[2] The prevalence of mental health issues for athletes is starting to be taken seriously. Research shows that 33 percent of college athletes experience mental health issues and that up to 35 percent of professional athletes do.[3]

These are several of the most significant sports social problems that will be examined in the present chapter. They are pervasive in American sports, and they have troubling consequences for the participants, fans, and others associated with sports.

VIOLENCE IN AMERICAN SOCIETY

Understanding the ways and means by which violence has come to play such a salient role in sports requires historically situating and culturally locating it within the larger culture in which sports are embedded.

Violence in Historical Context

The United States was literally born through violence. Early colonists in America encountered a native population whom the colonists systematically imprisoned, killed, or placed on reserved lands. Thus, it was mostly through violent means that European settlers acquired almost all of the land in the North American continent. In the case of the American colonists, the Declaration of Independence literally furnished the rationale for the legitimate use of violence by the colonists.

Over the past two centuries, oppressed groups in America have been subject to the violence of their oppressors and have used violence to struggle against them. Many Africans brought to America throughout the colonial period and up to the U.S. Civil War were victims of daily violence by slave owners. Concomitantly, African Americans have resorted to violence in every era of American history to redress their grievances. As one African American civil rights activist said in justifying the use of violence, "Violence is as American as apple pie."

Every ethnic and racial minority group in the United States has encountered hostility and violence and has also resorted to violent means to protect itself or to gain a measure of revenge. Asians, Latinx, Irish, you name it: every newly immigrated ethnic and racial group has been subjected to violence in some form.

Throughout the nineteenth century, capitalism brought wage labor, horrible working conditions, and autocratic, sometimes brutal, bosses. By the later nineteenth century, workers had begun to organize into unions for collective action against the policies and practices of the industrialists. Such organizations were often met with force, which in many cases turned to violence by both capitalists and workers.

The expansion of the U.S. territories, which began in the early nineteenth century, has been mostly accomplished through violent military actions. Native Americans had most of their land taken away by violent means. Mexicans were driven out of what is now the southwest United States. Cuba and the Philippines were invaded and subjected to U.S. control.[4]

In summarizing the history of violence in American society, sociologists D. Stanley Eitzen, Maxine Baca Zinn, and Kelly Eitzen Smith explain: "Violence was necessary to give birth to the United States. Violence was used both to keep the blacks in servitude and to free them. Violence was used to defeat rebellious Indians and to keep them on reservations. Additionally, violence has been a necessary means for many groups in American society to achieve equality or something approaching parity in power and in the rights that all Americans are supposed to enjoy."[5]

This heritage of violence is learned in informal and formal ways by each new generation of young people, and it becomes embedded in their understandings about the culture of which they are a part. For the past century, the United States has had the highest homicide rate of all the "developed" countries—from four to twenty times the rates in other industrial nations. Americans living in cities report an alarmingly high rate of fear of being involved in a violent confrontation—that is, robbed, burglarized, or raped.[6]

Contemporary Violence in the United States

It is not only the historical legacy that shapes the violent characteristics of Americans. All anyone has to do is read each day's newspaper or watch the daily television news to get the latest stories of gruesome violence. The phrase "If it bleeds, it leads" captures television news directors' preference for opening newscasts with the most violent stories they can find.

Many popular films are violent. Recent examples include the movies *Inglourious Basterds*, *The Invitation*, and *The Purge*. No other nation comes close to the United States with respect to TV violence: children's daytime programs average 24 violent acts per hour, and evening prime-time programs average 7.5. The TV series *Game of Thrones* and *The Walking Dead* are prime examples. Content analyses of widely popular video games—*Grand Theft Auto V* and *Saints Row: Gat out of Hell*, for example—have as much as 89 percent based on violent actions. In such games, the video player controls the weapons of murder and destruction, with bullets, missiles, and other lethal objects producing spectacular explosions and bloody images as they hit their targets. The overall ambiance is one of extreme, violent imagery. People do not have to leave their living rooms to witness massive doses of violence.

Several media studies over the past decade estimated that by the time the typical American reaches the age of eighteen, they have witnessed 200,000 dramatized acts of violence and 40,000 dramatized murders—not counting video games. A number of noted scholars from a variety of fields of study have reported a connection between movie–TV–video viewing and proviolence attitudes and aggression in childhood and later aggressive behavior in adulthood among both males and females.[7]

More than any other Western nation, the culture of the United States promotes and glorifies violence; indeed, people in other countries are astounded by the salience of violent behavior and imagery in U.S. culture. A telling statistic is the number of mass shootings in the U.S. (a mass shooting is where 4 or more people are shot): in 2020 there were 610; in 2021 there were 692; and in the first 5 months of 2022 there have been 246.[8] Returning to the basic theme of this chapter—the connections between sport and American society—we conclude that sporting practices would be an anomaly if violent behaviors did not play a prominent role.

VIOLENCE IN SPORT: TERMINOLOGY, THEORIES

IS IT VIOLENCE OR AGGRESSION? CONFUSION IN THE LITERATURE

Before focusing directly on aggression and violence in sport, it is necessary to begin with a brief excursion into the meaning of these two key concepts that will be used in this section; there is no uniform definition for aggression among psychologist and sociologists, but there are similar words, terms, and characterizations used by these scholars. To have a specific statement that we can use in this chapter to portray aggressive behavior, we synthesize a statement by a well-known social psychologist. He states that aggression is human behavior delivered to another person with the intent to cause harm, and the aggressor must believe the aggressive act will harm the victim and that the victim will attempt to escape or avoid the aggression. As for the word violence, we prefer the World Health Organization's definition: "Violence is the intentional use of physical force or power, threatened or actual, against oneself, another person, or against a group or community, which either results in or has a high likelihood of resulting in injury, death, psychological harm, maldevelopment, or deprivation."[9] We do not claim that these are the "correct" definitions, but these descriptions contain the essence of common depictions.

Despite the variety of definitions and meanings assigned to the two concepts, we believe that a definition of aggression and violence in sport, what sport sociologist Kevin Young calls sports-related violence and which encompasses notions of both aggression and violence, is appropriate for use in this chapter. He asserts that sports-related violence is defined in a twofold fashion:

- Direct acts of physical violence contained within or outside the rules of the game that result in injury to persons, animals, or property; and
- Harmful or potentially harmful acts conducted in the context of sport that threaten or produce injury or that violate human justices and civil liberties.[10]

A former NFL linebacker put an amusing interpretation on sports-related violence, saying, "When I played pro football, I never set out to hurt anybody deliberately . . . unless it was, you know, important, like a league game or something."

In this chapter we shall use these two words—aggression and violence—in the way we just described, but when referring to other theorists' and researchers' works, it will be necessary to employ their terminology.

THEORIES ABOUT THE CONNECTION BETWEEN AGGRESSIVE BEHAVIOR AND SPORT

Two theories of human aggression dominated the scientific literature during the twentieth century: instinct theory and frustration–aggression theory. The first postulated that aggressive behavior is based in human instincts. This notion owed its popularity to two major proponents: Sigmund Freud, the founder of psychoanalysis, and Konrad Lorenz, a world-renowned ethologist. Both claimed that aggression

is instinctive in humans and that humans can do little to change or control this aggressive impulse. See Box 4.1 for additional descriptions of these theories.

Basing his theory of aggression on his studies of various animal species, Lorenz concurred with the outlines of Freud's notion that humans possess an aggressive impulse that requires periodic release and that by venting aggressive energy we become less aggressive, an effect known as *catharsis*. Aggressive releases of energy can take benign forms or destructive forms, and Lorenz believed that sports can help channel aggressive behavior into benign forms. Although this model of aggression sounds plausible, it has been roundly attacked by both social and biological scientists.

A second theory of aggression that generated much interest and research is called frustration–aggression (F-A) theory. This theory proposed a specific process by which the underlying instinct to aggression is triggered: when an individual is frustrated by someone or something, he or she will aggress to purge the pent-up frustration. In other words, the existence of frustration leads to some form of aggression, although not necessarily an overt act of violence, which, as in the instinct theory, then produces a catharsis, a reduction in the instigation to further aggression.

When examined by the methods of empirical research, the Freud–Lorenz instinct theory, like the F-A hypothesis, has not stood up. Most studies show that aggression does not always occur when a person has been frustrated and that there is no cathartic effect

---

BOX 4.1 *THINKING ABOUT SPORT:* THEORIES ABOUT AGGRESSION/VIOLENCE

Instinct Aggression Theory

Aggressive behavior is based in human instincts; humans cannot change or control this aggressive impulse. Aggressive impulse requires periodic release; sports can help channel aggressive behavior into benign forms.

Frustration–Aggression Theory

When an individual is frustrated, he or she will aggress to purge the pent-up frustration; the aggression then

produces a catharsis, which reduces the likelihood of further aggression.

Aggression Socially Learned Theory

Emphasis is on the learning of aggression via vicarious or observational learning and reinforcement through the interaction–socialization process. There is a focus on learning, thinking, and interacting with peers, family, community, social institutions, and cultural practices in shaping aggressive behavior.

after aggression is employed. One of the most telling arguments against the F-A hypothesis is research that has persuasively shown that not all aggressive behavior stems from prior frustrations and that the linkage between frustration and aggression is not as close as the theory claimed.[11]

The most recent theorizing about aggressive behavior has come from scholars who postulate that aggression is a learned social behavior (e.g., social learning theory, social cognitive theory, and social interaction theory). These theories emphasize the learning of aggression via vicarious or observational learning and reinforcement and through the interaction–socialization process. A major assumption of these models is that individuals who observe esteemed others (parents, teachers, peers, coaches) exhibiting aggressive behavior and being rewarded for it will experience a vicarious reinforcement that has the same effect as personally receiving the positive reinforcement. Moreover, individuals who exhibit aggressive behavior and receive approval for it will tend to employ aggressive behavior in future situations that are similar.

In both cases, the prediction is that continued rewards for aggressive acts will eventually form a tendency to respond to various situations with aggressive actions. According to these socially grounded theories, the conditions most conducive to the learning of aggression seem to be those in which the individual is rewarded for his or her own aggression, has many opportunities to observe aggression, or is the object of aggression. Individuals who mature under such conditions learn to assume that violent behavior is natural and, thus, an appropriate interpersonal response in many situations. These individuals will continue to rehearse violent actions both in actual situations and in fantasy. They will dismiss alternative actions as inappropriate or inadequate. They will also come across situations in which such responses are readily elicited because of the similarity of cues to former situations in which a violent response was learned.

The converse is also true—that is, if an individual receives, or observes esteemed others receiving, some form of negative sanction or punishment, that aggressive behavior will be inhibited. Thus, negative reinforcement will eventually form a habit or tendency to respond to various situations nonaggressively.

It may be seen, then, that social learning, social cognition, and social interactionist theories depart drastically from the older models for explaining aggression. Whereas the instinct and F-A models ground aggression in biological explanations, the socially grounded theories focus on learning, thinking, and interacting with peers, family, community, social institutions, and cultural practices in the environment as shaping aggressive behavior.[12]

Socially based theories and cultural explanations have much more research support than the other aggression models, and we will describe some of that research in the next section. This is not to say, however, that the issue of the roots of aggression has been settled once and for all. Scientists of several disciplines continue to probe for answers to the mysteries surrounding the pervasiveness of human aggression.

AGGRESSION THEORIES AND RESEARCH ON SPORTS

Advocates of the instinct and F-A theories have often claimed that participation in and observation of aggressive activities have a cathartic effect by allowing one to discharge pent-up aggressive energy, and sporting activities have often been suggested as a means of dispelling aggression in a socially healthy way. One disciple of Freud called sports "a salutary purgation of combative instincts," and he claimed that if those instincts are dammed up within, they will break out in disastrous ways. Konrad Lorenz wrote, "The most important function of sport lies in furnishing a healthy safety valve for that most indispensable and, at the same time, most dangerous form of aggression that I have described as collective militant enthusiasm."[13] He even suggested that if nation-states would devote more energy to sporting activities, the chances for war between countries would be reduced.

The basic problem with the notion that sports provide an outlet for the aggressive instinct is that it does not have a confirming empirical basis. Freud, Lorenz, and anyone else can make claims about the connections among instinct, aggression, and sport, but for the claims to be credible they need scientific confirmation. No empirical findings, from Freud, Lorenz, or any others, have provided compelling research evidence in support of their claims.

On the one hand, applying the F-A theory to sport suggests that these activities provide a setting for expressing aggression, thus producing a catharsis—a reduction in aggressive inclinations. On the other hand, it has been observed that frustrations that often accompany sporting contests can trigger aggressive and violent behaviors. In what has become a classic test of the prediction of theories about sport having cathartic effects, researchers assessed the hostility of male spectators before and after a football game and a gymnastics meet. They found that, contrary to the predictions of these theories, hostility increased significantly after observing the football game (a violent event), regardless of the preferred outcome of the game. However, there was no increase in hostility from spectators after observing the gymnastics meet (a nonviolent event).

In a follow-up to that study, the researchers studied men and women who were exposed to a professional wrestling match, an ice hockey game, or a swimming event. General support was found for the previous finding of increased spectator hostility as a result of observing violence. Hostility among subjects increased at the wrestling and hockey events, but such increases did not occur at the swimming competition.

A meta-analytical research study of data from ninety-eight independent studies with 36,965 participants revealed that there was a significant association of social outcomes with violent video games. Violent video games increased aggression and aggression-related outcomes. Several other research studies over the past decade have reached similar conclusions. These findings are exactly the opposite of what should happen according to the cathartic effect of aggression. Overwhelmingly, the findings suggest that, contrary to the predictions of instinct and F-A theories, aggression tends to produce more aggressive predispositions and actions rather than serving as a catharsis.[14]

Several studies seem to support the view of socially oriented scientists that learned cultural behavior patterns explain aggressive behavior rather than aggressive behavior being the result of an innate drive within humans. A unique and interesting study by an anthropologist focused on the relationship between war and sport forms in different types of cultures. He assessed the correlation between types of societies, warlike and nonwarlike, and the existence of combative sports. Using cross-cultural data on ten warlike and ten nonwarlike cultures, the researcher found that warlike societies and combative sports were positively correlated—90 percent of warlike societies had combative sports, but only 20 percent of nonwarlike societies had combative sports.

This same anthropologist did a time-series case study of the United States to see whether the popularity of combative sports (e.g., boxing, hockey, and football) rose or fell during times of war. He found that during wartime, combative sports indeed rose in popularity and noncombative sports declined. Both investigations led to the conclusion that war and combative sports are found together in societies. Both studies were published about forty years ago, but there has been no research more recent that contradicts them.[15] It is not too farfetched, then, to say that combative sports are not channels for the discharge of aggressive tensions but rather seem to promote aggression.

Directly and indirectly, sports research studies have found no support for the instinct and F-A theories of aggression. At the same time, support for the socially oriented theories has accumulated from a variety of sources.

VIOLENCE IN SPORT

Violent actions have been a part of sporting practices for as long as we have records of organized sports. In the ancient Olympic Games, the Greeks had boxing and pankration as a regular part of the program of events. In the former, there were no rounds and no weight classifications. The boxers continued to pummel each other until one boxer was hurt so badly that he could not continue or acknowledged defeat. The pankration was a brutal, all-out combination of wrestling and what we would call street fighting. The rules permitted almost anything, including kicking, choking, hitting, and twisting of limbs. Gouging of eyes and biting were illegal. The object was to maim the opponent so badly that he could not continue or to force him to admit defeat, as in boxing.[16]

Physical tests of strength, endurance, and skill were popular in the Roman civilization and the Middle Ages, and many, such as gladiator spectacles, chariot races, jousts, and tournaments, were quite violent; indeed, deaths were common in these events. The irrepressible bare-knuckle boxing and the precursors to team sports, such as soccer and football, were popular in England and Europe during the eighteenth and nineteenth centuries; all were extremely violent.[17]

VIOLENCE AS PART OF U.S. SPORTS

Just bring along the ambulance
And call the Red Cross nurse,
Then ring the undertaker up,
And make him bring a hearse;
Have all the surgeons ready there,
For they'll have work today,
Oh, can't you see the football teams
Are lining up to play.

—A popular jingle in the 1890s

Aggressive and violent actions in sports have always had a special meaning separate from violence in the wider social context. On the one hand, violent behavior in the larger society, except for a few situations such as war, typically carries with it negative sanctions in the form of norms or laws; violent behavior is punished. On the other hand, violent actions are encoded into the rules of some sports, and there are sport-specific techniques, tactics, and strategies that are quite violent but considered perfectly appropriate in playing the sport. Violent actions have consequences, and regardless of where they occur, they frequently lead to injuries to those subjected to the violence. One of the most common is concussions occurring from injuries to the head.

There is no issue in American sport that cuts across all levels and ages, from youth through high school, intercollegiate, and professional sports, more than concussions. Concussions have become the most dominating and important issue in all of sports. It is being called a "concussion crisis" throughout the spectrum of writers, coaches, athletes, broadcasters, parents, and so forth, and all agree that it is a pressing public health crisis, and for good reason. In the following paragraphs we are going to describe the ways in which the concussion issue is present at each level of sport, from the professional to the youth.

- Within the past several years, many former NFL players have committed suicide or died an early death and were found to have shown evidence of *chronic traumatic encephalopathy* (CTE), a degenerative neurological disorder caused by repeated hits to the head

suffered while playing football. Shockingly, researcher Ann McKee, at the Boston University Center for the Study of Traumatic Encephalopathy, has found evidence of CTE in over 70 of the athletes that she has examined, including 3 NHL enforcers and 18 NFL players. She has also studied 46 brains of deceased football players and found evidence of chronic encephalopathy in 45 of them In a 2007 survey of 2,552 retired NFL players, almost 61 percent of them indicated that they had suffered a concussion in their career; 595 of them had three or more. In 2013, former NFL stars such as Brett Favre, Tony Dorsett, Terry Bradshaw, and Harry Carson all came out to discuss how concussions have affected their postfootball lives. *Sports Illustrated* writer S. L Price recently described how Nick Buoniconti, once the heart of the Miami Dolphins defense, is now experiencing the symptoms of CTE, which are the long-term effects of the concussions he suffered during his playing career, from youth to high school, to college, to professional.[18] See Figures 4.1 and 4.2 for data about increasing high school injuries and concussions.

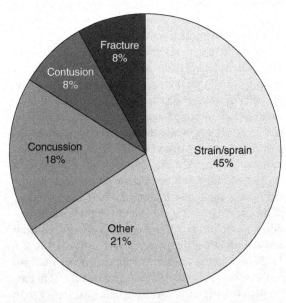

FIGURE 4.1 The Ratio of High School Injury Diagnoses, 2020. Source: Author created with data from: Christy Collins, Hannah Robison, Todd Burus, National High School Sports-Related Injury Surveillance Study 2019-20 School Year. Indianapolis: Datalys Center for Sports Injury Research and Prevention, 2021.

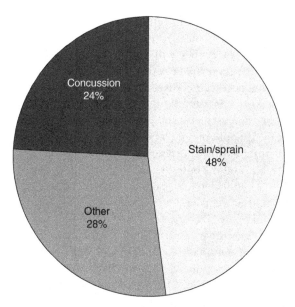

FIGURE 4.2 The Ratio of High School Girls' Soccer Injury Diagnosis, 2020. Source: Author created with data from: Christy Collins, Hannah Robison, Todd Burus, National High School Sports-Related Injury Surveillance Study 2019-20 School Year. Indianapolis: Datalys Center for Sports Injury Research and Prevention, 2021.

- In negotiations with former NFL players during 2013–2016, the NFL reached a tentative $765 million settlement over concussion-related brain injuries among retired players, agreeing to compensate victims suffering from a variety of brain conditions that they blame on blows to the head. In addition, the suit also claimed that the league had concealed the dangers of concussions while glorifying and profiting from hits that made for spectacular highlight-reel footage.
- It is not just NFL players. Concussion-related lawsuits have been filed by more than a dozen former NHL hockey players against the NHL They, too, accuse the league of neglecting to protect players from the dangers of repeated head hits and promoting violence to the fans.[19]
- At the next level down—the intercollegiate level—in 2013 the NCAA reported that its football players experienced more than 3,000 concussions a year over a recent five-year span; some 16,000 occurred in football. Although much of the research

on concussions focuses on men's intercollegiate football and hockey, there are medical analyses of concussions in women's sports. In a ranking of women's college sports on the basis of concussions as a percentage of all injuries, women's soccer and basketball ranked highest. As a consequence of the hundreds of concussions that occur in intercollegiate sports each year and the research over the past decade on brain damage from concussions in sports—particularly in football—in May 2014 the NCAA announced a $30 million effort to fund the most comprehensive clinical study of concussion and head impact exposure ever conducted and issued an educational grand challenge aimed at changing important concussion safety behaviors in college sports. In 2019 the NCAA settled a suit and will now pay up to $70 million for medical diagnosing and treatment for former NCAA athletes.[20] As of 2020, the NCAA has developed concussion protocol guidelines and a system for each member school to report the number of concussions.[21]

- The Datalys Center for Sports Injury Research and Prevention, Inc., used data collected as part of three large injury surveillance programs: the NCAA Injury Surveillance Program; the National Athletic Treatment, Injury and Outcomes Network, which included 96 secondary school football programs providing 11,957 athlete-seasons; and USA Football, called the Youth Football Safety Study. The Datalys study found that during the 2012 and 2013 seasons there were 1,198 concussions reported, with 795 (66.4 percent) in high school athletes.[22] During the 2017–2018 school year, football was still the number one sport for concussions, followed by girls' soccer and then boys' ice hockey. Cheerleading was the activity that resulted in the most concussions during practice.[23]
- In a groundbreaking study at Virginia Tech, researchers placed instrumented helmets on seven- and eight-year-old football players. They then collected data on more than 750 hits to the head over the course of a season. The lead researcher reported that some of the head impacts in youth football in the youth sport group were equal in

force to some of the more vicious hits he has seen in his studies at the college level.[24]

- Beyond the various levels of sports, researchers have begun to focus on age and sex differences in concussion outcomes. Data came from 300 concussed athletes from multiple states over two years. The researchers found that there were indeed age and sex differences. Studies of high school and college athletes have shown that girls and women suffer from concussions at higher rates than boys and men in similar sports, and female athletes take longer to recover from concussions than adult male athletes.[25]
- But concussions are not just a football issue. "Every year boys and girls in youth and high school sports are getting concussions in lacrosse, soccer, wrestling, and ice hockey, as well as football."[26]

Most states have laws with requirements for concussion education for athletes and parents, criteria for removal from play, and medical clearance for returning to play. However, there is variation among states in the specific educational requirements for coaches, student athletes, and parents; qualifications of providers who are permitted to make return-to-play decisions; and populations to which the legislation applies. Research indicates that concussion education programs are effective for improving concussion knowledge and awareness, but there is little evidence that these programs change behavior.

The Institute of Medicine–National Research Council report on sports-related concussions in youth recommends that the NCAA and the National Federation of State High School Associations, in conjunction with other groups, develop, apply, and evaluate the effectiveness of efforts to increase understanding about concussions, with the goal of changing the culture about concussions among elementary school through college students and their parents, coaches, officials, educators, trainers, and health care professionals.

One major justification for the legitimate use of violence in sport is that participants play knowing the rules and therefore understanding that they will be subject to violent actions against them. Just the opposite is typically true in the larger society: people expect they will not be subject to violence and that there are laws that protect them from violent actions. Of course, as we have previously described, this has not always been the case. If, as some analysts have suggested, violence is as American as apple pie, violence in American sport is as natural as the knockout punch, the "bell-ringing" tackle, and the body check.

A Philadelphia Eagles football player once claimed, "People want to see violence, and every collision in the NFL is violent." An NFL Players Association executive asserted, "Typically the greater physical domination and degree of violence a team does to its opponent, the more likely that team will win the game." A *USA Today* editorial explained that "the fans have never complained about a little violence. They even enjoy it." Several years ago, the sports television network ESPN had entire segments of their shows glorifying bone-crunching hits. "Jacked Up!" was a regular feature on ESPN's Monday Night Football show, and it highlighted the most violent plays from the previous weekend of football; ESPN eventually cancelled this segment. And in action and lifestyle sports such as skateboarding and snowboarding, sponsored and self-made videos featuring crashes and injuries are considered key cultural elements. The quintessential skateboarding magazine, *Thrasher*, has regularly had a feature called the "Hall of Meat," where skateboarders are showcased taking painful falls. This type of risk-taking and injury-inducing behavior is indeed used by skateboarders to distinguish themselves as "authentic" participants within their social networks.

The inherent features of some sports—the skills required to achieve victory, the strategy and tactics, and the rules—literally demand violent actions. Several "body contact" sports include tackling, body checking, collisions, and legal "hits" of various kinds, so violence is intrinsic to their actions. Indeed, it is taken for granted that when athletes engage in these activities, they automatically accept the inevitability

High school athlete being attended to by her coach and peers. Studies of high school and college athletes have found that girls and women suffer from concussions at higher rates than boys and men in similar sports; furthermore, female athletes take longer to recover from concussions than male athletes. (Photo: skynesher/Getty Images)

of contact, the probability of some bodily injury, and even the prospect of serious injury.

Boxing is perhaps the most obvious example of a violent sport. The entire objective of a boxing match is for the two contestants to try to injure the other so severely that one cannot continue. A knockout, in which one's opponent is rendered unconscious (or at least semiconscious), is what every fighter strives for. In the past fifty years more than 500 boxers have died from injuries sustained in the ring, mostly from cerebral blood clots.

Ultimate Fighting Championship (UFC)—which combines the striking techniques of boxing and kickboxing with the ground techniques of jiu jitsu and wrestling—has recently become the most popular hand-to-hand combat sport. In recent years, UFC broke the pay-per-view industry's records for a single year, surpassing World Wrestling Entertainment and boxing. As of 2022, an estimated 900 million viewers of UFC programming are found in more than 170 countries.[27]

Significant health benefits are derived from sports and recreational physical activities. Americans, from young children to adults, take part in organized leagues and pickup games to play dozens of sports. But nearly 2 million of them suffer sports-related injuries and utilize the health care system for treatment of injuries resulting from playing sports. Of course, not all of these injuries are the result of aggressive or violent actions from athlete to athlete, but many of them are.[28]

The social consequences of these sports injuries are sometimes devastating. Some athletes sustain injuries that are chronic and cause pain throughout the individuals' lives. In other cases, injured athletes have become quadriplegic and are confined to a lifetime in a wheelchair. At the most extreme are the athletes who die from their injuries.

Still, few people understand the relationship between the violence of a sport and the frequency of injuries and how serious some of them are. But they are the markers of the violence in a sport. Injuries are so common in the NFL that during the season, newspapers publish a weekly "casualty" list of each team in the league. In a survey of 870 former NFL players, 65 percent reported they had suffered a "major injury," one that forced them to miss at least eight games. Seventy-eight percent reported some kind of physical disability from their pro football injuries. One retired player has had thirty knee surgeries, dating back to his college days. Another retired player suffered at least fifteen concussions while playing in the NFL. One Denver Broncos guard had twenty-eight surgeries and was still an active player. After thirteen surgeries on the ankle of another former NFL player, the physicians cut off his leg eight inches below the knee.[29]

College and high school football violence takes its toll too. According to the National Athletic Trainers' Association, about 37 percent of U.S. high school football players are injured badly enough each year to be sidelined for at least the remainder of the day. About eight high school football players die each year from football-related injuries.

A number of sports, such as baseball, basketball, soccer, NASCAR, and so forth, do not have the inherent violence found in others, but the methods employed and the way the rules are being interpreted are increasingly encouraging strategy and tactics resulting in violent actions.

Borderline Violence

What in the sports culture is called *borderline violence* is a category of violent actions that are prohibited by the official rules of a given sport but routinely occur and are more or less accepted by everyone; they have become the unofficial norms. Included here are the late hit in football, hockey fistfighting, the knockdown pitch in baseball, the high tackle in soccer, and the deliberate foul in basketball. All such actions occasionally produce serious injuries; they also occasionally trigger bench-clearing brawls among the athletes. Although penalties are often meted out for these actions, the punishments are typically not severe enough to deter their future occurrence.

Often the intent behind much of this type of violence in sport is to "get the edge" over an opponent through "intimidation." The fistfight in ice hockey, the "brushback" pitch and the "break-up-the-double-play slide" in baseball, "clotheslining" and hitting wide receivers even when they are not directly involved in the play in football—all are done with the intent of breaking opponents' attention and concentration on the tasks they are trying to perform. Indeed, in NHL hockey and NBA basketball it has been a common practice of teams to carry an "enforcer" or "intimidator" on the roster. General managers and coaches of NHL teams often acknowledge that every team likes to have one or two enforcers or designated hit men so that the rest of the team feels comfortable.

Although the objects of these tactics may not be physically harmed, there are cases in most sports where these enforcer tactics have extended beyond borderline violence and resulted in career-ending injuries: In 2004, the NHL's Todd Bertuzzi of the Vancouver Canucks punched Steve Moore of the Colorado Avalanche from behind and drove his face into the ice, causing three fractured neck vertebrae. Moore was wheeled off the ice on a gurney, and he never played another game in the NHL. Pittsburgh Penguins legendary player Sidney Crosby has been the target of enforcers throughout his career because of his status as "the best of the best." He has had at least four concussions during his NHL career, beginning in 2011, with the most recent one, at this writing, during the 2017 Stanley Cup playoffs.

These are, of course, only two of the most well-known examples of violent actions that have led to major injuries. There are literally hundreds of other incidents where the quasi-criminal violence shortened the victim's sports career or rendered him permanently impaired for the remainder of his career. Whenever current and former pro athletes get together to talk about their playing experiences, they recount stories about the "dirty play" or the "cheap shot" that had long-term consequences for the victim.

Although comparative figures are hard to come by, there is a widely held perception that all of the types of sports violence previously described are increasing in the United States. Articles deploring this trend regularly detail the latest incidents of sports violence, with pleas to everyone, from the athletes to the highest officials in government, to end the growing menace to the good health of athletes, officials, and fans.

FOSTERING AND SUPPORTING PLAYER VIOLENCE

Mediated Sports: Violence Is What the Viewers Want

Some of the most respected researchers of television's coverage of sports believe that the mass media highlight and foster violence in a number of ways. Focusing on rough play, replaying spectacular hits over and over, and sportscasters praising violent play are three prominent ways violent actions are promoted. Broadcast sports tend to be unrestrained odes to violent action; almost any violent behavior—the more spectacular, the better—is highlighted and given justifications.

In one NFL playoff game, an instant replay showed an offensive lineman clearly and deliberately delivering a viciously illegal elbow into the face of an opponent, virtually twisting off the victim's head. This graphic illegal violence was followed by a comment from one of the sportscasters: "Nobody said this was going to be a tea party!" A similar situation in a televised college football game drew this comment from one of the sportscasters: "Anything that is not called is legal." Camera crews and sportscasters are ever vigilant to the violent collision, the late hit, the shove in the back that can be replayed over and over via instant replay to the horrified fascination of viewers.

As if it were not enough that people see violent sport actions in person and on television and hear sportscasters praise sports violence, television also helps sponsor programs whose fundamental ethos is to present gratuitous violence. The highly popular World Wrestling Entertainment events are, as one commentator put it, "celebrations of violence"—the more outrageous the better—even if not strictly real. But it is a newcomer, mixed martial arts, the most popular variation of which is UFC, a full-contact combat sport that permits the use of both striking and grappling tactics, both standing and on the ground, and features movements of a variety of other combat sports and martial arts, that has captured the golden eighteen- to thirty-four-year-old male demographic. A match ends when one combatant cannot physically continue or gives up. Its program on Fox Sports 1 (although it has made frequent changes) has surpassed the TV ratings of the NBA and MLB playoffs. UFC events attract more pay-per-view than any pro wrestling or boxing event.[30] (More about UFC can be found in Chapter 12.)

During the NFL season, daily and weekly ESPN segments, as well as other networks, often highlight the previous weekend's most violent legal, noninjury hits. The large voyeuristic audience for shocking, even horrifying, violence is obviously the target audience for these segments. However, some critics of these TV segments argue that it glorifies the violent aspects of football and celebrates cheap shots or injuries. Nevertheless, ESPN, as well as other TV networks, routinely plays and replays the most violent actions of college and professional sports events.

Sports video games, staples for teenage and young adult males, graphically emphasize violent actions. *Madden NFL*, the most popular of these video games had sold over 130 million copies. As of 2021, sales of this game have generated more than $7 billion in revenue since the game was introduced in 1988, making the series one of the best selling in the video game industry's history.[31]

Fans: Violence Reigns

Corporate sports are commercial endeavors, and those who produce the sporting events (professional franchise owners, university athletic departments, etc.) are dependent on fan support. Surveys of fans indicate that spectator enjoyment of games is related to the amount of violence in them. Research findings about viewers' enjoyment of televised sports events clearly indicate that increased player aggressiveness enhances spectators', especially male spectators', enjoyment of watching sports contests. Also, those who perceive high levels of violence in sports events report greater enjoyment than those who perceive low levels of violence.[32]

Related evidence reveals that broadcast commentary stressing roughness of actions facilitates viewers' perceptions of the violence of the event, which, in turn, can lead to greater enjoyment of the sports contest. Finally, play-by-play and color commentary that stresses hostility and animosity between opponents, causing spectators to perceive players' actions as more violent than they really are, can result in greater enjoyment for spectators.[33]

Given the preferences that fans seem to have for violent action, and given that commercial sports must depend on the fans to stay in business, it should not be surprising that the sports industry is quite willing to make sure that violent play is a salient feature of the events. Professional sports executives, coaches, and players frequently exclaim, "We depend on the fans for our existence."

Pressures on Athletes to Be Violent

Pressures exist in sports to use violence, legal and illegal, in the quest for a victory. At all levels of play, incentives exist for athletes to be violent. Coaches teach players the use of intimidating and violent tactics, and peer pressure inspires players to use violence. Athletes are unanimous in saying that the best way to gain coaches' recognition and praise is through aggressive play and, in contact sports, to become known for violent hits.

The folklore of the sports world is that aggressive play yields positive results. Youth, high school, and college athletes often either secure a place on the team or are cut from it depending on the amount of aggressiveness they display. College athletic scholarships are often awarded by coaches based on the aggressive tendencies shown by recruits. Various financial incentives promote aggressive actions by professional athletes. For example, the NFL's New

Orleans Saints were penalized after it was revealed that they had a "bounty hunting" program during the 2009-2011 seasons that gave cash rewards to players whose hits injured other players.

Coaches, Owners, Commissioners: Enablers of Violence

Beginning with their first organized sports experience, athletes learn that they must please their coaches if they expect to remain a member of the team. Pleasing the coach often means doing "whatever it takes" to win. Many coaches firmly believe that the most aggressive team wins games; therefore, athletes quickly learn that being aggressive gains the coach's approval. A former NFL player said the message that coaches repeat over and over is that if you are going to make a mistake, make an aggressive one.

Welcoming violent play also applies to dealing with injuries. As one NFL lineman asserted, "If it's not bleeding and it's not completely broken, rub dirt on it and let's go." As we have noted previously in this chapter, concussions are an epidemic in the NFL. Still, one NFL linebacker had this to say about the prospect of incurring a concussion when getting hit: "That's football. It's what makes the game so popular. People love the battle! People love the violence."[34]

Professional team owners refuse to condemn violence because they are convinced it attracts spectators. Among owners and general managers of professional sports franchises, there is a tacit agreement that it is hard to justify making changes in the rules to reduce violence because the bottom line is that there are many fans who like it. It boils down to this: there is no economic incentive to curb violence on the playing field.

Athletes who refuse to participate in violent actions often find themselves demoted on the team roster or even dropped from the team. In professional ice hockey the expectation is that players will participate in fights. One NHL player argued, "The game of hockey is special. Its blend of physical play, intensity and emotion is what makes players such as myself love it. But I think it is important to realize that fighting plays a role in—and enhances—all of those aspects. Would hockey still be a good game without fighting? Yes, I think so. But it is a great game with it!"[35]

VIOLENT BEHAVIOR OF COACHES AND ADMINISTRATION

We have discussed how athletes are in environments that encourage them to be violent to each other. But it is important to note that violence has been perpetuated by coaches and medical staff and that these types of behaviors are often hidden by organizations whose reputations could be hurt by it. Two notorious examples include sexual assault of minors. USA Gymnastics faced a huge scandal when it was found that one of their team doctors, Larry Nassar, was accused of sexually abusing nearly 200 young female gymnasts over a period of fourteen years. Many top gymnasts, including Simone Biles, publicly testified about their abuse at his hands. Nassar pleaded guilty to sexual assault and was sentenced in 2018. This investigation ultimately pointed to a whole environment that was neglectful. USA Gymnastics was headquartered at Michigan State University. Since the trial and conviction of Nassar, several head administrators of Michigan State resigned, as well as top officials at USA Gymnastics.[36] The second example is Jerry Sandusky, who was a coach at Pennsylvania State University. He was convicted of sexual assault of minors who were part of his youth camp. The majority of the crimes were after his tenure with Penn State, but he was given permission to use Penn State facilities for the youth camp. Again, the abuse was over a long period of time, 1994–2009. He was convicted of assaulting ten boys over a fifteen-year period. Many people who were connected to the program, including the head coach, Joe Paterno, were fired because they were held responsible for not creating a safe environment.[37]

The significance of the social context and power dynamics for understanding how and why nonaccidental violence in sport occurs was highlighted by the International Olympic Committee's consensus statement:

> The cultural context of harassment and abuse is rooted in discrimination based on power differentials across a range of social and personal factors. . . . All athletes have a right to engage in "safe sport," defined as an athletic environment that is respectful, equitable and free from all forms of non-accidental violence to athletes. Yet, these issues represent a blind spot for many sport organisations through fear of reputational damage, ignorance, silence or collusion. . . . Sport stakeholders are encouraged to consider the wider social parameters of these issues, including cultures of secrecy and deference that too often facilitate abuse.[38]

In sum, those who have more social and organizational power are both responsible for creating a safe environment and, paradoxically, more often the perpetrators of harm. Thus, it is vital that athletes have support and advocates inside and outside their sport organizations.

VIOLENT BEHAVIOR OF ATHLETES IN THEIR PERSONAL LIVES

The majority of an athlete's life is lived off the field of play. Even on days in which they practice or play sports, these activities will typically take less than 20 percent of their waking hours. Beyond their role as athletes, athletes do most of the same things that other young people do. They have friends they hang out with, they party, they drink, they develop sexual relationships, they marry and have families, and so forth.

At one time, little was known by the public about what athletes did on their "own" time, nor was it reported by the media. Moreover, if athletes got into trouble of any kind, coaches, owners, administrators, and the media covered it up; "taking care of the athlete" was the explanation given for this action (others have called it a "conspiracy of silence"). In effect, athletes' misbehavior, even unlawful action, was protected from public scrutiny and the criminal justice system.

At the same time that athletes of previous eras were being protected if they ran afoul of the law, they were portrayed as honest, sober, upstanding pillars of the community and role models to be emulated. However, the accumulating literature makes it clear that in reality many of them engaged in behavior ranging from fun-loving mischief to violent criminal behavior when they were not playing their sport.

Currently, the private lives and escapades of college and professional athletes in many sports are being spelled out in detail through various mass media. In many cases, it has not been a pretty story because violent criminal behavior, especially sexual assault and spousal abuse by the athletes, has been a persistent theme. The following examples illustrate this point.

- During the last month of 2012, Kansas City Chiefs linebacker Jovan Belcher killed his girlfriend and fatally shot himself in the head while he was drunk. About a week later, Dallas Cowboys defensive tackle Josh Brent drove drunk and crashed his car, killing his teammate Jerry Brown, who was in the car. Between the 2013 Super Bowl on February 3 and September 5 that same year, NFL players were arrested or accused of crimes some 37 times; 10 were accused of driving drunk. Between September 2006, when Roger Goodell became NFL commissioner, and late 2015, NFL players have been arrested or charged with crimes over 400 times; more than 110 were drunken-driving arrests, 43 were domestic abuse cases, 34 were incidents involving guns, and more than 90 were cases that involved fighting or disorderly conduct. During that block of years, there was an average of 56 arrests per year.[39]
- NFL player Rae Carruth was found guilty of conspiracy to commit murder, shooting into an occupied vehicle, and using an instrument to destroy an unborn child. He was sentenced to eighteen to twenty-four years in prison.
- In 2007 NFL Atlanta Falcons quarterback Michael Vick admitted that he was involved in an illegal interstate dog-fighting operation. He pleaded guilty to federal felony charges and served twenty-one months in prison, followed by two months in home confinement.
- In 2014, Baltimore Ravens running back Ray Rice was arrested and subsequently indicted for third-degree aggravated assault related to an incident in which he hit his then-fiancée with his fist. The incident went viral after celebrity news website TMZ released a video of the encounter. Rice's contract was terminated by the Ravens, following the release of an additional video of the incident. Rice was then suspended indefinitely by the NFL league, but was later reinstated after he successfully appealed the decision in federal courts.
- In 2021, former Portland Timbers soccer player Andy Polo was accused of domestic violence. According to Polo's former partner, Génessis Alarcón,

"He pulled my hair. I fell to the floor. He slapped me in the face and gave me a black eye." This led to Polo's eventual dismissal from the team and from the American first division soccer league, MLS, although there has been substantial controversy regarding how the team handled this case. Main supporter groups including the Timbers Army and the Rose City Riveters have been highly vocal in protesting team leaders and their practices.[40]
- Former New England Patriots player Aaron Hernandez was given a life sentence for killing a semi-professional football player, Odin Lloyd, in 2013. In April 2017 Hernandez was acquitted in a separate murder case stemming from the deaths of two men in a 2012 drive-by shooting that prosecutors felt were linked to Lloyd's death. While the acquittal did not affect the Lloyd case directly, some legal experts felt it could have assisted Hernandez's chances in an appeal of the Lloyd decision. But a week later, Hernandez was found dead of an apparent suicide in his jail cell.[41]

There are quite different views about whether athletes as a group, especially athletes in contact sports, commit a greater share of domestic violence and sexual assaults than nonathletes. On one side, largely represented by the sports industry, is the view that the private lives of today's athletes are being scrutinized more closely by the media, and the private-life behaviors of athletes that prevailed for a long time are just now being reported. In this view, big-time college athletes and pro athletes have become celebrities and, as with other celebrities, there is fierce competition among the media to satisfy the public's appetite for scandal. Finally, it is alleged that many of the reports of athletes' violence against women are inaccurate, charges are dropped, or athletes are not convicted of the charges.

On the other side, there is an acknowledgment that high-profile athletes in the past received special coddling by the media, and their transgressions were ignored or just not reported. But that view does not change the empirical evidence in recent years showing that athletes, especially in contact sports, have indeed been overrepresented in domestic violence and sexual assaults. Behavioral and social theories have been employed that suggest that the norms and values of the sport culture socialize athletes into attitudes that valorize male power and control over females, and one outcome is male athletes' propensity toward committing violence against women.

Having said that, we want to emphasize that athletes are not the only assailants and abusers of women. We focus on athletes because this book is about sports. According to the Rape, Abuse & Incest National Network, the nation's largest anti–sexual violence organization, nearly 250,000 sexual assaults occur annually, and one in six women has been the victim of an attempted or completed rape in her lifetime, with college women four times more likely than nonstudents to be sexually assaulted. These statistics leave little doubt that male sexual assault against women and spousal abuse are major national social problems and are not unique to the sport world.[42]

SOURCES FOR VIOLENCE BY MALE ATHLETES IN THEIR PRIVATE LIVES

What accounts for this rather alarming trail of violence by male athletes in their private lives? There is, of course, the fact that they live in a violent culture and that their lives are much more under the media's scrutiny than the average person's. These factors have been previously discussed, but are there other factors? We believe there are at least three other factors that might contribute to this subculture of violence: male bonding rituals, preconditioning to aggressive behavior, and steroid use by many athletes.

Sport Culture and Male Bonding

As part of gender development, both males and females learn culturally prescribed attitudes, rituals, symbols, and behaviors for their sex. Much of this learning, and exhibiting the effects of the learning, takes place in sex-segregated activities. Sports teams provide fertile ground especially for male bonding, fostering a spirit of exclusivity, camaraderie, and solidarity among males. Given traditional masculine prescriptions of toughness, dominance, repression of empathy, and competitiveness, athletes may display the effects of this socialization by engaging in reckless and violent behavior as proof of their masculinity. One aspect of this socialization is the attitude that men have a right to dominate women. Sport studies researchers have found that the language of locker room male bonding is a language of power and control over women, and of violence against women.

Preconditioning Males for Violence

A number of behavioral and social scientists contend that male socialization tends to be a preconditioning to aggressive behavior as an appropriate response for achieving one's goal, whether it is defending oneself in the streets, making a tackle, or satisfying one's sexual desires against a woman's wishes. Society's concept of masculinity is inextricably woven into aggressive, forceful, physical behavior. Physicality and masculinity have meant the same things for men and male dominance: force, coercion, and the ability to subdue and control the natural world.

The epitome of socially appropriate physical dominance, use of force, and violent action occurs in various sports. Pulitzer Prize–winning journalist H. G. Bissinger spent a year in a Texas community studying its high school football team. His book, *Friday Night Lights: A Town, a Team, and a Dream*, was turned into a movie and then into a popular TV series. All three describe what the players did and what they talked about, much of which was about "hitting" or "sticking" or "popping" someone. These were the things that coaches exhorted players to do. The supreme compliment was to be called a "hitter" or "headhunter." A hitter made bone-crushing tackles that knocked out or hurt his opponents. The book was about something rather small—the culture of high school football in a Texas town—but it and the movie and TV series ended up being about something large—the core values in the United States.

Sociologist Derek A. Kreager studied whether participation in contact sports by teenagers also promoted violence off the field and found that involvement in contact sports such as football and wrestling did indeed increase the likelihood of off-field violent behavior.[43] This suggests that a culture of violence can be nurtured on the sporting field. Behavior learned in one context, where it is appropriate, can be transferred to another, where it is not.

Steroid Use and Male Violent Behavior

There is a myriad of evidence that anabolic steroid use is widespread in many sports at the high school, collegiate, and professional levels, especially in sports involving physical contact and feats of strength. There is also convincing anecdotal as well as some empirical evidence showing that the regular use of anabolic steroids can trigger episodes of aggressive behavior in users. Researchers who have studied the effects of steroid abuse agree that athletes who are steroid users seem more inclined to extremely violent behavior than nonusers.[44] The issue of steroid use in sports is taken up again in the section "Substance Abuse and Sport" in this chapter.

Concluding Thoughts on Violence by Male Athletes in Their Private Lives

Undoubtedly, these and other factors can interact in any given situation or incident that ultimately leads to violent, even criminal, behavior by athletes. We want to emphasize, however, that we recognize that the actual percentage of athletes at any level and in any sport who are involved in violence off the field is small. Nevertheless, there are enough incidents, and they are serious enough, for all of us to be concerned. Concerted efforts must be made by everyone involved in sport to find ways and means to reduce, even eliminate, sexual assault and domestic violence by athletes that has become all too familiar.

One effort to do something about this problem has been initiated by a woman who was raped by a football player while she was a college student. She has formed the National Coalition against Violent Athletes (NCAVA), now called the WeLEAD Project. The purpose of the WeLEAD Project is to educate the public on various issues involving athletes and violence, while also providing support to the victims. See Box 4.2 for more information about the WeLEAD Project.

ATHLETES' VIOLENCE AGAINST TEAMMATES: HAZING

Rites of passage are a common feature of many cultures. They are rituals and ceremonies through which people must pass in the transition from one group to another within the culture. Perhaps the most common rites of passage are those that young boys and girls must pass through to become recognized as full-fledged adult men and women of that society. The rites-of-passage principle has also been adopted by many organizations—military, business, social, sport—and specific rituals and ceremonies are established to initiate new members.

BOX 4.2 *THINKING ABOUT SPORT:* THE WELEAD PROJECT

One of the valuable roles increasingly being played by the Internet—especially Facebook and Twitter—is providing a means by which fledgling organizations can quickly communicate with large numbers of people about a social problem, educate them about that social problem, bring those who wish to do something about the problem into contact with one another, and even mobilize people into action to resolve the problem. Those are the purposes behind the founding of the National Coalition against Violent Athletes (NCAVA). This organization recently changed its name to the WeLEAD Project. The website of WeLEAD states the following:

> WeLEAD works to eliminate off the field violence by athletes through the implementation of prevention methods that

recognize and promote the positive leadership potential of athletes within their communities.

Started by Katherine Redmond in 1997 after the conclusion of her Title IX lawsuit against the University of Nebraska, WeLEAD was formed to address toxic sports culture and empower survivors to come forward.

Athletes are role models and leaders in our communities who carry heavy influence over societal standards, especially with children. WeLead strives to promote positive athlete development through education, support and accountability. We also work to advocate for and support survivors. Because we work with survivors and athletes, we are uniquely able to aid in prevention.

Source: WeLEAD Project, https://weleadproject.org/about. Accessed June 17, 2022.

Rites of passage, in the form of initiation ceremonies and rituals, became a popular part of belonging to a sports team from the beginning of modern organized sports. But also from the beginning many teams employed a variation called *hazing*. Sport hazing involves humiliating, degrading, or endangering the initiate, and it predominantly operates as a male-defined, male-dominated practice. Nevertheless, hazing has been a normalized practice (especially in high school and college sports) that resists pressures to change. Hazing rituals tend to reinforce the power structure of the group: newbies must conform to traditions and prove their dedication to the status quo by going through trials for the team. Yet, many initiates have been seriously harmed physically and/or psychologically.

Administrators periodically attempt to put an end to hazing, but their efforts have been largely unsuccessful. In a survey in three western Canadian cities with amateur and professional teams competing in eight contact sports and three non-contact sports, two sport sociologists found that hazing occurred routinely but in varying degrees across the sports. They concluded that despite increasing social disapproval and closer policing, hazing continues to play a significant role in both men's and women's sports teams. In related research, two University of Northern Iowa investigators obtained corroborating evidence, noting that "athletes reported engaging in risky, hazing behaviors and that both the values of sport as well as the desire to be accepted by teammates encouraged hazing."[45]

In the past few years dozens of high schools and colleges have had hazing incidents in which school officials placed teams on probation, required that team members perform community service, or suspended team members from school or college. To give the reader some understanding of the kinds of hazing incidents that have occurred, several examples follow.

- In 2021, the University of California Davis found in their investigation that the baseball team had created a culture of rookie hazing over the course of a decade. Activities included excessive drinking, threats of sexual assault, and evidence of illegal drug usage. This led to the resignation of coaching staff including the head coach and new restrictions were placed on the team.[46]

- In 2012, eight freshmen on the State University of New York Geneseo women's volleyball team were summoned via text message to an off-campus house party in the Livingston County village. The hosts were upperclassmen players, and a dangerous game was about to be played. "I was expecting to be at a volleyball party, like the previous weekend," one freshman said in a police deposition. This time, it was a hazing ritual—an initiation onto the team. Before the night was over, one freshman was near death with a blood-alcohol content of 0.266 percent—saved only by passers-by as she lay unconscious on the grass. Within days, eleven young women were charged with hazing, and the volleyball season was shut down for the year.

- In 2016, three seniors at a Philadelphia-area high school were charged with assaulting another student in the locker room during a hazing ritual called "No-Gay Thursday." According to the county district attorney, "No-Gay Thursday" is a hazing ritual that involves incidents such as students in upper grades forcing students in lower grades to take off most of their clothes and clean the locker room. The older students then place their genitals on other students' heads. In this particular case a football player was allegedly held down by two other football players while a third player penetrated him with a broom handle. Three players were all seventeen years old at the time of the incident and have been charged as juveniles with assault, unlawful restraint, making terroristic threats, and related offenses.[47]

Similar incidents have occurred in virtually every corner of the United States, where initiates have been showered with mixtures of urine and vomit, brutally paddled, or sodomized.

Because hazing has historically been prominent at the high school and college levels, in recent years governing bodies throughout the United States have been furiously busy developing no-hazing policies. The NCAA recently published a manual for its member institutions and athletes that includes guidelines on hazing.[48] Their efforts are commendable, but individuals and organizations that develop no-hazing policies face several barriers to eliminating hazing: denial of the problem, arguments that hazing is harmless, silence among victims, fear among victims, and cultural norms that perceive hazing as normal.

SPORTS FANS: VIOLENT AND ABUSIVE ACTIONS

Spectators at a sporting event are not usually passive observers. Typically, they like to "get into it," to become part of the game, as it were. But sometimes their enthusiasm turns into violent and abusive actions. And this is not merely a contemporary phenomenon, nor is it confined to American sports.

The word *fan* is short for *fanatic* and comes from the Latin word *fanum*. The Romans used the word to describe persons who were overly zealous while attending the chariot races. In one renowned spectator riot at the chariot races in ancient Rome, some 30,000 fans were killed. In 1969 in a World Cup soccer series between El Salvador and Honduras, spectator violence accompanied each of the games. Finally, the riot that followed the third game resulted in the two countries severing political and economic relations and mobilizing their armies against each other; this has been called the "soccer war" between El Salvador and Honduras.

Traditional but typically good-natured heckling of players, coaches, officials, and opponents has taken on a completely new attribute in the past decade. Fans—especially at professional and collegiate sports events—are increasingly resorting to abusive and obscene language. In addition to vocal communication, placards and apparel emblazoned with obscenities are displayed. Student sections at some universities compete to be the most outrageous, vicious, obscene, and offensive, and they believe they have a constitutional (First Amendment free speech) right to engage in such behavior.

Those who follow American sports may be quite aware of the many incidents of spectator violence. Several years ago, *Sports Illustrated* took what it called an "unscientific poll of fans" and reported that everyone who confirmed having ever been to a sporting

event had witnessed one or more acts of violent behavior by fans. Within the past decade, major fan violence has erupted across all the major professional team sports. It became so bad that several years ago management at eight NFL teams created a class that ejected fans are asked to complete, called the NFL's Fan Code of Conduct policy. Hundreds of fans have completed the class, and the psychotherapist who oversees the program claims, "There hasn't been a single repeat offender."

Fan violence has also penetrated high school and university campuses, where football and basketball games have been marred by riots. Indeed, because of frequent spectator riots at high school sports events, several large city school systems have imposed strict limits on the number of spectators admitted to basketball games in an effort to prevent fights between fans and opposing teams. Several universities have stopped scheduling games against traditional rivals because of fan violence that has accompanied the contests.[49]

Newspaper and magazine articles describing, and usually condemning, a seemingly escalating amount of fan violence are common. "Sports in USA Sick: Violence out of Hand," "Fans Behaving Badly," and "Uncivil Disobedience" are examples of article titles found in the popular press. The theme of all of these is a contention that an excessively violent equilibrium exists in sports today at almost all levels.

Factors Associated with Fan Violence

Behavioral and social scientists seeking to understand and explain spectator violence and abusive actions tend to center their explanations on fans' social learning and experiences in the wider society. In support of this, there is widespread agreement—and a burgeoning list of recent books to support it—that there is an increasing lack of civility in the United States. This is manifested in growing violence and incivility in all of the major social institutions, including family, schools, business, politics, and media.

Hardly a week passes without some major incidence of violence or interpersonal abuse in these social arenas. All of the major sports themselves have become more violent, not only in the games but also

The fan experience at stadiums across the United States shows a disturbing trend of violence. American sports fans, especially at professional and collegiate sports events, are gradually resorting to abusive and violent behavior. Both researchers and mass media who follow American sports have been increasingly reporting incidents of spectator violence. Newspaper and magazine articles describing a seemingly escalating amount of fan violence are common. There is a persisting theme in all of these reports pointing to an excessively abusive and violent fandom that exists in sports at almost all levels in the early twenty-first century. (Photo: AP Photo/Ben Margot, File)

in the alarming lack of sportsmanship on the field and the widespread trash-talking among the athletes. Given the cultural background pervading fans' general social experiences, it is hardly a coincidence that fan violence and obnoxious actions are escalating.[50]

Although actions during sporting events may play a contributing role in fans' violent and abusive behavior, most behavioral scientists reject cathartic explanations. Instead, they contend that violence viewed in sport contributes to violence in the crowd. A fundamental principle of social learning is that people learn what they observe, and if what they observe goes unpunished, they are likely to consider it appropriate for themselves.

The sequence of witnessing violence–learning–acting might proceed in this manner: fans watching a violent sporting event are likely to become more aggressively inclined themselves; as they witness violent behavior, they might, in the right circumstances, act violently themselves. Of course, as we emphasized earlier in this chapter, learning the heritage and culture of violence is the lived experience of everyone in the United States, so sports fans have more than their immediate experiences in the stadium or arena mediating a mindset for violence.

There are other factors that can precipitate spectator violence and abusive behavior that go beyond just broad enculturation and witnessing these behaviors in sports. Two forms of "perceived injustice" can trigger fan anger and abuse. The first form occurs when fans believe that officials have applied a rule unfairly or inaccurately; the second occurs when fans believe that a rule itself is unfair, regardless of how accurately it is employed.[51]

An example of the first form would be bad calls by officials, such as calling a batted baseball foul when it was fair or calling a made basket from three-point range two points. An example of the second might occur when a penalty kick is awarded near the end of a tie game in soccer; since it is such a high-percentage kick, it will almost always result in a victory for the kicking team. The penalty kick in soccer is uniformly condemned as unfair by soccer fans, so a situation as just described may precipitate fan violence.

Social scientists have suggested five social situational factors that can be conducive to spectator violence. They are as follows:

1. A large crowd, because of a perceived power inherent in a mass of people, and the anonymity foments irresponsible behavior;
2. A dense crowd, because annoyance and frustration build when one's comfortable space is violated and when one is forced to be near strangers;
3. A noisy crowd, because noise is itself arousing, and arousal is a common precondition to violence;
4. A standing crowd, because standing for long periods is tiring, jostling is common, and the lack of an assigned space is frustrating; and
5. Crowd composition, because drinking crowds, young male crowds, and crowds made up of people who are oppressed in the larger society are more predisposed toward violent behavior than more diverse crowds.

Game and Postgame Violence

Recent years have witnessed several violent incidents involving athletes and fans during or immediately after a sports event. There are far too many of these incidents each year to list all of them. But here we summarize a few examples from recent years.

- After a home game at the Los Angeles Dodgers' Stadium, two men in Dodgers clothing followed three men in San Francisco Giants gear as they walked to their car after the game. Witnesses said the attackers yelled slurs against the Giants and began kicking and punching the men. One victim suffered a head injury and was hospitalized in critical condition with a severe skull fracture and bad bruising to his brain's frontal lobes. He remained in a coma for weeks. He was left with disabling brain damage following the attack in the stadium parking lot. In July 2014, a jury awarded the San Francisco Giants fan beaten at Dodger Stadium $18 million in damages and found the Dodgers organization partially to blame for the incident.[52]

- After one preseason NFL football game between the Oakland Raiders and San Francisco 49ers at Candlestick Park, mayhem between fans erupted in the stands. Seventy were ejected from the park, twelve were arrested, two were shot in the parking lot, and one was savagely beaten in a restroom. The president of a sports consulting firm noted, "The viciousness, the escalation of violence is what is so striking. It's escalated, perhaps, as a reflection of society."

- During a recreational soccer game in Taylorsville, Utah, a seventeen-year-old player punched the referee in the head after the referee issued a yellow card. After a week in a coma, the referee died. The president of the National Association of Sports Officials said, "It's a response to the environment in which we find ourselves. That environment is growing increasingly violent."

Player–fan incidents are not new to sports, but the frequency of these types of violent incidents has been on the upswing for years.

There is a lengthy tradition of sports fans celebrating the winning of a championship, tournament, or contest against a bitter rival. Violence often accompanies these celebrations in stadiums and arenas, as fans storm the playing area. In football, fans tear down the goalposts; in basketball, they clip the basket nets; in hockey, they throw objects onto the ice; and so forth. Frequently these celebrations become violent because security officials attempt to thwart such actions and fans of the losing teams resent the celebrations and taunt and start fights with the celebrants. Sometimes celebratory stampedes move to city streets after an important victory.

Violent incidents involving athletes and fans during or immediately after a sports event have become more frequent in recent years. Newspaper and magazine articles describing fan violence are becoming common. This photo illustrates a fight during an NFL football game between the San Diego Chargers and Oakland Raiders. (Photo: Thearon W. Henderson/Contributor/ Getty Images)

Revelers set bonfires, destroy property, turn over automobiles, and attack police and security personnel. Conversely, crucial losses by a home team have triggered similar violent street actions.

A unique form of fan celebration that has become widespread in recent years is called court or field storming. Fans pour out of the stands in celebration of an exciting victory, applauding the players, back-slapping them, and sometimes lifting them into the air. With the popularity of these stormings, injuries to fans and players have occurred. One of the most shocking and disturbing took place several years ago after a high school basketball game in Tucson, Arizona. A player dunked the ball at the end of a big home win, igniting a frenzied fan celebration. The player was grabbed, tackled, and trampled. He suffered a stroke and paralysis on his right side and has never fully recovered his physical and mental health. Dozens of court/field storming incidents like this one have resulted in injuries to players and fans.

Up to this point, American sport studies scholars have done little research on these forms of sports violence. Most British and European research on sports crowd violence has centered on soccer riots and "hooliganism." Several have explained this behavior in terms of the working-class roots of soccer fans, their team loyalties, and their resentment of and alienation from the larger society. Informal analyses of postgame crowd violence at American sports events suggest that there is little commonality between the European and British soccer fans and American college and professional sports fans.[53]

Reducing Fan Violence and Abusive Behavior

Numerous suggestions for reducing spectator violence have been proposed by researchers of violence. Common suggestions include improving the physical facilities and appearances of stadiums and arenas, making them more attractive and less foreboding places; increasing the numbers of security forces at sporting events; limiting the sale of alcohol (already done in some stadiums and arenas); changing the rules of some sports, such as soccer, to make scoring easier; keeping violence under control on the field by preventing fights, excessive displays of anger or aggression by athletes, and arm-waving displays of disapproval of officials' calls by coaches and athletes; and severely punishing offenders.

Sports administrators at all levels have been considering various options to stop court/field stormings. Professional sports and university attorneys have been asked to seek legal opinions regarding whether they can eject fans from games for abusive actions. University presidents, coaches, and athletic directors have been trying moral suasion, asking for civil behavior among student fans. Several university conferences have considered disbanding student sections.

All of these strategies might indeed reduce fan violence abuse to some extent. However, none of them deals with the larger, structural issue of the heritage and culture of violence and incivility that underlie much of the culture of contemporary American society beyond the confines of sports but nevertheless affect both athletes and fans alike.

SUBSTANCE ABUSE AND SPORT

Substance abuse is considered such a significant social problem that the U.S. government has pursued a "war on drugs" for more than forty years. But according to experts who study the importation and use of drugs, drug abuse is still widespread. A recent survey by the Centers for Disease Control found that nearly one in ten Americans twelve years and older regularly uses illicit drugs. Drug use among young adults between eighteen and twenty-five years of age is double that of the general population.[54]

Newspaper and magazine headlines tell of substance abuse in sports: "Steroids Are Just a Click Away," "Drug-Free Sports Might Be a Thing of the Past," "Tour de France's Downhill Slide: Doping Scandals Sully World's Biggest Bike Race." The stories that follow these headlines poignantly tell of American athletes' involvement with substance abuse. Athletes use a myriad of performance-enhancing drugs, and the laboratories and agencies that test for and regulate athletes' use of these substances find it almost impossible to detect and control all the drugs used, despite the advanced technologies they are able to employ. Perhaps the most disturbing feature of this scenario is the indifference of fans to doping by athletes, making it doubtful that sports will ever be drug free.

Substance Abuse Not New to Sports

The use of substances to enhance performance has been present throughout the history of organized sports. The ancient Greek athletes consumed mushrooms in the belief that they improved performance, and Roman gladiators used a variety of stimulants to hype them up and forestall fatigue. Athletes throughout the nineteenth century experimented with caffeine, alcohol, nitroglycerine, opium, and strychnine. Strychnine, cocaine, alcohol, and caffeine mixtures were used by boxers, cyclists, and British and European soccer players before World War II. Amphetamines and steroids began their rise to the drugs of choice among athletes in the years immediately after World War II.

The Scope of Current Substance Abuse in Sport

As anyone who has followed sports in the past few years knows, any short list of drug-use issues will represent only a speck of dust in the universe of substance abuse in the sports world. Indeed, some knowledgeable authorities believe that substance use by athletes is epidemic in scope, all the way from high school to the Olympic and professional levels.

The variety of substances that athletes use in hopes of improving their performance has become astounding: growth-retardant hormones are used by female gymnasts to prolong their careers; archers and shooters use beta blockers to slow their heart rate for steadier aiming; swimmers use nasal decongestants to enhance airflow through their lungs; weight lifters

TABLE 4.1 PERFORMANCE-ENHANCING SUBSTANCES MOST COMMONLY USED BY ATHLETES

Substance	Expected benefit	Users	Side effects
Steroids	Promotes muscle growth	Speed, power, endurance athletes	Impacts sex organs such as reduction in sperm production or abnormal menstrual cycles, liver and heart damage, mood changes
Testosterone	Promotes muscle growth	Speed, power, endurance athletes	Same as steroids
Human growth hormone	Promotes muscle growth	Speed, power athletes	Acromegaly, joint and jaw enlargement, high blood pressure and heart failure
Erythropoietin	Produces red blood cells	Endurance athletes	Thickened blood leading to stroke or heart problems
Androstenedione	Promotes muscle growth	Speed, power, endurance athletes	Similar to steroids
Creatine	Energizes muscle function	Quick, power, speed athletes	Dehydration, muscle cramping, intestinal problems

Source: Adapted from Johnston, Lloyd D.; O'Malley, Patrick M.; Miech, Richard A.; Bachman, Jerald G.; Schulenberg, John E. *Monitoring the Future National Results on Drug Use: 1975–2016: Overview, Key Findings on Adolescent Drug Use* (Ann Arbor: Institute for Social Research, University of Michigan, 2016).

use amphetamines to release vast amounts of adrenaline into the blood and speed up the systems used for strength activities; endurance athletes use recombinant erythropoietin to stimulate the production of red blood cells that transport oxygen throughout the body, thereby improving endurance; wrestlers and boxers use diuretics for weight loss to compete at lower weight classes; and drug-using athletes in many sports use diuretics to minimize detection of other drugs by diluting the urine.[55] Table 4.1 lists the performance-enhancing drugs most commonly used by athletes.

Anabolic Steroids: Promises Big and Strong

Anabolic steroids have been a popular drug of choice for athletes for several decades. For several years the U.S. Department of Health and Human Services has been surveying secondary school students who admit to using steroids. Typically, some 40,000 students in more than 400 schools are surveyed each year. Table 4.2 shows the trend for steroid use over the period from 2000 to 2020. These students might not all be athletes; indeed, if only athletes were surveyed, the percentages would likely be much higher.[56] However, an accurate assessment of steroid use by secondary school athletes is difficult. Converting the percentages to numbers of

TABLE 4.2 TRENDS IN ANNUAL PREVALENCE OF USE OF STEROID DRUGS AMONG SECONDARY SCHOOL STUDENTS IN GRADES EIGHT, TEN, AND TWELVE (IN PERCENTAGES OF TOTAL NUMBER OF STUDENTS PER GRADE)

Grade level	2000	2006	2010	2015	2020
Eighth-graders	1.7	0.9	0.5	0.5	1.1
Tenth-graders	2.2	1.2	1.0	0.7	.9
Twelfth-graders	1.7	1.8	1.5	1.7	1.2

Sources: Lloyd D. Johnston, Patrick M. O'Malley, Richard A. Miech, Jerald G. Bachman, and John E. Schulenberg, *Monitoring the Future: National Survey Results on Drug Use: 1975–2015: Overview, Key, Findings on Adolescent Drug Use* (Ann Arbor: Institute for Social Research, University of Michigan, 2015). Also, Johnston, Lloyd D.; O'Malley, Patrick M.; Miech, Richard A.; Bachman, Jerald G.; Schulenberg, John E. *Monitoring the Future Study: Trends in Prevalence of Various Drugs for 8th Graders, 10th Graders, and 12th Graders; 2017–2020,* https://www.drugabuse.gov/drug-topics/trends-statistics/monitoring-future/monitoring-future-study-trends-in-prevalence-various-drugs.

steroid users, eminent expert on sports and steroids Charles Yesalis estimates that well over 1 million young people in the United States have used steroids at one time or another.

Studies of steroid use in intercollegiate athletics vary widely in their results. One study reported that 9.7 percent of college football players acknowledged using the drug. At the other extreme, the NCAA has released reports indicating that positive drug tests for steroids have minimally increased in recent years.

But, according to a report by Minnesota Public Radio, "an investigation by The Associated Press—based on interviews with [major college football] players, testers, dealers and experts and an analysis of weight records for more than 61,000 players—revealed that while those running the multibillion-dollar sport say they believe the problem is under control, that control is hardly evident." The report goes on to say, "The sport's near-zero rate of positive steroids tests isn't an accurate gauge among college athletes. Colleges . . . are reluctant to spend money on expensive steroid testing when cheaper ones for drugs like marijuana allow them to say they're doing everything they can to keep drugs out of football."[57]

From these figures and others from the study of drug abuse in college sports, the NCAA's claim that steroid use has only minimally increased displays complete naiveté about the sophisticated methods athletes use to avoid testing positive. Physicians who have experience with steroid users say that users have found numerous ways to beat the drug-testing systems; drug testing is not the threat to drug-using athletes that sport organizations often portray it to be.

The situation is similar with professional and Olympic-level athletes. Use is greatest in athletes for whom power, strength, speed, and bulk are important. NFL athletes, coaches, and trainers have claimed that up to 75 percent of NFL players use or have used steroids. It has become clear in the past few years that steroid use is still present in the MLB too, despite a stepped-up testing program now employed. It has been estimated that three to eight players per major league team are using or have used steroids.

Alex Rodriguez, once the MLB's biggest star, was given a historic drug suspension that included all of the 2014 season, including the postseason; it was estimated it cost the Yankee slugger $25 million in salary.[58] Despite the increase in testing athletes for steroid use by sport organizations at every level, use of steroids continues and is no longer limited to elite athletes or men.

One of the newest trends in sport substance abuse is the use of nutritional supplements. By 2024, the nutritional supplement market is projected to reach more than $56 billion in the United States.[59] Several experts on the sports supplement industry have claimed that it operates as a Pandora's box of false claims, untested products, and bogus science.

But nutritional supplements are touted by their manufacturers, and hyped by many athletes, as muscle-building aids for increasing muscle size and strength. Many are not banned by most sport governing bodies, nor are they illegal drugs. One in five Ohio high school athletes said that they used supplements to enhance performance. At the national level, between 8 and 12 percent of high school male athletes have said they were using creatine. As many as 60 percent of collegiate male and female athletes report having used nutritional supplements, creatine being one of them.

It has been estimated that up to 50 percent of professional athletes in some sports have used creatine. Creatine is thought to improve strength, increase lean muscle mass, and help the muscles recover more quickly during exercise. Despite creatine's popularity among young athletes, there has been very little research conducted about creatine's alleged beneficial effects on physical performance. The use of this substance seems to have peaked in recent years, primarily because it has become associated with more dangerous performance-enhancing substances, such as anabolic steroids. Other nutritional supplements that are popular in the athlete culture include cold medications, diet pills, energy pills, and sports drinks, most of which contain ephedra, or synthetic forms of ephedrine. Ephedrine stimulates the central nervous system and thus is an amphetamine-like stimulant.

Human growth hormone releasers and gene therapy doping are two other performance enhancers. The first stimulates the pituitary gland into overproducing the natural form of the hormone, which influences the body's growth, cell production, and metabolism. This can boost muscle growth, decrease body fat, and aid in recovery from strenuous sports competition. Gene doping is considered by many experts the next frontier for athletes seeking a biologic edge.[60] The experts also agree that it is years away, but the World Anti-Doping Agency, which sets the rules on banned substances, has already outlawed gene doping.

In addition to using performance-enhancing substances, athletes, like the general population, are deeply involved in what are called *recreational* drugs. The main culprit has historically been alcohol—serious enough, to be sure, but not as deadly or debilitating a substance as cocaine, crack, heroin, or speed. The extent of cocaine, crack, heroin, and speed usage is minuscule compared to that of alcohol usage. Alcoholic beverages have long been one of the most widely used substances by young people. A 2019 national Center for Disease Control and Prevention youth behavior study found that 29% of high school students had drank alcohol and 14% had even binge drank in the thirty-day period prior to the survey. [61]Then, in terms of high school sport, a survey of almost 800 coaches asked them what they considered the greatest threat to athletes on their teams. Their responses: alcohol, 88 percent; cocaine/crack, 6 percent; marijuana, 3 percent; steroids, 1 percent.[62]

In a 2017 study, the NCAA surveyed roughly 23,000 student-athletes about their substance use habits including alcohol consumption. The study found that 77 percent of student-athletes had drank in the previous year, while 42 percent of these student-athletes had engaged in binge drinking within the past year.[63] It was also noted in the study report that 36 percent of student-athletes reported drinking on a weekly basis while nearly 2 percent reported drinking daily. Lacrosse, hockey and swimming reported the highest rates of binge drinking amongst all collegiate sports, while Division III student-athletes had the highest overall percentage of alcohol consumption in comparison to other divisions of competition.[64]

Although the actual incidence of alcohol consumption by professional athletes has not been studied, so many pro athletes have been arrested for drunkenness that eyebrows are hardly raised anymore when such incidents are reported on television or in newspapers. Several high-profile pro athletes have been involved in fatal accidents in which alcohol played a role.

The use of cocaine, crack, heroin, and speed by athletes may be small compared to that of alcohol, but this does not mean it is insignificant. In the 2017 study of intercollegiate athletes, 3.8 percent acknowledged using cocaine in the prior year with lacrosse being the found to have the highest consumption rates (22 percent for men, 6 percent for women). Compared to cocaine, smaller percentages of student-athletes had reported using amphetamines, LSD or Ecstacy/Molly.[65] Players representing nearly all of the professional sport leagues have been involved with cocaine use in criminal cases, with some teams having several players arrested.

And it is not just team sport athletes who use performance-enhancing products. Lance Armstrong won the Tour de France a record seven consecutive times between 1999 and 2005. However, in 2012, the U.S. Anti-Doping Agency announced that because of the use of illegal drugs, Armstrong had been issued a lifetime ban from competition, applicable to all sports that follow the World Anti-Doping Agency code. The agency also stripped Armstrong of his seven Tour de France titles.

Several organizations have been created to control—even eliminate—the use of performance-enhancing products and practices. The NCAA does random drug testing of athletes. A small percentage of high schools also randomly test for illicit drug use. The most comprehensive organization in the United States is the U.S. Anti-Doping Agency, which runs the anti-doping programs including education, sample collection, results management, and drug reference resources for athletes in the U.S. Olympic, Paralympic, Pan American, and Parapan American sport, including all Olympic sport national governing bodies, their athletes, and events. It works to preserve the integrity of competition, inspire true sport, and protect the rights of athletes in this movement.

Social/Cultural Influences and Substance Abuse among Athletes

Why do athletes risk their health and their opportunity to compete by using performance-enhancing drugs? There is, of course, no single answer to this question because athletes have different reasons. But athletes are a part of a much larger social community, wherein substance abuse is rampant. Athletes are not immune to the societal influences under which they live. In their world, athletes see drug use all around

Lance Armstrong won the Tour de France a record seven consecutive times between 1999 and 2005. However, in 2012 the United States Anti-Doping Agency announced that because of his use of illegal drugs, Armstrong had been issued a lifetime ban from competition, applicable to all sports that follow the World Anti-Doping Agency code. The agency also stripped Armstrong of his seven Tour de France titles, concluding that Armstrong engaged in "the most sophisticated, professionalized and successful doping program that sport has ever seen." (Photo: © miqu77/Shutterstock.com)

them: aspirin, tranquilizers, amphetamines, heroin, opioids, diet pills, and so forth.

Drug use among athletes must be understood in the context of an increasingly drug-obsessed society. It is not realistic to expect athletes to insulate themselves from a culture in which pharmacists and doctors supply medicines for all symptoms, both physical and psychological. Indeed, some experts on drug abuse refer to the United States as a "drug nation," and that

portrayal seems accurate. If the world's countries are divided into those with high-, medium-, and low-level drug problems, the United States is the only developed country that falls into the high-level category.

Young athletes are especially susceptible to what they see and hear from high-profile athletes. They often hear TV sportscasters report that an athlete was given pain suppressants, such as morphine, so that he could play in the game that day. During a Monday Night NFL football game, one of the sportscasters commented approvingly about a quarterback: "Here's a guy who probably had to take a painkiller shot in his lower back so he could play tonight." Many young athletes have seen athletic trainers' rooms, rooms that are filled with all kinds of salves, ointments, and pills, all used to help athletes perform at their best. Is it any wonder that young athletes believe that drugs are widely used in sports? The sports culture itself promotes drug usage.

Another factor that motivates young athletes to turn to chemicals for performance enhancement is that there is enormous social status that goes with being an athlete; as we will explain in Chapter 9, being an athlete is admired by both males and females. Most people do not understand how or the extent to which the system of sport and its status-conferring and rewarding properties often lead athletes to a commitment in which they are willing to risk anything, even their lives, to achieve their goal. A hypothetical scenario was posed to 198 U.S. Olympians and aspiring Olympians who were sprinters, swimmers, powerlifters, and other assorted athletes: "Suppose you are offered a performance-enhancing substance with two guarantees, if you choose to use it: You will win every competition you enter until you win an Olympic Gold Medal. But the substance will cause your death within a year after your achievements. Would you take it?" More than 50 percent of the responding athletes said yes![66]

There are other temptations. The best high school athletes are recruited to colleges with "full-ride" scholarships—a college education with basic expenses paid. Although few ultimately become professional athletes or Olympic champions, there are millions of young athletes who devote themselves to years of training and personal sacrifice in attempting

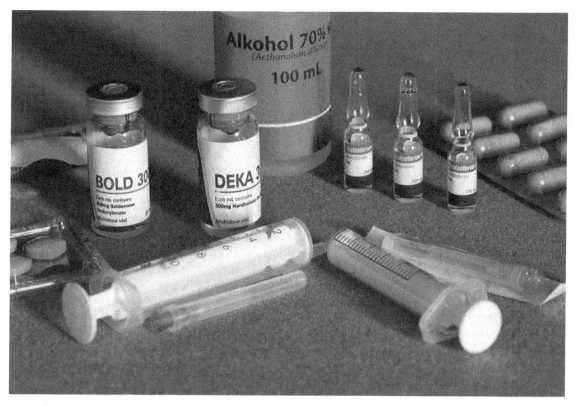

Some athletes take anabolic steroids to increase their muscle mass and strength. The main anabolic steroid hormone produced by the human body is testosterone. Steroids appeal to athletes because they make muscles bigger, and they seem to help athletes recover from a hard workout more quickly by reducing the muscle damage that occurs during the session. This enables athletes to work out harder and more frequently. Some athletes report they like the aggressive feelings they get when they take anabolic steroids. (Photo: © iStock/vuk8691)

to attain this lofty goal. At every level the competition is keen, and athletes know that they must continue to improve if they are to move to the next rung of the ladder.

Many literally devote their lives to the quest to move onward and upward, and they will try anything that will aid them in their quest. Thus, athletes striving to improve often believe that any substance that could give them even the slightest advantage over their opponents is worth trying. Rather than depending on legitimate training methods and developing a sound approach to their sport, some athletes choose to rely on drugs to improve their performance.

It is difficult for young athletes to do their best when they know they might be competing against athletes who are using substances that may be performance enhancing. During the time Dr. Robert Voy was director of drug testing for the U.S. Olympic Committee, he claimed that most of the athletes did not want to do drugs. They would come to him and say that unless drug abuse in sport was stopped, "we *have* to do drugs." Their argument was that if they did not use drugs, after years of training to be an Olympian they would be cheated out of a medal by athletes from Europe or Asia who *were* doing drugs.

Another factor in substance abuse among athletes is that at the high school, college, and professional levels, coaches pressure athletes to improve their performance. Some coaches put demands on athletes to increase their strength and endurance, reduce or increase their weight, and play while injured, knowing such conditions can only be met through the use of substances that are banned. These coaches want world records and bigger-than-life athletes with tremendous physical capacities that yield medals and championships. To meet these demands, some athletes resort to drugs to enhance their performance or to allow them to play when hurt.[67]

Finally, there is the ambiguity (perhaps hypocrisy) in the links athletes see every day between sports and substance abuse. They see the cozy financial connection between alcohol and tobacco and big-time sports. Beer and tobacco companies are the number one sponsors and underwriters of sporting events. Beer ads dominate concession stands and scoreboards at sports venues; beer commercials dominate TV and radio advertising during sports events. It is virtually impossible to watch or listen to a sporting event in the United States without feeling overwhelmed by beer ads. Many stadiums are sponsored by beer companies, including Coors Field, where the Colorado Rockies baseball team plays.

As we noted previously, alcohol is without question the most abused drug in sport, and a number of college sport officials acknowledge that alcohol is a much more pervasive problem for collegiate athletes than other substances. Still, professional leagues, American Olympic sports organizations, and the NCAA happily accept advertising money generated by alcohol companies.

It is little wonder that athletes resort to using performance-enhancing substances. When the rules and customs governing drug use in both the larger society and the sports world itself seem arbitrary and inconsistent, it is easy to understand why athletes may view the use of these substances as acceptable and normative behavior, despite the distortions they bring to the ethics of sport competition and their potentially devastating consequences to health and well-being.

CAN SUBSTANCE ABUSE IN SPORTS BE REDUCED, EVEN PREVENTED?

Although the evidence, incomplete as it is, strongly suggests that in terms of percentages only a minority of athletes at any level have a substance abuse problem, there is still the question of what is to be done with the small number who are substance abusers.

There are several options, but the one that has received the most attention is the drug-testing programs of the various sports' governing bodies. But these programs have had limited success and many failures at this point. To a large extent this is because they have been implemented without fully resolving at least two important questions: (1) What are the athletes' individual rights? and (2) What are the athletes' responsibilities?

Drug Testing and Athletes' Rights

With respect to athletes' rights, the Fourth Amendment to the U.S. Constitution forbids any unreasonable searches and seizures, or any intrusions on human dignity and privacy, simply on the hunch that incriminating evidence might be found; this protects all U.S. citizens, including athletes. The U.S. Supreme Court has ruled that extracting bodily fluids—such as urine tests—constitutes a search within the meaning of this amendment. The U.S. Constitution, however, protects persons only from intrusion by government, and furthermore, because there can be different interpretations of "reasonableness," this has become a complicated issue involving a balancing of the invasion of personal rights and the need for the search.

Determination of reasonableness requires that the court balance an individual's privacy rights against the government's legitimate interests in deterring drug use. The U.S. Supreme Court has twice made exceptions to students' privacy rights to enable schools to make random drug tests of athletes and other students who participate in extracurricular activities. Still, mandatory, random drug testing is not a fully settled issue in the U.S. court system.[68]

Although some of the major sport organizations, such as the International Olympic Committee, the NCAA, and the NFL, have taken the lead in mandatory and random drug testing, considering it necessary and appropriate, there are many critics as well. Several health scientists have argued that invasion of privacy initiated by effective anti-doping measures cannot be justified solely by the good those actions seek to attain. For drug-free sport, what is needed is effective enforcement. But the methods required for effective enforcement can be invasive of athletes' rights, especially the personal right to privacy.[69] They propose an alternative, a way that shares ownership of the rules of sport, and the methods for enforcing those rules, with those most affected by them: the athletes.

Several unresolved issues exist where drug testing has been implemented. The validity and accuracy of the tests have been a continuing controversy, and rightly so, because the test results are not infallible. Drug-testing programs in professional sports have been frequently found to be misleading to the public and unfair to the players. Several sport organizations that now routinely test their athletes do not even have an appellate process in place; thus, an athlete who tests positive does not have a process for appealing the results of the tests.

Another unresolved issue is that sport organizations do not seem to understand or acknowledge that the social conditions of high-pressure sports may contribute to drug abuse by athletes. There is a substantial literature documenting the pressures and incredible time demands that go with being a high school, major university, or professional athlete. It does not appear to be stretching the imagination to think that some of these pressures contribute to substance abuse by athletes.

Medical professionals, health educators, and other knowledgeable professionals who have been critical of drug-testing programs acknowledge the social structural factors that cultivate drug abuse by athletes, but they are skeptical about any immediate changes that will discourage athletes from abusing drugs. They are also scornful of random drug testing as a viable tool for behavior change. Instead, many believe that drug education programs can make a better contribution as a key component of drug abuse prevention. Not just any drug education program will do, however; certainly the "one-shot" efforts used by many high schools, universities, and professional teams are largely a waste of time. The fundamental strength of any substance abuse prevention program for athletes should be through education, and drug education must include more than just giving information or threatening athletes with punishment for substance abuse. Such programs must help athletes avoid making decisions about drugs that they may regret for the rest of their lives.[70]

What Are the Responsibilities of Athletes?

Regarding athletes' responsibilities to abstain from substance abuse, various lists have been compiled that range from the personal responsibility that athletes have for keeping their bodies in excellent physical condition to their responsibilities as society's role models to their responsibilities to spectators who pay money to watch their performances. These appear to be good "common-sense" reasons for athletes to abstain from drug abuse, but they ignore a number of related issues. For example, it does not take in-depth investigating into equitable treatment provisions in sports to see how blatantly athletes are victimized by the drug-testing system. Although athletes often must undergo mandatory, random drug testing, there is no provision for coaches, athletic directors, sports information directors, athletic trainers, athletic secretaries, and various and sundry others who are part of the big business of sports to undergo the same testing. Instead, the public is encouraged to dwell only on drug use by athletes.

The structure of society, especially at the level of its political and economic institutions, is responsible for many of the problems associated with drug abuse among Americans. At a more microsocial level, the political economy of sports has contributed to drug abuse among athletes. Thus, solutions to drug abuse among athletes must begin with structural modifications in the larger society as well as in sport culture; when this happens, serious amelioration of drug abuse among athletes will occur.

In the best of all possible worlds—a world for which we should all be striving—there would be no place for drug abuse among athletes. Use of performance-enhancing drugs corrupts the essence of fair sporting competition; it is cheating. As serious as this is within the bounded world of sport, performance-enhancing and recreational drug abuse is improper for a more important reason: it is dangerous to personal health; its use is an unnecessary health risk.

SPORT AND MENTAL HEALTH ISSUES

The recent decade has witnessed elite athletes speaking out about mental health issues. NBA player Kevin Love, swimmer Michael Phelps, and, most recently, tennis player Naomi Osaka and gymnast

Simone Biles have all publicly acknowledged their own struggles. Their public disclosure was, in part, an effort to encourage others to identify and discuss their own mental health. This is evidenced in a Tweet Michael Phelps shared in May of 2019: "I struggled with anxiety and depression and questioned whether or not I wanted to be alive anymore. It was when I hit this low that I decided to reach out and ask for the help of a licensed therapist. This decision ultimately helped save my life. You don't have to wait for things."

Mental health is defined by the World Health Organization as "a state of well-being in which every individual realizes his or her own potential, can cope with the normal stresses of life, can work productively and fruitfully, and is able to make a contribution to her or his community."[71] Thus, it goes beyond the absence of disease and relates more holistically to being an active and valued member of society and of a sport organization.

Using the sociological imagination, we must move from thinking of mental health as solely an individual's problem and examine the social context and social factors that impact mental health. First, it is important to address the prevalence of mental health issues in the United States. The National Institute of Health statistics for 2019 noted that 20 percent of adults have experienced some mental illness and that young adults (ages eighteen to twenty-five) had the highest prevalence (nearly 30 percent of that age group).[72] Research shows that cumulative stress around social factors of poverty, sexism, racism, and acute stress such as being a victim of violence leads to more mental health problems.[73]

With regard to elite athletes, it has been noted that 33 percent of college athletes experience mental health issues and that up to 35 percent of professional athletes do.[74] Now, we turn to the structure of high-performance sport and look at what social factors researchers have identified that influence mental health problems. Researchers point to the "win at all costs" expectations as a threat to mental health because it is tied to sporting environments that push athletes to an extreme. In some cases, those environments allow bullying, fail to prevent sexual abuse, or condone excessive weight control.

Researchers also ask practitioners to reflect on the more common practices of pressuring athletes to compete and train while injured and to pressure young people to specialize at an early age. They remind us that it is an accumulation of all these factors that can impact mental health.[75] Of course, there are factors external to sport, too, such as an athlete's personal and social background. Some have pointed to the prevalence of social media in athletes' lives. Athletes are under pressure to use social media to develop their personal brands—this means a constant attention to their platforms.[76] With this dependence on social media to promote their brand, athletes open themselves up to many negative messages that can take a toll on mental health.

One of the most important steps in addressing mental health is to acknowledge that one is having problems—and this is what much of the impetus was for the athletes who publicly shared their own issues. Christine Press, a U.S. national soccer player, addressed her motivation for making her mental health a priority: "We all have history and baggage. And I think as people, knowing our responsibility is to take care of ourselves and love ourselves first, can help us take care of each other in a more beautiful way."[77] From a sociological perspective, it is important to create social structures and sporting organizations that respect and support the development of the whole person.

SUMMARY

It is not surprising that violent behavior and substance abuse are conspicuous problems in American sports, given the close connections between sport and society. Three theories of human aggression dominate the scientific literature: the instinct theory, the frustration–aggression (F-A) theory, and the socially grounded theory. Advocates of the instinct and F-A theories have often claimed that participation in and observation of aggressive activities have a cathartic effect by allowing one to discharge pent-up aggressive energy, and sporting activities have often been suggested as a means of dispelling aggression in a socially healthy way. Research findings suggest that, contrary to the predictions of the instinct and F-A theories, aggression tends to produce more aggressive predispositions and actions rather than serving as a catharsis.

Another theory about aggressive behavior has come from scholars who advance a perspective that postulates that aggression is learned in the social environment. This perspective places emphasis on learning aggression through the socialization process. Socially based explanations have much more research support than the other aggression models. Directly and indirectly, sports research has overwhelmingly supported this perspective of human aggression.

Violent behavior has been part of sporting practices for as long as we have records of organized sports. The nature of some sports literally demands violent actions. Other sports are not inherently violent, but the tactics employed and the way the rules are interpreted increasingly encourage violent actions.

Violence on the playing field is often mirrored by sports fans in the stadium, arena, or the environs, and it is not merely a contemporary phenomenon, nor is it confined to American sports. Those who follow American sports are aware of the many incidents of spectator violence. Within the past decade, major fan violence has erupted at all levels of competition—high school, collegiate, professional.

The use of substances to enhance performance has been present throughout the history of organized sports. Some behavioral and social scientists believe that drug use by athletes is an epidemic, from high school to the professional level. The variety of substances athletes use in the hopes of improving their performances is astounding.

There is no single answer to the question of why some athletes risk their health and their opportunity to compete by using drugs, because athletes have different reasons. Athletes are a part of a much larger social community, within which substance abuse is rampant. There is enormous social status that goes with being an athlete, and undoubtedly that is one factor that motivates young athletes to turn to chemicals for performance enhancement. There is also the potential of the fulfillment of young athletes' dreams

of being a professional athlete or an Olympic gold medalist.

Only a small minority of athletes at any level have a substance abuse problem. However, the question of what is to be done with those who are drug abusers remains. There are several options, but the one that has received the most attention is the drug-testing programs of the various sports governing bodies. Two questions that have been raised about drug testing are, What are the athletes' individual rights? and What are the athlete's responsibilities? Also, several unresolved issues exist where drug testing has been implemented. The validity and accuracy of the tests have been a continuing controversy.

The social problems that face athletes are ultimately manifested in mental health issues. It is apparent that elite athletes are not often in environments that focus on the development of the whole person. With more attention paid to mental health, it will be important to go beyond a focus on the individual to address their own health and incorporate a focus to reform the sport organizations these athletes spend so much of their time with.

Learn more with this chapter's digital tools, including web resources, video links, and chapter self-assessment quizzes at www.oup.com/he/sage-eitzen-beal-atencio-12e.

NOTES

1. Quoted in Kate Dailey, "NFL Safety: Is American Football Too Violent?" *BBC News Magazine*, September 13, 2012, http://www.bbc.com/news/magazine-19549703.
2. Jenna Fryer, "'OK Not to Be OK': Mental Health Takes Top Role at Olympics," Associated Press, July 28, 2021, https://apnews.com/article/2020-tokyo-olympics-swimming-gymnastics-sports-mental-health-0766e3e512f877254b11b1cf99710473.
3. https://www.athletesforhope.org/2019/05/mental-health-and-athletes/; see also https://www.ncaa.org/about/resources/media-center/news/survey-shows-student-athletes-grappling-mental-health-issues.
4. For other historical examples of violence in North America, see John Smolenski and Thomas J. Humphrey, eds., *New World Orders: Violence, Sanction,*

and Authority in the Colonial Americas, Kindle ed. (Philadelphia: University of Pennsylvania Press, 2013); Ned Blackhawk, *Violence over the Land: Indians and Empires in the Early American West* (Cambridge, MA: Harvard University Press, 2008); Douglas Brinkley, *American Heritage History of the United States* (Rockville, MD: American Heritage Publisher, 2017).

5. D. Stanley Eitzen, Maxine Baca Zinn, and Kelly Eitzen Smith, *In Conflict and Order: Understanding Society*, 14th ed. (Boston: Pearson, 2016), 57.

6. Bureau of Justice Statistics, *Bureau of Justice Statistics: Criminal Victimization, 2015*, https://www.bjs.gov/index.cfm?ty=pbdetail&iid=5804.

7. Sylvie Mrug, Anjana Madan, Edwin W. Cook III, and Rex A Wright, "Emotional and Physiological Desensitization to Real-Life and Movie Violence," *Journal of Youth and Adolescence* 44 (May 2015): 1092–1108; see also Maren Strenziok, Frank Krueger, Gopikrishna Deshpande, Rhoshel K Lenroot, Elke van der Meer, and Jordan Grafman, "Fronto-Parietal Regulation of Media Violence Exposure in Adolescents: A Multi-Method Study," *Social Cognitive and Affective Neuroscience*, October 7, 2010, http://scan.oxfordjournals.org/content/early/2010/10/07/scan.nsq079/.

8. 22 weeks into the year, American already seen at least 246 mass shootings. June 5, 2022, NPR https://www.npr.org/2022/05/15/1099008586/mass-shootings-us-2022-tally-number accessed June 11,2022

9. Gordon W. Russell, *Aggression in the Sports World: A Social Psychological Perspective* (New York: Oxford University Press, 2008); WHO, *Health Topics: Violence* (New York: World Health Organization, 2014).

10. Kevin Young, *Sport, Violence and Society*, 2nd ed. (New York: Routledge, 2019), 16.

11. David Churchman, *Why We Fight: Theories of Human Aggression and Conflict*, 2nd ed. (Lanham, MD: University Press of America, 2013); see also Theodore Avtgis and Andrew S. Rancer, eds., *Arguments, Aggression, and Conflict: New Directions in Theory and Research* (New York: Routledge, 2010), especially ch. 14, "Trash Talk and Beyond: Aggressive Communication in the Context to Sport."

12. Ronald L Akers, *Social Learning and Social Structure: A General Theory of Crime and Deviance* (Piscataway,

NJ: Transaction, 2009); see also Patricia Adler and Peter Adler, *Social Construction in Context*, 8th ed. (Boston: Cengage Learning, 2015).

13. Konrad Lorenz, *On Aggression* (New York: Harcourt, Brace & World, 1963), 281.

14. Rachel Kowert and Thorsten Quandt, eds., *The Video Game Debate: Unravelling the Physical, Social, and Psychological Effects of Video Games* (New York: Routledge, 2015); see also Tobias Greitemeyer and Dirk O. Mügge, "Video Games Do Affect Social Outcomes: A Meta-Analytic Review of the Effects of Violent and Prosocial Video Game Play," *Personality and Social Psychology Bulletin* 40 (May 2014): 578–589; see also Teena Willoughby, Paul J. C. Adachi, and Marie Good, "A Longitudinal Study of the Association between Violent Video Game Play and Aggression among Adolescents," *Developmental Psychology* 48, no. 4 (2012): 1044–1057.

15. Richard G. Sipes, "Sports as a Control for Aggression," in *Sports in Contemporary Society: An Anthology*, 6th ed., ed. D. Stanley Eitzen (New York: St. Martin's Press, 1996), 154–160.

16. Donald G. Kyle, *Sport and Spectacle in the Ancient World*, 2nd ed. (Malden, MA: Wiley–Blackwell, 2014); see also Judith Swaddling, *The Ancient Olympic Games*, 3rd ed. (Austin: University of Texas Press, 2015).

17. Charles River Editors, *The Roman Gladiators: The History and Legacy of Ancient Rome's Most Famous Warriors* (New York: CreateSpace Independent Publishing Platform, 2013); see also Robert Crego, *Sports and Games of the 18th and 19th Centuries* (Westport, CT: Greenwood Press, 2002).

18. Ann McKee et al., "Clinicopathological Evaluation of Chronic Traumatic Encephalopathy in Players of American Football," *Journal of the American Medical Association* 318, no. 4 (2017): 360–370; see also S. L. Price, "Man in the Middle," *Sports Illustrated*, May 15, 2017, 102–111; see also James A Holstein, Richard S. Jones, and George E. Koonce Jr., *Is There Life after Football? Surviving the NFL* (New York: New York University Press, 2014).

19. Maryclaire Dale, "Judge Gives Preliminary OK to NFL Concussion Settlement," *Huffington Post*, July 8, 2014, http://www.huffingtonpost.com/news/nfl-concussions/; see also Mark Fainaru-Wada and Steve Fainaru, *League of Denial: The NFL*,

Concussions and the Battle for Truth (Danvers, MA: Crown Archetype, 2013); Greg Bishop, Jonathan Jones, Kalyn Kahler, and Robert Klemko, "Brain Check," *Sports Illustrated*, December 18, 2017, 36–37; Gay Culverhouse, *Throwaway Players: Concussion Crisis from Pee Wee Football to the NFL* (Burlington, IA: Behler, 2011).

20. Craig Lyons, "$75 Million NCAA Settlement to Fund Concussion Screening for 4 Million Former Athletes," *Lansing State Journal* (Lansing, MI), August 15, 2019, https://www.lansingstatejournal.com/story/news/2019/08/15/ncaa-concussion-settlement-athlete-medical-testing/2012186001/. Accessed June 23, 2021.

21. NCAA, "Concussions," NCAA Sports Science Institute, July 29, 2022, https://www.ncaa.org/sports/2021/2/10/sport-science-institute-concussion.aspx.

22. Andy Martino, "Football's Concussion Crisis Is Killing Former High School Players, Too," *HUFFPOST*, August 15, 2017; see also Thomas P. Dompier, "Study Examines Incidence of Concussion in Youth, High School, College Football," *For the Media*, May 4, 2015, http://mediajamanetwork.com/news-item/study-examines-incidence-of-concussion-in-youth-high-school-college-football/.

23. Zachary Y. Kerr, Avinash Chandran, Aliza K. Nedimyer, Alan Arakkal, Lauren A Pierpoint, and Scott L. Zuckerman, "Concussion Incidence and Trends in 20 High School Sports," *Pediatrics* 144, no. 5 (2019): 2019–2180.

24. National Research Council, *Sports-Related Concussions in Youth: Improving the Science, Changing the Culture* (Washington, D.C.: National Academies Press, 2014); see also Robert Cantu, *Concussions and Our Kids* (Boston: Houghton Mifflin Harcourt, 2012); Stone Phillips, "Hard Hits, Hard Numbers: The First Study of Head Impacts in Youth Football," *Stone Phillips Reports*, February 2013, http://www.stonephillipsreports.com/2013/02/hard-hits-hard-numbers/.

25. Patricia Salber, "Girls Suffer Concussions at a Higher Rate Than Boys, Study Reveals," *The Doctors Weigh In*, April 1, 2017, https://thedoctorweighsin.com/girls-suffer-concussions-at-a-higher-rate-than-boys-study-reveals/; see also Marjorie A Snyder, "Girls Suffer Sports Concussions at a Higher Rate Than Boys. Why Is That Overlooked?" *The Washington Post*, February 10, 2015, http://www.washingtonpost.com/posteverything/wp/2015/02/10/our-effort-to-reduce-concussions-in-youth-sports-overlooks-the-biggest-victims-girls/.

26. Quoted in Christine Brennan, "Obama: Stop the Head Games," *USA Today*, May 30, 2014, 1C–2C.

27. "UFC Kickstarts Journey on Discovery+ and Eurosport in the Netherlands and Spain," UFC News, January 10, 2022, https://www.ufc.com/news/ufc-kickstarts-journey-discovery-and-eurosport-netherlands-and-spain.

28. Heather Clemons, "National Injury Surveillance System for Youth Concussions—When Will It Happen?" *Athletes Saving Athletes*, January 15, 2016, http://injuredathletes.org/blog/2016/national-injury-surveillance-system-for-youth-concussions—when-will-it-happen-/.

29. Mark Fainaru-Wada and Steve Fainaru, "League of Their Own," *Sports Illustrated*, October 7, 2013, 62–69; see also Culverhouse, "Throwaway Players."

30. See, for example, the Ultimate Fighter website, 2014, http://msn.foxsports.com/watch/the-ultimate-fighter/.

31. Kellen Browning & Kevin Draper, Dec 29, 2021, "How John Madden Became the 'Larger-than-Life' Face of a Gaming Empire, https://www.nytimes.com/2021/12/29/sports/football/john-madden-nfl-video-game.html accessed June 11, 2022

32. Daniel L Wann, Stephen Weaver, Brian Belva Sagan Ladd, and Sam Armstrong, "Investigating the Impact of Team Identification on the Willingness to Commit Verbal and Physical Aggression by Youth Baseball Spectators," *Journal of Amateur Sport* 1, no. 1 (2015): 1–28; see also Y. Choi, J. J. Martin, M. Park, and T. Yoh, "Motivational Factors Influencing Sport Spectator Involvement at NCAA Division II Basketball Games," *Journal for the Study of Sports and Athletes in Education* 3 (2009): 265–284.

33. Arthur A Raney and Anthony J. Depalma, "The Effect of Viewing Varying Levels of Aggressive Sports Programming on Enjoyment, Mood, and Perceived Violence," *Mass Communication and Society* 9, no. 3 (2009): 321–338; Arthur A Raney and W. Kinnally, "Examining Perceived Violence in

and Enjoyment of Televised Rivalry Sports Contests," *Mass Communication and Society* 12 (2009): 311–331.

34. Ken Belson, "Brain Trauma to Affect One in Three Players, N.F.L. Agrees," *The New York Times*, September 13, 2014, A1; see also Sammi Silber, "War on Ice: The Chilling Truth of Enforcers, CTE, and Fighting in the NHL," *The Hockey Writers*, October 3, 2016, http://thehockeywriters.com/war-on-ice-the-chilling-truth-of-enforcers-cte-and-fighting-in-the-nhl/.

35. Jarome Iginla, "Hockey Is Better, Safer with Fighting in It," *Sports Illustrated*, November 15, 2013, http://www.si.com/nhl/news/20131115/jarome-iginla-hockey-fights/.

36. Associated Press, "How the Larry Nassar Scandal Has Affected Others," February 25, 2021, https://apnews.com/article/larry-nassar-forced-labor-michigan-sexual-assault-crime-be07cdaaa3b0ce8ae87f37e b0ee04cc2.

37. Bill Chappell, "Penn State Abuse Scandal: A Guide and Timeline," National Public Radio, June 21, 2012, https://www.npr.org/2011/11/08/142111804/penn-state-abuse-scandal-a-guide-and-timeline.

38. Margo Mountjoy et al., "The IOC Consensus Statement: Harassment and Abuse (Non-accidental Violence) in Sport," *British Journal of Sports Medicine* 50, no. 17 (2016): 1–11. https://doi.org/10.1136/bjsports-2016-096121.

39. Brent Schrotenboer, "Arrests a Big Test for League's Image," *USA Today*, September 5, 2013, 1A–2A

40. Jeff Carlisle, Feb 10, 2022, ESPN, "Portland Timber ruminate Andy Polo's contract after domestic violence allegations, https://www.espn.com/soccer/portland-timbers/story/4590641/portland-timbers-terminate-andy-polos-contract-after-domestic-violence-allegations, accessed June 1, 2022

41. Peter Jacobs, "Ex-NFL Star Aaron Hernandez Has Killed Himself in Prison," *Business Insider*, April 19, 2017, http://www.businessinsider.com/aaron-hernandez-killed-himself-in-prison-2017-4.

42. Rape, Abuse & Incest National Network, https://www.rainn.org/about-rainn/; see also Brooks Barnes, "An Unblinking Look at Sexual Assaults on Campus," *The New York Times*, September 13, 2014, A1; this article describes the documentary film *The Hunting Ground*, which is a shocking exposé of sexual assault on U.S. campuses, institutional cover-ups, and the terrible social toll it takes on the victims and their families.

43. Kevin M. Beaver, J. C. Barnes, and Brian B. Boutwell, "School Sports, Peer Networks, and Male Adolescent Violence," *Youth & Society* 48, no. 6 (2014): 786–809; see also Derek A. Kreager, "Unnecessary Roughness? School Sports, Peer Networks, and Male Adolescent Violence," *American Sociological Review* 72 (October 2007): 705–724.

44. Kevin M. Beaver, Michael G. Vaughn, Matt DeLisi, and John Paul Wright, "Anabolic–Androgenic Steroid Use and Involvement in Violent Behavior in a Nationally Representative Sample of Young Adult Males in the United States," *American Journal of Public Health* 98, no. 12 (2008): 2185–2187; see also "The Behavioral Effects of Anabolic Steroid Use," *Dartmouth Undergraduate Journal of Science*, April 29, 2012.

45. Jay Johnson and Margery Holman, "Gender and Hazing: The Same but Different," *Journal of Physical Education, Recreation and Dance* 80 (May/June 2009): 6–9; Jennifer J. Waldron and Christopher L. Kowalski, "Crossing the Line: Rites of Passage, Team Aspects, and Ambiguity of Hazing," *Research Quarterly for Exercise and Sport* 80, no. 2 (2009): 291–302.

46. UC Davis says Baseball Team Hazed Students with Alcohol, Sports Illustrated, November 13, 2021 https://www.si.com/college/2021/11/13/uc-davis-says-baseball-team-hazed-students-with-alcohol; accessed June 1, 2022

47. Bob Cook, "'No-Gay Thursday'—Another Horrible Chapter of High School Sports Hazing," *Forbes*, March 5, 2016, https://www.forbes.com/sites/bob-cook/2016/03/05/no-gay-thursday-another-horrible-chapter-of-high-school-sports-hazing/#1e10e66b2e4b; see also Jim Mandelaro, "Hazing Continues Despite Efforts to Change," *USA Today*, January 12, 2014, https://www.usatoday.com/story/news/nation/2014/01/12/hazing-continues-despite-efforts-to-change/4434379/; Casey Quinlan, "These High School Football Players Have Been Charged with Assault during Hazing Ritual," *ThinkProgress*, March 7, 2016.

48. Susie Bruce and Holly Deering, "Addressing Student-Athlete Hazing," *National Collegiate Athletic Association* (Indianapolis, IN: National Collegiate Athletic Association, 2016); Susan H. Murphy and David J. Skorton, "Dismantling the Hazing Culture," *USA Today*, August 20, 2013, 8A

49. Quoted in Mike McCarthy, "Teams Asking Disruptive Fans to Take Lesson in Class," *USA Today*, April 17, 2012, 4C; also see Eric Simons, *The Secret Lives of Sports Fans* (New York: Overlook Hardcover, 2013); Adam C. Earnheardt, Paul Haridakis, and Barbara Hugenberg, eds., *Sports Fans, Identity, and Socialization: Exploring the Fandemonium*, reprint ed. (Lanham: MD: Lexington Books, 2013).

50. Justine Gubar, *Fanaticus: Mischief and Madness in the Modern Sports Fan* (Baltimore, MD: Rowman & Littlefield, 2016); see also Jim Chernesky, *Once a Fan: Why It Is So Hard to Be a Sports Fan* (Bloomington, IN: iUniverse, 2012).

51. Eric Simons, *The Secret Lives of Sports Fans: The Science of Sports Obsession* (New York: Overlook Press, 2014); see also Kevin G. Quinn, *Sports and Their Fans: The History, Economics and Culture of the Relationship between Spectator and Sport* (Jefferson, NC: McFarland, 2009).

52. Lee Jenkins, "The Day That Damned the Dodgers," *Sports Illustrated*, August 29, 2011, 50–58; Robert Klemko, "Ominous Signs in Stands," *USA Today*, August 30, 2011, 1C–2C; Corina Knoll and Victoria Kim, "Dodgers Likely to Pay About $13.9 Million in Bryan Stow Verdict," *Los Angeles Times*, July 9, 2014, http://www.latimes.com/local/lanow/la-me-ln-dodgers-partly-liable-in-attack-on-giants-fan-bryan-stow-20140709-story.html.

53. Matt Hokins and James Treadwell, eds., *Football Hooliganism, Fan Behaviour and Crime: Contemporary Issues* (New York, Palgrave Macmillan, 2014); see also Daniel G. Renfrow, Terrence L. Wissick, and Christopher M. Guard, "(Re)Defining the Situation When Football Fans Rush the Field," *Sociology of Sport Journal* 33 (2016): 250–261; Anastassia Tsoukala, *Football Hooliganism in Europe: Security and Civil Liberties in the Balance* (New York: Palgrave McMillan, 2009).

54. Center for Disease Control and Prevention, "Illicit Drug Use," January 27, 2022, https://www.cdc.gov/nchs/fastats/drug-use-illicit.htm.

55. John Allen, *How Harmful Are Performance-Enhancing Drugs?* (New York: Referencepoint Press, 2016); see also Tony Khing, *Performance-Enhancing Drugs in Sports* (Edina, MN: Abdo, 2014); Chris Cooper, *Run, Swim, Throw, Cheat: The Science behind Drugs in Sport* (New York: Oxford University Press, 2012); Simon S. Outram and Bob Stewart, "Enhancement Drug Use in Society and in Sport: The Science and Sociology of Stimulant Use and the Importance of Perception," *Sport in Society* 16, no. 6 (2013): 789–804.

56. Quoted in Matt Apuzzo, Adam Goldman, and Jack Gillum, "Steroids Loom in Major-College Football," *MPR News*, January 1, 2013, http://www.mprnews.org/story/2013/01/01/news/steroids-in-college-football; see also Lorraine Savage, "What to Know About Doping in College Athletics," *Cengage Learning*, August 12, 2016.

57. Matt Apuzzo, Adam Goldman, Jack Gillum, "Steroids Loom in Major-college Football," MPR News, January 1, 2013, https://www.mprnews.org/story/2013/01/01/steroids-loom-in-major-college-football.

58. Teri Thompson, Michael O'Keeffe, Christian Red, and Nathaniel Vinton, "Alex Rodriguez Gets SLAMMED! Arbitrator Hits Yankees Slugger with Full-Season Ban, Plus Postseason," *New York Daily News*, January 12, 2014, http://www.nydailynews.com/sports/baseball/yankees/breaking-a-rod-slammed-full-season-ban-postseason-article-1.1576281/.

59. Matej Mikulic, "Total U.S. Dietary Supplements Market Size 2016-2024," Statista, Inc., September 19, 2019, https://www.statista.com/statistics/828481/total-dietary-supplements-market-size-in-the-us/.

60. Michael Le Page, "Gene Doping in Sport Could Make the Olympics Fairer and Safer," *New Scientist*, August 5, 2016, https://www.newscientist.com/article/2100181-gene-doping-in-sport-could-make-the-olympics-fairer-and-safer/.

61. Center for Disease Control and Prevention, "Underage Drinking," Alcohol and Public Health, April 14, 2022, https://www.cdc.gov/alcohol/fact-sheets/underage-drinking.htm.

62. Johnston et al., *Monitoring the Future: National Results on Drug Use: 1975–2015*.

63. NCAA National Study on Substance Use Habits of College Student-Athletes Executive Summary June

2018, https://ncaaorg.s3.amazonaws.com/research/substance/2017RES_SubstanceUseExecutiveSummary.pdf, accessed June 3, 2022

64. Brian Burnsed, "Rates of Excessive Drinking among Student-Athletes Falling," National Collegiate Athletic Association, July 22, 2014 (Indianapolis, IN: National Collegiate Athletic Association), http://www.ncaa.org/about/resources/media-center/news/rates-excessive-drinking-among-student-athletes-falling.

65. Chris Jastrzembski, SBNation, June 12, 2018, Alcohol, marijuana, cocaine use highest among college lacrosse players in new NCAA study https://www.collegecrosse.com/2018/6/12/17456412/alcohol-marijuana-weed-cocaine-college-lacrosse-men-s-women-s-ncaa-study-yearly-research; accessed June 1, 2022

66. Michael Bamberger and Don Yaeger, "Over the Edge," *Sports Illustrated*, April 14, 1997, 60–70.

67. David R Mottram and Neil Chester, eds., *Drugs in Sports*, 6th ed. (New York: Routledge, 2015); Mark Johnson, *Spitting in the Soup: Inside the Dirty Game of Doping in Sports* (Boulder, CO: VeloPress, 2016).

68. Mary Pilon, "Differing Views on Value of High School Tests," *The New York Times*, January 6, 2013, SP 6; see also Tiffany John, "Should Students Be Drug Tested at School?" *The Buzz* (The National Center on Addiction and Substance Abuse), January 29, 2016, https://www.centeronaddiction.org/the-buzz-blog/should-students-be-drug-tested-school.

69. Nicole Greenstein, "Privacy and the Law: How the Supreme Court Defines a Controversial Right," *Time Magazine*, July 31, 2013, http://nation.time.com/2013/08/01/privacy-and-the-law-how-the-supreme-court-defines-a-controversial-right/slide/student-drug-testing; Associated Press, "Athletes Say Drug-Test Rule Violates Right to Privacy," *The New York Times*, February 24, 2009, B12.

70. Nicole Greenstein, "Privacy and the Law: How the Supreme Court Defines a Controversial Right," *Time Magazine*, July 31, 2013, http://nation.time.com/2013/08/01/privacy-and-the-law-how-the-supreme-court-defines-a-controversial-right/slide/student-drug-testing; Associated Press, "Athletes Say Drug-Test Rule Violates Right to Privacy," *The New York Times*, February 24, 2009, B12.

71. World Health Organization. *Promoting Mental Health: Concepts, Emerging Evidence, Practice: Summary Report* (Geneva: World Health Organization, 2004).

72. National Institute of Mental Health, "Mental Illness," Mental Health Information, January 1, 2022, https://www.nimh.nih.gov/health/statistics/mental-illness. .

73. World Health Organization, "Mental Health: Strengthening Our Response," Newsroom, June 17, 2022, https://www.who.int/news-room/fact-sheets/detail/mental-health-strengthening-our-response.; see also Ella McLoughlin, David Fletcher, George Slavich, Rachel Arnold, and Lee Moore, "Cumulative Lifetime Stress Exposure, Depression, Anxiety, and Well-Being in Elite Athletes: A Mixed-Method Study," *Psychology of Sport Exercise* 52 (2021): 101823.

74. https://www.athletesforhope.org/2019/05/mental-health-and-athletes/; see also https://www.ncaa.org/about/resources/media-center/news/survey-shows-student-athletes-grappling-mental-health-issues.

75. Kristoffer Henriksen, Robert Schinke, Karin Moesch, Sean McCann, William D. Parham, Carsten Hvid Larsen, and Peter Terry, "Consensus Statement on Improving the Mental Health of High Performance Athletes," *International Journal of Sport and Exercise Psychology* 18, no. 5 (2020): 553–560, https://doi.org/10.1080/1612197X2019.1570473.

76. Guillaume Dumont, "The Working Lives of Professional Rock Climbers: An Ethnographic Exploration of Multilayered Labor," in *Lifestyle Sports and Identities: Subcultural Careers through the Life Course*, ed. Tyler Dupont and Becky Beal (London: Routledge, 2021), ch 8.

77. Anne Killion, "Simone Biles Isn't Alone: Olympic Athletes Face a Mental Health Crisis," *San Francisco Chronicle*, July 31, 2021, https://www.sfchronicle.com/sports/annkillion/article/Simone-Biles-isn-t-alone-Olympic-athletes-face-16353587.php.

SPORT AND STRUCTURED INEQUALITY IN SOCIETY

CHAPTER 5

SPORT, SOCIAL STRATIFICATION, AND SOCIAL MOBILITY

Americans are coming to realize that their cherished narrative of social and economic mobility is a myth. Grand deceptions of this magnitude are hard to maintain for long—and the country has already been through a couple of decades of self-deception.

—JOSEPH E. STIGLITZ, *recipient of the Nobel Memorial Prize in Economic Sciences*[1]

Sport is generally assumed to be an egalitarian institution that promotes interaction across social class and racial lines. But sport, like the larger society, is highly stratified, and like all social institutions, sport accommodates and reinforces the existing structure of social inequality. Many sports activities, such as equestrian training and competition, are too expensive for the less well-to-do. (Photo: © Hvatio|Dreamstime)

Sport is generally assumed to be an egalitarian and a meritocratic institution. It is accepted as egalitarian because it purportedly promotes interaction across social class and racial lines and because interest in sport seemingly transcends class and social boundaries. Sport is also believed to be meritocratic because within this context it is widely assumed that persons who have talent, regardless of social background, can be upwardly mobile. The argument is that when athletes compete together, socioeconomic status disappears. Black or White, Christian or Jew, rich or poor—socioeconomic locations are irrelevant. All that matters is that everyone is giving their all, and high fives are exchanged by all when a victory is achieved.[2]

Similar assertions reinforce conventional wisdom about how sport transcends social class in the United States and elsewhere around the world. However, empirical examinations of the sports world clearly demonstrate that sport, like the larger society, is highly stratified. Like all institutions, sport is a powerful contributor to the existing structure of social stratification and social inequality. There are exceptions, as we will note, but as exceptions they prove the rule.

TERMINOLOGY AND THEORY IN SOCIAL STRATIFICATION AND MOBILITY

BASIC TERMINOLOGY IN SOCIAL STRATIFICATION

If members of a social grouping have differing amounts of wealth, power, or prestige, a condition of social inequality is said to exist. When these attributes are ranked hierarchically in that grouping— from lower to higher—sociologists call the situation *social stratification*; by this they mean that inequality is present in the system of social relationships that determines who gets which of the rewards and power in a society and why. Although social inequality benefits some members of a society while oppressing others, it is acknowledged as the way things are.[3]

When a group of people occupy the same relative economic rank in a stratified social system, they form what is frequently referred to as a *social class*. Although there can be some fluidity here, as complex humans can have dynamic backgrounds and futures, members of a society are often socially located in a class position on the basis of income, occupation, and education, either alone or in combination. One's placement in the class hierarchy determines access to the rewards and resources of society, such as wealth, power, and privilege. And, crucially, differential access to these societal resources and rewards produces different life experiences, lifestyles, and life chances.

The chances one has to live and experience good things or bad things in life are called *life chances*. The affluent members of society and their children will have a good education, good medical care, comfortable homes, safe neighborhoods, expert services of all kinds, the best in leisure activities, and, likely, a longer life span—all of which could be called favorable life chances. The converse is that the poor and the near-poor members of society will often have inadequate health care, shelter, and diets. Their lives will be potentially more difficult, and they will have shorter life expectancies—unfavorable life chances, to be sure.

In addition to class, race, gender, and ableness are structured systems of inequality that organize society as a whole and create varied environments for individuals and families through their unequal distribution of social opportunities. They are also structured systems of exploitation and discrimination in which the affluent dominate the poor, men dominate women, Whites dominate people of color, and the disabled are dominated by the general public.

Functional Theory and Social Stratification

On the one hand, functional theorists insist that a differentiated system of rewards and privileges is essential for the efficient processes of society, so functionalism is replete with explanations for the existence and necessity of social inequality and stratification. Without incentives for achievements, functionalists argue, people would not seek to discover, develop new and better products, strive for medical advances, and work for better livelihoods. Rewards and the power and prestige that go with these achievements function to make a better society.

Advocates of a functionalist viewpoint argue that without this inequality, division of labor would be difficult (not everyone can be an owner, boss, or team captain). They also maintain that attracting people to important social roles and positions requires variation in rewards that motivate individuals to make the effort needed to gain these top positions.

Conflict/Cultural Theories and Social Stratification

On the other hand, conflict/cultural theorists contend that in a competitive capitalist system—which exists in the United States—capitalist interests dominate both the economy and the social culture. Capitalism enables business owners and corporations to employ and, often, to exploit workers and employees, who must sell their labor—that is, their ability to work—in return for wages. The consequence is that social inequality and exploitation become inherent in capitalism.

According to this theoretical perspective, exploitation of the working class has resulted in members of each social class possessing large differences in income, power, and social prestige, resulting in distinctive social classes and cultures. The current manifestation of this in the United States and elsewhere in the Western world is the huge gap between the wealthy and the poor and the enormous differences in lifestyles and therefore life chances. Moreover, because they are the beneficiaries of the status quo, those with wealth, power, and prestige have a clear interest in resisting social change.

DIMENSIONS OF INEQUALITY

Americans rank differently from one another on a number of socioeconomic dimensions, such as wealth, income, education, and occupation. Wealth and income, the bases of social class, are concentrated among individuals and families. The following facts illustrate the range on each of these dimensions:

1. In 2016 some 14.3 percent of Americans were below the poverty line, and one-third say they are "just getting by."[4]
2. Thirty-five percent of African Americans and 33 percent of Hispanic Americans are now living below the federal poverty line.[5]
3. In 2016 the top 1 percent of wealth holders controlled nearly 38 percent of total net worth and the top 20 percent owned 84 percent of the nation's wealth; the bottom 21 percent accounted for just 1 percent of the wealth.
4. In the United States, 49 percent of aggregate income went to upper-income households in 2016, up from 29 percent in 1970. The share accruing to middle-income households was 43 percent in 2016, down substantially from 62 percent in 1970.
5. The mean income of American households headed by persons identifying as African American or Black represents only 61 percent of the mean income in households headed by persons identifying as White.

During national crises, these types of societal inequalities between groups can become more pronounced. For example, in 2020 during the outset of the COVID-19 pandemic, households from lower social class backgrounds, often representing racial minority groups, struggled to pay for housing, maintain employment, and feed their families. In this regard, upper-class households were much more insulated from the effects of the pandemic.[6]

Taken together, these facts make it clear that the United States and other Western nations are certainly not classless societies. In these nations, a form of economic structuring called neo-liberalism prevails, in which the free market has become the prioritized means for economic and social development, rather than government-led social welfare. As a result of this economic view and the policies that accompany it, there are wide disparities in economic resources and what those resources can yield. The remainder of this chapter deals with two issues involving inequality and sport: (1) the influence of stratification on sports participation and spectatorship and (2) the idea that sport can help individuals move up (increase their upward social mobility) in the stratification hierarchy.

SOCIAL CLASS AND SPORT

Americans enjoy playing and watching sports. The question thus becomes, How are their sporting engagements related to their socioeconomic status?

TABLE 5.1 NUMBER OF RESPONDENTS REPORTING PARTICIPATION IN SELECTED SPORTS ACTIVITIES

Sports	Household income (in dollars)						
	Under 15,000	15,000– 24,999	25,000– 34,000	35,000– 49,000	50,000– 74,999	75,000– 99,000	100,000– and over
Baseball	573	456	1,076	1,772	2,473	2,366	2,791
Basketball	1,816	1,078	1,852	3,702	5,068	4,738	6,154
Bicycling	2,433	1,894	2,529	5,268	8,321	8,850	10,837
Golf	606	675	1,078	3,061	4,614	4,589	7,693
Soccer	956	539	727	1,644	2,527	2,803	4,583
Tennis	411	436	509	1,301	2,149	1,955	4,058
Weightlifting	2,029	2,123	2,330	5,224	6,976	7,192	8,631
Snowboarding	91	150	826	503	1,358	1,415	1,767
Exercise w/equipment	2,917	2,885	4,423	8,112	12,151	10,707	16,001

Source: U.S. Census Bureau, *Statistical Abstracts of the United States: 2012*, 131st ed. (Washington, D.C.: 2012), Table 1249. Data are based on a questionnaire mailed to 10,000 households.

Looking first at participation, we find that the data from empirical research provide consistent support for the generalization that the higher the socioeconomic status of the individual, the more likely that individual will be to participate actively in leisure activities.

ADULT PARTICIPATION PREFERENCES FOR SPORTS BY SOCIOECONOMIC STATUS

The evidence is clear that high-income, high-education, and high-status occupational groups have the highest rates of active sport participation and attendance at sports events. Consider first the data in Table 5.1, which show a consistent and strong pattern in the relationship between social class and involvement in sports. That is, the higher a person's income, the more likely a person is to attend sports events and to participate in sports.

Similarly, Table 5.2 illustrates that for all types of individual and team sports activities, the higher the income, the greater the rate of participation. This trend can be seen by scanning left to right across Table 5.2.

There are several bases for this tendency. The most obvious is that many activities (e.g., skiing and

TABLE 5.2 PARTICIPATION IN SELECTED SPORTS ACTIVITIES BY HOUSEHOLD INCOME (IN PERCENTAGES)

Activity	Under $25,000	$25,000– $74,000	$75,000+
Team sports			
Basketball	8.3	11.3	12.2
Baseball	4.4	5.6	6.4
Volleyball	2.0	4.4	6.0
Soccer	4.0	5.3	7.3
Individual sports/ leisure			
Aerobic exercise	9.4	12.2	17.3
Running/jogging	7.2	12.8	17.5
Golf	2.9	8.1	15.0
Tennis	1.7	3.9	7.4
Swimming	14.8	23.0	29.5
Weightlifting	7.8	13.1	18.4

Source: U.S. Census Bureau, *Statistical Abstract of the United States: 2012*, 131st ed. (Washington, D.C.: 2012), Table 1248. Percentages calculated from data in table.

golf) are too expensive for the less well-to-do. The affluent also have access to private clubs and resorts where golf, tennis, skiing, and swimming are available. Communities rarely provide inexpensive access to these activities, other than tennis and swimming in some cases.

An interesting speculation as to why the affluent are disposed toward certain sports was presented in *The Theory of the Leisure Class* by sociologist/economist Thorstein Veblen near the beginning of the twentieth century, at a time when organized sports were becoming widely popular. Veblen argued that the affluent engaged in leisure activities to impress on observers that they can afford expensive and time-consuming activities. In other words, sport is used by these persons as a form of *conspicuous consumption*, to prove that they can spend great amounts of money and time away from work.[7]

This rationale explains why the upper class has held amateur sport as an ideal and why Olympic competition was traditionally limited to the more well-to-do. Another explanation for the greater likelihood of the affluent to engage in sports is that their occupations, unlike lower-income jobs, offer more flexible schedules. This allows them more freedom to go to the gym, club, or golf course whenever they wish.

The affluent and educated are more prone than lower socioeconomic groups to engage in health and physical fitness activities such as running, aerobics, swimming, and bicycling. An interesting difference between white-collar and blue-collar workers involves participation in workplace-centered fitness programs. Many corporations provide sports equipment and facilities for their workers and encourage them to participate. The typical reaction is enthusiastic support from the salaried professionals and relative nonsupport from the hourly workers.[8] It has been demonstrated that these types of activities can be used by managerial-level workers to obtain certain workplace culture values and attributes that will be recognized and valued by the employer.[9]

There are several reasons for this difference in perception between social classes. First, the lower the social status, the less likely the individual will be to exercise regularly, to regularly participate in health and wellness programs, to maintain what is considered a proper weight, and to stop smoking and drinking. Second, the activities provided (e.g., running, swimming, cycling, adventure racing) are of more interest to higher-status workers. Third, blue-collar workers may mistrust such programs because they suspect that management provides exercise programs to serve the interests of management, not the workers. Finally, many blue-collar workers may resent the money spent on exercise equipment and the like because it does not address their real needs (e.g., the monotony of repetitive work, the need for above-minimum wages, desire for consistent full-time employment and benefits, and the negative physical effects of hands-on shift work). Health promotion is thus often viewed as a luxury, not as a relief from the stress and demands of much blue-collar work. In other words, when blue-collar workers are encouraged to become more self-reliant and to take charge of their health, they see this as "blaming the victim" because it refocuses the need for changes in the job environment to be the responsibility of individual workers.

At the lowest end of the stratification hierarchy—the working poor or the unemployed poor—participation in organized team sports occurs much less frequently. Their access to organized sports is severely limited by their lack of resources and the unavailability of teams, equipment, or facilities. This situation worsened during the recent COVID-19 pandemic lockdowns when organized sport provision for the public was scaled back.

One prominent French sociologist, Pierre Bourdieu, developed a conceptual framework that delves into the differing ways that social class groups invest in and gain value from sport participation. In his book called *Distinction*, Bourdieu contends that people from different social classes utilize lifestyle activities such as sport to gain certain benefits, or capitals, as he calls them. These various capitals can be in the form of *social* networks and connections, *cultural* values and attributes, and direct *economic* gains.[10] The upper-class members of society are especially able to develop these capitals and, in so doing, are able to distance themselves from lower-class members and keep "exclusive access to the most valued and valuable resources, positions, activities and institutions" in our society.[11]

From Bourdieu's perspective, sport is the vehicle to maintain class distinction, and we therefore can understand how and why upper-class members of society use certain sporting contexts that are considered more elite or "high class" to gain these types of benefits. We can see that golf, for example, is one such activity where upper-class members can gain new social networks, obtain cultural styles and attitudes, and also find ways of generating financial benefits. In this way, playing golf becomes more than simply getting the lowest score over eighteen holes, because it provides various capital benefits that translate into broader societal status and achievements. Conversely, sports such as boxing, weightlifting, and basketball are generally associated with lower-class members of society, because these types of physical sports seem aligned with hard labor and instrumental body orientation. These sports may in rare cases lead to economic success (e.g., professional contracts or prize money); however, these sports do not generally provide substantial social and cultural benefits that translate into other important sectors of society, such as higher education and professional employment. Once again, these translatable benefits are obtained more frequently and profoundly by those participating in more "distinguished," upper-class activities. Overall, Bourdieu's work has been highly influential to sociology of sport scholars examining social class differences and reproduction.[12] Bourdieu's ideas about capital generation are indeed useful to understand sport participation trends that exist between different social classes.

YOUTH SPORT PARTICIPATION BY SOCIOECONOMIC STATUS

There are several tendencies concerning sports participation by the children in low-income households. First, they are more likely than the children of the affluent to engage in physical contact sports (wrestling, boxing, basketball). This is a social arena where they can be somebody, where they can achieve respect they otherwise do not get.[13] This argument has been poignantly illustrated by micro-level sociological researchers who have immersed themselves in such sporting cultures.

Indeed, research evidence confirms the generalization that athletes from lower social origins are much more likely to compete in contact sports and to gravitate to sports that emphasize physical strength (e.g., weightlifting or arm wrestling) and physical toughness (e.g., boxing or wrestling).

A second tendency for children of low-income families is to engage in sports that require little equipment or that are publicly funded, such as those found in community youth programs and schools. Basketball, both the playground variety and school teams, is one sport at which urban children of the poor tend to excel. Prowess in basketball begins for these youngsters not in organized leagues or teams, but as individuals joining with other individuals to challenge another loosely organized group of individuals. This formative type of basketball activity can often occur in streets, parks, or empty school playgrounds. More than twenty years ago, sportswriter Pete Axthelm sensitively characterized it in a way that is as applicable today as when he wrote it:

Basketball is the city game. Its battlegrounds are strips of asphalt between tattered wire fences or crumbling buildings; its rhythms grow from the uneven thump of a ball against hard surfaces. It demands no open spaces or lush backyards or elaborate equipment. It doesn't even require specified numbers of players; a one-on-one confrontation in a playground can be as memorable as a full-scale organized game.

Basketball is the game for young athletes without cars or allowances—the game whose drama and action are intensified by its confined spaces and chaotic surroundings. . . .

The game is simple, an act of one man challenging another, twisting, feinting, then perhaps breaking free to leap upward, directing a ball toward a target, a metal hoop ten feet above the ground. But its simple motions swirl into intricate patterns, its variations become almost endless, its brief soaring moments merge into a fascinating dance. To the uninitiated, the patterns may seem fleeting, elusive, even confusing; but on a city playground, a classic play is frozen in the minds of those who see it—a moment of order and achievement in a turbulent, frustrating existence. And a one-on-one challenge takes on wider meaning, defining identity and manhood in an urban society that breeds invisibility.[14]

The prolonged fiscal crisis at all levels of government (federal, state, and local) has had a negative impact on sports programs for the children of the poor. Municipal governments often cannot fund recreational programs at an appropriate level. City schools are especially hard hit as their funds, which come mostly from property taxes, diminish and federal and state assistance programs are reduced or eliminated.

The children of the affluent, in contrast, go to either private schools or public schools in wealthier districts. Wealthy districts provide more sports opportunities, more coaches, and better facilities and equipment than do the poorer districts. When sports in the more affluent areas are threatened by cuts, the shortfall can usually be saved by installing "participation fees"—an arrangement that increases the gap between sports participation possibilities for the children of the poor and the affluent. In some cases, local business sponsors, parent groups, alumni, or boosters will step in to provide significant financial assistance to school sport programs in these wealthier communities.

For youngsters growing up in a country club milieu, interest in the sports provided there is natural, and they tend to develop the skills, enhanced by coaches at the clubs and even in private training sessions, that are essential to successful sports performance. Children of the poor, in contrast, often do not have access to golf courses, tennis courts, swimming pools, and traveling sports club teams (except in rare "scholarship" arrangements that are problematic for various reasons). Nor do they receive trained or certified coaching in these sports, often relying on parents or other volunteers. The only sports in which they tend to receive experienced coaching outside schools are track and field (through community track clubs) and boxing, because gyms are located in the poorest and racially segregated urban areas.

SPECTATOR PREFERENCES FOR SPORTS BY SOCIOECONOMIC STATUS

The mass media have been instrumental in generating an interest in professional football, basketball, baseball, and hockey that transcends social class, since the overwhelming majority of American households have access to live sport either through mobile phones, computers, or television.

There are three kinds of spectators—those who attend in person, those who watch on television or listen to radio, and the more than 40 million people in the United States who spend many hours each week on their fantasy sports teams.[15] Examining first the attendance at a live sporting event, we find that the data show a consistently strong relationship between sports attendance and social class. For example, as shown in Table 5.1, those respondents whose household income was from $50,000 to $100,000 and above reported greater sports participation in every sport listed than respondents earning below $50,000. Clearly, the higher the income, the educational attainment, or both, the more likely it is that individuals will attend and participate in sports.

During the past twenty years, overall participation in and attendance of sporting events in general have shifted toward more educated and affluent people. This is not surprising, given the relatively high costs of travel, tickets, parking, and concessions. In 2021, for example, the average price of a ticket was $107.05; the Las Vegas Raiders games were the most expensive, with $153.47 being charged on average per ticket. The high cost of attendance is ironic because many stadiums were built with public funds, yet only the affluent can often afford to attend.[16]

Statistics on sports watching on television reveal these patterns:

- The affluent are much more likely than the poor to watch golf and tennis;
- The college educated are more likely to watch college sports than those who did not attend college; and
- High school graduates or those who have less education are overrepresented among those watching auto racing, demolition derbies, tractor pulls, bowling, and professional wrestling.

An excellent indicator of what type of audience watches a sporting event on television is the sponsors who have purchased advertising for them. Advertisers for golf events include corporations such as IBM, Xerox, Prudential, and United Airlines; professional wrestling is typically sponsored by used-car dealers, beer distributors, and country music record companies. Clearly, advertisers have researched sports audiences and have discerned that for some sports activities, the audiences are disproportionately from certain social classes.

SEGREGATION IN SPORTS BY SOCIAL CLASS

We have previously noted that the different social strata have some unique preferences in sport. Although they enjoy some of the same sports (especially the mass media presentations of professional football, basketball, soccer, and baseball), the self-selection process in sports tends to segregate by social class. Let us look beyond this process to ascertain whether there are any other barriers that separate the social classes.

At the participatory level, some barriers serve to segregate the social classes. As we noted earlier in this chapter, in sports such as swimming, golf, and tennis, the affluent compete in private clubs or at facilities limited to residents in an exclusive academy/club facility or neighborhood or condominium complex (at some of these, access is controlled by fences with locked gates, walls, and even armed guards). The middle and lower classes may participate in these sports only at public facilities. In a given city, then, a dual system of competition often exists—tournaments or competitions for the wealthy and a separate set of events for the general public. The quality of play at these two levels varies, with the wealthy usually rated better because of their access to better facilities, equipment, and private trainers/coaches. This difference in skill also serves to segregate affluent from less affluent players.

Spectators, too, are often segregated by social class at general-interest sporting events. This is accomplished in several ways. First, as we noted previously, ticket prices for professional sports often exclude the poor, especially when season tickets are considered. The common practice of different prices according to seating location also tends to segregate persons by socioeconomic status. The affluent rarely sit in the relatively low-cost bleacher seats, and the poor rarely purchase "lower deck," reserved seats, or box seats and do not have access to seats in the skyboxes.

The ultimate in differentially priced seating locations, and thus segregation by social class, is the purchase of skyboxes. These exclusive luxury suites are typically outfitted with expensive furniture, a bar, and other luxuries. They are purchased by individuals or corporations for very high prices, as we will note in Chapter 11. For example, the price of luxury suite rentals at NFL individual games can be in the five figures while suite rental at special events such as the Super Bowl far exceed this cost (between $1 million and $2.5 million in 2022).

This ostentatious display of wealth is an example of *conspicuous consumption*, the purchase and display of expensive items to flaunt one's high status. From Bourdieu's perspective, this practice also simultaneously distinguishes one from lower-class members and potentially leads to further benefits. Although several sports offer the opportunity for conspicuous consumption spectating, it is most commonly found at the premier events—for example, at the Super Bowl, the Stanley Cup Championship, the World Series, and the Kentucky Derby, as well as heavyweight boxing and MMA championship bouts.

At the other end of the stratification hierarchy are the poor and near-poor, who often cannot afford to attend sports. The high costs likely keep the poorest away from the sports arenas, except as workers (vendors, janitors, parking attendants). Even when the poor can afford seats for regular events, they are often priced out of premier events. Since these events are sold out (with corporate sponsors holding huge blocks of seats), scalpers sell the precious few remaining seats at premium prices. The high cost of going to sports events has prevented the local poor and the working poor from attending them, and some of these individuals may actually work in entry-level jobs within stadiums and arenas. The poor have, instead, become that huge mass of television fans. For more on this, see Chapter 12.

SOCIAL MOBILITY IN THE UNITED STATES

Social mobility is the term used to describe the movement of individuals from one social location in a society's stratification system to another. Income mobility is the most common measure of social mobility. *Intra*generational mobility refers to people who move from one social class to another during their life. Those whose income and financial resources increase within their lifetime are said to be upwardly mobile, whereas those whose income and resources decrease are said to be downwardly mobile. A second commonly measured form of social mobility is *inter*generational mobility, which refers to sons and daughters whose lifetime income and financial standing are upward or downward relative to that of their parents.

Typically, Americans believe that the United States has a fluid, socially mobile class system—in other words, that positions of high pay and prestige are open to those with the requisite talents and aptitudes, regardless of their social origin. Indeed, a central creed of the so-called American dream is a vision of a society in which one becomes upwardly mobile by working hard and competing to become wealthy, and this article of faith is reinforced by rags-to-riches successes that do, rarely, occur. This view is often linked with the neo-liberal economic view, which purports that all members of society have the ability to achieve success through participation in the free market.

Although there are certainly opportunities to be upwardly mobile in the United States, citizens of Denmark, Austria, Norway, Finland, Australia, and Spain have higher rates of socioeconomic mobility than U.S. citizens. Moreover, social mobility in the United States has been declining in the past three decades. The data in Figure 5.1 show that in 2011 about 53 percent of sons ended up in a similar social class as

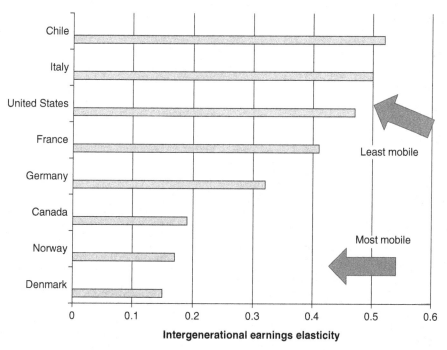

FIGURE 5.1 Intergenerational Correlations between the Earnings of Fathers and Sons in Organisation for Economic Co-operation and Development Countries. *Note*: The higher the intergenerational elasticity, the lower the extent of social mobility. *Source*: Adapted from Miles Corak et al., "Economic Mobility, Family Background, and the Well-Being of Children in the United States and Canada," in *Persistence, Privilege and Parenting: The Comparative Study of Intergenerational Mobility*, eds. Timothy Smeeding, Markus Jäntti, and Robert Erickson (New York: Russell Sage Foundation, 2011), 73–108.

adults as their fathers. A senior writer at the *New York Times* declared that "many researchers have reached a conclusion that turns conventional wisdom on its head: Americans enjoy less economic mobility than their peers in Canada and much of Western Europe." Isabel Sawhill of the Brookings Institution's Center on Children and Families agrees, saying, "The simple truth is that we have a belief system about ourselves that no longer aligns with the facts."[17]

More than almost any other cultural practice, the sports world has been one of the most influential contributors to shaping the belief about widespread social mobility in the United States through sport. This belief has been reinforced by the stories of a few youth from poor rural and urban areas, whether White or Black, skyrocketing to fame and fortune through success in high-profile professional sports. This is the quintessentially American "hoop dream."[18] The next section investigates the extent to which social mobility operates in the sports world—and if so, to what extent. Let us first examine the arguments and evidence supporting this belief.

SPORT AS A MOBILITY ESCALATOR

Involvement in sport is no guarantee of upward social mobility. However, there are examples of sports participation facilitating upward social mobility of athletes from several sports from low socioeconomic backgrounds who have become wealthy and famous because of their sports achievements. Most typically, this has occurred in boxing, where young athletes are recruited almost exclusively from the lower socioeconomic levels, and a few do earn many millions of dollars during their careers—very few. Loïc Wacquant, a sociologist who spent three years studying boxing in a boxing gym, quotes a veteran boxing trainer as having told him, "If you want to know who's at d'bottom of society, all you gotta do is look at who's boxin'."[19] Successful professional athletes in some sports (football in particular) must attend both high school and college. In this way, sports participation has the effect of encouraging or (in some cases) forcing young athletes to attain more education than they might otherwise achieve. This, in turn, increases their opportunities for success outside the sports world.

At the high school level, athletic participation appears to have positive consequences for mobility, as we revisit in more detail in Chapter 9 ("Interscholastic Sports"). Research shows consistently that, compared to their nonathlete peers, high school athletes as a category have better grades, more positive attitudes toward school, and more interest in continuing their education after high school. One recent study found that White and African American males who played school sports stayed in school longer than students of similar racial backgrounds who did not play sports, and African American, Hispanic, and White athletes who played high school sports were more likely to graduate from college.[20]

Although this research literature suggests that sport is a mobility escalator, there are three confounding problems with these findings. First, researchers have found it difficult to determine whether sports participation makes the difference or whether there are qualities that successful athletes have that give them an edge in academic achievement, such as willingness to work hard and follow orders, as well as a strong goal orientation. There is also a powerful selection factor at work here, inasmuch as coaches have been known to weed out certain types of problematic students. These are more likely to be academically low-performing students. Thus, where this happens, the grade point average for the sports team tends to rise.

Second, perhaps the differences are effects of family background and social class. Third, there is a problem with comparing athletes with nonathletes on grades, delinquency, and the like, given that athletes must maintain a minimum grade point average to remain athletes. Similarly, students can lose their athlete status if they get into serious trouble in school or in the community. Again, removing problem students from the athlete category "loads the dice" in favor of finding positive results when comparing athletes with nonathletes.

For these reasons we should be wary of research comparing athletes with nonathletes. That said, the research shows that there are positive consequences for participation in high school sports. Sports success often translates into high social status in the school, which has positive benefits for self-concept and for identifying positively with the school. Athletes are less likely than nonathletes to drop out of school. And athletes who believe that they will get a scholarship to college will be motivated to prepare for post–high school education.

Limited research has examined the question of whether success in high school sports enhances the probability of attending college and attaining high-paying, high–social status occupational positions. We summarize two of them.

In one study comparing male athletes and nonathletes six years after their class graduation from college, the researchers found that former athletes working in business, military, or manual labor occupations were better off financially than former nonathletes. The exception was that former athletes who had become high school teachers lagged behind nonathletes in income.[21]

A second study focused on high school seniors and compared the educational and labor market outcomes for athletes and nonathletes eight years after their scheduled high school graduation. The findings were that high school athletes, compared to nonathletes, were more likely to (1) have attended college and earned a bachelor's degree, (2) be employed full-time, and (3) be earning a higher income.[22]

Each study suggests that athletes possess achievement indicators for more upward social mobility than nonathletes. These studies lead to the tentative conclusion that male high school and college athletes are upwardly mobile. The actual ways and means by which sport may account for these findings remains problematic. There are some possible reasons for the findings.

First, athletic participation may lead to various forms of "occupational sponsorship." The male college athlete is a popular hero and can often access new higher-status social and cultural networks that are generally unavailable to the average nonathlete. For example, well-placed alumni often offer former athletes positions in their businesses after graduation. This may be done to help the firm's public relations, or it may be part of a payoff in the recruiting wars that some alumni are willing to underwrite.

A second reason athletes may fare better is that the selection process for many jobs requires the applicant to be "well-rounded," that is, to have had a number of successful experiences outside the classroom. An extreme example of this is in the selection of Rhodes scholars, which requires, in addition to superior grades, participation in extracurricular activities and demonstrated athletic ability. Some employers also target athletes for employment directly because of the perception that they are well-rounded, especially in their ability to multitask and work within team environments under pressure.

Finally, there is the possibility that participation in highly competitive sports situations will lead to the development of attitudes and behavior patterns highly valued in the larger occupational world. If attributes such as leadership, human relations skills, teamwork, good work habits, strategic decision-making, and a well-developed competitive drive are acquired in sports, they may indeed help athletes succeed in other endeavors.

Considerable debate surrounds the issue of whether sports build character or whether only certain kinds of personalities survive the sport experience. There may be a self-fulfilling prophecy at work here, however: if employers assume that athletes possess these valued character traits, they will make their hiring and promotion decisions accordingly, giving athletes the advantage.

DEMYTHOLOGIZING THE SOCIAL MOBILITY-THROUGH-SPORT HYPOTHESIS

Although there is evidence suggesting that involvement in high school and college sport may facilitate upward social mobility, that notion must be balanced with the reality that much of the upward social mobility acquired through sport is constructed on a succession of *myths*. The most prominent myths are as follows:

1. Sport provides a free college education.
2. Sport leads to a college degree.
3. A professional sports career is readily possible.
4. Sport is a way out of poverty, especially for working-class racial minorities.
5. Because of Title IX, women now have many opportunities for upward mobility through sport.
6. A professional sports career provides security for life.

Myth: Sport Provides a Free College Education

One assumption of the "social mobility-through-sports participation" position is that involvement in high school sport leads to college scholarships, which is especially helpful to poor youth who could not afford college otherwise. The problem with this assumption is that few high school athletes actually receive athletic scholarships, especially "free-ride" scholarships. Consider the following facts:

- NCAA Division I and II universities offer athletic scholarships. Division III schools do not offer athletic scholarships; they offer academic scholarships only. According to the NCAA, only about 2 percent of high school athletes are awarded athletic scholarships to compete in college.
- Fewer than 3.5 percent of male high school basketball players will go on to play at an NCAA university. Four in one hundred, or 4 percent, of female high school basketball players will go on to play women's basketball at an NCAA member institution.
- About 6.7 percent, or about one in sixteen, of all high school football players will go on to play football at an NCAA member institution. Less than three in fifty, or about 5.6 percent, of high school soccer players will go on to play men's soccer at an NCAA member institution. About six in seventy-five, or about 7 percent, of high school baseball players will go on to play men's baseball at an NCAA member institution.[23]

As these figures clearly show, the notion that if one is a good high school athlete an athletic scholarship to a reputable university will likely follow—a belief held by many high school athletes and their parents—does not correspond to reality.

Myth: Participation in Sports Leads to a College Degree

A problem with the assumption that sports participation leads to a college degree is that fewer than half of college athletes graduate with college degrees (see Chapter 10). This is especially true for those athletes who aspire to become professional athletes. Data show that, among the small percentage of college athletes who do become professional athletes, many

have not graduated from college. The percentages fluctuate from year to year, but figures in recent years have shown that only about 50 percent of NFL players have college degrees, and only 20 percent of NBA players are college graduates; the rate is even lower for professional baseball and hockey, where more than 90 percent of MLB and NHL players have not graduated.

There are a number of barriers to graduation for athletes. One obvious problem is the inordinate demand on their time and energy for practices, meetings, travel, and other sport-related activities. Indeed, former UCLA basketball player Ed O'Bannon once stated, "I was an athlete masquerading as a student. I was there strictly to play basketball. I did basically the minimum to make sure I kept my eligibility so I could continue to play."[24] Many college athletes, because of these pressures, are counseled to take easy courses that maintain eligibility but that may not meet graduation requirements. The result is either to delay graduation or to make graduation an unrealistic goal. Another barrier to graduation for many college athletes is that they are recruited for athletic prowess rather than for academic achievement. Athletes from low-income families who have typically attended inferior high schools, for example, are generally not prepared for the intellectual demands of college. As noted in Chapter 6, after six years, only about four of ten Black football players and three of ten Black basketball players in big-time programs graduate. Put another way, whereas about one-half of White players do not graduate, two-thirds of Black players do not graduate.

A third barrier to graduation for college athletes is their own behavior, because many of them do not take advantage of their scholarships to work toward graduation. This is the case for those who perceive their college experience merely as preparation for their professional careers in sport. Study for them is necessary only to maintain their eligibility, as the previous quote from the former UCLA basketball player suggested. An NBA rule change in 2006 mandates that players be at least one year removed from high school and at least nineteen years old to be drafted. For many basketball players, that has meant attending at least one year of college and then entering the NBA draft. In basketball circles this rule change is known as the "one and done rule." Between 2006 and 2016, over sixty players who were one year out of high school have been drafted by NBA teams.[25]

These attitudes and practices by college athletes are shortsighted because even a successful professional athletic career is limited to a few years, and not many professional athletes are able to translate their success in the pros to success in their postathletic careers. Such a problem is especially true for African Americans, who often face employment discrimination in the wider society.

Myth: A Professional Sports Career Is Probable for Successful High School and College Athletes

When queried about their aspirations as athletes, many youth sport and high school athletes say that they believe they can become a professional in their sport. A survey by the Center for the Study of Sport in Society found that two-thirds of African American males between the ages of thirteen and eighteen believed that they could earn a living playing professional sports. Slightly less optimistic were the more than 30 percent of young White males who held such a belief. Moreover, African American parents were four times more likely than White parents to believe that their children were destined for careers as professional athletes. Obviously, for both young athletes and their parents, the higher echelons of sport are readily available and thus will lead to upward social mobility.[26] The reality is quite different:

- Of the 535,289 boys playing high school basketball each year, 0.03 percent will be drafted by an NBA team. Of some 435,885 high school girls playing interscholastic basketball, 0.02 percent will eventually be drafted by a WNBA team.
- Of the approximately 4,155 college male basketball players who are eligible for the NBA draft each year, 1.1 percent are drafted by an NBA team. In women's college basketball, 3.0 percent of the draft-eligible players are chosen in the WNBA draft; typically, all will come from Division I colleges. Of the approximately 16,175 college football players who are eligible for the NFL draft each year, some 256, or 1.6 percent, will be chosen in the NFL draft. When the calculation includes NFL,

Canadian Football League, and Arena League draft slots available for first-year professionals, the percentage of football players drafted rises to 1.9 percent.

- Similar percentages are found for high school baseball and soccer athletes.

The basic fact is that a small percentage of high school athletes become college athletes, and an infinitesimally small percentage become professional athletes. Furthermore, this pipeline ideal was recently impacted by COVID-19, since this pandemic interfered with high school, collegiate, and professional seasons of play, as well as the recruitment processes for potential student-athletes. So the notion that being a high school athlete positions one for a career as a professional athlete, with all of the social mobility that entails, is a myth.[27]

If these young athletes do play as professionals, the economic rewards are excellent, as shown in Chapter 11. The dream of financial success through a professional sports career is, however, just a dream for all but an infinitesimal number. Not only are the odds long of making it to the professional level, if one is good enough and lucky enough to make it, but also the career will be short, averaging three to seven years in team sports and three to twelve years in individual sports. So, in light of what is obviously a false ideology of guaranteed upward mobility for poor youth who excel at sport, the vast majority of youth would stand a better chance of achieving social mobility by focusing their time and energy on their education rather than on sport.

Myth: Sport Is a Way out of Poverty, Especially for Racial Minorities

Sport appears to be an important avenue out of poverty for African Americans. Several professional sports are dominated numerically by Blacks. Although they comprise only 13.5 percent of the U.S. population, African Americans constitute around 82 percent of the players in professional basketball and about 70 percent of the players in professional football. Moreover, Blacks are high on the list of the highest moneymakers in sport (salaries, commercial sponsorships). At first, these facts seem impressive, but they are illusory. Consider the following:

- There are fewer than 2,500 African American athletes playing in the most popular professional team sports leagues—NFL, NBA, WNBA, MLB, NHL, and Major League Soccer (MLS). There are approximately 14.3 million African Americans aged eighteen to forty years old, the age range of pro athletes; thus, only approximately 0.0002 percent of African Americans in that age range (2 in 10,000) are professional athletes in those sports.
- African Americans are rarely found in certain sports (automobile racing, swimming, tennis, golf, bowling, hockey).
- African Americans are rarely found in positions of authority in sport (head coaches, athletic directors, league officers, general managers, owners).

These figures clearly show that only a small percentage of African Americans make it to the professional level as athletes. Several African American scholars have noted that, statistically, young African American athletes have a better chance of being hit by a meteorite than of getting work as an athlete, and the prospects for African American women are much worse than for men.

Nevertheless, this myth is pervasive in the African American community. Despite the low odds of making it as a professional athlete, many poor African American boys—and increasingly girls—see sport as their only hope to escape a life of crime, poverty, and despair. They latch onto the dream of sport success partly because they have limited opportunities for middle-class success. That is why many African American youth spend countless hours, year in and year out, developing their speed, strength, or "moves" to the virtual exclusion of developing capabilities that have a greater likelihood of paying off in upward mobility—mathematical competence, communication skills, computer literacy, and so on.

It is true that some gifted athletes make out all right, but what happens to the thousands of young unathletic African Americans and poor children whose only heroes are sports stars? How many brilliant doctors, lawyers, teachers, poets, and artists have been lost because intelligent but uncoordinated youth were led to believe that their only chance for getting ahead was to develop a thirty-foot jump shot, throw a ninety-mile-per-hour fastball, or run the hundred meters in 9.3?

This largely futile pursuit of sports stardom is of serious consequence, especially in the African American community. Foremost, the strong belief in the "sports as a way up" myth causes young players to spend their energies and talents on athletic skills rather than on pursuing occupational skills that would help them meet their political and material needs. In short, because of belief in the sports myth, they remain dependent on Whites and White institutions.[28]

The conventional rhetoric that sports are an avenue of upward social mobility is accompanied by assertions about how sport plays a progressive role for African Americans. The success of African Americans in the highly visible sports gives White America a false sense of Black progress and interracial harmony. But the social progress of African Americans in general has little relationship to their achievements on America's playing fields.

Several sport sociologists have argued that the numerical superiority of African Americans in several of the most popular sports, coupled with their disproportionate underrepresentation in other professions, reinforces the racist ideology that African Americans are physically superior to Whites but are inferior to them intellectually. In short, sport harms African Americans by serving up imagery and metaphors that reinforce racism and the racial divisions that continue to plague American society.

We are not suggesting that talented African American athletes should not seek a career in professional sport. Professional sport is a legitimate career with the potential for exceptional monetary rewards. What is harmful, to reiterate, is that the odds of success are so slim—rendering extraordinary, sustained effort futile and misguided for the vast majority. If this effort were directed at areas having better odds of success, then upward mobility would occur for many more.

Myth: Women Now Have Sport as a Vehicle for Upward Mobility Because of New Opportunities

Since the passage of Title IX in 1972 (see Chapter 7), sports participation by women in high school and college has increased dramatically. In 1971, for example, there were 294,000 high school girls' sport participants; during 2018-2019 there were some 3.4 million. The number of NCAA women's teams has increased each year since 1984, and women now receive about 47 percent of the money allotted to athletic scholarships (still less than half, but a considerable improvement). This has allowed many women to attend college who otherwise could not have afforded it. That is positive because of the indirect educational benefits accruing from athletic ability.[29]

Upward mobility through sport is another matter for women. Women have fewer opportunities than men in professional team sports. But a few women in individual professional sports have recently done well financially—Serena Williams and several other tennis players, Paula Creamer in golf, Danica Patrick in automobile racing, and a relative handful of women in other sports. Ironically, the sports with the greatest monetary rewards for women are those associated with the middle and upper classes. These sports are expensive, and they require considerable individual coaching as well as access to private facilities. In short, sport offers poor women limited opportunities for upward mobility.

Opportunities in sport apart from the athlete role (trainers, scouts, referees, sports journalists, and coaches) are more limited for women than for men. Ironically, with the passage of Title IX, which increased the participation of girls and women so dramatically, there has been a decline in the proportion of women as coaches and athletic administrators. We will have more to say about women in sport in Chapter 7.

Myth: A Professional Sports Career Provides Lifelong Security

Even when a professional sports career is attained, the probabilities of fame and fortune are limited. The average length of a career in professional sport is short—three to five years in the popular team sports. The pay for professional athletes may be relatively high, but their employment does not last long. Professional athletes leave sport, on average, when they are in their late twenties or early thirties, at a time when their nonathlete peers have begun to establish themselves in occupations leading toward retirement in thirty years or so. Of course, some pro athletes make an income from salaries and endorsements that, if invested wisely, provides financial security for life. But many have not planned for the future beyond sports or do not invest wisely and wind up in financial trouble.

Some professional athletes do plan ahead, preparing themselves for other careers in sport (coaching, scouting, reporting, administering) or for a nonsport occupation. Others do not prepare themselves for this abrupt change. Exiting the athlete role is difficult for many because they lose (1) what they have focused on for most of their lives, (2) the primary source of their personal identity, (3) their physical prowess, (4) adulation bordering on worship from others, (5) the money and perquisite

In New York City, West 4th Street's iconic basketball court, "the cage," has been a proving ground for NBA stars. Many people consider sport to be a major way for poor White and African American youth to escape their social conditions. Because several of the popular professional sports are dominated numerically by African Americans, young Black youth buy into the myth that with dedication and the development of superior skills in a sport, they can become pro athletes. But fewer than 1 in 7,000 African Americans become professional athletes. (Photo: © pio3/Shutterstock.com)

fame, (6) the camaraderie with teammates, (7) the intense "highs" of competition, and (8) status (most ex-athletes are downwardly mobile on retirement from sport).[30]

Ex–professional athletes frequently do not know what to do with their remaining working years. Consequently, many of them have serious personal, social, and economic troubles. Most of us can think of media accounts of ex–professional athletes in trouble as a result of drug addiction, domestic violence, criminal activity, and so forth. Studies of former pro athletes have found that emotional difficulties, divorce, and financial strain were common problems for retired professional athletes. There are also those athletes we discussed in Chapter 4 who have experienced multiple concussions during their playing career and in retirement are found to have evidence of the degenerative brain disease chronic traumatic encephalopathy.[31]

For most former pro athletes, entry into the "real world" is a step down. Big-time pro athletes are pampered like royalty. They fly first class while hired hands pay the bills and tote the luggage. High-powered executives and heads of state fawn over them. "You begin to feel like Louis XIV," said a former pro athlete. He continued, "Step off the pedestal and everything changes. It's like being dipped into hell."

There is some potential for a sports-related career after one's playing days are over: coaching, managing, scouting, sportscasting, public relations, and administration are all possibilities for former athletes, but the opportunities are severely limited, especially if the athlete is a minority group member (see Chapter 6) or a woman (see Chapter 7).

A major theme of this chapter is that sport contributes to the ideology that legitimizes social inequalities and promotes the myth that all it takes to succeed is extraordinary effort. In another publication one of us has made this point forcefully. We think it bears repeating here: "The overall effect of the few athletes who do become professional athletes reproduces the belief system among the general public that the American social class system is more open to social mobility than it really is. Because the few rags-to-riches athletes are made so visible,

the social mobility theme is maintained. This reflects the opportunity structure of society in general—the success of a few reproduces the belief in social mobility among the many."[32]

SUMMARY

Two themes dominate this chapter. The first is that sport, like the larger society, is stratified. Socioeconomic status is related to the types of sports one participates in and watches. The lower one's status, the more one is inclined toward high-contact sports with intensive physical demands. Higher socioeconomic strata are segregated in sport by their ability to dominate sporting activities that provide rich social, economic, and cultural benefits, or capitals, thus benefiting them in other key life endeavors. Those in upper-class positions are also able to reinforce and enhance their status through economic barriers such as entrance requirements and prohibitive participation costs that exclude lower-class members of society from participating in these lucrative activities.

The second theme is that sports participation has limited potential as a social mobility escalator. There is evidence that being a successful athlete enhances self-confidence and the probability of attending college. Thus, social mobility is accomplished through sport indirectly because of the increased employment potential from educational attainment. Social mobility through sport is limited, however, by failure to graduate and extremely low number of positions in professional sports that are available for aspiring athletes each year. Moreover, social mobility is limited, even almost nonexistent, for women. Even for those who attain major league status, the probabilities of fame and fortune are small because of the comparably limited funding resources found in these activities and the tendency for relatively short careers and injuries.

The myth that sport is a mobility escalator is especially perilous for minority racial and ethnic youth. The mass of these youngsters from poor or near-poor family backgrounds who devote their lives to the pursuit of athletic stardom will, except for the fortunate few, become disappointed when their specialized sports skills fail to provide them

Junior Seau was inducted into the San Diego Chargers Hall of Fame in 2011. Seau was a linebacker in the National Football League; he was a ten-time All-Pro and twelve-time Pro Bowl selection. Seau committed suicide in 2012 at the age of forty-three. Studies by the National Institutes of Health concluded that Seau suffered from chronic traumatic encephalopathy (CTE), a type of chronic brain damage caused by repeated trauma to the head. CTE has also been found in other deceased former NFL players. (Photo: AP Photo/Denis Poroy)

with significant educational and occupational opportunities.

Another negative consequence is more subtle but very important. Sport contributes to the ideology that legitimizes social inequalities and promotes the myth that all it takes to succeed is extraordinary effort.

Learn more with this chapter's digital tools, including web resources, video links, and chapter self-assessment quizzes at www.oup.com/he/sage-eitzen-beal-atencio-12e.

NOTES

1. Joseph E. Stiglitz, "Equal Opportunity, Our National Myth," *New York Times*, February 17, 2013, SR4.
2. For an in-depth discussion of this topic, see Howard L Nixon II, *Sport in a Changing World*, 2nd ed. (Boulder, CO: Paradigm, 2015); for an international perspective on this topic see Ramón Spaaij, *Sport and Social Mobility: Crossing Boundaries* (New York: Routledge, 2013).
3. Good discussions of this topic can be found in Kasturi DasGupta, *Introducing Social Stratification: The Causes and Consequences of Inequality* (Boulder, CO: Lynne Rienner, 2015); see also Christopher B. Doob, *Social Inequality and Social Stratification in U.S. Society* (New York: Routledge, 2012); Dennis L Gilbert, *The American Class Structure in an Age of Growing Inequality*, 9th ed. (Thousand Oaks, CA: Sage, 2015).
4. Jonathan Morduch and Rachel Schneider, *The Financial Diaries: How American Families Cope in a World of Uncertainty* (Princeton, NJ: Princeton University Press, 2017); see also Carol Graham, *Happiness for All? Unequal Hopes and Lives in Pursuit of the*

American Dream (Princeton, NJ: Princeton University Press, 2017).

5. *Poverty Rate by Race/Ethnicity*, Kaiser Family Foundation, 2014, http://kff.org/other/state-indicator/poverty-rate-by-raceethnicity/.
Brian Root and Lena Simet, "United States: Pandemic Impact on People in Poverty," Human Rights Watch, March 2, 2021, https://www.hrw.org/news/2021/03/02/united-states-pandemic-impact-people-poverty.

6. Center on Budget and Policy Priorities, "Tracking the COVID-19 Recession's Effects on Food, Housing, and Employment Hardships," August 9, 2021, https://www.cbpp.org/research/poverty-and-inequality/tracking-the-covid-19-recessions-effects-on-food-housing-and.

7. Thorstein Veblen, *The Theory of the Leisure Class* (New York: Create Space Independent Publishing Platform, 2013; originally published in 1899).

8. Ilona Bray, *Healthy Employees, Healthy Business: Easy, Affordable Ways to Promote Workplace Wellness*, 2nd ed. (Berkeley, CA: NOLO, 2012); see also Laura Putnam, *Workplace Wellness That Works: 10 Steps to Infuse Well-Being and Vitality into Any Organization* (New York: Wiley, 2015).

9. Joanne Kay and Suzanne Laberge, "The 'New' Corporate Habitus in Adventure Racing," *International Review for the Sociology of Sport* 37, no. 1 (2002): 17–36.

10. Pierre Bourdieu, *Distinction: A Social Critique of the Judgement of Taste* (Cambridge, MA: Harvard University Press, 1984).

11. Carl Stempel, "Adult Participation Sports as Cultural Capital," *International Review for the Sociology of Sport* 40, no. 4 (2005): 411–432.

12. Alan Tomlinson, "Pierre Bourdieu and the Sociological Study of Sport: Habitus, Capital and Field," in *Sport and Modern Social Theorists*, ed. Richard Giulianotti (London: Palgrave Macmillan, 2004), 161–172.

13. Michael S. Kimmel and Michael A. Messner, eds., *Men's Lives*, 10th ed. (New York: Oxford University Press, 2018); several articles in this book are relevant to the topic of youth sport participation by socioeconomic status.

14. Pete Axthelm, *The City Game: Basketball from the Garden to the Playgrounds* (Lincoln, NE: Bison Books, 1999); see also Darcy Frey, *The Last Shot: City Streets, Basketball Dreams* (New York: Mariner Books, 2004).

15. For four interesting publications about sports fans, see Jim Chernesky, *Once a Fan: Why It Is So Hard to Be a Sports Fan* (Bloomington, IN: iUniverse, 2012); Bill Ordine, *Fantasy Sports, Real Money* (Las Vegas: Huntington Press, 2016); see also Kevin Bonnet, *Essential Strategies for Winning at Daily Fantasy Sports* (New York: CreateSpace Independent Publishing, 2015); Matthew Berry, *Fantasy Life: The Outrageous, Uplifting, and Heartbreaking World of Fantasy Sports from the Guy Who's Lived It* (New York: Riverhead Books, 2013).

16. "National Football League Average Ticket Price from 2006 to 2016," Statista, Inc., https://www.statista.com/statistics/193425/average-ticket-price-in-the-nfl-since-2006; also Christina Gough, "Average NFL Ticket Price," Statista, Inc., February 10, 2021, https://www.statista.com/statistics/193595/average-ticket-price-in-the-nfl-by-team/. Accessed June 11, 2022

17. Jason DeParle, "Harder for Americans to Rise from Economy's Lower Rungs," *The New York Times*, January 5, 2012, A1; Sawhill quoted in Rana Foroohar, "What Ever Happened to Upward Mobility?" *Time*, November 14, 2011, http://content.time.com/time/subscriber/article/0,33009,2098584,00.html; Alan Krueger, *The Rise and Consequences of Inequality in the United States* (Washington, D.C.: Center for American Progress, 2012).

18. See *Hoop Dreams* film from 1994.

19. Loïc Wacquant, *Body & Soul: Notebooks of an Apprentice Boxer* (New York: Oxford University Press, 2006), 42.

20. D. Stanley Eitzen, "Sports as a Path to Success: Myth and Reality," in *Foul and Fair: Beyond the Myths and Paradoxes of Sport* (Lanham, MD: Roman & Littlefield, 2016), ch. 11; see also Robert Sean Mackin and Carol S. Walther, "Race, Sport and Social Mobility: Horatio Alger in Short Pants," *International Review for the Sociology of Sport* 47, no. 6 (2011): 670–689.

21. Daniel J. Henderson, Alexandre Olbrecht, and Solomon W. Polachek, "Do Former Athletes Earn

More at Work?" *Journal of Human Resources* 41 (Summer 2006): 558–577.

22. Devon Carlson and Leslie Scott, "What Is the Status of High School Athletes Eight Years after Their Senior Year?," NCES 2005–303, National Center for Education Statistics, "Statistics in Brief," September 2005.

23. "Estimated Probability of Competing in College Athletics," National Collegiate Athletic Association, last updated March 10, 2017, http://www.ncaa.org/about/resources/research/estimated-probability-competing-college-athletics.

24. Lee Romney, "Ed O'Bannon Testifies in Lawsuit against the NCAA," *Los Angeles Times*, June 9, 2014, https://www.latimes.com/sports/sports-now/la-sp-sn-ed-obannon-ncaa-20140609-story.html.

25. Dylan Hernandez, "College Basketball's So-Called One-and-Done Rule Needs Revisiting," *Los Angeles Times*, March 24, 2016, http://www.latimes.com/sports/la-sp-college-one-and-done-hernandez-20160324-story.html.

26. Stanley Eitzen, *Fair and Foul: Beyond the Myths and Paradoxes of Sport*, 6th ed. (Lanham, MD: Rowman & Littlefield, 2016), ch. 11.

27. "Estimated Probability of Competing in College Athletics."

28. Gary Sailes, *Modern Sport and the African American Experience*, 2nd ed. (San Diego, CA: Cognella Academic, 2015); Gary Sailes, *Sports in Higher Education: Issues and Controversies in College Athletics* (San Diego, CA: Cognella Academic, 2013).

29. *2016–2017 High School Athletics Participation Survey* (Indianapolis, IN: National Federation of State High School Associations, 2017).

30. Emma Vickers, "Life after Sport: Depression in the Retired Athlete," *Sport in Mind*, October 14, 2013, http://www.thesportinmind.com/articles/life-after-sport-depression-in-retired-athletes/; see also Robert Laura, "How Star Athletes Deal with Retirement," *Forbes Magazine*, May 22, 2012, http://www.forbes.com/sites/robertlaura/2012/05/22/how-star-athletes-deal-with-retirement/#2160d6a71601.

31. Elena Schneider and Cara Cooper, "After Final Whistle, Former College Athletes Face Relief, Depression," *Helix Magazine*, June 18, 2013; see also S. L. Price, "Man in the Middle," *Sports Illustrated*, May 15, 2017, 102–111; see also James A. Holstein, Richard S. Jones, and George E. Koonce Jr., *Is There Life after Football? Surviving the NFL* (New York: New York University Press, 2014).

32. George H. Sage, *Power and Ideology in American Sport*, 2nd ed. (Champaign, IL: Human Kinetics, 1998), 53.

CHAPTER 6

RACIAL-ETHNIC MINORITIES
AND SPORT

Nowadays, except for members of white supremacist organizations, few whites in the United States claim to be "racist." . . . Most whites believe that if blacks and other minorities would just stop thinking about the past, work hard, and complain less (particularly about racial discrimination), then Americans of all hues could "all get along." But regardless of whites' "sincere fictions," racial considerations shade almost everything in America

—EDUARDO BONILLA-SILVA[1]

Jack Johnson in the ring. In 1908 Johnson became the first African American world heavyweight champion. (Photo: George Grantham Bain Collection [Library of Congress])

Racial domination is fundamentally maintained in the United States through economic, political, social, and ideological social institutions. Racial minorities continue to face systematic and pervasive discrimination against them. Although most Americans agree with this sociological fact, there are some who believe that sport is an oasis free of racial problems and tensions. After all, the argument goes, sports are competitive; fans, coaches, and players want to win; clearly, the color of the players involved is not a factor, only their performance. A further argument is that the proportion of African Americans in the major team sports, which far exceeds their proportion in the U.S. population, indicates an absence of racism. The facts, however, lead to a very different conclusion. Rather than being free from racism, sport as a microcosm of the larger society reflects many of the same racial problems as society. In this chapter we will document through various forms of evidence that prejudice and discrimination based on race and ethnicity are prevalent in sport. In doing so, we hope to alert readers to this continuing societal problem and to challenge the popular belief that sport is a meritocracy in which skin color is disregarded.

RACIAL-ETHNIC MINORITIES: SOCIAL THEORIES AND RELEVANT CONCEPTS

SOCIAL THEORIES AND RACE AND MINORITIES

The topics of prejudice and discrimination in connection with race and minorities are found in the social theories we have described in this volume. The functionalist perspective emphasizes that personal and social practices and values must contribute to social order and harmonious societal stability, so the role of racial and ethnic minorities, like that of other constituents of a society, is to assimilate and integrate socially, economically, and culturally into the general social system. Starting in schools, workplaces, churches, and political activities, the minority racial and ethnic factions must acquire the language, customs, and aspirations for success in the dominant social order and lose, or give up, much of their own culture, mannerisms, customs, rituals, values, and so on.

Race theory was identified in Chapter 1 as one of the conflict/cultural social theories. We introduced concepts such as CRT and racial formation theory to set up the idea that race is a social rather than biological construct that profoundly influences sport practice in the United States. For instance, CRT is a theoretical perspective whose premise is that racism is thoroughly rooted in the social fabric of American society (as well as in other societies) and that it "privileges whiteness as it disadvantages others because of their 'blackness.'"[2] CRT theorists emphasize the socially constructed nature of race and consider it based on inherently racist social assumptions. Therefore, they contend that society-wide actions are needed to change these endemic cultural attitudes and values. Analyses of racial inequity as the social construction of race and discrimination are present in the scholarship of CRT theorists. A racial formation perspective likewise views race as a social construction, generated over time through social, economic, and political structures that exist relative to prevailing racial identities and categories. Under this racial formation viewpoint, we constitute prevailing understandings about race through systemic/institutional as well as everyday human relations.

A variation, called the intersection perspective, claims that the effects of race and gender are interlinked unto themselves as well as interlinked with the effects of social class. Thus, class conflict is an integral part of race and gender differences in society.

RELEVANT CONCEPTS ABOUT RACE

Race is a social category regarded as distinct because the members supposedly share some genetically transmitted traits.[3] The races, however, are socially constructed categories. People have arbitrarily placed others into racial categories based on their physical attributes (most notably skin color). But these differences are minor attributes and can vary greatly within each category. Moreover, the categories used to divide people into races are not fixed; they vary from society to society.

Historically, in the United States the laws defining who is Black, for example, have varied from state to state. Tennessee law once defined as Black anyone who had at least one great-grandparent who was Black. Other southern states defined as Black any person who had Black ancestry (the "one drop of Black blood" rule). By either of these laws Tiger Woods would be Black, because he is one-fourth African American, one-fourth Thai, one-fourth Chinese, one-eighth Native American, and one-eighth White European. In Brazil he would be considered White; in the U.S. media he is described as Black.

Social scientists reject race as a valid way to define human groups. The accepted view in the scientific community is that races are a social invention. They do not exist biologically. Scientific examination of the human genome finds no genetic differences among the so-called races. Fossil and DNA evidence shows that humans are all one race, evolved in the past 100,000 years from the same small number of tribes that migrated out of Africa and colonized the world. Although there is no such thing as biological race, races are real insofar as they are *socially defined*. In other words, races are real because people believe they are real. Worldwide, and certainly within the United States, race divides people between "us" and "them."[4]

Ethnicity, unlike race, refers to the cultural heritage of a group rather than biology. An ethnic group is a category of people who share a common culture (language or dialect, religion, customs, and history). Examples of ethnic groups in the United States are Italian Americans, Arab Americans, Greek Americans, Irish Americans, and Mexican Americans.

In the United States, race and ethnicity both serve to mark groups as different and typically as "others." Groups labeled "races" by the larger society are bound together by their common social and economic conditions. As a result, they develop distinctive cultural (ethnic) characteristics. Thus, we often refer to them as *racial-ethnic groups* (or racially defined ethnic groups). The term racial-ethnic group refers to groups that are socially subordinated and culturally distinct in society. It is meant to include (1) the systematic discrimination of socially constructed racial groups and (2) their distinctive cultural arrangements. The categories African American, Latino/a, Asian American, Native American, First Nations, and Indigenous Peoples of America have been constructed as both racially and culturally distinct.

Different racial and ethnic groups are unequal in power, resources, and prestige. Why are some groups dominant and others subordinate? The basic reason is power—power derived from technology, weapons, property, or economic resources. Those holding superior power in a society—the *majority group* or *dominant group*—establish a system of inequality by dominating less powerful groups. A *minority group* is any distinct group in society that shares common group characteristics and is forced to occupy low status in society because of discrimination. A group may be a minority on some characteristics such as race, ethnicity, sexual preference, disability, or age. Crucially, the distinction between a majority and a minority is not numerical superiority, but power—with the minority having less power, and therefore low status, relative to other groups in society.

The key to understanding the personal and social issues and problems arising about race and other minorities is that they have structural foundations, which, in turn, debunk conventional misperceptions about race and minority relations. Many Americans believe that discrimination has disappeared and that racial-ethnic minorities are no longer disadvantaged. But as Eduardo Bonilla-Silva, a prominent scholar of race and ethnicity, contends, "regardless of whites' 'sincere fictions' [meaning unconsciously misrecognizing the reality of the situation or condition—in this case, brutal race relations], racial considerations shade almost everything in America. African Americans and dark-skinned racial minorities lag well behind whites in virtually every area of social life."[5] For example,

- According to the 2019 Survey of Consumer Finances, "White families have the highest level of both median and mean family wealth: $188,200 and $983,400, respectively. Black and Hispanic families have considerably less wealth than White families. Black families' median and mean wealth is less than 15 percent that of White families, at $24,100 and $142,500, respectively. Hispanic families' median and mean wealth is $36,100 and $165,500, respectively."[6]
- In 2019, the poverty rate for Blacks was 18.8 percent, for Hispanics it was 15.7 percent which indicated a reduction from past years, yet the poverty

rate for non-Hispanic Whites was only 7.3 percent.[7]

- With each step up the ladder of academic achievement, the gap in lifetime income between African Americans and Whites increases. Over a work life, African American high school graduates earn $300,000 less, African American college graduates earn $500,000 less, and African Americans with advanced degrees earn $600,000 less than comparably educated Whites.

- At every level of educational achievement, African Americans and Latino/as have higher rates of unemployment than Whites.[8]

- In 2015, 35 percent of the prison inmates in the United States were African American men and women, while only 14 percent of the U.S. population were African American. There were some 2,000 Latino prisoners for every 100,000 Latino residents. In sharp contrast, only 800 Whites per 100,000 were in prison during that year.[9]

Bonilla-Silva concludes, "Whites have developed powerful explanations—which have ultimately become justifications—for contemporary racial inequality that exculpates them from any responsibility for the status of people of color. These explanations emanate from a new racial ideology that I label *colorblind racism*."[10]

These differences between the racial-ethnic groups are not the result of deliberate decisions by racial-ethnic minorities. Instead, the problems lie in social institutions—the common way things are done, such as the way schools are financed by local taxes, using class-based testing to place children in tracks, bank lending practices, "racial profiling" by the police, bias in the criminal justice system, the eligibility requirements for jobs, the informal requirements for job promotion, and the seemingly fair practice of "last hired, first fired"—all of which prevent racial and ethnic "others" from achieving economic and social parity with the dominant Whites. This pattern of negative treatment and oppression by society's institutions is called *institutional racism*. This form of discrimination can occur without prejudice or malice toward minorities.

In their well-known text about diversity in society, sociologists Margaret Anderson and Howard Taylor put it this way: "Consider this: Even if every White person in the country lost all of his or her prejudices, and even if he or she stopped engaging in individual acts of discrimination, institutional racism would still persist for some time. Over the years, it has become so much a part of [fundamental social] institutions (hence, the term *institutional racism*) that discrimination can occur even when no single person is causing it. Existing at the level of social structure rather than at the level of individual attitude or behavior, it is 'external' to the individual personality."[11]

This chapter focuses on institutional racism in sport and is divided into several parts: (1) sports participation by the various racial-ethnic groups, (2) explanations for the dominance of African Americans in many sports, and (3) discrimination against minority group members in sport. Although the discussion refers to a variety of minorities, a disproportionate amount focuses on African Americans because they comprise the most prominent racial-ethnic minority in American sport.

As a useful background for these topics, we refer the reader to Figure 6.1, which contains demographic data about the population for 1990 and 2000 and projected data for 2025 and 2050. Note that (1) in 2025, Latino/as will have surpassed African Americans as the largest racial-ethnic category (in 2003 Latino/as became the largest racial-ethnic minority); (2) Latino/as will be about one-fourth of the U.S. population in 2050; and (3) minorities will be about one-half of the U.S. population in 2050. These trends have important implications for sports participation and the popularity of particular sports.

SPORTS PARTICIPATION AMONG RACIAL-ETHNIC MINORITIES

THE HISTORY OF AFRICAN AMERICAN INVOLVEMENT IN U.S. SPORT

Until the past decade, African Americans were the largest minority group throughout the history of the United States. Although they were involved in sports in every era of American history, it has only been in the past sixty years that they, or any racial-ethnic minorities, have become a major part of

Percent of the Population, by Race and Hispanic Origin: 1990, 2000, 2025 and 2050
(Middle-series projections)

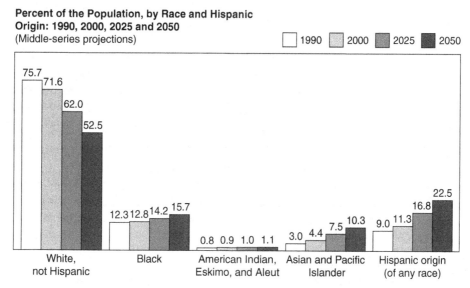

FIGURE 6.1 Percentage of the Population by Race and Hispanic Origin: 1990, 2000, 2025, 2050 (Middle-Series Projections). *Source*: U.S. Census Bureau, Population. Division, Population Profile of the United States.

America's organized sports. However, African Americans continue to be marginalized in some sports and underrepresented in leadership in most sport organizations—from coaching to management to ownership.

Historically, Africans were brought to the United States as slaves throughout the colonial period and into the first half of the nineteenth century. They were concentrated in the southern states because of the plantation system. Despite systematic and pervasive discrimination against African Americans throughout their history in the United States, they have played a continuing and significant role in the rise and development of modern sport.

The history of African American involvement in sport can be divided roughly into four stages: (1) exclusion before the Civil War, (2) breakthroughs following the Emancipation Proclamation, (3) racial segregation between the two world wars, and (4) racial integration after World War II. This last period is especially interesting and significant from a sociological standpoint, and we will focus on it during this chapter.

Plantation owners often used Black slaves to stage boxing matches, and they also used them as jockeys in horse races. Occasionally in boxing, when a slave boxer won an important bout and won his owner a lot of money, he might be set free. Tom Molineaux, a Black slave, was a beneficiary of such an arrangement. In the early nineteenth century, after gaining his freedom, he attained a respected reputation in boxing circles in the northern states and in England.

After the Civil War, African Americans made contributions to the rise of spectator sport as boxers, jockeys, and team players, but they were clearly exceptions. Society and sport remained racially segregated by custom and in some places by law (e.g., Jim Crow laws in the South). Between the first Kentucky Derby in 1875 and about 1910, African American jockeys dominated the sport of horse racing. Of the fifteen jockeys in the first Kentucky Derby, fourteen were African Americans, including the winner. By the first decade of the twentieth century, however, horse owners and trainers had succumbed to the segregationist doctrine and no longer employed African American jockeys. African Americans did remain in much lower-status positions around racing, such as exercising the horses, grooming the horses, and cleaning out their stalls.

When African Americans were barred from professional baseball, football, and basketball in the late nineteenth and early twentieth centuries, they formed all-Black teams and leagues.[12] The Harlem Globetrotters and the famous players of the African American baseball leagues such as Satchel Paige and Josh Gibson emerged from this segregated situation. When Jackie Robinson broke the color barrier, first in 1946 in the minor leagues (the first African American in the International League in fifty-seven years) and then in 1947 in the majors, he received much verbal and physical abuse from players and fans who resented an African American playing on an equal level with Whites. The great MLB player Rogers Hornsby uttered the common attitude of the time: "They've been getting along all right playing together and they should stay where they belong in their league."[13]

Although some champions would not fight them, African Americans made early gains in boxing and increased their numbers over the years, even when they were excluded from other professional sports. Perhaps boxing was the exception because it has typically recruited from the most oppressed social groups. Although African Americans were allowed by the boxing establishment to participate continuously during the early 1900s, they were still the objects of discrimination. One of the most significant historical figures in the early decades of the twentieth century was Jack Johnson, an African American who won the world's heavyweight boxing championship in 1909, becoming the first African American to win this title. Johnson was more than just a boxer; his lifestyle challenged the racialized social system in the United States, and it also challenged the prevailing dogmas of White supremacy and Black inferiority throughout the world.

Largely because of Jack Johnson, boxing achieved a major symbolic role in the sporting lives of African Americans. That was sustained during the 1930s, largely because of the popularity of Joe Louis, who in 1937 became the second African American to win the world heavyweight championship. Nevertheless, even Louis was the target of the same kinds of racist verbal abuse that other African American athletes encountered. Consider, for example, the following comment from Paul Gallico, a noted sportswriter of that era, writing about the world champion boxer Joe Louis: "Louis, the magnificent animal. . . . He eats. He sleeps. He fights. . . . He is as tawny as an animal. . . . He lives like an animal, fights like an animal, has all the cruelty and ferocity of a wild thing."[14]

Throughout the twentieth century African Americans steadily increased their numbers in boxing. But White boxers almost always received more money than African Americans. The White promoters, because of the great-White-hope myth, liked to match Whites against Blacks in the ring, and African Americans often consented to lose just to obtain a match.

It was not just in boxing that sportswriters referred to African American athletes in racist terms. Consider, for example, the prediction of Jimmy Powers, sports editor of the *New York Daily News*, about Jackie Robinson, the first African American to play major league baseball, and who became a Hall-of-Fame major leaguer: "[Jackie] Robinson will not make the grade in major league baseball. He is a thousand-to-one shot at best. The Negro players simply don't have the brains or skills."[15]

African Americans were absent, with a few exceptions, from intercollegiate sports for the first half of the twentieth century. A few Ivy League and other eastern colleges had African American athletes at an early time, but they were exceptions. For the most part, however, prior to World War II African American athletes played at so-called Black colleges in Black conferences. Although the system was segregated, it did provide many African Americans with the opportunity to play intercollegiate sports.

College sports remained segregated, except for isolated instances, until after World War II. In 1948, for example, only 10 percent of college basketball teams had one or more African Americans on their rosters. The last major conference to integrate was the Southeastern Conference. The University of Tennessee broke the barrier by signing an African American football player to an athletic scholarship in 1966, and Vanderbilt signed an African American basketball player in that same year. By 1975, African American athletes were common in the Southeastern Conference and in all the other conferences. However, a fan of Louisiana State University summed up the prevalent attitude toward African Americans playing college football in the South, saying, "I'm all for segregation until it interferes with something important[,] like football."

The transition from a segregated program to an integrated one is perhaps best illustrated by the University of Alabama: in 1968 there were no African Americans on any of its teams, but its 1975 basketball team had an all–African American starting lineup.

As more and more colleges searched for talented African Americans to bolster their athletic programs, Black colleges lost their monopoly on African American athletic talent. The best African American athletes found it advantageous to play at predominantly White schools because of greater visibility, especially on television. This visibility meant, for the best

athletes, a better chance to become professional athletes. The result of this trend was a depleted athletic program at Black colleges, forcing some to drop their athletic programs and some previously Black college conferences to disband.

Since World War II, African Americans have made tremendous strides in professional team sports (except for hockey). From 1940 to 2020 the percentage of African Americans playing in professional football went from 0 to 57.5 percent, in professional basketball from 0 to 74.2 percent, and in baseball from 0 to nearly 8 percent (with another 30 percent Latino in baseball) (see Box 6.1).[16]

Black head coaches in professional football, basketball, and baseball are now common but still

Runners come around for the final lap of the Women's 800-meter final at the 2016 Olympic Trials. Discrimination in sport against African Americans has been pervasive, just as it has been in other social institutions and cultural practices; indeed, in some sports there was complete segregation. Nevertheless, African Americans have played a significant role in the development of modern sport and currently have a dominant presence in several of the most popular sports in North America. (Photo: Joshua Rainey/Alamy Stock Photo)

BOX 6.1 *THINKING ABOUT SPORT: AN ANOMALY: THE DECLINING PROPORTION OF AFRICAN AMERICANS IN MAJOR LEAGUE BASEBALL*

Baseball has been known as America's National Game for over one hundred years, but like other popular sports it was rigidly segregated before World War II. Talented African Americans were limited to playing in the Negro Leagues. But in 1947, Branch Rickey, owner of the Brooklyn Dodgers, integrated Major League Baseball (MLB) when he played Jackie Robinson over the vehement opposition of his fellow owners. Beginning with Robinson's playing excellence, African Americans soon achieved prominence in baseball and ultimately were accepted by White players and fans.

By 1975, 27.5 percent of all baseball players were African American. Since then, the numbers—in sharp contrast to what has happened in professional basketball and football—have dwindled at a stunning rate. By 2020, this percentage of players had declined to about 8 percent, and only one of the thirty MLB managers was African American.

Something is going on to suppress the number of African American players. Like most social change, there are a variety of reasons for it; several have been advanced for the declining proportion of African Americans in the national pastime.

It is estimated that African American turnout at major league games is only 8 percent of total attendance. That is below what one might expect, considering that African Americans are about 13 percent of the population and constitute almost half of the population in central cities where more than a third of major league teams are located. For example, only 4.5 percent of those attending Chicago White Sox games are African American in a city with an African American population of 37 percent. The high price of tickets might be a factor, but the cost for MLB tickets is considerably less than for professional basketball, which African Americans attend in much greater numbers.

It is not a case of discrimination against players of color, as was the case until Jackie Robinson's breakthrough. In 2020, about 40 percent of the players in the MLB were people of color, mostly Latinos. What has occurred is a major influx of Latino players into professional baseball, who have replaced African Americans as the dominating force in MLB. Teams are devoting much more in resources to find and recruit Latino players because those from Latin American countries are much cheaper to sign. Also, MLB teams have established baseball academies in Latin America to locate talent and hone baseball skills. They have not established similar academies in inner cities where African Americans are located.

Another possible reason for the decline of African Americans in the MLB is that the inner cities do not have the space for baseball fields, a luxury found in abundance in the White suburbs. Although this does not explain the large proportion of African Americans playing football, it does explain the African American interest in basketball. Clearly the sport of basketball is more accessible than baseball to urban youth in terms of facilities and equipment.

Football and especially basketball are indeed more appealing to African American youth. When baseball was becoming integrated, there were great African American players for African American youth to emulate, such as Jackie Robinson, John Roseboro, Bob Gibson, Willie Mays, and Hank Aaron. Two of the best young MLB African American players of the past decade—Tony Gwynn Jr. and Eric Young Jr.—are sons of excellent MLB players from an earlier era. Young African American athletes today are looking elsewhere for sports to follow. About the time African American participation began to decline, NBA basketball players became the sports idols of youth—most notably Michael Jordan and LeBron James.

Another factor mediating this social change, according to some baseball analysts, is that young African Americans began abandoning baseball in large numbers in the 1980s precisely when flashier African American athletes were rising to megastardom in football and basketball. Michael Jordan, and more recently LeBron James, with their high-flying dunks and widely popular line of shoes, epitomized the intoxicating blend of money, talent, power, and fame that kids wanted to copy.

Finally, the route to athletic stardom is longer for professional baseball than for either professional football or basketball. For aspiring MLB players there are two routes to the major leagues. One is to play in college. But baseball is a minor sport in most schools, so fewer scholarships (many are partial) are available for football and basketball players. The other route is to play in the minor leagues for several years. In either case, the rewards are few. In football and basketball, in contrast, there are full college scholarships. The truly gifted in those two sports can become superstars in the professional ranks at age twenty or so, an extremely rare feat in baseball.

So, it appears that discrimination does not explain the relative paucity of African Americans in the MLB. Although there are some structural barriers to African American participation, young African American athletes seem to be choosing basketball and football over baseball. To change this, the MLB has established its Reviving Baseball in Inner Cities program and urban youth academies. But many years will likely pass before it is known whether those efforts are paying off.

Sources: Bob Nightengale, "Can MLB Boost Black Ranks?" *USA Today*, April 14, 2017, 1C, 5C; Richard E. Lapchick, *2020 Racial and Gender Report Card* (Orlando: Institute for Diversity and Ethics in Sport, University of Central Florida, 2020); Bob Nightengale, "On Jackie Robinson Day, MLB Diversity Is Lagging," *USA Today*, April 15, 2014, 1C, 4C.

underrepresented. African Americans now officiate games; they are now part of the media reporting the games in newspapers, magazines, and television. Discrimination remains, however, as we will document in the final part of this chapter. Moreover, African American women face dual barriers: racism and sexism.

Discrimination in sport against African Americans has been pervasive, just as it has been in other social institutions and cultural practices; indeed, in some sports there was complete segregation. Nevertheless, African Americans have played a significant role in the development of modern sport and currently have a dominant presence in several of the most popular sports in North America.

LATINO/A INVOLVEMENT IN U.S. SPORT

We use the terms *Latino* and *Latina* to describe those whose heritage is traced to Spanish-speaking countries. This is an inclusive category that shares the Spanish language, but the category is quite heterogeneous. For example, among this group there are Mexicans, Mexican Americans, Puerto Ricans, Dominicans, Nicaraguans, Venezuelans, and Cubans, each group with its own cultural heritage. But even within these subdivisions, there are often crucial differences. For instance, Cubans who left Cuba for the United States when Batista ruled Cuba are quite different in social class, occupations, and political behaviors from those who left Cuba later, fleeing Castro. Differences can also be found, for example, among those who self-identify as having Mexican heritage in this nation; some are descended from families who moved to the U.S. Southwest beginning in the 1700s, while others have immigrated to this region and others in the United States only during recent decades.

Latino participants in American sport are found most notably in baseball, soccer, and boxing; they are also prominent as fans of these sports. Let's begin with baseball. Latino players have been in the major leagues since 1902, with at least forty-five Latino athletes, mostly Cubans, playing before Jackie Robinson's breakthrough for African Americans in 1947. Darker-skinned Latino players whose

African ancestry was evident—such as the legendary player Josh Gibson—were barred from major league baseball.

Latino players in major league baseball constituted nearly 30 percent of 2020 opening-day rosters (up from 13 percent in 1990), with many also plying their trade in the minor leagues. Major league players come from several Caribbean and Latin American countries; the Dominican Republic leads the way, with roughly one in seven of all players (Venezuela has half as many players, followed in order by Puerto Rico [technically a U.S. territory], Mexico, Cuba, Colombia, and Nicaragua).[17]

Many Latino major leaguers were born outside the United States and were discovered by major league scouts as teenagers; they faced language barriers, social isolation, and culture shock when they moved into the Anglo world of U.S. baseball. Although most came to the United States through normal immigration patterns, the players from Cuba have arrived by defecting (they left Cuba illegally but were welcomed in the United States because they provide evidence of the "evils" of the Castro regime).

There are two reasons for the overrepresentation of foreign-born Latino players in the MLB. First, baseball is an extremely popular sport in many Latin American countries, where young boys play year-round developing their skills. Many of the poor youth believe that the way out of the barrio is to play baseball in the United States. They are motivated by the success of previous Latino players, such as Mariano Rivera, the son of a poor Panamanian fisherman. When first scouted by the Yankees, he did not even own his own glove. Latinos such as Miguel Cabrera, Robinson Cano, and Albert Pujols have been among the highest-paid athletes in the MLB.

The second reason for the expanding Latino presence in baseball is that MLB teams have found a lot of raw but talented athletes whom they can sign much more cheaply than U.S.-born athletes. All thirty major league teams scout talent in Latin America (referred to by owners as "the Republic of Baseball"), and many teams have elaborate multimillion-dollar baseball academies there.[18]

More than 90 to 95 percent of Latino baseball players who sign professional baseball contracts never reach the major leagues. The ones who make it to the United States but fail to make a team tend to stay in the country as undocumented immigrants, working for low wages rather than returning home as "failures." These castoffs represent the other side of the Latino professional baseball hopeful, the rule rather than the exception in the high-stakes recruitment of ballplayers from Latin America and the Caribbean.

In terms of soccer, Major League Soccer (MLS) teams in the United States include a number of foreign players, with many of them hailing from Latin American countries. Unlike other professional team sports in the United States, in soccer the players sign a contract with the league, which then assigns players to a franchise. Not surprisingly, Latino players are often assigned to franchises in cities with large Hispanic populations such as Los Angeles, Chicago, and Washington, D.C. MLS games are televised on Univision, the nation's largest Spanish-language television company. With the Latino/a population in the United States expected to triple to around 100 million by 2050, the popularity of MLS should grow just as rapidly.

Boxers have always typically come from poor or near-poor family backgrounds. Poor racial-ethnic minorities with little hope for upward mobility other than through sport are likely candidates to become boxers. Thus, African Americans and Latino athletes are heavily overrepresented among boxers and spectators of boxing. A few boxers (e.g., Oscar De La Hoya) have done extraordinarily well financially. Most, however, do not. Many are exploited by unscrupulous promoters. For example, promising U.S. boxers must build a history of wins to become known and command higher purses. Many promoters bring overmatched boxers from Mexico (the most important supplier of boxing opponents to the United States) to lose to their boxers. The unknown Mexican boxers are paid $100 for each three-minute round. This is more than they can make in Mexico as boxers or laborers, so they risk injury for the money and the hope of making it.

Young male Latino high schoolers often gravitate toward the school's soccer team. That is one of the reasons why soccer has spread throughout high schools and has become one of the most popular high school sports. Some local clubs with lower costs associated with participation are also frequently considered valuable for these young men. A popular talent identification program aimed at Latino soccer players, Alianza de Futbol, regularly hosts tryout events across major cities in the United States. When it comes to adults, many Latino players participate in informal yet regular park games or semistructured "Mexican" leagues. In this regard, a recent book revealed the importance that a daily pickup soccer game in a public Los Angeles park has for a group of Latino men in terms of creating social ties and work opportunities.[19]

Several popular Spanish-language channels, such as Telemundo, UniMás, and Galavisión, devote much of their programming to covering the latest soccer from Mexico, Spain, and South American nations. Thus, TV viewership of club and international soccer teams from these regions is at an all-time high for soccer aficionados.

Compared to their peers, high school–age Latinas are underrepresented in sports. It is often the case that Latinas in the United States are first- or second-generation immigrants and can bring with them the traditional cultural expectations that girls are supposed to do household tasks or help their families by working. Nationally, the U.S. Centers for Disease Control and Prevention found in 2017 that overall 54.6 percent of high school girls played on at least one sports team, and yet only 48.4 percent of Hispanic/Latina girls participated.[20] Latinas who do participate in interscholastic sports participate mainly in soccer, track and field, and softball. A research study conducted by Vera Lopez at Arizona State University used focus groups and interviews to ascertain why Latina girls regularly feel excluded from participating in sports. Girls in Lopez' study felt that they did not belong in sport because of several reasons: girls are physically different compared to boys (e.g., boys are bigger and more capable of playing traditional sports), coaches treat girls differently (e.g., girls are considered emotional and fragile), and boys get more support (e.g., funding, recognition, and fans). Latina girls in this study also noted that they would like to participate in sport to feel connected like a family when part of a team.[21]

ASIANS AND ASIAN AMERICAN INVOLVEMENT IN U.S. SPORT

Participants identified as Asian (including both foreign born and Asian American) have become stars in several American sports. Some examples include figure skaters Kristi Yamaguchi and Michelle Kwan; speed skater Apolo Ohno; basketball players Yao Ming and Jeremy Lin; MLB players Ichiro Suzuki, Shohei Ohtani and Daisuke Matsuzaka; street skateboarder Eric Koston; and golfers Tiger Woods (whose mother is Thai) and Collin Morakawa, who at a young age already has won several Professional Golfers Association (PGA) tour events. Asians have also recently been making remarkable inroads in women's golf. For example, in 1998 Se Ri Pak was the only South Korean on the Ladies Professional Golf Association (LPGA) tour; by 2001 there were ten South Koreans on the tour, and in 2016, forty of the top one hundred were Asians. In the 2016 season, twelve of the top twenty money winners among LPGA golfers were Asian, most typically of Korean heritage.[22] Recent U.S. Women's Open champion Lee Jeong-eun is also known as "Jeongeun Lee6" to avoid confusion with five other golfers of the same name.[23] In cycling, Filipina American Coryn Rivera has captured more national titles than any other cyclist in the United States and she competed in the 2020 Tokyo Summer Olympic Games. Other sports where Asians tend to excel include diving, gymnastics, and the various martial arts (karate, tae kwon do, and judo, sports with Asian origins).

A recent trend is for athletes born in Japan, where baseball is popular, to make it in the U.S. MLB. For example, Daisuke Matsuzaka (his American nickname is "Dice-K") was a superstar in Japan. His rights, owned by the Seibu Lions, were sold at auction to the Boston Red Sox for $51 million. He then signed a six-year, $52 million contract, beginning in 2007; in 2014 he was with the New York Mets, but after that season Matsuzaka returned to Japan to pitch in his home country.

The most recent high-profile Japanese player to sign an MLB contract is Shohei Ohtani, who had never thrown a pitch or made a plate appearance in an MLB game before 2017, yet in 2017 he was perhaps the biggest prize of the offseason. Amid the desperation across MLB to sign him, Ohtani chose the Los Angeles Angels. Ohtani's agent has said Ohtani wanted to be used as both a pitcher and a hitter. The Angels play in the American League, so Ohtani could pitch and dabble with hitting in the designated hitter spot.

Matsuzaka followed the Japanese superstar Ichiro Suzuki of the Seattle Mariners, who in 2001 won both the American League's Rookie of the Year and the Most Valuable Player award. Suzuki's location in Seattle, where there is a significant Asian population (including in nearby Vancouver, British Columbia, where the population is 25 percent Asian), was important because it changed the racial-ethnic composition of spectators at Mariners games (at home and away) and even affected the media (there were Japanese-language broadcasts of Mariners games in Japan). It is a long story, but Suzuki was traded to the New York Yankees in 2012. He went to the Miami Marlins in 2015 and eventually returned to Seattle in 2018.

When considering the sports participation patterns of Asian Americans in the United States, there are differences depending on two diversity dimensions. First, there is immigration history—that is, the length of time that the immigrant group has been in this country. Some Chinese, Filipino, and Japanese families have been in the United States for many generations and therefore have been assimilated into the culture (including mainstream sports) of the United States (see Box 6.2 which illustrates how Americans of Japanese descent played baseball during their isolation within internment camps that were established during World War II). This is in sharp contrast to many South Asian immigrants (Thai, Vietnamese, Cambodian), who are typically first or second generation and are tugged in different directions by their culture of origin and the new culture in which they are immersed.

A second dimension is the social class of recent Asian immigrants. Some were successful in their country and arrived with resources and skills that gave them advantages over other migrants. Others came from poorer villages or cities destined, at least initially, to work at entry-level and low-paying jobs. The greater the economic resources of the family, the greater the likelihood that the children will receive sports lessons, attend sports camps, and purchase the

BOX 6.2 *THINKING ABOUT SPORT: "BOB AND BASEBALL"*

Bob Hayashida and his family ended up at the Tule Lake camp, far north in California and close to the Oregon border. It was a large camp, and the size meant Bob had a lot of peers, because there were children and youth of all ages imprisoned there with their families. With the number of people and varying age groups, it also meant that there were a lot of sports and teams formed, including for baseball. Bob had played a little bit of baseball as a young boy, often with other Japanese American youth who inhabited the farming towns in Placer County, just north of Sacramento. With no "little leagues" in the area at the time, and with scant resources, Bob recalls wearing adult-size catcher's gear as a child, along with uniforms that were too big. Remembering such details causes him to pause and then continue with a laugh, "Everything was huge, you know?!"

Bob also remembers that teams and leagues formed quickly at Tule Lake, not long after he and his family had arrived there. There were teams formed from each block of barracks, and it did not take long before there were a good number of players involved, along with a decent level of competition. When asked how important baseball was as part of his camp experience, Bob replied, "I think that it was really important . . . yeah, I mean, everyone had fun playing, you know? Well, there were fights too, but . . . I think it made camp more enjoyable for us. You know, playing sport, what else was there to do . . . so there were all kinds of sports being played."

It was not long before Bob's abilities and baseball prowess became evident to him, as well as to teammates and opponents. After a year in camp, and now an eighteen-year-old playing catcher on a team with older men, he recalls an early competition: "They said, we're going to play the . . . Klamath Falls Pelicans, a semi-pro team from Klamath Falls. So we were going to pick out a team to play those guys. I tried out, I made it . . . pretty fair team. So the Klamath Falls Pelicans came into camp . . . I think we beat them sixteen to nothing."

As we chuckled about his remembrance, I realized it was refreshing to hear Bob's laughter in the context of recounting his experience of being displaced, moved, and eventually imprisoned, with uncertainty about his future . . . but perhaps that was due to the outlet that baseball became for so many young Japanese American men and why it became so significant to them as part of their camp experience and in maintaining a sense of community. Many parents tried to shield their children

Young Japanese American player, Bob Hayashida, in his internment camp team uniform. (Photo: From bobandbaseball.com)

from the unpleasantness of the situation, and it may be that such a notion carried over to young adults, like Bob, as well. Regardless, his journey as a Japanese American man learning the game of baseball, while imprisoned by his government, was only just beginning.

Source: Courtesy of Matt Bell and Bob Hayashida, from bobandbaseball.com.

requisite equipment. The poorer the family, the greater the probability that the children will have to forgo sports participation and instead work to support the family.[24]

People from India and the entire Indian subcontinent (including Pakistan, Bangladesh, Sri Lanka, and others) are also officially identified under the Asian racial category in the United States. In terms of their sport participation patterns, generational differences play a pivotal role here as well. More established families from this region who have been in the United States for several decades, usually from India, often follow traditional American sports such as basketball, soccer, or football. Meanwhile, newer immigrants from these regions are usually fans and participants of cricket. Avid interest in this latter sport on behalf of this recently immigrated segment of society is reflected in a recent $1 billion investment in Cricket USA from wealthy Indian backers to grow the sport in this nation.[25] These newer immigrants typically work in professional jobs and thus can have disposable income to participate in activities such as tennis and golf, while also enrolling their children in these activities, too.

NATIVE AMERICAN INVOLVEMENT IN SPORT

In 2020 there were about 3.7 million Native Americans (in the continental United States) and Native Alaskans (approximately 1 percent of the U.S. population). The tribes located in the United States were and are heterogeneous, with major differences in physical characteristics, language, and social organization. When Europeans arrived in North America, there were as many as 7 million indigenous people, but disease, warfare, and in some cases genocide reduced the Native American population to less than 250,000 by 1890.

In the first half of the nineteenth century the U.S. government forced Native Americans to leave their homelands and move to areas with marginal land and other resources. The government also developed a reservation system that subordinated Native Americans. By the end of the twentieth century, Native Americans, although better off than they were in the early 1900s, ranked at the bottom on most indicators of well-being (life expectancy, per-capita income, employment, and education).

A few Native Americans have been recognized nationally for their sports prowess. Most notably, more than a century ago Jim Thorpe won gold in the pentathlon and decathlon; he also played for the MLB and professional football (see Chapter 2 for more about Jim Thorpe). More recent Olympic medalists are Billy Mills, who won the 10,000 meters gold medal, and Billy Kidd, who won silver and bronze medals in downhill skiing. Joe Tompkins, a U.S. Paralympian, gold medaled in downhill skiing in the 2005 and 2010 Paralympic World Cup. More recently, Notah Begay III, a Navajo, played on the PGA tour.

Native American athlete Jim Thorpe, two-time All-American in college football and Olympic gold medal winner in the pentathlon and decathlon, played Major League Baseball and professional football. He is considered by many sport historians to be the greatest athlete of the twentieth century. (Photo: AP Photo/Pro Football Hall of Fame)

But only six Native Americans have ever played in the NBA. And in 2020 only 0.4 percent of student-athletes in Division I were Native Americans in both men's and women's sports.

There are athletically talented Native American high school athletes, as evidenced by many state basketball championships and cross-country and track titles, but many choose not to attend college, or, if they do, return home rather than play at the college level. Some of the reasons for this are the racism they experience away from home, their lack of economic resources, and not fitting into another social world. Most important, there tends to be a tension between White American and Native American cultures. The first values the individual above all else; the other values the tribe. For the latter, going away to college means largely forgoing what is good about reservation life: the land, the hunting and fishing, the ceremony, the ties to family, community, and history. It also means giving up, at least temporarily, much of what one has learned is the very essence of Native American life. As gold medal Olympian Billy Mills observed, "If you go too far into society, there's a fear of losing your Indianness. There's a spiritual factor that comes into play. To become part of white society you give up half your soul."[26]

As we noted in Chapter 2, lacrosse was played by tribal warriors for training, recreation, and religious reasons. Lacrosse has undoubtedly been the Native American sport that is most well known and currently widely played throughout the United States. It has recently developed into a popular interscholastic, professional, and international sport. Interestingly, despite its humble Indigenous origins, the youth version of this sport has become quite popular in White and wealthier suburban areas of the United States.

Thousands protest the "Redskins" name. The Washington Redskins name controversy involved the name and logo of the NFL franchise located in the Washington, D.C, metropolitan area After eighty-seven years, the name of this team was finally changed in 2020 to the "Washington Football Team" and the team is now known as the "Washington Commanders". Many Native American, civil rights, educational, athletic, and academic organizations consider the use of Native American names or symbols by non-Native sports teams to be a hurtful form of ethnic stereotyping that contributes to many of the other problems faced by Native Americans. (Photo: *The Washington Post*/Getty Images)

BOX 6.3 *THINKING ABOUT SPORT:* THE NEGATIVE IMAGES OF NATIVE AMERICANS IN CERTAIN SPORT NAMES, LOGOS, AND MASCOTS

Sports teams use symbols (team names, logos, colors, and mascots) to evoke strong emotions of solidarity among the team members and their followers. Most teams use symbols of aggression and ferocity for their athletic teams (birds such as hawks, animals such as tigers, human categories such as pirates, and even otherworldly beings such as devils).

There is a potential dark side to the use of these symbols: the names, mascots, and logos selected for some teams might be derogatory to some groups. Such symbols might dismiss, demean, and trivialize marginalized groups such as African Americans, Native Americans, and women. These symbols then serve to maintain the dominance of the majority and the subordination of groups categorized as "others." That may not be the intent of those using negative symbols, but the symbols diminish these others nonetheless and help maintain the racial and gender inequities found in the larger society.

Native Americans are the racial-ethnic group most commonly demeaned by sports team names. Many professional sports teams have previously used or are still using Native American names—for instance, the Atlanta Braves, Kansas City Chiefs, Golden State Warriors, Chicago Blackhawks, Cleveland Indians, and Washington Redskins. High school, college, and university teams have been known as Redmen, Seminoles, Hurons, Choctaws, Utes, Fighting Illini, and Savages. Many Native American, civil rights, educational, athletic, and academic organizations consider the use of Native American names or symbols by non-Native sports teams a hurtful form of ethnic stereotyping that contributes to many of the other problems faced by Native Americans.

However, defenders of Native American names claim that the use of Native American names and mascots is no different from the use of names and mascots that represent other ethnic groups, such as the Irish or the Vikings, and that people from those heritages accept the use of their names.

But many Native Americans do object to the use of their symbols by athletic teams. Although some names such as Indians, Braves, Warriors, and Chiefs are not manifestly offensive, other names, logos, and mascots project a violent caricature of Native Americans (e.g., redskins, scalpers, warriors, savages).

Clyde Bellecourt, national director of the American Indian Movement, summarizes the complaints:

If you look up the word "redskin" in both the Webster's and Random House dictionaries, you'll find the word is defined as being offensive. Can you imagine if they called the Washington team "Jews" and the team mascot was a rabbi leading them in [the song] Hava Nagila, [with] fans in the stands wearing yarmulkes and waving sponge torahs? The word "Indian" isn't offensive. "Brave" isn't offensive, but it's

the behavior that accompanies all of this that's offensive. The rubber tomahawks; the chicken-feather headdresses; people wearing war paint and making these ridiculous war whoops with a tomahawk in one hand and a beer in the other. All of these things have significant meaning for us. And the psychological impact it has, especially on our youth, is devastating. (p. 53)

After numerous protests, many high school and college teams have dropped their racially insulting Native American nicknames (e.g., Stanford, Syracuse, Dartmouth, Marquette, St. John's, Siena, Miami of Ohio, and the University of North Dakota). Recently, professional sports teams have begun to take initiative in changing their racially demeaning names and mascots. For instance, Cleveland's Major League Baseball team has been known as the Indians since 1915, and this organization recently announced that they will now be called the Guardians. This name change came into effect at the end of the 2021 season. Another prominent example of change is reflected in the case of the Washington Redskins NFL football team name. Opposition to this team name once included a letter signed by fifty members of the U.S. Senate, a letter from the members of the Congressional Native American Caucus, a plea from former President Obama, and resolutions passed by organizations representing more than 2 million Native Americans and 300 sovereign tribes. Moreover, the U.S. Patent and Trademark Office once canceled six federal trademark registrations for the name of the Washington Redskins, arguing that the name is "disparaging to Native Americans." Despite this array of powerful forces opposing the name, the team owner, Daniel Snyder, previously resisted efforts to change the team name, once arguing that the name honored Native Americans and that it was not intended in a negative manner. About the Redskins name in 2013, he stated "I'll never change it. . . . It's that simple. NEVER—you can use caps."

However, social justice protests held across American cities beginning in early 2020 once again brought attention to the problematic usage of the Redskins name. The following timeline provided by the *Sporting News* reveals how this team's Redskins name was eventually removed and replaced as the Washington Football Team; the team is currently known as the Washington Commanders[27]:

July 1, 2020: Investors worth over $620 billion send letters to Nike, Pepsi, and FedEx calling for the end of their sponsorships of the team.

July 3, 2020: FedEx, which holds naming rights to the franchise's stadium, formally asks the Redskins to change their name. Nike, meanwhile, pulls Washington gear from its website. The team says it will review its name.

July 13, 2020: Responding to mounting pressure to change its name that for the first time includes significant financial stakes, the team announces its severance from the Redskins

(continued)

(continued)

name and logo. The moniker is replaced by Washington Football Team until a permanent name is agreed on and trademarked.

July 16, 2020: The popular Madden video game series announces it will not feature the Redskins in *Madden 21* despite having the old logo in initial promotional materials. It will instead promote the organization as the Washington Football Team.

July 23, 2020: The Washington Football Team unveils its updated uniforms.

A number of prestigious organizations have publicly opposed the negative use of Native American symbols, including the National Congress of American Indians, the National Education Association, the U.S. Commission on Civil Rights, the American Sociological Association, and the North American Society for the Sociology of Sport. Most significantly, the NCAA ruled in 2005 that member colleges and universities could not display hostile and abusive racial/ethnic/national origin mascots, nicknames, or imagery at any of the eighty-eight NCAA championships. This also meant that the NCAA would not conduct championships on the campuses of member institutions where the use of nicknames and mascots representing Native Americans is considered hostile and abusive. Several institutions with Native American symbols subsequently appealed this decision, although Illinois, North Dakota, and Indiana University of Pennsylvania eventually lost their appeals. As a consequence, the University of Illinois announced that Chief Illiniwek will no longer perform at athletic events on the Urbana–Champaign campus, and the university is now eligible to host postseason NCAA championship events.

Sources: Erik Brady, "The Real History of Native American Team Names," *USA Today*, August 24, 2016, S; see also C. Richard King, ed., *The Native American Mascot Controversy: A Handbook* (Lanham, MD: Rowman & Littlefield, 2015); Jennifer Guiliano, *Indian Spectacle: College Mascots and the Anxiety of Modern America* (New Brunswick, NJ: Rutgers University Press, 2015); A. J. Perez, "MLB, Indians in Talks to End Chief Wahoo Use," *USA Today*, April 13, 2017, 2C; Bob Nightengale, "Chief Wahoo Is Gone, Now It's Time to Drop Nickname," *USA Today*, 30, 1, 2018, 1C, 4C; Associated Press, "Cleveland Changing Name from Indians to Guardians after 2021 Season," ESPN, July 23, 2021, https://www.espn.com/mlb/story/_/id/31868331/cleveland-changing-name-indians-guardians.

THE EFFECTS OF GLOBALIZATION ON ETHNIC DIVERSITY IN AMERICAN SPORT

Political boundaries across the globe are becoming increasingly blurred by the ease of communication and transportation and the easing of trade restrictions among nations. One consequence of this trend toward globalization is the movement of athletes from nation to nation. Some of these migration patterns are seasonal, as athletes move from one climate area to another. North American skiers, for example, might train in the Southern Hemisphere in places such as South America or New Zealand during its winter (and the Northern Hemisphere's summer). Many world-class runners go to Colorado, locating in Boulder or the San Luis Valley, so that they can train at high altitude. U.S. universities are eager to give scholarships to foreign-born athletes who can help their programs. This is true for both male and female athletes, most notably in sports such as track and field, basketball, soccer, and volleyball.

Some foreign-born athletes become U.S. citizens and compete for the national teams in the Olympics and in the World Cup. The 2014 U.S. Men's World Cup soccer team had seven players who played on the U.S. team despite being born or raised outside the country; these team members came from places such as Norway, Iceland, and Germany. Professional sports, with the exception of American football, are becoming increasingly stocked with foreign-born athletes. In 2020, 44 percent of the MLS's players were born outside the United States and teams in this league have designated "International Roster Slots". And the MLB has had an enormous influx of players from the Dominican Republic, Cuba, Venezuela, Colombia, Japan, and South Korea.

The NBA, which has franchises in the United States and Canada, often has players from many foreign countries, including Germany, the Czech Republic, Russia, Australia, and Serbia. At the beginning of the 2021-2022 NBA season, there were 39 different nations represented in team rosters. The Toronto Raptors franchise alone had 10 international players hailing from 9 different countries on their team. [28]

BOX 6.4   *THINKING ABOUT SPORT:* DIRK NOWITZKI'S INFLUENCE CANNOT BE OVERSTATED

Dallas Mavericks star Dirk Nowitzki is a former German-born NBA basketball player who entered the league in 1998 and played for only the Mavericks for eighteen years. When Nowitzki entered the NBA, he was 1 of 38 international players from twenty-seven countries on NBA rosters. When the 2016–2017 season started, he was one of an NBA-record 113 international players—a total of 25 percent—from an NBA-record forty-one countries. According to the NBA Commissioner Adam Silver, the league will not be surprised if that roster number climbs to 30 percent within five seasons—an average of almost 4 to 5 international players per team.

Jeff Zillgitt, *USA Today*'s NBA reporter, argues that "Dirk Nowitzki helped open gates for foreign players" and his "influences are simple, extensive and far-reaching." Dallas Mavericks director of player personnel asserts, "When Dirk came

over, there were a few Europeans who tested the waters, but to me, he was the first to make it and become a star in the NBA. He also helped the league spread word of the NBA globally."

Dirk redefined the power forward position, patented the one-legged fadeaway, and mastered the three-point shot for big men, all of which have been copied by European (as well as North American) basketball players. Not all of that is Nowitzki's influence alone, but his impact is significant, because he became the NBA's highest-scoring non–U.S. born player ever, and it puts him sixth on the NBA's all-time-scoring list behind Wilt Chamberlain, Michael Jordan, Kobe Bryant, Karl Malone, and leader Kareem Abdul-Jabbar.

Sources: Jeff Zillgitt, "Nowitzki's Influence Can't Be Overstated," *USA Today*, March 9, 2017, 1C–2C; John Denton, "Magic's European Players Take Pride in Dirk Nowitzki Surpassing 30,000 Points," NBA, March 8, 2017, http://www.nba.com/magic/news/magics-european-players-take-pride-dirk-nowitzki-surpassing-30000-points.

In the NHL, U.S.-based teams are usually dominated by Canadians, and players from nations such as Sweden, Finland, the Czech Republic, Hungary, and the various countries that once were part of the Soviet Union play on Canadian-based as well as U.S.-based teams. Professional golf and tennis are also truly global sports. At one point in 2022, for example, the top ten ranked golfers on the LPGA tour included four South Koreans, one Korean-born New Zealander, one Australian-born Korean, one Japanese, four Americans, and one Thailander.[29]

These athletes are a form of global migrant workforce. Many come to play in these major leagues to learn and live in a new society and there are opportunities for significant economic rewards compared to their home nations. Both are possible, but so, too, are the sorts of exploitation experienced by foreign-born boxers and baseball players. At a personal level, many of these "migrant workers" find it difficult to adjust to living in a new society, with its language barriers, cultural differences, social isolation, and various forms of racial and ethnic bigotry. Some teams expect their foreign-born athletes to adjust on their own; others provide support to help them learn English and understand the norms and values of their new cultural setting.

AFRICAN AMERICAN DOMINANCE IN SPORT

Since World War II, the number of African Americans in major team sports has increased dramatically. The watershed year in professional sports (when the proportion of African Americans approximated their proportion in the national population) was, for baseball, 1957; for basketball, 1958; and for football, 1960. Since then, however, the rate, except for baseball, has virtually exploded compared to that for Whites and other races and ethnic groups. In 2020, African Americans constituted only around 13 percent of the general population, but they were 74.2 percent of all NBA players, 69.4 percent of all WNBA players, 57.5 percent of all professional football players, and 7.5 percent of MLB players.[30]

Over the past half century an enormous literature has accumulated regarding the proportion of African Americans at the highest levels of American sports—intercollegiate, professional, and international. During the past five decades African American athletes have achieved a prominence in some sports that, in terms of numbers, far exceeds their percentage of the general population, as noted previously. In other sports they are rarely seen at the upper levels.

This situation has fascinated people in all walks of life, from curious sports fans to social, physical, and biological scientists. Consequently, a variety of speculations and educated (and uneducated) hypotheses, but little empirical research, have accumulated to explain African American overrepresentation in certain sports and underrepresentation in others. In trying to sort out and provide some organization to this issue, we have come to the conclusion that there are three hypotheses—genetic, cultural, and social—that best explain the disproportionate presence of African Americans in American team sports. We examine the genetic hypothesis first.

RACE-LINKED PHYSICAL DIFFERENCES

One explanation for the overrepresentation of African Americans in certain sports is that they are naturally better athletes than Whites and that their predominance in sports is therefore attributable to innate physical supremacy. There are some problems with this biological determinism argument. First, there is the issue of who is Black. Racial categories in any society, but particularly in the United States, where the amalgamation of Africans, Caucasians, and Native Americans continues, are ill-defined and, of course, socially defined. The point is that racial categories are not fixed, unambiguous, and dichotomous.

Because African Americans, like Whites, exhibit a wide range of physical builds and other physiological features, sampling becomes a problem. Does the scientist compare randomly selected Whites with randomly selected Blacks? More logically, to answer the question of athletic superiority, does the researcher compare a random selection of superior White athletes with superior African American athletes? But how useful would that be? We noted that African Americans are not a homogeneous physical category. In fact, the recent Human Genome study found that, genetically speaking, there are greater ranges of differences within races than between races.

The word *Black* provides little information about anyone or any group. Of the 100,000 genes that determine human makeup, only one to six regulate skin color, so we should assume almost nothing about anyone based on skin color alone. West Africans and East Africans are both Black, but in many physical

ways they are more unlike each other than they are different from most Whites. When it comes to assumptions about Africans, we should make just one: that the peoples of Africa, short and tall, thick and thin, fast and slow, White and Black, represent the fullest and most spectacular variations of humankind to be found anywhere.

Another problem in comparing races on some behavioral pattern is the impossibility of eliminating social variables (social, cultural, and political factors) from consideration. Why, for example, do Blacks from Kenya tend to excel in distance running whereas Blacks from Nigeria do not? Is this major difference explained by differences in diet, cultural emphasis, geography, or what? Whatever the explanation, it is not racial difference.

Some scholars argue that although genes are important, they do not work independent of the environment. Genes are influenced by environmental factors that trigger chemical changes. In general, they conclude that biology alone cannot explain human differences.[31] Hence, perhaps the issue is not nature versus nurture, but how nature interacts with nurture.

The biological determinist explanation for Black athletic superiority also has racist implications. First, as Harry Edwards, an African American and former professor of sociology at the University of California at Berkeley, points out, "What really is being said in a kind of underhanded way is that blacks are closer to beasts and animals in terms of their genetic and physical and anatomical make up."

Second, this explanation implies that African American athletes do not have to work hard to be successful in sport and that White athletes achieve success because of hard work and intelligence.

Third, such beliefs reinforce an ideology that seeks to explain and justify the political status quo where Blacks are second to Whites in power, authority, and resources. The problems with existing empirical studies on racial differences lead us to conclude that they are (1) meaningless, on the one hand, that is, they make assumptions that obscure the realities of race as a social rather than biological category, and (2) dangerous, that is, racist, on the other. Moreover, whatever differences are found to exist among the races are explained not by genetic advantages of one social category over another but by cultural and social reasons.

RACE-LINKED CULTURAL DIFFERENCES

Variations in the prominence of Black athletes in some sports and not in others have often been explained through cultural differences. The Kalenjin tribe of the Great Rift Valley, in Kenya, represents 2,000 of the earth's population of more than 6 billion, yet they win 40 percent of the top international distance-running honors. With all of their physical advantages for endurance sports, why are Kenyans missing from such endurance events as the Tour de France bicycle competition and other endurance bicycle races, which are dominated by Whites? Similarly, if Blacks are so good at jumping, as evidenced by their basketball prowess, why don't they dominate the high jump and the pole vault in track? If Blacks are superior in physical strength, why don't they excel in the shot put, discus, and weightlifting events? Why do Russians dominate chess? Why in the music world are there so many superstar Italian tenors? The answer to each of these questions is that categories of people with a similar culture place a greater emphasis on some activities while ignoring others.

African Americans may be overrepresented in some sports because of the uniqueness of the African American subculture in the United States. Some social analysts argue that African American subculture places a positive emphasis on the importance of physical (and verbal) skill and dexterity. Athletic prowess in men is highly valued by both African American women and African American men. The athletically superior male is comparable to the successful hustler or rap singer; he is something of a folk hero. He achieves a level of status and recognition among his peers, whether he is a publicly applauded sports hero or not. There is ample evidence of just such adulation accorded African American basketball players, regardless of age, in the urban playgrounds of the United States.

Cultural differences probably do account for the differences in sport performance between Black Africans and African Americans. Here, where physical differences are more or less controlled (although African Americans are more racially mixed), there are great variances. At elite-level track events, on the one hand, Black Africans excel in distance running but not in the sprints and jumping events. African Americans, on the other hand, have dominated the sprints, hurdles, and long and triple jumps but have had negligible success in the distance events. Clearly, something other than the physiology of race must explain this variance. Cultural differences, along with differences in history and geography, account for much of the sharp contrast.

Unique forms of dance, music, art, and humor have emerged from the African American subculture. Perhaps that subculture also accounts for the interest and ability of African Americans in basketball, where moves, speed, and aggression predominate. The interest of other groups in particular sports is easily explained that way. For example, Japanese Americans, who constitute less than 0.3 percent of the total population, are greatly overrepresented among the top Amateur Athletic Union judo competitors. Although African American culture might similarly contribute to Black excellence in athletics, especially in certain sports, there is little systematic empirical evidence at present to substantiate the claim.

SOCIAL STRUCTURE CONSTRAINTS

Many analysts contend that the most plausible reasons for African American dominance in some sports are found in the structural constraints on African Americans in American society. These constraints can be divided into two types: (1) occupational structure and (2) sports opportunity structure.

African Americans may perceive sport to be one of the few means by which they can succeed in the highly competitive American society because their opportunities for upward mobility in the economic system are limited. A young African American male's primary role models are much more likely to be sports heroes than are a young White male's role models. The determination and motivation devoted by young African American adolescents in the pursuit of a sports career may, therefore, be more intense than those of White adolescents, whose potential career options are broader.

In every society, people are taught to strive for that which is considered the most desirable among potentially achievable goals. With highly rewarding sports opportunities and all the apparent influence, glamor, and so forth that accompany being a successful African American athlete, the talents of African American males are likely disproportionately concentrated toward achievement in this one social domain.

In high-prestige occupational positions outside sports, African Americans have role models in entertainment, such as music, acting, comedy, and so forth. Still, given the popularity of sports, and given the competition among sport organizations for the best athletes, it is reasonable that a high proportion of the extremely gifted African American athletes would be in sports. Whites have a broader range of visible alternative role models and greater access to alternative high-prestige positions, so they can aspire to a broader range of occupational alternatives. Thus, the concentration of highly gifted White athletes in sports is proportionately less than the number of highly gifted African American athletes. Under these conditions, African American athletes dominate sports in terms of excellence of performance, where both groups participate in large numbers.

Occupational limitations for African Americans do not fully explain why they tend to gravitate toward some sports, such as boxing, basketball, football, and track, and why they are underrepresented in others, such as soccer, swimming, golf, skiing, tennis, and polo. It has been argued that the reason African Americans tend to be attracted to certain sports lies in what is called the "opportunity structure" of sports. That is, African Americans tend to excel in those sports in which facilities, coaching, and competition are available to them—namely, sports in schools and community recreation programs.

African Americans are not prominent in those sports that require the facilities, coaching, and competition usually available only in private clubs. There have been a few excellent African American golfers, for example, but they had to overcome the disadvantages of being self-taught and limited to playing at municipal courses—perhaps with the exception of Tiger Woods. Few African Americans are competitive skiers for the reasons that most African Americans live far from snow and mountains and that skiing is expensive.

Social structural reasons help to explain why African Americans outperform Whites in certain sports. Basketball provides an excellent example because the style of African American basketball players differs so significantly from that of White players. African American college and professional players learn the game under substantially different conditions than White players. The inner-city basketball courts frequented by African Americans are generally crowded with many players competing for valuable playing time on the limited facilities. The norms that prevail under these conditions shape the skills and behaviors of the inner-city players in predictable ways. The games are intensely competitive, with winning teams staying on the court to meet the next challengers. Players must learn to dribble, pass, and shoot in close quarters against a tight person-to-person defense. Players in these circumstances learn to fake and to alter shots in midair. Players are expected to score without much help from teammates. They accept contact as routine. The spectators present at inner-city games often encourage flair and flamboyance.

In contrast, most White college and professional players developed their basketball talents in rural, small-town, and suburban community traveling clubs. Basketball in these settings is characterized by player scarcity rather than by a crowding of players on outdoor courts. White players tend to develop excellent passing and shooting skills, mostly in team play rather than in aggressive one-on-one play. The paucity of players leads to a playing environment that encourages the participation of marginal players, makes use of skills developed in team practice, and keeps the pace relatively controlled. Thus, Whites develop pure shooting skills and the ability to score when wide open. In sum, the differences in play between Whites and Blacks are not found in racial differences but in the social structural conditions under which they develop their basketball skills.

Another social basis for racial differences in participation is that, for economic and social reasons, African Americans have been denied membership in private clubs—and thus, they have been denied access to the best facilities and coaching in sports such as swimming, golf, and tennis. The economic barrier to membership is the result of the discriminatory practices (in types of jobs, salaries, and chances for promotion) that deny most African Americans affluence. The social barriers have occurred because of the discriminatory practices of many private clubs that exclude various racial and ethnic groups. Sports that are often learned and played in private clubs where social interaction is common, and typically include social relationships between males and females—namely, sports such as golf, tennis, and swimming—exclude or discourage racial and ethnic diversity.

There is still another type of discrimination implied in the sports opportunity structure: the powerful in some sports have denied access to African Americans, even to African Americans with the requisite skills and financial support. Certain golf tournaments (the Masters, for instance) have only begrudgingly admitted African Americans.

Just as golf once allowed African American caddies but not African American golfers, horse racing allowed African Americans as exercise boys but not as jockeys. Automobile racing is another sport in which African Americans have had great difficulty participating. The Indianapolis 500 waited until 1991 for its first African American driver. The explanation for this delay surely lies not in the limitations of African Americans in driving fast or having inferior skills but rather in the reluctance of corporate sponsors to give financial support to African American drivers.

RACIAL DISCRIMINATION IN SPORT

American sport in the twenty-first century is not free of racial discrimination. However, the dominant presence of African Americans in the three major team sports appears to belie the existence of racism in sport. Moreover, the prominence and huge salaries of minority superstars such as LeBron James, Miguel Cabrera, and Kevin Durant have led many Americans to believe that collegiate and professional sports now provide a broad avenue of upward social mobility for racial-ethnic minorities, thus illustrating, it is often argued, that racial discrimination is a thing of the past.

But this is not true, according to many commentators—social scientists, journalists, and the athletes themselves. They contend that African American visibility in collegiate and professional sports merely serves to mask the racism that pervades the entire sport establishment. Although there is broad acknowledgment that American society has transformed greatly over the past four decades and that much of the societal discrimination that existed in the 1970s is no longer present, there is a research tradition in the sociology of sport that clearly shows a pattern of racial discrimination in sport that has been persistent. We review this research tradition because it demonstrates the myth perpetrated by promoters and commentators on sports who have made sport sacred by projecting its image as the single institution that is relatively immune from racism.

The following sections focus on two aspects of the research tradition that illustrate a pattern of racial bias in sports: the assignment of playing positions and the rewards and authority structures. The analysis is limited to the major professional team sports (baseball, basketball, and football) in which minorities are found most prominently. In addition to describing and explaining this research tradition, we assess whether any substantial changes have occurred or can be anticipated in the future.

STACKING

One of the best-documented forms of discrimination in both college and professional ranks is popularly known as *stacking*. The term refers to situations in which racial minority group members are disproportionately found in specific team positions and underrepresented in others. Racial stacking was first empirically verified about fifty years ago. Although stacking is less prominent in college and professional baseball, basketball, and football compared to how it once was, we describe and discuss this phenomenon to illustrate how racism in the general society has historically been incorporated into sport. Indeed, the stacking trend in sport over several decades is indicative of the slogan "sport is a mirror of society."

Research on Stacking

Analysis of the stacking phenomenon was first undertaken by John W. Loy Jr. and Joseph F. McElvogue, who argued that racial segregation in sports is a function of centrality, that is, spatial location in a team sport unit.[32] To explain positional racial segregation in sport, they combined organizational principles advanced by two social scientists, one of whom argued that (1) the lower the degree of purely social interaction on the job, the lower will be the degree of (racial) discrimination, and (2) to the extent that performance level is relatively independent of skill in interpersonal relations, the degree of (racial) discrimination is lower. The second argument was similar but centered on the formal structure of organizations; it reasoned that, all else being equal, the more central one's spatial location, (1) the greater the likelihood dependent or coordinative tasks will be performed and (2) the greater the rate of interaction with the occupants of other positions. Also, the performance of dependent tasks is positively related to frequency of interactions.[33]

Combining these propositions, Loy and McElvogue hypothesized that "racial segregation in professional team sports is positively related to centrality." Their analysis of football (in which the central positions are quarterback, center, offensive guard, and linebacker) and baseball (in which the central positions are catcher, pitcher, shortstop, second base, and third base) demonstrated that the central positions were indeed overwhelmingly held by Whites and that Blacks were overrepresented in the peripheral (noncentral) positions.

Subsequent empirical research during the 1970s and 1980s corroborated this relationship in other sports. For example,

- In women's intercollegiate volleyball, African Americans were overrepresented at the hitter position and Whites at setter (the central position) and bumper.
- In Canadian hockey, French Canadians are overrepresented at goalie (the central position), and English Canadians are disproportionately represented in defensive positions.[34]

The previous situation for the NFL and MLB in 2014 is found in Table 6.1. Examination of Table 6.1 is instructive because data at this time reveal that (1) stacking remained in practice more than forty years after Loy and McElvogue's original research; (2) in football, African Americans have usually been found

TABLE 6.1   POSITIONAL BREAKDOWN BY RACE/ETHNICITY, 2014 (IN PERCENTAGES)

National Football League	White	Black	Other[a]	
Offensive positions				
Quarterback	78	21	3	
Running back	10	89	2	
Wide receiver	13	86	2	
Tight end	57	41	2	
Offensive tackle	48	51	1	
Offensive guard	49	46	7	
Center	82	14	7	
Defensive positions				
Cornerback	2	97	0	
Safety	18	79	3	
Linebacker	25	73	4	
Defensive end	19	81	3	
Defensive tackle	10	85	5	
Major League Baseball	**White**	**Black**	**Latino**	**Asian**
Pitcher	68	4	26	2
Catcher	65	1	33	1
Infielder	59	8	32	9
Outfielder	52	22	23	4

[a] Pacific Islander, Latino, or Asian.

Source: Richard E. Lapchick, *2014 Racial and Gender Report Card* (Orlando: Institute for Diversity and Ethics in Sport, University of Central Florida, September 2014).

more commonly on defense (where the requisite requirement is "reacting" to the offense) than on offense (which is control oriented); and (3) Whites have typically been found disproportionately at the thinking, leadership, and most central positions, whereas African Americans have been mostly found at those peripheral positions requiring physical attributes (speed, quickness, strength).

Even within more recent years, the NFL and MLB have exhibited the stacking phenomena, but basketball, which once did, is no longer characterized by racial segregation by position—at either the college or the professional level. This appears to be related to the proportion of a racial-ethnic minority in a sport.

When college and professional basketball were dominated numerically by Whites, stacking occurred (with Whites disproportionately at the point guard and African Americans overrepresented at the strong forward position). This trend is no longer the case in college men's basketball, where African Americans are now a majority. In professional basketball, where about 80 percent of the players are African American, stacking has ceased to exist. These patterns substantiate the social–psychological hypothesis that the greater the numerical proportion of a minority in a social organization, the more likely genuine integration will occur.

Explanations for Stacking

The discovery of a social condition, such as stacking, raises the question of why. In the case of stacking, asserting that it is merely a case of racist stereotyping and discrimination is inadequate. Several of the social scientists who have reported stacking in their research findings have advanced their interpretations for the stacking phenomenon. Loy and McElvogue, the first investigators to articulate stacking, interpreted it as resting primarily on a position's spatial location in a team unit. However, other scholars have argued that the actual spatial location of a playing position is an incidental factor; for them the crucial variable involved in positional segregation is the degree of *outcome control* or *leadership responsibility* found in each position. In football, for example, quarterbacks have greater team authority and ability to affect the outcome of the game than players who occupy noncentral positions. Thus, it is the leadership and the degree of responsibility for the game's outcome built into the position that account for the paucity of men of color in central positions.

A historical ideology underpinning the world of professional football is that various football positions require specific types of physically—and intellectually—endowed athletes. When these beliefs are combined with the stereotypes of racial minorities and Whites, groups such as African Americans are excluded from certain positions. Warren Moon, the African American Hall of Fame quarterback, recently recounted that his coaches believed the central positions (e.g., quarterback and center on offense, middle linebacker on defense) "were the

'thinking positions.'" "We (African Americans) were good for the athletic, reaction positions: run, jump, block."[35] We will explicate this belief system next.

Normal organizational processes when interlaced with racist conceptions of the world spell out an important consequence—namely, the racial basis of the division of labor in professional football. This view, then, posits that it is the racial stereotypes of African Americans' natural abilities that lead to the belief that they are more ideally suited to those positions labeled "noncentral." For example, in an early study of stacking in football, a researcher compared the requirements for the central and noncentral positions in football and found that the former require leadership, thinking ability, highly refined techniques, stability under pressure, and responsibility for the outcome of the game. Noncentral positions, in contrast, require athletes with speed, aggressiveness, "good hands," and "instinct."

Using those positional requirements, the researcher collected data on NFL teams and found evidence for the racial-stereotype explanation for stacking in the small number of African Americans at the most important positions of outcome control in football. The conclusion seems inescapable: African Americans have historically been relegated to noncentral positions that require speed, strength, and quick reactions and are precluded from occupying leadership positions (such as the quarterback and the center, who calls out the blocking assignments) because subtle but widely held stereotypes of African American intellectual and leadership abilities have persisted in the sports world. Yet, it might be the case that change is on the horizon. In 2020, there were an unprecedented ten black quarterbacks in the NFL.[36] Researchers will be keeping an eye on whether this trend continues and whether there are parallel examples emerging in other major sports.

Another explanation for the historical practice of stacking is that African American youths may segregate themselves into specific sport roles because they wish to emulate African American stars. Contrary to the belief that stacking can be attributed to discriminatory acts by members of the majority group, this interpretation holds that the playing roles to which African American youths aspire are those in which African Americans have previously attained high levels of achievement. The first positions to be occupied by African Americans in professional football were in the offensive and defensive backfield and in the defensive line; therefore, subsequent imitation of their techniques by African American youths has resulted in African Americans being overrepresented in these positions.

Although there is no empirical research confirming that socialization variables contribute to the racial stacking patterns historically found in baseball and football, it seems reasonable to suggest that socialization processes are involved, but in a negative sense. That is, given historic discrimination in the allocation of playing positions (or at least the belief in its existence), young African American males may consciously avoid those positions for which opportunities are (or are believed to be) low (e.g., catcher, pitcher, quarterback) and will select instead those positions where they are most likely to succeed (e.g., outfielder, running or defensive back). Trends such as the recent increased number and visibility of African American quarterbacks as noted can begin to change this type of socialization.

Consequences of Stacking

Regardless of the reasons for stacking, its effects are far-reaching. First, the historic stacking of Whites in "thinking/leadership" positions and African Americans in "physical" positions reinforces negative stereotypes about African Americans and the ideology of White supremacy. Second, professional football players in those positions requiring speed, quickness, and agility have shorter careers than those in highly skilled positions requiring technique and thinking. The shortened careers that result for African Americans mean lower lifetime earnings and more limited benefits from the players' pension fund, where the amount of payment is based on longevity. Also, as we will see shortly, playing at noncentral positions significantly reduces the chance of a career as a coach or manager.

LEADERSHIP, ADMINISTRATION, AND AUTHORITY

Despite the spectacular achievements that minority athletes, especially African American athletes, have made in sports during the past twenty-five years, the paucity of minorities in positions of leadership in professional and college sports continues to be a reality. The reasons proposed for this underrepresentation of racial minorities in leadership positions have centered on two forms of access discrimination. The first is overt discrimination. This is proposed to occur when franchise owners and team executives ignore competent African Americans for coaching and management because of their prejudices or because they fear the negative reaction of fans to African Americans in leadership positions.

The second form of access discrimination is more subtle and applies especially to coaching. Here it is proposed that African Americans are not considered for coaching positions because they did not, during their playing days, play at highly interactive positions requiring leadership and decision-making. We know that MLB managers, for example, tend to have played as catchers or infielders. African Americans, because of stacking, have tended to play in the outfield and therefore do not possess the requisite infield experience that traditionally has provided access to the position of manager.

The situation is similar in football. Research has shown that the majority of coaches played at the central positions of quarterback, offensive center, guard, or linebacker. African Americans have historically been underrepresented at these positions and are thus almost automatically excluded from head coaching responsibilities. And the same pattern has been found for basketball, in which two-thirds of professional and college head coaches played at guard (the most central position). Once again, since African American athletes in the past were underrepresented at guard, they have been less likely than Whites to be selected as coaches when vacancies occur.

Although the percentage of minority players in the NFL and NBA greatly exceeds their percentage of the total population, few opportunities are available to them in coaching and managerial roles. For example, in 2020, only four of the head coaches in the NFL were racial minorities (Latino and African Americans) and only nine of the head coaches in the NBA were racial minorities (African American, Latino/Hispanic, and Asian). In baseball, there were only six MLB managers from racial minority backgrounds. All of these leagues have more than thirty teams. (For a race-ethnicity breakdown of executive leaders, managers, coaches, and players in these major professional sports, refer to Table 6.2.)

TABLE 6.2 PLAYERS, EXECUTIVE LEADERSHIP, AND COACHING POSITIONS IN PROFESSIONAL SPORTS BY RACE/ETHNICITY, 2020 (IN PERCENTAGES; NOT 100 PERCENT IN ALL CASES)

League	White	Black	Latino	Asian
National Football League				
Players	25	58	.4	.1
Chief executive officers/presidents	85	3	3	6
Head coaches	88	9	3	0
Assistant coaches	64	31	1	1
National Basketball Association				
Players	17	74	2	.4
Chief executive officers/presidents	89	7	4	0
Head coaches	70	23	3	3
Assistant coaches	54	37	4	.6
Major League Baseball				
Players	60	8	30	2
Chief executive officers/presidents	97	0	0	0
Managers	80	3	13	0
Coaches	54	6	33	1

Source: Richard E. Lapchick, *2020 Racial and Gender Report Card* (Orlando: Institute for Diversity and Ethics in Sport, University of Central Florida, 2020).

Shoni Schimmel of the New York Liberty is a Native American professional basketball player. She was an All-American college player at the University of Louisville and a first-round draft pick of the WNBA's Atlanta Dream. In 2016 Schimmel suffered a concussion that caused her to miss part of the season, including the playoffs. In May 2017 it was announced that Schimmel would be sitting out the 2017 WNBA season because of personal issues. (Photo: Patricia Tanewasha, "Making It Patti Photography")

During the past decade, a number of sports franchise owners and their executives have vowed that hiring of coaches, managers, and league officials of color was a top priority. Moreover, the NFL adopted the Rooney Rule in 2002 (named after the owner of the Pittsburgh Steelers, Dan Rooney), which mandated that any team with a head coach opening must interview at least one racial minority candidate for the job unless it was promoting one of its own assistants. That rule initially made a difference, but it has stalled in recent years. Whereas the league had only two African American head coaches in 2002, by 2007 there were six, and two of those coached the competing teams in the 2007 Super Bowl. We noted earlier that in 2020 only four head coaches in the NFL came from racial-ethnic minority backgrounds.

There is also a dearth of racial minorities in professional sports ownership and administrative roles.

In the NFL, four of the thirty-two teams had a majority owner of color in 2020, while only 14.5 percent of vice presidents and above in the NFL's League Office were people of color. In the MLB Central Office, people of color represented 17.6 percent of those holding positions at the senior executive level (vice president or above). Meanwhile, thirty-nine of forty majority owners of MLB teams were White. In 2020, four of thirty-five majority owners in the NBA were people of color. However, the NBA League Office continues to have the best record for people of color (39.4 percent) in men's professional sports.[37]

Thus, although athletes of color have made significant advances in the past quarter century, they have not gained comparable access to ownership and decision-making positions at the executive level. With the exception of professional basketball in some cases, the corporate and administrative decision-making structure of most professional sports is still about as White as it was before Jackie Robinson entered the MLB in 1947.

Officiating is another area that is disproportionately White, if the number of players is taken as the reference. The NFL employs mostly White game officials (59 percent) even though the majority of league players are African American. Meanwhile, the NBA has 67 White referees of 147 total officials (46 percent), although only 17 percent of league players are White.[38]

Leadership in college sports is also predominantly a domain for White males. Although some progress in racial minority hiring has been made in certain intercollegiate sports and institutions, leagues, and conferences, it is still the case that coaching and athletic directorship positions tend to be filled by White males. The *2020 Racial and Gender Report Card: College Sport* reported data about NCAA-sanctioned sports at all levels. Highlights of this reported data are summarized as follows:

- In 2020, Whites dominated the head coaching ranks in men's sports, holding 85.3, 86.2, and 89.6 percent of all head coaching positions in Divisions I, II, and III, respectively.
- White people made up 82.3, 90.7, and 94.3 percent of men's basketball, football, and baseball head coaching positions, respectively, in all divisions combined during the 2019–2020 season.
- Whites held approximately 90 percent of all head coaching positions in women's teams competing in Divisions I, II, and III.
- In 2019–2020, 72.3, 70.8, and 61.6 percent of all the athletic director positions were held by White men in Divisions I, II, and III, respectively.
- Only four people of color served as conference commissioners in all of Division I sports, of thirty conferences.
- At the NCAA National Office, people of color in the positions of executive vice president, senior vice president, and vice president were found to comprise 31.6 percent.

The distribution of minorities in the sports world is therefore not unlike that in the larger society. Minorities are admitted to lower-level occupations but are often excluded from positions of authority, power, and prestige. Despite some indications of change, because of ideology shifts and concomitant policymaking, in most cases discrimination against racial minorities continues in American collegiate and professional team sports.

SUMMARY

Participation in sports continues to increase, even though racial minorities continue to face systematic and pervasive discrimination against them. Although most Americans agree with this sociological fact, there are some who believe that sport is an oasis free of racial problems and tensions. This has led many observers to conclude incorrectly that sports participation is free of racial discrimination, that discrimination has disappeared, and that people of color are no longer disadvantaged. But the reality of the situation or condition is that racial considerations conceal almost everything in America. Racial minorities lag well behind Whites in virtually every area of social life. As our analysis has demonstrated, stacking in major sports such as football and baseball, although occurring less now than twenty-five years ago, remains an issue worth monitoring. African Americans have traditionally been disproportionately found in those positions requiring physical rather than cognitive or leadership abilities. Racial-minority athletes in America's major team sports have generally been found disproportionately in peripheral positions and are relatively absent from central positions. There has been some evidence of positive change here recently, with recent data indicating that patterns have been substantially altered in collegiate and professional basketball, and there are now more African American quarterbacks in the NFL than ever before. Only time will tell whether these positive trends continue.

The sporting histories of Asian Americans, Latino/a Americans, and Native Americans are marked by rich, and often unique, participation experiences and achievement. Yet prejudice and discrimination toward all these groups has occurred through sport just as in American society more broadly. Sport is not a meritocratic, neutral realm where race and ethnicity are ignored. Equality of opportunity is not the rule if race or ethnicity is a variable. Even where there have been significant positive changes, it is still the case that discrimination based on race and ethnicity continues and must be addressed in all the major forms of American sport.

Learn more with this chapter's digital tools, including web resources, video links, and chapter self-assessment quivzzes at www.oup.com/he/sage-eitzen-beal-atencio-12e.

NOTES

1. Eduardo Bonilla-Siva, *Racism without Racists: Color-Blind Racism and the Persistence of Racial Inequality in America*, 5th ed. (Lanham, MD: Rowman & Littlefield, 2018), 1–2.

2. Richard Delgado and Jean Stefancic, *Critical Race Theory: An Introduction*, 2nd ed. (New York: New York University Press, 2012); Billy J. Hawkins, Akilah R Carter-Francique, and Joseph N. Cooper, eds. *Critical Race Theory: Black Athletic Sporting Experiences in the United States* (New York: Palgrave Macmillan, 2017).

3. This section on definitions draws on D. Stanley Eitzen, Maxine Baca Zinn, and Kelly Eitzen Smith, *In Conflict and Order: Understanding Society*, 14th ed. (Boston: Pearson, 2017), ch 9, and Anthony Giddens, Mitchell Duneier, Richard P. Appelbaum, and Deborah Carr, *Introduction to Sociology*, 10th ed. (New York: W. W. Norton, 2016), ch 11.

4. Carol C. Mukhopadhyay, Rosemary C. Henze, and Yolanda T. Moses, *How Real Is Race? A Sourcebook on Race, Culture, and Biology*, 2nd ed. (Lanham, MD: Rowman & Littlefield, 2013).

5. Eduardo Bonilla-Silva, *Racism without Racists*, 2.

6. Neil Bhutta, Andrew C. C. Chang, Lisa J. Dettling, Joanne W. Hsu, and Julia Hewitt, "Disparities in Wealth by Race and Ethnicity in the 2019 Survey of Consumer Finances," *The Fed—Disparities in Wealth by Race and Ethnicity in the 2019 Survey of Consumer Finances*, Board of Governors of the Federal Reserve System, accessed July 28, 2021, https://www.federalreserve.gov/econres/notes/feds-notes/disparities-in-wealth-by-race-and-ethnicity-in-the-2019-survey-of-consumer-finances-20200928.htm.

7. John Creamer, "Poverty Rates for Blacks and Hispanics Reached Historic Lows in 2019," U.S. Census Bureau, April 14, 2021, https://www.census.gov/library/stories/2020/09/poverty-rates-for-blacks-and-hispanics-reached-historic-lows-in-2019.html.

8. "African American Income," Black Demographics, 2015, July 29, 2022, http://blackdemographics.com/households/african-american-income/.

9. U.S. Census Bureau, "Quick Facts, Black or African American Alone, Percent," July 1, 2015, https://www.census.gov/quickfacts/table/PST045216/00; Catherine McIntyre, "Canada Has a Black Incarceration Problem," *Torontoist*, April 21, 2016, http://torontoist.com/2016/04/african-canadian-prison-population/.

10. Bonilla-Silva, *Racism without Racists*, 2.

11. Margaret L Anderson and Howard F. Tayler, *Sociology: Understanding a Diverse Society*, 4th ed. (Belmont, CA: Wadsworth, 2008), 280.

12. Frank Foster, *The Forgotten League: A History of Negro League Baseball* (New York: CreateSpace Independent Publishing, 2012); see also Claude Johnson, *Black Fives: The Alpha Physical Culture Club's Pioneering African American Basketball Team, 1904–1923* (Greenwich, CT: Black Fives, 2012).

13. Quoted in Ocania Chalk, *Pioneers of Black Sport* (New York: Dodd, Mead, 1975), 78; see also Gary Sailes, ed., *Modern Sport and the African American Experience*, 2nd ed. (San Diego, CA: Cognella Academic, 2015); see also Benjamin Compall, "Remembering Jackie Robinson: Racial Equality in Sports," *Washington University Political Review*, February 9, 2015, http://www.wupr.org/2015/02/09/remembering-jackie-robinson-racial-equality-in-sports/; Janelle Joseph, Simon Darnell, and Yuka Nakamura, eds., *Race & Sport in Canada: Intersecting Inequalities* (Warsaw, NY: Brown Bear Press, 2012).

14. Quoted in Richard Bok, *Joe Louis: The Great Black Hope* (Cambridge, MA: Da Capo Press, 1998), 99; see also Randy Roberts, *Joe Louis: Hard Times Man* (New Haven, CT: Yale University Press, 2010);

Theresa Runstedtler, *Jack Johnson Rebel Sojourner: Boxing in the Shadow of the Global Color Line* (Berkeley: University of California Press, 2012).

15. Quoted in Phillip M. Hoose, *Necessities: Racial Barriers in American Sports* (New York: Random House, 1989), xviii; see also Lori Latrice Martin, *Out of Bounds: Racism and the Black Athlete* (New York: Praeger, 2014); Earl Smith, *Race, Sport and the American Dream*, 3rd ed. (Durham, NC: Carolina Academic Press, 2013).

16. "Quick Facts," U.S. Census Bureau, https://www.census.gov/quickfacts/fact/table/US/PST045219; Richard E. Lapchick, *2020 Racial and Gender Report Card: Major League Baseball* (Orlando: DeVos Management Program, University of Central Florida, 2020).

17. Richard Lapchick, *The 2020 Racial and Gender Report Card: Major League Baseball the Institute for Diversity and Ethics in Sport* (Orlando: University of Central Florida, 2020); see also Alan M. Klein, *Dominican Baseball: New Pride, Old Prejudice* (Philadelphia: Temple University Press, 2014); George H. Sage, *Globalizing Sport: How Organizations, Corporations, Media, and Politics Are Changing Sports* (Boulder, CO: Paradigm, 2010), ch. 3.

18. Klein, *Dominican Baseball*; see also John Wertheim, "Futures Market," *Sports Illustrated*, April 14, 2014, 46–49; see also Tony Dokoupil, "Does Major League Baseball Exploit Latino Players?" NBC News, October 21, 2014, http://www.nbcnews.com/news/latino/does-major-league-baseball-exploit-latino-players-n228316.

19. David Trouille, *Fútbol in the Park: Immigrants, Soccer, and the Creation of Social Ties*, (Chicago: University of Chicago Press, 2021).

20. "Adolescent and School Health," Centers for Disease Control and Prevention, https://nccd.cdc.gov/Youthonline/App/Results.aspx?TT=A&OUT=0&SID=HS&QID=QQ&LID=XX&YID=2017&LID2=&YID2=&COL=S&ROW1=N&ROW2=N&HT=QQ&LCT=LL&FS=S1&FR=R1&FG=G1&FA=A1&FI=I1&FP=P1&FSL=S1&FRL=R1&FGL=G1&FAL=A1&FIL=I1&FPL=P1&PV=&TST=False&C1=&C2=&QP=G&DP=1&VA=CI&CS=Y&SYID=&EYID=&SC=DEFAULT&SO=ASC.

21. Allison Torres Burtka, "Understanding the Barriers That Get in the Way of Latina Girls Playing Sports," Global Sport Institute, November 17, 2020, https://globalsport.asu.edu/blog/understanding-barriers-get-way-latina-girls-playing-sports.

22. "LPGA Tour Official 2016 Money List," *Golf Today*, November 14, 2016; Neha S. Contractor, "South Asian Women in Sports: Overcoming Obstacles and Building Support," *The Aerogram*, February 11, 2014, http://theaerogram.com/south-asian-women-sports-building-support-network/.

23. "Jeongeun Lee6," LPGA, https://www.lpga.com/players/jeongeun-lee6/99109/bio.

24. Stanley I. Thangaraj, Constancio Arnaldo, and Christina B. Chin, eds., *Asian American Sporting Cultures* (New York: New York University Press, 2016).

25. Tristan Lavalette, "How a $1 Billion Investment into American Cricket Will Kick Start a Professional U.S. T20 League," *Forbes*, May 24, 2019.

26. Frank A Salmone, ed., *The Native American Identity in Sports: Creating and Preserving a Culture* (Lanham, MD: Scarecrow Press, 2012); see also Kevin Simpson, "Sporting Dreams Die on the 'Rez,'" in *Sport in Contemporary Society*, 10th ed., ed. D. Stanley Eitzen (New York: Oxford University Press, 2015), 224.

27. Dan Bernstein, "Redskins Name Change Timeline: How Daniel Snyder's 'NEVER' Gave Way to Washington Football Team," *Sporting News*, November 26, 2020, https://www.sportingnews.com/us/nfl/news/redskins-name-timeline-washington-football-team/1uk394uouwi631k7poirtq1v1s.

28. "NBA Rosters Feature 109 International Players from 39 Countries," NBA.com, October 19, 2021, https://www.nba.com/news/nba-rosters-feature-109-international-player.

29. "Women's World Golf Rankings," Rolex, June 1, 2022, https://www.rolexrankings.com/rankings.

30. "Quick Facts," U.S. Census Bureau, https://www.census.gov/quickfacts/fact/table/US/PST045219. Lapchick, *2020 Racial and Gender Report Card*.

31. David Epstein, *The Sports Gene: What Makes the Perfect Athlete* (Yellow Jersey, 2013); see also Edward Dutton and Richard Lynn, *Race and Sport: Evolution and Racial Differences in Sporting Ability* (London:

Ulster Institute for Social Research, 2015); Ian B. Kerr, "The Myth of Racial Superiority in Sports," *The Hilltop Review* (Spring 2010): 19–29.

32. John W. Loy Jr. and Joseph F. McElvogue, "Racial Segregation in American Sport," *International Review of Sport Sociology* 5 (1970): 5–24.

33. Hubert M. Blalock Jr., "Occupational Discrimination: Some Theoretical Propositions," *Social Problems* 9 (Winter 1962): 246; and Oscar Grusky, "The Effects of Formal Structure on Managerial Recruitment: A Study of Baseball Organization," *Sociometry* 26 (September 1963): 345–353.

34. Stanley Eitzen and David Furst, "Racial Bias in Women's Intercollegiate Sports," *Journal of Sport and Social Issues* 13 (Spring 1989): 46–51; Marc Lavoie, "Stacking, Performance Differentials, and Salary Discrimination in Professional Ice Hockey," *Sociology of Sport Journal* 6 (1989): 17–35.

35. Michael Powell, "Warren Moon, Who Helped Clear Way for Black Quarterbacks, Recalls His Struggles," *New York Times*, February 5, 2016, https://www.nytimes.com/2016/02/06/sports/football/warren-moon-clearing-way-for-black-quarterbacks-recalls-his-struggles.html.

36. Doug Farrar, "10 Black Starting Quarterbacks in Week 1 Marks the Most in NFL History," *USA Today*, September 13, 2020, https://touchdownwire.usatoday.com/2020/09/13/10-black-starting-quarterbacks-in-week-1-marks-the-most-in-nfl-history/.

37. Lapchick, *2020 Racial and Gender Report Card.*

38. Lapchick, *2020 Racial and Gender Report Card.*

CHAPTER 7

GENDER IN U.S. SPORT

Continuity and Change

I think in this generation, I think it's going to be important for us to continuously celebrate our women as they step up to different platforms. Women have so many great qualities, and it's time to let them stand right beside us and make sure that they're seen as equal.

—MICHAEL BENNETT, *Nfl Player And Activist*[1]

College women's basketball game. Historically, sport has been a major cultural practice of gender inequality against females. Females have fought against this prejudice and discrimination for several decades and are now successful and admired athletes in many sports. (Photo: Eric Harding, California State University East Bay)

The word *gender* is capricious. More than one social scientist has called it a word without a meaning; other scholars have called it a word whose meaning changes every year. Notwithstanding the inconsistent meaning of gender, we believe there is a need for a chapter dealing specifically with gender and sport, particularly because we have only briefly commented on gender topics and issues in chapters throughout this book. We believe that despite the tremendous social changes that have taken place over the past twenty-five years, with respect to the meaning of gender, the sport world continues to promote and preserve traditional gender inequalities in many ways. As a consequence, a focused and in-depth analysis must be provided about gender in a way that has not been possible in the other chapters.

We have divided this chapter into two major sections. In the first section of this chapter, the primary focus will be on gender injustices and inequities that are present in sports. In the second major section, our focus turns to issues about gender identity and sexual orientation.

Before we begin our examination of the two substantive sections in this chapter, we wish to clarify several of the concepts and terms that are frequently in use with the main subject of this chapter. We understand that many readers have heard, read, and used some of these concepts and terms, but we believe some explanation is necessary to clear up ambiguities that may be out there, and that is what we hope to do.[2]

A person's sex is ascertained by biological features such as one's reproductive system and the sex chromosomes of XX and XY. Commonly, we think that sex is a binary category: one is born either with all the biological male or with all the biological female traits. The assumption of a gender binary implies that to be male means you are not female—that sex categories are exclusive realities. Importantly, biologists are now arguing that male and female categories are not binary or exclusive. In fact, sex is more akin to "race," representing a biological continuum whose features are in flux and complex. For example, biological characteristics that are commonly seen as sex specific, such as testosterone and estrogen, are present in all people.[3] And chromosomes do not always line up as either XX or XY. For example, some folks have XYY chromosomes. Additionally, some people are born with reproductive systems or genitalia that do not fit neatly into a traditional male or female category. The umbrella term for people who do not fit the conventional standards of one of the two sex categories is "intersex." Historically, people identified as intersex have often been forced to identify and live as either male or female. Thus, humans become the arbitrators of the binary sex classifications. The history of sex in the Western world is one that clearly demarks and polices the boundaries, and sport has been used to reinforce these binary categories (see Box 7.1 on sex testing).

Intersex is a different classification from transgender. Those who do not identify with their sex

---

BOX 7.1 *THINKING ABOUT SPORT:* POLICING WOMEN'S BODIES THROUGH THE PRACTICE OF SEX-TESTING FEMALE ATHLETES

Policing female athletes, and intersex women in particular, has a long and despicable history. For nearly a century, international sports organizations have monitored women for "masculine" qualities, and throughout the twentieth century, as women athletes' strength, endurance, and confidence grew, some observers speculated whether a fast, powerful female athlete could even *be* "a woman." By the mid-1960s, amid complaints that some successful female athletes were actually biologically men, the International Association of Athletics (track and field in the United States) Federations (IAAF) and International Olympic Committee, in response to complaints about

genital checks, introduced a "gender verification" strategy—a chromosome test—and when questions about a female athlete's sex arose, international sport organizations asserted the right to employ the chromosome test, while also retaining the right to use a hormone test, a gynecological exam, and a psychological evaluation.

Dutee Chand, an elite running champion while still a teenager, was born in 1996 in India to a desperately poor family of weavers. In 2012 she became an Indian national champion in the under-eighteen category. In 2013 she became the first Indian to reach the final in the World Youth Championships. But her running accomplishments ensnared her in the "but is she a woman?" controversy.

Born with a condition in which Chand's body produces a high level of testosterone, she was banned from participating

(continued)

(continued)

in the 2014 Commonwealth Games in Glasgow, Scotland. The IAAF stated that hyperandrogenism (an excessive level of androgens in the body) made her ineligible to compete as a female athlete. Her levels of testosterone were higher than the guidelines acceptable for female athletes according to the IAAF's rules. Ostensibly, this gave her an unfair advantage over other female athletes. Chand was given two options; she could undergo surgery or fight the decision. She refused the surgery option, saying, "I feel that it's wrong to have to change your body for sport participation. I'm not changing for anyone."

Dutee Chand immediately initiated an appeal against the validity of the IAAF's hyperandrogenism regulations at the Court of Arbitration for Sport (CAS)—the supreme court for sports disputes—against her ban from competition. Chand won her appeal. In July 2015, the CAS ruled in her favor in a judgment saying there was no evidence that she had an unfair advantage over other female athletes as a result of her condition. Chand was allowed to "continue to compete" throughout the world of IAAF championship events until a final decision was made on her appeal against IAAF's hyperandrogenism policy. This was done by the CAS in order to provide the IAAF with an opportunity to accumulate further evidence as to the degree of performance advantage that hyperandrogenic female athletes have over athletes with normal testosterone levels. CAS also gave the IAAF until July 24, 2017, to provide new scientific evidence supporting their claims. If new evidence was not provided, then IAAF's rules and regulations would be declared null and void.

CAS's ruling came as an enormous boost for Chand, who looked forward to finally resuming her career. She admits that, at times, it was "heartbreaking," but she was happy that she was finally free to pursue her passion for running.

While waiting for the IAAF to collect data, Dutee competed in a variety of competitions. In 2016 she won the gold 2016 Federation Cup National Athletics Championships in New Delhi. In June 2016, Dutee broke the national record twice in one day at the XVI International Meeting G Kosanov Memorial in Almaty, Kazakhstan, and thereby qualified for the Rio Olympic Games. She was the first Indian woman to run the 100 meters in the Olympics since 1980.

Just as Chand prepared to compete at the Asian Athletics Championships in Bhubaneswar in July 2017, the IAAF announced its decision to reopen Chand's "gender case." The IAAF now must now return to CAS with new evidence in support of its hyperandrogenism policy. In 2018, the IAAF (now called, World Athletics) narrowed their restriction on testosterone levels to apply only to the women's running events from 400 meters to one mile.

CAS's initial ruling in support of Dutee Chad came as a boon not just for Chand but also for female athletes all over the world who have faced "sex-testing" discrimination through no fault of their own. It should be noted that men are not subject to sex testing, which illustrates the gendered assumption that men's superior performance is expected while women's outstanding accomplishments are "suspect."

An accumulating trend about "gender verification" in sports suggests it should be abolished. Several reports have shown that the tests have adversely affected women athletes in a variety of ways. For example, physical and psychological harm has been documented in a number of cases. These include severe sex and gender identity crisis, social isolation, depression, and suicide. Benefits are dubious because most cases of intersex are considered irrelevant to sports competition. In fact, many international human rights organizations have identified sex-testing as violating many fundamental human rights. In 2021, the IOC released a document to address this historical discrimination. That document is called: "IOC Framework on Fairness, Inclusion and Non-Discrimination on the Basis of Gender Identity and Sex Variations.

Sources: Rebecca Jordan-Young, Peter Sönksen, and Katrina Karkazis, "Sex, Health, and Athletes," *BMJ*, April 28, 2014, http://www.bmj.com/content/348/bmj.g2926; Claudia Wiesemann, "Is There a Right Not to Know One's Sex? The Ethics of 'Gender Verification' in Women's Sports Competition," *Journal of Medical Ethics* 37, no. 4 (2011): 216–220; "Sprinter Dutee Chand 'Not Worried' About Reopening of Gender Case," *The Quint*, July 5, 2017, https://www.thequint.com/athletics/2017/07/05/dutee-chand-gender-case-reopened. Ruth Padawer, NYTimes, June 28, 2016, The Humiliating Practice of Sex-Testing Female Athletes, https://www.nytimes.com/2016/07/03/magazine/the-humiliating-practice-of-sex-testing-female-athletes.html, accessed May 15, 2017.; Human Rights Watch, December 4, 2020, "They are chasing Us Away from Sport," https://www.hrw.org/report/2020/12/04/theyre-chasing-us-away-sport/human-rights-violations-sex-testing-elite-women, accessed June 10, 2022; Lindsay Parks Pieper, November 29, 2021, Washington Post, The new Olympic policy that undoes a half-century of bigotry, https://www.washingtonpost.com/outlook/2021/11/29/new-olympic-policy-that-undoes-half-century-of-bigotry/; accessed June 10, 2022

assigned at birth are transgender. Although the concept of a person's sex is complicated, gender is even more fluid and complex; gender refers to individuals' roles and stereotypes that are considered normal or acceptable behaviors for males and females in a given society, whereas gender identity is a person's innate, deeply felt psychological identification as a man, woman, nonbinary, or some other gender, and it may or may not correspond to the sex assigned to an individual at birth.

Beyond gender, sexual orientation refers to the direction of one's sexual interest toward members of the various sex categories. The acronym LGBTQ is now well known to stand for gay, lesbian, bisexual, transgender, and queer and has become adopted by much of the sexuality and gender identity–based community and the media in the United States, and it is now used in everyday conversation. LGBTQ is intended to emphasize a diversity of sexuality and gender identity–based communities.

SOCIAL THEORIES AND GENDER RELATIONS

A major belief of functional theory is that society is composed of groups or societies that are cohesive, share common norms, and have a stable culture. Gender inequality has been explained from a functionalist perspective as a "natural" and necessary division of labor. Because only females give birth and nurse infants, there is a natural division of labor in which women are more involved in child raising and domestic activities of the home. Historically, male role identifications have been as the economic breadwinners and protectors of the family. Thus, the division of labor in families was based on sex, with females being subordinate to males. This allowed the components of society to function smoothly because everyone in a society knew their respective position in the social hierarchy. The ultimate implication was that when a society functions smoothly with gender stratification, gender inequality is acceptable and efforts should not be made to change it. This example illustrates that functionalism is commonly supportive of the status quo.

Industrialization and modernization made historical gender differentiation less functional, but remnants of that traditional system can still be found today and are viewed by functionalists as contributing to social order, integration, and stability. Conflict/cultural theorists argue that gender inequality rooted in the male–female power relationship from preindustrial societies is unsuitable for contemporary societies. However, domination by males over females has been reproduced and continues because of males' greater control over the major social institutions, especially the family, education, economic, political, religious, and social resources. Thus, female subjugation and inequality are prevalent in the social structures and processes of most human societies today.

Feminist theories began as critiques of patriarchy, stereotyping, discrimination, and oppression of females and as a commitment to change those conditions. Feminism is grounded in a belief in the social necessity of gender equality and challenges the patriarchal gender ideas that prevail in other social theories.

CONSTRUCTING AND REPRODUCING GENDER RELATIONS THROUGH SPORT

American society prides itself on its concern for the fullest development of each person's human potential, but historically it has been quite insensitive to the social injustices and inequality toward females. A fundamental feature of American society is the pervasiveness of male privilege. Male/female disparities in wealth, power, and prestige are ubiquitous social phenomena. Men are privileged throughout the occupational structure, and they dominate hierarchies of public, institutional power; thus, they experience greater material rewards, a higher level of deference and esteem, and a more dominant position in the control of both their personal lives and their social activities.

That is only one of the issues that require attention. Another involves the processes of the social construction of gender relations and understanding how meanings about masculinity and femininity serve to promote and sustain gender inequities and injustices, thus creating problems for both males and females. One cultural practice that is most influential in the construction of meanings about masculinity and femininity is sport. Historically, it has been a significant cultural practice in constructing and reproducing gender inequalities.

THE HERITAGE OF GENDER INEQUALITY IN SPORT

During childhood, adolescence, and early adulthood, there is a tendency to believe that current social conditions have always existed. There is typically a lack of understanding that current social conditions are historically rooted and have emerged out of quite different conditions in the past. This is certainly the case with gender relations and sport. Young people today see girls playing a variety of youth sports, girls on high school teams winning state championships, women in intercollegiate athletics capturing NCAA national championships, and professional women athletes earning incomes of more than a million dollars a year. Little do they realize that such opportunities and achievements were unheard of only fifty years ago.

Here is a tip for college-age readers of this book: ask your grandmothers to tell you what conditions were like for females in sport when they were growing up. We think you will be amazed at what you will hear.

To develop an understanding about contemporary gender relations, it is helpful to place social relations between the sexes in historical perspective. For the past 3,000 years, Western cultural ideology has been firmly grounded in patriarchy, which is a set of personal, social, and economic relations that enable men to have power over women and the services they provide. Patriarchal ideology defines females as inferior to and dependent on men, and their primary gender-role prescriptions are seen as childbearers, childrearers, homemakers, and sex objects.

The traditions of Western civilization have been preserved in the United States with respect to the status of females. The overemphasis on the historical socialization pattern of preparing women for their adult role as passive helpmates of men—standing on the sidelines of history and cheering men on to their achievements and successes—was persistent. When the framers of the U.S. Declaration of Independence wrote that "all men are created equal" (excluding Black and Native American men, of course), that is literally what they meant, and it was not until 144 years later—in 1920, with the passage of the Nineteenth Amendment to the U.S. Constitution—that women were even considered worthy of the right to vote.

As modern sport began to develop in the latter nineteenth century, it served as one of the most powerful cultural forces for reinforcing the ideology of male superiority and dominance. Organized sport created symbols, rituals, and values that preserved patriarchy and women's subordinate status

in society. By celebrating the achievements of males through their sporting achievements and marginalizing females into the roles of spectators and cheerleaders, sport reproduced the male claim to privileged status. The overriding societal attitude with respect to sport was that it was for males and not for females.[4]

The combined role of female and athlete was virtually unthinkable in the United States in the nineteenth century. Women who wished to participate in competitive sports and remain "feminine" faced almost certain social isolation and censure. By choosing the physically active life, a woman was repudiating traditional female gender-role expectations. It seemed, therefore, that females would have little role to play in the burgeoning expansion of sport. Notwithstanding the cultural obstacles females had to overcome, their increasing presence and persistent involvement in sport in the late nineteenth and early twentieth centuries made a significant contribution to the rise of modern sport.

Social changes were numerous during the late nineteenth century, as industrialization brought new wealth and more leisure to Americans. Middle- and upper-class women experienced more freedom than they had ever known. Their interests expanded to activities outside the home, and as organized sport grew, women were often some of the most ardent participants. Croquet, roller skating, ice skating, bowling, archery, lawn tennis, golf, and bicycling were a few of the sports that captured the interest and enthusiasm of women during the latter part of the nineteenth century.[5]

One important trend in sport in the late nineteenth century took place at women's colleges. Several of the best-known women's colleges began including sports as part of their physical education programs. Boating, skating, bowling, horseback riding, swimming, tennis, and golf were all popular on campuses, and they were respectable because participants were protected from public view while they played. When basketball was created as a sport in the 1890s, it quickly became popular at women's colleges. The British game of field hockey was introduced into the United States in the early twentieth century, and it too became immediately popular in the eastern women's colleges.

Throughout the twentieth century, females faced a continuing struggle for equality and justice in sports. This is obvious from the following statement made by two *Sports Illustrated* writers in 1973 about females still encountering oppression and inequality in the world of sport: "There may be worse (more socially serious) forms of prejudice in the United States, but there is no sharper example of discrimination today than that which operates against girls and women who take part in competitive sports, wish to take part, or might wish to if society did not scorn such endeavors."[6]

This statement makes it clear that the sport culture was pretty much the exclusive domain of males. Men typically engaged more often in sports and manifested greater interest in sporting achievements. Sports heroes and superstars were mostly males, and male dominance was notable in the administrative and leadership branches of sports, where men clearly overshadowed women in power and numbers. Female athletes did not suit the ideal of femininity, and those who persisted in sport suffered for it. These same *Sports Illustrated* writers characterized the prevailing view in the 1970s: "Sports may be good for people, but they are considered a lot gooder for male people than for female people."[7]

SOCIAL SOURCES OF GENDER INEQUALITY IN SPORT

The ultimate basis of gender inequality in U.S. sport is embedded in the sociocultural milieu of and in the traditions of Western societies that are foundational to the United States. The historical foundations of the American gender system and how it has specified behaviors, activities, and values of the sexes were described previously. We showed how the gender system has operated as a mechanism of inequality by ranking women as inferior and less able and by conferring privilege and status to males. In addition to the historical sociocultural influences, more specific socialization agents and agencies tend to reproduce the gender system with each new generation. We now turn to an examination of some of these influences, emphasizing the role of several social institutions in gender socialization.[8]

PARENTAL CHILDREARING PRACTICES AND GENDER CONSTRUCTION

Sex is a biological characteristic, whereas gender refers to an ongoing cultural process that socially constructs differences between men and women (and, as noted previously, socially constructs only two binary sex categories). Each culture *constructs and teaches its young* the social role expectations for males and females, about what is considered masculine and what is considered feminine. Thus, humans are immersed in a complex network of sex and gender norms throughout life. Almost everything is gendered, and all societies have attitudes, values, beliefs, and expectations based on sex.[9]

The teaching of gender-role ideology comes from a range of social sources, including peers, teachers, faith leaders, mass media, and so forth, but the earliest and most persistent instruction takes place in the family. Parents are major contributors to the shaping of gender-role ideology by acting differently toward sons and daughters as early as their first exposure to them and throughout the remaining years of their rearing. From infancy, there are both marked and subtle differences in the way parents speak to sons and daughters, the way children are dressed, the toys they are given, and the activities in which they are encouraged and permitted to engage. A certain amount of aggression is not only permitted but also encouraged in boys; much less is tolerated in girls. Techniques of control tend to differ also: praise and withdrawal of love are used more often with girls, and physical punishment is used relatively more often with boys.

Children rapidly learn the difference in parental expectations concerning gender-appropriate behavior. Studies of the childhood experiences of female and male athletes have found that in a variety of ways, parents, especially fathers, encourage sport involvement of their sons more than that of their daughters.[10]

THE SCHOOL AND GENDER CONSTRUCTION

The school serves to reinforce and extend the gender-role stereotyping that begins in the home. Teachers are in close contact with students throughout the day, day after day, year after year; therefore, they are a major influence on children and youth. Teachers mold the traditional gender-role differences both directly and indirectly.

An indirect means by which the school reinforces traditional gender roles is through its own authority structure. Whereas some 80 percent of all elementary/middle school teachers are women, more than 44 percent of elementary school/middle school principals are men, and about 67 percent of secondary school principals are men, although some 64 percent of the teachers at this educational level are women. Fewer than 25 percent of all superintendents are women. Thus, children learn the differential status of men and women simply by attending school.[11]

Another mechanism of gender-role reinforcement is sex-segregated, or at least single sex–dominated, classes. Subjects such as math and science are often viewed as male subjects, and English and fine arts are regarded as female subjects. We realize that educators have made a concerted effort to "degender" these courses during the past several decades.

Some textbooks, one of the basic sources of learning in schools, perpetuate gender-role ideology. In studies of the treatment of gender roles in textbooks, investigators have found that females tend to be marginalized in the world of politics, science, and sports, with their future presented as consisting primarily of homemaking, glamor, and service.[12]

Hours of every school day are lived outside the classrooms in hallways, on the playgrounds, and going to and from school. It is during these times that a great deal of interaction takes place between classmates. Much of this time is spent in conversations, informal fun and games, and just plain horsing around. These interactions between boys and girls turn out to be what some researchers call *power play*. By that they mean that through these school-related ritualized interactions, gender inequality is socially constructed.[13]

A lot has changed in high school sports in the past thirty years, and we will discuss those changes in more detail later in this chapter. Despite the greater opportunities for females in interschool sports, these programs are still testimony to the importance of boys and the secondary status of girls. Thus, extracurricular activities, like school athletics, play an important role in the production and reproduction of gender differences. Having said that, this gender differentiation in school sports is not nearly as conspicuous as it once was.

THE MASS MEDIA AND GENDER CONSTRUCTION

As we emphasize in Chapter 12, social contexts and descriptions of females in the mass media—including newspapers, magazines, radio, television, and motion pictures—generally reinforce gender-role stereotypes. Coverage of women in sport historically tended to reinforce the stereotypes firmly embedded in the cultural heritage regarding women. However, considerable change has taken place in media coverage of women's sports in the past decade.

Despite increasing respect given to women athletes in mass media, there are still major differences in women's and men's sports coverage. Male sports still dominate sports sections in newspapers, and the content of the vast majority of sport magazines focuses on males. Recent research on representation of gender on the covers of two of the most popular U.S. sport magazines, *ESPN: The Magazine* and *Sports Illustrated*, shows a continued pattern of favoring male athletes. From 2013 to 2018, *ESPN: The Magazine* had 115 covers, on which a total of twenty-eight women appeared. Importantly, fifteen of the twenty-eight were featured on an annual Body Issue, where the emphasis is on the beauty of the body. Only five women were featured on the cover for their athletic skills. The remainder were pop culture stars such as Nicki Minaj. In the same time frame, *Sports Illustrated* had 233 covers, 36 of which featured women. Only 8 covers featured women for their athletic skills (others depicted cheerleaders, fans, or team photos).[14]

Television, because of its omnipresence, plays a powerful role in depicting gender relations. Studies extending over twenty years convincingly show the unequal treatment of women's sports on TV (see Chapter 12 for a discussion of these studies). Gender stereotyping and sexist commentary, once rampant on TV sports programs, has become less frequent. However, commentary during a women's sports event will still occasionally focus on the physical attractiveness of the performers, their fashionable attire, their grooming, or their "cute" personality characteristics; commentary on such subjects is rarely part of a men's event. See the "Media Sport and Gender Inequities" section in Chapter 12 for a more detailed account of this topic. Motion pictures also play a powerful role in reinforcing the secondary status of women. An analysis of the top money-making movies of 2020 by the Center for the Study of Women in Television & Film found that men had 64 percent of the speaking roles whereas women had about 36 percent. The findings also revealed that females accounted for only 38 percent of major characters.

Movie producers have tended to project two identities for women: as a sex object and as a wife/mother figure, but seldom as a competent athlete. Movies about women in sports have been rare. In the past thirty years, a few films on this subject were not only memorable but also commercially successful. The first, *A League of Their Own*, is a 1992 American comedy–drama that gives a fictionalized account of the real-life All-American Girls Professional Baseball League. In 2002, *Bend It Like Beckham*, a British film about women navigating their ethnic, class, and gender identities in soccer, was released and received critical acclaim. The third, a 2004 film titled *Million Dollar Baby* starring Hilary Swank, is about a woman boxer; it won an Academy Award for Best Picture, and Swank took the Oscar for Best Actress in a Leading Role. Although these films represent breakthroughs, there is still a major discrepancy between the number of films that feature male and female athletes.

NICKNAMES, MASCOTS, AND HEROINES

One vestige of the past that is gradually disappearing is the trivialization of female sports teams through the nicknames and mascots used for high school girls' and college women's teams. Although the nicknames and mascots are chosen by the institutions, it is through the mass media that they are largely communicated to the public. Tigerettes, Rambelles, Teddy Bears, and other "cutesy" mascot names may seem harmless, but they have the effect of defining female athletes and females' athletic programs as frivolous and insignificant, even trivial.[15]

Through media accounts of their achievements, athletes become widely known to the public and become role models. Media portrayals of them tend to link their personal lives with their sports achievements; if a socially positive character is created, they become heroes and heroines, especially to children and adolescents. Historically, there have been few feminine counterparts to sport superstars LeBron James, Tom Brady, and Cristiano Ronaldo. Boys are bombarded with daily accounts of high school, college, and professional athletes, but until the past decade girls rarely read, heard, or saw reports about the feats of outstanding female athletes. Today, several women have become visible role models, including Serena Williams, Megan Rapinoe, Simone Biles, and Naomi Osaka (who has a Barbie doll in her image).

FEMALES SURMOUNT SOCIAL BARRIERS TO PARTICIPATION IN SPORT

Gender inequality directed against females, like prejudice and discrimination of any kind, is insidious and denigrating. For females, it has taken many forms: the perpetuation of myths about the biological and psychological weaknesses of females (for example, see Box 7.1 about sex-testing female athletes), unequal opportunity for participation in many activities, and unequal access to the authority and power structure. Each of these forms of gender inequality has been used to discourage women and girls from participating in sports and to deny them equal access to the rewards that sport has to offer.

NEGATIVE MYTHS

A variety of folklore, myths, and slogans traditionally prevalent in American society supported sport as an exclusively masculine activity and served as barriers to female participation in sport until recently.

Myth: Athletic Participation Masculinizes Females

One of the oldest and most persistent notions about female participation in sport, and a main deterrent, was the idea that vigorous physical activity tended to "masculinize" the physique and behavior of girls and women. For years, women of physical competence were stigmatized as "masculine" by claims that women who engaged in physical activities were not "feminine." This acted to discourage female interest and involvement in sport.

From the beginning of modern sport, sport was a male preserve, and images of ideal masculinity for males were culturally constructed through sports. The cultural script was that males validated their masculinity through athletic endeavors. Females had no place there; it could only make them masculine, as it does males. The founder of the modern Olympic Games and an influential leader in sport, Pierre de Coubertin, opposed what he called the "indecency, ugliness and impropriety of women in . . . sports [because] women engaging in strenuous activities were destroying their feminine charm and leading to the downfall and degradation of . . . sport."[16] At another time, de Coubertin drove home the same point: "Would . . . sports practiced by women constitute an edifying sight before crowds assembled for an Olympiad? Such is not [the International Olympic Committee's] idea of the Olympic Games in which we have tried . . . to achieve the solemn and periodic exaltation of male athleticism with internationalism as a base, loyalty as a means, art for its setting, and female applause as its reward."[17]

The impression that physical activity produces masculine body types is undoubtedly a result of the fact that females who become serious athletes do indeed develop muscular and movement characteristics appropriate for performing the skills of a sport. Such muscle development and movement patterns have nothing to do with maleness or femaleness but are merely the most efficient use of the body to accomplish movement tasks. Nevertheless, the threat of masculinization was sufficiently terrifying to discourage many females from becoming physically active, and those who did become athletes often lived with the fear of becoming masculine.

Even in the twenty-first century, many female athletes attempt to maintain a "ladylike" appearance in deference to the ideology that sport masculinizes females. By wearing ruffles, pastel colors, or lacy designs and styles, they seem to be saying, "Even though I'm a highly skilled athlete, I'm still feminine." There seems to be a growing trend for female athletes to not create a dichotomy between femininity and athleticism. One researcher has suggested that many younger women have moved from seeing themselves as either pretty *or* powerful and now see themselves as pretty *and* powerful.[18] In short, for many women being strong and feminine is no longer seen as a contradiction. For example, sociologist Nancy Theberge studied the sources of pleasure and satisfaction in women ice hockey players and found that many of them were attracted to ice hockey because of the physicality involved in playing it. One of the players told Theberge, "I like the fight for the puck; it's who's going to fight for the puck . . . . That's where the competitiveness comes in, that's where my aggressiveness comes from: this [the puck] is mine and I'm not giving it to you kind of thing. . . . I like a physical game."[19] Box 7.2 describes how women use rugby to create a strong body.

BOX 7.2   *THINKING ABOUT SPORT:* ANYONE FOR RUGBY?! CHALLENGING DISCOURSES OF FEMININE BODIES IN AMERICAN CULTURE

The sport of rugby presents a cultural site, where the shape and size of the female sporting body often contradict dominant ideas of feminine bodies in American culture.

Tackling Normative Femininity

Rugby provides women with the opportunity to participate in an aggressive, physically demanding collision sport. For many of them it is the first time they have participated in an organized collision sport. A few of them may have tried or considered playing high school football because of the tackling and physicality required in football. But the majority of these women are usually actively searching for an outlet for their physicality.

One study of women playing rugby discussed how their participation in rugby had changed how they thought and felt about their bodies and their performance. One of the smaller players addressed rugby's impact on the way she feels about her body:

> Definitely I want to be stronger. Since I started playing rugby and lifting weights I want big shoulders. There is some gene in me that says you're not going to have big shoulders because I've been trying for a long time and I haven't gotten them yet. But I want to be stronger and fitter. I don't want to be, you know I used to want to be thin, everybody wants to

(continued)

(continued)

be skinny, now I don't want to be that, I want to look, I want to be muscular. I want to look like I have muscles. I want to be able to see definition in my arms or my legs. I want that. I don't care if I have a six-pack, but I want muscle there. If you can't see it I at least want it to be there anyway. I just want to be strong.

Another player also revealed that playing rugby had changed the poor relationship she had with her body. She wanted to look like a muscular, professional female athlete instead of an emaciated supermodel. This suggests that she had become aware that idealizing a supermodel body was problematic and that desiring an ultrathin body was not healthy. Her involvement in rugby significantly changed how she felt about her body.

Resisting Dominant Female Body Ideals

Many women recognize that by playing rugby they are challenging images of the ideal female body and using their bodies in ways that disturb the boundaries of what is appropriate for women. One player effectively described the pleasure some of the women take in resisting these boundaries. She said,

I mean that's body on body, women pushing, determination, everything they've ever been told that they can't ever do,

they are doing right then. I mean everything, I mean you're not supposed to be tough, you're not supposed to get dirty, you're not supposed to bleed, you're not supposed to whatever, you know don't perspire, what is that? You don't sweat, you glisten, my ass, you know you've got women over there with their ears taped down, and their hair flopping out of their ponytails. I'm sure not everybody thinks about it when they are out there playing, but like everything we've been told we can't do, it's like you know what, fuck you, I'm doing it, and it's like, I'm going to kick mud in your face, and I'm going to breathe and I'm going to be dirty and I'm going to love it, and it is the best, to have your body hurt like that, to push it all the way past the end, I mean beyond the end.

Women who play rugby actively work to construct athletic and powerful bodies that challenge ideals of normative feminine bodies, and they display a critical awareness of how their bodies challenge these ideals.

Source: Adapted from Laura Frances Chase, "(Un)Disciplined Bodies: A Foucauldian Analysis of Women's Rugby," *Sociology of Sport Journal* 23 (2006): 229–247; see also Chad Wise, "USA Rugby Names 2016 U.S. Olympic Women's Rugby Team," *USA Rugby*, July 18, 2016, https://www.usarugby.org/2016/07/usa-rugby-names-2016-u-s-olympic-womens-rugby-team/.

Myth: Sports Participation Is Harmful to the Health of Females

From the beginnings of modern sport forms in the mid-nineteenth century, women were cautioned about participation in sport. It was widely claimed that sport was harmful to female health. Principally concerned with physical injury to the reproductive organs and the breasts and with possible effects on the menstrual cycle, pregnancy, and the psychological well-being of females, the literature of the past one hundred years is laden with such opinions. Early in the twentieth century, a Harvard physical educator discouraged women from engaging in competitive sports because of "the peculiar constitution of [a female's] nervous system and the greater emotional disturbances to which she is subjected."[20]

Currently, physical activity and sports competition are being touted as positive for girls and women of all ages. In fact, there is a growing literature around older women participating in all sorts of sports, including skateboarding, windsurfing, mountain biking, and surfing, alongside "fitness" activities such as yoga and jogging.[21]

Myth: Women Are Not Interested in, or Very Good at, Sports

A generation ago, male domination of sport culture was so complete that females could be denied opportunities in sport by those asserting that women were not really interested in or very good at sports. Those who made this point typically referred to the paucity of women in sports and claimed that the best performances of those who did participate in sport were inferior to men's performances. Such arguments, like all cultural norm explanations of social regularities, tended to ignore social structure.[22] Females were simply socialized out of sport by a variety of powerful social agents and agencies. Without interest and encouragement, few indeed did play or play very well.

Female achievements in sport during the 1990s and the first two decades of the twenty-first century are too numerous and too remarkable to list. In ultra-distance running, swimming, and cycling, as well as equestrian events, dogsled racing, and horse and auto racing, women and men now compete together, even at the highest levels of competition. Women win their share of those events, too. World and Olympic records once set by male athletes in swimming, distance running, cycling, and other sports have been broken by female athletes.

The remarkable achievements of female professional, collegiate, and elite amateur athletes in recent years have provided a foundation for role modeling by young female athletes. As briefly noted earlier in the chapter, athletes such as tennis superstars Serena Williams and Naomi Osaka, basketball All-Star Maya Moore, gymnast Simone Biles, and soccer champion Abby Wambach have achieved celebrity status comparable to that of many male athletes, and many women's teams—such as the America's World Cup women's soccer team and the women's basketball teams at the University of Connecticut—are world renowned. Thus, "name" female athletes do exist in several sports, and girls of the present generation now have sport heroines to admire. The interest in women's elite sport is demonstrated by the over 4 million television viewers of the 2021 NCAA women's basketball championship game.[23] Clearly, the argument that females are not interested in sports and that they do not play them well enough to be taken seriously has been put to rest for even the most hardened skeptics of women's potential.

WOMEN'S STRUGGLE FOR OPPORTUNITY AND EQUALITY IN SPORT

The progress that females have made in overcoming gender inequality during the past three decades did not come without a struggle. Their targets for change varied from the kinds of legal and extralegal restrictions that prevented females from having equal access to sport opportunities to attempts to elevate the social and political consciousness of women as a group. However, prejudices are not altered by courts and legislation, and culturally conditioned responses to gender ideology are ubiquitous and resistant to sudden changes. Therefore, despite laws that have forced compliance in equality of opportunity for females in the world of sport, inequities in sport continue, albeit in more subtle and insidious forms, as has been the case with racism.

In the following sections we will describe some of the continuing legal and extralegal struggles females have encountered as opportunities have opened up for women to experience the access to and rewards of sports participation at all levels.

FROM BOYS-ONLY YOUTH SPORTS TO OPPORTUNITIES FOR BOTH SEXES

As we note in Chapter 8, youth sports programs introduce most children to the experience of organized sports. The Little League, Babe Ruth, and Connie Mack baseball leagues are three of the most popular baseball programs. Pop Warner football, Junior Hockey, and Biddy basketball initiate youngsters into tackling, blocking, ice skating, and jump shooting. Age-group programs in swimming, track and field, and gymnastics are only a few of the more than twenty-five youth sports programs that involve millions of youth annually.

Until the mid-1970s, Little League baseball had an all-male policy as part of its federal charter that prevented girls from playing on its teams. This policy was challenged by several girls or their representatives, and it was reluctantly rescinded by Little League officers. But it was not just Little League that opened up for girls. Girls and women are participating in a wide variety of sports and physical activities buttressed by policies and social support. A 2019 report by the Aspen Institute's Project Play found that 31.4 percent of girls aged six to twelve played sports on a regular basis and about 43 percent of high school girls played a sport.[24] To a large extent this is because the parents of these children are from the generations since the modern women's movement began. Thus, these parents are part of the generations that renounce the traditional cultural edicts of strict gender differentiation in social life. They tend to have a more favorable attitude toward gender equity, including equity in sport.

TITLE IX: FEDERAL GOVERNMENT SUPPORT FOR GENDER EQUITY

When the Educational Amendments Act of 1972 was passed, Title IX, a key provision in that law, required schools that receive federal funds to provide equal opportunities for males and females. It constituted a considerable weapon against sex discrimination in the American public school and collegiate sports programs, because some 16,000 public school districts and more than 2,600 colleges and universities benefit from federal funds.[25]

A note of explanation to readers: In the next few pages, we make several references to Title IX. Some readers will wonder, "Why so much attention to a fifty-year-old education law?" Our answer: Title IX has been the most significant factor in the liberation of gender inequality in the United States. Without Title IX, it is unlikely that females currently would have the sports opportunities in schools and colleges it made possible. Moreover, Title IX has had the effect of opening up opportunities in sport organizations beyond just public education. It has been an essential civil rights force for female sports.

TOWARD GENDER EQUITY IN HIGH SCHOOL SPORTS

A little more than forty-five years ago, a high school with ten or twelve teams for boys might have had no teams, or only a few teams, for girls. Boys' sports seasons might have run three months with fifteen or twenty-five scheduled contests; the season for a girls' sport would typically have extended a mere three to four weeks, with two or three contests. But Title IX was proving to be the beginning of a sports revolution for girls and women. Table 7.1 illustrates the staggering increases that have occurred in girls' high school athletic participation. In the past thirty years, the number of girls participating in high school athletic programs throughout the nation has increased by more than 900 percent.

Despite a federal law requiring schools to treat the sexes equally, the transition from a predominantly male athletic program to a two-sex program did not occur without controversy and litigation. Title IX was silent or vague on some issues; therefore, high school girls had to challenge the discrimination in their school sports programs through legal and legislative action. A number of lawsuits were brought by girls against school districts or state high school athletic regulatory bodies. In general, the cases fell into two categories: (1) a girl desired to participate on the boys' team when a girls' team was not

TABLE 7.1 HIGH SCHOOL SPORTS PARTICIPATION SURVEY TOTALS

Years	Boy participants	Girl participants
1971–1972	3,666,917	294,015
1975–1976	4,070,125	1,645,039
1989–1990	3,398,192	1,858,659
2000–2001	3,921,069	2,784,154
2006–2007	4,321,103	3,021,807
2016–2017	4,563,238	3,400,297
2018–2019	4,534,758	3,402,733

Source: National Federation of State High School Associations, "Participation Statistics," 2018–2019, https://www.nfhs.org/media/1020412/2018-19_participation_survey.pdf.

provided at her school, or (2) a girl wished to be on the boys' team although her school provided a girls' team. In the first type of case, the courts generally ruled in favor of the girl, although some of these suits required appeals. In the second type of case, the girl was usually not successful because the court reasoned that equal opportunity had not been denied her.

High school wrestling illustrates the trend that has been taking place with regard to girls' participation. When high school girls first came out for wrestling, they found various legal and policy barriers. They also found social objections. In the case of one girl who was a member of a high school wrestling team in Arizona, a fundamentalist religious group protested, saying it was immoral for a boy to wrestle a girl. One coach protested because a girl did not weigh in with the rest of the boys, stripped of all clothing. At the 2011 Iowa State High School Wrestling Tournament, a high school female wrestler won by default because her opponent, a male wrestler, refused to wrestle her, saying, "Wrestling is a combat sport. . . . As a matter of conscience and my faith, I do not believe that it is appropriate for a boy to engage a girl in the manner."[26] Despite such objections, more than 17,000 girls now participate on high school wrestling teams across the country annually.[27]

A development that has shown increasing strength involves requests by boys to be allowed to participate on girls' high school teams. In almost every case, the boys have wanted to take part on the girls' team because the school did not have a boys' team in that sport. Volleyball, soccer, gymnastics, field hockey, and swimming have been the sports that have most commonly drawn requests.

In several instances boys have won the right to play on the girls' team. According to the National Federation of State High School Associations (NFHS) participation survey, about 175 boys were playing high school field hockey in 2016. Throughout the nation, it is clear that boys do not wish to play on girls' teams in large numbers, but the situation does illustrate the unintended consequences of efforts to address gender equity against one sex. Each fall a few girls go out for high school football teams. Some states have ruled that they may not become members of the team. Others have ruled that if they can make the team, they may remain.[28]

In 2018–2019, about 43 percent of all high school sport participants were female, and the number of sports available to them was more than twice the number available in 1980.[29] Girls' high school sports have become so popular that they rival boys' high school sports for attention in many communities. Indeed, in some communities the girls' teams have a larger following of fans because of their winning records.

GENDER EQUITY IN INTERCOLLEGIATE SPORTS

Chapter 10 is devoted to intercollegiate sport, but in that chapter gender inequality is not one of the topics we focus on because we think gender inequality in intercollegiate sports is more properly located in this chapter, where gender inequality is a main feature. For readers to comprehend the current status of gender inequity in American intercollegiate sports for women, we must describe some of the specific struggles that have been intricately bound to Title IX in the United States for the past fifty years. So before we turn to an examination of gender in equity in intercollegiate sport, we explain the legislative and legal incidents surrounding Title IX.

Legislative and Legal Incidents Involving Title IX

Title IX specifies, "No person in the United States shall, on the basis of sex, be excluded from participation in, be denied the benefits of, or be subjected to discrimination under any education program or activity receiving Federal financial assistance." Although the clear intent of this legislation is to provide equal educational opportunities to females and males where federal funds are being used, Title IX has not brought about the goal of gender equality. A variety of legal challenges to it have been mounted by various groups, including the federal government, the NCAA, and individual universities, many of which still resist, or at least resent, complying with the intent of the legislation.[30]

The Office for Civil Rights (OCR) in the U.S. Department of Education (DOE) issued what became known as the "three-part test" policy. It is titled "Intercollegiate Athletics Policy Clarification: The Three-Part Test," which provides that a university sponsoring an athletic program must provide equal athletic opportunities for members of both sexes. Among other factors, the regulation requires that an institution must effectively accommodate the athletic interests and abilities of students of both sexes to the extent necessary to provide equal athletic opportunity. The OCR indicated that it will apply the three-part test to assess whether an institution is providing nondiscriminatory participation opportunities for individuals of both sexes. Readers interested in the details of the OCR three-part test may download it.[31]

Although the three-part test for compliance with Title IX has been in place for more than forty years, resistance to full compliance and the achievement of gender equity in college sport persists well into the twenty-first century. Resistance to gender equity in intercollegiate athletics has been met by complaints filed with the DOE's OCR and by legal action through the courts. More than a thousand complaints have been filed with the OCR involving sports. Dozens of lawsuits have been filed on behalf of gender equity in college sports, and in most cases the party or parties claiming discrimination have won.

Over the past fifteen years, the OCR has issued several clarifications about the three-part test for compliance with Title IX. The most recent clarification was published in 2010, and it goes to great lengths to clarify the meaning and implementation of the Title IX three-part test, but concludes with this statement: "The three-part test gives institutions flexibility and affords control over their athletics programs. This flexibility, however, must be used consistent with Title IX's nondiscrimination requirements."[32]

Although progress has been made, there are still some discrepancies in support for women's programs and women's opportunities in collegiate sport. Take into consideration the following:

- Females comprise nearly 60 percent of the college student population, but only 44 percent of NCAA participants are women.
- A law firm found the NCAA spent $4,285 for each men's Division I and national championship participants, excluding basketball. For each female participants, the NCAA spent about $1,700 less that same 2018-19 season. The gap is even larger when it comes to the six single-gender sports, like wrestling and beach volleyball. The NCAA spends $2,229 more per student-athlete for the men's championships than for the women's.[33]
- The NCAA started sponsoring women's sports in 1981. In that year, the average NCAA institution sponsored approximately 15 teams: 9 for men and 6 for women. In 2020-21, the average NCAA member institution sponsored approximately eighteen teams: eight for men and 10 for women.[34]
- Even though there are more sports sponsored for women, men participants still outnumber women. In 2021, the number of men participating in NCAA sports was 278,988 and the number of women was 219,177.[35]
- "In 2019-20, male athletes received $252 million more in athletic scholarships than female athletes received. If athletic departments offered athletic opportunities to female athletes proportional to enrollment, they would have had to award an additional $750 million in athletic scholarship assistance."[36]
- "In 2019-20, of the $241,40,778 spent on recruiting athletic talent to compete at the college level (in both two-year and four-year institutions), 30% was spent on recruiting female athletes ($75,290,142)."[37]

It is clear from this information that although women have been making gains toward gender equity in U.S. intercollegiate athletics, progress is being made much too slowly, and there are still inequities that must be abolished.

Governance and Control in Intercollegiate Sports: Post–Title IX

Governance of women's sport in colleges has been male dominated. Leadership opportunities for women have lagged far behind those for men. Even into the third decade of the twenty-first century, only about 14.3 percent of intercollegiate athletic director positions in Division I are held by women. The percentages increase in the other divisions: Division II is 21.9 percent and Division III is 32.6 percent. The executive director position, the highest position in the NCAA, has never been occupied by a woman; opportunities for women to serve on the elite Executive Committee have been limited. In 2021, six of the eighteen committee members were women. Each NCAA institution has a faculty athletics representative to the NCAA. Faculty athletics representatives represent their university on issues regarding athletics. Women from Division I universities held only 36 percent of these posts; 30 percent were from Division II and 40 percent from Division III institutions.[38]

During the past two decades, concern has arisen that an elite, professionalized approach similar to that of the men's athletic programs was emerging. It has now become clear that despite some protests by women's coaches and athletic directors, many of them embrace the NCAA commercial model of college sports and see the NCAA as providing the best avenue for getting on with the "business" of women's collegiate athletics. Indeed, this is exactly the direction that most major university athletic programs have taken. At the University of Connecticut, where the women's basketball team had won more than 110 consecutive games in recent years, average attendance at women's basketball games has been more than 8,500; at the University of Tennessee it has been more than 10,000. Several other universities report an average basketball attendance of more than 8,000. Other women's sports, especially volleyball, soccer, and softball, have experienced escalating spectator appeal.

With the professionalization of women's intercollegiate athletics, involving money, prestige, and popularity, have come falling graduation rates and violations of NCAA rules similar to the kind prevalent in men's programs. In the spring of 2017, over forty NCAA women's sports teams were on probation. Several others have received reprimands for NCAA rule violations—and not just in one or two sports. The teams involved include basketball, softball, tennis, golf, track and field, volleyball, and swimming.

Some sportswomen are distressed about what has happened to women's collegiate sports. They see the control of women's programs being absorbed into male-dominated sporting structures and losing their chance to advance a different ethic and form for intercollegiate sport. It appears that such a structure is already well advanced, and there is no discernible sign that women's athletic leaders have any plan for creating a different model of college sports.

Consequences of Title IX for Men's Intercollegiate Sports

Not all gender equity complaints and lawsuits have come on behalf of women. University officials, principally presidents and athletic directors, have refused to rein in the extravagant expenditures of football and men's basketball; therefore, athletic budgets have been under pressure as women's sports teams have been added to meet gender equity provisions of Title IX. Consequently, universities throughout the country have dropped some men's "minor" sports (e.g., swimming, gymnastics, golf, wrestling). The cuts in men's sports have led to wide-ranging claims that compliance with Title IX will be the death knell of men's intercollegiate sports and that women's sports leaders are just greedy and out to abolish men's sports.

The National Wrestling Coaches Association charged that Title IX has been hijacked, diverted from its original purpose of eliminating gender-based discrimination, and fashioned into a handy weapon to enforce a de facto quota system. The assistant secretary of civil rights responsible for dealing with Title IX cases has been accused of being a bureaucrat who is notorious for indifference to the imminent extinction of male sports programs. Many critics assert that Title IX is being misinterpreted, arguing that Title IX was not designed to require that a high school or college sports program reflect the male:female ratio of its student body because males are more interested in sports than are females. Thus, males should have more sport opportunities than females, but institutions are dropping male sports to add female sports just to meet Title IX standards. Although NCAA institutions have certainly dropped many sports teams over the past twenty years, research by the NCAA shows clearly that male athletes have not lost *opportunities* as a result of Title IX.

- During the 2005–2006 year, NCAA universities sponsored 8,137 championship teams for men, with 224,926 athletes playing on those sports teams. During 2019–2020, NCAA universities sponsored 9,235 teams for men, with about 282,411 athletes on those teams.
- During the 2005–2006 year, NCAA universities sponsored 9,150 teams for women, with 168,583 women athletes playing on those teams. During 2019–2020, NCAA universities sponsored 10,682 teams for women, with 221,212 athletes playing on those teams.

With NCAA universities adding and dropping teams between 2006 and 2019, there was an increase of around 1,100 men's teams and an increase of over 1,500 women's teams, a net gain of nearly 400 for women's teams. However, from 2006 to 2019, there was a net gain of 4,687 male athletes over female athletes on NCAA championship teams.[39]

Over the period just cited, about 1,500 NCAA women's sports teams were added. However, the figures show that increases in women's sports teams have not been accompanied by the downsizing of men's sports teams, as is often claimed by intercollegiate athletic directors and coaches of men's teams; indeed, during this fifteen-year period, male athletes increased by 4,687 more than women athletes.

The controversy over the effects of Title IX on men's intercollegiate athletics continues to be perhaps the most contentious issue in intercollegiate sports. In the summer of 2007, the College Sports Council (CSC), an advocacy group for men's sports, filed a petition asking the DOE for additional clarification of Title IX because the CSC believes the first test of the three-part test—proportionality—that the DOE uses for compliance with Title IX has led to fewer athletic opportunities for men in college and that the same thing could happen to boys in high schools.

Within the year, the DOE denied the CSC petition. Although there is no disputing that hundreds of men's teams have been abolished throughout the nation in the past forty years, there is also no disputing that 56 percent of NCAA student-athletes remain men while only 44 percent are women and that the average NCAA member institution currently sponsors approximately seventeen teams, eight for men and nine for women, in colleges and universities where nearly 60 percent of the students are women.

Most of those who defend the progress toward gender equity in women's intercollegiate sports do not advocate eliminating men's sports teams to achieve that end. They contend that universities and their athletic departments make decisions to drop men's sports or reduce the squad sizes for a number

Females have taken up sports that at one time were considered too rough and violent for women. They have been able to get sports such as lacrosse, rugby, and wrestling adopted into the regular high school and college sports programs. (Photo: Rich Barnes/USA Today Sports)

It is impossible to nail down how many high school girls are wrestling in the United States right now, thanks in large part to the lack of state associations sanctioning the sport. It seems clear that the number is at least 17,795 and may be higher, depending on the population of girls that age who are exclusively wrestling for clubs. In the end, all we really know is that the number of high school girls wrestling is growing and the participation numbers are higher than reported. Thirty colleges now sponsor a varsity wrestling program. Since 2004, women's wrestling has been a recognized Olympic sport. (Photo: Courtesy of Jordan Alves)

of reasons, not always just to increase the number of women's teams. So to blame Title IX for universities' decisions to drop some men's sports is misleading and untrue. Moreover, they argue that universities have other options to achieve gender equity.

For example, they argue that men's sports are eliminated largely because of fiscal mismanagement: Schools spend enormous sums of money for revenue-generating, but overwhelmingly non-profit-making, football and basketball programs. Indeed, fewer than 10 percent of intercollegiate football and basketball teams generate a profit; most are by far the biggest financial drain on athletic department budgets when revenue and expenditures are both considered.

Several sport studies scholars have questioned why Division I-A football teams need ten assistant coaches, why football and basketball coaches must be paid more than $5 million annually, and why Division I-A football teams need eighty-five scholarship players when NFL teams have only fifty-man rosters. They argue that ways and means could be found to reduce spending in areas such as these and divert the savings into preserving men's sports teams.

For their part, most male administrators, coaches, and athletes agree with the spirit behind Title IX. For them, it is the strict gender-based quota they object to. Although one can empathize with the male athletes and coaches who feel that their sports programs face restrictions, and who in some cases see gender equity as the cause of those restrictions, the good news is that recent trends in intercollegiate sports show that the gap between men's and women's intercollegiate sports—in terms of participation, teams, operating expenses, and so forth—is narrowing, without the elimination of men's teams, and that is the intent of Title IX—to end gender-based discrimination.

MEN RULE IN THE COACHING AND ADMINISTRATION OF WOMEN'S SPORTS

First, it is important to recognize that men dominate the professional/occupational structure in the United States. Overwhelmingly, they hold the most prestigious positions, occupy the most powerful leadership roles, and command the highest salaries. A report by the Joint Economic Commission of Congress found that women accounted for only about 40 percent of managers in the U.S. workforce. So throughout the professional/occupational structure there are differentiated opportunities and rewards for men and women, and management careers in sports follow the same patterns found elsewhere. *The Benchmarking Women's Leadership in the United States* report of 2014 asserts, "Results revealed that women are outperforming men, but they are not earning salaries or obtaining leadership roles commensurate with their higher levels of performance." It is the twenty-first century, and this report shows that women comprise, on average, less than 20 percent of positional leaders across fourteen sectors in the United States.[40]

High School and College Women's Coaching Positions

Title IX does not apply to coaches and administrators, so gender equity is not required with respect to the employment or salaries of high school and college women coaches and administrators. One ironic consequence is that as opportunities for female athletes opened up and high school and college sports programs expanded, positions in coaching and athletic administration formerly held by women were sought and filled by men. In high school, for example, at the time Title IX became law, 80 to 90 percent of high school girls' sports were coached by women; within fifteen years, only 35 to 42 percent were coached by women.

This trend has slowly reversed itself, and a majority of girls' high school sports are now being coached by women. There were even several dozen women among the more than 60,000 or so coaches of boys' high school sports teams across the United States during the 2017–2018 school year. For example, Nederland High School in Colorado hired the first female head football coach in state history. About achieving this coaching position, she said, "I was just following my passion."[41]

The coaching pattern that has just been described for high school girls' sports has been duplicated at the collegiate level. In the early 1970s almost all coaches of women's intercollegiate teams were women, but the situation changed rapidly, and by 1990 only

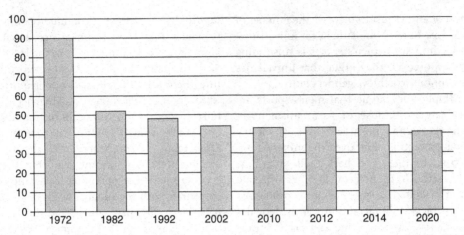

FIGURE 7.1 Percentage of College Women's Teams Coached by Women. Sources: R Vivian Acosta and Linda Carpenter, "Women in Intercollegiate Sport: A Longitudinal Study—Thirty-Seven Year Update, 1977–2014" (Acosta/Carpenter, P.O. Box 42, West Brookfield, MA, 2014). Updated to 2020 and the percentage is at 41 percent for all three divisions. Richard Lapchick, *The 2020 Racial and Gender Report Card: College Sport, The Institute for Diversity and Ethics in Sport* (Orlando: University of Central Florida, 2020).

48 percent of coaches of women's intercollegiate teams at four-year institutions were women. By 2020 this figure had declined to 41 percent (see Figure 7.1).

Even more disturbing, the percentage of African American women head coaches of women's basketball teams in Division I was 14 percent, which contrasts starkly with the nearly 41 percent of student-athletes playing women's basketball who were African American.

Assistant coaching positions are often seen as a stepping-stone to the position of head coach. There is a marginally higher percentage of college women assistant coaches than head coaches—about 53 percent across the three divisions of the NCAA—hardly an impressive figure when one considers that females have been involved in high-level college sports for more than forty years. In fact, in 1990 the men's basketball coach at the University of Kentucky, Rick Pitino, hired Bernadette Mattox as an assistant coach. Since then, other women have become full-time assistants on several Division I men's teams' staffs, such as swimming, volleyball, and soccer. Currently, about 4 percent of head coaches for men's Division I teams are women and about 8.5 percent of assistant coaches for men's Division I teams are women.[42]

The long-term trend in hiring practices remains unclear, but every year there are more women who are experienced and successful coaches, and it will be increasingly difficult for higher education officials to hire men for positions for which women are as qualified as (or better qualified than) male applicants. Indeed, there are some women coaching men's teams. However, there is a growing belief that in the not-too-distant future one of the highly successful women basketball coaches will be hired to coach a men's college basketball team.

Another issue for women college coaches involves payment for services rendered. In a 1992 NCAA survey, the average salary for male coaches was almost twice that of women coaches. That shocking finding caused universities throughout the country to reassess their salary structures because gender equity can never be achieved as long as there are such wide differences in salary for men and women doing essentially the same tasks. Nevertheless, even in the second decade of the twenty-first century, Division I head coaches of women's basketball teams earn only about 47 percent of the salaries of head coaches of men's teams. There is a wide range of salaries for both men and women basketball coaches, but at the upper extremes in 2017, several Division I men's basketball coaches had annual salaries between $4 and $7.2 million, while in 2016 the women's basketball coach at the University of Connecticut, Geno Auriemma, signed a five-year agreement that is scheduled to pay him about $13 million, or about $2.6 million annually. Kim Mulkey, who is now the Louisiana State University head coach, is purported to make $2.5 million annually.

Those defending the difference in salaries for men and women coaches contend that many men's programs generate more money than women's programs, so differential salaries are justified. That argument is countered with claims that because women's programs receive far less for their operating budgets, women are not given equal opportunity to promote and market their programs, factors essential to generating equal revenue in return (see Chapter 10 for further discussion on this).

High School and College Administrative/ Management Positions

Administrative/management positions in high school sports have remained overwhelmingly held by men. The NFHS was founded in 1920 and has led the development of education-based interscholastic sports. Throughout its more than one hundred years, it has just recently appointed its first woman as executive director (its chief operating officer), Dr. Karissa L. Niehoff.

High school athletic directors (sometimes called athletic coordinators) are typically men, with a woman as the assistant, when there is such a position. As of 2017, fewer than ten of the fifty-one directors of state high school associations were women, and only four women served on the NFHS's twelve-member board of directors.

Female athletic administrators have also lost out during the past forty years. Women's intercollegiate sports programs in the mid-1970s were administered almost exclusively by women with the title of athletic director. Then, as women's programs grew, many colleges combined their men's and women's athletic departments into one. Most such mergers followed a pattern: after the merger, there emerged a male athletic director and several assistant directors, one of whom was often a woman in charge of women's athletics or the less visible sports.

According to R. Vivian Acosta and Linda Jean Carpenter, two researchers who had been conducting a longitudinal study of colleges and universities for thirty-seven years, in 1972 more than 90 percent of women's intercollegiate programs were headed by a female administrator; more recently, data collected by the Institute for Diversity and Ethics in Sports found that within Division I, 14 percent of the head athletic directors were women and the majority were White. This decrease reflects the barriers to leadership women have faced in the era of the dominance of the governance of collegiate sport by the NCAA (since 1982). There are signs that the trends in the employment of women in intercollegiate sports are improving. In 2016 more than 13,950 females were employed in intercollegiate sports in positions such as athletic directors, assistant/associate athletic directors, head coaches of men's or women's teams, paid assistant coaches, head athletic trainers, and sports information directors. Their demonstrated competence and accomplishments show convincingly that in this industry, just as in many others that have opened up to women, they are capable of performing just as well as men.

In a later section of this chapter we will discuss some of the reasons why women are underrepresented in college athletics. To highlight some of the discrepancies that continue, data from a study sponsored by the Global Sport Institute at Arizona State University is insightful. The study looked at the 385 athletic director changes across 248 NCAA Division I schools over a ten-year period from 2010 through 2019. The study found the following:

- Incoming college athletic directors were overwhelmingly White (77 percent) and male (88 percent).
- Women and people of color made small gains over the decade, with the overall percentage of Black athletic directors rising from 17 percent to 19 percent and the percentage of women rising from 8 percent to 12 percent.
- The majority of women who were athletic directors had NCAA coaching experience, but the majority of their male counterparts did not.
- Athletic directors of color were more likely than their White counterparts to have attained graduate and doctoral degrees, and women athletic directors were more likely to have attained those degrees than their male counterparts.
- No Asian American women or Latinas were hired in seven of the ten years studied.

- Historically Black Colleges and Universities accounted for 36 percent of the Black women hired as athletic directors over the period studied.[43]

Thus, the practice of predominantly White institutions hiring White men as athletic administrators continues. It can be inferred from the findings that women and people of color had to have more credentials (i.e., coaching experience and education) than their White male counterparts to be seen as qualified. Women have been underrepresented in other leadership opportunities in collegiate governance. In 2021, six of the twenty NCAA Board of Governors members were women, and women held only 35 percent of all administrative jobs within all divisions of the NCAA, at a time when 43 percent of the student-athletes were women.

OWNERSHIP, MANAGEMENT, AND COACHING IN PROFESSIONAL AND OLYMPIC SPORTS

The pattern of men dominating the leadership of women's sport prevails at the professional level, just as it does at the other levels of sport. Women are scarcely found in leadership positions in professional team sports. Of all of the women's professional team sports, the WNBA has perhaps the highest profile. It operates under the auspices of the NBA—although seven of the WNBA franchises are independently owned in 2020—and is the beneficiary of the NBA's marketing and promotional resources. During the 2020 season, seven women held chief executive officer/president positions, while 40 percent of the head coaches and 62 percent of the assistant coaches were women. WNBA players are some of the most recognizable and popular athletes in our society—women or men. But WNBA salaries are a far cry from NBA salaries; in 2020 the average salary for the NBA was $7.7 million, while the WNBA average was $100,500.

Shortly before the NBA 2014–2015 preseason practices began, the San Antonio Spurs announced the hiring of Becky Hammon, the first full-time, paid female assistant coach in the NBA. She is a six-time WNBA all-star. Spurs coach Gregg Popovich told her, "I'm hiring you because you're a good fit here and you just happen to be a woman."[44] Hammon has recently taken the head coaching job for the WNBA team, the Las Vegas Aces. With regard to women coaching in

the NFL, the Buffalo Bills made Kathryn Smith the first female full-time assistant coach in 2016. Other women include Katie Sowers, who has been an assistant coach in the NFL for the San Francisco 49ers and the Kansas City Chiefs. Maral Javadifar and Lori Locust were assistant coaches for the Tampa Bay Buccaneers and Jennifer King was a coach for the Washington Commanders.

Beyond coaching and ownership, men have a commanding presence from top to bottom in most women's professional sports, and women's involvement in professional men's sports is extremely rare. Of the professional sport leagues, the NBA and WNBA have been the most responsive to advancing diversity. A good example was the selection of Laurel Richie in 2011 to be the president of the WNBA, making her the first African American woman named president of a U.S. professional sports league. Another African American woman, Lisa Borders, replaced Laura Richie in 2016. Currently, a White woman, Cathy Engelbert, is the president.

In 1997 Violet Palmer was the first woman given an officiating assignment in the NBA. She continued to referee until 2016, when she retired from on-court duties with the NBA. At the time of her retirement, she had refereed 919 NBA games. During the 2016–2017 NBA season, one woman, Lauren Holtkamp, was the only full-time female referee. Currently five of the sixty-five referees for the NBA are women.

In the summer of 2015, the NFL formally announced that Sarah Thomas had been selected as the first full-time female official in the league's history and she was the first woman to officiate the Super Bowl (2021). Maia Chaka is the second woman, and first African American woman, to referee in the NFL.

Several women have umpired in the minor leagues, and two have umpired major league spring training games, but no woman has been an umpire for a regular-season MLB game. As Lucy McCalmont, the sports editor at the *Huffington Post*, claimed, "Anyone hoping for a . . . milestone in the MLB sometime soon shouldn't hold their breath."[45]

Women are greatly underrepresented as sportswriters. Despite the addition of a few women sports reporters to the staffs of television networks and a

The Los Angeles Clippers guard was unhappy with the way Lauren Holtkamp, currently a full-time female official in the NBA, called a play. In the 2014–2015 NBA season Lauren Holtkamp became a full-time NBA referee, becoming the third woman to ref NBA games full-time, joining Dee Kantner and Violet Palmer. In 1997 Violet Palmer was the first woman given an officiating assignment in the NBA. She officiated in the NBA until the 2014–2015 season. (Photo: AP Photo/Mark J. Terrill, File)

few newspapers, there are still relatively few women in the field. Women are also underrepresented as sports officials, judges, commissioners, athletic trainers, racehorse trainers, and most other sports-related occupations.

Fortunately, many barriers to women's involvement in sport leadership careers are falling, and it is becoming more difficult each year to keep women from fulfilling their sport career goals. Still, optimistic accounts of progress and equality serve to obscure long-term structural inequalities between men and women that are not only about gender but also about general social inequality.

Coaching and Administration/Management in U.S. Olympic Organizations

The Olympic organizations continue to be bastions of male dominance. There are hundreds of coaches with the U.S. Olympic teams, and the fluid movement into and out of those positions makes it difficult to determine the percentage of men and women with any accuracy. One generalization is possible, however: the overwhelming majority of coaches are men. Men coach all of the men's U.S. Olympic teams, and men coach many of the women's teams as well. Where the head coach of a women's team is a woman, there are often men holding positions as assistant, or special position, coaches.

Board of director positions with the U.S. Olympic Committee are predominantly male too. In 2021, eight (44 percent) of the eighteen members of the U.S. Olympic Committee were female. Of the fifteen members of the International Olympic Committee's (IOC) Board of Directors in 2021, only five are women, representing 33 percent.

Reasons for the Persistence of Men in Coaching and Administering Women's Sports

Considerable speculation has centered on why girls' and women's sports coaching and administration have been dominated by men. Some have suggested that higher salaries are attracting men into coaching and administration careers; others have suggested that men have greater access to the hiring system through an "old boys" network. A woman who is the director of membership engagement for the National Association of Collegiate Women Athletics identifies one of the most likely reasons; she said, "It goes back to a long history. The people in these positions, which are predominantly white males, have built a system. Those men who have built this system know people, and the people they know are the ones who get these jobs."[46] Others contend that when men and women apply for coaching and/or administering women's sports jobs, men are perceived to be better qualified because sport has traditionally been a male domain. This is a prototypical gender assumption, that men are somehow more qualified to lead sports organizations. Drawing on sociologist Pierre Bourdieu's ideas (see Chapter 5) about capital reproduction, we can see that having certain types of sporting social networks and cultural capital enhances one's chances to be promoted. This facilitation of men's advancement is illustrated in the study mentioned earlier in this chapter: the Global Sports Matter research on hiring practices and qualifications found that the majority of women applicants had more athletic experience and more education than the men who were hired.

However, there are those who maintain that the changing social and occupational conditions for women in the past twenty years have enabled women to have a much greater menu from which to choose a career. They argue that women who have the drive, determination, self-confidence, and intelligence to make good coaches and sports administrators also now have the option to become physicians, lawyers, and business leaders. These positions often pay better than coaching or administering sports programs, especially when women's salaries for coaching and sports administration lag behind men's in those positions.

For these and other reasons, more job opportunities in women's sport are left open to male applicants. In a recent study, to ascertain why more than 120 female former college coaches had withdrawn from coaching, the investigator found that in addition to gender discrimination, homophobia, and the centrality of male coaches, "conflict between working as a coach and motherhood, or women with children as being 'distracted' by motherhood . . . revealed that women have multiple, complex, and overlapping reasons for leaving collegiate coaching."[47]

WOMEN ATHLETES' CAREERS AT THE PROFESSIONAL AND OLYMPIC LEVELS OF SPORT

As one might expect, opportunities for women to engage in sports at the highest levels have been severely restricted historically, and differential rewards have been the norm. However, progress has been made toward expanding opportunities for females in top levels of sport during the past two decades. The most popular professional sports for women have traditionally been individual sports, especially golf and tennis, because they have traditionally been "socially approved" sports for women, particularly by the affluent social classes.

Professional women's team sports have been less successful in their struggle for acceptance. Some examples are listed here. As you read the list, use the sociological perspective we introduced in Chapter 1 to try to understand why some efforts to form stable women's professional sport organizations have succeeded, whereas others failed.

- *Tennis*: Currently, there are some 2,500 women representing more than ninety nations on the Women's Tennis Association Tour. They are competing for more than $50 million in prize money at the tour's events and grand slams. The top five to ten women on the pro tennis circuit typically win about half as much prize money as the men on its Association of Tennis Professionals World Tour. However, men's and women's championship prize monies are the same at the U.S. Open, French Open, Wimbledon, and Australian tennis tournaments.

- *Golf*: Founded in 1950, the LPGA currently has more than 260 players on the LPGA tour. In 2016, the top 5 female money leaders earned an average of about one-half of the amount that the top 5 male money leaders earned. A report noted that the average take-home pay (after expenses) for a PGA player was approximately $1,300,00 compared to the LPGA player at $183,000.[48]

- *Baseball*: As far back as World War II, there was a women's professional baseball—yes, baseball—league. It remained a viable league until 1954. Several efforts have been made to establish professional baseball for women, but all have been short-lived.

- *Softball*: The Women's Professional Softball League was formed in the mid-1970s but was disbanded after four years. As in baseball, several unsuccessful attempts have been made to establish a stable women's professional softball league. In 1997 the Women's Pro Softball League was formed, but it folded in 2001. In 2004 the Women's Pro Softball League was revived under the name National Pro Fastpitch League but had to suspend activities indefinitely after canceling two seasons due to COVID-19.

- *Volleyball*: Women's professional volleyball has had a number of leagues and several formats during the past twenty-five years. Some of the leagues were mixed gender, some have been indoor, and some have been outdoor. But there has been little stability in any of them. The Association of Volleyball Professionals beach volleyball tour is the nation's most prominent professional volleyball tour. It features more than 150 of the top beach volleyball players in the world. In 2021, a player-run pro sport league, Athletes Unlimited, partnered with USA Volleyball to launch a pro indoor women's league in the United States.

- *Basketball*: Between the mid-1970s and mid-1990s several attempts were made to make a go of women's professional basketball in the United States. All of those efforts ultimately failed. Then, in the mid-1990s, two professional leagues began play: the American Basketball League and the WNBA. The former lasted a little less than three years before going out of business. Meanwhile, the WNBA has flourished, having grown to a thirteen-team league by 2011. Despite its seeming success, its financial viability is heavily dependent on the financial backing, marketing, and promotions of the NBA. The structure of WNBA players' salaries is paltry—compared to NBA salaries. In 2021 the average salary was about $100,500, whereas in the same year the average NBA salary was $7.7 million, with thirty teams in the NBA, more than twice the number of WNBA teams. Another notable feature of the WNBA is the diversity of its players. During the 2021 season, 19.5 percent of players were white and 74.5 percent were African American. In 2021, five of the twelve head coaches were African American and five of the head coaches were women.[49]

- *Soccer*: When American women won the Women's World Cup in 1999, interest in women's soccer skyrocketed. Women's soccer organizations immediately began talking about forming a women's professional soccer league. But the reality of having to raise a minimum of $30 to $50 million to get even a modest league off the ground stalled the formation of a league. It was not until the spring of 2001 that the Women's United Soccer Association launched its inaugural season of play, but within a year it failed. A new league, Women's Professional Soccer (WPS), began playing in the spring of 2009. The WPS was composed of six teams during the 2011 season, based solely on the East Coast. About 25 percent of WPS players were from outside the United States, and virtually the entire world is represented among these players. The WPS folded in 2012 and a new league started in 2013, called the National Women's Soccer

League, which is spread throughout the United States, with twelve teams currently in operation. Again, the stunning play of the U.S. women's national soccer team at the Women's World Cup in 2015 and 2019 in winning the championship triggered a renewed enthusiasm for women's soccer in the United States. According to the Sports and Fitness Industry Association, there are more than 5 million females playing organized soccer in the United States, nearly 70 percent of whom are under the age of seventeen.

- *Football*: There have been several unsuccessful efforts to develop a viable women's football league. The Women's Professional Football League "kicked off" in the fall of 2000 with eleven teams; fifteen teams competed in the league during the 2006 season. Within the past few years, the United States Women's Football League has attempted to form a stable women's football organization, with little success. The Independent Women's Football League has managed to remain solvent from 2000 to 2018, when it was founded by a group of players dedicated to providing women's tackle football teams that play at the top competition tier of their sport. The most current and viable iteration is the Women's Football Alliance, which is also a nonprofit organization. It started in 2009 and played national championships in 2021. Money problems forced the earlier leagues to fold, and the newest league seems saddled with the same problems. None of the athletes earns enough money to make a living, so the league is more like

The Women's World Cup is the most important international competition in women's soccer (football). The first Women's World Cup tournament was held in 1991, sixty-one years after the men's first FIFA World Cup tournament in 1930. The United States won the Women's World Cup in 1991, 1999, 2015, and 2019. (Photo: AP Photo/Patrick Semansky)

"semi-pro" operation than a full-blown professional one.

- *Foreign professional sports*: Opportunities to play on foreign teams in Europe and Asia have opened up for women in several team sports, and more than 300 American female athletes currently participate in foreign leagues. Top players can earn good salaries. For example, two-thirds of the WNBA's players spend the off-season playing in basketball leagues in foreign countries, where salaries range from $250,000 to $1 million.

- *Other professional sports*: Professional opportunities in sports are continuing to diversify for women. Professional ice skating has provided a chance for a few skaters to make high salaries, and more than one hundred women are doing well as jockeys in thoroughbred horse racing. A few female track-and-field athletes, distance runners, triathletes, and race car drivers are making six-figure salaries.

The reality is that except for a few hundred female professional athletes, few women make a living in pro sports (see Table 7.2), and with the current social and economic conditions for female professional athletes, the day when more than a handful of women can make sports a full-time job is far away.

TABLE 7.2 2020–2021 PROFESSIONAL ATHLETES' AVERAGE ANNUAL SALARIES OR EVENT PURSES (IN U.S. DOLLARS)

Sport	Men	Sport	Women
NBA (basketball)	$7.7 million	WNBA	$100,500
MLS (soccer)	$400,000	NWSL	$22,000–$52,500 (range)
MLB (baseball)	$3.89 million	National Pro Fastpitch	$6,250
U.S. Open Golf	$2.25 million		$1 million
British Open Golf	$2.07 million		$1 million
NYC Marathon	$100,000		$100,000
Boston Marathon	$150,000		$150,000

Female Olympic Athletes

Gender inequality has prevailed in the Olympic Games since the modern Games began in 1896. The quotes by the founder of the modern Olympics, Pierre de Coubertin, in an earlier section of this chapter make clear his belief that females did not belong. However, despite de Coubertin's belief, which was shared by many of his cohorts, sports events for females have gradually been added to both the Summer and the Winter Olympic Games over the past one hundred years.[50] Yet substantial gender inequities remain. For example, in the 2004 Athens Summer Olympic Games, among the more than 120 women's events and more than 170 men's events (about a dozen were mixed), 41 percent of the total participants were women and 59 percent were men. Thus, although there were more women's events than ever before, the gap between the number of men's and women's events narrowed to an all-time low. More recently, women comprised more than 40 percent of the approximately 10,500 athletes at the 2012 London Olympic Games, roughly the same percentage of women who participated in the 2010 Winter Games in Vancouver. For the first time, all 200-plus participating nations had female athletes. Also, for the first time, the U.S. team had more women than men. The Summer 2020 Games (which were delayed because of the COVID-19 pandemic, taking place in 2021 in Tokyo) were purported to have 49 percent women athletes. This captures the sea change occurring across the global sports landscape.

Along with the increase in female competitors, new opportunities are opening up for women in the Olympics. In 2000 and 2004, several new sports and more than twenty new events for women were added to the Summer Olympic Games. In 2008, in Beijing, women competed in the same number of sports as in 2004 (26), but in two more events (137). For the 2012 London Summer Olympics, the IOC voted to include women's boxing. New women's sports events have been added to recent Winter Olympic Games, such that the percentage of female athletes participating rose from 27 percent at the 1992 Winter Olympics in Albertville to 40.4 percent at the 2014 Sochi Winter Olympics (see Figure 7.2).[51]

Although professional women athletes' opportunities have increased, their average salary is still significantly less than men's. (See Table 7.2) (Photo: AP Photo/Patrick Semansky)

But even as the percentage of women has been increasing in every Olympiad for the past fifty years, there are wide variations in the percentage of women representing each country at every Olympic Games.

The U.S. Olympic Committee and their many sport federations provide various kinds of subsidies to Olympic athletes—from training expenses to grants of money. Some members of U.S. women's teams, as well as female athletes in individual sports, have been paid more than $50,000 annually while they were preparing for the next Olympic Games. This practice was first adopted for male Olympians, but widespread objections to male-only subsidies resulted in opening them up to women.

Gender Equality in Sport?

We have demonstrated that gender inequality has been the social cultural norm in sport since organized sports became a popular social practice. It was pervasive at all age levels, from youth to professional to Olympic, but over the past forty years, sports involvement for females has witnessed an extraordinary increase, largely boosted by legal requirements—such as Title IX in the United States—but also by a social acknowledgment of gender equality in all social institutions in the United States.

We now turn to the second major section of this chapter, which focuses on gender identity and sexual orientation.

SPORT, GENDER IDENTITY, AND SEXUAL ORIENTATION

In an article titled "Infinite Identities" in the March 2017 issue of *Time* magazine, the author synthesizes and summarizes research by the LGBTQ advocacy

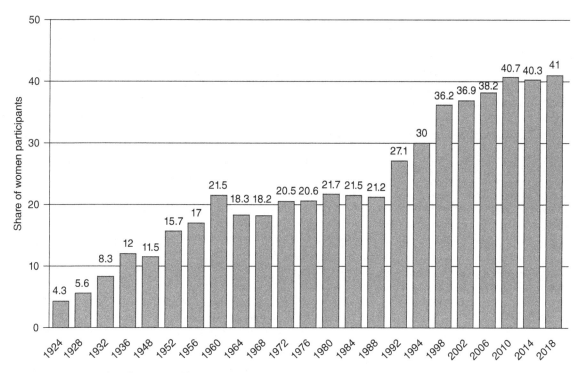

FIGURE 7.2   Percentage of Women Athletes Competing in Winter Olympic Games

organization GLAAD as well as several scholarly journals devoted to gender issues. Based on these sources, the *Time* author declares that an increasing number of young people are thinking beyond the idea that when it comes to gender and sexuality there are only two options for each—male or female, gay or straight—but about 20 percent of millennials identify as something other than strictly straight and cisgender (one whose gender is in line with the sex they were assigned at birth). In contrast, only 7 percent of boomers identify similarly.[52] Even though younger generations are more comfortable identifying within the LGBQT community, it does not translate into widespread acceptance.[53]

In a 2017 Harris Poll, some three-fourths of over 2,000 respondents believed that it feels like "more people than ever" have "nontraditional" sexual orientations and gender identities. It is clear that various expressions of gender and sexuality are progressively moving from the margins to the mainstream. Facebook now has about sixty options for users' gender,

and there are more than 200 regular or reoccurring LGBTQ characters on cable TV and streaming series.[54]

We will briefly review some key terms that we introduced earlier in this chapter. First, a person's sex is not a binary of either male or female. Instead, one's sex is more complex, as illustrated by those who are identified as *intersex*, meaning they are born with either ambiguous sex traits or both male and female biological traits. Sexual orientation is the direction of one's sexual interest toward other people. Finally, the term *gender identity* is distinct from the term *sexual orientation* and refers to a person's innate, deeply felt psychological identification as a man, woman, or some other gender, which may or may not correspond to the sex assigned to them at birth, such as the sex listed on their birth certificate. In these cases, the acronym LGBTQ has come into popular usage, standing for gay, lesbian, bisexual, transgender, and queer.[55]

Although we have focused on the gender minorities in this chapter, women and LGBQT, it is important to reiterate the central role sport has played in the social construction of masculinity. In doing this we show how traditional gender-role prescriptions have perpetuated problems for both females and males involved in sports, especially for those whose sexual orientation or gender identity does not conform to society's norms (see Box 7.3 for a discussion of trans and nonbinary athletes).

There are social sanctions against active females that are closely linked to the "sport masculinizes females" argument that we described previously and that constitute a charge about female athletes and

---

BOX 7.3 *THINKING ABOUT SPORT*: TRANS AND NONBINARY ATHLETES CHALLENGING THE BINARY STRUCTURE OF SPORT

The relationship of gender and sport is profound and well established. Throughout the modern era sport has been widely used to "discipline" sporting bodies into culturally appropriate masculinity and femininity. In turn, masculinity has been linked to athleticism and seen as an appropriate cultural activity for boys and men to express themselves (see Chapter 2 for more details on this). Additionally, sport has been organized around the notion that sex is a binary (which is no longer an accepted biological fact). Thus, when women were formally allowed and encouraged to participate in sport, it was nearly always in gender, segregated sport. Many have noted this sex segregation is to create more equitable competition because adult male bodies tend to have a physical advantage. On average, men are taller, have higher muscle mass, and have denser bones than women. Yet, when similar (but separate) sports are played, there has been a history of creating different rules for women that mark their bodies as less competent. For example, we can see this in the history of basketball. For women, the court was divided into three sections. Players could not leave their designated section, the players were only allowed three dribbles, and they were not allowed to have physical contact (not to mention their uniforms often consisted of a long skirt). Today, there are different standards in tennis, golf, and gymnastics that mark women's bodies as "weaker." In short, sport has been organized around patriarchal norms, which reinforces "common-sense" notions about sex, gender, and the value of different bodies' capacities.

As more people express their gender identity in a variety of ways, it challenges the binary assumptions about sex and gender and complicates how we think about sport. Trans identities are most commonly explained as a disconnect between the sex one is assigned at birth and one's personal gender identity. Thus, in the example of a child who was born and identified by a doctor as a boy, a trans person would have a sex identity that does not align neatly to "male." Trans identities are not tethered to one's physical body and often represent nonbinary notions of gender. Some trans folks want and undergo gender-affirming surgery. There are also people who identify as nonbinary, which has a variety of specific meanings for each individual, but generally comprises the notion that one does not identify completely as either a man or a woman.

Trans folks have requested participating in sport that matches their gender identity. Currently, there is substantial debate about the inclusion of trans folks in sport. In particular, two issues stand out. First, for those who have gender-affirming surgery, there is concern that trans women will have an unfair advantage competing with other women since they were born with male characteristics. There is very little concern about the fairness of trans men competing with other men. This reinforces the notion that men are always better athletes than women. We know that many factors are important in determining athletic prowess and that within each sex category there is a wide range of body types. Those who compete at the highest level are, by definition, outside the normal curve on physiological characteristics. Take Michael Phelps, one of the most decorated swimmers. There is no doubt he trained hard and has impeccable technique, but his anatomy and physiology have also been discussed as giving him an advantage. For example, it is purported that he produces half the lactic acid of his competitors.

Most international sport organizations and national governing bodies have policies in place for determining when a trans person can compete in their chosen gender category. As of June 16, 2021, the U.S. Department of Education's Office for Civil Rights expanded interpretation of Title IX applies to transgender people. The second issue is for trans folks who do not have surgery. Their gender identity may not fall neatly into either category and, therefore, they have few options to participate in organized sport. According to a systematic review of whether transgender people have an advantage in sport, several sport medicine researchers concluded, "Currently, there is no direct or consistent research suggesting transgender female individuals (or male individuals) have an athletic advantage at any stage of their transition (e.g. cross-sex hormones, gender-confirming surgery) and, therefore, competitive sport policies that place restrictions on transgender people need to be considered and potentially revised."

As sport organizations work to create policies for trans athletes, there is still more work to be done for nonbinary athletes. One recent example of athletes butting up against the binary structure of sport is Layshia Clarendon of the WNBA. Clarendon is openly trans and nonbinary (Layshia uses the pronouns she/he/they). Clarendon has acknowledged the strain of being nonbinary and not fitting in: "Right now, you either fit in or you get lost. Like, you meet the NCAA or IOC

(continued)

(continued)

standards that make you eligible to play on the men's or women's side, or you don't. Or you transition and you get lost, forced to move on with your life."

Some scholars and practitioners have been working on ways to create trans- and nonbinary-inclusive sport. These efforts are grounded in the evidence that participation in physical activity and sport has many physical and mental health benefits. Are there different ways for organizing sport besides a gender binary? Do we use weight and height categories? Do we develop gender-inclusive sports? It will be important to listen to the voices of those who have been historically left out in order to develop a sustainable practice.

Sources: Jamie Schultz, *Qualifying Times* (2014) Champaign Urbana, IL: University of Illinois Press; Catherine Phipps, "Thinking beyond the Binary: Barriers to Trans* Participation in University Sport," *International Review for the Sociology of Sport* 56, no. 1 (2021): 81–96; Madeleine Pape, "Ignorance and the Gender Binary: Resisting Complex Epistemologies of Sex and Testosterone," in *Sports, Society, and Technology*, ed. J. Sterling and M. McDonald (Singapore: Palgrave Macmillan, 2020), https://doi.org/10.1007/978-981-32-9127-0_10; Janet S. Hyde, Rebecca S. Bigler, Daphna Joel, Charlotte C. Tate, and Sari M. van Anders, "The Future of Sex and Gender in Psychology: Five Challenges to the Gender Binary," *American Psychologist* 74, no. 2 (2019): 171–193, http://dx.doi.org/10.1037/amp0000307; Bethany Alice Jones, Jon Arcelus, Walter Pierre Bouman, and Emma Haycraft, "Sport and Transgender People: A Systematic Review of the Literature Relating to Sport Participation and Competitive Sport Policies, *Sports Medicine* 47 (2017): 701–716, quote is on page 701, https://doi.org/10.1007/s40279-016-0621-y; Britini De La Cretaz, "Living Nonbinary in a Binary Sports World," *Sports Illustrated*, April 16, 2021, https://www.si.com/wnba/2021/04/16/nonbinary-athletes-transgender-layshia-clarendon-quinn-rach-mcbride-daily-cover.

their sexuality. Two interrelated arguments fuel the supposed connections between sports and lesbianism. One is that there is a profusion of women athletes who are lesbians. The second is that sports participation converts females to lesbianism. Although there is no scientific evidence for the perpetuation of these myths, it has had the effect of producing homophobic (meaning dislike and intolerance of homosexuals) claims about rampant lesbianism among female athletes. Given the widespread homophobic public attitudes that prevail in the United States, this charge has had ominous consequences for females who might wish to become involved in sports and for those who are involved in sports. It has certainly had a profoundly stigmatizing effect on them.

The claims about sport's presumed "masculinizing" and "lesbianizing" of females have been vigorously attacked by a broad spectrum of scholars and scientists who have exposed the ideological foundations of these arguments. They have emphasized that definitions of feminine and masculine behavior are culturally constructed—that they are not natural, biological characteristics at all. Moreover, they emphasize that sexual orientation is irrelevant with regard to sport participation, and there are heterosexual, bisexual, as well as homosexual males and females in sport just as there are in every other sector of social life.

Martina Navratilova, one of the greatest tennis players of all time, was the first well-known female athlete to openly acknowledge she was a lesbian. Since then, a number of other top women athletes have done likewise. In the fall of 2005, WNBA star Sheryl Swoopes publicly announced that she was lesbian. In a *Sports Illustrated* interview with Swoopes, she was asked whether the public's reaction was what she expected. Swoopes replied that the support she had gotten had been phenomenal and that on the first five road trips after her announcement there were standing ovations when she was introduced, and not just from lesbians and gay men. Currently, there are many athletes who are publicly acknowledging their lesbian or queer identities, including soccer players Megan Rapinoe and Kelly O'Hara; basketball players Sue Bird, Brittney Griner, and Diana Taurasi; and track-and-field athletes Erica Bougard and Raven Saunders.[56] Swoopes and other women athletes maintain that contemporary women are no longer willing to have traditional definitions of masculine/feminine and sexuality imposed on them, especially when such definitions prevent females from experiencing highly valued social activities.[57]

It is now clear that the presumptions that women become masculinized and that their sexual orientation is influenced by sports participation have served as social weapons to reinforce cultural traditions of male privilege and female subordination, but they are now widely rejected. Indeed, some women have completely repudiated the traditional definitions that identify muscles with masculinity and homosexuality, and such sports as bodybuilding, weightlifting, and boxing are growing rapidly among sportswomen. Women bodybuilders and weightlifters are judged much like male bodybuilders and weightlifters. Furthermore, their sexuality is no more important than is men's.[58]

Of course, there are females in sports who are lesbians, just as there are homosexuals in every other walk of life. They suffer many of the social troubles that all LGBTQ individuals live with. These include a sense of isolation, feelings of loneliness, fear of being outed, and, if they do come out, prejudice and discrimination among friends and family. Despite pervasive homophobia within sport and the wider society, LGBTQs in increasing numbers are deciding to come out and live their sexual orientation openly and with pride in the honesty of their decision.[59] The 2020 Summer Olympics (held in 2021 in Tokyo) was called the "queerest" ever because over 180 athletes openly acknowledged that their identities were under the LGBTQ umbrella.[60]

Sport is one way in which feminist cultural politics are being employed as a form of organized opposition to the domination of men in sport through empowering women from diverse backgrounds. It may be seen, then, that contemporary women refuse to be locked into outmoded role prescriptions and baseless assertions, especially those that limit their physical potential.

At the same time that various social barriers have discouraged females from sport involvement to preserve their feminine identity, males have been socialized into attitudes, values, and behaviors in which sport plays a dominant role in shaping their masculine identities. Sport has been the cultural activity that makes it seem natural to equate masculinity with competition, physicality, aggressiveness, movement skills, and physical achievements. Two of the best-known slogans that reinforce this are "Sports make men out of boys" and "Sport builds character."

The competitive structures of the sports world socialize young boys into the exciting world of physical skills, tactics, and strategy in the pursuit of victory, but they also introduce them to the structured world of autocratic leadership, hierarchical organization, bureaucratic relations, and homophobia. That is how the current institution of sport is organized at every level.

Sports teams are commanded by strong, forceful male coaches, whose word is taken as incontestable. Sports rules and coaches' orders are understood to be followed without question. Athletes are expected to sacrifice their individual interests, skills, and goals for the benefit of the team. Personal relations are structured around competition against teammates for positions on the team, as well as competition against opponents. Although friendships and feelings of connection often develop among teammates, these are not deliberately structured in sport organizations. Instead, what develops from an interpersonal connectedness standpoint is a conditional self-worth, meaning masculine identity and personal value are dependent on one's individual achievements.

Along with other attitudes and values boys acquire through their sport experiences, they learn about masculine sexuality. One of the most profound things they learn about masculine sexuality through the sport culture is that to be homosexual, or even to be suspected of it, is unacceptable. Males who have been uninterested in sport or unwilling to allow dominant gender definitions of masculinity to force them into sport or into "appropriate" masculine attitudes, values, and behaviors have often faced gender bigotry from both males and females. They have been the butt of jokes about their "effeminacy," and they have been labeled "fags," "queers," and "fairies." Many times they have been physically abused in various ways. Thus, gender inequality and injustice have been directed at males who for one reason or another do not conform to dominant cultural definitions of masculinity.[61]

Although there is growing evidence that gay athletes have competed, and continue to compete, at all levels of sport, mostly closeted, the sports world has remained predominantly homophobic. Only a handful of male collegiate and professional athletes have come out, and until recently all of them were retired when they made their sexual orientation public. In 2007, on ESPN's *Outside the Lines*, former NBA player John Amaechi came out as gay shortly after retiring. Amaechi followed up the announcement with a memoir titled *Man in the*

Middle. In reaction to Amaechi's announcement, NBA superstar LeBron James stated that an openly gay person could not survive in the NBA. James went on to say, "With teammates you have to be trustworthy, and if you're gay and you're not admitting that then you are not trustworthy." More directly homophobic attitudes still exists; in 2017 former NBA player Amar'e Stoudemire commented that he would "shower across the street" if he learned a teammate was gay."[62]

Despite homophobic attitudes and behavior toward gays, the 2016 version of the Pew Research Center's survey of attitudes about homosexuality documented an increase in public acceptance of gay relations between 2007 and 2016, finding that 63 percent of Americans in 2016 supported the proposition that homosexuality should be accepted by society. In 2007, the same proposition only garnered 49 percent support. By 2017, Katie Sowers exemplified an unusual social acceptance for women in coaching professional sports—she was a San Francisco 49ers assistant coach—and she has publicly acknowledged being openly LGBTQ, becoming the first openly LGBTQ coach—male or female.[63] (See also Box 7.4.).

Confirming constitutional support for equitable homosexuals' public interests, in June 2015 the U.S Supreme Court handed down a ruling regarding same-sex marriage. The high court ruled that same-sex couples have the right to marry in all fifty states.[64] Although the broader issue of LGBTQ is still a source of controversy, there is increasing support for giving

---

BOX 7.4 *THINKING ABOUT SPORT:* MALE ATHLETES CHIPPING AWAY AT THE HOMOPHOBIC WALL

With few exceptions, gay male athletes have remained closeted, but a new era in "coming out" for male athletes emerged beginning in 2013, when a veteran but still-active player in the NBA publicly announced he was gay. The overwhelming social force keeping gay male athletes closeted has been the stigma associated with same-sex sexual attraction because it is contrary to the societal norm of compulsory heterosexuality. This widely held belief assumes that same-sex eroticism is aberrant behavior and thus deviant. In the past, this meant shame for a gay athlete, ostracism by peers and family, and the strong propensity to hide their sexual feelings from public view. Exacerbating this closeting of gays is the homophobic culture of the athletic world. There is the typical male locker room climate, where homophobic slurs are common and suspected gays are bullied. Within the world of sport, gay men are much less likely than women to be public about their gay, bi, or queer sexuality.

A common motivational ploy by some coaches is to question a male athlete's heterosexuality if they feel he is too passive. Another important sports-related factor that keeps gays closeted is the difficulty in attaining one of the few playing slots in such a fiercely competitive activity/occupation. At the professional level, there are 3,436 jobs available in the four major sports. Coming out reduces one's chances of making the final roster in this dog-eat-dog contested terrain because owners, general managers, and coaches are likely to avoid situations that they believe might lead to distractions that will negatively impact team unity.

Although various manifestations of homophobia remain in society and the sports world, the past several years have been a pivotal time as the acceptance of gay athletes increased and, for the first time, some broke the barrier by publicly acknowledging their sexuality while they were still active athletes. Notable active gay athletes breaking down the walls of homophobia in those years include the following:

- Carl Nassib became the first active NFL player to publicly announce his sexual identity. He played for the Las Vegas Raiders.
- Jason Collins, the first openly gay NBA player, stated in a 2013 *Sports Illustrated* article, "I'm a 34-year-old NBA center. I'm black. And I'm gay." About his announcement, Collins said, "I want to do the right thing and not hide anymore. I want to march for tolerance, acceptance and understanding. I want to take a stand and say, 'Me, too.'"
- Robbie Rogers of the Los Angeles Galaxy became the first openly gay professional soccer player.
- Orlando Cruz, a top-ranked featherweight, was the first active professional boxer to declare publicly that he was gay.
- Derrick Gordon, a starter on the University of Massachusetts men's basketball team, became the first openly gay male NCAA Division I basketball player.

Given all of the reasons for male athletes to stay in the closet, what factors converged to start the breaking down of the sexual orientation barriers in sport? Several lesbian athletes have come out since the 1980s. More recently, former male gay athletes became open about their sexual orientation after their playing days. Support also came from the NFL collective bargaining agreement in 2011, which stated for the first time, "There will be no discrimination in any form against any player by the Management Council, any Club or by the NFL Players Association (NFLPA) because of race, religion, national origin,

(continued)

(continued)

sexual orientation, or activity or lack of activity on behalf of the NFLPA."

Most significant, sport as a microcosm of society is in tune with changing public opinion about gay rights. The majority of Americans now favor gay marriage. Young people, and today's athletes who are young people, are more accepting than older cohorts of differences in sexual orientation. Popular movies and television shows portray gays and lesbians favorably. Many nonathlete celebrities are open about their sexual preferences. And more and more people outside the sports world are coming out to their families, peers, and fellow workers without repercussions. Nonetheless, in our broader society many social issues are contentious and, thus, it is important to note that

there are special interest groups and some state legislatures that are currently challenging the rights of LGBTQ folks.

These societal trends made it easier (but still difficult) for gay athletes to acknowledge their sexuality publicly. As Dave Zirin has put it, "Every time a top athlete comes out of the closet, it chips away at one of the foundations of homophobia."

Sources: Jason Collins, with Franz Lidz, "I'm a 34-Year-Old NBA Center. I'm Black. And I'm Gay," *Sports Illustrated*, May 6, 2013, 34–41; see also Dave Zirin, "Knocking Out Homophobia," *The Progressive* 66 (December 2012/January 2013): 66; Jason Collins, "Why NBA Center Jason Collins Is Coming Out Now," *Sports Illustrated*, May 13, 2013, 15–16.

members of the LGBTQ community the same legal rights that other citizens enjoy. Homophobia has not disappeared, but a growing sense of social humanitarianism has weakened it.[65]

One of the outcomes of the gay/lesbian liberation movement has been the founding of sport organizations by and for gays and lesbians. LGBTQ sports clubs are now found in most major cities of the United States; also, a wide variety of LGBTQ sports, fitness, and recreational organizations—camping groups, bicycling tours, skiing, hiking, canoeing, and so forth—are popular in urban areas. Gay-governed organizations have developed in a variety of sports; they include the International Gay and Lesbian Aquatics Association, the Gay and Lesbian Hockey Association, and the International Gay Bowling Association.

The most prestigious gay sport organization, and event, is the Federation of Gay Games, which governs the Gay Games. The first Gay Games were founded by a former Olympic decathlete, Tom Waddell, and held in 1982 in San Francisco. The Gay Games are held every four years as a celebration of the international gay community. Athletes and teams compete in a variety of sports, and many of the routines and ceremonies are patterned after the International Olympic Games.[66]

SUMMARY

In this chapter we have examined the social bases for the gender inequality and injustice that have traditionally confronted females in sport, the consequences

of the processes, and the developments in this topic. Gender inequality and injustice against females in sport have taken many forms. First, a number of myths about the biological and psychological effects on women of competitive sports effectively discouraged their participation. Second, unequal opportunity for participation in sports existed for a long time. Finally, women had unequal access to the authority and power structure of sport. Patriarchal ideology was employed to socialize females out of sports and to deny them equal access to its rewards.

Title IX has been the most important factor in the lessening of gender inequality in the United States. It has had the effect of opening up opportunities in sport organizations beyond just public education. It has been an essential civil rights force for female sports. Without Title IX, it is improbable that females would have the sports opportunities in schools and colleges currently available.

Making discrimination illegal does not eliminate it, however, as previous experiences with civil rights legislation so clearly illustrate. Socially conditioned attitudes are slow to change. In some individual cases, they cannot be changed. Stereotypes are persistent and feed on the examples that confirm them. Nevertheless, attitudes and behaviors have changed in remarkably significant ways in response to challenges and demands as well as federal legislation.

Gender inequality and injustice involve males as well as females. Traditional masculine identity is closely bound with sport culture, and males who do not conform to the social prescriptions face a variety of negative social sanctions.

Learn more with this chapter's digital tools, including web resources, video links, and chapter self-assessment quizzes at www.oup.com/he/sage-eitzen-beal-atencio-12e.

NOTES

1. Lois Nam, "Seahawks' Michael Bennett Is an Activist Disguised as a Football Player," *The Undefeated*, September 2017, http://theundefeated.com/features/seahawks-michael-bennett-is-an-activist-disguised-as-a-football-player/.

2. For a more detailed discussion of this topic, see Maxine Baca Zinn, Pierrette Hondagneu-Sotelo, Michael A Messner, and Amy M. Denissen, eds., *Gender through the Prism of Difference*, 6th ed. (New York: Oxford University Press, 2019); and Hilary Lips, *Gender: The Basics*, 2nd ed. (New York: Routledge, 2019).

3. See Rebecca M. Jordan-Young and Katrina Karkazis, *Testosterone: An Unauthorized Biography* (Boston: Harvard University Press, 2019).

4. Jaime Schultz, *Qualifying Times: Points of Change in U.S. Women's Sport* (Champaign: University of Illinois Press, 2014); see also Jean O'Reilly and Susan K Cahn, eds., *Women and Sports in the United States: A Documentary Reader* (Boston: Northeastern University Press, 2007), pt. 1.

5. Jon Sterngass, "Cheating, Gender Roles, and the Nineteenth-Century Croquet Craze," in *Sport in America*, Vol. 2, *From Colonial Leisure to Celebrity Figures and Globalization*, 2nd ed., ed. David K Wiggins (Champaign, IL: Human Kinetics, 2010), 85–104.

6. Bil Gilbert and Nancy Williamson, "Sport Is Unfair to Women," *Sports Illustrated*, May 28, 1973, 90.

7. Gilbert and Williamson, "Sport Is Unfair to Women"; see also Betsy Ross, *Play Ball with the Boys: The Rise of Women in the World of Men's Sports* (Cincinnati: Clerisy Press, 2010).

8. Margaret Andersen and Dana Hysock Witham, *Thinking About Women*, 11th ed. (Boston: Pearson, 2020); see also Martin N. Marger, *Social Inequality: Patterns and Processes*, 6th ed. (New York: McGraw–Hill, 2013).

9. Andersen and Witham, *Thinking About Women*.

10. Travis E. Dorsch, Emily Wright, Valerie C. Eckardt, Sam Elliott, Sam N. Thrower, and Camilla J. Knight, "A History of Parent Involvement in Organized Youth Sport: A Scoping Review," *Sport, Exercise, and Performance Psychology* 10, no. 4 (2021): 536–557, https://doi.org/10.1037/spy0000266.

11. Swapna Venugopal Ramaswamy, "School Superintendents Are Overwhelmingly Male. What's Holding Women Back from the Top Job?" *USA Today*, February 20, 2020, https://www.usatoday.com/story/news/education/2020/02/20/female-school-district-superintendents-westchester-rockland/4798754002/; and National Center for Education Statistics, "Characteristics of Public School Teachers," May 2021, https://nces.ed.gov/programs/coe/indicator/clr.

12. See Lauren Camera, "How Children around the World Learn to Be Sexist: Gender Bias Is Rampant in Textbooks in Multiple Countries, Researchers Argue," *U.S. News and World Report*, March 6, 2016, https://www.usnews.com/news/articles/2016-03-08/sexism-in-textbooks-a-worldwide-problem.

13. See Victoria Cooper and Naomi Holford, *Exploring Childhood and Youth* (London: Routledge, 2020).

14. Kate Harmon, "Jumping through Hoops; A Post-Structural Gender Critique of Magazine Covers Depicting Female Athletes," in *Sportswomen's Apparel in the United States: Uniformly Discussed*, ed. L K Fuller (London: Palgrave Macmillan, 2021), 111–128.

15. D. Stanley Eitzen and Maxine Baca Zinn, "Language and Gender Inequality: Change and Continuity in the Naming of Collegiate Sports Teams," in *Sport in Contemporary Society: An Anthology*, 10th ed., ed. D. Stanley Eitzen (New York: Oxford University Press, 2015), 94–107; see also D. Stanley Eitzen, *Fair and Foul: Beyond the Myths and Paradoxes of Sport*, 6th ed. (Lanham, MD: Rowman & Littlefield, 2016), ch. 3.

16. Pierre de Coubertin, quoted in Sheila Mitchell, "Women's Participation in the Olympic Games, 1900–1926," *Journal of Sport History* 4 (Summer 1977): 211.

17. Quoted in Ellen Gerber, Jan Felshin, and Waneen Wyrick, *The American Woman in Sport* (Reading, MA: Addison–Wesley, 1974), 137–138.

18. Toni Bruce, "New Rules for New Times: Sportswomen and Media Representation in the Third

Wave," *Sex Roles* 74 (2016): 361–376, https://doi.org/10.1007/s11199-015-0497-6.

19. Nancy Theberge, *Higher Goals: Women's Ice Hockey and the Politics of Gender* (Albany: State University of New York Press, 2000), 113; see also Scott Rawdon and N. Stanley Nahman Jr., *Women's Rugby: Coaching and Playing the Collegiate Game* (Terre Haute, IN: Wish, 2005); and Lisa Taggart, *Women Who Win: Female Athletes on Being the Best* (Emeryville, CA: Seal Press, 2007).

20. Dudley A. Sargent, "Are Athletics Making Girls Masculine?" *Ladies Home Journal* 29 (1912): 72; and Ethel Perrin, "A Crisis in Girls Athletics," *Sportsmanship* 1 (December 1928): 10–12.

21. See Tyler Dupont and Becky Beal, eds., *Lifestyle Sports and Identities: Subcultural Careers through the Life Course* (London: Routledge, 2021); also Belinda Wheaton, "Staying 'Stoked': Surfing, Ageing and Post-youth Identities," *International Review for the Sociology of Sport* 54, no. 4 (2019): 387–409.

22. See Cheryl Cooky, "'Girls Just Aren't Interested': The Social Construction of Interest in Girls' Sport," *Sociological Perspectives* 52, no. 2 (2009): 259–284, for an illuminating discussion of how this assumption still impacts girls in sport.

23. Kimberly Elchlepp, "Women's Championships Cap Impressive Season of Growth across ESPN Networks with Women's College World Series," *ESPN*, June 14, 2021, https://espnpressroom.com/us/press-releases/2021/06/womens-championships-cap-impressive-season-of-growth-across-espn-networks-with-womens-college-world-series/.

24. Aspen Institute, *State of Play: Trends and Developments in Youth Sports*, 2019, https://www.aspeninstitute.org/wp-content/uploads/2019/10/2019_SOP_National_Final.pdf; and Allison Torres Burtka, "Girls Play Sports Less Than Boys, Miss Out on Crucial Benefits," Global Sport Matters, October 11, 2019, https://globalsportmatters.com/youth/2019/10/11/girls-play-sports-less-than-boys-miss-out-on-crucial-benefits/.

25. Deborah L. Brake, *Getting in the Game: Title IX and the Women's Sports Revolution* (New York: New York University Press, 2012); Linda Jean Carpenter and R. Vivian Acosta, *Title IX* (Champaign, IL: Human Kinetics, 2005).

26. Jim Halley, "By Default, Girl Wins in State Wrestling Meet," *USA Today*, February 18, 2011, 11C.

27. Rachel Jessen, "Photos: Why Is Girls' High School Wrestling on the Rise?" *ESPN*, April 12, 2019, https://www.espn.com/high-school/story/_/id/26438471/why-girls-high-school-wrestling-rise.

28. "High School Sports Participation Increases for 27th Consecutive Year," National Federation of State High School Associations, Athletics Participation Totals, September 12, 2016, https://www.nfhs.org/articles/high-school-sports-participation-increases-for-27th-consecutive-year/; see also Burtka, "Girls Play Sports Less Than Boys"; see also Cam Smith and Josh Barnett, "Girls Making Their Presence Felt on Gridiron," *USA Today*, December 23, 2016, 3C.

29. Smith and Barnett, "Girls Making Their Presence."

30. Brake, *Getting in the Game IX and the Women's Sports Revolution*; see also Pamela Grundy and Susan Shackelford, "The Fight for Title IX," in *Sport in America*, Vol. 2, *From Colonial Leisure to Celebrity Figures and Globalization*, ed. David K. Wiggins (Champaign, IL: Human Kinetics, 2010), 359–375; Kelly Belanger, *Invisible Seasons: Title IX and the Fight for Equity in College Sports* (Syracuse, NY: Syracuse University Press, 2017); Amanda L. Paule-Koba, Othello Harris, and Valeria J. Freysinger, "'What Do You Think About Title IX?,' Voices From a University Community," *Research Quarterly for Exercise and Sport* 84 (2013): 115–125.

31. U.S. Department of Education, Office for Civil Rights, *Intercollegiate Athletics Policy: Three-Part Test—Part Three*, last modified April 16, 2010, https://www2.ed.gov/about/offices/list/ocr/docs/title9-qa-20100420.html.

32. U.S. Department of Education, *Intercollegiate Athletics Policy*; for an example of one of the many court rulings about the three-part test, see Claire Darnell and Jeffrey Peterson, "Eliminating Sports for Title IX Compliance," *Journal of Physical Education, Recreation and Dance* 82 (February 2011): 9–10.

33. Jaclyn Diaz, "The NCAA's Focus on Profits Means Far More Gets Spent on Men's Championships," October 27, 2021, NPR.Org, https://www.npr.org/2021/10/27/1049530975/ncaa-spends-more-on-mens-sports-report-reveals

34. "NCAA Sports Sponsorship and Participation Rates Report," NCAA, January 6, 2022, https://ncaaorg.s3.amazonaws.com/research/sportpart/2021RES_SportsSponsorshipParticipationRatesReport.pdf.

35. NCAA, "NCAA Sports Sponsorship and Participation Rates Database," NCAA Research, December 1, 2022, https://www.ncaaorg/sports/2018/10/10/ncaa-sports-sponsorship-and-participation-rates-database.aspx.

36. Women's Sports Foundation, *50 Years of Title IX: We're Not Done Yet*, May 2022, https://www.womenssportsfoundation.org/wp-content/uploads/2022/05/13_Low-Res_Title-IX-50-Report.pdf, accessed June 16, 2022

37. Women's Sports Foundation, *50 Years of Title IX: We're Not Done Yet*.

38. Richard Lapchick, *The 2020 Racial and Gender Report Card: College Sport* (Orlando: University of Central Florida, 2020), https://43530132-36e9-4f52-811a-182c7a91933b.filesusr.com/ugd/8af738_3b5d1b6bdb10457ebe8d46cc5a2fcfd0.pdf.

39. NCAA, "NCAA Sports Sponsorship and Participation Rates Database," NCAA Research.

40. *Benchmarking Women's Leadership in the United States* (Denver: University of Denver–Colorado Women's College, 2013); see also Adrienne N. Milner and Jomills H. Braddock II, *Sex Segregation in Sports: Why Separate Is Not Equal* (Santa Barbara, CA: Praeger, 2016); Cheryl Cooky and Michael A. Messner, eds., *No Slam Dunk: Gender, Sport and the Unevenness of Social Change* (New Brunswick, NJ: Rutgers University Press, 2018).

41. John Rosa and John Bear, "Historic Hiring at Nederland," *Denver Post*, July 4, 2017, 2B.

42. Women's Sports Foundation, *Beyond X's & O's: Gender Bias and Coaches of Women's College Sports*, Women's Sports Foundation Report, June 2016, 1–6; see also Kelly Belanger, *Invisible Seasons: Title IX and the Fight for Equity in College Sports* (Syracuse, NY: Syracuse University Press, 2017). See also Lapchick, *2020 Racial and Gender Report Card*.

43. Patrick Hruby, "Lonely at the Top: Few College Athletic Directors Are Women and People of Color," Global Sport Matters, https://globalsportmatters.com/business/2021/05/07/few-college-athletic-directors-minorities-ncaa/.

44. Joe Nguyen, "Hammon Hired by Spurs," *Denver Post*, August 6, 2014, 2B; WNBA, "Coaches," http://www.wnbacom/coaches/coaches.html/.

45. Lucy McCalmont, "MLB Probably Won't Have a Female Umpire for at Least 6 Years," *The Huffington Post*, April 16, 2015, http://www.huffingtonpost.com/2015/04/16/baseball-female-umpire_n_7064220.html.

46. Ashley Mikelonis, "Women Hold Few Top Jobs in NCAA Division I Athletics," *Ahwatukee Foothills News*, March 15, 2017, 54–55.

47. Quoted in Nicole M. LaVoi, *Head Coaches of Women's Collegiate Teams: A Report on Select NCAA Division-I FBS Institutions, 2013–2014* (Minneapolis: Tucker Center for Research on Girls & Women in Sport, January 2014), the report and infographic can be downloaded free of charge at http://z.umn.edu/womencoachesreport/; Cindra S. Kamphoff, "Bargaining with Patriarchy: Former Female Coaches' Experiences and Their Decision to Leave Collegiate Coaching," *Research Quarterly for Exercise and Sport* 81, no. 3 (2010): 360.

48. Steve DiMeglio and Beth Ann Nichols, "Truth behind Tournament Paychecks: Financial Scorecards Go beyond Money Lists," *USA Today*, January 11, 2020, https://golfweek.usatoday.com/2020/01/11/truth-behind-tournament-paychecks-pga-tour-lpga/.

49. WNBA, "Coaches"; Richard Lapchick, *The 2021 Racial and Gender Report Card: Women's National Basketball Association* (Orlando: University of Central Florida, 2021).

50. For an interesting account of U.S. women and their struggles with the Olympic leadership during the 1920s, see Mark Dyreson, "Icons of Liberty or Objects of Desire? American Women Olympians and the Politics of Consumption," *Journal of Contemporary History* 38, no. 3 (2003): 435–460.

51. Lindsay Hock, "From Vancouver to London to Sochi: How Do Women's Participation Numbers Stack Up?" *Women's Sports Foundation*, February 12, 2014, http://www.womenssportsfoundation.org/en/sitecore/content/home/she-network/education/from-vancouver-to-london-to-sochi.aspx/; Peter Donnelly and Michele K. Donnelly, *The London 2012 Olympics: A Gender Equality Audit*, Centre for Sport Policy Studies Research Report (Toronto: Centre for Sport Policy Studies, Faculty

of Kinesiology and Physical Education, University of Toronto, 2013); Michele Donnelly, Mark Normen, and Peter Donnelly, *The Sochi 2014 Olympics: A Gender Equality Audit*, Centre for Sport Policy Studies Research Report (Toronto: Centre for Sport Policy Studies, Faculty of Kinesiology and Physical Education, University of Toronto, 2015).

52. Katy Steinmetz, "Infinite Identities," *Time*, March 27, 2017, 48–54; see also Lisa Wade and Myra Marx Ferree, *Gender: Ideas, Interactions, Institutions* (New York: W. W. Norton, 2014).

53. Matthew Lavietes and Hugo Greenhalgh, "Most U.S. LGBT+ Students Face Homophobic or Transphobic Abuse," Reuters, October 19, 2020, https://www.reuters.com/article/us-education-lgbt-students-trfn/most-u-s-lgbt-students-face-homophobic-or-transphobic-abuse-idUSKBN2741GO.

54. Catalina Gonella, "Survey: 20 Percent of Millennials Identify as LGBTQ," NBC News, March 31, 2017, http://www.nbcnews.com/feature/nbc-out/survey-20-percent-millennials-identify-lgbtq-n740791.

55. Amy S. Wharton, *The Sociology of Gender: An Introduction to Theory and Research*, 2nd ed. (New York: Wiley–Blackwell, 2011); see also Todd W. Reeser, *Masculinities in Theory: An Introduction* (New York: Wiley–Blackwell, 2010); Victoria Robinson, *Everyday Masculinities and Extreme Sport: Male Identity and Rock Climbing* (London: Berg, 2008).

56. OutSports, "At Least 182 Out LGBTQ Athletes Were at the Tokyo Summer Olympics, More Than Triple the Number in Rio," August 8, 2021, https://www.outsports.com/olympics/2021/7/12/22565574/tokyo-summer-olympics-lgbtq-gay-athletes-list.

57. Schultz, *Qualifying Times*; see also David C. Ogden and Joel Nathan Rosen, eds., *A Locker Room of Her Own: Celebrity, Sexuality, and Female Athletes* (Jackson: University Press of Mississippi, 2013); Lori Selke, "11 Powerful Lesbians in Sports," *Curve Magazine*, February 2, 2011, http://www.curvemag.com/Curve-Magazine/Web-Articles-2010/The-11-Most-Powerful-Lesbians-in-Sports/.

58. Kristin Kaye, *Iron Maidens* (New York: Indie Media Ventures, 2011); see also Sarah Fields, *Female Gladiators: Gender, Law, and Contact Sport in America* (Champaign: University of Illinois Press, 2008).

59. Jodi Mailander Farrell, "Sexism, Softball and the Supreme Court," *Miami Herald*, May 30, 2010, L1; see also Sherry Wolf, "America's Deepest Closet," *The Nation*, August 15/22, 2011, 29–31.

60. OutSports, "At Least 182 Out LGBTQ Athletes."

61. Chris Knoester and Rachel Allison, "Sexuality, Sports Related Mistreatment, and U.S. Adults' Sports Involvement," *Leisure Sciences* (2021): 1–23. DOI: 10.1080/01490400.2021.1895009; Sam Dolnick, "Openly Gay in the Bronx, but Constantly on Guard," *New York Times*, October 16, 2010, A13

62. John Amaechi, *Man in the Middle* (New York: ESPN Books, 2007); LeBron James quoted in Gene Farris, "Amaechi Takes Bold Step," *USA Today*, February 8, 2007, 11C; quote of Stoudemre in Paola Boivin, "Gay-Athlete Debate Calls for Tact and Compassion," *The Arizona Republic*, March 2, 2017, 1C, 7C; Micah A. Jensen, *Off the Bench—Gay Athletes in Professional Sports: A Look at Gay Athletes Entering the Fraternity of Professional Sports, and What It Means for the Players, the Games, and Society at Large* (Alpharetta, GA: MPB Publishing, 2014).

63. Scott Gleeson, "San Francisco 49ers Assistant Katie Sowers Comes Out, Becomes NFL's First Openly LGBT Coach," *USA Today*, August 23, 2017, 2C; see also Andrew Kohut, *The Global Divide on Homosexuality Greater Acceptance in More Secular and Affluent Countries* (Washington, D.C.: Pew Research Center, 2013).

64. Bill Chappell, "Supreme Court Declares Sam-Sex Marriage Legal in all 50 States," NPR, June 26, 2015, http://www.npr.org/sections/thetwo-way/2015/06/26/417717613/supreme-court-rules-all-states-must-allow-same-sex-marriages.

65. Pew Research Center, "Majority of Public Favors Same Sex Marriage, but Divisions Persist, May 14, 2019, https://www.pewresearch.org/politics/2019/05/14/majority-of-public-favors-same-sex-marriage-but-divisions-persist/

66. Caroline Symons, *The Gay Games: A History* (New York: Routledge, 2010).

FROM ORGANIZED SPORT TO CORPORATE SPORT: YOUTH TO COLLEGE SPORT

CHAPTER 8

YOUTH AND SPORT

The days of simply playing ball with your friends is over and the age of the youth sports industrial complex featuring pay-to-play leagues is here. Club sports is where adults make a living putting on tournaments for 7- to 15-year-olds, and parents pay good money for the right to join the team. Club sports are a for-profit venture with coaches making money from the skills of 7- and 10-year-olds.

—JOE EPSTEIN, *"Pay-To-Pay Leagues," Kqed Radio*

If I can't win I don't want to play.
—*Slogan on the T-Shirt of a Fourteen-Year-Old Girl Training at the International Performance Institute at Img Academies tn Bradenton, Florida*

Little League baseball is a major youth sport organization in the United States and in over eighty countries. Initially, Little League baseball was for boys only, but after several lawsuits challenging the ban on girls, the boys-only rule was dropped and girls legally won the right to participate in Little League. (Photo: mTaira)

More people participate in sport during their youth than at any other time in their lives. In the United States, nonschool youth sports programs have been created to include a bewildering variety of sports, and more than twenty-five agencies and thousands of local and regional sports organizations sponsor teams. Indeed, youth sports constituted a $19 billion market in 2021, with projections that it will become a $77.6 billion industry by 2026.[1]

YOUTH SPORTS PROGRAMS: SOMETHING FOR EVERYONE

The National Council of Youth Sports alone represents more than 200 organizations/corporations serving 60 million registered participants in organized youth sports throughout the United States. Clearly, then, a large number of youths under the age of seventeen participate in organized and team sports as they pass through childhood and adolescence.

Little League baseball is the largest youth sports organization, with leagues in every U.S. state and in eighty countries (160,000 teams at present) and with more than 2.5 million youngsters engaged in Little League annually. There are several baseball divisions for boys and girls based on age. Some 360,000 girls play Little League softball on more than 24,000 softball teams in more than twenty countries, whereas other girls choose to play on baseball teams with boys.

Pop Warner football was founded over ninety years ago and is the nation's largest youth football program. However, while other youth sports programs are proliferating, community and club youth football programs have seen a precipitous drop in participation over the past decade. The discovery of chronic traumatic encephalopathy, a progressive degenerative disease that afflicts the brains of people who have suffered repeated concussions and traumatic brain injuries, has created a concussion predicament for youth football players, parents, and boosters, who have become seriously concerned with the problem of maintaining confidence in youth football's safety. According to a survey of 1,003 adults

by the Robert Morris University Polling Institute, "more than 40 percent of Americans support a ban on youth playing contact football up until entering high school."[2]

In terms of participants, soccer has been growing faster than any other youth team sport during the past decade. The largest youth soccer organization, US Youth Soccer, registers nearly 3 million players annually and oversees 10,000 clubs and leagues and nearly 1 million administrators, coaches, and volunteers.[3]

As shown in Table 8.1, the regular participation of youths six to twelve years of age in team and organized sports fell or stagnated between 2008 and 2018 in some of the major sports listed.

More than 3,000 YMCAs in the United States and Canada provide some 8 million boys and girls the opportunity to participate in organized sports. The Junior Olympics Sports Program sponsors more than 2,000 local, state, regional, and national events in twenty-one different sports.

The emerging popularity of ESPN's X Games in the late 1990s stimulated the rise of several new youth-oriented extreme sports, such as in-line

TABLE 8.1 CORE PARTICIPATION IN TEAM SPORTS: PERCENT OF CHILDREN AGES SIX TO TWELVE PLAYING THESE SPORTS ON A REGULAR BASIS (2008–2018)

Sport	2008	2013	2018	2008–2018
Basketball	16.6	16.0	14.1	▼
Baseball	16.5	14.2	13.6	▼
Outdoor soccer	10.4	9.3	7.4	▼
Tackle football	3.7	3.5	2.8	▼
Gymnastics	2.3	2.9	3.4	▲
Volleyball	2.9	2.7	2.8	▼
Ice hockey	0.5	1.1	1.1	▲
Track and field	1.0	1.1	1.0	=
Wrestling	1.1	0.7	0.7	▼
Softball (fast pitch)	1.0	1.1	1.2	▲

Source: "Youth Sports Facts: Participation Rates," Aspen Institute, https://www.aspenprojectplay.org/youth-sports-facts/participation-rates.

skating, freestyle bicycling, BMX racing, snowboarding, and skateboarding, all having had explosive growth. There is even a National Hot Rod Association Jr. Drag Racing League and go-kart racing with more than 55,000 youngsters ages eight to seventeen competing at 130 National Hot Rod Association member tracks throughout the United States and Canada. Girls' participation in organized sports in the United States and other Western nations has experienced dramatic increases over the past forty years.

There is a well-organized outlet for almost every child who has an interest in being involved in sports. Parents can enroll their children in age-group gymnastics and swimming programs at three years of age; ice hockey, soccer, football, T-ball, and a half-dozen other sports usually begin at age four. Indeed, an early start is considered essential when parents or children have professional or Olympic-level aspirations.

The major promotional forces behind these youth sports programs have been parents and interested laypersons, whereas educators, physicians, and psychologists have tended to be less enthusiastic. Indeed, educators have rather effectively prohibited interscholastic sports in elementary schools and have severely restricted school sports in middle and junior high schools. They have, however, been ineffectual in controlling nonschool programs.

As sports for children and adolescents have expanded and diversified, a wide variety of sponsors have emerged. The types of agencies that sponsor youth sports in the United States are quite varied, reflecting public and private interests, and examples of each are shown in Table 8.2. We can compare this type of American youth sport sponsorship with the example of youth sport in France. In this European nation, most young people practice competitive sports activities in local municipal associations and their facilities, which are supported by city, regional, and national funding streams. National sport federations in respective sports provide oversight to these activities, which are generally low cost and volunteer driven, with few paid coaches and administrators.

Such a bewildering number of American youth sports programs with varying structural arrangements

TABLE 8.2 CATEGORIES OF AGENCIES THAT ORGANIZE YOUTH SPORTS

Type of agency	Example of type
National youth sport organization	Little League Baseball
National youth agency	Boys and Girls Clubs of America
National governing body	U.S. Wrestling
National service organization	American Legion Baseball
National religious organization	Catholic Youth Organization
Regional youth sport organization	Cal North Youth Soccer
State school activity association	Ohio High School Activities Association
Local school district	Norton, Kansas, public school
Local service club	Greeley Lions Club
Municipal recreation department	Portland Parks and Recreation Department
Private sports club	Del Mar Water Polo Club

exist that it is somewhat foolish to talk about them as though they were all alike. On the one hand, there are programs that emphasize participation and carefully regulate the type and extent of stress placed on the players. On the other hand, there are programs in which adults intrude enormously on the play of the youngsters; in many of these the purpose is simply to train children to become champions. An example of the former is the IMG Sports Academies in Florida, which are clearly devoted to producing champions in several sports.

There are many academies and clubs devoted to a variety of sports scattered across America training athletes to become pros or Olympic-level competitors. In 2007, the governing body of soccer in the United States established a program called the Development Academy to recruit and train young soccer players with the aim of helping them become established professionals and participate in the World Cup. This project ended in 2020 as a result of the financial situation under COVID-19 and now this mission falls under the purview of domestic professional clubs and leagues.

SOCIAL THEORIES AND YOUTH SPORTS

A major role of every social institution and organization, according to a functionalist social theory, is maintaining the social system as a whole and promoting a social value consensus and stability. Social activities that do this, functionalists argue, help to create a high degree of support for societal goals and cultural values. Despite variations in youth sports forms and functions, functionalist advocates of youth sports programs claim that they provide a means for the development of such personal–social attributes as self-discipline, cooperativeness, achievement motivation, courage, persistence, and so forth. Thus, proponents of organized youth sports typically view them as good preparation for appropriate adjustment to the realities of adult life. Additionally, advocates contend that the physical activity involved in playing sports promotes health and fitness. These are all attributes, attitudes, and values that functional theorists view as socially efficient and useful for socializing youth to perform cooperatively and consensually with others, thus promoting social stability.

In contrast, a conflict/cultural perspective emphasizes that highly organized sports frequently place excessive psychological and physical demands on young athletes. A conflict/cultural perspective contends that the encroachment of adults into the world of young people reduces the value of play as a spontaneous, expressive experience. Advocates of this social theoretical perspective make a case that youth sports frequently seem to be conducted for the self-serving needs of parents and youth sports leaders. Pressure from parents and coaches forces many elite child athletes to strive for perfection, and that pressure is responsible for dropping out, burnout, overuse injuries, and a host of other physical and psychological ailments.

THE RISE OF YOUTH SPORTS PROGRAMS: THE TAKEOFF AND EXPANSION OF A NEW FORM OF SPORT

Two independent but interrelated developments in the sociocultural milieu of the United States during the past two generations were primarily responsible for the rise and expansion of youth sports programs. The first was the rise of organized and corporate sport in all parts of the United States. Throughout the twentieth century there was enormous growth in popular spectator sports, such as major league baseball, collegiate football, professional ice hockey, and boxing. High school athletics became an integral part of American education, and the overall obsession with these forms of organized sport eventually trickled down to preadolescent youth.

The second development promoting the growth of youth sports programs was that childhood was seen as a particularly opportune time for nurturing attitudes and cultivating habits that would prepare youth for adulthood. Youth leaders urged the use of sports for the development of desirable personal and social skills. When the schools refused to sponsor sports for preadolescent youth, the task was left to voluntary agencies, and responsibility for sport competition for preadolescents was assumed by child-oriented organizations outside the educational framework.[4]

Until the 1970s, most organized youth sports programs were for boys only, but growing out of the attack on gender discrimination in all aspects of social life by the women's movement, exclusion of girls from organized sport became unacceptable. The Little League's ban against participation by girls was challenged in 1973, and after several lawsuits girls legally won the right to participate in Little League baseball.

Over the past thirty years organized youth sport has become available in almost every sport in which girls have wished to participate. The initial reservations, and even objections, to girls' sports participation gradually declined and have been replaced by enthusiastic endorsement by almost everyone. However, there are those who question the wisdom of merely incorporating girls into the traditional youth sport system. They argue that the structure of mainstream youth sports programs, where participation reflects the division of genders, inhibits more innovative ways of organizing sporting activities.

It often seems that there is a youth sport for every boy and girl in the United States. Youth sports programs are organized by thousands of local and regional sport organizations and numerous national agencies. (Photo: Courtesy of Kelly McCann)

OBJECTIVES OF YOUTH SPORTS PROGRAMS

Regardless of the sponsoring organization, the objectives of most youth sports programs are quite similar. They are intended to provide young boys and girls with opportunities to learn culturally relevant sports skills. Inasmuch as sport is such a pervasive activity in the United States, developing sports skills becomes almost a public duty. Equally important in the objectives of these programs, however, is the transmission of attitudes and values through interpersonal associations with teammates and opponents and through deliberate actions on the part of coaches, officials, and parents.

Thus, youth sports are viewed as an environment for promoting attitudes and values about such things as competition, sportsmanship, discipline, authority, and social relationships. The original certificate of the federal charter granted to Little League baseball illustrates the objectives of most youth sports programs: "To help and voluntarily assist boys in developing qualities of citizenship, sportsmanship, and manhood. Using the disciplines of the native American game of baseball to teach spirit and competitive will to win, physical fitness through individual sacrifice, the values of team play, and wholesome well-being through healthful and social association with other youngsters under proper leadership." As we noted, girls are now participants in Little League, but otherwise its objectives remain the same.

WHAT DO YOUNG ATHLETES, THEIR PARENTS, AND COACHES WANT FROM SPORTS?

Many books and articles for parents, coaches, and athletes about youth sports have enumerated the benefits of sports for young athletes. The most commonly listed benefits are the following:

- Helps a child's overall physical development.
- Gives the child the opportunity to become familiar with his or her body and to learn the body's needs and limitations.
- Is social as well as physical and thus teaches young athletes how to interact with his or her peers.
- Teaches cooperation, teamwork, and how to follow rules.
- Helps the child learn for him- or herself whether winning or losing is important.
- Gives parents the opportunity of offering the child unqualified support.
- Helps the child gain acceptance and credibility among his or her peers.

Beyond the benefits that youth sports are believed to provide for participants, a functionalist perspective views community-based youth sports programs as bringing together members of a community, thus functioning to satisfy a need by contributing a link with symbols of stability, order, tradition, and a communal focus.

The extent to which youth sports serve these functions is hard to quantify, but there is little doubt that substantial community financial and human resources are poured into the programs. Local merchants sponsor teams; coaches volunteer their time; groundskeepers, concession-stand operators, scorekeepers, and so forth facilitate the ongoing operations of the programs; and parents turn out in large numbers to cheer for their children. In addition, playing fields are built and maintained largely with taxpayers' money and other community contributions.

According to research at Utah State University, the growing business of youth sports has almost doubled in the past ten years. The researchers found that the average family spends $2,292 per year on sports, with a maximum expenditure close to $20,000 for families with children on traveling teams or employing personal trainers.[5]

Conflict/cultural theorists agree with some of these communal outcomes of youth sport, but they contend that youth sports also serve to divert attention away from many community problems and social issues prevalent throughout the United States. It has also been argued that the structures and practices found in youth sport contribute to social divides and inequities.

SOCIALIZATION AND SPORT: INVOLVEMENT IN SPORT AND ITS CONSEQUENCES

With youth sports as pervasive as they are in the United States, issues about the social forces promoting youth sports involvement are important for understanding how youngsters get into organized sports and what the consequences of these experiences are. In the broadest sense, the process of becoming a young athlete is part of a socialization process.

Socialization is the process of learning and adapting to a given social system. In the context of society, the activity of socialization is called cultural transmission and is the means by which a society preserves its norms and perpetuates itself. At birth, infants are certainly living organisms, but they are not social beings. Humans raised under daily social interaction demonstrate the impact of their culture on them, and this is called socialization.

Socialization continues throughout an individual's life cycle, but the years from birth to adolescence are considered critical because in these years the basic cultural transmission takes place. Numerous people are involved in the socialization of an individual, but because of their frequency of contact, their primacy, and their control over rewards and punishments, the primary agents and agencies for socialization are families, peer groups, schools, churches, and various media forms.

The outcomes of the socialization process are attitudes, values, knowledge, and behaviors related to the culture of which individuals are a part and to the roles that they will play in it. Thus, as children in a society interact with others through language, gestures, rewards, and punishments, they learn the attitudes, the values, and the expectations of various individuals in that society as well as the behaviors considered appropriate to the various situations of their social life.

As we noted in Chapter 1 and in an earlier section of this chapter, social theorists view the process and outcomes of socialization quite differently. The functionalists emphasize the importance of the social structure to socialize each new generation toward maintaining the existing social order. Conflict/culturalists tend to problematize the existing social order, especially the undemocratic social practices, inequalities, injustices, and various forms of discrimination present within the existing social organization. They simultaneously accentuate the need for opportunities for human agency, meaning the power people have to think for themselves and act in ways that shape their experiences and life skill trajectories. So, while peoples' lives are shaped by the existing social order, they nonetheless have the capability—*the agency*—to make decisions and express them through behavior.

Socialization is not merely a one-way process from socializers (parents, peers, and so forth) to the children; instead, a reciprocal interaction process is at work, and youngsters actually influence the attitudes, values, and behaviors of adults. Often-heard comments among parents include "I've certainly learned some things from my kids" and "My kids have made me change my mind about _____." There is little doubt that young athletes continually influence the attitudes and behaviors toward sport of various socializing mediators, including parents, coaches, teachers, and peers.

The topic of socialization and sport may be divided into two subtopics for analysis: (1) socialization into sport and (2) socialization via sport. In the first, the focus is on the agents and agencies that attract, or draw, children into sports, that is, an analysis of the ways in which children become involved in sports. An analysis of socialization via sport concentrates on the consequences, or outcomes, of sports involvement. First, we direct our attention to socialization into sport; socialization via sport is addressed later in this chapter.

SOCIALIZATION INTO SPORT: WHY DO CHILDREN BECOME INVOLVED IN ORGANIZED SPORTS?

An analysis of socialization into sports is concerned with who becomes involved in sport, which social agents and agencies are responsible for guiding young people into such involvement, how persons learn sports roles, and what the social processes for becoming involved are. One thing is clear: an enormous variety of individuals—parents, friends, siblings, coaches, even friends of the family—are involved in the socialization process of individuals becoming involved in sport.

FAMILIES

The family is the first and perhaps the most important social environment in a young person's life, and there is overwhelming evidence that the family—its social status, its structure, and its patterning of activities—is a significant influence in socializing their children in a variety of ways.

One important factor in the sport involvement of youngsters is the structure of the family. Families vary in size from a single child to sometimes more than a dozen offspring; following divorce or the death of one parent, some families become single-parent families. According to Child Trends Data Bank, in 2015 the proportion of traditional families, meaning married couples with or without children, is nearly at its lowest—65 percent—in at least 200 years. Black children are significantly less likely than other children to be living with two married parents. Only 34 percent of Black children and 60 percent of Hispanic children were living with two parents.

Participation in youth sports programs cuts across all socioeconomic strata; however, children from working-class families are overrepresented in some youth sports and children from upper-middle-class families in others. Parents socialize their children into sports that are deemed most appropriate for their socioeconomic status. For example, tennis players, skiers, gymnasts, golfers, swimmers, and sailors tend to come from upper-middle-class families; these families consider these activities instrumental in cultivating certain embodied ways of being that are useful for other important life contexts, such as schooling and professional work. It is arguable that participation in these sports also serves to reinforce high family status compared to others. One recent research article about youth sailing presented the following quote from an upper-class father when discussing his family's participation: "You're sitting on a hot soccer field drinking Gatorade . . . I'm sitting in a yacht club just enjoying the view, enjoying the drinks."[6]

In contrast, youth baseball, boxing, wrestling, and football programs tend to attract youngsters from middle- and working-class families, because these are considered more physically demanding endeavors that are prioritized by these families. (Chapter 5 dealt with the social stratification aspects of sports in more detail.)

PARENTS

Children tend to adopt the attitudes and values of their parents. Parents who themselves engage in sporting activities tend to socialize their children to have an interest in physical activity. Several investigators have indeed conducted research projects seeking to discover how individuals became involved in sport. They have found strong evidence that parents are a chief force for socializing their sons' and their daughters' involvement in sport.[7] Parental influence appears to occur through their own participation (the modeling influence) and through their interest in and encouragement of their offspring's involvement in sport. Research suggests that parental encouragement and actual participation are primary sources of sport socialization. For instance, a high percentage of fathers and mothers of young female athletes engage in sport themselves, and overall, parents are the most salient social agents in encouraging female athletes to participate.[8]

Although parents have received considerable attention as a factor in influencing the sport involvement of their offspring, little is known about the specific contributions that each parent makes. Some investigators have reported that the father is frequently the most significant socializing agent in the family and the most important predictor of sport participation for both boys and girls. In one research paper titled "The Good Father," sport sociologist Jay Coakley argues that "fathers are more likely than mothers to have or claim expertise in sports," and thus "the development of athletic skills among children is often monitored by fathers who act as coaches, managers, agents, mentors, and advocates for their child athletes."[9] Others have reported a tendency for the same-sex parent to have greater influence on sport involvement than the opposite-sex parent. More specifically, they have found that fathers' sports interests are more strongly related than mothers' interests to direct primary participation for both males and females.

Mothers have recently become more involved in their children's sports, reflected in the popular characterization of the "soccer mom" in American culture. This type of involvement can be underpinned by different motivations and lead to various outcomes. For instance, a study of wealthier mothers whose sons played soccer found that these women were using their economic capital "to produce, in their words, 'good boys.'" These mothers' involvement in soccer resulted in the reproduction of their social class perceptions and lifestyle patterns in their sons.[10]

Parents who have been asked about their children's involvement in organized sports programs have often expressed strong support for this participation, and parents of youth sport athletes have usually rated the coaches as excellent or good. They generally view sports as having had a positive effect on family life and as helping parents in socializing their children, in that they teach youngsters useful personal and social skills. In the case of the soccer moms discussed above, the mothers were enthusiastic about their sons' soccer experiences because soccer participation provided a space that reinforced certain preferred values and identities.[11]

For those parents whose children are training for elite status—for instance, to be a collegiate scholar-athlete, Olympic-level athlete, or professional athlete—there are fears, sacrifices, and constant pressures. Is the child being robbed of his or her childhood in the tightly structured training environment? Are the sacrifices of the child living away from home year-round worth it? Are the costs for coaching worth it? There is also the constant realization that unless the child continues to improve against the competition, he or she will be dropped by the coach or the program or both. When parents set for their child the goal of achieving professional standing, pressures are inevitably applied to the child's performance.[12]

In the literature on socialization into sport, little attention has been given to the ways in which youths influence their parents to become involved. Instead, most research has presented a one-dimensional socialization process in which the offspring are the learners and the parents are the socializers. Some sociologists have called for greater attention to the symbolic interactionist perspective, which sees social interacting as reciprocal and negotiable. In this view, analysis of parent effects must be balanced by analysis of child effects and of the two-way *reciprocal-effects synthesis*. With respect to sport, in addition to parental encouragement of offspring, some family adjustments may produce reverse socialization, with parents being socialized into sport through their children's participation. Indeed, many parents learn about sport and become involved in sport from their children. This often occurs when parents become volunteer coaches of their children's sport teams. Therefore, the socialization between parents and their children is frequently bidirectional. Sport studies scholars recently reported research in which they found that both moms and dads picked up the practice of skateboarding with their children. It was precisely because their kids skated that they started too. They therefore found that there are skate parents like there are soccer or baseball parents. Thus, although parents may initially steer their children into sport, the child's involvement often has behavioral and attitudinal consequences for the parents.[13]

SIBLINGS

A rather consistent association has been shown between parents' sports involvement, support, and encouragement and the involvement of their children

in sport, but the influence of siblings is not so clear. Still, a number of studies examining factors that affect the sport and physical activity participation of youngsters have identified siblings as a positive social influence. It is probable that the example of an older brother or sister participating in organized sport spurs younger children to become involved. In a TV interview, NBA basketball star Derrick Rose said he and his three older brothers used to play basketball together. The older brothers were sports inspirations for Derrick, and he said that when he was little he tried to do everything they would do. Siblings certainly play a positive role in influencing the social environment apart from parents.

PEERS

As important as the family is, the neighborhood and the peer group also serve as powerful socializing agents for sport involvement, especially as youngsters move into adolescence. Typically, during adolescence less time is spent with the family, and more time is spent with peers. Interactions with peers in the neighborhood and at school almost force compliance with their interests and activities. When peers are involved in sports, young people frequently experience a great deal of pressure to become involved also or else give up cherished social relationships. Few studies have examined the influence of socializing agents on the process of socialization of boys and girls into sports, but research in other physical activity contexts has found that peers are a major influence throughout childhood and adolescence.[14]

COACHES

Coaches are not often the persons responsible for initiating young boys and girls into sports, but for many youngsters an extremely close, emotional bond develops between athlete and coach, a bond that frequently becomes the main reason for continuing involvement. From the huge number of volunteer coaches to those who make their living coaching, coaches exert a tremendous influence on young athletes. Most young athletes perceive the role of coach in terms of someone to be socially admired. Also, for many young athletes the sports skills they have acquired, an important source of self-esteem, have been learned and developed under the leadership of their coaches. Their coaches are therefore seen as people who have helped young athletes acquire some of their most important possessions. Many ex–youth athletes, years after they have stopped competing, still consider their former coaches the most significant adults in their lives. It can often be the case that former coaches who are respected and admired will influence new generations to become coaches, even within the same programs.[15]

Interestingly, although coaches make vital contributions to children's lives, serving as inspirational mentors and role models, it has been found that most American coaches have limited or no training. According to Project Play, "unlike other educators, youth sports coaches are often unpaid or underpaid volunteers, with little training." Their conclusion is that training more American coaches will lead to even better sport experiences for youths.[16]

SCHOOLS

Of course, the school, with its physical education classes, is a significant socializing agent for North American children. Thanks to universal education and a physical education curriculum that typically puts a great deal of emphasis on learning sports skills, most children are taught the rudiments of a variety of sports in school. (Chapter 9 deals in depth with interscholastic sport.)

MASS MEDIA

The mass media are a powerful force for the sport role socialization of young boys and girls. Youngsters are virtually inundated with sports via newspapers, magazines, the Internet, and especially television. It is obvious that the mass media bring sports to the attention of the young. Few youngsters do not know the names of the NFL, NHL, NBA, MLS, and MLB teams. A great many boys and girls have heroes among professional and Olympic athletes, and many of them have plastered their bedroom walls with sports posters or follow these athletes on various social media platforms.

Sports video games emerged early in the history of television, and their popularity continues to grow as new sports games and new platforms come into the market. They now emulate more than two dozen traditional and action/lifestyle sports. Although sports video games are played by people of all ages, the most frequent players are children and adolescents. In the process of playing these games, young boys and girls are socialized into the skills, strategies, and tactics of sports, and some will even go on to become associated with professional sport franchises that sponsor video game competitions. Furthermore, many youths are motivated to try those same sports in their social environments. One study found that children who play sports-themed video games were likely to participate in real sporting activities as well.[17]

During the past decade, television programming has expanded to include a number of youth sports events. Perhaps the most prominent of these is the Little League World Series. Several days of the series are shown on TV. Many other youth championship events also are now televised. *USA Today*, which is sold worldwide, has a prominent place in its sports section for high school sports—including state-by-state results of high school championship events and a national ranking of the top twenty high school teams in several sports. Many young readers of *Sports Illustrated Kids*, *USA Today*, and SIKIDS.com are undoubtedly influenced to become involved in sports because of the media coverage. After all, the most immediate role models and heroes of younger athletes are the athletes featured on TV, on the Internet, and in magazines and newspapers.

Parents, siblings, peers, coaches, schools, and the media, then, are the main sport socializing agents and agencies that act on youth. They are so influential that it is a rare youngster who is not affected in some way by sport as he or she passes through childhood and adolescence.

PARTICIPANTS: YOUTH ATHLETES

Studies of participants in youth sports programs usually find that they have positive attitudes toward their experiences. When asked what they like most about their sports experiences, young athletes typically list the fun of being on an organized team, the chance to meet others and make friends, and the opportunity to improve their skills. Comprehensive analyses of

TABLE 8.3 THE TEN MOST IMPORTANT REASONS WHY YOUTH PLAY SPORTS

Boys	Girls
1. To have fun	1. To have fun
2. To improve skills	2. To stay in shape
3. For the excitement of competition	3. To get exercise
4. To do something I'm good at	4. To improve skills
5. To stay in shape	5. To do something I'm good at
6. For the challenge of competition	6. To be part of a team
7. To be part of a team	7. For the excitement of competition
8. To win	8. To learn new skills
9. To go to a higher level of competition	9. For the team spirit
10. To get exercise	10. For the challenge of competition

Source: Compilation from various youth sport publications; John O'Sullivan, "Why Kids Play Sports," Changing the Game Project, January 9, 2017, http://changingthegameproject.com/kids-play-sports/; see also John O'Sullivan, *Changing the Game: The Parent's Guide to Raising Happy, High Performing Athletes, and Giving Youth Sports Back to Our Kids* (New York: Morgan James, 2013).

youth sports have found there is a common cluster of the most important reasons kids play organized sport (see Table 8.3). A close examination of Table 8.3 shows that, while both boys and girls have many of the same important reasons for playing youth sports—they cite eight of the same ten reasons—they do rank the important reasons differently. Perhaps the most surprising difference is that "winning" ranks number eight with boys, but it is not one of the ten for girls who play youth sports.

Although millions of youngsters enthusiastically participate in organized youth sports each year and many continue for as long as they are eligible, a surprisingly large number do not continue to take part in sport; they become dropouts. Indeed, as many as one-third of youth sports participants voluntarily drop out of sport each year. Various studies have reported that between 50 and 70 percent of children drop out of organized sports before the age of thirteen.

Researchers have tried to ascertain the motives for sports withdrawal. They have found that the disappointment of not getting to play, poor umpiring, and being scolded for mistakes by coaches, parents, or both are the things young participants dislike most.[18] In studies that asked participants why they discontinued youth sports involvement, the ten most often cited reasons for both boys and girls were these:

1. I lost interest.
2. I was not having fun.
3. It took too much time.
4. Coach played favorites.
5. Coach was a poor teacher.
6. I was tired of playing.
7. Too much emphasis on winning.
8. Wanted a nonsport activity.
9. I needed more time to study.
10. Too much pressure.

The picture that emerges from studying young athletes and their views of participation in youth sports is that they want to have fun and learn skills, but since many of them encounter pressures to train and win, some simply drop out of organized sport programs. For them, the promise of fun, sociability, and skill acquisition through sports is lost.

SOCIALIZATION VIA SPORT: PROCESS AND OUTCOMES

Globally, there is a growing body of micro-level research that examines the attitudes, values, beliefs, and behaviors of young people participating in both traditional and action/lifestyle sports. This type of research reveals how these youth engage and interact in sports participation. For instance, Lisa Wood and her colleagues recently conducted a community survey and found that participation in skateboarding in Australia fostered young peoples' social skills, self-esteem, cooperative behavior, and respect for self and others.[19]

This type of empirical evidence is necessary to substantiate the many claims that have been made about the contributions of sport to psychological and social development of youth participants. Indeed, it is worth keeping in mind that sport constitutes only one of many developmental forces operating on young people. Every child is subjected to a multitude of social experiences that are not sport related. Thus, much of what we think we know about the effects, or consequences, of sport participation is impressionistic, and more research is required to understand the specific contributions of sport to youth.[20]

There are several principles of socialization theory, however, that likely hold true with regard to youth sports. In general, the influence of sports experiences will be stronger:

- when the degree of involvement is frequent, intense, and prolonged;
- when the participation is voluntary rather than involuntary;
- when the socializer (e.g., the coach) is perceived as powerful and prestigious; and
- when the quality of relationships is highly meaningful.

TWO FORMS OF PLAY: PEER GROUP AND ADULT ORGANIZED

Several social scientists have suggested that the social context in which a sport activity takes place determines its social outcomes. The observational studies of several sport sociologists who have studied children and adolescents and their sports involvement indicate that there are two distinct social contexts in which sports activities take place: *peer group* and *adult organized*. They have characterized and contrasted the potential socialization outcomes for these two forms of play in terms of their organization, process, impetus, and social implications.

Organizational Differences

In organized team sports the most salient characteristics are that both action and involvement are under adult control and that the actions of the players are strictly regulated by specialized rules and roles. For example, Little League games are organized as performances rather than play. They are modeled after professional sports. Young athletes on organized sports teams are subject to the direct influence of adult coaches who have substantial power to determine whether participation will be either positive or negative in nature.

Youth sport coaches have traditionally been remarkably similar in the way they organize practice sessions. Activities during practice tend to be discipline oriented and performative. That is, coaches may allow little flexibility in the executing of skills or in the performing of other tasks associated with practice. The youngsters tend to wait to be told what to do, often waiting for directions on how to do things according to coaching plans. Spontaneous behavior, both during performance and while waiting to practice some given task, is usually discouraged. Therefore, few decisions on any aspect of the practice are made by the youngsters themselves. Most decisions and rules are made by the coaches, and the participants are expected to carry them out obediently. The emphasis in this organized sport team setting tends to be on the development of sport skills, not on the facilitation of social and emotional learning.

With respect to play, before the age of seven children rarely play games spontaneously; if they play them at all, it is usually on the initiative of adults or older children. Thus, organized sports programs for youngsters under the age of seven are not organized extensions of what children of that age would be doing anyway; they are simply testaments to the power and influence adults have on young children. For example, out of a desire to make sure their children do not get behind, many parents are enrolling offspring as young as four years of age in organized sports or in "personal training" skill development sessions.

When peer play is found, usually among youngsters over the age of seven, it is player controlled. In one study, researchers observing children's play on a public school playground found that "children's choices of what to play, which games or sports, were influenced by a number of considerations: what was 'going on,' the equipment available, novelty, the weather, friendship groups . . . and, finally, those mysterious fads and fashions that cause a game to be hugely popular for a period until it loses appeal and another takes its place."[21]

Players rely on informal norms of conduct and informal rules to regulate the game. The youngsters make consensual decisions on groupings and game rules. Teams are usually organized informally; this is done quickly and typically with little friction. The games children choose in free play generally have fewer rules and fewer specialized roles than the games organized by adults, and children vary the rules in the process of play to suit the situation. In informal peer "sandlot" or "street" games, the authority structure operates uniquely. There is an authority structure, but the structure works through moral suasion rather than role occupancy.

Process Differences

The process of play in peer-group sport and adult-organized sport is also quite different. In the former, teams are chosen, and the game usually begins quickly. Field researchers of children's informal sports frequently note the efficiency with which the youngsters go about getting the teams chosen and the game underway. Arguments about rule interpretations or a "call," such as whether a player is "safe" or "out" or if a ball is "in" or "out," when they do occur, usually cause only minimal delays. Shouts of "Let them have it" or "Play it over" usually settle the debate, and play is resumed.

In the informal peer-group games the primary focus tends to be on a combination of action, personal involvement, keeping the game close, and the reaffirming of friendships. The quest for victory, or a "win," may be a secondary outcome here; while more intense games such as park soccer or street basketball may involve determining winners and losers, there is often a search for self-mastery—that is, attempting to create situations that require performing up to a personal standard of satisfaction. The public-school-playground researchers quoted previously stressed that "in the end, what the players most enjoyed, beyond winning, was the exhilaration of exercising skill, strength, speed, and coordination along with teammates."[22]

By contrast, in the play process of organized youth sports, there tends to be an emphasis on order, punctuality, respect for authority, obedience to adult directions, and a strict division of labor. Coaches typically insist on order, sometimes prohibiting participants from talking unless the coach speaks to them. The coach's concern for order and discipline often reduces the amount of playing time. Organizing the practice session or stopping practice to discuss mistakes or to punish misbehavior sometimes takes up significant portions of the practice session. The participants become so accustomed to following orders in an organized sport setting that they frequently will cease to play altogether if the coach is absent or not directly supervising. Close observation and directing by the coach are required to keep them playing.

In organized youth sports the participants have very little say in determining the rules; adults make the rules. In the programs of national sports agencies (such as Little League baseball), a national rulebook is published to which all participants must conform. Thus, in this form of sport, participants are merely followers, not makers or interpreters, of the rules.

Winning is frequently the overriding goal in formal youth sports programs. By striving for league standings, by awarding championships, and by choosing all-star teams, such programs send the not-so-subtle message to youngsters that the most important goal of sports is winning.[23]

Impetus Differences

The impetus of peer play comes entirely from the youngsters; they play because they enjoy it. They are free to commence and terminate a game based on player interest. Conversely, the impetus of play in organized sports programs comes from the coaches; they schedule the practices for a given time and end practices when they see fit. Games are scheduled by a league authority and are played in a rigid time frame. The youngsters have no choice but to play in the manner the adults wish them to play. Their own enjoyment is often determined by the nature of adults and their approaches. Coaches and many players expect participants to adhere to a Puritan work ethic, and the word *work* is ever-present in practices and games. "Come on, work hard!" and "Take pride in your work!" are proddings frequently used by coaches and parents.

Social Implications of the Two Forms of Play

On the one hand, adult-sponsored youth sport is basically an organized structuring of groupings, activities, and rules imposed on the participants. Peer play, on the other hand, is a voluntary activity with a flexible process of social exchange based on consensus. Youngsters are therefore exposed to quite different experiences in what appear to be similar sport activities.

What are the social implications of these two different forms of organization of play activities for the socialization of youngsters? The application of arbitrary, adult-imposed rules in organized youth sport markedly contrasts with the spontaneous group-derived rules in peer-group play. This contrast is a function of the different roles of the peer group and of adults in the socialization process. The role of the peer group serves to bridge the gap between the individualistic world of children and the orientations of the wider society. The role of the organized team serves to emphasize the adult, universalistic-achievement orientations deemed appropriate by the society.

The differences between the goals of peer-group play and organized team effort become apparent in their emphasis on means and ends. In the peer context, play is not overly concerned with ends; the essence of the play is the play—its skillful fun, decision-making, ritualistic practices, and personal interactions. In contrast, in organized sports, play tends to be more incidental.

For the adults who organize sport programs, play is identified with ends—that is, to win; to teach youngsters specific skills and rules needed to play soccer, baseball, and so forth in the short run; and to develop certain attitudes and values toward social relationships and activities that in the long run tend to reproduce the requirements of occupational life by emphasizing punctuality, periodicity, and performance. Indeed, it has been argued that organized sport socializes young athletes to accept authoritarian leadership and carry out coaches' directions without question, thus suppressing their own creative initiatives and personal growth.[24]

In peer play, there tends to be an elaboration of means through varying the rules, particularizing relationships, or encouraging novelty. The games chosen in free play (in which less specialization of roles tends to occur) permit more elaboration of means. For example, the youngsters find many creative ways to modify space and equipment in their games. In organized sports the codified rules (enforced by coaches and officials) emphasize rigidity within the space of sport, permitting only one way to use a ball, utilization of a one-size field, allocating a certain number of players to a side, and so forth. In organized sports programs, disputes about calls or about rules do not occur between players because they are made and applied by referees and coaches. Therefore, the experience in peer play emphasizes interpersonal skills (negotiations and compromise) and spatial/task adaptability, whereas the sociospatial experience in organized sport is marked by a knowledge of and dependence on strict rules and with the acceptance of the decisions of adults, who are in positions of legitimate authority.

Research on formal and informal sport settings finds that enjoyment of social experiences has a high positive correlation between challenges and skills in informal sports settings, but not in adult-supervised settings. This is often interpreted as suggesting that enjoyable social experiences are easier to achieve when adolescents are in control of the activity, probably because they can manipulate the balance between challenges and skills more easily in an informal setting. Unfortunately, casual/pickup play in youth continues to decline, primarily because more young athletes are specializing in one sport at an earlier age.

To summarize, what is implied by an analysis of these two play forms is that play behavior in the peer group is quite different from play behavior in youth sports programs. We are not arguing in a "black or white" fashion that one of these forms of play is good and the other bad. In fact, some criticisms have been raised in terms of youth-driven sporting activity, where sometimes stronger and more skillful athletes (often experienced males) are able to determine codes of behavior and create social hierarchies. Simultaneously, some organized sport contexts featuring adult leaders can provide safer and more inclusive spaces for females, in particular.[25]

What we are emphasizing is that the variations in the social organization of youthful play generally have different processes and values, and thus social consequences, for these participants.

DEVELOPMENT OF PERSONAL–SOCIAL ATTRIBUTES THROUGH SPORT

As noted earlier in this chapter, the primary justifications of youth sports programs are the opportunities they provide for young boys and girls to learn culturally relevant sport skills and to develop desirable personal and social characteristics. "Sport builds character" is one of the most frequently recited slogans for the supposed outcomes of sport for youth. It inevitably is used by community leaders, school officials, parents, coaches—virtually everyone—when a discussion turns to the purpose of organized sports for children and adolescents.

YOUTH ORIENTATION TOWARD SPORT

There has been a sustained professional and scholarly interest in the effects of sports experiences on the orientations youth have toward sport. One of the orientations sport sociologists have focused on is whether participation in organized sport influences what participants think is most important about playing. Specifically, they have studied orientations that emphasize the process (playing fair, playing for fun) and orientations that emphasize the product (playing to win).

Researchers have found, overall, that there is a strong tendency for both males and females who have been involved in organized sports to have more professionalized orientations than peers who have not been involved in organized sports. Elite athletes, both males and females, display a strong professional orientation toward sport. These findings are probably not surprising, given the structural conditions of organized sport, which socializes youngsters into accepting and internalizing values of success striving, of competitive achievement, of personal worth based on sports outcomes, and of subjection of self to external control. Although it is difficult to credit (or discredit) sports participation entirely for greater professionalized attitudes toward sport, it does seem that sport for fun, enjoyment, fairness, and equity is often sacrificed at the altar of skill and victory as children continue their involvement in organized sports.[26]

SPORTSMANSHIP IN YOUTH SPORTS

Sportsmanlike behavior—striving to succeed but committed to playing by the rules and observing ethical standards that take precedence over strategic gain when the two conflict—is universally admired, but it sometimes conflicts with the quest for victory.

In the sport culture at all levels, good sportsmanship and fair play are the accepted standards and are overwhelmingly practiced by those involved in organized sports. But the prevalence of good sportsmanship throughout sports is rarely noted in the public discourse or in the media. This is true because it is the expected, the normative, behavior. In contrast, poor sportsmanship, like deviant behavior in most social settings, gets noted, gets attention, gets reactions, and therefore often seems to overshadow good sportsmanship in personal conversations and in media stories. In the following paragraphs on this topic, we will describe some findings about poor sportsmanship, but the reader should keep in mind what we have said here about good sportsmanship.

On the one hand, sportsmanship and fairness underlie the social convention of virtually all youth sports programs, but on the other hand, victory in organized sports competition often carries more salient rewards. The slogan "It's not whether you win or lose but how you play the game," although never universally embraced in the culture of organized sport, is acknowledged by many coaches, athletes, and parents as an appropriate attitude for playing well, playing within the rules, and playing in a sportsmanlike manner rather than for the mere winning of a sporting event.

That standard is challenged by the slogan "Winning isn't everything, it's the only thing." When taken seriously, this latter slogan suggests that any means or methods are legitimate in the pursuit of victory. It has been accompanied with practices like trash-talking, intimidating opponents, taunting and ridiculing opponents, and deliberately violating the rules of the sport—all in the interest of "getting the edge" and winning the sporting event. For example, a study of youth sports conducted by researchers at the University of Missouri at St. Louis, the University of Minnesota, and Notre Dame involving 803 young athletes ages nine to fifteen, along with 189 parents and 61 coaches, found, according to the athletes:

- Two in ten admitted to cheating often.
- Nine percent cheated to help the team win.

- Thirteen percent had tried to hurt an opponent often.
- Twenty-seven percent had acted like "bad sports" after a loss.
- Seven percent of their coaches had encouraged the athletes to cheat.
- Eight percent of their coaches had encouraged the athletes to hurt an opponent.[27]

These percentages may seem low, but they are made up of hundreds of individual respondents, so the sum of the incidents is actually quite large and thus disturbing. See Box 8.1 for further discussion on this topic.

There are a number of sources illustrating a trend toward increasingly unsportsmanlike attitudes and behaviors in youth sports. Professional and college athletes have always profoundly influenced young athletes, because they are the role models and heroes of youth sport athletes. Young athletes adopt the attitudes, manner, and behavior of their heroes.

Unfortunately, those heroes often display the trash-talking, intimidating, ridiculing, and rule breaking that have cascaded down to youth athletes.

CHARACTER DEVELOPMENT IN YOUTH SPORTS

From the beginning of organized youth sports forms there has been a prevailing impression that the sporting environment is particularly useful for young athletes to learn moral values and principles. The slogan often used to affirm this is "sport builds character." Like most slogans, this one is not grounded in empirical findings, and when research has been conducted to ascertain the effects of sport involvement on character development, the findings have provided little in the way of specific or consistent answers.

Because the word *character* is so ambiguous and has so many meanings to people, over the past decade the literature on "character development through

---

BOX 8.1 *THINKING ABOUT SPORT:* WHICH IS IT, POOR SPORTSMANSHIP OR JUST BEING A GREAT COMPETITOR?

As the emphasis on winning and "doing whatever it takes" to win has become more prevalent in youth sports, the line between good and poor sportsmanship has become blurred for many youth sport coaches, athletes, and parents. Here is an example: Referring to one of his young pitchers, a coach explained, "He's just a fierce competitor. Nobody competes better." The coach went on to recount how once when this pitcher lost his bid for a perfect game in the sixth inning, "he didn't get upset. He didn't say anything. You couldn't tell by his demeanor, but he wound up and hit the next batter right between the shoulder blades." The coach proudly exclaimed, "I love to have pitchers who are great competitors like that." The young pitcher was praised for deliberately hitting a batsman for something he had nothing to do with—spoiling the pitcher's perfect game. What did the young pitcher learn from his coach about sportsmanship in this episode?

Coaches and parents are other powerful sources for socializing young athletes about sportsmanship attitudes and behaviors. Many coaches and parents are aware of their influence and make a valiant effort to make sport a positive experience, emphasizing fun, fair play, and good sportsmanship. Regrettably, a growing number of other coaches and parents are out of control. Many have become models of bad sportsmanship for

young athletes. More about this can be found in the "Adult Intrusion in Youth Sports" section of this chapter.

An ominous societal trend might be contributing to the growing unsportsmanlike behavior of young athletes. There is widespread acknowledgment that acts of "incivility" between people have become more common in North American culture (more about this in Chapter 15). Such actions undoubtedly influence the culture of sport and become translated into poor sportsmanship at all levels.

Efforts are being made to counteract the trend toward unsportsmanlike conduct. The Positive Coaching Alliance, a national nonprofit organization with the mission to transform the culture of youth sports so that youth athletes can have a positive, character-building experience, through partnership with more than 1,100 youth sports organizations, leagues, schools, and cities nationwide, has conducted 10,000-plus workshops for youth sports coaches, parents, organizational leaders, and athletes. Its website has this statement: "Our Mission: Better Athletes, Better People by working to provide all youth and high school athletes a positive, character-building youth sports experience." Also, the National Alliance for Youth Sports has publicly affirmed good sportsmanship and committed to developing policies to reward sportsmanlike behaviors and punish unsportsmanlike actions in events under their jurisdiction. Although these efforts are against the prevailing trend, there are encouraging signs that they are having some positive effects on sports at all levels.[28]

youth sports" has been largely replaced by literature using the term *life skills*. Life skills are conceptualized as the psychosocial abilities for adaptive and positive behavior that enable individuals to deal effectively with the demands and challenges of everyday life. They are a set of human skills acquired via teaching or direct experience used to deal with problems and questions commonly encountered in daily life. When applied to youth sport athletes, the attention is on athletes developing and acquiring life skills, such as responsibility, self-confidence, leadership, self-esteem, teamwork, and decision-making through involvement in sport. Of course, they do not inherently occur just by playing a sport; positive life skills outcomes must be taught to young athletes. Youth sport researchers often emphasize that "life skills are taught, not caught."

Whether it is called character development or life skills, learning attitudes, values, and moral behavior is a core aim of youth sports, and there is growing research literature on the outcomes of sports participation—that is, the effects of sport involvement on the personal and social development of children. Indeed, given the popularity of the "sport provides character" ideal, the processes and effects of sports involvement on young athletes' social and moral development will be a topic for future researchers to unravel. Although many families, schools, program leaders, and government representatives believe that sports can be used to create personal and social attributes that young people need to achieve success, there remains a need for more critical research regarding youth development claims.[29]

A question often asked about the social outcomes of playing sport for young boys and girls is, Are there experiences during sports participation that *might* hamper their social development? If we accept the notion that children learn normative behavior from sports and if we agree that social-norm deviance is present in sport, youth sports programs may be providing patterned reinforcement of attitudes, values, and behaviors that are at variance with social development as well as social values. Clearly, deviations from the ideal social values and norms do occur in youth sports (e.g., incidents of athletes physically attacking one another during games, the booing of

officials, and even the incorporation of deviance as part of the strategy of the game, such as spearing in football, illegal body checking in hockey, and so forth). But such incidents and events are rarely condoned, and most youth sport leagues and broader sport organizations (e.g., Little League) have patterned methods for discouraging them. One may question the extent to which social learning of life skills in sports generalizes to larger social relations, but it is certainly necessary to consider the possible social effects on athletes who play under coaches who encourage unethical behavior. Convincing evidence from social learning experiments demonstrates that youngsters do model the attitudes and behaviors of people they respect and admire, and young athletes almost universally have high regard for their coaches.

Besides life skills development, there are other social outcomes to which sports involvement during youth may contribute. Competence in sports skills apparently does influence self-evaluation and social esteem with peers. Sports provide innumerable opportunities for the individual to perceive the feelings of others and their judgments. Thus, experiences in sports may be instrumental in the development of a self-image or self-concept. Several investigations have shown that sports abilities and interests are related to a positive self-concept, and research has consistently shown that young sports participants score higher on a variety of tests that measure mental health. Finally, but no less important, research suggests that encouraging sport participation during childhood and adolescence may result in an increase in the likelihood of participation later in life. However, we want to emphasize that most of the research on these topics is designed to measure relationships between the variables, not causal outcomes.

POTENTIAL PSYCHOSOCIAL PROBLEMS IN YOUTH SPORTS

A variety of social problems have arisen with the growth and expansion of organized youth sports, and there is increasing apprehension about potential harm to youngsters in these sports programs. There is little doubt that some abusive practices are taking place in the world of youth sports. Having said this, we wish to re-emphasize the point we made in the previous section, namely, that many young people experience positive personal–social growth experiences through youth sports. The kinds of outcomes experienced by youngsters are primarily contingent on parents and coaches because they are the most powerful "significant others" in the lives of young boys and girls.

In this section we discuss some of the most common problems of youth sports with a view to improve the nature of this widespread activity, for all participants. It is not our intent to make specific accusations or to condemn all youth sports. We merely suggest that the social experiences of some youth sports athletes may have social consequences that are perhaps unintended and unwanted.

ADULT INTRUSION IN YOUTH SPORTS

The rationale behind the organization of youth sports programs is admirable: to provide young boys and girls with structure for their sports, opportunities for wide participation, proper equipment for their safety, and adult coaching to help them learn the fundamental skills and strategies. But there is overwhelming agreement that one of the major problems of youth sports is the intrusion of adults into the sports life of youngsters. According to the National Alliance for Youth Sports (NAYS), "twenty-eight percent of adults say they've witnessed a physical confrontation involving coaches, officials or parents during a youth sporting event, and . . . say [there] is a 'growing epidemic' of bad behavior in youth sports."[30] *USA Today* sportswriter Christine Brennan recently provided several examples: "A mother in New York has received a 60-day sentence for threatening a Little League official after her son failed to make a summer travel team. A grandfather in Alabama is facing felony charges after punching a 20-year-old umpire in the nose at his granddaughter's softball game. A Babe Ruth League coach in Pennsylvania was charged with reckless endangerment and harassment after allegedly trying to run someone over with his pickup truck. A . . . man in Massachusetts allegedly punched and then bit off part of the ear of the winning coach after his son's team lost a sixth-grade basketball game."[31]

Parents and Coaches: Expectations and Pressures

The evidence is clear that many parents and coaches are living out their sports dreams through young athletes. Hundreds of communities complain about parents and volunteer coaches who are overly involved in their youth sport programs.[32] It appears that these adults expect a payoff, and that payoff is athletic achievement by way of victories and championships. When a youngster achieves, parents and coaches see that success, in a way, as their personal achievement. If the young athlete fails to live up to performance expectations, he or she may feel like a personal failure, as well as feeling he or she did not fulfill the expectations of others. These pressures on a young athlete are exemplified by the practice of parents employing personal trainers for their offspring. In the past decade, the number of parents employing professional trainers for their grade-school athletes has multiplied. Parents willingly pay $100 or more for an hour of individual coaching. One coach, Steve Clarkson, whose young athletes include sons of former NFL players and more than 200 of whom have become major college football players, charges parents $700 an hour for private training sessions.[33]

For parents, athletes, and coaches whose aspirations are national rankings and a professional sports career for the youngsters involved, youth sports are not about fun and play. As one of the most published authors about youth sport, Mark Hyman, argues, "Commercialization is obscuring the life lesson of youth sports. . . . we've been brainwashed to believe that excellence in sports is a product on a shelf, like laundry soap or a necktie. It isn't, and commercialization is drowning out a vital truth."[34]

The parents of Venus and Serena Williams have become the role models for thousands of parents throughout the United States. They have devoted most of their adult lives, and the childhood lives of these athletes, to the pursuit of their daughters' professional sports careers. Their success in achieving professional sports careers for their offspring, and the celebratory status accompanying it, has set a course that countless parents now follow for their children. "If the Williamses can do it, we can too" seems to be the attitude of parents who adopt this course. In addition to professional careers, some parents aspire for their child to receive a college athletic scholarship, whereas others aspire to their child winning a professional contract or even an Olympic berth.

Because such aspirations have become so commonplace, they have changed the structure of youth sports and some families' lives. In previous generations children and youth played year-round, alternating the sport with the season. That is not the case anymore as parents let unrealistic dreams shoehorn their children into one-sport specialization. The day of the three-sport high school athlete is disappearing as even ten-year-olds who show some promise in a particular sport are told to stick to that sport year-round. But children focusing on one sport to the exclusion of all others and at younger and younger ages is considered a troubling trend by a broad spectrum of developmental and sport psychologists.[35]

Among the reasons for such early specialization, college coaches now recruit middle school athletes as young as thirteen and fourteen years old. For example, David Sills V, a seventh-grader, verbally committed to attend the University of Southern California and play quarterback. He never became a major university quarterback. In July 2017, a Mississippi youth reported he had received scholarship offers from three Division I universities, and he had not yet started the eighth grade. As pressures to win increase and competition for the top prospects grows fiercer, college coaches justify recruiting pre–high school athletes by arguing "You've just got to be first" to go after them.[36]

Traveling Teams and Club Teams

Now it is *traveling teams* or *club teams* that have become a popular form of youth sport organization. Specialization into one sport and belonging to a traveling team has become a popular choice for many young boys and girls. The procedure varies; some specialize in one sport and then join a traveling team, others join a traveling team but then they must specialize in the sport of the traveling team. These young athletes are drawn from mostly suburban neighborhoods and towns in a given region.

The main reason for the attraction of travel teams, which can cost $2,000 or more a year in coaching,

equipment, and tournament fees, is that most successful traveling teams offer better coaching than recreational league sports, players wear top-rate uniforms, they play on well-kept facilities, there is year-round training, there is "elite" competition, and there is the enjoyment of travel to various state tournaments. There is often little regard for anything but winning and the development of individual talent in one sport. Travel team coaches and parents of travel team athletes paint a rosy picture of their character-building goals, but all too often this is empty rhetoric.[37]

The extremes to which traveling youth sports go are illustrated in the saga of a boy who played 127 baseball games in one year in the ten-and-under leagues. The consequences? An increasing number of Tommy John surgeries on youth/high school baseball pitchers. One famed orthopedic surgeon has called it an epidemic. He elaborated, "There [has been] a tenfold increase in Tommy John [surgeries] at the high school/youth level in my practice since 2000."[38]

For both the young athletes and their families, the commitment to traveling teams is almost total. The young athletes must abandon other organized sports and life activities to concentrate on the travel team. They must commit to specializing in one sport and often must compete with their team year-round. Family lives must be recentered around the sports world of the traveling teams. The new breed of sports parents are road warriors who drive thousands of miles every season and spend weekends and evenings watching their kids practice and play. And as noted, it is expensive to support a traveling or club team athlete. The founder of the NAYS feels that the point of saturation has been reached—a revolving door of never-ending seasons for traveling team athletes and their parents.[39] Traveling teams will also be discussed in Chapter 9.

Sports Academies and Youth Olympic Games

The trends of parental intrusion into youth sports, traveling teams, hyperorganization, and hypercompetitive youth sports have spawned a commercial industry devoted to coaching and training young athletes for the lofty sports goals they and their parents often have. This new industry goes way beyond the traditional sports camps that have been held by college coaches and professional athletes for the past twenty-five years. Although the daily or weekly sports camps are still popular throughout the United States, sports academies have become the ultimate in coaching and preparing young athletes whose parents strive for athletic excellence in their children.

IMG Academies, headquartered on a sprawling 400-acre campus in Bradenton, Florida, is the elite model of the academies. According to its website, "IMG Academies is the largest, most successful multi-sport training and education institution in the world. More than 12,000 junior collegiate, adult and professional athletes from over 75 countries attend each year." IMG Academies offer programs throughout the year for the IMG Bollettieri Tennis, IMG Golf, IMG Baseball, IMG Basketball, IMG Soccer, IMG Football, IMG Track and Field and Cross Country, and IMG Lacrosse academies as well as the IMG Performance Institute. A one-year, full-time boarding plan costs about $75,000. With the addition of special private lessons, some parents pay up to $100,000 per year. Some children remain at IMG Academies for several years.[40]

Similar high-tech sports performance training centers are popping up, mostly in suburbs, across the country. Some cater to young athletes who want to become "the best" in specific sports; others focus on arcane skills designed to improve agility, strength, speed, and power—the fundamentals of all sports. This trend has even reached sports once deemed alternative or countercultural. Camp Woodward, for instance, provides expensive training across several national "world-class" facilities for sports such as skateboarding, parkour, BMX, mountain biking, and snowboarding.[41]

Overwhelmingly the athletes who attend specialized training programs come from affluent families. Sports academy and sports performance training center athletes tend to be members of middle- and upper-middle-class families. Parents of these athletes report annual expenses for their athlete son or daughter ranging from $12,000 to more than $100,000.

IMG Academies officials admit that the real basis for admission is parents' ability to pay, not physical prowess. At the time, the IMG Golf Academy was named the David Leadbetter Golf Academy, and the renowned teaching pro said, "We don't want only rich kids to come here." But, he acknowledged, "There's certainly a class factor. It's expensive to play golf." Poor families cannot afford such expenses for their children's sports programs. In recent years public money for recreation centers and after-school sports programs has declined, and for children growing up in poor families in their communities, youth sports opportunities are severely limited.

Commenting on how the academy system training centers put youth from poor families and the school sports teams they belong to at a disadvantage, the former commissioner of one of the high school activities associations claimed, "They bust their butt at [inner-city schools] and once in a while put together good teams. But mostly, they get kicked; they have no chance. It's totally a case of haves and have-nots. You can almost name the sport; even volleyball and basketball. These are inner-city games, but it's the well-heeled suburban schools that have the best teams."

Household income is one major indicator of sports participation. Simply put, families that can afford more can allow their kids to play more (see Table 8.4). One infamous exception to this system of social class privilege is youth basketball. Basketball shoe corporations Nike, Adidas, and Under Armour, working with the Amateur Athletic Union and sport

TABLE 8.4 INCOME IMPACT ON YOUTH SPORT PARTICIPATION: PERCENTAGE OF PARTICIPANTS BY HOUSEHOLD INCOME

Sport	Under $25K	$25–$49.9K	$50–$74.99K	$75–$99.9K	$100K+
Football (tackle)	16	24	20	13	27
Baseball	12	23	22	16	27
Basketball	16	21	19	15	29
Soccer (outdoor)	13	19	16	17	35
Swimming (team)	8	16	12	21	43
Lacrosse	4	10	16	14	56

Source: "State of Play 2017 Trends and Developments," Aspen Institute, 2017, https://www.aspeninstitute.org/publications/state-of-play-2017-trends-and-developments/.

shoe–sponsored coaches, seduce young, mostly poor inner-city kids to play in tournaments all over the United States. According to *USA Today* sportswriter Jim Halley, the young players play more than eighty games in a summer. One Amateur Athletic Union basketball official admitted, "Teams are probably playing too many events." But he rationalizes, "There's so much pressure from parents and players to play more events for exposure that it takes away from what we're about—and that's developing players."[42]

The young athletes and their parents are showered with merchandise, flown to tournaments, fawned over, and then subtly steered toward high schools whose teams happen to have lucrative shoe deals with the companies. Even some of the driving forces behind this system are calling it the "cesspool of amateur basketball."

In a seemingly never-ending search for higher and higher levels of competitive sports for youth, adult intrusion into youth sports has gone global with the creation of the Youth Olympic Games, an international multisport event first held in Singapore in 2010. These games have been held since 2010 every four years in staggered summer and winter events, in nations such as Switzerland, China, Argentina, and Norway, similar to the current Olympic Games format. They are designed to be a media-driven extravaganza that will boost Olympic enthusiasm and participation among younger fans and athletes worldwide.

Like Mount Everest climbers, a few youth sport athletes do make it to the top and become professional athletes or Olympians. They become celebrities, and newspaper and magazine stories about them frequently report their odyssey through youth sports programs. But they are the few of millions of youths who play sports each year and whose parents fantasize that their son or daughter will become the next LeBron James, Serena Williams, Mike Trout, or Michelle Wie.

Unfortunately, despite thousands of dollars spent by parents and untold hours of practicing and playing games by young athletes, fewer than 1 percent of them will even receive a college athletic scholarship. And less than 1 percent of those who play college sports will become professional or Olympic athletes.

Occasionally the stories of athletes who did not fulfill their, or their parents', dreams of sporting fame come to light. There are even the sad stories of successful professionals and Olympians who publicly share their experiences of pressure, abuse, depression, and the loss of childhood through the years of struggling to achieve sporting prominence.

Children who are sent to train in sports academies in another part of the country and who are coached by well-known coaches, compete in national and international sports events, or turn professional during their adolescence are under immense pressures. In such cases, they are competing to live up to the expectations of their parents, their coaches, the media, and themselves. Sport participation, then, for these youth, can become a heavy burden.

Many former youth sports athletes remember their years in youth sports programs as being fun, exciting, and even, for some, the best years of their lives with their family. However, several writers have documented these years as being filled with stress, fear, abuse, and torment for some young athletes. Tom Farrey's book *Game On: The All-American Race to Make Champions of Our Children* details the impact of parents who lose perspective and, driven by their own aspirations and goals for their children, subject their kids to unrelenting pressure and anxiety. Farrey offers many excellent suggestions that will lead to better sports for youth.[43]

Adult intrusion into the world of youth sports can rob the young participants of some of the greatest potential of sports: the opportunity to have fun and to develop self-discipline and responsibility for one's own actions. Many youth sports programs are dominated by the coaches, who make all the decisions; they decide who plays, where they play, what tactics to employ, and what plays to run. In effect, the youngsters are the "hired help" who carry out the orders and do not ask questions if they do not want to be labeled "problem athletes." Thus, the imposition of adult dominance and decision-making in youth programs can sometimes do little to develop self-discipline and self-responsibility in children.

We want to make clear that we do not condemn all youth sports programs, but dominance by some dominating parents, coaches, personal trainers, and

BOX 8.2 *THINKING ABOUT SPORT:* A TEACH-ABLE MOMENT OR A REACTION BY THE COACH?

Behind by one run in the fifth inning of the Colorado state-qualifying American Legion B District Tournament baseball game against an arch-rival, the coach yanked his centerfielder from the game after the player threw his glove twice in a fit of anger when he failed to make a play and allowed a run to score.

The coach's action may not seem unusual, but in this case the coach showed the extent of his priorities inasmuch as he did not have another player to replace the one who was pulled. The team had no substitutes on the bench.

With only eight players to finish the game, the disciplinary action put the coach's team at a huge disadvantage because the team had to finish the game with only two outfielders and accept an automatic out every time the yanked player's place in the lineup came up.

The coach said he did what he did because he thought it was important to show the disciplined player the value of "trusting your teammates and not being an individual. If we didn't care about him or we didn't think he was a player then you just let that kind of stuff go. When you know he's a player and he's a good kid you can't let it go."

Postscript: After prolonged discussion by the umpires, and over the vigorous objection of the coach, the umpires ruled—incorrectly, it turns out—that a coach cannot remove a player from a game if the team does not have another player to replace the removed one.

Source: One of the authors of this book witnessed this incident.

---

private sponsors/boosters tends to conflict with the true spirit of play by exaggerating the importance of technique, efficiency, and winning—such programs can deprive youngsters of the fun and play elements of sport (see Box 8.2).

Violent Behavior and Sexual Abuse toward Athletes, Parents, and Coaches

Perhaps the most objectionable forms of adult intrusion into children's sports involve violent behavior: physical assaults by parents and coaches and sexual abuse of young athletes by youth sport coaches. With regard to physical assaults, youth sport administrators admit they are dealing with what many call *sideline rage,* and they say it is at epidemic levels. Recent reports from more than 2,000 chapters of the NAYS have indicated that about 15 percent of youth games involve some sort of verbal or physical abuse from parents or coaches. The specific incidents vary, but they are widespread throughout the United States, and they all involve assaultive actions.

A reader survey by *Sports Illustrated for Kids* reported that 74 percent of more than 3,000 respondents said they had witnessed out-of-control adults at their games. A similar survey by *Sporting Kids Magazine,* with 3,300 coaches, parents, youth sports administrators, and youth athletes responding, found that 84 percent said they had seen parents acting violently, such as shouting, berating, and using abusive language. Here are accounts of a few recent incidents:

- After a basketball game between ten- and eleven-year-olds in Iowa, the mother of one of the players attacked a pregnant referee. According to police reports, the attacker grabbed the referee by the hair, threw her to the ground, and kicked her.
- At a girls' rugby tournament game in California, a coach and several parents beat the opposing coach unconscious with kicks to the head and face, according to witnesses.
- Coaches of the Tri-Community YMCA basketball program in Southbridge, Massachusetts, sent letters to parents telling them that they were barred from attending the final game of the season because of continued unruly behavior.

Social scientists who have tried to explain these violent incidents point to the culture of violence in the wider society. Richard Lapchick's Institute for Diversity and Ethics in Sport at the University of Central Florida studies the interrelationships between society and sport. Lapchick blames the increase in parental violence on the rise of violence in other sectors of society. Indeed, one of the most hotly discussed current social issues is the rise in interpersonal incivility today. Other social analysts suggest that the excesses, aggression, and "in-your-face" actions that characterize contemporary cultural behavior are at work in professional sports for all to see: NFL players spitting in the face of opponents; NBA players charging into the stands to punch fans; NHL players sucker-punching opponents and, in one case, knocking an opponent unconscious and then driving him headfirst into the ice.

Parents and coaches are part of a social system that is larger than just sport; they are not immune to happenings in the broader society and in professional sports. There is also an additional factor for them. Many parents and coaches have become so emotionally involved with their children's sports or with the kids they are coaching that they have lost control over their own behavior. After spending a year examining the landscape of youth sports, the *Columbus* (Ohio) *Dispatch* reported that more than 40 percent of the youth sports athletes they interviewed said their parents pressured them to play, and 10 percent said their parents' behavior during games embarrassed them.

Social problems typically produce collective actions aimed at remedying them. Various efforts are being made to stem the tide of escalating parent and coach sideline rage. The goal is to educate parents and coaches and hold them accountable for their actions. As we noted earlier in this chapter, for the past decade the Positive Coaching Alliance has been holding workshops for youth sport coaches to transform the culture of youth sports to provide all young athletes the opportunity to have positive, character-building experiences. It has three national goals:

- To replace the "win-at-all-costs" model of coaching with the "double-goal coach" who wants to win but has a second, more important, goal of using sports to teach life lessons;
- To teach youth sports organization leaders how to create an organizational culture in which honoring the game is the norm; and
- To spark and fuel a "social epidemic" of positive coaching that will sweep this country.

Over the past two decades the Positive Coaching Alliance has conducted thousands of workshops nationwide for roughly 200,000 youth sports leaders, coaches, parents, and athletes that have helped create a positive sports environment for more than 1 million youth athletes.[44]

The NAYS is another organization that advocates for positive and safe youth sports. It created the Parents Association for Youth Sports to give parents a clear understanding of their roles and responsibilities in youth sport. It does that through a thirty-minute program that teaches parents sportsmanlike behaviors they can then pass on to their children. Parents access the program through a participating sports organization or online. More than 500 organizations are currently using the Parents Association for Youth Sports in an effort to prevent parent behavior problems in their programs.[45]

Some communities have begun hiring paid, trained supervisors to oversee all youth sports in the community. Other communities now require parents and coaches to sign an agreement spelling out a code of conduct. Without the signatures, parents' children cannot play in the programs and coaches are not able to coach.

As serious as the physical assaultive behavior of some parents and coaches is, surely the most distressing and odiously violent adult in youth sports is the child molester, the pedophile (a Greek word literally meaning "lover of children"). Until a few years ago, molestation was a nonissue in youth sports. The few scattered reports of sexual abuse of young athletes had been so rare that the media had largely ignored them.

However, the world of youth sports has been riddled with sexual abuse of young athletes by their powerful and often publicly respected coaches in a variety of sports, regardless of sex. Although there are no definitive data on the prevalence of these episodes, there is reason to believe that data from national sport governing bodies represent the proverbial "tip of the iceberg." Here are two examples that illustrate the magnitude of this problem:

- In 2011 USA Swimming listed fifty-nine coaches who have received a lifetime ban, permanently resigned their membership, or been declared permanently ineligible for membership, all but six with code of conduct violations.
- In 2011 USA Gymnastics listed eighty-two coaches permanently ineligible for membership because of conduct determined to be inconsistent with the best interest of the sport and the athletes being served.

Clearly, coaching behavior of this kind continues in youth sports.[46]

The fact that sexual molesters are found in youth sport is just another example of the linkages between the sports world and the broader society. But these recent revelations and frightening truths about child molestation in youth sports have made everyone connected to youth sports more vigilant in the selection and monitoring of coaches.

DISRUPTION OF EDUCATION

Another major social problem for young boys and girls who are being groomed for professional careers and Olympic status is that normal school attendance becomes impossible. At first the sports career and school may coexist peacefully, but when young athletes must practice six to eight hours per day, travel to distant cities and even foreign countries to participate in competition, and perhaps move from one region of the country to another to receive the desired coaching, normal educational routines must be disrupted. One example of this situation is sports academies, where more and more of the young athletes are being groomed for pro sport careers, Olympic berths, and a shot at fame and fortune. A relative of one of this book's authors regularly missed around thirty annual high school days as a result of his commitments to various club and select sports team duties. He eventually enrolled in a club-supported tutoring program until graduation. This type of alternative high school experience is becoming commonplace for high school–aged athletes who are seen as elite prospects.

Tennis, golf, swimming, figure skating, speed skating, skiing, soccer, and gymnastics require most of those who hope to become national- and international-level performers to train with the best coaches. There are so few of them in each sport that most athletes have to leave their homes and take up residence sometimes thousands of miles away to be near the best coaches and facilities.

Several solutions have emerged to meet the needs of young athletes who are in full-time training. One solution is the employment of tutors for the youngsters. Increasingly, however, such informal arrangements are giving way to more formal academies where children live, train, and go to school in one complex.

Most of the sports academies point with some pride to the academic records of their students. Some youth sports academies are subsidized by parent professional teams, such as those in Major League Soccer, and can afford to draw from a wide pool of athletes, regardless of social class background. Meanwhile, other academies that are more "pay to play" in nature draw uniformly from upper-middle-class families, and they receive tutorial instruction or are in classes with a low student-to-teacher ratio. In both scenarios, these alternatives may result in a good education for such youngsters, yet a question can be raised about the disruptive effects of going to school in an environment dominated by sport practices and competition and about the restricted interpersonal relationships present in such an environment.

This leads to a fundamental question: Is sport involvement so important during the growing-up years that children must be robbed of the normal experiences of childhood? Undoubtedly, some parents and coaches answer yes, and for those very, very few who become national team members, Olympic champions, or successful professionals, this assessment may be justified. For the vast majority of young athletes who endure this lifestyle and do not achieve the desired goal, however, a childhood may be lost. Examples of this abound in the stories of former athletes who spent their youth in sports academies and never reached their goals.

RISK OF INJURY

Daily living has risks and the potential for injury. Going through childhood and adolescence without risk and injury would be like missing a part of one's life. Given this, there are nevertheless some activities in which the chance of injury is greater than normal, and when these activities are forced on youngsters by adults, the issue of abuse is present.

Sport specialization and year-round play have long been linked to burnout in sports such as tennis, gymnastics, and figure skating. But doctors now also recognize a physical toll, suggesting that overtraining is behind an increase in physical injuries. Medical concern for young athletes has a long history, and most persons associated with youth sports have heard the arguments about "Little League elbow" and the dangers of tackle football and ice hockey for preadolescent youngsters.

There is, however, a growing concern that goes beyond Little League elbow and broken bones and concussions in football or hockey to "swimmer's shoulder" and "gymnast's back." Dr. James R. Andrews, president of the American Orthopedic Society for Sports Medicine, says that 60 percent of the athletes he operates on these days are high school athletes or younger. He argues, "I don't think epidemic is too strong a word. . . . We're seeing kids hurt before they even have a chance to become athletes." That organization has launched a campaign to curb sports injuries in children called STOP (Sports Trauma and Overuse Prevention). According to Andrews, the main culprit is sport specialization: "You just have this enormous pressure nowadays on kids to play one sport year-round."[47]

Along with a steady flow of reports on the long-term effects of concussions and repeated head injuries in several sports, especially football, hockey, soccer, and lacrosse, public awareness has spiked as parents, coaches, and medical experts now approach the injury with greater urgency. In *The Concussion Crisis*, the authors assert, "A silent epidemic of these unseen brain injuries among kids has been exploding right under our noses . . . . We underestimated the damage resulting from jolts to the head and . . . scientists, over the last couple of decades, began to recognize that there was an emerging epidemic of brain injuries . . . in sports."[48] To better understand the causes and effects of brain injuries, in 2013 the U.S. government launched a sweeping study of the rising number of sports-related concussions among youth sport athletes.

There are reports that some parents are forbidding their sons to play football, and some are considering the same for their daughters with soccer. Pop Warner football established a policy that players with suspected concussions cannot return until evaluated by a licensed medical professional. Youth soccer's governing body has banned or limited heading the ball for certain younger age groups because of concerns about head injuries.

The accelerated training regimens of many current youth athletes that extend up to eight hours per day, six—even seven, in some cases—days a week, throughout the year, raise serious questions about physical injury. Physicians are seeing a dramatic increase in overuse injuries among children in organized sports. Dr. Andrews alone is "seeing four times as many overuse injuries in youth sports than five years ago and more kids are having surgery for chronic sports injuries." There is widespread agreement among orthopedic professionals attributing this increase to the fact that more youth today are specializing in one sport at an early age and training year-round. According to Dr. David Frumberg, an orthopedic surgeon from the Yale School of Medicine, "The problem is that when children do the same thing, like pitch a baseball—over and over again—and don't play other sports, they continually stress the same body part," says Dr. Frumberg. "Five or 10 years ago, coaches didn't realize this was such a problem. But now it's a public health issue."[49]

THE "WINNING-IS-THE-ONLY-THING" ETHIC AND YOUTH SPORTS

The final topic we discuss in this section on potential psychosocial problems of youth sports is one that lurks throughout youth sports. We call it the "winning-is-the-only-thing" ethic. To understand this ethic in youth sports, it is helpful to understand its linkages to the broader culture of the United States.

The United States' form of capitalist economy came into prominence with the robber barons of the latter nineteenth century and continues today, with most industries dominated by huge corporations that have driven other enterprises out of business. The major form of testing in America's educational system is based on competition against other students or against standardized norms for good grades and educational advancement. America's media compete vigorously against each other for readers, listeners, and viewers. The political system is democratic, and citizens have an opportunity to vote for the candidates of their choice, but the candidates compete fiercely to win the election.

It is perhaps not surprising, then, that hypercompetitiveness has permeated U.S. sports since the rise of organized sports forms. Social analysts and researchers

Every year, more than 3.5 million children aged 14 and younger are treated for sports injuries.*

Sports injuries can cause permanent damage and increase the chances of surgeries and arthritis later in life. If an injury does occur, early identification and proper treatment is the key to a successful recovery. Armed with the correct information and tools, today's youth athletes can remain healthy, play safe, and stay in the game for life.

Become an advocate for safe sports participation.

For more information, visit www.STOPSportsInjuries.org

* American Academy of Orthopaedic Surgeons. Play it Safe. 1999

Medical concern for young athletes is growing, and parental concern has been growing as well. Most persons associated with youth sports have heard the rather shocking statistics about the number of young athletes treated each year for injuries. (Photo: With permission from American Orthopedic Society for Sports Medicine) have indeed found that Americans strongly believe that competition is a national way of life, and that this cultural trait is prominently promoted through sporting endeavors.[50] At every level of organized sports, winning has been richly rewarded, either in monetary form or in social status. Some of the most admired sports celebrities have exuded a win-at-all-costs attitude. The slogans of sports culture have emphasized an uncompromising attitude about winning: "Winning isn't everything, it's the only thing"; "Show me a good loser, and I'll show you a loser"; "*Lose* is a four-letter word"; "Not every kid should get a winner's trophy."

As we have previously noted, coaches and athletes at the professional, college, and high school levels are the role models and heroes of youth sport athletes, who tend to internalize the attitudes, values, and behaviors of older athletes. Their other role models and heroes are parents and coaches who are in daily contact with them and are powerful and direct in their socializing influence. Young athletes form fundamental attitudes, values, and beliefs from these interactions.

Although "winning is the only thing" is widely accepted for child athletes thrown into the big business of elite sports, such an ethic can become a terrible burden for young athletes. Win–loss records define them. Winners are accorded prestige and honor; losers suffer disdain and ridicule. Because being labeled a loser is the epitome of criticism in our society, many young athletes experience stress and develop anxiety and other forms of psychosocial trauma.

With more and more professional athletes making huge salaries and with top amateur athletes earning money and getting considerable media attention, more and more junior and age-group athletes are in training to become scholarship, professional, or Olympic-level athletes, and the pressures have become even more intense on these youngsters. What for most boys and girls is play becomes a job for some young athletes. Despite the hours, even years, of hard work put in by these ambitious youth (and their parents), the issue of child labor has rarely come up, and the laws prohibiting child labor have never been applied to elite youth athletes.

There is no safety net protecting youth athletes—not the parents, not the coaches, not the sport organizations where they play. Child labor laws prohibit a twelve-year-old from working forty hours a week at a McDonald's restaurant, but that same boy or girl can labor for forty hours or more at a gym or a tennis court or an ice skating rink without drawing any attention from the government.

The extent parents, coaches, and young athletes will go to, when winning becomes the only thing, has been well documented. The types of behaviors, with the attitudes toward sports to which they have been conditioned, do little to promote personal and social growth as well as the "character traits" that are universally endorsed as outcomes of sports involvement.

We wish to re-emphasize that we are not denying that the quest for victory has its place in youth sports. Striving for victory in a competitive situation is a perfectly legitimate goal. We do think, however, given the organizational nature of many youth sports programs and the emphasis on winning for elite-level young athletes, that there is a tendency to allow winning to become the only goal. When this happens in youth sports, the enormous potential benefit of sport involvement for a healthy self-concept development is jeopardized.

EMPHASIZING PERSONAL GROWTH AND SELF-ACTUALIZATION

Our major contention in this book is that sports for youth have virtually unlimited potential for promoting personal growth, self-actualization, and social competency. Therefore, the goal of youth sports should be nothing less than self-fulfillment of the individuals engaged in and influenced by them. The emphasis of such programs should be on personal expression and the value of participation, on offering everyone the opportunity to engage in sports in such a way that youngsters experience no feeling of humiliation if a contest is lost. Why must sport be justified on the basis that it does things other than providing joy and self-fulfillment for the participants?

An increasing number of attempts have been made to improve youth sports by designing programs based on principles that place the personal–social needs of the participants first and the mindsets of adults far behind. There is a growing literature describing these programs and discussing ways and means by which parents and coaches can improve the quality of the sporting experience for young boys and girls (see Box 8.3).[51]

LIFESTYLE/ACTION SPORTS

Baseball, football, and basketball were the dominant sports when organized youth sports programs were first getting started in the United States. Although these are still popular youth sports, there is now much more variety in the sports available for kids. The newest trends in youth sports are coming from what are called lifestyle/action sports that youngsters are developing largely themselves. Historically many youngsters have become involved in them as a rejection of the norms and values of traditional youth sports.

In contemporary society, then, youths are turning to participate in activities such as skateboarding, parkour (free running), and surfing, where values such as creativity, fun, and self-determination prevail. Then, although not a new sport, Freestyle football/soccer has been gaining popularity around the globe and in the United States. The sport involves competitors doing a short performance of creative ball skills involving juggling and other acrobatic moves, and there is even a World Freestyle Football Association that organizes events and educates the public about this growing sporting movement.[52]

One concern that many of these emerging sports face is increasing corporate intervention: advertisers and television executives discovered they could package these sports to make them attractive to young television audiences and that they could sell TV commercial time to advertisers with products appealing to teenage and young adult male audiences. The X Games were created by ESPN to capture the growing popularity of action/lifestyle sports among the young for the purpose of generating profits for ESPN and the advertising corporations. ESPN's X Games will be discussed in more detail in Chapter 12. The 2020 Tokyo Summer Olympic Games also hosted lifestyle/action sport competitions, with inaugural surfing, climbing, and skateboarding events, presumably to attract a more youthful global audience and consumer base.

YOUTH SPORTS COACHES

It is estimated that there are some 7.5 million volunteer youth sports coaches in North America, most of whom have had no formal instruction in the developmental or educational aspects of teaching/coaching. Thus, there is agreement by almost everyone associated with youth sports that the vast majority of youth sports coaches are ill-equipped for their role. Without them, however, millions of boys and girls would not have the opportunity to participate in organized sports.

In an effort to help volunteer coaches become more knowledgeable, some youth sports programs have instituted mandatory clinics, workshops, and certification programs for all of their coaches. The American Sport Education Program (ASEP) is a complete education package that has been adopted by many youth sports organizations throughout the United States. Since its founding in 1976, ASEP has

A coach reviewing strategies with her team. There are millions of volunteer youth sports coaches in the United States. (Photo: Monkey Business Images)

been a valuable education training tool for youth sports coaches. ASEP coaches learn to teach skills and strategies, plan effectively for their season, prepare athletes for competition, and understand the developmental needs of young athletes. Its curriculum is built on the philosophical foundation of "Athletes First, Winning Second."[53]

The National Youth Sport Coaches Association (NYSCA) has been a pioneer in the development of a national training system for volunteer coaches. More than 3 million coaches have attended NYSCA clinics since the program began in 1981. At the end

of each NYSCA clinic, coaches must (1) pass an exam that tests their understanding of the information conveyed in the clinic and (2) sign a pledge committing them to uphold the association's code of ethics. The NYSCA Coaches' Code of Ethics is shown in Box 8.4.

BILL OF RIGHTS FOR YOUNG ATHLETES

Guarantees of personal liberty for all U.S. citizens are found in the Bill of Rights, which are the first ten amendments to the Constitution of the United States. Similar safeguards have also been written into most state constitutions. Many business organizations have also developed a bill of rights for their employees as a commitment to employees that they will be treated with dignity and respect and that their needs and interests will be protected.

In an attempt to protect youth from adult exploitation in sports, a group of medical, physical education, and recreation leaders formulated a Bill of Rights for Young Athletes several years ago. The ten rights are targeted to coaches, leaders of recreation programs, officials, and parents in the hope that their implementation will promote the beneficial effects of athletic participation for all who are involved. These rights are as follows:

1. The right to participate in sports.
2. The right to participate at a level commensurate with each child's maturity and ability.

BOX 8.4 *THINKING ABOUT SPORT:* NYSCA COACHES' CODE OF ETHICS

I hereby pledge to live up to my certification as a NYSCA Coach by following the NYSCA Coaches' Code of Ethics.

- I will place the emotional and physical well-being of my players ahead of a personal desire to win.
- I will treat each player as an individual, remembering the large range of emotional and physical development for the same age group.
- I will do my best to provide a safe playing situation for my players.
- I will promise to review and practice the basic first aid principles needed to treat injuries of my players.

- I will do my best to organize practices that are fun and challenging for all my players.
- I will lead by example in demonstrating fair play and sportsmanship to all my players.
- I will provide a sports environment for my team that is free of drugs, tobacco, and alcohol, and I will refrain from their use at all youth sports events.
- I will be knowledgeable in the rules of each sport that I coach, and I will teach these rules to my players.
- I will use those coaching techniques appropriate for each of the skills that I teach.
- I will remember that I am a youth sports coach, and that the game is for children and not adults.

Source: National Alliance for Youth Sports, http://www.nays.org/.

3. The right to have qualified adult leadership.
4. The right to play as a child and not as an adult.
5. The right to share in the leadership and decision-making of their sport participation.
6. The right to participate in safe and healthy environments.
7. The right to proper preparation in sports.
8. The right to an equal opportunity to strive for success.
9. The right to be treated with dignity.
10. The right to have fun in sports.

Many youth sport organizations have adopted the Bill of Rights for Young Athletes as a guarantee to the young athletes and their parents that the athletes' development and welfare will be protected. Typically, the bill of rights is included in materials given to the athletes and their parents when they sign up to play in a particular sports program.[54]

YOUTH SPORT AND THE COVID-19 PANDEMIC

American youth sports have been undoubtedly impacted by the COVID-19 pandemic, which has required program and societal leaders to re-envision the place, provision, and meanings of these popular American youth activities. Here are some key statistics that provide a snapshot of the negative impacts of COVID-19 on youth sports participation during the onset of the pandemic in 2020[55]:

- The average child spent about 6.5 hours less per week on sports during COVID-19.
- Free play, practices, and competitions all significantly declined.
- Time spent on games declined by 59 percent.
- Practice hours were down 54 percent during the pandemic.
- Youth sports became less accessible to lower-income youth. In 2020, children from a household making $100,000 or more spent more than two hours additional time on sports each week compared to children from homes making under $50,000. That gap between these different groups of children was less than one hour before COVID-19.

Furthermore, in terms of the pandemic's consequences on children's experiences, it has been reported that 72 percent of parents reported that the inability to play sports has caused their child stress or anxiety.[56]

Given these stark findings surrounding the COVID-19 pandemic, numerous discussions have taken place regarding the future provision of and participation in youth sports. These conversations implicate a raft of public health, social, educational, and economic issues. Indeed, many scholars, observers, and even program leaders themselves believe that youth sports will never be the same again. It has thus been suggested that youth sports need to become more sustainable given the problems that emerged during the pandemic. Project Play of the Aspen Institute, for instance, contends that "the COVID-19 pandemic has laid bare fundamental flaws in our sport system . . . without coordinated leadership, organized youth sports were the last to shut down and the first to start back up. And it came back mostly for youth with access to private club teams. Left out are many younger children and vulnerable populations who rely on public recreation, YMCAs, in-town leagues and school sports, whose offerings have diminished due to budget constraints or COVID-19 mitigation concerns."[57]

During one event on June 12, 2020, hosted by the Global Sport Institute of Arizona State University, "COVID-19 & the Future of Youth Sport," several innovative ideas were proposed and discussed. Panelists raised the possibility that youth sport could refocus on its core values, including the development of life skills. A more local, community-based approach that would forego extensive travel and logistics was also proposed. At the same time, given economic disparities exacerbated by the pandemic, it was once again suggested that youth sport needed to avoid a situation whereby "the haves" with resources could continue to participate while the "have-nots" would be left out. In this regard, a social justice approach could serve as a key point of emphasis in future youth sport provision, in order to better include and engage underserved youth.[58] We will delve further into these issues of sustainable youth sport participation in Chapter 15.

SUMMARY

There has been an enormous increase in community-sponsored youth sports programs. There has also been a growth in elite youth sport in which the youngsters train and compete with aspirations of becoming professional or Olympic-caliber athletes. An estimated 60 million American boys and girls participate in these programs each year. Two of the most salient factors contributing to the growth of these programs are (1) the rise of organized and corporate sport, followed by the desire to participate and to spectate on the part of large numbers of people, and (2) the realization by Americans of the importance of providing varied opportunities for their children.

The objectives of most youth sports programs are to provide participants with an opportunity to learn culturally relevant sport skills and to develop attitudes and values about such things as competition, cooperation, sportsmanship, discipline, authority, and social relationships. There are, however, programs that are blatant career-training programs.

The extent to which the attitudes, values, beliefs, and behaviors of participants are influenced by organized youth programs is largely unknown. Most studies of attitudes toward youth sports suggest that parents and participants believe that they are more beneficial than detrimental to the development of young boys and girls. Participants in these programs are socialized into them by a variety of social agents and agencies, parents, siblings, peers, coaches, the mass media, and so forth.

The social context of informal, peer-organized sports activities is vastly different from that of adult-organized youth sports programs. Thus, the play behavior in the two social contexts is likely to lead to quite different learning.

There are a number of problems in organized youth sports. One is that the intrusion of adults into the play of youngsters may rob the young participants of many of the values of play. A second is that the norm learning involved may be at variance with American social norms. A third is that normal educational experiences may become impossible. A fourth is that intense training and competition for prolonged periods of time may cause both acute and chronic injury. Finally, the overemphasis on winning in some youth programs threatens to overshadow the expressive, self-fulfilling potential of sports participation.

A number of interesting efforts have been made to develop alternative youth sports programs; in most cases the emphasis of these programs is on fun, participation, and skill learning. One group of researchers has developed a system for helping coaches improve their coaching behavior, and courses have been developed to help coaches become more effective. In an attempt to protect young athletes from adult exploitation in sports, a Bill of Rights for Young Athletes and Fair Play Codes have been formulated. The advent of the COVID-19 pandemic and subsequent youth sport program shutdowns has also raised crucial questions regarding the future of youth sports in terms of providing more equitable access to participation, for all members of society.

Learn more with this chapter's digital tools, including web resources, video links, and chapter self-assessment quizzes at www.oup.com/he/sage-eitzen-beal-atencio-12e.

NOTES

1. Christopher Bjork and William Hoynes, "Youth Sports Needs a Reset. Child Athletes Are Pushed to Professionalize Too Early," *USA Today*, March 24, 2021, https://www.usatoday.com/story/opinion/voices/2021/03/24/youth-sports-competitive-covid-19-expensive-column/4797607001/.

2. "Head Injuries in Mind, RMU Survey Shows Strong Support for Ban on Youth Contact Football," PR Newswire/Robert Morris University, November 14, 2013, https://www.prnewswire.com/news-releases/head-injuries-in-mind-rmu-survey-shows-strong-support-for-ban-on-youth-contact-football-231895261.html.

3. US Youth Soccer, "Who Is US Youth Soccer?," https://www.usyouthsoccer.org/about/who-is-us-youth-soccer/. Accessed July 1, 2022.

4. Steve Silverman, "The History of Youth Sports," Livestrong, September 1, 2015, http://www.livestrong.com/article/353963-the-history-of-youth-sports/; see also David K Wiggins, "A Worthwhile Effort? History of Organized Youth Sport in the United States," *Kinesiology Review* 2, no. 1 (2013): 65–74.

5. Emily Barone, "The Astronomical Cost of Kids' Sports," *Time*, August 24, 2017, http://time.com/4913284/kids-sports-cost/; Sean Gregory, "How Kids' Sports Became a $15 Billion Industry," *Time*, August 24, 2017.

6. Anne Schmitt, Matthew Atencio, and Gaëlle Sempé, "'You're Sitting on a Hot Soccer Field Drinking Gatorade . . . I'm Sitting in a Yacht Club Just Enjoying the View, Enjoying the Drinks': Parental Reproduction of Social Class through School Sport Sailing," *European Physical Education Review* 26, no. 4 (2020): 987–1005.

7. Marlene A Dixon and Stacy M. Warner, "More Than Just Letting Them Play: Parental Influence on Women's Lifetime Sport Involvement," *Sociology of Sport Journal* 25, no. 4 (2008): 538–559; Michael Zito, "Family Systems Interventions in Sport," in *Routledge Handbook of Applied Sport Psychology: A Comprehensive Guide for Students and Practitioners*, ed. Stephanie Hanrahan and Mark B. Andersen (New York: Routledge, 2012), 177–185.

8. David King and Margot Starbuck, *Overplayed: A Parent's Guide to Sanity in the World of Youth Sports* (Harvey, ND: Herald Press, 2016); see also John O'Sullivan, *Changing the Game: The Parent's Guide to Raising Happy, High Performing Athletes, and Giving Youth Sports Back to Our Kids* (New York: Morgan James, 2013); Jack Perconte, *Raising an Athlete: How to Instill Confidence, Build Skills and Inspire a Love of Sport* (Chicago: Second Base Publishing, 2009).

9. Jay Coakley, "The Good Father: Parental Expectations and Youth Sports," *Leisure Studies* 25, no. 2 (2006): 153–163.

10. Lisa Swanson, "Soccer Fields of Cultural [Re]Production: Creating 'Good Boys' in Suburban America," *Sociology of Sport Journal* 26, no. 3 (2009): 404–424.

11. Swanson, "Soccer Fields."

12. Camilla J. Knight, Travis E. Dorsch, Keith V. Osai, Kyle L Haderlie, and Paul A Sellars, "Influences on Parental Involvement in Youth Sport," *Sport, Exercise, and Performance Psychology* 5, no. 2 (2016), 161–178; see also Camilla J. Knight, Travis E. Dorsch, Keith V. Osai, Kyle L Haderlie, and Paul A Sellars, "The Importance of Parents' Behavior in Their Children's Enjoyment and Amotivation in Sports," *Journal of Human Kinetics* 36 (March 2013): 169–177; L Gottzén and T. Kremer-Sadlik, "Fatherhood and Youth Sports: A Balancing Act between Care and Expectations," *Gender & Society* 26 (2012): 639–664; Michael A Messner, *It's All for the Kids: Gender, Families, and Youth Sports* (Berkeley: University of California Press, 2009).

13. Mathew Atencio, Becky Beal, ZaNean McClain, and Missy Wright, "'No One Wants to Mess with an Angry Mom': Females' Negotiation of Power Technologies within a Local Skateboarding Culture," in *Women in Action Sport Cultures: Identity, Politics, and Experiences*, ed. Holly Thorpe and Rebecca Olive (New York: Palgrave Macmillan, 2016), 175–191.

14. For a penetrating and sobering series of stories about youth in sport at various ages, see Jay Atkinson, "How Parents Are Ruining Youth Sports," *Boston Globe*, May 4, 2014, https://www.bostonglobe.com/magazine/2014/05/03/how-parents-are-ruining-youth-sports/vbRln8qYXkrrNFJcsuvNyM/story.html; Mark Hyman, *Until It Hurts: America's Obsession with Youth Sports and How It Harms Our Kids* (Boston: Beacon Press, 2010).

15. James McKeever, "Park 'Rats' to Park "Daddies": Community Heads Creature Future Mentors," in *Child's Play: Sport in Kids' Worlds*, ed. Michael A Messner and Michela Musto (New Brunswick, NJ: Rutgers University Press, 2016).

16. "Play 7: Train All Coaches," Project Play, Aspen Institute, n.d., https://www.aspenprojectplay.org/the-8-plays/train-all-coaches. Accessed June 1, 2022

17. P. J. Adachi and T. Willoughby, "Does Playing Sports Video Games Predict Increased Involvement in Real-Life Sports over Several Years among Older Adolescents and Emerging Adults?" *Journal of Youth and Adolescence* 45, no. 2 (2016): 391–401; Bart Sullivan, "Youth Sports and Video Games," *Sport IQ*, January 9, 2015, http://www.getsportiq.com/2015/01/youth-sports-and-video-games/.

18. Julianna W. Miner, "Why 70 Percent of Kids Quit Sports by Age 13," *The Washington Post*, June 1, 2016, https://www.washingtonpost.com/news/parenting/

wp/2016/06/01/why-70-percent-of-kids-quit-sports-by-age-13/?utm_term=.60525167d73c; Kelly Wallace, "How to Make Your Kid Hate Sports without Really Trying," CNN, January 21, 2016, http://www.cnn.com/2016/01/21/health/kids-youth-sports-parents/; Michael A Messner and Michela Musto, "Where Are the Kids?" *Sociology of Sport Journal* 31, no. 1 (2014): 102–122.

19. Lisa Wood, May Carter, and Karen Martin, "Dispelling Stereotypes . . . Skate Parks as a Setting for Pro-Social Behavior among Young People," *Current Urban Studies* 2, no.1 (2014): 62–72.

20. Melissa A Chase and Moe Machida, "The Role of Sport as a Social Status Determinant for Children," *Research Quarterly for Exercise and Sport* 82, no. 4 (2011): 731–739.

21. Deborah Meier, Brenda S. Engel, and Beth Taylor, *Playing for Keeps: Life and Learning on a Public School Playground* (New York: Teachers College Press, Columbia University, 2010), 83.

22. Meier, Engel, and Taylor, *Playing for Keeps*, 88.

23. For a persuasive account of how adults are turning youth sports into a high-pressure, big-money enterprise, see Hyman, *The Most Expensive Game in Town*; see also Hyman, *Until It Hurts*.

24. Sandra Spickard Prettyman and Brian Lampman, eds., *Learning Culture through Sports: Perspectives on Society and Organized Sports*, 2nd ed. (Lanham, MD: Rowman & Littlefield, 2010).

25. See Matthew Atencio and Jan Wright, "'Ballet It's Too Whitey': Discursive Hierarchies of High School Dance Spaces and the Constitution of Embodied Feminine Subjectivities," *Gender and Education* 21, no. 1 (2009): 31–46; also see Mathew Atencio, Becky Beal, E. Missy Wright, and ZaNean McClain, *Moving Boarders: Skateboarding and the Changing Landscape of Urban Youth Sports* (Fayetteville: University of Arkansas Press, 2018).

26. For a review of the professionalization research, see David Light Shields and Brenda Light Bredemeier, "Advances in Sport Morality Research," in *Handbook of Sport Psychology*, 3rd ed., ed. Gershon Tennenbaum and Robert C. Eklund (New York: Wiley, 2007), 663–664.

27. David Light Shields, Brenda Light Bredemeier, Nicole M. LaVoi, and F. Clark Power, "The Sport Behavior of Youth, Parents, and Coaches: The Good, the Bad, and the Ugly," *Journal of Research in Character Education* 3, no. 1 (2005): 43–59; see also David Light Shields and Brenda Light Bredemeier, *True Competition: Guide to Pursuing Excellence in Sport & Society* (Champaign, IL: Human Kinetics, 2009); "Lack of Sportsmanship Exposed in New Athletic Survey Points to Changing Attitudes among Today's Young Athletes," *American Chronicle*, August 9, 2010, http://www.americanchronicle.com/articles/yb/147394879/.

28. Fred Engh, "The Immature Parent in Youth Sports," *The Huffington Post*, March 30, 2016; Kim Payne, Luis Llosa, and Scott Lancaster, *Beyond Winning: Smart Parenting in a Toxic Sports Environment* (Guilford, CT: Lyons Press, 2013); Staff Report, "Youth Football Coaches Physically and Emotionally Abusing Their Players in the Pursuit of Wins," *National Alliance for Youth Sports*, February 11, 2015, http://www.nays.org/blog/youth-football-coaches-physically-and-emotionally-abusing-their-players-in-the-pursuit-of-wins/.

29. Jay Coakley, "Youth Sports: What Counts as 'Positive Development?'" *Journal of Sport and Social Issues* 35 (2011): 306–324.

30. Hyman, *The Most Expensive Game in Town*.

31. Christine Brennan, "'Rec Rage' Is Unfit for Youth Sports," *USA Today*, May 17, 2012, 3C; Fred Mann and Rick Plumlee, "Passionate Parents Can Mean Trouble for Youth Sports," *The Wichita Eagle*, September 13, 2014, http://www.kansas.com/news/local/crime/article2101296.html.

32. Engh, "The Immature Parent in Youth Sports."

33. Andy Staples, "Tis Better to Receive," *Sports Illustrated*, August 28, 2017, 46–49.

34. Hyman, *The Most Expensive Game in Town*.

35. Malcolm Conway, *Raising Elite Athletes* (Tulsa, OK: Total Publishing and Media, 2011); see also *State of Play 2017 Trends and Development*, Aspen Institute Project Play (Washington, D.C.: Aspen Institute, 2017); Atkinson, "How Parents Are Ruining Youth Sports."

36. Staples, "Tis Better to Receive"; see also Chris Johnson, "Early Daze: Why Do Coaches Offer Scholarships to Kids?" *Sports Illustrated*, August 28, 2017, 49.

37. Ron Filipkowski, *Travelball: How to Start and Manage a Successful Travel Baseball Team* (Palmetto, FL: Harmonic Research Associates, 2011); see also Brian T. Feeley, Julie Agel, and Robert F. LaPrade, "When Is It Too Early for Single Sport Specialization?" *American Journal of Sports Medicine* 44, no. 1 (2016): 234–241; David McCoy, "As Competition Rises, Team Sports Decline but Traveling Teams Soar," CBS Minnesota, November 16, 2015, http://minnesota.cbslocal.com/2015/11/16/as-competition-rises-team-sports-decline-but-traveling-teams-soar/.

38. Laken Litman, "Youth Pitchers Feel Pinch of Surgery," *USA Today*, July 23, 2014, 4C; Jeff Passan, "Under the Gun," *Sports Illustrated*, April 4, 2016, 56–64; Adam Shell, "Fitting High-Priced Elite Sports into the Family Budget," *USA Today*, September 5, 2017, 1B–2B.

39. Bob Cook, "What Drives Parents' Youth Sports Spending? Don't Underestimate Peer Pressure," *Forbes Magazine*, August 1, 2016, https://www.forbes.com/sites/bocook/2016/08/01/what-drives-parents-youth-sports-spending-dont-underestimate-peer-pressure/#36d66cb7325b; see also Fred Engh, "Travel Teams: Youth Sports' New Headache," *The Huffington Post*, March 18, 2015, http://www.huffingtonpost.com/fred-engh/travel-teams-youth-sports_b_6887720.html.

40. Quoted in Clay Latimer, "Under a Nonstop Watch," *Rocky Mountain News*, December 19, 2005, 8C.

41. For more information see Camp Woodword web page, https://www.worldofwoodward.com/.

42. Jim Halley, "New Rules Create Hoops Overload," *USA Today*, August 2, 2010, 8C; see also Kevin McNutt, *Playing Time: Tough Truths About AAU Basketball, Youth Sports, Parents, and Athletes* (Chicago: African American Images, 2015); George Dohrmann, *Play Their Hearts Out: A Coach, His Star Recruit, and the Youth Basketball Machine* (New York: Ballantine Books, 2012).

43. Farrey, *Game On.*

44. Positive Coaching Alliance, http://www.positive-coach.org/; see also Payne, Llosa, and Lancaster, *Beyond Winning.*

45. Parents Association for Youth Sports, http://paysonline.nays.org/.

46. "Confronting Sexual Abuse and Harassment by Sport Coaches: A Need for a National Effort," in *Make Sport Safe for Athletes*, 2014, https://safe4athletes.org/wp-content/uploads/2022/02/whitepaper-final-4-25-11-.pdf, accessed June 17, 2022; see also Margo Mountjoy, Celia Brackenridge, Malia Arrington, Cheri Blauwet, Andrea Carska-Sheppard, Kari Fasting, Sandra Kirby, Trisha Leahy, Saul Marks, Kathy Martin, Katherine Starr, Anne Tiivas, & Richard Budgett, The IOC Consensus Statement: harassment and abuse (non-accidental violence) in sport, (2016), Vol 50, issue 17 1–11. British Journal of Sports Medicine; see also Randy Nathan, *Bullying in Sports: A Guide to Identifying the Injuries We Don't See* (Boston: Pearson, 2014).

47. Quoted in Mark Hyman, "A Children's Crusade," *Sports Illustrated*, June 7, 2010, 18; see also Loyola University Health System, "Intense, Specialized Training in Young Athletes Linked to Serious Overuse Injuries," *ScienceDaily*, April 19, 2013, https://www.sciencedaily.com/releases/2013/04/130419132508.htm; Nikki Work, "Reaching a Healthy Goal," *The Greeley Tribune*, August 16, 2015, D1, D5.

48. Robert Graham, Frederick P. Rivara, Morgan A. Ford, and Carol Mason Spicer, *Sports-Related Concussions in Youth: Improving the Science, Changing the Culture* (Washington, D.C.: National Academies Press, 2014); see also William White, Alan Ashare, and Katharine White, *Winning the War against Concussions in Youth Sports: Brain & Life Saving Solutions for Preventing & Healing Middle-High School & College Sports Head Injuries* (New York: Create Space Independent Publishing Platform, 2014).

49. Kathy Katella, "Kids' Sports Injuries: What Parents Need to Know," Yale Medicine, January 29, 2019, https://www.yalemedicine.org/news/kids-sports-injuries.

50. Chris Knoester and Evan A Davis, "Patriotism, competition, nationalism, and respect for the military in US sports: Public recognition of American institutionalized sports nationalism," *International Review for the Sociology of Sport* (2021), DOI: 10.1177/10126902211048769.

51. Child Trends, "Family Structure," 2015, http://www.childtrends.org/indicators/family-structure/.

52. World Freestyle Football Association, "About the Association," accessed July 28, 2022, https://thewffa.org/about-%20association-wffa/.

53. American Sport Education Program, http://www.asep.com/; Wade Gilbert, *Coaching Better Every Season: A Year-Round System for Athlete Development and Program Success* (Champaign, IL: Human Kinetics, 2017); Holt, *Positive Youth Development through Sport*.

54. Mathias Teglbjaerg, "Children's Rights Are Still Widely Ignored in Sport," *Play the Game*, February 12, 2017. http://www.playthegame.org/news/news-articles/2015/0011_children-s-rights-are-still-widely-ignored-in-sport/; John O'Sullivan, "The Enemy of Excellence in Youth Sports," Changing the Game Project, January 8, 2015. http://changingthegameproject.com/the-enemy-of-excellence-in-youth-sports; Francesco Duina, *Winning: Reflections on an American Obsession* (Princeton, NJ: Princeton University Press, 2010); Nicholas L Holt, *Positive Youth Development through Sport*, 2nd ed. (New York: Routledge, 2016).

55. "State of Play 2020: Pandemic Trends," Aspen Institute's Project Play, 2020; https://www.aspenprojectplay.org/state-of-play-2020/pandemic-trends.

56. Global Sport Institute, Arizona State University, "GSM Live (video): COVID-19 & the Future of Youth Sport," https://globalsport.asu.edu/resources/gsm-live-video-covid-19-future-youth-sport. Accessed July 20, 2022.

57. "State of Play 2020: Pandemic Trends," Aspen Institute's Project Play, 2020, https://www.aspenprojectplay.org/state-of-play-2020/pandemic-trends. Accessed July 21, 2022.

58. Global Sport Institute, Arizona State University, "GSM Live (video): COVID-19 & the Future of Youth Sport," https://globalsport.asu.edu/resources/gsm-live-video-covid-19-future-youth-sport. Accessed June 15, 2022.

CHAPTER 9

INTERSCHOLASTIC SPORTS

Sportsmanship is extremely valuable in the role of providing education-based values through activities. . . . The life skills students learn through participation are accentuated best by competing in a fair, positive environment.

—JON OGLESBY, *from speech before the Utah High School Activities Association*

Interschool high school sports in the United States have become vitally important as a means of unifying the entire school in a common cause—supporting the local teams. While historically high school sports were exclusively a male preserve, Title IX of the Educational Amendments Act of 1972 has moved high school sports toward gender equity. (Photo: DonLand)

The formal systems of education in the United States are the foundational social institution for preparing each generation to take its place in preserving and advancing its nation. It is here that the young people learn cultural values and roles and acquire the skills that will be necessary throughout their adult lives. In the United States more than 90 percent of adolescents between the ages of fifteen and eighteen are enrolled in high schools.

SOCIAL THEORIES AND INTERSCHOLASTIC SPORTS

Social theorists have differing interpretations about the role of high schools. A functionalist perspective of the high school views it as the primary social institution for performing a number of social reproduction functions: transmitting knowledge and conveying the dominant culture, promoting social and political integration, providing a common moral code for social cohesion, maintaining social control, and sorting and selecting students for their adult roles in society.

This last function typically plays out through competition for grades, with intellectually brighter and more socially competent students earning higher grades and thus having better potential for high-status occupations as adults. Beyond that, in the functionalist viewpoint schools are sites of teaching and learning social skills and thus places where young people learn the "rules" of larger society; for the benefit of these individuals *and* society as a whole.[1]

While recognizing the importance of a high school education in the United States, conflict/culturalists view high schools as organizations with a distinctive elite orientation, with sharp inequalities in the educational opportunities available for students from different minority racial and ethnic groups and for female students. They stress that the sorting and selecting of pupils are highly biased according to students' socioeconomic backgrounds, giving students from affluent and wealthy families a variety of advantages on achievement tests; these enable such students to qualify for the best universities, which, in turn, increases the likelihood of their economic and social success in adulthood. Although some children from poor families do well in school, most economically disadvantaged students are denied the same educational opportunities afforded to children of affluent parents. The consequence is that schools tend to serve a social reproductive role that preserves a variety of social and economic inequalities from one generation to the next.[2]

The social theoretical positions we have identified thus far can be directly or indirectly applied to the topics we examine in this chapter. First, we describe the status of sport in American education; next, we explore the positive and negative consequences of secondary school sport for the school, the community, the individual, and the society; finally, we assess the relationship between sport and education by examining inherent problems and dilemmas.

THE STATUS OF SPORT IN SECONDARY SCHOOLS

Interschool sports are an extracurricular program that is inexorably intertwined in high schools of the United States. They have become vitally important as a means of unifying the entire school in a common cause—supporting the local teams. Although historically high school sports were exclusively a male preserve, congressional legislation in the United States has moved high school sports toward gender equity. More recently, legislation is supporting the inclusion of youth with disabilities in high school sport.

In the 2018-2019 school year, about 7.9 million boys and girls in the United States were involved in sports at the high school level. Of this total, 3.4 million were girls and 4.5 million were boys (see Table 9.1). This high level of involvement, however, is not the case elsewhere in the world. In most countries, sports programs for high school–age youth are organized through community-based sports clubs, not through the high schools.

In 2013 the Department of Education issued a "Dear Colleague" document telling public school administrators that they must "afford qualified students with disabilities an equal opportunity for participation" in sports. One education policy analyst said,

TABLE 9.1   NATIONAL FEDERATION OF STATE HIGH SCHOOL ASSOCIATIONS ATHLETICS PARTICIPATION SUMMARY, 2018–2019

Year	Participants		
	Boys	Girls	Total
1990–1991	3,406,355	1,892,316	5,298,671
1995–1996	3,634,052	2,367,936	6,001,988
2000–2001	3,921,069	2,784,154	6,705,223
2005–2006	4,206,549	2,953,355	7,159,904
2010–2011	4,494,406	3,173,549	7,667,955
2013–2014	4,527,994	3,267,664	7,795,658
2018–2019	4,534,758	3,402,733	7,937,491

Source: National Federation of State High School Associations Athletics Participation Data (2019), https://www.nfhs.org/media/1020412/2018-19_participation_survey.pdf.

"This will do for students with disabilities what Title IX did for women and girls." The new policy requires that schools provide "reasonable modifications" to ensure equal sports access. How this will be accomplished will be revealed in future years.[3]

According to the National Federation of State High School Associations, there are currently fourteen sports for youth with disabilities sponsored by high schools. Basketball, bowling, track, and soccer are the most popular sports. These programs are only sponsored in fourteen states and each state can have different programs and standards. For example, the California Interscholastic Federation has partnered with the U.S. Special Olympics and U.S. Paralympics to offer inclusive sports. They have two sports for para-athletes and three sports in a category called *unified sports,* where athletes with and without intellectual disabilities play on the same team.

Ascertaining the degree to which interschool sports contributes to the educational mission of U.S. schools is difficult. The debate over school sports is filled with fervent anecdotes. The conventional view is that participation in sport has educational benefits. High school athletes benefit, it is commonly argued, by learning about dedication and sacrifice, by learning to play by the rules, by working together with teammates toward a common goal, by learning

achievement orientation, and by meeting school academic requirements to stay eligible.

A less popularly held view is critical of high school sports programs as they are now conducted. From this perspective, school sports are believed to be detrimental to core educational goals. Moreover, spokespersons for this view assert that although sport participation may lead to positive behaviors, it is also an environment where some individuals learn bad behaviors. For example, although some athletes and coaches play by the rules, others circumvent them; sports experiences can teach good sportsmanship, but they can also teach poor sportsmanship; and although there is integrity in some high school sports programs, there is hypocrisy in others. For those who have witnessed a growing trend in the negative outcomes in high school sports programs, they often believe that sport and education have become incompatible, and some have even advocated abolishing high school sports programs.

Both views about the consequences of high school sports have its advocates. Amanda Ripley, an analyst of educational systems globally, has made a forceful case against high school sports. As she points out, U.S. high schoolers test far lower in reading and math than students from Finland or Singapore, where participation in sports is not connected to high schools. Ripley has claimed that, "sports are embedded in American schools unlike the way they are anywhere else. Yet this difference hardly ever comes up in domestic debates about America's international mediocrity in education." She also observed that the United States habitually spends more tax dollars per high school athlete than per high school math student—unlike most countries worldwide.[4]

But Daniel Bowen and Colin Hitt, two professionals in educational research, declare, "We have consulted the research. We examined many of the more popular theories about the role of sports in education. Student-athletes generally do better in school than other students—not worse. . . . Despite negative stereotypes about sports culture and Ripley's presumption that academics and athletics are at odds with one another, we believe that the greater body of evidence shows that school-sponsored sports programs appear to benefit students. Successes on the playing field can carry over to the classroom and vice versa."[5]

As for long-term consequences of being a high school athlete, several research studies suggest that student-athletes do better than their nonathlete peers. Specifically, researchers have found that student-athletes are significantly more likely to go to college, score higher on standardized achievement tests, and earn higher wages in their employment careers.[6]

THE CONSEQUENCES OF SPORT FOR SCHOOLS, COMMUNITIES, AND INDIVIDUALS

Interschool high school sports in the United States are so ubiquitous that high schools might appear to an outsider to be more concerned with sports than with scholarly endeavors. Social analysts who have studied the social climate of high schools have remarked about the prominent role of sports. They invariably comment about the presence of trophy cases near the main entrance to the high school buildings. The gold and silver trophies, as well as the footballs, basketballs, baseballs, and track batons, are, with rare exceptions, the hardware symbolizing sports victories and championships. The overall display suggests that one is entering a sports club rather than an educational institution.

In the hallways, student conversations and activities are dominated by talk about the outcomes of the school's sports teams during the previous week or about the upcoming Friday football or basketball games. All-school pep rallies are regularly held to allow students and cheerleaders to practice school cheers for the upcoming sporting events. The persistent social ambiance of the typical high school is about sports.

Academic matters seem to be of secondary importance to students, teachers, and administrators. Indeed, school administrations and communities are usually much more willing to spend large sums of money for sports teams and sports facilities than they are for academic equipment and buildings. They are also willing to allow a disproportionate amount of time to be spent on sports and related activities. Why are athletes and sports teams given such extraordinary importance? The reason is that they are believed to have positive consequences for the high schools, the communities, and the participants.

THE CONSEQUENCES OF SPORT FOR THE HIGH SCHOOL

All organizations require a minimum amount of unity; members must give an organization some allegiance for it to survive. Allegiance can stem from pay, ideology, chances for promotion, or the cooperative need to accomplish a collective goal. High schools, however, do not have the usual means to promote unity among their members. Grades, the equivalent of pay, do not always work because part of the school population is indifferent to them and because they are so often dependent on defeating one's peers. Moreover, students are forced by custom and by law to attend school; this ensures their physical presence but not their involvement in the school's academic objectives.

Sports contests are one of few collective goals found in schools, where it is mostly individual performance that is prioritized. Therefore, any activity that promotes loyalty to the school serves a useful and necessary purpose. Interschool sports provide a unique means of unifying the entire school. Different races, social classes, teachers, school staff, and students unite in a common cause—the defeat of a common opponent, sports teams from other high schools. The collective following of a sports team can also lift morale, thereby unifying the school (although we should remember that unity is usually accomplished when teams win; losing teams may increase the possibility of division).

Athletics serves not only to unify student bodies but also to minimize conflict between students and teachers. High school population segments often become fragmented into cliques, thus preventing a collective morale from arising and sometimes becoming conflict groups. Interschool sports programs can sometimes alleviate problems of this sort and become a powerful factor in building up school spirit, unifying various student groups as well as teachers and students.

The number of sports now sponsored by high schools has grown dramatically over the past generation. Soccer has been one of the fastest growing sports in the United States and is now a core high school sport for both men and women. (Photo: Courtesy of Shokie Lopez)

In addition to the unifying function of high school sports, they serve a social control function, which has several facets. First, many sport programs that were introduced in the early twentieth century were intended as a means to keep children out of trouble and to assimilate newly immigrated people into an "American" way of life. This idea of using sport to funnel young people's energies into "positive" channels still carries weight today.[7] For example, many believe that sports activity may make students more mannerly, inasmuch as it drains athletes' surplus energies. Likewise, it gives students something to converse about and something to do with their time, thereby keeping them from mischief and from questioning school rules and policies. For athletes and nonathletes alike, sport may serve as a diversion from undesirable activities. Second, athletes, because they must obey training rules if they want to compete, serve as examples of good behavior. Within the high school student culture, athletes have high status, and by virtue of their favored position, they may tend to have a modeling role favored by school administrators and teachers. If this assumption is correct and nonathletes tend to admire them, then athletes may preserve harmony in the school.

School boards and school administrators support high school sports programs for self-serving reasons—school and community cohesion, financial support, and social control. They encourage sports participation not only because they want to encourage physical fitness but also, more important, because they believe that sports involvement socializes students into the values of the nation. Schools want students to follow rules, to be disciplined, to work hard, to fit in—all of which are virtues in terms of learning their place in the hierarchical society where they will live as adults (as discussed in Chapter 3).

Sports, it is believed by those who organize and manage high schools, accomplish these aims. Functional social theorists approvingly point to interschool sports as a perfect venue for reproducing cultural values and promoting social consensus and stability.

A final social control function of high school sports is their use by school administrators and teachers to encourage intellectual activities among the students. A contingency for participation in sports is the maintenance of a certain grade point average, so athletes must at least meet this minimum. Consequently, the high school sports programs may have the concomitant effect of keeping some youngsters from dropping out of school because of their desire to participate.

THE CONSEQUENCES OF SPORT FOR THE COMMUNITY

We have already noted that school athletics appears to be an effective means for channeling the interest and loyalty of the community. Clearly, this enthusiasm generated by sports is a unifying agent for the community. Regardless of occupation, education, race, or religion, residents can and do unite in backing a school's teams. In addition, high school sports are entertaining. They provide action, excitement, fantasy, and escape in the otherwise humdrum world of many rural small towns and even urban communities.

Of course, communities vary in their attachment to high school athletic teams. Typically, the community members concentrate their interests around boys' football and basketball. Most often, individual sports are ignored by communities, and girls' games are often minimized, too. Small communities are generally more involved in high school sports than are large urban communities.

The focus on a sport may also vary by geographical location, with high school basketball the rage in Indiana, hockey in Minnesota, and football in Texas. In *The Fields of Fall*, Todd Weber follows several high school football dynasties in Iowa for a year, dissecting the teams' philosophies and recounting stories of the people and the communities that make the game so special for the towns. He cites one of the diehard fans as saying, "Life really wouldn't be worth livin' if you didn't have a high school football team to support."[8]

THE CONSEQUENCES OF SPORT FOR PARTICIPANTS

High school students participate in sports for a variety of reasons. One important reason is the extraordinary popularity of high school sports and its ability to generate high social status for males and, increasingly, for females. High school athletes receive fame and acclaim from peers, neighbors, teachers, and even strangers. A high school star (especially a male) can become a legend, a deity canonized in newspapers and immortalized through countless retold exploits. Even nonstar athletes have celebrity status. They enjoy praise and honor, special favors from businesses and the community, and popularity with their peers.

A socially defined position within a large group or society is called a *status*, and statuses are hierarchically ranked from low to high. Achievement in high school sports is for the most part the basis for high status among male peers. The athlete, regardless of other attributes, is favored over the nonathlete, with the highest preference being "scholar-athlete." For young females, popularity is judged more by their being in the "in-group" than by their scholarship. Membership in the in-group is crucial, and being an athlete is not sufficient for inclusion. For females, social background and physical appearance are more important for social status than sports achievement. Social scientists have suggested that this may be changing for high school girls because their participation in sports has increased rapidly during the past two decades and is becoming more and more acceptable; nonetheless, prototypical gender expectations seem to be stable.[9]

But popularity and social status are not the only reasons high school boys and girls play sports. Many participate because they enjoy the physical activity and because they derive great pleasure from being part of a cohesive unit striving for a common goal. Sometimes forgotten, however, is that many students participate because all of the normative influences pull them in that direction. There are many pressures to participate in high school sports. Of course, if students are socialized to desire participation, they may not feel the demands.

Regardless of the motivation for participation in sport, there are other potential consequences of participation. Several are considered here: academic benefits, character development, and adjustment to failure and life after sport.

Academic Benefits

Does participation in high school sports help or hinder the academic achievement of athletes? Arguably, no topic in sociology of sport has generated more speculation than the impact of high school athletics on academic achievement without, unfortunately, definitive empirical research on the issue. For almost half a century, researchers in sociology of sport, secondary education, sociology of education, psychology, and sport management have studied this topic, but most of the research has methodological problems, making it deficient in generalizability. We summarize here two key publications on this topic.

The National Federation of State High School Associations (NFHS) and its member state associations administer interscholastic sports in the United States for over 11 million students who participate nationwide. In a report, NFHS summarized several of the studies related to participation in high school sports and academic achievement. One study of about 140,000 Kansas high school athletes found that athletes earned higher grades, graduated at a higher rate, dropped out of school less frequently, and scored higher on state board examinations than nonathletes. Also, student-athletes of color had much higher grade point averages. Two other studies summarized by NFHS, one done in Minnesota and one in North Carolina, corroborated the Kansas study.[10]

These and other reviews of the research studies of the effects of playing high school sports on the academic achievement of athletes suggest that students who are involved in high school athletics tend to have higher academic achievement and better earnings later in life.[11] But empirical researchers and research interpreters caution that statistical correlation between high school sports participation and educational outcomes does not "prove" that participation

as a student-athlete automatically or inevitably leads to improved academic achievement. Correlation, in short, does not necessarily indicate causation. In this case, the relationships between high school sports participation and academic achievements are much more multifaceted than this.[12]

The relationship is contingent on a variety of social factors, such as socioeconomic background, type and intensity of sports participation, and the ways in which sports are contextualized and connected to academic attitudes and activities. Furthermore, other issues exist whenever athletes are compared with nonathletes. The two categories differ not only in terms of sports involvement but also with respect to academic achievement. First, athletes may have a higher grade point average because they are required to meet a minimum grade level to be eligible for sports. This grade barrier can prevent students with low academic performance from attempting to participate in athletics, thus increasing the likelihood that the athlete group will have higher average grades than the nonathlete group.

Second, either rebellious students may choose not to participate in sport or coaches may dismiss them from teams because they do not fit in. Under these circumstances, too, the athlete group will likely have better grades.

Third, athletes may get extra help from tutors and teachers, take easier courses to handle the rigors of being athletes, or receive outright gifts of good grades from sympathetic teachers. Where such conditions exist, the result may be better grades for an athlete group but not because being an athlete makes one a good student.

Finally, there is the question of whether athletes may differ from nonathletes in ways unrelated to sport. For example, there is a retention process that takes into account who enters and who drops out of high school athletics between the sophomore and senior years. Research findings across several social science disciplines clearly show that those who begin and remain in high school sports tend to be economically privileged in terms of family social class, cognitive ability, academic achievement, and self-esteem. In short, high school athletes possess a number of personal, social, and academic advantages over their nonathlete peers even before they participate in high school sports.[13]

Because there are significant differences between athletes and nonathletes that could affect their academic performance, without statistically taking those variables into account we cannot determine whether the differences found in much of the research on athletes versus nonathletes result from playing sports or are merely correlational. Thus, we should not infer that sports participation makes athletes perform better in the classroom.

Character Development

We noted in Chapter 8 that there are a number of questionable assumptions about the claim that "sport builds character." Although many people take this slogan for granted, there have been few well-conceived and implemented empirical research studies on the effects of high school sport involvement on the social development of athletes. We can suggest several reasons for this. First, the word *character* is vague; character is a socially constructed concept amenable to a variety of meanings and interpretations. When left unspecified, there is no way of knowing which meaning or interpretation is intended. To be amenable to verification, the definition of character must be anchored to a set of specific attitudes, values, and behaviors.

Second, there are differing cultural ideas about which character traits are considered "good." After all, the exhibition of a particular behavior or trait in a specific situation might be considered a demonstration of good character in one culture but bad character in another.

Third, even if one clearly defines what one means by character in a given setting, it is extremely difficult to empirically verify the character-building effects of sport involvement. Traditional experimental designs are impractical because it is almost impossible to arrange the necessary controlled conditions for relevant data collecting. Cross-sectional research designs, which provide data about relationships between variables, are worthless in the context of substantiating causal effects. Some studies have attempted to analyze the effects of sport involvement on a single discrete variable such as courage or self-discipline, but at the expense of almost trivializing the symbolic interactions that occur in a complex social setting like sport. So, such an approach is too simple to yield any meaningful information.

Because statistically verifying that sport builds character is so difficult, those who advocate this approach are reduced to relating anecdotes such as how particular athletes displayed courage, perseverance, or self-discipline in the course of a game or how a team showed dedication and teamwork. But a perusal of the nation's newspapers on any given day will reveal stories of courage, loyalty, perseverance, and so on by people who have never participated in sport. So character qualities often attributed to athletes are neither confined to nor peculiar to them.

Another common form of anecdotal evidence is the personal account of "what sport did for me." Such testimonials are often given by former athletes who attribute their postplaying achievements to their sport experiences. Regardless of the form, anecdotal evidence is unacceptable as scientific proof.

To these problems we can add the question of whether the character displayed by athletes or former athletes was present before they played organized sport or whether their particular preexisting character dispositions may have predisposed them to take up sport in the first place. Several sport studies researchers have suggested such possibilities.[14]

Our comments about the problems of empirically supporting claims that sport builds character should not be misunderstood. We are not asserting that high school sports participation has no effect on the personal and social development of athletes. Indeed, there is convincing, empirically grounded evidence that salient social experiences are powerful socializers. Sport involvement is an exciting form of human expression; many people find sports a source of great fun, joy, and self-satisfaction, and young athletes' values and beliefs are undoubtedly shaped by their experiences. But the exact effects of high school sports on attitudes, values, and behaviors (character) depend greatly on the social contextual conditions of the sporting experience, and the social contexts in which sports take place vary widely. Moreover, perhaps the sport setting is merely a particularly good setting for enabling persons to exhibit preexisting character traits; the fact that some athletes or former athletes display culturally valued personal and social characteristics cannot be wholly attributed to their sport experiences without an enormous leap of faith.

The overarching question is this: Does sports participation make a difference in character? As we have said, the data are contradictory. It is difficult to make the causal link. We believe that sports participation does not *build* character, discipline, and other achievement-related qualities in young men and women. Instead, there is a social dynamic that we feel may be working whereby, on the one hand, high school boys and girls are weeded out by coaches or drop out voluntarily because they do not possess the personal and social traits needed, whereas on the other hand, those who are imbued with the positive traits of hard work, discipline, goal orientation, and willingness to obey orders remain on high school sports teams.

Adjustment to Failure and Life after School Sport

Two problems for individual high school athletes are often overlooked. First, for many, sport leads to a series of failures. They fail to make the team, or if they make the team, they sit on the bench or their team loses many more times than it wins. In a success-oriented society, what are the effects of all the failures that sport often generates? At the individual level, failure can be devastating for some. They may be defined by others and by themselves as losers, which is a strong negative label in a society that places such high value on winning. This may negatively impact their self-esteem, confidence, and assertiveness. It may lead to mental health problems.

Another problem is one of adjustment after a career in sport is finished. The odds of making a team at the next level are remote: 6.8 percent of high school football players, 3.4 percent of male high school basketball players, and 3.9 percent of female high school basketball players will participate in college; the odds of making it from college into the pros in these sports are even lower (see Table 9.2). These long odds mean that most high school athletes will end their sports careers at the conclusion of high school.

After the glory years, what happens to former athletes when they are considered has-beens? Does

TABLE 9.2 LONG SHOTS: ODDS OF HIGH SCHOOL ATHLETES PLAYING IN COLLEGE AND PROFESSIONALLY

High school sport	Odds of playing in college (%)	% High school to NCAA Division I	% College to top pro league
Men			
Baseball	7.1	2.2	9.9
Basketball	3.5	1.0	1.2
Football	7.3	2.9	1.6
Ice Hockey	12.3	4.8	7.4
Soccer	5.6	1.3	1.4
Women			
Basketball	4.1	1.3	0.8
Soccer	7.2	2.4	1.0
Volleyball	3.9	1.2	Negligible
Softball	5.6	1.8	Negligible
Tennis	4.5	1.65	Negligible

Source: NCAA, "Estimated Probability of Competing in College and Professional Athletics," 2020, https://www.ncaa.org/about/resources/research/estimated-probability-competing-college-athletics. Accessed June 22, 2021.

participation in sport have carryover value to other endeavors where there is no hero worship, no excitement, and no fame? What happens to the athlete who finds himself or herself suddenly outside the world that has until now been at the center of his or her life and the principal source of identity and social status? Do former athletes become embittered and turn away from sport, or do they fill their time reliving the past, attending games, Monday-morning quarterbacking, and watching sports on television? How does the athlete, when compared to the nonathlete, adjust to job, marriage, and upward or downward mobility? Unfortunately, little research has been done on the effects of this shift away from the limelight when high school sports participation has ended. For those few athletes who make the transition and become professional athletes, there are a few mostly anecdotal accounts about their retirement experiences.[15] Recently, there has been some research on the process by which young athletes disengage from their athletic career.[16]

PROBLEMS, DILEMMAS, AND CONTROVERSIES

We have noted that sport in secondary schools has a variety of consequences for the schools, the community, and the participants, but many people wonder about the educational benefits of these sports programs. In this section, we focus on some of the problems, dilemmas, and controversies of interscholastic sport as it is currently organized.

THE SUBVERSION OF EDUCATIONAL GOALS

It is often argued that time-consuming, commercially oriented, expensive high school sports programs consume an inordinate amount of time in the school day and that the large amounts of money devoted to sports could be better spent on academic matters. There is also objection to the tendency to give star athletes preferential treatment in their schooling. Athletes may pass courses although they have not mastered the subject matter. The qualifications of coaches are also often questioned. It is estimated that only about 50 percent of high school coaches are high school teachers; indeed, many have never taught in the classroom and have little training or legitimate certification in coaching. In short, the coach in many high schools has no connection with the academic institution.

Increasingly, high school sports have come under criticism for becoming less about education and more about entertainment. This is coupled with the charge that high school sports now have no connection with lifelong health and income in the labor market. The argument is that skills emphasized in football and basketball, the objects of most public attention, are irrelevant beyond the school years. The existing research on this topic is inconclusive about whether high school sports participation has a significant effect on labor market income.

For example, Frank Howell and his colleagues used data from the Youth in Transition Study, a national sample of male youth, and did not find a significant effect of high school sports participation on income. More recently, Heidbreder used data from the National Longitudinal Survey of Youth and reported that participation in high school sports yielded higher income in the labor market, even after controlling for other determinants of earnings.[17]

REPRODUCTION OF SOCIAL CLASS AND WHITE PRIVILEGE

It is important to note that participation in high school sports may be a means of reproducing class and racial privilege. In this way, it is not that sport has a unique and neutral role of social mobility; instead, sport becomes a pipeline to college that is mainly used by wealthier (and White) families. In an in-depth study of athletes at an elite academic and athletic university, sociologist Kirsten Hextrum documented how this high school to college sport pipeline worked. The research found five key mechanisms that were more impactful than pure athletic talent in receiving a scholarship. And, significantly, these mechanisms favored White, middle-class families. First is community access, which refers to a family's wealth and institutional support for the sport in that community. Second are the sport bureaucracies and their rules and regulations that govern that sport. Third are the social relationships and connections that are developed in the community through the sport experience. Fourth is the knowledge that is circulated in these communities and how that can be leveraged to get an athletic scholarship. Fifth is how the athletes are able to use that knowledge to negotiate with university athletic departments. These five factors work together to privilege those with the type of "capitals" that sociologist Pierre Bourdieu identified with regard to enhancing social mobility: economic, social, and cultural resources (see Chapter 5). For example, if a family had access to good facilities, good coaching, and a sport community that knew how to negotiate bureaucracies such as the NCAA, then they were able to more successfully navigate and negotiate with university athletic departments. The outcome of these mechanisms can be seen by examining gender, racial, and class makeup of NCAA athletes. As noted by Hextrum, in 2017 in Division I athletes, 60.4 percent of scholarship athletes were White. Black athletes account for only 14 percent across all sports, but Black males are nearly half of all revenue athletes (football and basketball). With respect to women's scholarship athletes, 67 percent are White. Although the NCAA does not look at social class directly, they do identify first-generation college students, which can be used as an indicator. In 2015, only 14 percent of college athletes were first generation. It is no surprise that the country club sports had the lowest number of first-generation students.[18]

THE REINFORCEMENT OF GENDER INEQUITIES

In Chapter 2 we described how sport in American schools has historically been almost exclusively a male preserve. This is evident as one compares by gender the number of participants and facilities. We examined sexism in sport in greater detail in Chapter 7; therefore, the discussion here is limited to only

several unintended ways in which school sport works to maintain the conventional expectations for masculine and feminine roles (see Box 9.1).

With the implementation of Title IX (see Chapter 7) and the efforts to bring gender equity to school athletic programs, the number of female sport participants increased dramatically—from 294,015 girls involved in high school sports in 1971 to more than 3.4 million in 2019. Put another way, the growth in girls playing high school sports rose from 7.5 percent in 1971 to 42 percent in 2019. Also, in 2019 girls comprised nearly 9 percent in high school wrestling, a sport that is traditionally male.[19]

Although attempts have been made to equalize female and male programs in facilities, equipment,

---

BOX 9.1 *THINKING ABOUT SPORT AND GENDER:* CHEERLEADING AND THE DEVELOPMENT OF A SPORT

"Two-four-six-eight, who do we appreciate?" This familiar cheerleader yell is usually directed to a particular athlete, but cheerleaders also need appreciation. They are the "spirit-makers" of the high school and the spectator entertainers at sporting events in the United States. Cheerleading has a long history in the United States. When it started in the mid-1850s, it was an all-male activity because women were officially banned from it. In fact, some presidents of the United States were cheerleaders, including Dwight Eisenhower, Franklin Roosevelt, Ronald Reagan, and George W. Bush. It was not until World War II that cheerleading became more female as women filled in for the men who served in the war. When the gender composition changed, the values of the activity changed as well. When males dominated cheerleading it was touted as a means to develop leadership skills. When females have dominated cheerleading it has been framed as a means to develop fitness and support skills, including upbeat and well-mannered personalities.

Today, cheerleading ranks as one of the most popular extracurricular activities for girls: an estimated 400,000+ cheerleaders over the age of fourteen—96 percent are females—participate in year-round programs paralleling the fall, winter, and spring sports. Originally, cheerleading was merely a matter of leading the crowd in supportive cheers, but it currently entails complex, orchestrated performances involving advanced tumbling and acrobatic stunts. Many cheerleaders also attend summer training camps and state/province and national competitions.

The popularity of cheerleading, the practice and training needed to acquire advanced skills, and the widespread competitions have led to the demand that cheerleading be granted the status of a sport. This came to a head when Quinnipiac

University wanted to include cheerleading as a sport and, thus, include it in Title IX gender equity requirements for the athletic department. This was challenged by those who claimed it was not a sport. Ultimately, the courts determined that traditional cheer was not a sport, and, in so doing, clearly identified the criteria needed for an activity to be considered a sport under the federal law of Title IX. This decision inspired a national federation, USA Cheer, to develop a sport version of cheer. STUNT cheer is competitive and is judged on athletic and technical skills as opposed to the team's ability to rally crowds. It has been active since 2011. The NCAA's Committee on Women's Athletics has recommended to add STUNT as an NCAA emerging sport, which indicates that it has significant support to become an official NCAA sport in the future. In the summer of 2021, cheerleading was granted Olympic status and could be included as soon as the Summer 2024 Games. Additionally, USA Cheer includes divisions in their national and international championships for Adaptive Abilities and Special Olympics. It is apparent that competitive cheerleading as a sport is emerging and gaining popularity. This activity also represents a trend that females (and the males who do participate) can present themselves in ways that integrate some traditional masculine characteristics, such as a strong body and competitiveness, with more traditionally feminine, "sexy" appearance.

Sources: Lisa Wade, "The Manly Origins of Cheerleading," *The Society Pages*, December 28, 2012, https://thesocietypages.org/socImages/2012/12/28/the-manly-origins-of-cheerleading/; Nancy L. Malcom, Christina Gipson, Kristen S. Pirie, and Rachel Miller Wood, "The Creation of Stunt Cheer: A Story of Innovation, Cheerleading and Gender Politics of Sport," in *Social Innovation in Sport*, ed. Anne Tjonndal (Cham, Switzerland: Palgrave Macmillan, 2021); Alexandra Zdunek, "Who Knows the Difference between Competitive Cheerleading, Sideline Cheerleading, Acrobatics and Tumbling? Why This Distinction Is So Important for Title IX," *Marquette Sports Law Review*, 31, no. 1 (2020): 175–192.

coaching, and transportation, inequities remain. Football, with its high cost and large number of participants, continues to skew budgets in favor of males. The scheduling of games and media attention also stress male sports.

Finally, a major trend in high school sports is that as women's sports have gained in popularity, money, and respect, men have gained more and more control over them. Men are more likely than women to be athletic directors and coaches of women's sports at the high school and college levels. Male athletes see male role models exclusively as coaches and administrators, but female athletes are usually denied female role models in positions requiring decisiveness, confidence, and self-assurance. Thus, females once again receive the unambiguous message that the more responsible a position is in an organization, the more likely men are to occupy it. Occasionally, however, breakthroughs occur and challenge old gender traditions. There are now a handful of women coaching boys on varsity high school basketball and football teams.[20]

CHEATING

Cheating involves a violation of the rules to gain an unfair advantage over an opponent. It occurs at all levels of sport and may be done by individual players, teams, or coaches. Baseball historian John Thorn claims that "cheating is not merely countenanced in baseball, it is loved."[21] The types of cheating depend on the sport and the ingenuity of the participants.

Cheating is antithetical to educational values and should have no place in educational programs. However, as high school sports victories have become increasingly important to the school and community, as well as to the job security of high school coaches, cheating has become inevitable. Some high school players are coached to use illegal but difficult-to-detect techniques. One example is holding or tripping by offensive linemen in football. In basketball it is often advantageous to touch the lower half of the shooter's body because the referee usually watches the action around the ball. A form of cheating often taught to basketball players is to fake being fouled. The intent is to fool an official who is out of position and to receive an undeserved free throw. Similar faking of an injury to get an advantage occurs commonly in soccer

when a player is bumped during play and then acts as if he or she has been fouled, writhing in pseudo-pain in the hope that the referee will award him or her a penalty kick for the phony injury. This happens, too, in football when punters act as if they have been hit by an onrushing lineman.

Coaches sometimes break the spirit of a rule, if not the rule itself. For example, some high school governing organizations prohibit teams from having organized practices before a certain date, yet coaches insist on players practicing, with captains in charge or coaches at a distance yelling orders. Most secondary school governing organizations prohibit the inducement of athletes to transfer from one high school to another. But stories abound throughout secondary education about coaches who have recruited athletes or lost athletes to coaches who recruited them away. It has become so frequent in the state of New Jersey that the high school basketball coach at St. Mary's of Elizabeth asserted, "Transferring has just gone rampant."

Sports writers for the *Dallas Morning News* called it a "free-agent system" in which some teams will lose one player and simply plug in a transfer from another high school. They elaborate: "The high school transfer system has been abused for decades, and there's no sign of that trend ending anytime soon. . . . The rampant transferring in all sports, the result of a combination of factors that has led to what some coaches describe as a 'free-agent mentality' among athletes, has changed the landscape of high school sports." *USA Today* writer Jim Halley described the well-traveled journey of one high school player: he grew up in Inglewood, California, but played his freshman year at Calabasas, California, his sophomore year at Bishop Gorman in Las Vegas, Nevada, was back at Calabasas for his junior year, and in the fall of 2017 played his senior year at IMG.[22]

Coaches typically claim it was the athletes who initiated the transfer, whereas athletes say they were recruited, so it is always difficult to know what the truth is. Either way, this form of cheating has been widespread.

The Colorado High School Activities Association has reduced the likelihood of this kind of thing by allowing students to transfer before the start of the school year even if their only reason for transferring is sports. But such a rule invites recruiting and various inducements to athletes and their parents to change schools.

Paul Angelico, the commissioner of the Colorado High School Activities Association, is often asked why the organization has a statewide transfer rule. He said, "People not associated with high school sports wonder why such a big deal is made about a student changing schools." Here is how he has publicly replied: "We can't continue to have such imbalance in our haves and have nots in our high school programs, and expect our high school programs to survive. . . . So our job is going to be to figure out how to keep like schools together in terms of competitive balance."[23]

A different form of cheating involves the use of drugs so that an athlete may compete at a higher-than-normal level of ability (see Chapter 4). This is sometimes done at the insistence of trainers and coaches and sometimes by an athlete's own decision. A 2020 national survey found that for high school seniors, some 2 percent of boys and girls had taken anabolic steroids in their lifetime; this reflects a recent trend in the reduction of their use.[24] Even though steroid use is illegal and a form of cheating, other substance use and concomitant health concerns are more common. Athletes tend to have higher levels of binge drinking and marijuana use than nonathletes.[25]

UNSPORTSMANLIKE BEHAVIOR OF FANS

The intensity of sports competition sometimes leads some fans to cross the line. This may involve fighting, insulting opposing teams' players and fans, yelling obscenities, and other obnoxious behaviors.[26] Several unhealthy examples illustrate this point:

- In Phoenix, Arizona, when a football player was injured, fans from the opposing team shouted, "Broken neck, broken neck."
- Also in Phoenix, students wore green T-shirts implying that the players on the largely Latino team they were playing against had green cards and thus were foreigners.

- In Thomasville, Georgia, the police department issued a "brawl warning" after two incidents at high school basketball games where parents and grandparents went onto the court to enter into fights that broke out between opposing teams.

As more than one sports journalist has remarked, personal attacks, jeers, and politically incorrect insults can undermine the sportsmanship and camaraderie that high school athletics are supposed to promote. They can also lead to violence and distractions for players trying to focus on the game.

AUTOCRATIC COACHES

The authoritarian control by coaches that athletes experience in youth sports is often employed by high school coaches as well. So another criticism of high school sports is the almost total control that coaches exercise over their players' lives. Many coaches, for example, dictate hairstyles, clothing, dating, whom the players associate with, church attendance, and the like. Many also monitor their players' behavior off the field (bed checks) and restrict freedom of choice (what position to play, mandatory off-season weightlifting). Most coaches impose their will on their teams concerning team rules, discipline, play calling, and personnel decisions.

This model of leadership is a source of criticism from a conflict/cultural theoretical perspective because such behavior often becomes coercive and exploitive and is counterproductive for learning democratic actions and values by athletes. High school athletes have no control over the organized school athletics in which they participate. Instead, administrators, teachers, and coaches govern every facet of school sports programs: the rules of the games, who is eligible, who coaches, what constitutes practices, the number of games that can be played, and when and where those games take place. However, a functionalist perspective would view this model as appropriate for instilling habits and values for coping with the hierarchically structured organizations of contemporary life in the United States.

Whether coaches have the right to infringe on the civil liberties of their charges is certainly a legal question. Beyond that, there is the question of the educational value of controlling these teenagers on and off the field. A system that impedes personal autonomy, fosters dependence and immaturity rather than the presumed virtues of participation, which are leadership, independence, and self-motivation. Moreover, a relevant question is whether subservience to an autocrat prepares one for life in a democracy.[27]

We want to emphasize that we are not suggesting that all high school coaches are autocratic curmudgeons; they certainly are not. Indeed, many high school coaches use democratic and humanistic methods to coach.

EXCESSIVE PRESSURES TO WIN

Many of the problems found in high school sports result from the excessive emphasis on winning. The sociological explanation for coaches who are authoritarian, or cheat, or are hypocritical lies not in their individual psyches but in the intensely competitive system in which they operate.

In the United States, the success or failure of a team is believed by most persons to rest with the coach. This pressure to win brings some coaches to use illegal inducements to attract athletes to their schools, or to teach their linemen to hold without getting caught, or to look the other way when athletes (who face the same pressures to succeed) use drugs to enhance performance. The absolute necessity to win also explains why some coaches drive their players too hard. Thus, what some persons might label brutality has been explained by some coaches as a necessity to get the maximum effort from players.

Finally, authoritarianism can be explained by the constraints on the coaching role. Democracy is unthinkable to many in the coaching profession because coaches are liable for the outcome in an extremely uncertain situation. They cannot control injuries, officiating, mental lapses by athletes, or the bounce of the ball, so many coaches are convinced that they must seek to control as much else as possible.

Another consequence of the excessive stress on winning is that sports participation becomes work rather than play. The emphasis is on the outcome rather than on enjoyment of the process. Fun has become equated with winning rather than with pleasure in participating.

ELITISM

Interscholastic sport programs are elitist. That is, they are for the few, not the many. It is the experienced, the highly trained, and the physically gifted who make up high school sports teams. If sports participation is believed to have educational benefits, how can schools justify limiting teams to the most gifted athletes? Why should participation be restricted almost exclusively to the fast, the strong, or the tall? Several fitness and medical scientists have noted that high school athletes are more fit, more skilled, and have better training than ever before. But they say these top-notch athletes have become the singular focus of the high school sports system— whereas teenagers with average or low fitness and motor skills are given little attention in the high schools.

There are two reasons for limiting sports opportunities for high school students. One is that school boards and administrators funnel most of their limited funds toward those sports that entertain the public (football and basketball). In effect, then, the goal of high school sports has shifted from an educational endeavor to public entertainment. Second, because of limited financial resources, many schools have eliminated freshman/sophomore teams, some sports programs such as golf and tennis, and intramural sports programs. Even physical education classes have been cut from many schools.

The result is that high school sports and the use of high school sports facilities are increasingly being turned over to the elite performers in mainstream sport for the purpose of exhibiting their prowess publicly.

SPORT SPECIALIZATION

Not surprisingly, the growing trend in youth sport for one-sport specialization manifests itself in one-sport high school athletes who limit their participation and year-round training to that sport. This was first the case in individual sports (running, swimming, gymnastics, tennis), but it is now increasingly found in team sports as well, especially in large high schools. Leaders in both the Sports & Fitness Industry Association and the NFHS have noted that they are aware that a growing number of high school athletes are focusing on a single sport, but they feel strongly that it is important to promote high school athletes playing multiple sports. They are in agreement that more schools and coaches should encourage their student-athletes to play more than one sport (see also "Traveling Teams and Club Teams" in Chapter 8).

The arguments for this practice are that refined skill levels lead to optimal individual and team performance, encourage excellence, and increase the chances for obtaining a college athletic scholarship. The founder of the Colorado Chaos club basketball program, a high school–age traveling basketball team, boasted, "Our thing is, basketball is a tool to higher education," meaning a college basketball scholarship. Baseball's developmental system for high school athletes is almost indistinguishable from basketball's Amateur Athletic Union system, and it has a national organization named Perfect Game, which is devoted to furthering the development and career of talented high school baseball players. It organizes tournaments and showcases top traveling club teenage baseball players. According to *Sports Illustrated* writer Jeff Passan, teenage "travel baseball has become at least a nine-figure industry, preying on parents' insatiable desire to secure college scholarships and high-paying major league futures for their children."[28] The possible negative consequences of this practice include physical and psychological burnout, injuries from overuse, creation of a professional atmosphere for athletes that is inappropriate for adolescents, friction among coaches who compete for athletes, and the use of athletic facilities limited to the few.

ECONOMIC CLASS DIVISIONS AND BUDGET SHORTFALLS

Social scientists have pointed to a growing economic divide in the United States. In particular, there are a growing number of people living without economic security (see Chapter 5). These class divisions show up in different communities' ability to sponsor sport. The Women's Sports Foundation reported differences among high-poverty schools and low-poverty schools. In the 2015–2016 year, high-poverty schools offered 5 fewer sports than low-poverty schools (12.2 compared to 17.1). Accordingly, participation rates differed as

well. High-poverty schools had a 37.7 percent participation rate, whereas low-poverty schools had a rate of 57.2 percent.[29] This trend of differential access is reflected in all extracurricular activities. As noted by social science scholars, "Since the 1970s, upper-middle-class students have become increasingly active in school clubs and sport teams, while participation among working-class students has veered in the opposite direction. These growing gaps have emerged in the wake of rising income inequality, the introduction of 'pay to play' programs, and increasing time and money investments by upper middle-class parents in children's development."[30]

Many school districts have experienced a fiscal crisis with declining appropriations from federal and state governments. As noted previously, this has especially affected urban and poor rural school districts, because wealth has become more concentrated in the suburbs and particular urban neighborhoods. The trend appears to be toward even more budget tightening as the federal government shifts more programs to the states and the desire of the electorate is to reduce taxes. In particular, school districts must find new ways to fund sports in their districts.

Three strategies to overcome these declining revenues have been employed to continue the financing of interscholastic sports (and other extracurricular activities), each having negative consequences for high school sports programs. First, as noted, high schools have reacted to budget shortfalls by reducing or eliminating some sports (almost always individual sports with no potential for producing revenue) or the number of teams (eliminating sophomore or junior varsity teams). This solution reduces the number of participants and makes high school sports all the more elitist.

Football teams are typically not subject to elimination (although the number of players might be reduced). This is ironic because it is the most expensive sport in the number of coaches required, the cost of equipment (about $6,000 per player), and the cost of insurance. The sacredness of football poses another problem: because it is almost exclusively for males—although in 2018-2019 there were 2,404 females playing on high school football teams of the slightly more than 1 million football players—and as other sports are reduced or eliminated, the proportion of the athletic budget going for males becomes all the more unbalanced.[31]

A second solution to meager budgets is to charge a fee for all participants. Pay-for-play has become increasingly popular throughout the U.S., with the fees varying from $50 per sport to as much as $600. This practice has usually resulted in a reduction in numbers of participants. Most important, it has created difficulty for students from lower-income families, especially reducing their participation. It has been documented that "when fees were introduced, one in three sports-playing kids from homes with annual income of $60,000 or less dropped out because of the increased cost, as compared to one in ten kids from families with incomes over $60,000."[32] Thus, sport becomes not only elitist in skill level but also elitist in terms of socioeconomic class.[33]

The third strategy employed by some districts has been to seek corporate sponsorship. Corporations have been solicited to promote certain events, purchase advertising, and buy scoreboards, artificial turf, a track, or a team bus (a few schools in Texas have sold the naming rights of their stadiums for more than $1 million). Several questions arise when this practice occurs. Is the commercialization of high school sport compatible with educational goals? Will those who provide the resources for a program actually be in control? In other words, will companies that donate thousands of dollars to a high school program have an influence on schedules, coach selection, and use of the facilities? Will they encourage a win-at-any-cost philosophy, since they do not want to have their products associated with losers?[34]

CORPORATE HIGH SCHOOL SPORT PROGRAMS

There are five indicators that sport is already at the corporate level in some schools and moving generally in that direction across the United States.

First, as we have noted, some schools are closely resembling sports programs in big-time universities (see Chapter 10) by selling naming rights to stadiums and arenas, trademarking their names and logos, hiring coaches for salaries far exceeding those of

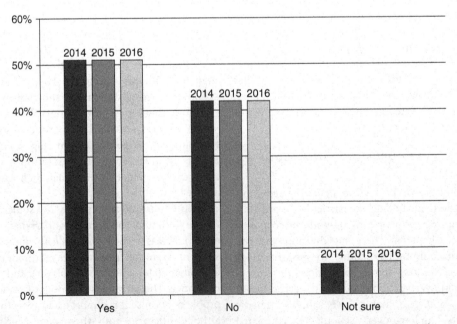

FIGURE 9.1 Do You Pay an Extra Fee for Your Child's School Sports? Source: 2017 Physical Activity Council, 2017 Physical Activity Council Report.

teachers, selling personal seat licenses (e.g., reserving seats for as much as several thousand dollars a season), and spending vast sums on football and basketball budgets. In the fall of 2012 the school district of Allen, Texas, opened a new football stadium that cost nearly $65 million. The stadium seats 18,000 fans, and that will merely tie Allen for the fifth-largest high school stadium in Texas. In 2017, another Texas high school district, Katy, opened a 70 million stadium that holds 12,000 spectators. This was matched by another 70 million dollar high school stadium, McKinney, in a suburb of Dallas that opened in 2018. Even in the outskirts of Dallas, school districts are pouring money into football stadiums. In 2018, Celina Independent School District approved $24.5 million for an athletic complex that includes a football stadium, field house, athletic

building, film room, and an $800,000 scoreboard. The state of Texas alone has at least nine stadiums that cost at least $40 million to construct.[35]

Although Texas provides some extreme examples, there are other high schools in Ohio, Pennsylvania, Louisiana, Georgia, Florida, Delaware, and elsewhere with similar outlays for their sports programs, revealing the priority of sport in these schools and making it clear that sport has taken on the characteristics of corporate enterprise.

A second indicator of the trend toward corporate sport at the high school level is the existence of fraudulent "prep schools" (mass media stories refer to them as "fake prep schools") that exist basically to inflate transcripts of those who are marginal students but excellent athletes. These high schools play the best schools around the country, providing their

The $60 million Allen Eagles Football Stadium in Allen, Texas, opened in August 2012. It is notable—and controversial—for its size, having a capacity of 18,000 spectators, and serves as home field for only one high school. (Photo: Courtesy of Mark Williamson)

athletes with exposure but also making their transcripts acceptable to big-time college sports programs.

In 2012 a *Sports Illustrated* article described Eastern Christian Academy, a Delaware academy without a field, no home uniforms, no listed phone number, and no permanent campus, that did have a "football training program" and recruited star athletes and was overseen by on-site instructors called "learning coaches." According to its president, the real teachers are the virtual ones, communicating with students through Adobe software.[36] In another case, a nationally televised game on ESPN featured IMG Academy defeating the "Bishop Sycamore" school from Ohio by 58-0. After some initial suspicions, it was soon uncovered that this latter school only had a post office box address as well as a phony address that was for a university's library, and that there were no academic lessons being provided to the athletes with basic education requirements at the school being called into question by the Ohio Governor.[37]

The NCAA has beefed up its transcript screening and inspection operation against questionable schools, disqualifying some, and announced that it would no longer accept transcripts from several nontraditional high schools that had failed to pass muster under a new academic review program. The *New York Times* editorialized that the problems may go deeper: "The storefront prep schools have been easy enough to identify. But the NCAA must now take a closer look at schools one level down that look legitimate but that may be just as willing to shortchange athletes' education as their fly-by-night counterparts. State departments of education also have a major role to play in curbing these abuses."[38]

A third indicator that sport in high school is becoming corporate is the combined effect of increased exposure and commercialization, which is moving high school sport to more closely resemble big-time college programs. High schools used to play games against league rivals and participate in tournaments at the state level. For many schools this continues to be the case, but some now participate in national tournaments in Hawaii, Florida, Las Vegas, and elsewhere.

These events are sponsored by various corporations. For example, the Burger King Classic (known as the McDonald's Classic from 1983 to 2010) is a high school boys' invitational basketball tournament held every year in Erie, Pennsylvania. Nationally ranked teams with NCAA Division I and NBA-bound players travel to Erie for the opportunity to play against other top teams for the championship and bragging rights. The annual National High School Invitational has been renamed the Dick's Sporting Goods High School National Tournament and is composed of eight of the nation's top boys' basketball teams and four of the top girls' teams. It is considered one of the leading high school basketball tournaments in the country. The games are played in Madison Square Garden and are broadcast on the ESPN network. With regard to football, there are several national all star games including the Under Armour Next Football game and Adidas All-American Game.[39]

Prior to national media coverage of high school sports, media attention tended to be local. Today, *USA Today* lists the twenty-five top-ranked high schools for the sport in season (separate lists for boys' and girls' teams) in the nation. *USA Today*, *Parade*, and other national publications select high school All-American teams and coaches of the year. SportsChannel, Madison Square Garden, Fox Sports Net, and ESPN now produce weekly "magazine" shows on high school sports.

Perhaps most surprising, in 2010 the NFHS, the umbrella organization for governing high school sports in the United States, published this statement on its website: "The National Federation of State High School Associations has led the development of education-based interscholastic sports [and] has joined with the sports and entertainment marketing giant IMG to establish and sanction national high school championships. Plans are underway to hold national championship events in boys' and girls' tennis, golf, lacrosse, and 7-on-7 football, and to ultimately stage championships in 20 sports." This shocked high school administrators and coaches throughout the country. Objections quickly piled up, and one year later, in February 2011, the following statement was made by the NFHS executive director and NFHS president: "After much debate and discussion during the past few years, the NFHS membership has continued to re-affirm the organization's longstanding stance against national championships in high school sports."[40]

As corporate ventures continue establishing national high school championships, Nike, Reebok, and Adidas are paying some coaches of the nationally ranked teams to outfit their teams with their products and to help steer their athletes to play in colleges that are "Nike schools" or "Reebok schools" or "Adidas schools."[41]

The fourth indicator of high school sports becoming corporate is the turning of young elite athletes into "professionals." It starts with some promising elementary and junior high school athletes being "grade retained" (held back a year) to give them an extra year before college to increase their skills, size, speed, strength, coordination, and maturity. Many young athletes are recruited to attend certain high schools. While in high school, some accept gratuities that technically make them professionals. Several educational administrators have asserted that elite high school athletes, by any honest measure, are professionals. They are routinely paid by coaches or agents and provided with cash, cars, and other gifts.

As we explained earlier in this chapter, top high school athletes play and train at their sport year-round. During the summers they play in high-level leagues and attend camps run by college coaches or shoe companies to hone skills and become recognized by agents, scouts, and coaches. This continues throughout the high school years, with increased pressure to succeed. What was once play has become work.

Finally, the fifth indicator of the corporatization of high school sports is that the elite high school athletes are the objects of intense recruitment by colleges throughout their high school career. One of the most recent trends of this recruitment process is high school athletes leaving high school early—for football, leaving in mid-year of their senior year—and enrolling in the university they have signed to play college football for. Early enrollees used to be the exception, but in early 2017 the University of Oklahoma football coach said, "I do believe it will start to become more of the norm."[42]

No doubt, the experience is flattering to the athletes, but it also likely makes them cynical about education because of the often-sleazy aspects of recruiting. A more important consequence is that these athletes are on the market. As such, they are being purchased by a university athletic department. For high school athletes to be treated as commodities is the essence of corporate sport.

EFFORTS TO REFORM HIGH SCHOOL SPORTS

Many educators and others are concerned about the path that high school sports are taking. As we have seen, there are school districts with 20,000-seat stadiums, there are high school coaches who do not teach in the classroom, some high school coaches make thousands of dollars from shoe companies, and there are nationally televised games. Under these conditions, the pressure on coaches and athletes has become intense.

The potential for abuse and exploitation of athletes has increased. We see more and more scandals involving payments and other gifts to high school players, recruiting, altered transcripts, and pressures on teachers to "give" athletes grades. The education of the athletes tends to become secondary. In short, high school sport is moving in the same direction as sport at the college level, that is, toward commercialization, exploitation, and elitism and away from the educational mission of schools.

What follows are suggestions for reforming high school sports. We are not public policy experts, but we think that we have some ideas that can promote discussion about changes in high school sports that, in turn, might lead to some reforms. The principle guiding our suggestions is that high school sports should be organized to maximize educational goals.

1. *Resist increasing efforts to "corporatize" high school sports.* High school sports should not be in the entertainment business. Nor should they allow the encroachment of corporations into their world. Moreover, high school sports should be kept in perspective; that is, they should not put undue pressure on coaches and players. In effect, to counter high school sport becoming corporate, several reforms must be instituted:

- Ban national televising of high school sports. High school should be a time for students to establish a sound academic foundation. High school sports should be seriously conducted as an extracurricular activity, not as a televised, overemphasized spectacle. The lure of national newspaper and television coverage is certainly distracting to the parents of athletes, the community, and the athletes themselves.
- Return to the practice of scheduling only teams within the high school's state or adjoining state. It has been suggested that high school sports introduce a "bus rule": if a team is able to travel comfortably in a bus to play another school, a game can be scheduled. Sending high school teams throughout the country to play is unnecessary and merely commercially exploits the athletes.
- Eliminate postseason all-star games. Their only intent is promotional and commercial.
- Do not permit athletic shoe companies and other corporations to intrude in high school sports. This means that corporations must not be allowed to have high school coaches on their payrolls or to sponsor summer camps.

2. *Enforce an educationally defensible standard of school academic performance for athletes to be eligible to participate in sports.* Many school jurisdictions have low academic requirements for athletes. Many accept a D average for sport eligibility. Low eligibility standards do not prepare athletes for college, and they convey the message that academics are not important. Some school districts and states (and provinces) have instituted a "No Pass No Play" rule, requiring at least a C in all subjects to be eligible to participate in extracurricular activities.

An effort intended to help reform school athletics through academic standards was instituted by the NCAA at the behest of the American Council on Education. The rules they first imposed have changed since their beginning some thirty years ago, but essentially they require a minimum grade point average in core high school courses and a minimum SAT score.

These NCAA eligibility rules seem to be working; that is, high school athletes are apparently better academically prepared for college than they were a generation ago. The number of new college recruits who are ineligible is diminishing. Again, caution should guide the interpretation of this apparent good news. This lower rate may not be a consequence of better preparation for students. The colleges may be less willing than in earlier years to offer scholarships to marginal students because their scholastic failures are embarrassing to the academic community. Another possibility is that marginal students opted to play in community colleges where the rules do not apply. Despite these cautions, it appears that the new academic demands are helping. High school athletes and their coaches are taking academics more seriously.

3. *Bring coaches back into the teaching profession.* High school coaches should be part of the faculty, teaching courses and being responsible for nonsport duties, just as are other faculty members. Coaches should be certified coaches, trained in first aid, the technical aspects of their sport, and the physiological and psychological aspects of adolescence. Coaches must be certified teachers, subject to the same rights and responsibilities as other teachers, including tenure. This will enhance the job security of coaches, thereby lessening somewhat the fanatical "win-at-all-costs" attitude.

4. *Minimize the elitism of sports: find ways to encourage more students to play on high school sports teams.* Schools should provide more school teams in more sports. Why not have two football teams, one for those weighing more than 150 pounds and one for those under that weight? Basketball could be divided into teams over and under a certain height. Consider this: parents, teachers, administrators, and even general sports fans uniformly claim that participation in sports promotes the physical and social development of athletes. Assuming there is some validity to that claim, isn't the logical conclusion that playing sports would be more valuable than merely watching them? If it is, high schools should provide sports opportunities for every student who wishes to participate.

5. *Increase student decision-making in sports programs.* One of the great ironies of school sports programs is that they are thought to enhance

In this photo a high school head coach gives last-minute instructions in a girls' basketball game. The majority of girls now playing high school sports in the United States are being coached by women. Furthermore, women are now beginning to coach boys' high school teams. (Photo: John McDonnell/*The Washington Post* via Getty Images)

responsibility, autonomy, and leadership qualities in participants. However, as currently organized with autocratic coaches, imposed rules, and all decisions made by adults, these goals are not being achieved.

Could sports be organized so that the athletes are involved in the rule making? Could they be organized so that elected player representatives could apply punishments for rule violations? Could team captains work with coaches on game strategies and make decisions during games?

Although rare, there have been some coaches who have experimented with promoting athlete involvement in decision-making. Those that have believe this system will do the following:

1. Increase confidence between players and coaches;
2. Promote team cohesion;
3. Teach responsibility, leadership, and decision-making, thereby fostering maturity rather than immaturity and independence rather than dependence;
4. Increase player motivation—instead of being driven by fear, harassment, and physical abuse by the coach, the players would have to impress their peers;

5. Free the coach to teach skills, techniques, and strategies; and
6. Allow the players to experience the benefits of democracy.

Many coaches insist football is not the place for social experimentation. But coaches are teachers, which is what they are being paid to do. Their job is to teach, to help athletes reach a level of independence. At any level, this is how democracy works and why it succeeds.

SUMMARY

The theme of this chapter has been the relationship among high school sport, educational goals, and in the United States. Our conclusion is that for sport to be compatible with educational goals, it should be structured as organized sport, not corporate sport. The data presented in this chapter, however, suggest that school sport is moving in the direction of corporate sport.

Sport at the elementary school level tends to accomplish educational goals (e.g., fostering good health practices, teaching skills, demonstrating the value of teamwork, and providing the experience of striving for a goal) in a playful, enjoyable atmosphere. However, school boards, superintendents, and teachers want students to follow rules, to be disciplined, to work hard, to fit in—all of which are virtues in terms of learning their place in the hierarchical society where they will live as adults. Thus, at each successive educational level the nature of sport changes; it becomes more serious, bureaucratized, and elitist, and its outcome becomes more crucial.

Historically, high school sports were exclusively a male preserve. Congressional legislation in the United States in the form of Title IX of the Educational Amendments Act of 1972 has shifted high school sports toward gender equity.

The serious question for educators is whether there is a place for corporate sport in education. This does reflect the corporate domination of American institutions, but is it appropriate for sport in high schools? To resist this trend is a form of emancipation with sport as the tool.

Learn more with this chapter's digital tools, including web resources, video links, and chapter self-assessment quizzes at www.oup.com/he/sage-eitzen-beal-atencio-12e.

NOTES

1. Jeanne H. Ballantine, Floyd M. Hammack, and Jenny M. Stuber, *The Sociology of Education*, 8th ed. (New York: Routledge, 2017); Alan R Sadovnik, ed., *Sociology of Education: A Critical Reader*, 3rd ed. (New York: Routledge, 2015); see also "High School Sports," in *The Routledge History of American Sport*, ed. Linda J. Borish, David K Wiggins, and Gerald R Gems (New York: Routledge, 2017), 70–94.

2. Marcia J. Carlson and Paula England, eds., *Social Class and Changing Families in an Unequal America* (Stanford, CA: Stanford University Press, 2011); Sara McLanahan and Christine Percheski, "Family Structure and the Reproduction of Inequalities," *Annual Review of Sociology* 34 (2008): 257–276.

3. Sean Gregory, "Disabled Kids Get in the Game," *Time*, February 11, 2013, 56.

4. Amanda Ripley, "The Case against High-School Sports," *The Atlantic*, October 15, 2013, 72, 74; see also Steven Overman, *Sports Crazy: How Sports Are Sabotaging American Schools* (Jackson: University of Mississippi Press, 2019)

5. see Daniel H. Bowen and Collin Hitt, "High School Sports Aren't Killing Academics," *The Atlantic*, October 2, 2013; Christine Brennan, "More Prep Football on TV? All About Networks, Not Kids," *USA Today*, August 22, 2013, 3C;.

6. Dara Shifrer, Jennifer Pearson, Chandra Muller, and Lindsey Wilkinson, "College-Going Benefits of High School Sports Participation: Race and Gender Differences over Three Decades," *Youth & Society* 47, no. 3 (2015): 295–318; see also J. M. Barron, B. T. Ewing, and G. R Waddell, "The Effects of High School Athletic Participation on Education and Labor Market Outcomes," *Review of Economics and Statistics* 82, no. 3 (2000): 409–421.

7. Peter Donnely and Jay Coakley, *The Role of Recreation in Promoting Social Inclusion*, (Toronto: Laidlaw Foundation, 2002).

8. Todd Weber, *The Fields of Fall: Small-Town High School Football in Iowa* (St. Petersburg, FL: Booklocker.com, 2011); see also Drew Jubera, *Must Win: A Season of Survival for a Town and Its Team* (New York: St. Martin's Press, 2012).

9. Margaret Kleiser and Lara Mayeux, "Popularity and Gender Prototypicality: An Experimental Approach," *Journal of Youth and Adolescence* 50 (2021): 144–158, https://doi.org/10.1007/s10964-020-01344-5.

10. NFHS, *The Case for High School Activities* (Indianapolis, IN: National Federation of State High School Associations, 2015), https://www.nfhs.org/articles/the-case-for-high-school-activities/; see also Angela Lumpkin and Judy Favor, "Comparing the Academic Performance of High School Athletes and Non-Athletes in Kansas in 2008–2009," *Journal of Sport Administration & Supervision* 4, no. 1 (2012): 41–62.

11. Daniel H. Bowen and Jay P. Greene, "Does Athletic Success Come at the Expense of Academic Success?" *Journal of Research in Education* 22, no. 2 (2012): 2–23.

12. For example, see Robert F. McCarthy, "Athletic Participation and Academic Achievement of High School Students: A Longitudinal Study of Athletic and Non-Athletic Participants," *Journal of International Education and Practice* 2, nos. 2 & 3 (2019); and also Overman, *Sports Crazy*.

13. See Ryan Yeung, "Athletics, Athletic Leadership, and Academic Achievement," *Education and Urban Society* 47, no. 3 (2015): 361–387.

14. Mark Edmundson, "Do Sports Build Character or Damage It?" *The Chronicle of Higher Education* 58, no. 20 (2012): B6–B9; see also Kirk Mango, "Character Building and Competitive Sports Participation—Do They Mix?" *ChicagoNow*, October 7, 2013, http://www.chicagonow.com/the-athletes-sports-experience-making-a-difference/2013/10/character-building-and-competitive-sports-participation-do-they-mix/.

15. Jill Martin Wrenn, "The End Game: How Sports Stars Battle through Retirement," CNN Living, January 7, 2013, http://www.cnn.com/2013/01/05/living/aging-athletes-retirement/; see also Robert Laura, "How Star Athletes Deal with Retirement," *Forbes*, May 22, 2012, https://www.forbes.com/

sites/robertlaura/2012/05/22/how-star-athletes-deal-with-retirement/#117467382a4e.

16. Inger Eliasson and Annika Johansson, "The Disengagement Process among Young Athletes When Withdrawing from Sport: A New Research Approach," *International Review for the Sociology of Sport* 56, no. 4 (2021): 537–557.

17. Brandin Heidbreder, "Does It Pay to Be a High School Athlete?" *The Park Place Economist* 15, no. 1 (2007), http://digitalcommons.iwu.edu/parkplace/vol15/iss1/10/.

18. Kirsten Hextrum, "Amateurism Revisited: How U.S. College Athletic Recruitment Favors Middle-Class Athletes," *Sport, Education and Society* 25, no. 1 (2020): 111–123, https://doi.org/10.1080/13573322.2018.1547962.

19. NFHS, participation survey, https://www.nfhs.org/media/1020412/2018-19_participation_survey.pdf. NFHS, "The Case for High School Activities" (Indianapolis, IN: National Federation of State High School Associations, 2015), https://www.nfhs.org/articles/the-case-for-high-school-activities/; see also Angela Lumpkin and Judy Favor, "Comparing the Academic Performance of High School Athletes and Non-Athletes in Kansas in 2008–2009," *Journal of Sport Administration & Supervision* 4, no. 1 (2012): 41–62.

20. Shira Springer, "Boys or Girls, It's All Basketball to Coach Kristen McDonnell," ESPNW, January 1, 2020, https://www.espn.com/espnw/culture/story/_/id/28377993/boys-girls-all-basketball-coach-kristen-mcdonnell; Andrew Ozaki, "Female Coach Breaks Down Boys Basketball Barriers," KEtv, March 14, 2014, http://www.ketv.com/sports/high-school-sports/female-coach-breaks-down-boys-basketball-barriers/24980838/.

21. Quoted in D. Stanley Eitzen, *Fair and Foul: Beyond the Myths and Paradoxes of Sport*, 6th ed. (Lanham, MD: Rowman & Littlefield, 2016), 65, see also 65–85.

22. Corbett Smith, Matt Wixon, Greg Riddle July 23, 2015, "Gaming the system: The high school transfer system has been abused for decades, and there's no sign of that trend ending anytime soon," https://www.dallasnews.com/interactives/2015/on-the-move/, accessed June 13, 2022; Nick Kosmider, "College Basketball Prep Can Be Spelled AAU,"

The Denver Post, July 20, 2015, http://www.denverpost.com/2015/07/20/college-basketball-prep-can-be-spelled-aau/; Jim Halley, "Spike in High School Football Transfers Concerns Some," *USA Today*, August 16, 2017, 8C.

23. Paul Angelico, "A Transfer's Paradise," *The Denver Post*, December 4, 2016, 1CC-10CC.

24. National Institute on Drug Abuse, "Monitoring the Future Study: Trends in Prevalence of Various Drugs," https://www.drugabuse.gov/drug-topics/trends-statistics/monitoring-future/monitoring-future-study-trends-in-prevalence-various-drugs. Accessed June 15, 2021. Lloyd D. Johnston et al., *Monitoring the Future National Survey Result on Drug Use, 1975–2020: Key Findings on Adolescent Drug Use*, sponsored by the National Institute on Drug Abuse and the National Institutes of Health, 2021.

25. Philip Velez, Marjorie Snyder, and Don Sabo, *The State of High School Sports in America: An Evaluation of the Nation's Most Popular Extracurricular Activity* (New York: Women's Sports Foundation, 2019), https://www.womenssportsfoundation.org/wp-content/uploads/2019/10/state-of-high-school-sports-report-final.pdf.

26. Eric Simons, *The Secret Lives of Sports Fans: The Science of Sports Obsession* (New York: Overlook Duckworth, 2014).

27. Eitzen, *Fair and Foul*, 123–139.

28. Jeff Passan, "Under the Gun," *Sports Illustrated*, April 4, 2016, 56–64; see also Halley, "Spike in High School Football Transfers Concerns Some."

29. Velez, Snyder, and Sabo, *The State of High School Sports in America*.

30. Kaisa Snellman, Jennifer M. Silva, Carl B. Frederick, and Robert D. Putnam, "The Engagement Gap: Social Mobility and Extracurricular Participation among American Youth," *Annals of the American Academy of Political and Social Science* 657, no. 1 (2015): 194–207.

31. Number of participants in U.S. high school football (11-player) 2018/19, by gender https://www.statista.com/statistics/267955/participation-in-us-high-school-football/#:~:text=The%20combined%20number%20of%20male,around%207.5%20percent%20to%202%2C404. Accessed June 12, 2022 Also, "Yes, Chapel Hill's Brooklyn Harker is a football player. Get used to it." North

Carolina Public Radio | By Mitchell Northam; Oct 21, 2021 https://www.wunc.org/sports/2021-10-21/chapel-hill-brooklyn-harker-more-girls-playing-tackle-football-tigers-marsh, accessed June 12, 2022

32. Snellman et al., "The Engagement Gap," 203.

33. Kyle Austin, "Now More Than Ever, Students and Families Are Paying to Participate in High School Sports," *The Ann Arbor News*, September 8, 2013, http://www.annarbor.com/sports/high-school/pay-to-participate-story/; see also Amy Donaldson, "High School Sports: What It Really Costs to Play High School Football," *Desert News*, September 2, 2013.

34. Mark Stewart, "Naming Rights Trickle Down to High School Level," *Journal Sentinel*, September 3, 2012, http://www.jsonline.com/sports/preps/naming-rights-trickle-down-to-high-school-level-tv6nn30-168421646.html/; Jim McConnell, "Selling the Rights to Friday Nights," *Chesterfield Observer*, September 11, 2013, http://www.chester-fieldobserver.com/news/2013-; see also Overman, *Sports Crazy*.

35. The crown jewel: All eyes on Katy ISD's $70M stadium, Thursday, August 17, 2017 https://abc13.com/sports/the-crown-jewel-katy-isd-unveils-new-$70m-stadium-/2319218/ Accessed on June 11, 2022; Matt Young, August 9, 2021, Most expensive high school football stadiums in Texas, chron.com, https://www.chron.com/sports/highschool/article/Most-expensive-high-school-football-stadiums-Texas-13145194.php accessed June 13, 2022; Erin Anderson, "Celina School Spending $25 Million on Sports Stadium Complex: A Small North Texas School District Is Spending Big Bucks on New Sports Facilities Instead of Classrooms," *TexasScorecard*, September 21, 2018, https://texasscorecard.com/local/celina-school-spending-25-million-on-sports-stadium-complex/.

36. Jeff Zillgritt, "Aspiring Power Has Doubters," *USA Today*, August 18, 2011, 1C–2C; see also Lee Jenkins, "Eastern Christian Academy Has No Field, No Home Uniforms, No Listed Phone Number. It Isn't Even a School, JUST A NATIONAL FOOTBALL POWER," *Sports Illustrated*, August 27, 2012, 47–51.

37. Andrew Lawrence, Sept 3, 2021, Was ESPN scammed by a fake high school? The real scandal goes much deeper, https://www.theguardian.com/sport/2021/sep/03/espn-bishop-sycamore-fake-high-school-allegation-football-img-academy, accessed June 12, 2022

38. Alexandra Starr, "Basketball Prep Schools: A World of Their Own, and Recruiting Worldwide," NPR, April 3, 2014; Brad Wolverton, "Basketball Academy's Empty Promises," *The Chronicle of Higher Education*, March 30, 2014, http://www.chronicle.com/article/Basketball-Academys-Empty/145597.

39. Derek Volner, "Eight of the Top-Ranked Boys Teams and Four of the Top-Ranked Girls Teams in the Country Set to Compete in the DICK'S Sporting Goods High School Nationals Basketball Tournament in New York City," ESPN Media Zone, March 16, 2017, http://espnmediazone.com/us/press-releases/2017/03/eight-top-20-boys-teams-four-top-20-girls-teams-country-compete-dicks-sporting-goods-high-school-nationals-basketball-tournament-new-york-city/.

40. Robert B. Gardner and Nina van Erk, "Associations Say 'No' to National Championships," *High School Today*, February 11, 2016, 1.

41. How Adidas, Nike and Under Armour have divvied up Major College Basketball, https://www.si.com/college/2017/10/02/adidas-nike-under-armour-contracts-schools-conferences, accessed June 17, 2022

42. George Schroeder, "Number of Early Enrollees on Rise," *USA Today*, January 30, 2017, 4C.

CHAPTER 10

INTERCOLLEGIATE SPORT

Despite the pretenses of U.S. intercollegiate sports to be educationally oriented, strictly amateur activities, the commercial aspects of college sports programs have progressively encroached on the educational terrain and, at the upper reaches of Division I, have subverted it.

—GERALD GURNEY, DONNA A. LOPIANO, AND ANDREW ZIMBALIST[1]

The Syracuse University lacrosse teams have won eleven national championship titles in the modern NCAA era. The Orange's eleven NCAA championship titles are the most since the NCAA began holding tournaments in 1971. (Photo: © Rich Barnes—USA TODAY Sports)

As we noted in Chapter 2, the system of intercollegiate sports that originated in the mid-nineteenth century and evolved into its current state is unique to the United States, and it has been one of the most significant forces in the development of American organized sports. It was the model for the development of high school sports, and many nonschool youth sports programs have been organized as feeder systems to the high school and college sports programs. Finally, the intercollegiate sports programs serve as a farm system for many of the professional sports.

We think it is important to point out that no other country in the world has a system of intercollegiate sports as elaborate and expensive as that in the United States. Most other countries separate their elite competitive athletics from their educational institutions. In most other countries, those who wish to pursue competitive sports join clubs.

Intercollegiate sports are not the only form of sports in higher education in the United States; sports are an enormously popular form of physical recreation in many high schools and on every college and university campus in the United States. Campus recreation facilities overflow with students playing pickup games of basketball, ice hockey, racquetball, volleyball, and a half-dozen other sports. Many college students participate in campus intramural sports programs. Sport club teams—teams that athletic departments refuse to fund—are funded by college student governments and compete against other institutions. Finally, there is the formal intercollegiate sports program. More than 500,000 young men and women participate on more than 22,800 teams, according to the NCAA and the National Association of Intercollegiate Athletics (NAIA).

The characteristics of intercollegiate sports programs in U.S. higher education vary widely. At one extreme, there are the programs where the student-athletes are an integral part of the student body, receiving no "athletic scholarships" for playing their sport. In these institutions, intercollegiate sports are primarily funded from general institutional accounts, games are played against colleges within the region, and spectator attendance at games is typically small, consisting mostly of students, parents of students, and alumni. Programs of this kind are classified as Division III by the NCAA, the major controlling body of intercollegiate sports. At the other extreme is Division I—so-called big-time intercollegiate sports—which is divided into two subdivisions (see Table 10.1). Sandwiched between those two is Division II. Here, member institutions are typically larger than Division III members and smaller than Division I institutions and with less funding and fewer facilities than Division I institutions. See Table 10.1 for a more complete explanation of the differences between the NCAA divisions.

Each of the NCAA divisions has a variety of unique rules and policies to which institutions must adhere to retain their membership in the division of their choosing. These are complex and complicated and need not concern us in this chapter. But, in general, to be considered a Division I (henceforth D-I) program, the NCAA requires that a university commit more resources than the other divisions in terms of scholarships and facilities in order to qualify. Essentially, the NCAA is requiring D-I schools to invest in creating more highly competitive programs, which, in turn, can be marketed to generate revenue for the schools and the NCAA. D-I is the division of NCAA intercollegiate sports—especially the sports of football and basketball—that garners the most media attention, and because so much money is associated with conducting D-I programs, they are commonly referred to as big-time college programs. That will be the main focus of this chapter.

BEGINNING AND DEVELOPMENT OF COLLEGE SPORTS

To recap what we said in Chapter 2, the first intercollegiate sports contest in the United States was a rowing race between Harvard and Yale in 1852. In 1869 the first intercollegiate football contest took place between Princeton and Rutgers. In 1891, James Naismith, a Canadian who was a theology graduate at the YMCA International Training School—now known as Springfield College—invented basketball to fill in the gap between the football and baseball seasons. It rapidly became a popular indoor winter sport for males and females in high schools and colleges.

TABLE 10.1 DIFFERENCES AMONG THE THREE NCAA DIVISIONS

Division I

Number of required sports: Division I programs must offer at least fourteen sports (at least seven for men and seven for women or six for men and eight for women). The institution must sponsor at least two team sports (e.g., football, basketball, or volleyball) for each gender.

Scheduling: Each Division I program must play a minimum number of contests against Division I opponents.

Financial aid: Division I institutions must offer a minimum amount of financial aid but may not exceed established maximums. Football Bowl Subdivision football, men's and women's basketball, women's gymnastics, women's volleyball, and women's tennis are considered head-count sports for financial aid purposes in Division I. Financial aid equivalencies (one grant-in-aid package divided into smaller pieces) may be offered in all other sports.

Subdivisions: Division I allows institutions to choose subdivisions based on the scope of their football programs. The three subdivisions are as follows:

1. Football Bowl Subdivision (FBS, 125 members): The FBS uses the postseason bowl system rather than a playoff to determine a national champion in football. FBS members must comply with higher standards for sports sponsorship (the overall program must offer sixteen teams rather than the fourteen required of other Division I members), football scheduling, and overall financial aid. In addition, FBS members must meet minimum attendance standards in football.

2. Football Championship Subdivision (124 members): Football Championship Subdivision members determine their football champion through an NCAA playoff.

3. Division I (98 members): The remaining programs of Division I do not sponsor football.

Total Division I membership: 309 members

Division II

Number of required sports: Division II programs must offer at least ten sports (at least five for men and five for women or four for men and six for women). The institution must sponsor at least two team sports for each gender. The school also must have participating male and female teams or participants in the fall, winter, and spring seasons.

Scheduling: Each Division II program must play a minimum number of contests against Division II opponents. The minimums vary by sport.

Financial aid: Division II institutions must offer a minimum amount of financial aid but may not exceed established maximums. Financial aid equivalencies are common in all Division II sports.

Total Division II membership: 311 institutions

Division III

Number of required sports: Division III programs must offer at least five sports for men and five for women.

Scheduling: Each Division III program must play a minimum number of contests against Division III opponents. The minimums vary by sport.

Financial aid: Division III student-athletes play for the love of the game, without an athletic scholarship.

Total Division III membership: 450 total members

Note: It must be understood that the NCAA's organizational structure and policies are constantly changing.
Source: NCAA, http://www.ncaa.org/.

These early collegiate sports events were organized and managed by students. The faculties, administrators, and alumni were not involved. The original form of governance was modeled after the well-established sports in the private secondary schools of England. In the British model the sports were for the students, and as student recreations they were expected to be organized, administered, and coached through student initiative, not adult intervention.

However, in the United States students soon began losing control over their sports. The first college faculty athletic committees were formed by Princeton in 1881 and by Harvard a year later. In 1895 the first league (later known as the Big Ten) was formed. By 1905 there was a need for a national organization to standardize rules and address problems associated with college sport. The Intercollegiate Athletic Association was formed in that year. In 1910 it became the NCAA, and that organization has controlled college sport ever since, except for colleges controlled by the NAIA, which has nearly 260 member institutions located throughout the United States. African American schools were blocked from the NCAA and NAIA, and in response, eight all-Black intercollegiate athletic conferences were formed between 1906 and 1923. Historically Black College and University athletic conferences were finally allowed access to the NAIA in 1953 and the NCAA in 1965.[2] Women also faced a history of exclusion and organized their own college sport organizations, such as the Association for Intercollegiate Athletics for Women, which lasted from 1971 to 1983. It was not until 1981 that the NCAA sponsored women's sports.

The NCAA does not sponsor championships for adaptive specific sports, such as wheelchair basketball. It does have a policy to provide reasonable accommodations for student-athletes with disabilities when they participate in NCAA athletics. There are some universities that support adaptive sports; often this happens in intramural or recreation departments. Even at well-known universities the programs are separate from varsity status sports. Not surprisingly, when these programs are not part of the athletic department, the funding for these sports is minimal. Essentially, most programs for students with disabilities run as separate and not equal.

Once intercollegiate sports were transformed so that students had virtually no voice in policymaking, control became vested in coaches, school administrations, athletic corporations, booster organizations, leagues, and national organizations. Moreover, college sport was converted from an activity for the participants to a large-scale commercial entertainment industry, at least at the NCAA D-I level.[3]

Along with this transformation of intercollegiate sport have come many abuses—illegal recruiting practices, altered transcripts, phantom courses, the physical and psychological abuse of athletes, and the exploitation of athletes.[4] These abuses occur for two related reasons: pressure to win on the field and pressure to succeed financially. A persuasive case can be made that big-time intercollegiate athletics has severely corrupted the goals and ideals of higher education.

This chapter is divided into five parts: (1) student-centered college sport remains, (2) college sport as big business, (3) the NCAA and student-athletes, (4) educational performance and student-athletes, and (5) reform initiatives and intercollegiate sports.

STUDENT-CENTERED COLLEGE SPORT REMAINS

With all of the public and media attention on big-time intercollegiate sports (televised games, national rankings, All-American selections, bowl games, etc.), outside higher education there is little awareness of a form of college sports that has many of the features of the original motivation for college students to form sports teams. It is found in the NCAA Division III (D-III) colleges. So as a contrast to the features of NCAA D-I sports, which will be the main focus of this chapter, we provide an outline of what D-III sports programs are like. They are characterized by the following:

- They feature student-athletes who are subject to the same admission standards, academic standards, housing, and support services as the general student body.
- They provide a well-rounded collegiate experience that involves a balance of academics, competitive athletics, and the opportunity to pursue the multitude of other co-curricular and extracurricular opportunities offered on the campus.
- Their playing seasons and eligibility standards minimize conflicts between athletics and academics, allowing student-athletes to focus on their academic programs and the achievement of a degree.
- They place primary emphasis on regional in-season and conference competition, while also offering thirty-six national championships annually.

- Athletic departments place special importance on the impact of athletics on the participants rather than on spectators. The student-athlete's experience is of paramount concern.
- The integration of athletics with the larger institution enables student-athletes to experience all aspects of campus life.
- They offer a competitive sports environment for student-athletes who play for the love of the game, without the obligation of an athletic scholarship.
- Perhaps the most surprising feature to those who are familiar only with big-time college sports, D-III has 450 institutional members—more than either of the other two NCAA divisions.

Our main reason for describing the fundamental features of D-III sports is to show readers that there is more than one viable model of intercollegiate sports. Throughout the remainder of this chapter, as you read our description of D-I sports, we suggest you compare and contrast that form of college sports with D-III sports.

COLLEGE SPORT AS BIG BUSINESS

It is indisputable that big-time college sports are an extremely popular cultural practice in the United States. In addition to the exciting matchups between teams representing highly esteemed universities, the sports events are accompanied by marching bands, cheerleaders, pom-pom groups, tailgate parties, and so forth. The enormously successful commercial entertainment business that has emerged from big-time college football and basketball is a popular cultural form of the same genre as theater, cinema, popular music, and, of course, professional sport. In each case, a group of talented persons, well

Scoreboard of a big-time university with all the corporate names, illustrating the commercialization of big-time intercollegiate sports. (Photo: AP Photo/David Stluka)

trained in their specialty, provide amusement and entertainment for audiences who pay to watch the performances.

We recognize the enthusiasm and loyalty of devoted fans of big-time intercollegiate sports. A hard-fought, well-played game provides entertainment and excitement. But the pageantry and hoopla of big-time intercollegiate sports tend to mask its underlying profit-oriented structure—the explicit fact that it is a big commercial business. The NCAA, which is the general corporate entity for its member universities, generated $1.15 billion in 2021. This type of income is mostly derived annually from the Men's Division 1 basketball tournament and associated media contracts. In 2020, during the COVID-19 pandemic, this basketball tournament ("March Madness") was canceled and the NCAA accordingly lost $800 million in revenue during this year.[5] This shows how dependent the NCAA is on media coverage of national championships—especially basketball and football.[6] It is an industry that is tightly integrated with three of the largest commercial industries: mass media, sporting goods and equipment, and entertainment. Other industries, such as transportation and hotels, have a significant footprint in the intercollegiate sports industry as well (see Box 10.1).

Big-time college sports are also about capital accumulation and the bottom line. All of the earmarks of capitalist enterprise have come to characterize the business of big-time collegiate athletics, and intercollegiate sport played for the personal, social, and emotional gratification of the participants has been jettisoned in the process. Many people view big-time intercollegiate sport as merely a form of fun and excitement, but people who work in that industry acknowledge its economic realities.

The following statements by various people associated with big-time college sports indicate the financial driver that is big-time collegiate sport. A former athletic director at the University of Michigan said, "This is a business, a big business. Anyone who hasn't figured that out by now is a damned fool." The University of Arizona athletic director concurred, saying, "I think it's important for people to realize that

BOX 10.1 *THINKING ABOUT SPORT:* THE IMPACT OF ESPN ON COLLEGE SPORT

ESPN's media empire includes 7 U.S. cable networks, 24 international stations, 350 full-time radio affiliates, one magazine with 2 million subscribers, and about 100 million households that pay cable providers for its productions. This media colossus has an enormous influence on big-time college football, which, according to the *New York Times*, is its chief empresario.

ESPN, and to a lesser extent other television networks, has flooded big-time college sports with money. In 2020, ESPN began a 12-year, $1 billion dollar contract with the American Athletic Conference (AAC). This deal infuses $7 million dollars annually to its member schools. Their contract with the Atlantic Coast Conference (ACC) extends over 20 years (ending in 2031-32) giving each school in that conference about $17 million annually. In 2024, ESPN will have exclusive rights to Southeastern Conference (SEC) football and men's basketball for ten years. It will provide $300 million annually for that league. By funneling billions of dollars to the NCAA and the power conferences, ESPN has created a behemoth that trumps academics, exploits athletes, and upends the power within universities.

Increasing the gap between the "haves" and the "have-nots," ESPN's money via the playoff system, the bowl system, and the payouts to leagues for television rights flows disproportionately to the dominant conferences. Besides the near-monopoly of television exposure, the major conferences use ESPN's money to upgrade their facilities (plush locker rooms, expansion of stadiums with more skyboxes), all of which advantage them in the recruiting wars and swell their coffers even more.

ESPN intrudes in the scheduling of big-time college sports. ESPN, under its contracts with conferences, has the power to determine kickoff times. Scheduling is also determined by ESPN as it moves away from the universality of Saturday games. To get television exposure, many lower-profile universities have agreed to play on Tuesday, Thursday, or Friday nights. These decisions disregard the academic side of these institutions, since games are often played during the school week, sometimes late at night.

In sum, we are left with the inescapable conclusion that there is no greater force affecting big-time college football than ESPN.

Sources: Travis Vogan, *ESPN: The Making of a Sports Media Empire* (Champaign: University of Illinois Press, 2015); Jeff Benedict and Armen Keteyian, *The System: The Glory and Scandal of Big-Time College Football* (New York: Doubleday, 2013); D. Stanley Eitzen, "ESPN: The Force in Sports," in *Sport in Contemporary Society*, 10th ed., ed. D. Stanley Eitzen (New York: Oxford University Press, 2015), 72–80. On3, *Here's a look at all the current conference TV deals*, August 2, 2021, https://www.on3.com/news/conference-tv-deals-current-status-college-football/

[NCAA Division I] sports is . . . a big business." The University of Minnesota president told a special convention of the NCAA, "We in Division I are in an entertainment business and we can't fool ourselves." A member of the University of Louisville's board of trustees argued, "College sports are a business, first and foremost. People in the Louisville community look forward to attending games and seeing a strong product on the field." The new director of the Pac-12 conference, George Kliavkoff, came from the hospitality sector, where he was a top executive at MGM Resorts International. One college sport analyst put it this way: "Big-time athletic departments [have become] franchises in College Sports Inc., a huge commercial entertainment enterprise with operating methods and objectives frequently opposed to the educational missions of the host universities." He went on to explain how one college athletic director "defined the motivation of the men directing big-time intercollegiate athletics: 'There are three definitions. . . . Greed, greed, and greed.'"

The intrusion of money into big-time college sport at that level is evident in the following representative examples:

- CBS and Turner Broadcasting will pay $10.8 billion from 2011 to 2024 to carry the NCAA men's basketball tournament. The broadcasting partners will show the fourteen versions of the tournament on four networks and carry each game nationally.
- Coca-Cola Company has an eleven-year, $500 million contract with the NCAA, giving it the exclusive right to advertise and promote its beverages at the eighty-six championships in twenty-two sports sponsored by the NCAA.
- In 2016 Texas A&M University had a total revenue of $193 million and employed more than 300 full-time workers and nearly 1,600 part-time employees.[7]
- College football's "Power 5" conferences that have contracts to send their champions to the Orange, Rose and Sugar Bowls, will each receive approximately $66 million.[8]
- The University of Alabama, one of the top collegiate teams in licensing revenue, has earned about $5 million in each of the past few fiscal years.

- T. Boone Pickens has donated more than $500 million to the Oklahoma State athletic department.

With a total fan base of more than 180 million, the college sports market is a prime target for corporate marketers. The president of IMG Sports and Entertainment has claimed that college sports has one of the most desirable fan bases available for corporate marketers, combining the overall appeal of college sports with top national universities. Corporate partners are thus considered vital to aid such universities in growing its athletic programs.[9]

Universities throughout the United States support naming rights of athletic facilities through one of two measures: a corporate sponsor or a philanthropic donor. Notice that the universities are merely considered as a "brand" name to IMG Sports, not a university or an institution of higher education. It is just another brand—another commodity—to be marketed and sold like other commodities. Indeed, some universities have contracted with corporations to extend naming rights to their sports venues in exchange for various sums of money. See Table 10.2 for examples. Selling their stadium's naming rights is a way to increase revenue for athletics departments.

Paralleling the corporatization of big-time college sports, the salaries of the men and women who coach these teams have skyrocketed in a manner similar to those of chief executive officers and top executives in other industries of the corporate world. The examples in Table 10.3 show how well the highest-paid coaches of big-time basketball and football programs are compensated.

The football coaches listed in Table 10.3 are only five of the approximately thirty head football coaches who made $4 million or more during the 2020 season. And lucrative college football salaries do not end there. In 2009, just one assistant football coach was compensated more than $1 million, but in 2018 that number had risen to fifteen.[10]

But compensation to coaches in big-time collegiate sports programs does not end with salaries. These coaches also receive gifts of housing, paid country-club memberships, use of private jets, travel allowances for family members, complimentary tickets in luxury boxes, use of vacation homes, free cars, and,

TABLE 10.2 EXAMPLES OF INTERCOLLEGIATE SPORTS VENUES WITH CORPORATE NAMING RIGHTS

University	Name of sports venue
University of Maryland football/lacrosse stadium	Capital One Field at Byrd Stadium: Began a twenty-six-year, $20 million contract in 2006
University of Memphis football	Simmons Bank Liberty Stadium 2022 deal that will bring 6,821, 009 over 10 years.
University of Minnesota football stadium	Huntington Bank Stadium (was TCF Bank Football Stadium until 2021): Will pay $35 million over twenty-five years for the naming rights and other agreements
James Madison University	Atlantic Union Bank Center
College of Charleston men's and women's basketball and volleyball arena	TD Arena: 5,100 seat multipurpose facility
University of Southern California football stadium	United Airlines Field at Los Angeles Memorial Coliseum 69 million for 16 years
Washington State football	Gesa Field at Martin Stadium 2021 deal guarantees at least 11 million to WSU
University of Houston football stadium	TDECU Stadium: Texas Dow Employees Credit Union, beginning in 2014, will pay $15 million over ten years to rebrand the Houston's new 40,000-seat on-campus football stadium

TABLE 10.3 COLLEGE FOOTBALL AND MEN'S BASKETBALL COACHES' COMPENSATION

Top compensation for Division I men's basketball teams in 2021		Top compensation for football bowl Division I coaches in 2020	
Kentucky	$8 million	Alabama	$9.1 million
Duke	$7 million	Louisiana State	$8.6 million
Villanova	$6 million	Clemson	$8.2 million
Texas Tech	$5 million	Michigan	$8 million
Tennessee	$4.9 million	Texas A&M	$7.5 million

Note: Keep in mind that college coaches' compensation is always in a state of flux, because some are being hired or fired or are being rewarded for some achievement of their team.

Sources: 2020 NCAAF coaches salaries, updated as of November 17, 2020, https://sports.usatoday.com/ncaa/salaries/; 2021 NCAA basketball coach pay, updated as of March 9, 2021, https://sports.usatoday.com/ncaa/salaries/mens-basketball/coach/.

in some cases, million-dollar annuities. In addition, rollover contracts give coaches "golden parachutes" if they are fired prematurely. In one prominent example of this practice, Texas A & M's football coach, Jimbo Fisher, was provided with a huge $95.6 million buyout clause in his latest contract extension from 2021.[11] At the same time, and by comparison, the average compensation and benefits for presidents at public doctorate-granting (the most prestigious) universities was about $450,000. Furthermore, the American Association of University Professors reported that the average

salary for full professors at those same universities was near $118,000.

These examples demonstrate clearly that big-time college sport programs are not amateur sports. They are big business. The money generated comes from gate receipts, student athletic fees, the educational budget of the university, booster organizations, individual contributors, advertising income, contracts with shoe and apparel companies, television, and league reimbursements for the television and bowl or tournament appearances by league members.

SOCIAL THEORIES AND THEIR ROLE IN COLLEGES AND UNIVERSITIES

FUNCTIONALISM AND BIG-TIME COLLEGE SPORTS

In the U.S. educational system, the progressive step beyond high schools is the college/university level. Students are older, but they are still part of the educational institution of their society. Colleges and universities are part of the social institution of education, the institution that formally socializes members of society. A functionalist perspective of the colleges/universities views them as a primary social institution and intercollegiate sport as an integral part of the process of cultural transmission, promoting social and political integration, maintaining social control, and contributing to social change while performing a number of social reproduction functions: transmitting knowledge and conveying the dominant culture, promoting social and political integration, providing a common moral code for social cohesion, maintaining social control, and sorting and selecting students for their adult roles in society.

Actual involvement in intercollegiate sports is viewed as providing learning experiences that create social solidarity. However, as we have shown, there are significant differences between the sports programs at D-III institutions and those at D-I institutions, so the functional consequences are quite different as well.

Although big-time college sports are part of the education institution, it has a huge footprint in the economic system and is clearly a commercial enterprise. In that role it functions to sponsor the production of an entertainment service. As we have noted, its revenues and expenses make it a multibillion-dollar industry.

Beyond its commercial role, big-time sports function in a variety of social, cultural, and public relations ways. For example,

- Administrators, faculty, and students at many universities believe sports teams are important parts of campus life and excellent vehicles for generating publicity and alumni support.

- These same groups believe that college sports add to campus spirit and unity, provide free advertising for the campus, help in name branding, and provide a link and outreach to alumni.

- Several years ago the student government president at Cincinnati argued, "There's a better feeling on campus, more pride for the university. It's something that connects students to the university other than going to class."

- About that same time, an athletic administrator said, "A strong successful athletic program is very important to the connection with alumni, donors and leaders in the state, and it magnifies the university . . . beyond the state. That's the visibility that the athletics program can have."[12]

CONFLICT/CULTURALISM AND BIG-TIME COLLEGE SPORTS

Conflict/cultural theorists believe that the colleges/universities reinforce and perpetuate social inequalities arising from differences in class, gender, race, and ethnicity. They view college/university education as largely preserving the status quo and reinforcing and reproducing the existing social system. Although recognizing the importance of a college/university education, conflict/culturists view them as organizations with a distinctive elite orientation, with sharp inequalities in the educational opportunities available for students from different minority racial and ethnic groups and for female students. They stress that the sorting and selecting of pupils are highly biased according to students' socioeconomic backgrounds, giving students from affluent and wealthy families a variety of advantages on achievement tests; these enable such students, in turn, to increase the likelihood of their economic and social success in adulthood. The consequence is that colleges/universities tend to serve a social reproductive role that preserves a variety of social and economic inequalities from one generation to the next.

BELIEFS AND REALITY ABOUT BIG-TIME SPORT FUNCTIONS

Despite the commonly held belief that college athletic departments are doing well financially, the fact is that big-time intercollegiate sports are not profitable—just the opposite. Only about 10 percent of the 229 NCAA D-I university athletics departments make more money than they spend each year. So at the same time that coaches' salaries are skyrocketing, many athletic departments have had to rely on general university and student fee subsidies.

According to several analyses in recent years, about $1.8 *billion* in student fees and general university subsidies prop up athletic programs at the nation's top sports colleges, including hundreds of millions in the richest conferences. The amount of student fees going to intercollegiate sports programs account for as much as 23 percent of the required annual bill for in-state students. Keep in mind that just 25 of approximately 1,100 schools across 102 conferences in the NCAA made a profit through collegiate sports in 2019. Thus, it is often the case that athletic departments in the United States require subsidies to remain operational (see also Figure 10.1).[13]

Perhaps just as troubling, investigators have found that among the twenty universities nationally that had the highest estimated per-student athletics fees, fifteen do not disclose their per-student athletics fee charges on their billing statements, on their websites, or in other official school publications.[14]

Without millions in subsidies from general university and student fees, universities could not pay their bills, so subsidies are being directed toward revenue-pursuing athletic departments and away from core academic uses. In 2019, ten public universities in Ohio spent $192 million of student fees and other nonathletic monies to cover costs of the athletic departments. This equated to $1,000 dollars for every student on campus, whether they were an athlete or not.[15] A few years ago, the University of California at Berkeley subsidized athletics in the amount of $8.1 million from its general fund and about that same time forgave $31.4 million in athletics debts. This is not unusual; the average public university subsidy for athletics has been $8.8 million in recent years. More than half of the athletic departments at public universities in the Football Bowl Subdivision (FBS) are subsidized by at least 26 percent.

At Rutgers University the athletics department received some $47 million in subsidies in 2013 from the university's general allocations fund to make up for a shortfall in the previous year's athletic budget; that was an increase of about 68 percent from 2012 (see Box 10.2 for more about Rutgers).[16] In regards to this type of scenario, a professor at Wake Forest University once remarked, "The word I would use is 'appalling.' It's appalling in the big picture and representative of what is going on in athletics with coaches' salaries and facilities."[17]

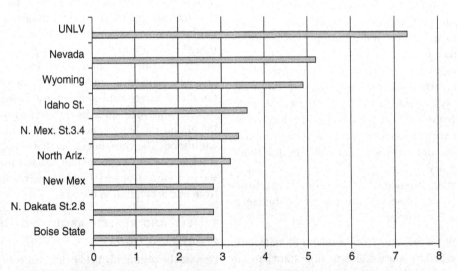

FIGURE 10.1 NCAA Division I Public University Athletic Departments Receiving Direct State or Other Government Support during the 2015–2016 Year (in Millions)

BOX 10.2 *THINKING ABOUT SPORT:* THE CONTRADICTIONS OF BIG-TIME COLLEGE SPORT

Big-time college sport is rife with contradictions that compromise the integrity of universities and their mission. In effect, these institutions of higher learning, organized for the best of reasons, allow blatant hypocrisy in their athletic programs. Consider the contradictions discussed next.

The overarching contradiction of big-time college sport is that as an organized commercial entertainment activity, it compromises educational goals. The actions of big-time college sport are antithetical to educational goals in the following ways:

1. Schools give disproportionately more per capita scholarship aid to athletes than to undergraduates with academic abilities and accomplishments.
2. Athletes are recruited as students, yet the demands of coaches and the athletic subculture are antithetical to the student role. The time demands on athletes (practice, lifting weights, meetings, studying playbooks, and travel), the spotlight of publicity and resulting pressures, and the sense of entitlement that ensues from their adoring fans diminish the importance of academics for the athletes.
3. In the search for success, big-time programs often enroll and subsidize ill-prepared and uninterested students solely for the purpose of winning games and producing revenue. Although some poorly prepared athletes find their intellectual footing in the academic environment, many do not. The "one-and-done" athletes who are recruited for just one year before they move on to the professional level, for example, are essentially poorly compensated migrant workers with no educational goals, making their year at school the height of educational hypocrisy. Related to this is the practice whereby some coaches at big-time programs recruit athletes with criminal backgrounds. Although the redemption of wayward athletes is a worthy goal, the object is to win games at whatever the cost.
4. Coaches, thought by many to be role models for building character, sometimes engage in breaking the rules in the process of recruiting athletes, keeping them eligible, or exceeding the rule limits for practice time.
5. Although big-time sports produce revenue for the athletic program, with few exceptions they lose money. To offset this, money is drained away from the educational functions of the university to subsidize athletic budgets. Although subsidies from student fees and university funds have decreased for some universities—for example, the University of California, Berkeley—they continue to increase for others. From 2005 to 2014, for example, Rutgers University's athletics program received subsidies of $238.6 million. In effect, the athletic departments are diverting money away from the educational mission to prop up athletic department budgets.
6. The final hypocrisy is that although big-time sport is a big business that benefits coaches, schools, television networks, advertisers, airlines, concessions, manufacturers of apparel and memorabilia, legitimate sports betting in the United States, and local businesses, the actual producers of the many millions are not paid. In short, the athletes are exploited. The fundamental question for alumni, boards of regents, and university administrators is, How is big-time college sports justified when the system is rigged in opposition to the academic mission of universities?

The subsidies to intercollegiate sports programs are much greater if the venues in which the sports events occur are taken into account. That is, college football and basketball teams play in multimillion-dollar stadiums and arenas paid for by taxpayers, contributors, and, more typically, bonds that are paid off by students' fees at no expense to the athletic departments.

There are several reasons for the financial plight of big-time intercollegiate sports. First, the revenue-producing sports (football and men's basketball and a few women's basketball programs) are expected to fund the entire athletic program, which may include more than thirty sports.

Second, there is a constantly escalating arms race in big-time college sport, as we noted earlier, to pay for raises to keep successful coaches. When a team succeeds, the coach's salary is raised by hundreds, sometimes by thousands, and the assistants' likewise. Typically, successful programs are constantly upgrading their facilities, including expanding the seating, adding luxury boxes, and improving weight rooms, locker rooms, and practice fields. For example, University of Georgia constructed an $80 million football operations building that is 165,000 square feet and has the nation's largest weight room, and in 2019 Kansas State committed $105 million to upgrading their athletic facilities.[18]

Third, the athletic departments spare no expense to fund the revenue-producing sports. A common practice, for example, is for the football team and some basketball teams to stay in a local hotel the night before *home* games. Travel budgets for these teams and for their recruiters are generous. The conventional wisdom throughout the universe of big-time intercollegiate athletes has always been that extravagant expenditures for football and basketball programs were necessary because they led to winning teams, and winning teams in turn led to increased revenue to the university.

Unfortunately, and as with so many other "wisdoms" about intercollegiate sports, the facts do not support the claim. According to a report commissioned by the NCAA titled *NCAA Athletic Departments: An Empirical Investigation of the Effects of Revenue and Conference Changes*, there is little difference in what a university pays to build its athletic program and what it gets back in new revenue. In other words, the empirical evidence showed that "for every one dollar increase in ticket sale revenue, total expenditures can rise by $0.83 and reduce a school's athletic subsidy by $0.19." Thus, there is virtually "no effect of changes in athletic expenditures at a given school on net athletic revenues at that school."[19]

Big-time intercollegiate sports even receive subsidies from the federal government. Analysts of college athletics have reported that athletic departments receive hundreds of millions in public support through federal tax deductions supporters can take for gifts to booster clubs. Athletic programs studied several years ago received about $1.04 billion in donations, which was probably translated into nearly a $200 million federal tax subsidy of the programs. A substantial portion of the money contributed to athletic programs gives the donors preferential seating at games and other "perks" such as access to coaches and players at special events. Several economists who have written about tax exemption and college sports contend that the government is essentially subsidizing expensive seats for wealthy football fans, as they receive a significant tax break on their donations.[20]

FURTHER CONSEQUENCES OF THE COMMERCIAL ORIENTATION OF BIG-TIME COLLEGE SPORTS

The other social theoretical orientation we have described, the conflict/cultural perspective, argues that big-time college sports are like any other form of commercial business, where capital accumulation interests are an adjunct to exploitation and coercion, and that sports events encourage people to focus on wins and losses, on coaches and standings, and on cheering and temporary excitement, while deflecting attention away from pressing social issues—inequality, injustice, racism, sexism, and violence.

Big-time college sports programs are a segment of the corporatized entertainment industry, and as with all the other enterprises in that industry, capital accumulation—making money—is paramount. There have been consequences: First, the lack of adequate revenue has led to budget cuts. Football and men's basketball produce revenue; therefore, they have been largely exempt from budget reduction. When the cuts are severe, some programs have been eliminated, and these casualties are in the so-called minor sports such as wrestling, lacrosse, gymnastics, swimming, water polo, tennis, and golf. For example, in the 1981–1982 season there were 146 D-I wrestling teams. Currently, there are 78 teams. During the COVID-19 pandemic, Stanford University, a very wealthy institution, announced that it would drop 11 sports (all "minor" or Olympic sports) because of budget constraints. Students and alumni rallied and put enough pressure on the institution that those sports were reinstated.

Women's sports have been less vulnerable than the men's minor sports because of the protection of Title IX (see Chapter 7), but their programs have historically been underfunded or have experienced cutbacks. The necessity of raising money through sports programs tends to make college sport more elitist (fewer and fewer participants) and limited to certain skills and physical types (the tall or the large or both). This commercial impetus reinforces the dominance of male sports, at least football and basketball. Concomitantly, when women's sports are not invested in to the same degree as men's, it has the effect of perpetuating secondary status (see Box 10.3).

A second consequence is that the commercial orientation of big-time college sport has prostituted the university and the purpose of sport. The necessity of making more and more money is a major source for the many abuses found in big-time college sport. Booster organizations that supply funds may influence which coaches are hired and when they will be fired. And corporate sponsors may intrude in various ways as they give or withhold their monies. In *Confessions of a Spoilsport: My Life and Hard Times Fighting Sports Corruption at an Old Eastern University*, William C. Dowling, a professor of English at Rutgers University, tells his story of mobilizing a group of students, faculty, and alumni who attempted to stop the move toward big-time sports at Rutgers, an institution with a distinguished Ivy League–type history. His explanation: big-time college athletics is filled with "corruption and hypocrisy and self-deception. [With] pious claims and brutally cynical behavior. [With] frightened faculty and powerful regents or trustees who see winning football and basketball teams as immeasurably more important than academic and intellectual values."[21]

A third consequence of an athletic department's search for money has meant that teams will reschedule games to fit the demands of television, even if it inconveniences their fans or interferes with athletes' studies. Football games are now played in the heat of

BOX 10.3 *THINKING ABOUT SPORT:* INVESTING IN WOMEN? THE NCAA BASKETBALL CHAMPIONSHIPS

During the 2021 NCAA Basketball Championships, a Stanford University sports performance coach, Ali Kershner, tweeted a picture showing the discrepancies between the practice facilities for men's and women's teams. In the women's practice facility was one rack of dumbbells, none of which weighed more than thirty pounds, along with a few yoga mats. In comparison, the men's facilities had fully equipped weight rooms. Oregon player Sedona Prince posted a thirty-seven-second video on TikTok that documented the same discrepancy and it went viral, with 10.8 million views and nearly 200,000 retweets. Arizona's women's coach, Adia Barnes, also posted a video showing the differences between men's and women's facilities and called for action. The NCAA responded quickly, admitted the problem existed, and upgraded the facilities, but there was no hiding the fact that the original discrepancies were dramatic. Other reports of the differences in the treatment of the men's and women's players followed: The men's teams were being tested for COVID-19 daily with highly accurate PCR tests, while the women's teams were receiving less accurate antigen tests. The meals provided and the swag bags were also clearly two different levels of quality. This sparked a conversation about the long-standing lack of equitable investment in women's basketball by the NCAA. The Women's Basketball Coaches Association asked the NCAA to create a Commission on Gender Equity in College Sports. It also created the website Our Fair Shot to document inequities and develop an activist strategy for change.

The NCAA hired a law firm to investigate these allegations. The report found, "With respect to women's basketball, the NCAA has not lived up to its stated commitment to 'diversity, inclusion and gender equity among its student-athletes, coaches and administrators.' " They found that the discrepancies of the 2021 basketball tournaments were a result of understaffing the women's event, but gender inequity runs deeper. The report stated that the NCAA makes the vast majority of its money from the men's basketball tournament. In 2019, the NCAA had revenues over $1 billion, and most of that came from the men's basketball tournament (especially the television contract). This profit encouraged them to put more resources into men's rather than women's basketball. The report noted this investment in the men's tournament, "over everything else in ways that create, normalize and perpetuate gender inequities." The report suggested merging the two tournaments and structuring the financial payouts similarly to promote investment into women's basketball.

(Photo: Courtesy of Ali Kershner and Quadrian Banks)

Source: Information taken from Andrea Adelson and Heather Dinich, "NCAA Women's Tournament 2021: Inside an Overdue Reckoning over Inequity in Basketball," ESPN, April 3, 2021, https://www.espn.com/womens-college-basketball/story/_/id/31182950/ncaa-women-tournament-2021-overdue-reckoning-inequity-basketball. Associated Press, "Long-Awaited NCAA Gender Equity Review Recommends Combined Final Four for Men's, Women's Basketball at Same Site," ESPN, August 3, 2021, https://www.espn.com/college-sports/story/_/id/31951330/long-awaited-ncaa-gender-equity-review-recommends-combined-final-four-mens-women-basketball-same-site.

August, on Tuesday, Thursday, and Friday nights, and any time on Saturdays from 11:00 a.m. to 9:00 p.m.

Smaller D-I teams (those in the Football Championship Subdivision) now schedule one or two games

The goal of many young boys and girls is to become an intercollegiate athlete. It is a worthy goal, but college athletes face unexpected challenges. Academic progress toward a degree must be pursued at the same time that demands to make the team and perform well enough to keep the athletic scholarship are ever-present. (Photo: Mark Herreid)

against major university programs to receive up to $2 million as a guaranteed payment. These are called *guarantee games*. They are also sarcastically called "body bag games" because the players from the smaller schools often incur an unusually large number of injuries in the game. But playing the national powerhouse universities provides a huge and much-needed revenue stream for the smaller D-I schools.[22] The same pattern is carried out in D-I basketball, but for smaller guarantee amounts and, in most cases, without the increased injuries.

A fourth result of "going after the money" is that when the pressure to win becomes too great, the result can be a sub rosa policy of cheating—that is, a policy of offering athletes more than the legal limit to lure them to a school and keep them there or using unethical means to keep them scholastically eligible.

This is not a new issue. In 1929, the Carnegie Foundation published a report that decried the widespread illegal recruiting practices of American colleges and universities. The problem has not only continued but also mega-intensified. The scandals involve illegal and immoral behavior of overzealous coaches, school authorities, alumni, and boosters. Athlete recruits not only are suspect academically but also sometimes go over the line in antisocial behavior.

Finally, perhaps the most serious consequence of the "winning-at-all-costs to generate money" mentality pervading many athletic departments is that the education of the athletes is secondary to their sports performances. Even sport as a pleasurable activity is an irrelevant consideration in the climate of big-time collegiate sport. Winning and making money are paramount.

Coaches proclaim that their athletes are students first and athletes only secondarily. This is the typical recruiting speech to prospects and their parents, but in practice the reverse is often true. The cynicism with which some coaches regard education is seen in the revelations concerning the enrollment of athletes in "phantom" courses (correspondence or residence courses that give credit for no work or attendance).

For decades college athletes have remained eligible by taking classes that can be described only as bogus, but the academic scandal in the athletics department at the University of North Carolina, with its reputation as one of the nation's finest public institutions of higher education, was unexpected. It began with a report by an academic tutor that football and basketball players were being steered into fake classes in the school's African American studies department to ensure that they remained eligible. After investigating the report, university officials acknowledged that more than 200 phony courses were offered, tutors wrote papers for students, and hundreds of grades were changed without authorization.[23]

This is only one recent scandal of this type. The swath of academic abuse, especially in big-time sports programs, cuts wide across intercollegiate athletics. But clearly, for coaches to permit this is to admit that the athlete's eligibility supersedes his or her learning. For the athlete, the message is equally clear. Yet it is erroneous to say all colleges participate in the sham. It is a minority of college sports programs in revenue-producing sports that taints the image for all. So, in this milieu the resulting evils are the result not of the malevolent personalities of coaches and athletes but of a perverse system. Achieving an education is incidental to the overriding objective of big-time sports.

A CONTRADICTION: ATHLETES AS AMATEURS IN A BIG-BUSINESS ENVIRONMENT

We have seen that large sums of money are generated by big-time college sports. University athletic departments act like corporations (indeed, many are organized separate from their universities as corporations). Many individuals in the athletic departments (athletic directors, coaches, trainers, accountants, groundskeepers, equipment managers,

academic advisors) make their living—some more than $5 million annually—from their employment in college sport.

The irony is that the athletes themselves—the major labor force in producing big-time college sport—have not been paid directly for their labor. The status of amateurism has recently come under scrutiny. New legislation will be discussed here, but it is important to know the long-standing claim by the NCAA that amateurism creates a different type of sport, one that people participate in for the love of sport, not money. The NCAA also has argued that it has a product that is different from professional sport, and amateurism is the foundation of their product. Historically, young people on athletic scholarships were limited by NCAA rules to tuition, room, board, and books but expected to bring honor and lots of dollars to their universities. By declaring that college sports are a form of amateur activity, the NCAA and its member universities were able to mystify the reality of big-time sports as professional and commercial enterprises.

A recent *NCAA Division I Manual* declares that student-athletes must be amateurs and that they "should be protected from exploitation by professional and commercial enterprises."[24] Remarkably, although such a statement completely discounts, even denies, the blatantly commercialized nature of big-time intercollegiate athletics, it is able to manufacture support for the economic exploitation of student-athletes. The reality is that the athletic scholarship is merely a work contract. What colleges are really doing is hiring entertainers. The deceit of claiming that educational purposes preclude salaried compensation for the sport performances of athletes is testimony to the extensive attempts of the collegiate establishment to avoid its financial responsibilities.

Athletic scholarships are a wage below poverty level for student-athlete-entertainers who directly produce millions of dollars for athletic departments. Big-time college sports are a big business for everyone except the athletes. Paying as little as possible to operate a business is called keeping overhead low; it is what every business owner strives to do. The NCAA and major universities have mastered this principle. No other American business operates so pretentiously, making huge sums of money while insisting the

College athletes in big-time, commercialized sports programs often have trouble balancing their academic and athletic responsibilities. Because of the pressures of maintaining their athletic scholarship, the athletic role often comes to dominate at the expense of the academic role. (Photo: ZUMA Press/Alamy Stock Photo)

enterprise be viewed as an educational service. The NCAA narrative and practice, that college athletes must remain amateurs, untainted by money, is being challenged by several groups (and will be described here).

It is important to discuss the amount of labor that scholarship athletes in big-time programs do. First, it has become a year-round commitment. Now that the football season has been extended to twelve games, some of the games are played in the last week of August, requiring that practices begin three weeks earlier. If a football team is successful, the players continue into a December or January bowl game. That, in turn, is followed six weeks later by a month of spring practice. And when that ends, players are expected to lift weights and spend their summers on campus with "voluntary" workouts. A UCLA quarterback explained his view of athletes playing D-I football: "Look, football and school don't go together. They just don't. Trying to do both is like trying to do two full-time jobs. . . . There's so much money being made in this sport. It's a crime not to do everything you can to help [athletes] who are making it for those who are spending it."[25]

Basketball players in big-time universities have similar demands, with practices beginning in early fall, games starting in November and continuing through thirty-plus games, and the national tournament in late March. But despite the increased workload and the great sums generated by big-time college sports programs, the athletes are just starting to gain rights that allow them to broaden their remuneration beyond tuition, room, board, and books. This shift reflects a growing awareness and willingness to fight for a more equitable distribution of huge sums of money generated by college athletics.

THE NCAA AND STUDENT-ATHLETES

The NCAA, or an organization like it, is necessary to provide a uniform set of rules for each sport, to adjudicate disputes among members, and to organize play-offs and tournaments. What has emerged, however, is a powerful monopoly, a monopoly that controls big-time college sport *for the interests of the universities, not the student-athletes.* This has occurred in two ways: through the enforcement of "amateurism" and through rules that limit athletes' rights.

THE ENFORCEMENT OF "AMATEURISM"

First, as we have just discussed, the NCAA rules have enforced a code of amateurism on student-athletes' labor, while the NCAA and its member institutions have raised millions of dollars off the student-athletes. It is common for powerful organizations to interpret reality and create normative prescriptions to serve their interests, and the NCAA and its member universities have done this by means of the amateur ideology. Although they have historically been able to argue the merits of amateurism, recent legislation (see the following) has challenged their assumptions.

By defining student-athletes as amateurs, schools have kept the costs of operation low by not paying the athletes what they are worth. Consider this: In 2017 the expenses for student athletic scholarships for public D-I universities were between 8 and 13 percent of the operating revenue of the university athletic departments. If the distribution of revenue of those athletic departments was similar to that of the main professional team sports, 50 to 60 percent of the revenue would go to the student-athletes. By NCAA rules, however, players are limited to their athletic scholarships. The universities obviously benefit from this arrangement.[26]

Universities benefit when intercollegiate athletes are defined as amateur because it enables the revenue generated from the sports programs to be free from taxation. Although the scholarship appears to be a payment to employees (athletes) for services rendered, it is called a "grant-in-aid" for educational purposes. This avoids the rules of the Internal Revenue Service stipulating that revenue generated by employees is taxable income.

The NCAA has done all it can to retain the amateur status of college athletes. Specifically, it has argued strenuously that college athletes should not be paid a stipend in addition to tuition, room, board, and books because that would lessen its case that the athletes are amateurs. This definition of amateurism has been successfully challenged, as will be discussed here. We think it is important to keep in mind how the NCAA *had prohibited* anything it considered "professional." Historically, those would include things such as the following:

- Athletes would lose their amateur status if they allow their pictures or names to be associated with commercial enterprise, whether they are paid for it or not.
- Athletes were not allowed to have a financial advisor (agent) until after their final college game.
- Athletes could not receive payment for their athletic skills. Using this principle, the NCAA ruled that a New Mexico State University basketball player who had won a car by making a half-court shot at halftime in a professional basketball game (he was one of two spectators chosen at random for the shot) could keep either the car or his senior year of eligibility, but not both.
- Athletes could not endorse products or otherwise use their name recognition for economic gain, but universities can use it in their publicity and can license and sell clothing, sports equipment, and souvenirs with the team logo.
- Athletes could not sell their complimentary tickets (in fact, they cannot give their tickets to anyone except family members, relatives, and students), yet coaches (some with hundreds of tickets) had no restrictions on their distribution.
- Coaches typically receive bonuses for taking their teams to a bowl or to the NCAA men's basketball tournament, but their players do not.
- Athletes could not be used to raise money for others, even charities. For example, the Lions Club of Alachua, Florida, was not allowed to raffle off a football signed by members of the University of Florida football team to raise money for its eye bank because, the NCAA ruled, the players were being exploited by selling their autographs.

These examples show the lengths to which the NCAA went to enforce the amateur status of college athletes. These examples also demonstrate the hypocrisy of the NCAA. While keeping their athletes pure, the NCAA, the universities, and the individual coaches are engaged in a relentless pursuit of revenue estimated at well over $1 billion annually. We emphasize again that this revenue is generated by the athletes. Athletes literally have been walking billboards by wearing shoes, for which the coach receives thousands of dollars, but the athletes cannot receive anything other than the free shoes.

The public may have a perception of a benevolent NCAA that protects young student-athletes. The reality is that what the NCAA protects is its own self-interest. Its rules have been created to protect the profit structure of big-time college sports, and more than one sport economist has expressed the opinion that the big-time intercollegiate sport system is one of the most obvious forms of labor exploitation in the United States. As elaborated on in the following, it appears that the parameters of amateurism in college sport are going to change as many entities are pushing for the rights of athletes. Perhaps amateurism in collegiate sport will follow the demise of requiring Olympic athletes to be amateurs. If you are under thirty-five years of age, you have never watched an Olympic Games that was composed solely of amateur athletes. The IOC required amateurism for nearly the first one hundred years of the Games. That requirement was dropped in 1971 and then the IOC fully opened the Olympics to professional athletes by 1986.

PRESSURE TO SHIFT THE LEGAL PARAMETERS OF AMATEURISM IN COLLEGIATE SPORT

It is apparent that many entities are concerned about the treatment of student-athletes. The power differential between athletes and the NCAA has been challenged by athletes in courts, it has been taken up by members of the U.S. Congress, and many states have passed laws giving student-athletes more ability to profit from their athletic skills, especially profiting from the name, image, or likeness (NIL). We will discuss several of the more groundbreaking examples here. One of the first serious challenges was Ed

O'Bannon's lawsuit against the NCAA. O'Bannon was a top basketball player for UCLA in the mid 1990s, named the most outstanding player in the NCAA basketball tournament in 1995. Years later, O'Bannon saw a video game of NCAA basketball and his image and likeness in it were unmistakable. Yet, he was not asked permission to use his image and he received no compensation for it. O'Bannon argued that a former NCAA player should be able to profit from their image once they were no longer an amateur collegiate athlete. The NCAA argued that once a player signs a NCAA contract, the NCAA may sell that athlete's image and likeness without asking permission or paying compensation to the ex-athlete. The original decision in 2014 was in favor of O'Bannon. The case wound up in the Supreme Court in 2016, where the court denied petitions from both parties.[27] Yet, the issue of who has rights to one's NIL has become a rallying point to break the NCAA's control over athletic compensation.

In 2019, California passed a law called the "Fair Pay to Play" Act, which made it illegal for state schools to prohibit athletes from making money off their NIL. It was set to be enforced by 2023. In the meantime, over twenty other states created similar legislation. It should be noted that there would be a recruiting advantage if some states allowed athletes to make money from the NIL and others did not. In July 2021, the NCAA responded to the growing legislative pressure and granted all collegiate athletes rights to their NIL. Students will now be able to profit from their athletic skills by sponsoring products such as athletic gear, local summer camps, or any product. This allows athletes to make money by being a social media influencer.[28]

Although this type of legislation was focused on NIL, another case was brought in front of the U.S. Supreme Court, *NCAA v. Alston*, that challenged the eligibility rules that restricted education-related compensation, such as post-eligibility paid internships or academic cash awards, violated antitrust laws. The NCAA continued to argue against extending education-related benefits, claiming that amateurism is what distinguishes college sports from professional sports. Therefore, the NCAA should be exempt from antitrust laws. The U.S. Supreme Court found in favor of Alston.[29] One of the justices, Brett Kavanaugh, wrote an opinion that was highly critical of the

NCAA's claims: "Nowhere else in America can businesses get away with agreeing not to pay their workers a fair market rate on the theory that their product is defined by not paying their workers a fair market rate. . . . And under ordinary principles of antitrust law, it is not evident why college sports should be any different. The NCAA is not above the law."[30]

Currently, there are many bills being introduced in the U.S. Congress that would protect the rights of athletes as students and workers. These include the Amateur Athletes Protection & Compensation Act, the College Athlete Economic Freedom Act, the Collegiate Athlete Compensation Rights Act, the Fairness in Collegiate Athletics Act, the Student-Athlete Equity Act, the College Athletes Bill of Rights, and the Student-Athlete Level Playing Field Act. It appears that there is legislative momentum to alter the current status of college athletes as amateurs.[31]

MORE CHANGES: INCREASED RIGHTS FOR STUDENT-ATHLETES AND DECENTRALIZATION OF THE NCAA

One of the prime examples of the NCAA limiting student-athlete freedoms was a rule that reduced the likelihood of student athletes transferring to other institutions. Previous to 2021, when young athletes signed letters of intent to play for a certain university, they made one-sided agreements. Foremost, these athletes agreed to play for four years at a given institution. Should they change their minds and decide to attend a different college or university, they had to spend one academic year in residence at the university to which they transfer before they may be eligible for competition. If they select a university because of a particular coach and the coach leaves before the athletes have enrolled in the school, under NCAA rules the athletes signed with the university, not the coach, and they must stay or lose a year of eligibility. This changed in April 2021, when the NCAA established a "one-time transfer rule," which allows student athletes to transfer once in their collegiate career without penalty. These changes represent the pressure the NCAA is facing to address the rights of student-athletes.

Another indicator of change is the prominence of a newly created committee in the NCAA called the Transformation Committee. Shortly after it was established the most recent president of the NCAA, Mark Emmert, resigned (although he will remain in his position until summer of 2023 while his replacement is being identified). In the meantime, the Transformation Committee is creating recommendations to update (or perhaps, deregulate) the NCAA's regulations. One of the speculations is that the NCAA will become decentralized, giving more power to the conferences to make policies.[32]

EDUCATIONAL PERFORMANCE AND STUDENT-ATHLETES

Research indicates that college athletes in big-time football and basketball programs do not perform at the same level academically as other athletes and the general student body. Their grades are lower, and they are much more likely to take easy courses in easy majors. Most significantly, they are much less likely to graduate. Before we examine the college performance of athletes, however, let's look at their preparation for college.

ACADEMIC PREDICTIONS FOR STUDENT-ATHLETES AT COLLEGE

There are three standard measures of student preparedness for college—the combined score on the SAT, the American College Testing (ACT) composite score, and the high school grade point average (GPA). Over the past twenty-five years the NCAA has enacted several policies designed to dictate minimum eligibility guidelines for freshmen in the association's D-I schools. These include minimum scores on the SAT or the ACT, a core group of high school courses, and a minimum GPA within that core.[33]

Despite efforts to discourage coaches in D-I sports from recruiting unqualified students, marginal students who were good athletes continue to be recruited. Research at a number of universities shows that in most big-time programs, athletes in the so-called revenue sports (men's football and basketball) have received special treatment in the admissions process; that is, they have been admitted below the standard requirements for their universities. Although the NCAA does not release information on athletes' SAT scores by sport, data from various public sources indicate that there are consistently gaps, in some universities large gaps, in SAT scores and GPAs between athletes and the nonathlete student body at public universities, among football and men's basketball. The gaps between athletes' and nonathletes' SAT scores and GPAs were less for women than for men.[34]

ACADEMIC ACHIEVEMENT AND COLLEGE ATHLETES

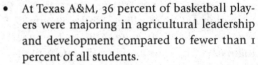

Regardless of the fact that young athletes have always been recruited by coaches for their athletic ability, they have always been required to enroll in academic programs and take courses of study. And institutions have always required that athletes maintain a certain level of academic progress toward graduation to continue participating in the intercollegiate sport program. No rational person would quarrel with holding athletes to academic standards.

However, focusing on athletes' academic achievement and seemingly demonstrating how athletes are being held to academic standards while ignoring the time demands on athletes—practices, games, weight training, video viewing, travel to sites of games, and so on—suggests to the public that social pathology is the reason for the recurring scandals involving student-athletes, not the social structure of which they are a part. Such thinking deflects attention away from the more endemic social structural problems of big-time college sports—including the question of whether it is appropriate for a commercialized sport system that does not pay its main workforce a livable wage to be operating on college campuses.

Research data on class grades are somewhat difficult to interpret. The reason is that athletes in the revenue-producing sports are more likely than other athletes and other students to receive grades fraudulently (e.g., through "shady" correspondence courses, "friendly" professors, and surrogate test takers or term paper writers) or to take easy courses and cluster in easy majors—also known as "jock majors." Examples include the following:

- As described previously, an academic tutor at the University of North Carolina reported that football and basketball players were being steered into fake classes in the school's African American

studies department to ensure that they remained eligible. After investigating the report, university officials acknowledged that more than 200 phony courses were offered and tutors wrote papers for students.

- The *Journal-World* analyzed the majors of big-time university basketball players. Several universities had a disproportionate number of players majoring in fields that few other students do. Here are several examples:

- At Texas A&M, 36 percent of basketball players were majoring in agricultural leadership and development compared to fewer than 1 percent of all students.

- At Iowa State University, 63.3 percent of basketball players were majoring in liberal studies, whereas 9.3 percent of all students do.

- At Indiana University, 52.9 percent of basketball players were majoring in sports communication, whereas 2.4 percent of all students do.

- At Syracuse University, 31.5 percent of basketball players were majoring in communication and rhetorical studies, whereas 1 percent of all students do.

- At Auburn, in a recent year, football players were thirty-five times more likely to major in sociology than the student body. Fewer than 1 percent of the student body choose that major.

- At the University of Alabama, the most popular football major in recent years has been general studies in the College of Human Environmental Sciences. Twenty-six percent of football players majored in this program compared with 2 percent of all Alabama students.[35]

Nationwide clustering extends far beyond the universities just identified. But we want to emphasize that we are not claiming that *all* football and basketball athletes at big-time sports universities are clustering or taking fake or phony courses. Many are taking a rigorous curriculum and expecting to graduate with a major that will serve them well in their future careers.

There are several possible reasons other than a genuine interest in the major for such clustering. The favored major may have fewer courses that conflict with practices and other sport-related demands, such as afternoon labs. The major may have less stringent admission requirements. And the major may be less demanding. For these reasons, the players may choose the easy route, or sometimes they are guided by academic advisors in the athletic department to keep them eligible. A former president of the National Association of Academic Advisors who has directed student-athlete support programs at two big-time sports universities put it this way: "Athletes are not representative of the general student body. Our population is apples; their population is oranges."

GRADUATION RATES AND STUDENT-ATHLETES

To its credit, over the past decade the NCAA—in conjunction with the Knight Commission on Intercollegiate Athletics—has made a significant effort to insist that universities hold their athletic departments responsible for the improvement of student-athletes' graduation rates. The NCAA Graduation Success Rate (GSR) and Academic Progress Rate were developed in response to college and university presidents who wanted graduation data that more accurately reflect the mobility among college students today. The GSR, similar to the Federal GSR, measures the proportion of a four-year institution's freshmen who earn a degree within six years at D-I institutions. The standard evaluations of NCAA student-athlete graduation rates involve comparisons with rates for the general student body.

Using the GSR measure, the NCAA reported that in 2021, overall, student-athletes in the class of 2021 at D-I institutions and earning their four-year degrees had a GSR of 89 percent. Although this GSR is impressive, it is important to note the trends for different gender and racial populations. In short, white athletes generally have higher GSR than athletes of color and women athletes tend to have higher GSR than male athletes. For example:

- The NCAA's reported GSR includes student-athletes from thirty-six sports, including both men and women. When all GSRs are considered, for D-I women athletes the GSR was 95 percent and for D-I men it was 85 percent.
- With regard to racial and ethnic groups participating in D-I sports, whites had a GSR of 94 percent; Latino/as had a GSR of 88 percent, and African Americans had a GSR of 80 percent.

- For D-I men's basketball the GSR was only 84 percent, whereas it was 94 percent for D-I women's basketball. But just 81 percent of African American male basketball players graduate compared to 94 percent of White male basketball players. Whereas the gap between African American women basketball players and their white counterparts was 5 percent: GSR of 92 percent compared to 97 percent.
- For D-I football the GSR was 81 percent.[36] African American football players had a GSR of 77 percent compared to their white counterparts whose GSR was 90 percent.

Reflecting on the racial discrepancy, Richard Lapchik, who is the director of the Institute for Diversity and Ethics in Sport, stated, "It's paramount that university hire more head coaches of color for men's and women's teams. We need to advocate to making education success equally represented across all students, including male and female student athletes of all races."[37]

The NCAA's method of calculating graduation rates (GSR) has been a source of controversy since it was formulated, primarily because critics believe it inflates and misrepresents college athletes' graduation rates in comparison to those of other full-time students. In 2016–2017, Richard Southhall, director of the College Sport Research Institute (CSRI) at the University of South Carolina, called the NCAA's GSR misleading. The CSRI claims FBS football players at 117 NCAA-member schools graduate at rates 18 percent lower than that for full-time male students. In addition, according to CSRI, the adjusted-graduation gap at "major" D-I basketball schools was even larger, with men's basketball players graduating at rates 34 percent less than that for full-time male students.[38]

THE IMPEDIMENTS TO SCHOLARLY ACHIEVEMENT BY COLLEGE ATHLETES

Many college athletes are not only ill-prepared for the intellectual demands of college but also face a number of obstacles that impede their scholarly achievement. The pressures on athletes, especially those in big-time, revenue-producing sports, are well known, including physical exhaustion, mental fatigue, media attention, and demanding coaches.

A university athlete competes during a NCAA college women's water polo match. Despite the rigorous training and the competition schedules of women participating in NCAA sports, the NCAA graduation success rate revealed that the graduation rate of Division I women was 10 percent higher than that of Division I men. (Photo: Hector Garcia-Molina/isiphotos.com)

The time demands alone are onerous. During the season, the athletes spend fifty to sixty hours preparing for, participating in, recovering from, and traveling to games. As described previously, big-time college revenue sports have become a year-round occupation for the scholarship players. The NCAA permits only "voluntary" workouts in the summer, but that requirement is a sham—the athletes know they must work out or risk losing favor with their coaches, at a minimum, or even risk losing their scholarships.

The athletes in commercialized, professionalized college sports programs often have trouble reconciling the roles associated with their dual statuses of athlete and student. The pressures of big-time sport and academic demands frequently result in the gradual disengagement of the athletes from their academic roles. Most athletes enter the university feeling idealistic about their impending academic performance; that is, they are optimistic about graduating, and many consider ambitious majors. For some, this idealism lasts until about the end of the first year and becomes replaced by disappointment and a growing cynicism, as student-athletes realize how difficult it is to keep up with their academic demands. The athletic role comes to dominate all facets of their existence.

Typically, student-athletes receive greater positive reinforcement from their athletic performance than from their academic performance, and they are increasingly isolated from the general student body. With respect to football and basketball players particularly, they become isolated culturally from the rest of the students by their racial and socioeconomic differences. They are even isolated from other students by their physical size, which others often find intimidating or exotic. They interact primarily with other athletes, who often demean academics.

As freshmen, athletes are frequently given courses with "sympathetic" professors, but this changes as the athletes move through the university curriculum. The academic expectations escalate, and the athletes are often unprepared. The resulting academic failure or, at best, mediocre academic performance leads to embarrassment and despair.[39]

The noneducation and miseducation of college athletes is especially acute for African Americans. Economic and racial realities in the United States have created barriers. Neighborhoods in the United States are commonly segregated by social class and race. African Americans are overrepresented in poorer neighborhoods, which, concomitantly, have fewer resources for local public schools. When African Americans attend colleges at predominantly White institutions (PWI), they are entering an environment that generally has few African Americans in leadership positions. For example, in 2019–2020, African American male students made up 53.2 percent of the basketball athletes in D-I, yet African American head coaches comprised only 22.7 percent. Athletic directors of D-I schools are overwhelmingly White, at 82.9 percent.[40] Simultaneously, African Americans are overrepresented as athletes in basketball, track and field, and football and seriously underrepresented in the general student body. For example, at a prestigious Pac-12 university, it was reported that 3.4 percent of the student body identified as Black, whereas 23.3 percent of the athlete population identified as Black.[41] Thus, the PWI is a stratified space that tends to reinforce hierarchies of race.

Along with the overrepresentation of White people at the leadership of sport, racial stereotypes that negatively impact African American students are still operating. For example, the social construction of the athlete as a "dumb jock" has been applied to all athletes, but it has had an accentuated application to African American athletes for several reasons. First, African American student-athletes must contend with two negative labels: the dumb athlete caricature and the dumb African American stereotype. These stereotypes impact how teachers, coaches, and fellow students interact with African American athletes by framing them as less academically inclined. These interactions, in turn, may impact how African American athletes see themselves as students.[42] Moreover, as soon as an African American youngster is viewed as a potential athletic star, many teachers, administrators, and parents lower their academic demands because they assume that athletic stardom will be the athlete's ticket out of the inner city.

In junior high school and high school, often little is demanded of African American athletes academically. These reduced academic expectations continue in college. The result? Many Black scholarship student-athletes manage to go through four years of college enrollment virtually unscathed by education.[43] A major unintended consequence of this situation is that, unwittingly, the universities with big-time programs that recruit marginal African American students and do not educate them offer "proof" for the argument that African Americans are inferior to Whites in intellectual potential. Thus, in PWI, African American athletes are navigating a space that "sees" and values Black students as athletes first and students second.

Importantly, more recent research shows that African American student athletes who attend Historically Black Colleges and Universities have a stronger sense of belonging and more holistic support, which translates into higher levels of academic success.[44] This points to a need to think through how race and racism are constructed and reinforced in PWI and how to develop better communities of support.

REFORM INITIATIVES AND INTERCOLLEGIATE SPORTS

Many who are familiar with intercollegiate sports are aware of the numerous scandals that have beset major university football and basketball programs during the past few years. Despite a continuing parade of committees, commissions, and task forces whose purpose has been to reform big-time college sports, horror stories persist in the form of reports about violations of NCAA rules, low graduation rates among football and basketball athletes, and athletes receiving illegal money from boosters.

Scandals develop with a frequency that is astonishing even to the most cynical of observers. Hardly a week goes by without the disclosure of new violations of NCAA rules. Each revelation is followed by righteous promises from university authorities and the NCAA that change is on the way—that collegiate athletics are going to be cleaned up. But the NCAA has been unable to stop these violations or the conditions from which they breed.[45]

One of the major attempts to address the endemic problems of major college sports has been the Knight Commission on Intercollegiate Athletics. The trustees of the Knight Foundation created this commission in 1989 and directed it to propose a reform agenda for college sports. During more than twenty-five years of work, the Knight Commission has produced various reports as solutions for abuses in college sports, and some strides have been made to reconnect intercollegiate sports with the educational mission of colleges and universities. Still, in many ways little has changed.

For all of the chest pounding about reform, an analysis of changes that have been made or proposed over the years shows that reorganization of existing structural relations is conspicuously absent from reform efforts in intercollegiate athletics. According to the NCAA infractions database, more than one-fourth of the major infractions cases in all of its divisions have involved football and basketball programs in universities from the six most prominent conferences.

The SEC has amassed the most major rules violations in D-I, the big league of NCAA sports. SEC schools have been found guilty of major violations more than forty times since NCAA records begin. Each SEC member has been accused of a major rules infraction at least once since 1990. Of over sixty NCAA schools with three or more major rules violations, eight are in the SEC. However, cheating is not limited to the SEC. The Southwest Conference had a reputation as an outlaw league by the time it disbanded; eight members of the Southwest Conference had twenty-seven major violations combined when the league fell apart; SEC schools had thirty-six total violations at the same time, records show.[46]

The structure of big-time, commercial college athletics—a structure that is largely responsible for the pervasive corruption and abuses—has been left intact, with no substantive changes. Hope for meaningful reform by the NCAA so that it would better serve the interests and needs of all college athletes has

been difficult to find. As noted earlier in this chapter, the pressure from external entities has forced some legal and procedural changes. In turn, these pressures have encouraged the NCAA to rethink its structure which is currently in process.

On the positive side, big-time college sports provide entertainment, spectacle, excitement, and festival-like atmosphere, along with excellence in sports. On the negative side, as we have seen, big-time athletics have severely compromised academe. Pursuit of educational goals has been superseded by the quest for big money. Winning big-time programs realize huge revenues from television, gate receipts, bowl and tournament appearances, and even state legislatures; therefore, many athletic departments and coaches are guided by a win-at-any-cost philosophy.

Can this fundamental dilemma be resolved? Can the corporate and corrupt sports programs at colleges and universities be changed to redress the wrongs that are making a mockery of their educational goals? Can the abuses be eliminated without sacrificing the high level of achievement by the athletes and the excitement of college sports?

We would like to think that having hope will bring about some necessary reforms in big-time college sports. After many years of studying college sports, we advance the following recommendations, which we hope will raise the consciousness of readers to begin thinking about how intercollegiate sports, especially at major universities, could be made more educationally focused, humane, and protective of the rights of student-athletes.

Specifically, reform must be directed at three crucial areas: the way sports are administered, the education of athletes, and the rights of athletes.

THE ADMINISTRATION OF INTERCOLLEGIATE SPORTS

As a beginning, athletic departments must not be separated from their institutions as self-contained corporate entities. They must be under the direct control of university presidents and boards of regents. Presidents, as chief executive officers, must be accountable for the actions of their athletic departments. They must set up mechanisms to monitor sports programs to detect illegal and unethical acts. They must determine policies to maximize the educational experiences of student-athletes.

Coaches must be part of the academic community and the tenure system, to provide them with reasonable job security and to emphasize that they are teachers too. As educators with special responsibilities, they should earn salaries similar to those of academic administrators. They should not receive bonuses for winning championships. Such performance incentives overemphasize winning and increase the likelihood of cheating.

The outside incomes of coaches should be sharply curtailed. Money from shoe companies should go to the universities, not the coaches. If coaches fail to keep their programs ethical, they should lose their tenure and be suspended from coaching at any institution for a specified period—even, in special cases, forever. Among the important criteria for evaluating coaches' performance should be the proportion of athletes who graduate within six years. The conditions we recommend in these two paragraphs already exist in more than 400 institutions—those in D-III.

Athletic departments must be closely monitored and, when warranted, sanctioned externally. The NCAA is not, however, the proper external agent, since it has a fundamental conflict of interest. The NCAA is too dependent on sports-generated television money and bowl contracts to be an impartial investigator, judge, and jury.

Accrediting associations should oversee all aspects of educational institutions, including sports, to assess whether educational goals are being met. If an institution does not meet those goals because of inadequacies in the sports program, then it should lose accreditation, just as it would if its library was below standard or if too few of its professors held doctorates.

EMPHASIZING THE EDUCATION OF STUDENT-ATHLETES

Institutions of higher education worthy of the name must make a commitment to their athletes as students. This requires, first, that only athletes who have the potential to compete as students be admitted. A few—very few—may be admitted as exceptions, but

they and other academically marginal students must receive the benefits of a concerted effort by the university to improve their skills through remedial classes and tutorials so that they can earn a degree.

Second, freshmen should be ineligible for varsity sports. Such a requirement has symbolic value because it shows athletes and the whole community that academic performance is the highest priority of the institution. More important, it allows freshman athletes time to adjust to the demanding and competitive academic environment before they also take on the pressure that comes from participating in big-time sports.

Third, colleges must insist that athletes make satisfactory progress toward a degree. There should be internal academic audits to determine whether athletes are meeting the grade point and curriculum requirements for graduation. Currently, schools must provide the NCAA with graduation rates based on how many athletes graduate in six years. They must also be required to make these rates public, including giving them to each potential recruit.

Fourth, the time demands of sports must be reduced. Analyses of the time that the average major college football and basketball players spend on their sport have found that football players devote about fifty-five hours per week and basketball players fifty hours per week practicing, weight training, watching films, traveling to games, and being away from campus and missing classes during their respective seasons. These figures are excessive and should be reduced by at least one-third. Finally, mandatory off-season workouts should be abolished, and spring football practice should be eliminated.

COMMITMENT TO ATHLETES' RIGHTS

The asymmetrical situation whereby universities have the power and student-athletes do not must be modified. First, athletes should have the right to fair compensation for the work they do as public entertainers and for the revenues they generate. Athletic scholarships are often called "free rides," but they are far from that. A joint study by Ithaca College and the National College Players Association revealed that student-athletes in D-I universities receiving so-called full-ride scholarships were left with an average shortfall of $3,250 per year in education-related expenses that they had to personally pay for. In the past decade, adjustments have been made to increase some support. For example, the Big 5 conferences increased their athletic scholarships to cover athletes' full cost of attendance. As noted previously, the most recent legislation will allow student athletes to benefit from their NIL. But there is also proposed legislation in the U.S. Congress that could have greater impacts. Because this legislation is new and other proposed legislation is in the process of being heard, it is too early to tell what may happen.

Second, the governing body of sports must establish a comprehensive athletes' bill of rights to ensure a nonexploitive context. Again, the pressure to do so may come from federal legislation. In 2020, U.S. senators Cory Booker (NJ), who was a football player at Stanford University, Richard Blumenthal (CT), Kirsten Gillibrand (NY), and Brian Schatz (HI) have proposed one version that, according to Booker, would "set a new baseline standard to expand protections and opportunities for all college athletes by providing fair and equitable compensation, ensure comprehensive health and safety standards, and improve education outcomes for college athletes. College athletes deserve better, they deserve justice, and they deserve to share in what they help create."[47] The bill included:

- *Fair and equitable compensation.* The College Athletes' Bill of Rights will allow college athletes to market their NIL, either individually or as a group, with minimal restrictions. It will also require revenue-generating sports to share 50 percent of their profit with the athletes from that sport after accounting for the cost of scholarships—for example, D-I women's basketball players will receive 50 percent of the total revenue generated by their play after deducting the cost of scholarships awarded to all D-I women's basketball players.
- *Enforceable evidence-based health, safety, and wellness standards.* Within 120 days of enactment, the Departments of Health and Human Services, along with the Centers for Disease Control and Prevention, will consult with the Sports Science Institution and the NCAA to develop industry-leading health, safety, and wellness standards addressing everything from

how to handle concussion and traumatic brain injuries to sexual assault and interpersonal violence to athletics health care administration.
- *Improved educational outcomes and opportunities.* While the NCAA often touts its near-90 percent graduation rate for college athletes, independent studies assert that number is far lower—roughly 70 percent of college athletes graduate in six years, while only 55 percent of Black male college athletes graduate in six years. Even more, many college athletes are pressured toward less challenging classes and majors to allow more time and focus on sport. Under the College Athletes' Bill of Rights, all college athletes would receive a scholarship for as many years as it takes for them to receive an undergraduate degree, while the coaches and athletic department personnel would be banned from influencing or retaliating against a college athlete for their choice of an academic course or major.
- *Establish a Medical Trust Fund.* The College Athletes' Bill of Rights will establish a Medical Trust Fund that athletes can use to cover the costs of any out-of-pocket medical expenses for the duration of their time as a college athlete for five years after their eligibility expires if used to treat a sport-related injury. Athletes can also draw from the Medical Trust Fund to treat certain long-term injuries, including CTE.
- *Accountability across college sports.* Each school will be required to provide annual public reporting that describes total revenues and expenditures, including compensation for athletic department personnel and booster donations as well as reporting on the number of hours athletes commit to athletic activities—including all mandatory workouts, "voluntary" workouts, film study, and game travel—and academic outcomes disaggregated by program, race, and gender.
- *Freedom for college athletes to attend the institution of their choice.* Our plan will ban restrictions and penalties that prevent college athletes from attending the institution of their choice, including penalties associated with transferring schools and penalties hidden behind National Letters of Intent.
- *Establish the Commission on College Athletics.* The Commission on College Athletics—composed of nine members including no fewer than five former

college athletes and individuals with expertise ranging from publicity law to Title IX—would ensure athletes are aware of their new rights and that those rights are upheld.

SUMMARY

Without designating them all as such, we have examined and demythologized several myths in this chapter. The first myth is that college athletic programs are amateur athletics. Big-time college sport is big business. The second myth is that the athletic programs in the various schools make money. Relatively few do; the rest depend on various subsidies to keep afloat. A related myth is that these programs help the universities. Almost always, the surplus monies are kept within the athletic departments. So, too, are the monies that sports attract from contributors. Also, when athletic departments are put on probation or otherwise punished for transgressions, the universities are hurt by the negative publicity.

Another myth is that the NCAA protects student-athletes. As we have seen, the NCAA rules are extremely one-sided in favor of the institutions over the athletes. We have shown that the term *student-athlete* in big-time athletic programs is an oxymoron. Scholarship athletes in the revenue-producing sports are employees of their athletic departments. Their role of student is surely secondary to the role of athlete in most big-time programs. Similarly, athletes are not amateurs. They are just poorly compensated professionals.

Finally, the notion that sport builds character is a myth at the big-time, big-business level of intercollegiate sports. Cheating in recruiting is commonplace. Payments to athletes outside the rules are widely dispensed. Athletes are sometimes pampered. Rules for admittance to schools are bent for them. They are enrolled in courses with professors who are friendly to the athletic department. Athletes hear the rhetoric about sport building character and that education is first, but they often see a different reality. In such a climate, cynicism abounds and the possibility of positive character development is diminished.

Learn more with this chapter's digital tools, including web resources, video links, and chapter self-assessment quizzes at www.oup.com/he/sage-eitzen-beal-atencio-12e.

NOTES

1. Gerald Gurney, Donna A. Lopiano, and Andrew Zimbalist, *Unwinding Madness: What Went Wrong with College Sports—and How to Fix It* (Washington, D.C.: Brookings Institution Press, 2017).

2. Joseph Cooper, Charles Macaulay, and Saturnino Rodriguez, "Race and Resistance: A Typology of African American Sport Activism," *International Review for the Sociology of Sport* 54, no. 2 (2019): 151–181.

3. Gilbert M. Gaul, *Billion-Dollar Ball: A Journey through the Big-Money Culture of College Football* (New York: Penguin Books, 2016); Charles T. Clotfelter, *Big-Time Sports in American Universities* (Cambridge, England: Cambridge University Press, 2011); see also Ronald A. Smith, *Pay for Play: A History of Big-Time College Athletic Reform* (Champaign: University of Illinois Press, 2010); John Watterson, *College Football, History, Spectacle, Controversy* (Baltimore: Johns Hopkins University Press, 2000).

4. There is an enormous literature about the problems endemic to contemporary big-time college sports. We are listing some of the most notable books on this topic that have been published. See Howard L. Nixon II, *The Athletic Trap: How College Sports Corrupted the Academy* (Baltimore: Johns Hopkins University Press, 2014); Frank Jozsa, *College Sports Inc.: How Commercialism Influences Intercollegiate Athletics* (New York: Springer, 2013); Gerald Gurney, Donna A. Lopiano, and Andrew Zimbalist, *Unwinding Madness: What Went Wrong With College Sports—and How to Fix It* (Washington, D.C.: Brookings Institution Press, 2017); William C. Dowling, *Confessions of a Spoilsport: My Life and Hard Times Fighting Sports Corruption at an Old Eastern University* (University Park: Pennsylvania State University Press, 2007); Jason Alsher, "College Sports: Schools That Bring in the Most Money," Sports Cheat Sheet, March 6, 2017, http://www.cheatsheet.com/sports/richest-athletic-departments-college-sports.html/?a=viewall. Aaron L. Miller, *Buying In: Big-Time Women's Basketball and the Future of College Sports* (Lanham, MD: Rowman and Littlefield Publishers, 2022)

5. Steve Berkowitz, "NCAA Revenue for 2020 Down 50% due to Pandemic-Forced Cancellation of Basketball Tournament," *USA Today*, January 25, 2021, https://www.usatoday.com/story/sports/college/2021/01/25/ncaa-revenue-decrease-due-to-no-basketball-tournament/6699352002/.

6. "NCAA earns $1.15 billion in 2021 as revenue returns to normal," Associated Press, Feb 2, 2022, https://www.espn.com/college-sports/story/_/id/33201991/ncaa-earns-115-billion-2021-revenue-returns-normal, accessed June 13, 2022;

7. "NCAA Finances," *USA Today*, 2016, http://sports.usatoday.com/ncaa/finances/. Accessed May 18, 2017

8. John Duffy, Dec 8, 2021, Bowl Game Payouts are Practically a Small Fortune in College Football, https://fanbuzz.com/college-football/bowl-game-payouts/, accessed June 6, 2022

9. Kenneth Cortsen, "IMG's Capitalization on Sport Stars and Other Assets—IMG College Is Meant for Success," August 16, 2013, http://kennethcortsen.com/imgs-capitalization-on-sport-stars-and-other-assets-img-college-is-meant-for-success/.

10. Tom Schad and Steve Berkowitz, "Quirks in Contracts of Assistants," *USA Today*, December 7, 2017, 6C

11. Tom Schad & Steve Berkowitz, USA Today, Oct 15, 2021, Jimbo Fisher's new buyout is the largest in college football history – and it's not close, https://www.usatoday.com/story/sports/ncaaf/sec/2021/10/15/texas-a-ms-jimbo-fishers-contract-buyout-largest-college-history/6003908001/, accessed June 2, 2022.

12. Quoted in Jodi Upton, Jack Gillum, and Steve Berkowitz, "Big-Time Sports: Worth the Big-Time Cost?" *USA Today*, January 14, 2010, 5C; see also Clotfelter, *Big-Time Sports in American Universities*.

13. Mark Drozdowski, Do Colleges Make Money From Athletics, November 16, 2022, *Best Colleges*, https://www.bestcolleges.com/news/analysis/2020/11/20/do-college-sports-make-money/ accessed June 13, 2022

14. Nixon, *The Athletic Trap*; Jozsa, *College Sports Inc.*; Clotfelter, *Big-Time Sports in American Universities*.

15. Rich Exner, "$192 Million in Student Fees, Other School Subsidies for Sports at Ohio Division I Public Universities," Cleveland, March 2, 2020, https://www.cleveland.com/datacentral/2020/02/192-million-in-student-fees-other-school-subsidies-for-sports-at-ohio-division-i-public-universities.html.

16. Keith Sargeant and Steve Berkowitz, "Subsidy of Rutgers Athletics Rises by 68%," *USA Today*, February 24, 2014, 7C; see also David B. Ridpath, Jeff Smith, Daniel Garrett, and Jonathan Robe, "Shaping Policy and Practice in Intercollegiate Athletics: A Study of Student Perceptions of Resource Allocation for Athletics and Its Effect on Affordability of Higher Education," *The Journal of SPORT* 4, no. 1 (2015): 19–46.

17. Brad Wolverton, Ben Hallman, Shane Shifflett, and Sandhya Kambhampati, "The $10-Billion Sports Tab: How Colleges Are Funding the Athletics Arms Race," *The Chronicle of Higher Education*, November 15, 2015; Harry Minium, "Proposed Bill Would Cap Student Fees for College Sports," *The Virginia-Pilot*, January 15, 2015, https://pilotonline.com/news/government/politics/virginia/article_929d6d05-5458-5045-921e-123d4d9a15b1.html; Will Hobson and Steve Rich, "Why Students Foot the Bill for College Sports, and How Some Are Fighting Back," *The Washington Post*, November 30, 2015.

18. Kristian Dyer, "College Football Arms Race: Georgia Football Announces New $80M Building," Fox Business, September 9, 2019, https://www.foxbusiness.com/features/university-of-georgia-football-new-facilities; https://www.foxbusiness.com/features/university-of-georgia-football-new-facilities. Harrison Reno, September 14, 2021 SI.Com, WATCH: Take a Tour Around UGA's $80m Indoor Facility, https://www.si.com/college/georgia/news/georgia-football-tour-80m-facility, accessed June 13, 2022; https://www.k-state.edu/presidential-search/position-profile/athletics/ accessed June 13, 2022

19. Adam Hoffer and Jared A Pincin, *NCAA Athletic Departments: An Empirical Investigation of the Effects of Revenue and Conference Changes* (La Crosse: King's College, University of Wisconsin–La Crosse, September 2013).

20. Gilbert M. Gaul, *Billion-Dollar Ball: A Journey through the Big-Money Culture of College Football* (New York: Penguin Books, 2016); see also Patrick Hruby, "How the NCAA Scams Taxpayers for Welfare Money," Sports Vice, March 31, 2015, https://sports.vice.com/en_us/article/kbvvjx/how-the-ncaa-scams-taxpayers-for-welfare-money.

21. Dowling, *Confessions of a Spoilsport*, 1.

22. Prez Ro, "Guarantee Money Games," Amateur Sports News Network, June 23, 2017, http://www.amateursports365.com/articles/CollegeGuarantee

Games.html; see also Steve Berkowitz, "Guarantee Games Grow in Stature," *USA Today*, August 29, 2017, 1C, 4C.

23. Jay M. Smith and Mary Willingham, *Cheated: The UNC Scandal, the Education of Athletes, and the Future of Big-Time College Sports* (Omaha, NE: Potomac Books, 2015); see also Glenn Harlan Reynolds, "Higher Ed Sports Lower Standards," *USA Today*, January 15, 2014, 10A

24. National Collegiate Athletic Association, *2016–17 NCAA Division I Manual* (Indianapolis, IN: National Collegiate Athletic Association, 2016), 4.

25. Kyle Fredrickson, "CU Coach Disagrees with Rosen," *The Denver Post*, August 10, 2017, 1B, 3B; for a scornful account of college sports, see Jesse Washington, "Big-Time College Athletes Should Be Paid with Big-Time Educations," *The Undefeated*, April 6, 2017, https://theundefeated.com/features/big-time-college-athletes-should-be-paid-with-big-time-educations/.

26. Nixon, *The Athletic Trap*.

27. Steve Berkowitz and A. J. Perez, "Supreme Court Passes on O'Bannon Case," *USA Today*, October 4, 2016, 6C; see also Michael McCann, "In Denying O'Bannon Case, Supreme Court Leaves Future of Amateurism in Limbo," *Sports Illustrated*, October 3, 2016, https://www.si.com/college-basketball/2016/10/03/ed-obannon-ncaa-lawsuit-supreme-court; Tom Dahlberg, "Judge Rules against NCAA," *The Denver Post*, August 9, 2014, 2B.

28. Tim Mullaney, "Supreme Court NCAA Ruling and the New Future of Paying College Athletes," *CNBC*, June 21, 2021, https://www.cnbc.com/2021/06/21/supreme-court-ncaa-decision-how-college-athletes-plan-to-cash-in.html.

29. *NCAA v. Alston*, 2021 Information from the Center for Leadership in Athletics, University of Washington, Seattle.

30. Paul Myerberg, "Supreme Court Justice Brett Kavanaugh Rips NCAA in Antitrust Ruling, Says It 'Is Not above the Law,'" *USA Today*, June 21, 2021, https://www.usatoday.com/story/sports/college/2021/06/21/justice-brett-kavanaugh-rips-ncaa-in-shawne-alston-opinion/7771281002/.

31. Legislations proposed by Congress, 2021, Center for Leadership in Athletics, University of Washington, Seattle.

32. Ross Dellenger, April 27, 2022, "College Power-Brokers Poised to Turn the NCAA Upside Down," https://www.si.com/college/2022/04/27/ncaa-new-transformation-committee-changes, accessed June 13, 2022

33. This may be changing due to a trend of many universities and colleges no longer requiring standardized tests for admissions. See Elissa Nadworny, "Colleges Are Backing Off SAT, ACT Scores—but The Exams Will Be Hard to Shake," NPR, June 12, 2020, https://www.npr.org/2020/06/12/875367144/colleges-are-backing-off-sat-act-scores-but-the-exams-will-be-hard-to-shake.

34. Sara Ganim, "CNN Analysis: Some College Athletes Play Like Adults, Read Like 5th-Graders," CNN, January 8, 2014, http://www.cnn.com/2014/01/07/us/ncaa-athletes-reading-scores/index.html; see also Ramsey Dahab, "Sacked for Dollars: The Exploitation of College Football Players in the Southeastern Conference," *Class, Race and Corporate Power* 4, no. 2 (2016), http://digitalcommons.fiu.edu/cgi/viewcontent.cgi?article=1067&context=classracecorporatepower; Shaun Hittle, "Athletes' Tendencies to 'Cluster' in Certain Academic Fields Problematic, Some Say," *Lawrence Journal-World*, June 15, 2012, http://www2.ljworld.com/photos/2012/jun/16/236266/.

35. NCAA Research Staff, *Trends in Graduation Success Rates and Federal Graduation Rates at NCAA Division I Institutions* (Indianapolis, IN: National Collegiate Athletic Association, October 2016).

36. NCAA Research Staff, December 2021, *Trends in NCAA Division I Graduation Rates; see also Maria Carrasco, December 3, 2021, NCAA Division I Athletes Maintain High Graduation Rate*, Inside Higher Ed, *https://www.insidehighered.com/quicktakes/2021/12/03/ncaa-division-i-athletes-maintain-high-graduation-rate, accessed June 13, 2022*.

37. Richard Lapchick, 2022, Keeping Score When It Counts Academic Progress/Graduation Success Rate Study of the 2022 NCAA Division I Men's and Women's Basketball Tournament Teams, https://www.tidesport.org/_files/ugd/403016_12af72184c504c4e9b86c4f8593ff506.pdf, accessed June 13, 2022

38. The College Sport Research Institute, *2017 Adjusted Graduation Gap Report: NCAA Division-I Football*, (Columbia: University of South Carolina, August 2017), http://csri-sc.org/; also, personal communication, August 19, 2017.

39. Nixon, *The Athletic Trap*; see also Yost, *Varsity Green*.
40. The Institute for Diversity and Ethics in Sport, 2019–2020 NCAA College Sport Association Racial & Gender Report Card.
41. Kirsten Hextrum, "Reproducing Sports Stars: How Students Become Elite Athletes," *Teachers College Record* 121 (April 2019).
42. Trajuan Briggs, Allison B. Smith, and Joseph Cooper, "They're Just Here for Ball: Proposing a Multi-Level Analysis on the Impact of Collegiate Athletics at Historically White Institutions on Black Male Collegiate Athletes' Holistic Identity & Transition out of Sport," *Journal of Athlete Development and Experience* 3, no. 1 (2021).
43. Gary Sailes, *Modern Sport and the African American Experience*, 2nd ed. (San Diego: Cognella Academic, 2015).
44. Joseph N. Cooper and Ajhanai Newton, "Black Female College Athletes' Sense of Belonging at a Historically Black College and University (HBCU)," *The Journal of Negro Education* 90, no. 1 (2021): 71–83.
45. Ronald A Smith, *Pay for Play: A History of Big-Time College Athletic Reform* (Champaign: University of Illinois Press, 2010); see also Jay M. Smith and Mary Willingham, *Cheated: The UNC Scandal, the Education of Athletes, and the Future of Big-Time College Sports* (Omaha, NE: Potomac Books, 2015); Jeff Benedict and Armen Keteyian, *The System: The Glory and Scandal of Big-Time College Football* (New York: Doubleday, 2013).
46. "Big-Money SEC Has NCAA's Worst Record for Violations," AccessNorthGa, 2014.
47. "Senators Booker and Blumenthal Introduce College Athletes Bill of Rights," Cory Booker, December 17, 2020, https://www.booker.senate.gov/news/press/senators-booker-and-blumenthal-introduce-college-athletes-bill-of-rights.

SPORT AND SOCIAL INSTITUTIONS

CHAPTER 11

SPORT AND THE ECONOMY

The National Football League remains the most popular and profitable sports league in America. Though it generates in the range of $10 billion annually, it's heavily subsidized by its fans, American taxpayers, who provide 70 percent of the capital costs in stadium construction. NFL headquarters, meanwhile, enjoys tax-free status as a non-profit organization.

—SAM RICHES, *Writer and Journalist*[1]

NASCAR racing is one of the most popular sports in the United States. Today's NASCAR drivers are covered from head to toe with the emblems of all their corporate sponsors. However, without the corporate sponsors, who donate their products and/or money to the drivers, many of the car owners could not afford to put their cars on the tracks. (Photo: David Banks/Getty Images)

Sociology and economics are distinctly separate academic fields of study, but in the real world of people, the social and the economic are closely intertwined. Our social lives are closely connected with our economic status in terms of lifestyle, education, occupation, health, and so forth. Sports are one of the most significant social/cultural practices in the United States, and they are associated with the economy in multiple ways. The major purpose of this chapter is to describe and illustrate the ways in which the social practices of sport are linked to the economic social institution. We will examine the intimate relationship between money and sports and the various consequences involved.

In Chapter 1 we characterized three levels of sport: informal sport, organized sport, and corporate sport, the latter referring to levels of sporting activity dominated by economic and political factors extrinsic to sport itself. Corporate sport contrasts with the relatively spontaneous, pristine nature of informal sport and is characteristic of sport in the United States today. Money is the foundation of corporate sport, even at the so-called amateur level. The profit motive usually shapes the decisions of sport organizations, franchise owners, school administrators, and the corporations that use sport. This raises the question of how fans are able to engage and be valued within corporate sport at all levels.

Scholars and journalists have criticized this trend, claiming that sport has been transformed into economic snake oil—indeed, that sport has been transformed by commerce from something wonderful to something instrumental. Going further, they argue that sport has been distorted and polluted by money and the never-ending quest for more.

Contemporary sport is certainly big business. Some relevant examples demonstrate this:

- According to Plunkett Research, the estimated size of the entire sports industry in 2018 was estimated to be $539 billion, making it one of the ten largest industries in the United States. The sports industry is twice the size of the U.S. auto industry and seven times the size of the movie industry.
- The American sporting goods and equipment manufacturing sector is currently a $125 billion industry. Nike, the world's leading manufacturer of athletic shoes and apparel and a major manufacturer of sports equipment, generated revenue in excess of $44.5 billion in its 2021 fiscal year. Thus, the manufacturing of sporting goods and equipment is a key economic component of American sport.[2]
- In the 1970s the prize money for the entire PGA tour was about $8 million. In 2022 the Players Championship—just one PGA event—offered the largest purse in golf at $20 million, with the winner taking home $3.6 million.
- The 2021 NCAA March Madness basketball tournament television rights cost $850 million.
- Boxer Floyd Mayweather's bouts have generated $756.5 million in pay-per-view revenues.
- About $4.7 billion has been bet on each recent annual Super Bowl, with a whopping $4.5 billion (97 percent) of such wagers being placed illegally.
- Sports video games represent a $1 billion industry, accounting for more than 30 percent of all video game sales.[3]
- The Denver Broncos were sold in 2022 to a Walmart heir for an American sport franchise record of $4.65 billion.

There is no longer any question that corporate sport is a business, although sports franchise owners and certainly big-time sport universities would like to perpetuate the myth that it is not.

PROFESSIONAL SPORT AS A BUSINESS

Contrary to what some owners would have the public believe, professional sport is overwhelmingly a big business structured to maximize profit. Business enterprises are part of America's economic systems, and the social theoretical perspectives we previously identified are applicable to the economy. So here we briefly explain how functionalism and conflict/cultural perspectives apply. We then describe the ways and means by which professional sports are made profitable by monopoly organization and the public subsidization of professional teams. We also consider the changes in the owner–player relationship in professional team sports brought about by players' motivation to increase their power and monetary rewards.

At age ten, Michelle Wie became the youngest player to qualify for a USGA amateur championship. She turned professional shortly before her sixteenth birthday in 2005, accompanied by an enormous amount of publicity and endorsements. She won her first major at the 2014 U.S. Women's Open. At one time or another her endorsement portfolio has consisted of Nike, Callaway Golf, Kia Motors America, Omega, McDonald's, and Sime Darby. In May 2022, Wie announced that she would stop touring and eventually retire from the sport after the 2023 U.S. Women's Open. (Photo: Tribune Content Agency LLC/Alamy Stock Photo)

SOCIAL THEORIES AND THE ECONOMY

Functionalism views the economy as a central social institution because it is the means by which vital goods and services are produced and distributed. Social stability requires a smoothly functioning economic system, which leads to confidence in the society's future. Functionalism views an industrious and committed workforce as being essential to society. A commitment to work ethic and productivity is considered a key societal value and one that integrates citizens within the social order.

A conflict/cultural position on the economic system considers it an instrument of powerful and wealthy social class domination, deriving its power from its ownership and control of the forces of production. The conflict/culture theory considers the dominant class exploitive and oppressive toward other social classes, thereby reproducing and perpetuating the economic class structure. The exploitative economic arrangements of capitalism are viewed by conflict/cultural theorists as the foundation on which the superstructure of social, political, economic, and intellectual consciousness is built. As a result, there is a basic conflict of interest between the two classes.

PROFESSIONAL TEAM SPORTS AS MONOPOLIES

A monopoly exists when a single business firm controls a market. Professional team sport leagues have been allowed to become monopolies over the years by the public and by the government—and they are not only monopolies but also unregulated ones. Unlike the broadcasting industry, for example, whose monopolistic practices are regulated by the Federal Communications Commission, the sport industry is left to regulate itself. Each professional league operates as a cartel, whereby competitors join together as a self-regulating monopoly. This means that the teams make agreements on matters of mutual interest (e.g., rules, schedules, promotions, expansion, and media contracts).

A recent effort by the NFL to be legally considered a single entity, and thus not a cartel and thereby immune from antitrust laws, was struck down by the U.S. Supreme Court (*American Needle, Inc., v. NFL et al.*). The court ruled that the NFL is a "cartel" subject to antitrust law.[4]

Monopolistic agreements are illegal for most businesses because they lead to collusion, price fixing, and restraint of trade, all of which are socially detrimental. Economists James Quirk and Rodney Fort have argued that professional sports teams create various social and economic problems from the monopoly power of the sports leagues. As they put it, "Eliminate the monopoly power of leagues and you eliminate the blackmailing of cities to subsidize teams. Eliminate the monopoly power of leagues and you eliminate the sources of revenue that provide the wherewithal for high player salaries. Eliminate the monopoly power of leagues and you eliminate the problem of lack of competitive balance in a league due to disparity in drawing potential among league teams. Eliminate the monopoly power of leagues and you transfer power from the insiders, owners and players alike, to the outsiders, fans and taxpayers."[5]

The enormous advantages to the league cartel are several. Foremost, each sport franchise is protected from competition. The owner of the Kansas City Royals, for instance, is guaranteed that no other MLB team will be allowed to locate in his or her territory. There are some metropolitan areas with two MLB teams, but these exceptions occurred before baseball had agreed to territorial exclusivity. Even in these cases, the teams are in different leagues, ensuring that, for example, Chicago baseball fans who want to see American League games can see them only by attending White Sox games.

This protection from competition eliminates price wars. The owners of a franchise can continue to charge the public a maximum without fear of price cutting by competitors. The league cartel also controls the number of franchises allowed. Each cartel is generally reluctant to add new teams because scarcity permits higher ticket prices, more beneficial media arrangements, and continued territorial purity.

In short, the value of each franchise is increased by the restriction on the number of teams. When new teams are added, such as the addition of the Denver and Miami franchises in 1993 to baseball's National League, they are selected with economic criteria paramount, especially concerning new television markets. (Neither the Rocky Mountain time zone nor Florida had a major league team at that time, making them attractive additions to the league.)

This monopolistic situation enables a league to negotiate television contracts for the benefit of all members of the cartel. The 1961 Sports Broadcast Act allowed sports leagues to sell their national television rights as a group without being subject to the antitrust laws. As a result, the national networks and cable systems may bid for the right to televise, for example, NFL football.

The final advantage of the monopoly is that the athletes are drastically limited in their choices and bargaining power. In football, players are drafted out of college. If they want to play in the NFL, they must negotiate with the team that drafted them. Their other choices are to play in the much less prestigious Arena League, to play in Canada (but the Canadian Football League limits the number of non-Canadian players per team, and the average pay is about one-third that of the NFL), or not to play that year. We will return to the owner–player relationship later in this chapter.

PUBLIC SUBSIDIZATION OF PROFESSIONAL TEAM FRANCHISES

Subsidies to franchise owners take two forms—tax breaks and the availability of sports venues at low cost. We examine these in turn.

The bleak financial picture typically painted by most owners of professional teams, when they seek tax breaks and other gratuities, suggests two things:

first it suggests that it is the responsibility of the local city or region to provide most of the funding for a venue for the professional franchise; two, it suggests that unless the owner is compensated for locating their franchise in that city or region, they will take the franchise to another city or region or not select that location for the team.

The tax benefits available to professional sports franchise owners have been largely unpublicized, even in those cases in which owners have not profited directly from having a largely public subsidized venue built for them. Owning a professional team is by no means the liability that owners often publicly state when they are seeking money for a new venue. In short, for many wealthy individuals, owning a sports franchise has lucrative tax advantages.

Investment in professional franchises enables a wealthy owner to offset the team's gate losses or to minimize taxable profits of the team or of other investments by large depreciation allowances. The purchase of a professional sports franchise includes (1) the legal right to the franchise, (2) player contracts, and (3) assets such as equipment, buildings, cars, and so forth. However, since the most valuable assets of a pro sports team are its players, most of the purchase cost will be attributed to player contracts, which, in turn, can be tax depreciated in the same way a steel company depreciates the investment costs of a new blast furnace.

Similarly, acquisition of a player from another team will enable the new owner to depreciate the player's value over a period of years, usually five. Thus, the player's status as property is readily apparent because no other business in the United States depreciates the value of human beings as part of the cost of its operation. There is an inconsistency here—the team is allowed to depreciate its players, but players are not permitted to depreciate themselves for tax purposes. This anomaly indicates the bias in the tax code favoring owners over players and that players are considered property.

Ownership of professional sports franchises provides this kind of tax shelter even if the team shows accounting losses. That is why it has become an attractive investment for many wealthy persons, who can use losses and player depreciation as a means of offsetting other taxes on individual income. For example, Steve Ballmer, the former chief executive officer of Microsoft and owner of the Los Angeles Clippers, has saved about $140 million in taxes because of the Clippers. Additionally, his federal income tax rate was 12 percent, which was less than a concession stand worker at the arena the Clippers play in. The owner of the hockey franchise Las Vegas Golden Knights was able to use his stake in the team to save more than $12 million in taxes over two years.[6]

These factors contribute to a relatively high turnover of professional team ownership. Since a team can depreciate the value of its players over a relatively short period (five years or less), expansion teams or newly franchised teams composed of players purchased from other owners can depreciate, but old leagues and established teams cannot, except with players purchased from previously established clubs. Thus, buying and selling teams is more profitable than retaining them for extended periods of time. Recently, rules have shifted to affect what other items can be depreciated. Currently, owners of teams can also write off television media deals and league franchise rights.[7]

Consider the example of the tax shelter benefits of the NFL Houston Texans franchise owned by Robert McNair, whose net worth in 2014 was $2 *billion*. Economist Andrew Zimbalist reported,

> Assuming McNair holds the team as a partnership or subchapter S corporation, the IRS will allow him to presume that up to 50 percent of the team's purchase price ($350 million) is attributable to the player contracts he will eventually sign. This amount is generally amortizable over five years, allowing McNair to add $70 million annually to the team's costs before calculating its tax liability. (Of course, McNair will also be allowed to expense players' salaries.) Then McNair can transfer any reported losses from the team to reduce his personal income-tax liability, potentially saving him some $28 million a year for five years . . . . On top of this, McNair will benefit from the pleasures, perquisites, and power that accrue to the elite owners of NFL teams.[8]

The second type of public subsidy to professional sport is the provision of sports facilities to most franchises at low cost. Adequate facilities are of great concern to sports franchise owners because they are essential to the financial success and spectator appeal of professional and big-time amateur sports. Conventional wisdom holds that the presence of the top professional major league sports teams enhances a city's prestige and generates considerable economic activity.

Regarding the former, image is important, especially to civic boosters, and having a top major league team conveys the impression of being a first-class city. Concerning the latter, the myth is that the presence of a major league team brings substantial economic growth to that city or region. This is a myth for at least three reasons. First, subsidizing a team drains government resources—the cost of building and maintaining arenas and of providing access roads and the loss of revenues because of "sweetheart deals" with team owners. Second, the deflection of government money toward a sport team often means that services to the poor may be reduced or dropped altogether. Third, the economic benefits are not spread equally throughout the community. The wealthy benefit (team owners, owners of hotels and restaurants), whereas the costs are disproportionately paid by the middle and lower classes.[9]

The empirical facts that never quite get communicated to the public about the claims touting the economic benefits of public subsidies to sports franchise owners are that no hard evidence exists to support the notion that public financing of these venues makes economic good sense for a community. The opposite is closer to the truth. In a comprehensive review of the empirical literature assessing the effects of subsidies for professional sports franchises and facilities, economists Dennis Coates and Brad Humphreys assert, "The evidence reveals a great deal of consistency among economists doing research in this area. That evidence is that sports subsidies cannot be justified on the grounds of local economic development, income growth or job creation, those arguments most frequently used by subsidy advocates." A University of Chicago economist eloquently summarized what empirical research suggests about the economic effects of building sports venues in cities: "If you want to inject money into the local economy, it

would be better to drop it from a helicopter than invest it in a new ballpark." An economist who has studied the economic impact of stadium construction for decades asserted, "The basic idea is that sports stadiums typically aren't a good tool for economic development." According to him, there is a simple rule for determining the actual return on investment: "Take whatever number the sports promoters say, take it and move the decimal one place to the left. Divide it by ten, and that's a pretty good estimate of the actual economic impact."[10]

As the boom in sports in America has increased, so also has the demand for facilities to accommodate the demands of fans for entertainment and of franchise owners for profits. During the past two decades, team owners of major pro sports leagues—the NFL, MLB, NBA, and NHL—have reaped some $20 *billion* in taxpayer subsidies for new sports venues.[11] Generally, these subsidies are from revenue bonds that allegedly are to be paid off with the revenue from the project. However, whenever a bond-financed public project cannot pay for itself, the obligation becomes a general public one. Other subsidies are indirect, such as providing light rail to the stadiums or access roads to interstate highways.

A Harvard University professor of urban planning calculates that league-wide, 70 percent of the capital cost of NFL stadiums has been provided by taxpayers, not NFL owners. That high percentage of public subsidy is because team owners do not just threaten to move their franchise if they do not get what they want in the form of public subsidies for venues for their team. They actually move their franchise to a welcoming city. We provide several recent examples from one league, the NFL (also, see Table 11.1).

- In 1995 St. Louis enticed the Los Angeles Rams to leave Los Angeles with a package that included a new $300 million stadium, all proceeds from concessions, parking, club seats, luxury suites, and a $15 million practice facility. To finance this largesse, Missouri taxpayers paid $24 million a year, St. Louis taxpayers paid another $12.5 million, and visitors to the county paid a 7.25 percent room tax to raise another $6 million annually. Twenty-one years later, in 2016, the owner of the St. Louis Rams, Stan Kroenke, moved the Rams back to

TABLE 11.1 NFL TEAMS THAT HAVE RELOCATED SINCE 1995

Team	Relocated	New City
Los Angeles Raiders	1995	Oakland
Los Angeles Rams	1995	St. Louis
Cleveland Browns	1996	Baltimore[a]
Houston Oilers	1997	Memphis[b]
St. Louis Rams	2016	Los Angeles
San Diego Chargers	2017	Los Angeles
Oakland Raiders	2020	Las Vegas

[a] Became Ravens.
[b] Tennessee Oilers moved to Nashville and became Tennessee Titans.

Los Angeles, despite the $447 million subsidy that St. Louis taxpayers were going to provide for a new stadium if the franchise remained in Missouri. But the Rams owner is worth in excess of $7.7 billion, and he scoffed at St. Louis's offer. Kroenke privately financed the new stadium in Los Angeles for his team and paid the NFL $650 million in relocation fees for the privilege, As a result of the move, the City of St. Louis and St. Louis County were left with over $100 million to pay on the municipal bonds used to finance the stadium[12] In 2021, St. Louis officials successfully won a $790 million settlement that was launched because of this stadium debt and also lost potential revenue.[13]

- In 2008 Lucas Oil Stadium in Indianapolis opened at an estimated cost of $720 million. It was financed with funds raised jointly by the state of Indiana and the city of Indianapolis, with the Indianapolis Colts providing $100 million. To supply funding for the stadium, Marion County (where Indianapolis is located) raised taxes for food and beverage sales, auto rental taxes, innkeepers' taxes, and admission taxes for its share of the costs. Meanwhile, an increase in food and beverage taxes in six surrounding counties and the sale of Colts license plates completed the total. Such taxes are regressive taxes, meaning that the burden of these taxes falls disproportionately on low-income citizens; moreover, none of the taxes contributes to the human needs of those who are paying most of them.

- The NFL's Atlanta Falcons new stadium, Mercedes-Benz Stadium, opened in the fall of 2017 at a cost of $1.4 billion. The city has agreed to contribute $200 million in stadium bonds, but with additional tax revenues, and with the state of Georgia contributing $40 million for parking expansion, public spending toward construction costs for the new stadium is expected to reach close to $600 million, and the state of Georgia is spending an additional $17 million on expanding a parking garage for the team[14]
- Both the city of Oakland and the ownership of the Oakland Raiders were in agreement that the Raiders needed a new stadium. The city presented a $1.3 billion plan for a stadium in Oakland that would be ready by 2021. But the NFL league and the Raiders were not satisfied with Oakland's proposals for a new stadium. At that point, Las Vegas stepped up to promise construction on a $1.9 billion stadium with $750 million from taxpayer money, and the Raiders eventually began playing in Las Vegas in 2020.[15]
- The San Diego Chargers tried for fifteen years to replace Qualcomm Stadium, but in 2016, 56 percent of the voters rejected a ballot measure that would have raised hotel room taxes to help build a $1.8 billion stadium in San Diego. The San Diego group that opposed a new stadium built largely with taxpayer money called themselves the "No Downtown Stadium—Jobs and Streets First" coalition and defined their central opposition as "We should not raise taxes to build a stadium and subsidize a billion-dollar corporation, especially when we have so many needs in San Diego, including street repairs. Additionally, this tax measure puts our economy and tourism jobs at risk, and it threatens an important revenue source the City relies on to pay for street repairs, 911 dispatchers, libraries and other neighborhood services. All this to help a billionaire build a new workspace for millionaires."[16] Because of San Diego's smaller market size, the team had said it needed public subsidies to build a new stadium there, but in Los Angeles, where the size and wealth of the market make such subsidies unnecessary and where the stadium construction debt could be shared by two teams, the

stadium needed no public funding for construction, instead relying on stadium naming rights, personal seat license sales, and other sources.

Franchise mobility in the search for public funding to build new venues is not limited to the NFL. Other professional sports owners employ the same tactics as the NFL in their search for public funding for new stadiums and arenas. Again, we describe examples:

- The move of an NBA team illustrates the kind of thing that happens when a franchise owner does not get what he or she wants from a city. The members of the Seattle Supersonics ownership group were unhappy with their former home, KeyArena, and petitioned the city of Seattle to build a new arena Their plea was refused, so the owners explored moving, which entailed breaking their lease with the city of Seattle for KeyArena The franchise moved to Oklahoma City as the Oklahoma Thunder for the 2008–2009 season. Oklahoma City attracted the team by promising to spend $100 million renovating its existing arena to bring it up to current NBA standards and an additional $20 million to construct a practice facility. Economists Dennis Coates and Brad Humphreys contend that the Seattle–Oklahoma City case suggests relevant lessons: "Professional sports leagues are able to restrict entry and play one city off against another to extract the best subsidy deal. In doing so, there is a significant positional element—one city's fan-base loses, another gains. And teams exploit the cities where politics most effectively taps the taxpayers."[17]
- In 2010 the MLB team the Minnesota Twins celebrated the opening of their $517 million stadium, Target Field—$350 million of which is to be paid by a 0.15 percent county sales tax. Meanwhile, the state of Minnesota was facing a $5 billion budget crisis, and the legislature was considering massive cuts to health and human services programs to help erase the state's budget deficit.
- In 2014 the Sacramento City Council voted approval of public financing and other terms for a new indoor arena for the NBA's Sacramento Kings. The new arena cost $557 million, with $255 million of that being funded by the city of Sacramento The rest of the arena ($222 million) was funded by the Sacramento Kings. The city also transferred $32 million worth of land

and allowed the team to operate six digital billboards. This vote was the culmination of a struggle to keep the Kings in Sacramento because the NBA had told the city that it had to have a new arena by 2017 or risk losing the Kings. Former Kings owners had considered moving the team to Las Vegas, Anaheim, and Virginia Beach and even had an agreement calling for an investor to buy the team and move it to Seattle.[18]

- In 2015, the Wisconsin State Assembly voted to pass a bill to help build an arena for the NBA's Milwaukee Bucks. Owners contributed $250 million, and $250 million came from public money. It was the typical case of public money being committed or the Bucks moving to another city. As a *USA Today* writer argued, "You can balk at the connections. You can balk at the use of public money for professional sports arenas for teams owned by billionaires and millionaires. But that's how it works, and if Wisconsin wanted to keep its NBA team, it did what it had to do."[19]
- In Atlanta, the MLB Atlanta Braves left Turner Field for a $1.1 billion suburban baseball field named Sun Trust Park, where the first regular-season game was held in April 2017. The move came at a heavy cost to Cobb County because taxpayers are on the hook for nearly $400 million that was approved by county commissioners without a public vote after holding secret negotiations with the team.[20]

It is clear that professional sports team owners are greatly subsidized, but to what extent do the communities that pay these subsidies benefit? Sociologists and economists argue that the benefits are not widespread for the following reasons: First, the wealthy benefit disproportionately when public municipalities use general taxes to build a sports venue. Although more jobs may be created while the venue is being constructed, the long-term profits accrue to the owners, not the general public. Team owners profit from fan attendance with little investment in the land or construction. They cannot lose financially because the burden is on the taxpayers. This is clearly a case of the wealthy receiving a public subsidy.[21]

The obvious beneficiaries of subsidized public sports venues are the owners of sports teams, as well as the owners of hotels, media, commercial modes of transportation, restaurants, construction firms, and property affected by the location of the new arena site. There is a strong relationship between professional team owners and the decision-makers at the highest political, corporate, financial, and media levels. These strong ties may explain the commonly found affirmative consensus among the political and economic elite for the building of public sports venues.

Second, the prices of individual and season tickets are usually too high for lower-income citizens. Ironically, bringing a major league team to an area (a primary reason for building a new stadium or arena) usually means that lower-income people see fewer games than before, primarily because building a new venue or refurbishing an old one invariably results in higher ticket prices.

Third, new stadiums, especially those built in downtown districts, are usually constructed as part of urban redevelopment agendas, which means that new, affluent professionals come to inhabit and utilize these areas. This gentrification increases rents and other costs, forcing the poor to live elsewhere.

Fourth, new publicly financed venues tend to be built with the purpose of appealing to the affluent fan with significant disposable income to spend on the game day experience, with increased luxury boxes, merchandise shops, and prime seating that comes at a high cost.

OWNERSHIP FOR PROFIT

The first thing to understand about ownership of sports franchises is that it requires enormous wealth. Many of the owners of professional team sports franchises are *billionaires*. To illustrate, Table 11.2 identifies the ten richest owners in sports. They bought sports franchise for various reasons. For those teams owned by individuals, psychological gratifications are inherent in owning a professional team. Many owners derive great personal satisfaction from knowing athletes personally. In addition, a great deal of social status comes with ownership of a sports franchise. Owners are feted by the community as service leaders and achieve a degree of celebrity status, social prestige, and publicity that can enhance other facets of their business ventures. Apart from the "psychological income" of team ownership, there are substantial

economic motives. Indeed, for most investors the primary motivation would seem to be a rationally economic one: ownership of a sports franchise is a profitable long-range investment.

The value of sports franchises has consistently increased. Several examples make this point: In 1949 the Philadelphia Eagles franchise was sold for $250,000. The value of the Eagles franchise in 2013 was estimated by *Forbes* magazine at $1.16 *billion*. In 1989 the Dallas Cowboys were purchased by Jerry Jones for an unprecedented $140 million. By 2021 that franchise had increased in value to $5.7 *billion*. Similar increases have occurred in the three other major professional team sports, with the increases correlating closely with new stadium and arena construction at taxpayers' expense. Table 11.3 lists the United States' ten most valuable teams. As we have seen, the main reasons for the great appreciation in franchise value are the advantages of monopoly, television revenues, tax breaks, and subsidized venues.

TABLE 11.2 AMERICA'S RICHEST SPORTS TEAM OWNERS, 2021

Name	Worth (in billions of dollars)	Team
1. Steve Ballmer	68.7	Los Angeles Clippers
2. Daniel Gilbert	51.9	Cleveland Cavaliers
3. Dietrich Mateschitz	26.9	New York Red Bulls, Red Bull Racing
4. Robert Pera	18.3	Memphis Grizzlies
5. Steve Cohen	16	New York Mets
6. David Tepper	14.5	Carolina Panthers
7. Joseph Tsai	11.6	Brooklyn Nets
8. Philip Anschutz	10.1	Los Angeles Kings, LA Galaxy
9. Jerry Jones	8.9	Dallas Cowboys
10. Hasso Plattner and family	8.3	San Jose Sharks

Source: Sergei Klebnikov, "The World's Richest Sports Team Owners 2021," *Forbes*, April 6, 2021, https://www.forbes.com/sites/sergeiklebnikov/2021/04/06/the-worlds-richest-sports-team-owners-2021/?sh=33daa6ab4153.

TABLE 11.3 UNITED STATES' MOST VALUABLE TEAMS, 2021

Team	Worth (in billions of dollars)
Dallas Cowboys	5.7
New York Yankees	5.25
New York Knicks	5.0
Golden State Warriors	4.7
Los Angeles Lakers	4.6
New England Patriots	4.4
New York Giants	4.3
Los Angeles Rams	4.0
San Francisco 49ers	3.8

Source: Mike Ozanian, "The World's 50 Most Valuable Sports Teams 2021," *Forbes*, May 7, 2021, https://www.forbes.com/sites/mikeozanian/2021/05/07/worlds-most-valuable-sports-teams-2021/?sh=4dcef44e3e9e.

That the structure of professional team sports tends to be lucrative is established, but the wealthy owners often downplay the business profit potential and highlight the notion that sports franchises are providing a service to their respective communities. This raises an important dilemma: If, on the one hand, a franchise's status is seriously considered that of a privately owned capitalist business enterprise, then special commerce concessions and subsidies for venue construction are inappropriate. If, on the other hand, professional team owners deserve these advantages because they are providing sport as a community service, then their profits should be scaled down and the major benefits should accrue to the players and the fans.

Perhaps the best test of the owners' primary motivation involves their policies regarding ticket prices. The test is simple. If the owner is basically civic minded, then the better the attendance during the season, the lower the prices should be. But the data on ticket prices consistently show that the greater the demand for tickets, the higher the price tends to be.

Consider, for example, the cost for attending a Washington Nationals game in 2017 in the Nationals Park venue against the Chicago Cubs, the World Series champions at the time. The high-end Delta Sky360 Club seat ran $450. The dugout box seats were $140 apiece, and the right-field terrace seat—that

cheap ticket was $35. These prices, by the way, do not include prices for the venue's sixty-six luxury suites, which start at $20,000 and go up to $30,000 per game. The stadium was built with $611 million in public funds. As Michael Friedman observes, an attractive "stadium typically gives professional teams an increase in ticket demand and a corresponding opportunity to increase prices to match that demand."[22]

The rationale usually offered to explain ticket price increases is that costs are skyrocketing, especially because of the high salaries of superstars. As a result, fans typically vent their anger on the athletes rather than on the owners. The anger seems misplaced; apparently, the fans do not recognize that greed motivates the owners as well as the players. Profit is, of course, the basic rule of capitalism. Still, the owners should not have it both ways. If they are capitalists, then subsidies are inappropriate. Their monopolies should not be supported by Congress and the courts. Their tax breaks should be eliminated. If public arenas are provided for professional teams, then the rent should be fair for both the owners of the teams and the citizens of the city.

A RADICAL QUESTION: ARE OWNERS NECESSARY?

Professional sport franchise owners receive anywhere from 50 to 75 percent of the profits from professional teams. What have they provided to receive such generous compensation? They did buy the teams from other owners, but what else? The stadiums and arenas, except on rare occasions, have been provided by taxpayers. So, too, the practice facilities. Sports analyst Dave Zirin argues, "Owners are uniquely charged with being the stewards of the game. It's a task that they have failed to perform in spectacular fashion. . . . Cities and city councils that allow their funds to be used by private franchises should, in turn, have some say in the relationship between team and fan."[23]

This leads to the question, Why don't the municipalities own these teams? They could hire competent general managers to sign players, make schedules, hire coaches and support staff, and negotiate for television and radio contracts. Indeed, that is exactly the way the Green Bay Packers professional football team has functioned since it began as the only professional sports team in the United States that is owned by the public, by shareholders—363,948 of them, representing 5,020,523 shares. As such, it provides a model for what could be. Following are some of its features:

- The Green Bay Packers football club was organized back in 1923 as a community-owned, nonprofit company. Today, some of the locals, including truckers, barkeeps, merchants, and bus drivers, can lay claim to part of the franchise ownership in the Pack.
- The stockholders draw no profit, and the locally elected board of directors that operates the team is unpaid, but all concerned draw great pleasure from knowing that the Packers are theirs.
- Home-game ticket prices are some of the lowest in the NFL.
- Parking is permitted on some lawns for home games. No, really. Residents will snow-plow their lawns and driveways and charge anywhere from $5 to $20 to park there, depending on walking distance.
- Nonprofit groups, which include service organizations and school groups, commit to working concessions at each game of the season.
- Off-duty police provide stadium security and are paid overtime by the team.
- Green Bay fans and citizens do not have to worry that some pirate of an owner is going to commandeer the Pack and haul their team to Los Angeles or some other big city, because Green Bay is their team. It stands as a shining model for how fans in other cities could control their sports franchises and stop corporate rip-offs.[24]

WHO BENEFITS ECONOMICALLY FROM SPORTS?

Only a small percentage of people participating in sporting activities derive direct economic benefits from them. As we documented more fully in Chapter 5, the number of professional athletes in elite sport competitions is extremely small. For instance, the total number of full-time players in major U.S. team sports—baseball, soccer, basketball, football, and hockey—is nearly 4,000 annually. Add to this the very few professional golfers who earn their living on

the PGA and LPGA tours and the handful of tennis players on the Women's Tennis Association and Association of Tennis Professionals tours, race-car drivers, boxers, and jockeys, and it is apparent that the business of professional sport is based on the performances of a small group of talented individuals.

PROFESSIONAL ATHLETES' EARNINGS

For those who do attain the elite status of professional athlete, the financial benefits can be substantial, but the well-publicized salaries of a handful of superstars have given the public a distorted and inflated idea of professional athletes' incomes. Moreover, professional athletes' salaries should be balanced against their generally brief, often tenuous, careers. For instance, the median length of an NFL player's career is 3.6 years, which does not even qualify the typical player for a retirement pension.

In addition to their salary, successful professional athletes often receive benefits gained through product endorsements, speeches and other public appearances, and jobs as actors, entertainers, and sports announcers. They are also well positioned to take advantage of opportunities for investments in business ventures as diverse as sports camps, real estate developments, quick-order franchises, motels, and restaurants.

Forbes magazine ranked the twenty-five top-paid athletes in the world in terms of income in 2021. Among U.S. professional team athletes, five of the top ten were NBA players. Naomi Osaka, a tennis player, was the only woman in the top ten. For most whose livelihoods are dependent on their sports abilities, the financial rewards are not nearly as great as they are for the publicized athletes.[25]

The following examples indicate players' salaries and income in several professional sports:

- In professional basketball a lucrative sports career awaits the successful athlete, but only about 276 players and approximately 40 rookies are hired each year. And although the average annual salary of NBA players in 2021-2022 was estimated to be $7.3 million, those just one rung below in the developmental league typically make between $35,000 and $50,000 a season.

- In professional golf some 350 men and 270 women pursue the multimillion-dollar prize money, but only about 200 make a living at it. The rest have trouble meeting expenses.
- More than 7,000 individuals play minor league baseball, and fewer than 7 percent of them will make it to the major leagues. None of these minor league players is covered by the minimum-salary scales of major league baseball. While a full-time minimum wage worker makes some $15,000 a year, the average minor leaguer earns $7,500. Without a "union to represent and advocate for minor leaguers, owners have leverage and no incentive to raise salaries."[26]
- In auto racing, winnings are split among owners, drivers, and their crew. Annual sponsorship revenue and the licensing market are other sources of income for racers, who need more than $1 million a year for expenses to be competitive on the auto-racing circuit. Meanwhile, unknowns, people of color, and women have great difficulty obtaining racing contracts, sponsorships, and licensing deals.
- The scholarship athlete in college is paid a paltry stipend for his or her services, even for those athletes who attend universities that now pay athletes annually to cover the full cost of attending college. Calculated on the basis of the room, books, meals, and tuition allowed by the NCAA, a college athlete's salary does not greatly exceed the federal government's stated poverty level and approximates the federally established minimum hourly pay scale. This is why there has been new legislation allowing student-athletes to profit from their NIL (see Chapter 10).

Professional athletes' salaries in the four historic major team sports in the United States have increased dramatically in the past two decades (see Table 11.4). As a result, the gap between the salary of the average professional athlete and that of the average worker has increased even more dramatically.

In the MLB, for example, the average baseball player in 1950 earned $13,300 a year, a little more than four times the median family income. By 2022, the average baseball player was earning $4.4 million, about fifty-five times as much as the median family income. These higher average salaries reflect the high salaries paid to superstars and do not reflect the

salaries for most players. In baseball, for example, the Los Angeles Dodgers had a total player payroll of $310 million in 2022. Overall, five teams exceeded payrolls of $230 million on opening day in 2022.[27]

Athletes of superstar status in individual sports sometimes receive even higher incomes than those in team sports. The most popular heavyweight boxers can make as much as $20 million for a single fight. The elite tennis players make more than $5 million annually. A few golfers approach $10 million a year in winnings, as do a few auto racers and jockeys.

These huge incomes, which are supplemented by endorsements and personal appearances, raise two important questions: (1) Are athletes paid too much? and (2) How do such enormous salaries for athletes affect the fans?

To the fans, their once-noble sports heroes are now businesspeople. Athletes are aware of the profits they are generating and, in turn, are seeking huge salaries to perform in games. They may threaten not to play. Their grandstand convictions are often regarded this way: "Players no longer have loyalty to their team or city," "Players have gotten too greedy," "They're all paid too much." We have all heard these complaints, and others, from disenchanted, angry people both inside and outside the sports world.

The high salaries are resented because many people view athletes as "merely" employees who are "playing" while others work. Fans see these athlete-employees as behaving like workers who are trying to acquire the most money, the most favorable working conditions, and the most favorable retirement benefits—even

TABLE 11.4 AVERAGE SALARIES IN SOME MAJOR PROFESSIONAL LEAGUES FOR SELECTED YEARS (IN U.S. DOLLARS)

Year	NBA	MLB	NFL	NHL
1976	110,000	51,500	63,200	90,000
1984	246,000	325,900	162,000	130,000
1991	990,000	850,000	355,000	370,000
2001	3,170,000	2,290,000	1,169,000	1,430,000
2007	5,200,000	2,920,000	1,400,000	1,600,000
2010	5,360,000	3,300,000	1,800,000	1,800,000
2019-20	8,320,000	4,003,000	3,2600,000	2,690,000

forming unions to collectively bargain to strengthen their demands, which is what the laboring workforce has done for more than 150 years. Although the labor union movement has been publicly supported for more than a century in its struggles, professional athletes and their player unions—using the same model for advancing their cause as trade and labor unions have employed to improve their incomes and working conditions—are criticized and resented for what they have accomplished. This is a perplexing reaction.

It is ironic that sports fans and the public have tended to take the side of the team owners in salary disputes, strikes, and other disruptions, although the owners over the years have had the monopoly, have taken economic advantage of the athletes, and have had the temerity to move franchises to more lucrative communities. Furthermore, fans resent the high salaries of athletes but take in stride the huge earnings of other entertainers. For some reason the huge monies collected by nonathlete entertainers are accepted by the public, but the lesser monies received by athletes tend to foster resentment.

In addition to the entertainment analogy, four other arguments justify the amounts paid to superstars for playing games. The first is that their salaries are paid on the basis of scarcity. There are some 400 NBA basketball players in a nation of over 320 million people, which makes NBA players about one in a million, and the capitalist principle of supply and demand—the economic foundation of the United States—suggests that they should be paid accordingly.

The second argument is that a typical pro sports career is brief, so players should be paid well (of all the players in the NBA, only thirty or so are thirty years of age or older). Third, the owners are paying the athletes what they are worth because the superstars bring out the fans. Finally, related to the last point, salaries have escalated but so have owners' and league office revenues from television, ticket sales, royalties from the sale of merchandise, and the like.

AUXILIARY PROFESSIONS AND OCCUPATIONS IN SPORT

In the sports industry numerous auxiliary professions and occupations are made up of persons who have knowledge and skills that facilitate the development and progress of athletes and teams. Unquestionably,

the most noted of these are coaches. Coaches are a universal component at all levels of organized sport, yet they are frequently overlooked in calculating the economic effects of sport in the United States. It is estimated that about 3,200,000 coaches are employed in secondary schools, and some 25,000 men and 4,500 women are engaged in coaching at the college level.

Umpires and referees constitute another sports occupational category. MLB umpires are the best paid, with salaries ranging from $104,704 to $324,545. The NHL and NBA also require full-time officials, but the pay is lower. Historically, the NFL paid its officials on a part-time, game-by-game basis, but an eight-year contract signed in 2011 allows the NFL to hire some officials on a year-round basis and hire additional referees so they can be trained.

Thousands more officiate at the other levels of sport for relatively low fees (e.g., in Class A minor league baseball, umpires receive less than $20,000 a season). At a lower level still, there are many thousands who officiate high school sports. In Colorado, for example, there are almost 5,000 registered officials for thirteen different sports. In recent years the per-game pay per official in Colorado high school sports has been $58 for varsity football, basketball, baseball, and ice hockey, and it is slightly less for other sports.

Another occupational category dependent on sport is the specialist in sports medicine. The treatment of sports injuries requires specialized education and training in treatment techniques, and sports medicine professionals are present at most sports events at all levels of organized sports. Sports medicine clinics are becoming relatively commonplace in metropolitan centers.

Another sports job is that of the player agent. With the advent of free agency in professional team sports and accelerated player incomes, agents for the players are performing an even greater function in professional and college sports. They provide a service to the players because they know the tax laws and the market value of the athletes. Their goal is to maximize monetary benefits for the athlete by extracting the most beneficial contract from management. For their services, the agents receive a percentage of the agreement (from 5 to 10 percent), which can be a considerable amount in this era of multimillion-dollar contracts. With the new changes to how NCAA athletes can profit from their NIL, there will be a new role for agents of college athletes.

This profession is so unregulated (and lucrative) that some agents have been able to take advantage of their naive clients, for example, by having them sign huge contracts with payments deferred over as many as forty years; in such instances, the agent takes a percentage of the total up front, while the player receives no interest on the deferred money, which is further devalued by inflation.

SPORT-RELATED BUSINESSES

In addition to those directly involved in producing the sport product, many businesses benefit from the sports industry—hotels, taxis, restaurants, parking, and other business establishments—and can thereby increase their volume of business. The presence of a major league team generates millions of dollars for a city's economy, and this is why cities are so generous to sports teams (in stadium rentals, concession revenues, and various tax subsidies). Huge sports spectaculars such as the Kentucky Derby, the Indianapolis 500, the World Series, and the Super Bowl are major tourist attractions bringing an economic bonanza to numerous ancillary businesses (hotels, restaurants, stores, casinos, caterers, florists). The 2020 Super Bowl, for example, seemingly poured an estimated $350 million net economic impact into the Tampa Bay, area economy. Some caution is needed here, according to sports economists, there are some hidden costs. For example, cities bid for the right to host the event and often provide incentives to the NFL which are often subsidized by the local taxpayers. One sports economist says his research shows an average impact of between $30 million and $130 million in overall spending at Super Bowl sites.[28] (See Box 11.1 for the numbers generated from recent Super Bowls.)

BOX 11.1 *THINKING ABOUT SPORT:*
THE SUPER BOWL

Watching huge men attack each has been popular since the Roman gladiators battled for their lives in the Colosseum. Now more than 100 million view Super Bowl football players generate big bucks, with spending topping $16 billion.

The Super Bowl is much more than a football game. The Super Bowl is a celebration of concentrated wealth—wealthy players and wealthy owners, corporate executives and their affluent clients, lobbyists and legislators, and high rollers of various stripes with money to spend on lavish parties, food, and lodging at inflated prices. One sports columnist described the situation just before each Super Bowl: an armada of Lear jets touch down, delivering dozens of America's corporate tycoons. Local streets are jammed with stretch limos; bars are stocked with $500 bottles of champagne to go with the epicurean dinners. Hotel suites are swarming with the rich, the celebrated, and the fortunate—an unadulterated symbol of class inequality.

The Super Bowl is business—big business—the magnitude of which is seen in these numbers:

- Hosting the game costs the city an estimated $6 million, primarily through increased need for police, fire, and emergency personnel. But in recent years, the game potentially brings at least $350 million to the local economy, according to the NFL, as visitors spend on hotels, entertainment, food, and drink.

- In 2022, the Super Bowl was held in SoFi Stadium. "SoFi Stadium in Los Angeles has a 70,000 seating capacity but can be expanded to 100,000 people. Standard ticket prices reportedly range from $950 to $6,200 (not counting the five-figure luxury boxes). Even at the lowest possible range that would value the tickets to this Super Bowl at $66.5 million in total."[29]

- Spending for commercials during the game has totaled almost $380 million in recent years. In 2022 the cost of a thirty-second spot was $6.5 million, which breaks down to $217,000 per second.

- In 2022, each member of the winning team received about $150,000, and each member of the losing team received around $75,000.

- "The American Gaming Association (AGA) estimates that a **record 31.4 million people** in the US would wager around **$7.61 billion** on this year's (2022) game between the Cincinnati Bengals and the LA Rams. The number of people expected to wager would be a 35 percent increase from last year's Super Bowl."[30]

Sporting goods corporations are some of the greatest beneficiaries of sport, both directly, through the sale of sports-related products, and indirectly, through the use of sports to generate interest in their products. Wilson, Spalding, Puma, Under Armour, Nike, Adidas, and Reebok are all global sporting goods firms selling dozens of sports products. (See Box 11.2, on Nike, for a look at the leading sports corporation.)

BOX 11.2 *THINKING ABOUT SPORT:* NIKE, THE SPORTS CORPORATE BEHEMOTH

In 1964, legendary University of Oregon track coach Bill Bowerman and one of his former distance runners, Phil Knight, formed a company called Blue Ribbon Sports to manufacture and sell running shoes. This company later became Nike, Inc., and today it is a huge global corporation with more than 500 factories and offices located in forty-five countries; 2021 revenues from continuing operations were $44.5 billion according to fiscal reporting. Nike's products have expanded to all types of athletic shoes, apparel, sports equipment, and accessories.

Nike has signed many of the world's major athletes to focus attention on its products—for example, Michael Jordan, LeBron James, and Kobe Bryant in basketball; Christiano Ronaldo and Neymar in soccer; golfer Tiger Woods; tennis players Roger Federer, Rafael Nadal, and Maria Sharapova; motorsport racer Michael Schumacher; and several Chinese athletes in basketball, track, and swimming.

In the United States Nike provides free equipment to professional, college, and some high school teams. Multimillion-dollar deals have been made with many major collegiate teams to supply equipment and supplements for coaches' salaries. Nike sponsors elite U.S. track-and-field athletes, allowing them to train without having to work at a job. Nike also sponsors high school tournaments and track meets and more than 500 sports camps in fifteen different sports.

There is a dark side to the Nike story. Most of its products are manufactured in low-wage countries in Asia, where not only is labor cheap but also regulations are scarce. There have been charges of exploitation of young women and children working under oppressive conditions for pennies an hour, making goods that sell for a huge profit in the United States. A Nike transnational advocacy network was formed to publicize these labor abuses and to mobilize efforts to pressure Nike

(and other sports manufacturing firms) to stop these human rights abuses. Nike has responded with some policy changes in recent years, although some controversies have continued to emerge.

Labor relations within the United States have also been a negative for Nike. For example, a class-action race discrimination lawsuit against Nike was filed on behalf of 400 African American employees of the company's Niketown Chicago store. Although Nike denied the allegations, it reached a $7.6 million settlement. Four women also filed a recent class-action lawsuit against Nike over systemic gender pay discrimination and ignoring sexual harassment. Previously, about ten top executives resigned due to allegations of a toxic boys' culture existing amongst Nike's corporate leadership.

Nike has also been accused of having an undue influence on college sports. By giving equipment and money worth millions to big-time college programs, Nike has increased the gap between the college haves and have-nots. There is also a Nike network, which means that when there is a coaching vacancy, a "Nike school" may be limited to selecting a "Nike coach"—that is, a coach who has a contractual agreement with Nike. Similarly, Nike's sponsorship of certain prominent high schools, Amateur Athletic Union teams, tournaments, and sports camps may have an influence on recruiting for colleges. In other words, "Nike high school coaches" or "Nike Amateur Athletic Union coaches" may steer their athletes to "Nike colleges."

Sources: George H. Sage, *Globalizing Sports: How Organizations, Corporations, Media, and Politics Are Changing Sports* (Boulder, CO: Paradigm, 2010), 118–126. https://investors.nike.com/investors/news-events-and-reports/investor-news/investor-news-details/2021/NIKE-Inc.-Reports-Fiscal-2021-Fourth-Quarter-and-Full-Year-Results/default.aspx, accessed June 16, 2022; Alexia Campbell, August 15, 2018, Why the gender discrimination lawsuit against Nike is so significant, https://www.vox.com/2018/8/15/17683484/nike-women-gender-pay-discrimination-lawsuit, accessed June 15, 2022

The concessions business provides sports spectators with food, drink, and merchandise. A concessionaire is typically given a monopoly by a team management, league, or city; in return, the grantor receives a percentage of the proceeds. The beer and hot dogs consumed by thousands of fans generate a lot of revenue for every team.

CORPORATE ADVERTISING IN SPORT

Commercial sports enhance big business in a variety of industries. Sports themes and prominent athletes are used in advertisements to sell products.

Companies are convinced that through the proper selection of sports and sports personalities, they can reach particular preidentified consumer categories or strengthen the general visibility of their products.

The commercialization of sport is also readily seen in the advertising at the ballparks, stadiums, and arenas of professional, college, and even high school sports. Many of these arenas have corporate names, purchased at significant cost, with over $1.1 billion in naming-rights revenue being pledged just from Jan. 1, 2020, to July 27, 2021, according to the *Sports Business Journal*.[31]

Nike factory in Vietnam. Much footwear purchased by Americans is manufactured in various low-wage countries in Asia, where labor is cheap and less regulated. Under this system, athletic products such as shoes are eventually sold for huge profits in the United States. (Photo: AP Photo/Richard Vogel)

In 2022 there were more than one hundred professional league North American sports facilities sponsored with corporate names. In 2009 the New York Mets began play in their new stadium, called Citi Field, which cost Citibank $20 million a year for twenty years for the naming rights. Newer NFL stadiums in Las Vegas (Allegiant Airlines) and Los Angeles (SoFi) have been named for $25 million and $30 million per year respectively.

Corporate naming rights contracts are not limited to professional sports venues. Corporate names are widespread on college sports venues. Some examples include the following:

- Desert Financial Arena—Arizona State University
- FCB Mortgage Stadium—University of Central Florida
- Capital One Field—University of Maryland
- Simmons Bank Liberty Stadium—University of Memphis
- JMA Wireless Dome—Syracuse University
- ExtraMile Arena—Boise State University
- Huntington Bank Stadium—University of Minnesota

Many companies and corporations have also paid to have their names associated with various college bowl games. A few examples of the games that were held in December 2021 and January 2022 are as follows:

- Lendingtree Bowl
- Radiance Technologies Independence Bowl
- Lockheed Martin Armed Forces Bowl
- Tony the Tiger Sun Bowl
- Allstate Sugar Bowl
- Cheez-it Bowl

Given the amount of bowl games with sponsorship deals, most of the 131 NCAA Football Subdivision teams in 2022 are able to play in a bowl.

The use of sport to promote business interests takes a number of other forms as well, some reciprocal. Corporations sponsor such sports as running, bowling, golf, rodeo, tractor pulls, tennis, and skiing. For example, becoming a "title sponsor" on a PGA tour event costs an estimated $7 million. Sponsorship has been especially crucial to the advances in women's professional sports: General Mills' MultiGrain Cheerios, Crowne Plaza Hotels and Resorts, Gillette's *Golf* magazine, J. M. Smucker Co., WorldTEK Travel, Usana Health Sciences, and Oriflame have all underwritten women's professional golf and tennis tournaments and have thus significantly raised both the prize money and the visibility of women's sports.

The most blatant expression of the commercial presence in sports occurs in automobile racing, because the races themselves are unabashedly organized to hype a variety of corporations such as the following:

- Bank of America—Official Bank
- Canadian Tire—Official Automotive Retailer of NASCAR in Canada
- Chevrolet—An Official Passenger Car
- Coors Light—Official Beer
- DuPont—Official Finish
- Exide—Official Auto Batteries
- MGM—Official gaming partner of MLB and NBA

Beyond that, drivers as well as owners of race cars receive a fee for using corporate logos on their racing vehicles and on the clothing of the drivers. These logos usually represent corporations involved in products for automobiles (e.g., tires, oil, auto parts, mufflers, shock absorbers), but they also include corporations selling chewing tobacco, cigarettes, clothing, soft drinks, and the like. The ubiquitous jumpsuits that drivers wear are the extreme in unabashed corporate advertising. Corporate logos adorn virtually every salable space of drivers' jumpsuits, making drivers appear to be walking sandwich boards.

A special relationship seems to exist between beer companies and sport. Beer is largely consumed by men, and men are overrepresented among the spectators at sporting events and among the avid followers of sport. The result is that the beer companies have partially subsidized sport. Some have owned teams: Coors Beer is part owner of the Colorado Rockies, and the venue is named Coors Field; the Molson (beer) family owns the Montreal Canadiens. Most sports teams have several sponsors for their local radio and television broadcasts, but a beer company is almost always one of them.

The major corporations of the United States have been active in the sponsorship of the U.S. Olympic team for the presumed benefits of public relations, advertising, and a generous allotment of tickets. In 2014 the International Olympic Committee announced it had agreed to a $7.75 billion deal with NBCUniversal for broadcast rights to all media platforms covering six Olympics to 2032, making it the most expensive television rights contract in Olympic history. Various corporations such as Panasonic, Bridgestone, Deloitte, Samsung, and Intel pay the International Olympic Committee for the right to be the corporate partners of the Olympics.

THE RELATIONSHIP BETWEEN OWNERS AND ATHLETES

One of the reasons ownership of a professional sports team has tended to be profitable is that the courts have allowed sport to be an exemption from U.S. antitrust laws. Early in the twentieth century Supreme Court justice Oliver Wendell Holmes ruled that major league baseball was a game that did not involve interstate commerce and was therefore exempt from federal antitrust laws. This enabled MLB sport team owners to function as a monopoly. As other professional team sports leagues developed, their franchise owners operated under the special legal status conferred on the MLB until the mid-1970s. The major consequence of professional team sports functioning as monopolies was the right of owners to own and control their players.

THE DRAFT AND THE RESERVE CLAUSE

The last couple of decades of the twentieth century were characterized by a concerted attack by athletes on the employment practices of professional team sports owners. Unlike employees of other businesses, athletes were not free to sell their services to whomever they pleased. Players' salaries were determined solely by each team's owner. In the MLB, before the landmark cases of the mid-1970s (to be discussed), once a player signed a contract with a club, that team had exclusive rights over him, and he was no longer free to negotiate with any other team. In succeeding years, the player had to sell his services solely to the club that owned his contract unless it released, sold, or traded him or he chose to retire. The reserve clause specified that the owner had the exclusive right to renew the player's contract annually, and thus the player was bound perpetually to negotiate with only one club; he became its property and could be sold to another club without his own consent.

The NFL was more restrictive in one respect and more open (at least on paper) in another. Unlike the MLB, the NFL had a draft of college players, and the selected athletes had no choice as to the team for which they would play. The player would play for the team that drafted him and at the salary offered or else join a team in the Canadian League (the number of foreign players allowed to play in Canada was limited, however, so that option was a real one only for the most sought-after football athletes). As in the MLB, after signing with a team, the NFL player was bound to that team. He could, however, play out his option, in other words, play a year at 90 percent of his previous salary without signing a contract, whereupon he would be free to negotiate with another team.

This apparent freedom of movement for the players was severely limited, however, by what was called the Rozelle Rule. This rule allowed the NFL commissioner at that time, Pete Rozelle, to require the team signing any such "free agent" to compensate (with other athletes or with money of equal value) the club the player had left. This rule made signing free agents rarely in a club's interest; therefore, the free agent did not in reality have full economic freedom.

These provisions in the NFL and MLB (and similar ones in the NBA and NHL) were clearly one-sided, giving all the power to the owners, binding the employees (athletes) without binding the employers. The owner was free to decide whether to continue the relationship; the player was not. It was sarcastically observed that after the Civil War settled the slavery issue, owning a professional team sport franchise was the closest one could come to owning a plantation.

PROFESSIONAL TEAM SPORT ATHLETES FIGHT FOR FREE AGENCY

In the 1960s, sometimes called the civil rights decade, various marginalized groups (racial minorities, women, LGBQT people) became militant in attempts to overcome social injustices and change existing power arrangements. Professional athletes, too, began to recognize their common plight and organized to change it. Most fundamentally, professional athletes felt that because the owners had all the power, players did not receive their true value in the marketplace. The result was that athletes, singly and together in player associations, began to assert themselves against what they considered an unfair system. The MLB is where the battle by athletes was waged most vociferously and over a period of decades. Their struggle is outlined in Box 11.3. Even a cursory study of this box should demonstrate the impressive persistence that was shown by MLB players to obtain their goals of free agency and fair salaries.

Victories for the MLB players were not won easily. Owners fought them at every instance. There were strikes by the players and lockouts by the owners. Most significant, the owners were found guilty of *collusion* by the courts—that is, they conspired not to sign free agents from 1985 to 1987. This was an attempt to stop the salary spiral in baseball by taking away the players' power. The arbitrator, George Nicolau, in his opinion found that "there was no vestige of a free market [during these years]. It was replaced by a patent pattern of deliberate contravention of baseball's collective bargaining agreement." As a result, the owners had to pay $280 million in damages to the players adversely affected by the owners' collusion. In 2000 a federal appeals court commented on this collusion in a case involving an ex-MLB player. The court wrote, "The scope of the owners' deceit and fabrications in their 1980s effort to cheat their employees out of their rightful wages was wholly unprecedented, as was the financial injury suffered by

BOX 11.3 *THINKING ABOUT SPORT:* THE BUSINESS OF BASEBALL: SHIFTING POWER AND INCREASED SALARIES

1879—Reserve rules instituted.

1922—The Supreme Court decided that baseball was not a trade in interstate commerce and therefore not subject to federal antitrust laws.

1953—A minor league player, George Toolson, wanted to change teams but was denied. The Supreme Court agreed with the owners that the players were bound to a club for life, citing the 1922 decision.

1966—Marvin Miller was elected executive director of the Players Association. At this time, the average player salary was $19,000, and the minimum for a major league player was $6,000 (an increase of only $1,000 since 1947).

1968—Players agreed not to sign 1969 contracts until a benefits plan (pensions and health insurance) agreement could be reached. This was the first mass holdout in baseball history. The minimum salary was increased to $10,000.

1970—The Players Association negotiated a grievance and arbitration procedure with the owners.

1970—Curt Flood refused to leave the St. Louis Cardinals for Philadelphia.

1972—The Supreme Court ruled 5–3 against Flood.

1972—The first strike in the history of professional sports, lasting thirteen days. (Overall, there were four strikes in the preseason and nine during the season.) As a result, the owners added $500,000 to the health care insurance and agreed to a cost-of-living increase in retirement benefits. The average salary was $22,000, and the minimum salary was $13,500.

1974—Jim "Catfish" Hunter became a free agent. As a result, he left his $100,000 salary with Oakland for $750,000 with the Yankees.

1975—Andy Messersmith and Dave McNally became free agents.

1976—Free agency rights were created in the contracts of baseball. The average salary at this time was $51,500.

1979—The average salary was $113,558.

1980—A new pension agreement increased all benefits. The owners' contribution to the pension plan was one-third of the national television and radio package.

1981—A strike occurred for fifty days because the owners demanded restricted free agency (compensation for the loss of a free agent), which would have lost what the players had won in 1976. The players lost $34 million (an average of $52,000 each) in the strike, but they won by retaining free agency. The average salary at this time was $186,000.

1985—The average salary was $371,000.

1989—The average salary was $489,000.

1990—The average salary was $597,000, with the minimum salary at $100,000. The combined salaries for major leaguers was $388 million, and the owners' combined revenues were $1.5 billion (players thus received 26 percent of the revenues they generated).

1992—The average salary was $1 million.

1994 to 1995—A 232-day shutdown of the MLB with no World Series in 1994. After a delay of the 1995 season and still no labor agreement, attendance for the season was down around 18 percent and television audiences were off by 11 percent.

1998—Congress passed the Curt Flood Act, a compromise that amended the special exemptions from antitrust for major league players but excluded minor league players and baseball owners from dealing with communities over franchise location.

2001—The owners voted to eliminate two teams.

2001—The average player salary was $2.29 million.

2006—The average player salary was $2.69 million.

2014—The average player salary was $3.9 million.

2017—The average player salary was $4.47 million.

2022—The average player salary was $4.41 million.

the players."[32] As recently as the 2022 season, there was an owner-imposed lockout in MLB which lasted 99 days.

The NFL did not have as far to go as the MLB did because players were already allowed to play out their option. The obstacle, as we noted earlier, was the Rozelle Rule, which was voided after two court cases. The first occurred when an NFL quarterback signed a nonstandard contract with the New England Patriots and it was voided by Commissioner Rozelle. The player gave up his career and sued the league. A district court judge ruled in the athlete's favor, saying that the standard player contract violated federal antitrust laws and that the Rozelle Rule was illegal.

That case involved an individual player rather than the entire NFL system and was subject to a prolonged appeal process, so the NFL Players Association brought suit to change the system for all players. A federal court judge decided that the Rozelle Rule was illegal. He directed the NFL and all of its teams to cease enforcing the rule. The result was that twenty-four new free agents began searching for the best offers.

The NFL Players Association conducted two strikes—one in 1987 missing forty-two games—demanding free agency and $18 million for the pension fund. The strike failed as the owners hired replacement players, the networks televised the games, and public opinion sided with the owners. The strike cost the players $79 million in lost salaries and the owners $42 million in fewer ticket sales and $60 million in rebates to the television networks.

Although the players lost this battle, in 2001 the owners and the players' union agreed to a three-year extension of the collective bargaining agreement that ensured labor peace until 2006. A war of words and actions over a new labor agreement began in earnest months before the 2006 contract expired. The owners threatened to lock out the players, and the union decertified and filed an antitrust suit against the owners. Despite their differences, the NFL commissioner and NFL Players Association negotiated a five-year contract that expired in 2011. Under that agreement players received 63 percent of the NFL's designated gross revenue and had a rich benefits package. This revenue sharing was especially lucrative given the multibillion-dollar television package that was in force.[33]

Another contentious round of negotiations took place in 2011 between NFL owners and the NFL Players Association over a new contract for future years. Once again, the owners imposed a lockout and the NFL Players Association decertified, as both groups struggled for the upper hand. This is not the place for a detailed account of the various strategies the two sides used in the negotiations that took place over several months; suffice it to say that the players and owners finally came to an agreement with a new ten-year collective bargaining agreement. Another agreement was made in 2020, in effect until 2030, although this only passed by 60 player votes; an item of contention was the potential that owners could schedule an additional game to the season which some viewed as too physically demanding.[34]

Historically, negotiations within the NBA, unlike those in the NFL and MLB, have been characterized by considerable cooperation between owners and athletes. Agreements have also been much more progressive. This spirit of cooperation on the part of the owners, however, has been prompted by the clear messages of the court decisions in the other sports: owners may no longer treat their players as highly paid slaves.

In 1995, after the NBA Players Association negotiated a deal with the league, a number of high-profile athletes (e.g., Michael Jordan, Patrick Ewing) led an attempt by the players to decertify the union. The union members voted against this effort, followed by the owners' ratification of the collective bargaining agreement. This new plan allowed a dramatic increase in the salary cap, taking the average player salary to nearly $3 million by the conclusion of the contract; decreased the amount of rookie contracts; and guaranteed all first-round choices three-year deals, after which they become free agents. A collective bargaining agreement made in 2005 expired following completion of the 2010–2011 season. After prolonged negotiations, a new ten-year NBA contract, due to expire in 2022, was made. In 2017, another agreement was made which runs through the 2023-2024 season.

AMATEUR SPORT AS A BUSINESS

The trend toward greater bureaucratization, commercialization, and institutionalism—the trend toward corporate sport—is not restricted to professional sports; it is also true of much of organized amateur sport. Analysis of the sports industry must therefore deal with both amateur and professional categories of sports, although in reality they are often virtually indistinguishable.

The amateur concept was a product of the late-eighteenth-century leisure class in Britain and the United States where the ideal of an aristocratic sportsman was part of the pursuit of conspicuous consumption. Consequently, to be a pure amateur required independent wealth because the true amateur derived no income from his sports participation. Explicit in the amateur ideal was the belief that one's sports endeavor must be unrelated to one's work or livelihood and that sport itself is somehow sullied, tarnished, or demeaned if one is paid for performing it.

In fact, the distinction between professional and amateur sport has always been largely artificial. Over the past century this has gradually been recognized throughout the sports world, and the archaic idea that amateurs and professionals cannot compete against each other has largely been laid to rest. Even the Olympic movement, through the various international sport organizations, has eliminated the requirement that competing athletes must be amateurs and not professionals. In a few other sport organizations, however, the distinction is still made, but it is usually applied inconsistently.

THE AMBIGUOUS CASE: INTERCOLLEGIATE SPORTS AND AMATEURISM

In Chapters 2 and 10 we described the rise of intercollegiate sports from a thoroughly amateur student-centered and student-controlled activity to the massive commercial industry that now exists. As college sports became more popular and more commercial, it became impossible to deny that they had become a big business enterprise. Its member institutions are dependent on attracting outstanding high school athletes for its sports teams, and this is done by subsidizing them with what is called an *athletic scholarship*. Ignoring for the moment the long-range value of a college degree, the typical U.S. athletic scholarship (a legal maximum of room, books, board, tuition, and fees, as specified by the NCAA) has an annual value of $25,000 at a state-supported school with low tuition and near $70,000 at a private school with high tuition.

College athletic scholarships do not constitute incomes comparable to professional contracts; nevertheless, college athletes are being compensated financially for their sports exploits. Thus, the distinction between amateur and professional sport is primarily one of degree. However, subsidization in the way of an athletic scholarship has not kept up with the colossal sums of money that currently characterize NCAA big-time college sports. For example, the NCAA's annual television rights alone will generate more than $870 million in 2022, and many coaches whose teams play in the NCAA Division I basketball tournament will have salaries exceeding $2 million. One coach, Bill Self from the University of Kansas, took home over $10 million in 2022, while John Calipari from the University of

Kentucky made over $8 million in this year. In terms of NCAA football, 86 head college football coaches in 2021 collected paychecks worth over $1 million; seven coaches pocketed more than $7 million in this year with Alabama's Nick Saban taking home close to $10 million.[35] Major university athletic departments currently manage yearly budgets in excess of $190 million.[36]

But the NCAA athletic scholarship status has changed significantly in the past decade. As we discussed in Chapter 10, a surprising action taken by the NCAA in 2014 scrapped the historical opposition to paying college athletes. The NCAA Division I Board of Directors passed a new model giving five major conferences—SEC, ACC, Big Ten, Pac-12, and Big 12—the authority to increase their athletic scholarships to cover athletes' full cost of attendance, which will be several thousand dollars more per athlete than colleges currently provide. The pay increase is structured as a stipend, not a formal system of salaries to athletes. More recently, the NCAA has been successfully challenged in court (see Chapter 10) and now athletes will be able to profit from their NIL. This is a huge shift for the NCAA and its version of amateurism and it is difficult to predict how this may change the business of collegiate athletics.

THE ECONOMICS OF COLLEGIATE SPORT

The intercollegiate sports system, initially student organized and student run, came under the control of school administrators early in the twentieth century. It has since become a major business industry, generating, as noted in this chapter and in Chapter 10, hundreds of millions of dollars in individual university budgets, millions of dollars for football bowl appearances, and lucrative television contracts for men's basketball.

Operating a big-time collegiate athletic program as a business proposition has not been profitable for most individual colleges and universities. Various responses to financial crises have been made by universities and the NCAA. The NCAA has responded by permitting first-year students to compete at the varsity level, reducing the maximum number of scholarships that each institution may annually award and eliminating the "laundry" allowance once given to scholarship athletes each month.

Some universities have even reduced their commitment to intercollegiate athletics, either by de-emphasizing the level of competition in their athletic programs or by dropping support for specific (typically nonrevenue) sports, such as golf, tennis, swimming, wrestling, soccer, rugby, and lacrosse. This was explained in Chapter 10.

In universities where sports have been dropped by university athletic administrations as financially prohibitive, some have been reinstituted as student-initiated "club sports," which are student run without any real institutional assistance, thus moving them back to their original level: organized sport.

When financial losses have occurred or have been impending, many athletic departments have redoubled their efforts to remain competitive and thus approach fiscal solvency. One common strategy has been to fire the incumbent coach, typically of football or basketball, and to replace him or her—often with a public statement that "we are moving in a different direction"—with another coach who promises to reverse the institution's athletic fortunes. The new coach inevitably negotiates an agreement that the institution intends to make a commitment of greater financial outlays to support the new and invigorated program. The characteristic consequence of this strategy of escalating financial costs is that it further intensifies the pressures on coaches to recruit athletes legally and illegally while the administrators at the institution often ignore what is happening.

The lure of money affects even athletic programs below the big-time level. A common practice is for institutions that devote fewer resources to intercollegiate sports to schedule major university football or

A Texas Christian University Horned Frogs guard makes a pass from the baseline as an Oklahoma Sooners forward defends it. (Photo: Cal Sport Media/Alamy Stock Photo)

basketball teams, so-called big-time teams, just for a guaranteed fee. Both institutions benefit from such an arrangement. The smaller universities make relatively big money, and the big-time university teams add to their winning records and pocket most of the gate receipts.

The extensive financial involvement of American colleges and universities in sports makes it difficult to distinguish their operations from openly professional sports enterprises. In fact, the average game attendance of many universities in football and basketball exceeds that of professional teams. As mentioned earlier, the money paid to college athletes in the form of athletic scholarships raises the question of how they are to be distinguished from professionals. In other words, the money an admitted professional athlete receives is merely greater than that paid the typical college player—although the professional player is not confronted with the necessity of diverting energies to studies or to the hassle of remaining academically eligible, and the professional is free to devote himself or herself solely to developing sports skills.

Not surprisingly, collusive practices have infiltrated college athletics because the professional–amateur distinction is difficult to make realistically. A free market does not exist for college athletes; they are subject to severe restrictions by the NCAA, which functions as a cartel. NCAA regulations regarding recruiting, scholarships, and eligibility are collusive, and as with the reserve clause in professional sports, their effect is to prevent one team from raiding another for players. Although colleges have not yet fully rationalized procedures to the point of instituting a draft of eligible high school and community college players, fierce competition exists. The national and conference letters of intent that all recruited athletes must sign require an athlete to declare his or her intention of enrolling in and competing for a specific university. This has the effect of insulating a given university from competition for an athlete by other universities in its conference.[37]

The effect of such practices is advantageous for competing universities; it enables them to restrict their feverish recruiting of high school talent to a few months of the year. NCAA rules also preclude "tampering" with athletes who have already committed to attend and play at a university. A university cannot recruit an athlete already attending another university unless the athlete is willing to be penalized by being declared ineligible for a year. Only recently have NCAA rules relaxed regarding student-athletes transferring between institutions, although there remain certain restrictions; it has generally been the case that control and restrictions have applied only to the athletes rather than to the coaches of intercollegiate teams. Indeed, coaches are even able to break their employment contracts at the university where they are coaching to accept better coaching offers at another university, hence the preponderance of high buyout clauses in coaching contracts.

In Chapter 10 we explained how NCAA regulations also seriously limit the freedom of college athletes. The effect of these NCAA regulations is to allow American colleges to conduct their sports programs in a monopolistic manner by regulating and limiting the freedom of athletes, which includes regulating the length of and criteria for participation and restrictions on player mobility.[38]

For the few who have the ability and skill, collegiate sports participation has historically been the prelude to professional competition in basketball and football, whereas this has been infrequently (although increasingly) the case in baseball and ice hockey. Although the minor league systems of the MLB and the NHL have diminished considerably from their heydays after World War II, they are still much more extensive than those of any other major professional team sports. For a professional baseball or hockey player not to have served at least a minimal apprenticeship in the minor leagues is highly atypical; however, for a professional basketball or football player to have done so is highly atypical.

Awareness of the commercialism that now exists in collegiate sports, and of their function as minor leagues, or training grounds, for a future professional sports career, has led to the suggestion that the professionalism of collegiate athletics be explicitly recognized. This would be accomplished by having a college athlete's letter of intent be considered a legal contract with the university in the same way that a professional athlete's contract is owned by his or her team. Professional sports league owners desiring the services of a college athlete would have to purchase the contract, thereby reimbursing that university for the cost of player development and training and simultaneously improving the financial position of the university team supplying the pro team with its raw material.

Recognizing this natural source of player development, professional basketball and football leagues have entered into informal agreements with colleges and universities. The NBA has established an age limit and a "one year out of high school" rule that prohibit teams from drafting players. Top high school players who qualify academically can enroll in college, play one year of college basketball—called "one and done"—and then bolt to the NBA. For a football athlete to be eligible for the NFL draft, at least three years must have passed since he graduated from high school. The NCAA allows college players to "test the waters" of the NFL draft once while they are in college. However, if a player makes any kind of agreement to be represented by a player agent or accepts anything from an agent or anyone working for an agent, the NCAA will void all his remaining college eligibility.[39]

The NCAA has always vigorously opposed college athletes leaving early for professional careers. It reluctantly allows this practice only because its legal advisors have cautioned that attempts to prohibit it would not stand up in court.

GAMBLING AND SPORTS

We now turn to a topic that has close connections with the highly competitive, commercial, and corporatized sport that is currently so popular in the United States—gambling. Sports gambling is an economic activity with a history that dates back to antiquity. Betting on sports events was popular with the ancient Greeks 500 years before the birth of Christ, and it was popular in all of their Pan-Hellenic Games—one of which was the Olympic Games. Gambling reached some incredible extremes at the Roman chariot races, with rampant corruption and fixed races. Horse racing was the most popular sport

in colonial North America, and one reason for its popularity was the opportunity the races provided to bet on the outcome.

Gambling is a form of entertainment with excitement, risk taking, and challenge that appeals to many people, and in the United States most moral sanctions against gambling and laws outlawing gambling have largely disappeared. More than 75 percent of North American adults gamble at least once each year. Until 2018, there were not many legal venues to participate in sports gambling in the United States. Nonetheless, people gambled and they annually bet at least $150 billion a year on sports illegally as a result of the 1992 federal prohibition on sports betting largely outside of Nevada. They wager an estimated $500 billion legally (not counting most sports gambling, Internet gambling, or poker). In the following, we will discuss the boom in legal sports betting since the 2018 Supreme Court ruling.

Gambling is growing at a phenomenal rate in the United States, and one reason for this is that there are now more opportunities to gamble than ever before. Some form of gambling is now legal in forty-eight states (gambling is completely illegal in Utah and Hawaii).[40]

Approximately 500 Native American gaming facilities dot tribal land in twenty-eight states. Forty-three states and the District of Columbia have enacted lotteries; more than eighty riverboat or dockside casinos ply the water or sit at berth in several states. The nation wagers more than $45 billion annually in state lotteries.

Internet wagering is the fastest-growing new form of gambling and has become a major force in the gambling industry. In 2013 Delaware, Nevada, and New Jersey became the first three states in the country to legalize Internet gaming. Total online gambling revenue generated from U.S. residents is estimated at nearly $11 billion annually.[41]

ISSUES ABOUT SPORTS BETTING IN THE UNITED STATES

Sports betting in the United States got a boon when the Supreme Court overturned the federal ban on it in 2018. At that point, only Nevada had legal status for sports betting. Currently, twenty-five states and

Washington, D.C., have legalized sport gambling. This means that since 2018, 100 million people now have legal access to sports gambling. The market generated $1 billion in 2020 and is likely to grow.[42] The 2021 Super Bowl had 4.3 billion bets on the game, while 47 million people placed bets on the NCAA's March Madness tournament in 2021.

The business around sports betting is booming. Two platforms, FanDuel and DraftKings, are prominent. DraftKings generated $614 million in 2020 and is expected to reach $1 billion in 2021. FanDuel's revenue for 2020 was $896 million, up 81 percent from 2019. Not surprisingly, others are interested in becoming part of the gambling industry. In fact, sport leagues are selling data to betting companies. It has been reported that the NBA has a six-year contract for more than $250 million with one such company but has contracts with many more. NFL franchises are following suit and have signed at least eleven deals.[43] For example, MGM became the "official gaming partner" of the New York Jets and of MLB and the LPGA. The NHL has a partnership with Sportradar and other sports betting companies. The WNBA's Phoenix Mercury have a contract with Bally's.[44] No doubt this trend will continue as the gambling industry grows. Additionally, sports betting could be a benefit to the mediated sport industry as more people may tune in to the games they are wagering on.

SPORTS GAMBLING AND COLLEGE STUDENTS

A recent study by the Annenberg Foundation reported that more than 47 percent of young people ages fourteen to twenty-two bet on sports events at least once per month. The National Council on Problem Gaming is concerned that gambling problems may rise since sports gambling is now legal and because access is facilitated through mobile and online means.[45] Even more troubling, sports gambling is rampant and prospering on campuses throughout the country, and the majority of bookies are students. One writer referred to this phenomenon as "the dirty little secret on college campuses"; another referred to it as a "silent addiction" for many college students. Estimates of sports betting by college students range between 30 and 50 percent of male

In 2018, the Supreme Court of the United States cleared the way for sports betting to become legal. This decision along with the new mobile apps such as FanDuel and DraftKings will increase the popularity of sports betting. (Photo: Bloomberg / Getty Images)

college students and between 10 and 20 percent of female students.

The NCAA has been a vigorous critic of all forms of legal and illegal sports gambling, but its football and basketball games are favorites of sports bettors. The NCAA prohibits athletics department staff members and student-athletes from engaging in gambling activities as they relate to intercollegiate or professional sporting events. But that policy has not deterred some student-athletes. One study of more than 600 Division I men's football and basketball players found that 72 percent had gambled in some form, 25 percent had gambled money on other college sports events, and 4 percent had bet money on a game in which they had played. Another study assessed gambling on college and professional sports by college students classified as athletes, sports fans, and other students at colleges with students expressing differing levels of "sports interest." All groups—athletes, sports fans, and other students—had higher rates of gambling at colleges with higher sports interest. Athletes and sports fans—both male and female—reported more sports gambling than other students. The NCAA still bans its student-athletes and those working in college sports from betting on NCAA sports. This is done to curb gambling problems, but also to reduce cheating. Nonetheless, others can bet on NCAA sports (depending on what state you live

Gambling on sports events dates back to the ancient Greeks and Romans. Sports gambling is popular with all adult age groups, and betting takes place on virtually every sport. A major problem with sports gambling is the inevitable issue of compulsive, addictive gambling. (Photo: AP Photo/*Las Vegas Review-Journal*, Chase Stevens)

in), but most states do not allow bets on in-state college teams.

The popularity of intercollegiate football and basketball, and the naiveté and financial desperation of many college athletes, have made these sports attractive for professional gamblers. College football and basketball have gone through a series of fixing and point-shaving scandals during the past decade. During the late 1990s thirteen Boston College football players were suspended for betting on college and pro football. Two players bet against their team in a loss to Syracuse University. Between 2003 and 2006 two University of Toledo football and basketball players were charged with attempting to fix games through bribes and shaving points in games. In 2019, two UNC Greensboro staff in the athletics department were placing bets on college sport. The athletics department was fined and put on three year probation because it was evident that others new of the gambling but did not report it.[46]

Wherever gambling on sports takes place, the specter of cheating is always a companion. A colonial America historian documented a horse-racing fix scandal in 1674. One of the most stunning professional sports fixing scandals occurred in the 1919 MLB World Series and involved Chicago White Sox players. Once the fixing was discovered, that team became known as the Black Sox. Pete Rose, the record holder for the most hits in the MLB, was banned from baseball when it was discovered he had bet on MLB games.

Considering their current popularity and the huge sums of money bet on them, professional sports have been relatively free of cheating scandals—Chicago

White Sox players conspiring to fix the 1919 World Series and MLB player Pete Rose being permanently banned from baseball for gambling on MLB games are the two most notorious cases. Other cases do exist and sometimes include referees. In 2007 NBA referee Tim Donaghy admitted that he had been making bets on NBA games—including games that he refereed—for four years and, furthermore, that he had tipped off professional gamblers with inside information.[47]

With sports gambling, just as with any other form of gambling, there is the inevitable issue of compulsive, addictive gambling. According to the National Council on Problem Gaming, sports bettors have higher rates (nearly twice the level) of gambling problems than other gamblers and they predict that gambling problems will increase with online betting.[48] Obtaining an accurate number of compulsive gamblers is extremely difficult, but several agencies and organizations that have conducted surveys of these conditions estimate that 1.0 to 3.5 percent of the U.S. population (3 million to 10.5 million) are pathological gamblers, and this disorder is more common in men than in women. Extensive research at the Center for Compulsive Gambling clearly shows that wherever there is availability and opportunity for gambling, compulsive gambling problems increase accordingly. Thus, current trends and future predictions suggest that a growing social problem for both sport and the larger society will likely be large numbers of tragic compulsive gamblers; many of these will be sports gamblers.[49]

SUMMARY

We have shown the economic side of American sport in this chapter. The message is clear: corporate sport is a multimillion-dollar enterprise selling sporting events and a variety of ancillary products. Indeed, it is big business. The owners of professional teams are in a constant search for better markets and higher profits. The possibility that a franchise will move increases the probability that municipalities will provide facilities or other inducements at taxpayers' expense to entice teams to their city or to encourage them to remain there.

Professional sports have sold out to the demands of television. In return for large TV rights contracts, the leagues allow the television networks to dictate schedules, time outs, and the like. But without those contracts, professional sports would be a small, struggling industry.

Professional sports owners seek as much money as they can from fans and taxpayers. The principle of supply and demand operates in setting admission charges for athletic events. If sport were truly a public service, as the sports industry often claims, rather than a business, the most successful teams would charge the lowest ticket prices, but this is not the case.

Professional athletes demand high salaries and other monetary inducements (bonuses, retirement benefits, insurance policies, interest-free loans, and so forth). The frequent result is pugnacious negotiations between owners and athletes. An ongoing struggle exists between athletes (through unionlike organizations) and entrepreneurs for the power to regulate sports and to apportion profits. This is manifested in court battles, player strikes, owner lockouts, and press agencies by both sides attempting to sway public opinion.

College sports have evolved from mostly a student recreation to a major business industry. Big-time intercollegiate sports are merely another form of professional sports. Intercollegiate sports serve not only as a minor league farm system for many professional sports but also as a public relations avenue for future pro stars.

Gambling has close connections with the highly competitive, commercial, and corporatized sport that is currently so popular in the United States. With the 2018 Supreme Court decision that struck down a federal ban on sports betting, the industry has grown and illustrates the interrelationship between entertainment, sport, and media. Sports gambling is common and prospering on college campuses, and the majority of bookies are students. In short, the economics of professional sport has become similar to that of the world of work. As such, it reveals, in microcosm, the values of the larger society. The result is the ultimate loss of sport as a meaningful, joyous activity in itself.

Learn more with this chapter's digital tools, including web resources, video links, and chapter self-assessment quizzes at www.oup.com/he/sage-eitzen-beal-atencio-12e.

NOTES

1. Sam Riches, "Imagining an America without Sports," *Pacific Standard*, January 20, 2015, https://psmag.com/social-justice/imagining-america-without-sports-98627.

2. "Nike, Inc. Reports Fiscal 2021 Fourth Quarter and Full Year Results," Nike.com, June 24, 2021, https://investors.nike.com/investors/news-events-and-reports/investor-news/investor-news-%ADdetails/2021/NIKE-Inc.-Reports-Fiscal-2021-Fourth-Quarter-and-Full-Year-Results/default.aspx.

3. "Sports Industry, Teams, Leagues & Recreation Market Research" (Houston, TX: Plunkett Research, 2017), https://www.plunkettresearch.com/industries/sports-recreation-leisure-market-research/.

4. *American Needle, Inc., v. National Football League et al.*, No. 08–661. U.S. (2010).

5. James Quirk and Rodney Fort, *Hard Ball: The Abuse of Power in Pro Team Sports* (Princeton, NJ: Princeton University Press, 2010), 9.

6. Robert Faturechi, Justin Elliott, and Ellis Simani, "The Billionaire Playbook: How Sports Owners Use Their Teams to Avoid Millions in Taxes," *ProPublica*, July 8, 2021, https://www.propublica.org/article/the-billionaire-playbook-how-sports-owners-use-their-teams-to-avoid-millions-in-taxes.

7. Faturechi, Elliott, and Simani, "The Billionaire Playbook."

8. Andrew Zimbalist, *The Bottom Line: Observations and Arguments on the Sports Business* (Philadelphia: Temple University Press, 2006), 29–30; see also Neil Longley, *An Absence of Competition: The Sustained Competitive Advantage of the Monopoly Sports Leagues* (New York: Springer, 2013).

9. Zimbalist, *The Bottom Line*, 130–170; see also Neil deMause and Joanna Cagan, *Field of Schemes: How the Great Stadium Swindle Turns Public Money into Private Profit*, revised and expanded ed. (Lincoln: University of Nebraska Press, 2008).

10. Quoted in Travis Waldron, "Should Taxpayers Subsidize Sports Stadiums?," ThinkProgress, February 11, 2013, http://thinkprogress.org/alyssa/2012/09/07/814991/should-taxpayers-subsidize-sports-stadiums/; see also Dennis Coates and Brad R Humphreys, "Do Economists Reach a Conclusion on Subsidies for Sports, Franchises, Stadiums, and Mega-Events?," *Econ Journal Watch* 5, no. 3 (2008): 294–315.

11. Gregg Easterbrook, "How the NFL Fleeces Taxpayers," *The Atlantic*, October 15, 2013, 44–50; see also Emily Maltby and Sean Gregory, "Loser's Game: The Public Cost of Pro-Sports Stadiums," *Time*, December 9, 2013, 14–15.

12. Brent Schrotenboer, "Abandoned Cities Woo Other Sports," *USA Today*, March 28, 2017, 6C; see also Associated Press, "Rams Headed Back to Los Angeles; Chargers Have Option to Join," ESPN, January 13, 2016, http://www.espn.com/nfl/story/_/id/14558668/st-louis-rams-relocate-los-angeles.

13. Jabari Young, November 24, 2021, NFL and Rams reach $790 million settlement in St. Louis relocation case, CNBC, https://www.cnbc.com/2021/11/24/nfl-and-rams-reach-more-than-700-million-settlement-in-st-louis-relocation-case-report-says.html accessed June 15, 2022

14. Meris Lutz and J. Scott Trubey, "A Tale of Two Atlanta Stadiums: Political Fortunes Rise, Fall in Deals," *Atlanta Journal-Constitution*, August 13, 2016, http://www.myajc.com/news/tale-two-atlanta-stadiums-political-fortunes-rise-fall-deals/y41UynoxhimNXt4VaDRIoO/.

15. Brent Schrotenboer, "Gambling Issues Await Raiders," *USA Today*, May 4, 2017, 1C, 6C.

16. Michael Farren and Thomas Savidge, "A Win for San Diego," *U.S. News and World Report*, November 14, 2016, https://www.usnews.com/opinion/articles/2016-11-14/san-diego-voters-wisely-reject-new-chargers-stadium; see also Brent Schrotenboer, "It's Time for Chargers to Decide Whether to Stay, Go," *USA Today*, January 11, 2017, 4C.

17. Coates and Humphreys, "Do Economists Reach a Conclusion," 296; Pat Garofalo and Travis Waldron, "If You Build It, They Might Not Come: The Risky Economics of Sports Stadiums," *The Atlantic*, September 7, 2012.

18. Judy Lin, "With Vote, Sacramento Kings to Build New NBA Arena," *Yahoo News*, May 21, 2014,

https://news.yahoo.com/vote-sacramento-kings-build-nba-arena-080350552–spt.html/.

19. Jeff Zillgitt, "Bill Passed, Bucks Gaining Momentum," *USA Today*, July 30, 2015, 9C.

20. Gabe Lacques, "From Baseball to Beer, Braves' New Home a Marvel," *USA Today*, April 14, 2017, 4C.

21. Quoted in Garofalo and Waldron, "If You Build It, They Might Not Come"; see also Brent Schrotenboer, "Taxing Tourists Has Critics," *USA Today*, August 23, 2016, 1C, 4C.

22. Michael T. Friedman, "'The Transparency of Democracy': The Production of Washington's Nationals Park as a Late Capitalist Space," *Sociology of Sport Journal* 27 (2010): 327–350.

23. Dave Zirin, "What Owners Owe Us," *The Progressive Populist*, September 1, 2010, 21; see also Sean Conboy, "Welfare Kings Roger Goodell and the NFL Owners Are Crying Poverty and Playing Politics Once Again," *Pittsburgh Magazine*, September 24, 2012.

24. Austin Smith, "The Lords of Lambeau," *Harper's Magazine*, January 2017, 51–63.

25. Brett Knight and Justin Birnbaum, "Highest-Paid Athletes: The Top 50 Sports Stars Combined to Make Nearly $2.8 Billion in a Year of Records," *Forbes*, 2021, https://www.forbes.com/athletes/. Accessed July 16, 2021

26. Jorge L. Ortiz, "Minor Leaguers Seeking Major Life," *USA Today*, April 23, 2015, 7C.

27. Associated Press, June 3, 2022, "Los Angeles Dodgers Open With $310 Million Payroll, Set to Pay Record $47 Million Tax Bill, https://www.espn.com/mlb/story/_/id/34033460/los-angeles-dodgers-open-310-million-payroll-set-pay-record-47-million-tax-bill, accessed June 15, 2022.

28. Andrew Lisa, February 7,2022, Is Hosting the Super Bowl Worth it for Cities?, gobankingrates, https://www.gobankingrates.com/money/economy/is-hosting-the-super-bowl-worth-it/ accessed June 15, 2022

29. Eric Reed & Kirk O'Neil, Feb 11, 2022, Super Bowl Revenue: How Much Does the Big Game Generate? https://www.thestreet.com/lifestyle/sports/super-bowl-revenue, accessed June 15, 2022

30. "How Much Money Will Be Bet on the Super Bowl in 2022?," The Lines, February 13, 2022, https://www.thelines.com/super-bowl-how-much-money-bet/.

31. David Broughton, Naming-rights deals thrive, Sports Business Journal, August, 2, 2021, https://www.sportsbusinessjournal.com/Journal/Issues/2021/08/02/Portfolio/Sports-marketing.aspx; accessed June 15, 2022

32. Quoted in "Court Says '80s Collusion as Bad as Scandal in '19," *Arizona Republic*, February 15, 2000, 6C; for an interesting account of one MLB player's fight for free agency and its widespread impact, see also Brad Snyder, *A Well-Paid Slave: Curt Flood's Fight for Free Agency in Professional Sports* (New York: Penguin, 2006).

33. Michael Oriard, *Brand NFL: Making and Selling America's Favorite Sport* (Chapel Hill: University of North Carolina Press, 2010).

34. Dan Graziano, March 15, 2020, NFL CBA approved: What players get in new deal, how expanded playoffs and schedule will work, ESPN, https://www.espn.com/nfl/story/_/id/28901832/nfl-cba-approved-players-get-new-deal-how-expanded-playoffs-schedule-work, accessed June 4, 2022

35. Jeff Faraudo, October 15, 2021, Sports Illustrated, Once Again, College Football Coaching Salaries Are Hard to Wrap Your Head Around, https://www.si.com/college/cal/news/2021-coaching-salaries accessed June 15, 2022. Ryan Hannable, *Top College Basketball Head Coach Salaries.* BETMGM, July 26, 2022, https://sports.betmgm.com/en/blog/ncaab/top-college-basketball-head-coach-salaries-bm10/.

36. Brad Crawford, "Ranking College Sports' Highest Revenue Producers," 24/7sports.com, July 17, 2020, https://247sports.com/LongFormArticle/College-football-revenue-producers-USA-Today-Texas-Longhorns-Ohio-State-Buckeyes-Alabama-Crimson-Tide-149248012/#149248012_1

37. Gilbert M. Gaul, *Billion-Dollar Ball: A Journey through the Big-Money Culture of College Football* (New York: Penguin, 2015); see also Jay M. Smith, *Cheated: The UNC Scandal, the Education of Athletes, and the Future of Big-Time College Sports* (Lincoln, NB: Potomac Books, 2015).

38. Howard L Nixon, *The Athletic Trap: How College Sports Corrupted the Academy* (Baltimore: Johns Hopkins University Press, 2014); see also Ronald A Smith, *Pay for Play: A History of Big-Time Athletic Reform* (Champaign: University of Illinois Press, 2010).

39. B. David Ridpath, "Ben Simmons Is Half Right, but 'One and Done' Is Not the Main Problem," *Forbes*, November 6, 2016, https://www.forbes.com/sites/bdavidridpath/2016/11/06/ben-simmons-is-half-right-but-one-and-done-is-not-the-main-problem/#31afd4201242.

40. Sam Skolnik, *High Stakes: The Rising Cost of America's Gambling Addiction* (Boston: Beacon Press, 2011); see also William N. Thompson, *Gambling in America: An Encyclopedia of History, Issues, and Society*, 2nd ed. (Santa Barbara, CA: ABC–CLIO, 2015).

41. Alexandra Berson, "So, You Think You Know the Gambling Business?" *Wall Street Journal*, September 14, 2016, http://graphics.wsj.com/quiz/index.php?standalone=1&slug=trquiz10192016.

42. Jeff Bell, "Not Just A Game: Online Sports Betting and the Rise of Corrosive Technology," *Forbes*, February 25, 2021, https://www.forbes.com/sites/forbestechcouncil/2021/02/25/not-just-a-game-online-sports-betting-and-the-rise-of-corrosive-technology/?sh=110853170ec. See also Marie Fazio, "It's Easy (and Legal) to Bet on Sports. Do Young Adults Know the Risks?" *NY Times*, April 1, 2021, https://www.nytimes.com/2021/04/01/sports/sports-betting-addiction.html.

43. Khristopher J. Brooks, "Sports Gambling Has Soared during the Pandemic and Continues to Climb," CBS News, March 29, 2021, https://www.cbsnews.com/news/sports-gambling-betting-draft-kings-fanduel-american-gaming-association/; see also Alice Hancock and Sara Germano, "Paying for the Pandemic: US Politicians Gamble on Sports Betting," *Financial Times*, April 12, 2021, https://www.ft.com/content/bb04b14c-e215-4ae8-a655-2bf85fcb73c0.

44. American Gaming Association, "Gaming-Sports Partnerships," July 6, 2021, https://www.american-gaming.org/wp-content/uploads/2021/07/Partnership-Tracker-7.9.21.pdf.

45. Bell, "Not Just a Game."

46. Grant Lucas, August 5, 2019, NCAA Drops Betting Hammer, Highlighting Who Exactly cannot Wager on College Sports, The Lines, https://www.the-lines.com/ncaa-sports-betting-rules/ accessed June 15, 2022

47. Sean Patrick Griffin, *Gaming the Game: The Story behind the NBA Betting Scandal and the Gambler Who Made It Happen* (Fort Lee, NJ: Barricade Books, 2011); see also Tim Donaghy, *Personal Foul: A First-Person Account of the Scandal That Rocked the NBA* (New York: Simon & Schuster, 2008).

48. Bell, "Not Just a Game."

49. Leighton Vaughan Williams and Donald S. Siegel, eds., *The Oxford Handbook of the Economics of Gambling* (New York: Oxford University Press, 2013); Hale Humphrey, *This Must Be Hell: A Look at Pathological Gambling* (Bloomington, IN: iUniverse, 2009); see also Rex M. Rogers, *Gambling: Don't Bet on It* (Grand Rapids, MI: Kregel, 2005).

CHAPTER 12

SPORT AND THE MASS MEDIA

Essentially, ESPN is in the business of building athletes into superheroes, because, like Walt Disney Pictures, it is in the business of building blockbusters.

—DEREK THOMPSON[1]

Television camera operators working from the playing field. The most dramatic programming trend in television during the past twenty years has been the enormous increase in sports coverage. All major sporting events
are covered with dozens of TV camera operators. (Photo: © Paul Brennan/Shutterstock.com)

Social institutions that appear to be independent of one another frequently are found, on closer examination, to be very interdependent. Such is the case of sport and the mass media, although the former is concerned with physical action, skill in a highly problematic task, and the outcome of a competitive event, whereas the latter communicates information and entertains. Both commercial sports and the printed and electronic media are preeminently commercial industries that constitute two of the most successful businesses in the United States. Thus, the goal (and logic) of both is mainly economic profit. As one sports management scholar noted, "We live in a world that is saturated by sport media, the result of a . . . cultural and commercial relationship between these two massive industries."[2]

SOCIAL ROLES OF THE MASS MEDIA

The term *mass media* refers to all of the print (newspapers, magazines, and books) and electronic (radio, satellite radio, television, movies, and the Internet) means of communication that carry information to widespread audiences. Advertising falls into both categories, and it is also a component of mass media.

Over the past decade, new technologies have changed the viewing and listening habits of people. For example, media consumers have shifted toward digital images on their computers and portable devices and away from radio and television. Social media—Facebook, YouTube, Twitter, Instagram, texting—and Internet browsing have become the preferred media sources, while most newspapers and magazines now have strong Internet presences.

PROMINENT AND SUBTLE ROLES OF THE MEDIA

One of the prominent roles of the mass media is the communication of information. Culture depends on communication; indeed, culture cannot exist without an effective system of transmitting and disseminating information. In small, primitive societies information is transmitted by direct one-to-one, face-to-face contact, but this form of information transmission is efficient only in a society of limited

geographical size with a sparse population. Modern societies require complex networks of printed and electronic media to keep people informed about other people and events. Information binds people to their friends, neighbors, cities, states, and other nations of the world.

Another prominent role of the mass media is to provide entertainment for people from all walks of life. Newspapers carry special features and the comics. Magazines and books offer stories of adventure, humor, and mystery. Radio and television provide a wide variety of entertainment, from music to sporting events. Internet technology, a key form of mass communication, offers everything that the other media offer and indeed often incorporates these platforms; the Internet offers such a stunning variety of everything that it is impossible to try to enumerate all of its entertainment forms.

In performing these two fundamental roles, the mass media fulfill two more subtle roles: providing collective experiences for the members of society and promoting social change. Shared information and entertainment via the media contribute to the socialization of citizens in a particular culture and thus serve to socially integrate persons into that culture. In effect, the messages and images that the media create help shape the national and international cultural environment. Indeed, COVID-19 coverage in the media, through news stories, feature reports, press conferences, and health promotion announcements, recently gripped the attention of most people in the United States and elsewhere. As for social change, media is one of the major features of modernization, on the forefront of reporting social change, while also contributing to it.

MASS MEDIA AND SOCIAL THEORIES

As we have emphasized in previous chapters, social functionalism views society as a vast network of interconnected parts, each helping to maintain the system as a whole. Each component of the system is expected to contribute to stability, social integration, and the promotion of value consensus within the society. To the extent that the mass media provide a collective experience for members of a society, they promote shared values and norms and secure a common consensus among citizens. Thus, they may be said to contribute to society's stability and integration. In short, the mass media are a powerful ideological institution because the messages and images that they create help shape and mold the national and international cultural atmosphere.

In the United States, the media present a more or less standardized version of culture by broadcasting important events and ceremonies, such as press conferences, political campaign debates, inaugurations, parades, and sporting championships, and by covering local, national, and international happenings. Collectively, these promote social cohesion by providing a collective experience for all citizens.

Print and electronic advertising in the media functions to sustain the economy, provide information about services and products, and finance the cost of the media. In this role the media contribute to a socially integrated consumer culture that constructs needs and beliefs about what is necessary to be content and satisfied, in accordance with functionalists' expectations.[3]

Conflict/cultural advocates recognize that the media are a powerful source for forming values and beliefs and for organizing consensus within the United States; indeed, the media are often labeled "the consciousness industry." But ownership of contemporary mass media is in the hands of a few huge corporations, which in turn are owned by wealthy stockholders who maintain close relations, through lobbying endeavors, with politicians at all levels. As Bernie Sanders stated, "Why does the mainstream media see politics as entertainment, and largely ignore the major problems facing our country? Because six multinational corporations control 90 percent of what we see, hear and read."[4]

Profits are paramount, and publishing and broadcasting decisions about what reaches the public are made by a small number of decision-makers who are overwhelmingly White, male, and wealthy. Those decisions often ignore subordinate groups and simultaneously reinforce many of the established attitudes, inequalities, and injustices found in the United States centered on race, gender, ethnicity, age, sexual orientation, disability, and social class.

Conflict/cultural theorists are in agreement with functionalists that the media tend to promote the established social order and reigning consensus, not necessarily out of cynical self-interest or subservience to particular group interests, but certainly as an instrument for the promotion of economically and politically powerful stakeholders. Whereas functionalists consider this arrangement appropriate for social stability, conflict/cultural advocates contend that it tends to promote and sustain the unequal distribution of power and wealth, as well as legitimize existing unequal social relations related to class, gender, and race.

Both functionalist and conflict/cultural theorists agree the mass media nevertheless promote social change as well. The media present information about cutting-edge research, new social practices and values, and critiques of contemporary attitudes and behaviors; in doing this they are supporting social change. The mere reporting of new ideas and events stimulates reinterpretations of the world and promotes changes in many spheres of life.[5]

THE SYMBIOSIS OF MASS MEDIA AND SPORT

All of the roles of the mass media are represented in their association with sports. First, the media supply information about sports—for example, game results and statistics about individual players and teams. Second, they provide exciting entertainment. Reading about, listening to, or watching sporting events allows individuals opportunities to temporarily escape the burdens and frustrations that bind them to reality. We can see this in the way many people acutely felt the absence of live sport programming during the onset of COVID-19 in early 2020, leaving networks consequently scouring the world to find live fare such as Korean baseball and Belarussian soccer.[6] Sport that is provided through various media platforms has the perfect combination for entertainment, including controlled violence, excitement, and lots of audio and visual power.

One of the media's subtle roles—providing collective experiences—is often played out through conversations, both in face-to-face talk and through mobile devices (Facebook, Twitter, Instagram, etc.) about sport. One can ask almost any stranger about sports or well-known sporting events and the stranger will likely know the relevant information because he or she has read about it, heard about it, or seen it in the media; consequently, the conversation can be sustained and sometimes transformed into a more enduring social relationship. Media sport, then, provides a communal focus whereby large segments of the population can share common norms, rituals, ceremonies, and values.

Finally, the media have played a significant role in social change as it relates to sports through the creation and/or promotion of new sports, which run the gamut from pro skateboarding leagues to the CrossFit Games. The media also strive to enhance the popularity of existing sports to the point that they may even initiate rule changes in some cases to serve their purposes (more about this later in the chapter). The media also play a role in promoting specific attitudinal and value changes in sport culture about competition, winning, losing, cheating, and so on.

ENDURING LINKAGES BETWEEN THE MASS MEDIA AND SPORT

Little did the inventors of our technical means of communication realize how their inventions would become associated with sport. Johannes Gutenberg invented movable type in the mid-fifteenth century. As his invention was refined during the following centuries, the ability of the printing press to produce reading material quickly and cheaply increased and made possible the growth of the publishing industry. Wireless telegraphy, invented at the end of the nineteenth century, served as the technological foundation for the various electronic media of today's world.

Newspapers

In the mid-nineteenth century U.S. newspapers began periodic coverage of sports events, but it was not until the 1890s that the first sports section became a regular feature of a newspaper. In 1895, William Randolph Hearst, publisher of the *New York Journal*, developed the first modern sports section.

Over the past hundred years the symbiosis between the newspaper and sport has become so well established that sports are one of the few industries that has its own section in almost every major daily newspaper in the United States. In many of the most popular newspapers, sports coverage constitutes almost 50 percent of the space devoted to local, national, and international stories, and the sports pages have about five times as many readers as any other section of the newspaper. So the newspaper sports section has not been curtailed by the growth of radio, television, or the Internet; instead, other forms of communication have strengthened rather than replaced the sports section of newspapers.[7]

Magazines

Today, magazines (in print and online versions) represent a large component of the media industry. Around 19,000 different titles exist in the United States. Historically, magazines and books chronicled the activities of athletes and teams before the newspaper sports sections existed. In the years between the American Revolution and the 1830s, there arose a widespread interest in journals of all kinds, and magazines cropped up everywhere to exploit the popular interest in horse racing, hunting, fishing, and athletic sports.

The momentum of sports literature accelerated in the 1830s, and the first prominent sports journal in the United States, *Spirit of the Times*, began publication in 1831. This journal featured horse racing in particular, but also reported on other sports and indirectly helped to establish what was to become "the national pastime"—baseball. Another popular nineteenth-century sports magazine, *The Sporting News*, began publication in 1886, and after one hundred years as a weekly publication, in 2008 the magazine switched to a biweekly publishing schedule; then in 2011 it became a monthly schedule. In 2013, the magazine converted to a digital-only publication, a trend that has been found with many other magazine titles recently.

Magazines specializing in sports have been standard fare in the publishing business for the past one hundred years, with almost every sport having its own publication. Indeed, one indication that a new sport is rising in popularity is the appearance of a magazine describing its techniques and strategies, profiling its best players, and advertising equipment and accessories for playing or watching the sport. *Sports Illustrated*, founded in 1954, is currently the bestselling sports magazine through both online and print platforms. It was reported in 2019 that *Sports Illustrated* had 2.75 million subscribers.[8] This magazine has numerous online news and feature pages covering collegiate, Olympic, and professional sports as well as many others. These pages offer thousands of video and written pieces and attract several million online visitors each month.[9]

Books

The first massive book wave in the United States began in the two decades before the Civil War as dime novels began to appear in large quantities. Numerous books on field sports, horse racing, boxing, and the increasingly popular team sports poured from the publishing houses throughout the late nineteenth century, but the youth literature contributed most significantly to arousing interest in sports among the youngsters of this era. Undoubtedly the most prolific of the youth literature authors was Burt L. Standish (whose real name was Gilbert Patten), who in 1896 began turning out a story every week about a fictitious schoolboy athlete, Frank Merriwell. In the early 1900s the Merriwell stories sold about 135,000 copies weekly. Youth athletic stories also streamed from the pens of many other authors.

Serious novelists tended not to focus on sport to any extent, although some of the most powerful passages in Ernest Hemingway's novels dealt with blood sports (e.g., bullfighting). A trend has now developed toward serious writing about sport, and novelists have increasingly employed sports themes in their works. A coalition of university professors and friends founded the Sport Literature Association in the early 1980s; it publishes *Aethlon: The Journal of Sport Literature,* a print journal designed to synchronize the intersection of literature with the world of play, games, and sport; it issues works about sport literature, including original fiction and poetry.

Perhaps the greatest impact of sport on the literary field has been made by former athletes and sports journalists. The United States and other Western countries have been virtually deluged with books by professional athletes (most of these are ghostwritten) who describe their experiences in sports. A number of former athletes have written "kiss-and-tell" books depicting the good, the bad, and the ugly of their sporting experiences. Sports journalists have also shared in the publishing windfall; several have written what might be called exposé, or muckraking, types of books while others have written books featuring compelling sport phenomena. The consequence: Most bookstores have an entire section devoted to sports books.

Radio

Although sports sections of newspapers, sport magazines, and books about sports continue to have significant linkages to sport, the electronic media—radio, motion pictures, television, and the Internet—have made dramatic inroads into the traditional information and entertainment functions of the printed media. Only a few years separated the invention of wireless broadcasting and the advent of radio sportscasts. The first permanent commercial radio station, KDKA in Pittsburgh, went on the air in 1920. Less than a year later, in July 1921, the first heavyweight championship boxing bout was broadcast. From the mid-1920s to the early 1950s, radio reigned supreme in broadcasting sports news and live sports events.

Radio's popularity as a medium for sport information and entertainment declined with the beginning of network television in the 1950s. Nevertheless, there are some 11,000 radio stations in North America that broadcast more than 700,000 hours of sport annually. Sports call-in shows and interviews with sports celebrities as well as play-by-play game reporting have sustained the role of radio in sports, and the twenty-four-hour-per-day, all-sports radio stations appear to have created excitement in this industry. In 2017, it was reported that there were 780 all-sports radio stations in the United States devoted almost solely to discussion, debate, and analysis of athletes and teams by both hosts and callers.[10]

Motion Pictures

Thomas Edison's rudimentary motion-picture camera, the kinetoscope, which he patented in 1891, marked the birth of the movie industry. Movies quickly became a favorite popular culture phenomenon. As popular as the movies were, however, sports stories were relatively rare before 1970, but in recent decades several sports films have received critical acclaim; *Rocky* and *Chariots of Fire* were awarded Oscars for best picture. The columnists and editors of ESPN recently ranked what they considered the top twenty sports movies of all time. The following were the top ten:

1. *Bull Durham* (1988)
2. *Rocky* (1976)
3. *Raging Bull* (1980)
4. *Hoosiers* (1986)
5. *Slap Shot* (1977)
6. *The Natural* (1984)
7. *Field of Dreams* (1989)
8. *Caddyshack* (1980)
9. *The Hustler* (1961)
10. *The Longest Yard* (1974)[11]

Of course, these ESPN selections are subjective. Increasingly, however, sports films tend to transcend mere entertainment and attempt to explore broader social issues of power, race, masculinity, and gender relations.

Television

Currently the predominant mass media presenter of sport is television. The technology to produce telecasts was developed during the 1930s, but World War II delayed the large-scale growth of commercial television for nearly a decade. When television began to grow, however, its rate of growth was staggering. In 1950 fewer than 10 percent of households had television; according to one media research group, approximately 87 percent of American homes had at least one connected television device in 2022. The average television viewer received only 4 or 5 channels in 1970, 3 of which were broadcast networks. By contrast, there are now about 11,000 cable TV systems offering more than 150 channels of programming. To watch this plethora of TV choices, Americans have nearly 500 million connected TV devices.[12]

Other Electronic Media

Other media viewership and multimedia viewership have increased rapidly. The amount of time spent consuming media in all its forms—digital, TV, radio, and print—is moving upward. Indeed, by 2020 U.S. adults' daily overall media engagement with these forms totaled 13 hours and 21 minutes. Digital media consumption, involving mobile and other internet-connected devices, is the most prevalent form of media consumption.[13] Given the popularity of "smart" and "online" devices in everyday life, it is to the point that 31 percent of American adults reported in 2021 that they went online "almost constantly."[14] See Table 12.1 to see how digital media usage increased compared to traditional media usage, between the years 2017 and 2022.[15]

A prevailing type of mass media takes the form of social interaction and is called *social media*. Social media are primarily Internet- and mobile-based digital content vehicles for sharing and discussing information. Among the various types of social media are forums, message boards, blogs, wikis, and podcasts. Social media applications include Facebook, Instagram, YouTube, Twitter, Flickr, and LinkedIn, each of which allows end users to engage in multidirectional conversations in or around the content on the website.[16]

There is little question that social media is transforming sport in a variety of ways. As Jimmy Sanderson, author of *How Social Media Is Changing Sports: It's a*

TABLE 12.1   TRADITIONAL VERSUS DIGITAL MEDIA USAGE: SHARE OF AVERAGE TIME SPENT IN THE U.S. ADULTS, 2017–2022 (PERCENT OF TOTAL MEDIA USAGE)

	Digital	Traditional
2017	49.2	50.8
2018	51.8	48.2
2019	55.1	44.9
2020	58.6	41.4
2021	60.5	39.5
2022	62.2	37.8

Note: Ages eighteen and over; time spent with each medium includes time spent with that medium regardless of multitasking. *Includes time spent on TV, newspapers, magazines, and radio.

Source: eMarketer, April 2021

Whole New Ballgame, asserts, "In some respects, it is difficult to imagine another industry that has been so dramatically altered by social media as the sports world."[17] Social media platforms have become a medium through which athletes and sport figures have discovered intriguing broadcast capabilities that have changed the ways that sports media is produced and consumed. In some instances, those athletes, sport figures, and sport organizations have emerged as a competitive force to mainstream media organizations. Sanderson also argues that although "the mass media still holds primacy in reporting stories, social media enable athletes and sport figures to circumvent the media and directly break news via their social media account."[18]

Sport fans and participants now have numerous devices from which to access various sources of sport information anytime, anywhere; consequently, sports organizations have come to realize this and are utilizing it by supplementing their TV broadcast instruments, through the implementation of various platforms that work in a synergistic manner.

TELEVISION: THE MONSTER OF THE SPORTS WORLD

Even with the growth of high technology and new forms of media, television still remains a key outlet for consumers. Television has historically had a major influence on sport, but the influence has been reciprocal; television programming is greatly influenced by sport as well.

Sport made a union with television while the tube was still in its infancy. The first televised sports event was a college baseball game between Columbia and Princeton in 1939. The announcer was located in the stands with the spectators; there was only one camera, and its range was so limited that it could not show the batter and the pitcher at the same time. Other technical difficulties made it almost impossible for viewers to know what was happening during the game. In describing the television coverage, the *New York Times* reported, "The players were best described by observers as appearing like white flies running across the screen. . . . When the ball flashed across the grass, it appeared as a comet-like white pinpoint. . . . The commentator saved the day,

otherwise there would be no way to follow the play or tell where the ball went except to see the players run in its direction."[19]

Despite the many problems encountered by the infant television industry, it grew enormously in a short time, and television watching is still the most popular and most time-consuming leisure activity in the United States.

INCREASING TV SPORTS COVERAGE

The most dramatic programming trend in television has been the enormous increase in sports coverage over recent decades. Spectators consume sport to a far greater extent through television than through personal attendance at events. Table 12.2 lists examples of the variety of sports television that now exists.

In the United States, tens of thousands of hours of sport are televised annually by four major free-to-air networks as well as pay-TV platforms such as cable, pay-per-view (PPV), and satellite television, along with various digital channels and local sports cable networks. In regards to this televised coverage of sports, the average American was reported in one study to watch 4 hours of live sports per week and

TABLE 12.2 EXAMPLES OF THE EXPANDING SPORTS TELEVISION MENU

Original major networks	ABC, *Wide World of Sports* (1961); NBC, Olympic Games (1980); CBS, Sunday afternoon football
New major networks	FOX, FOX Sports, formed in 1994
Cable television sports networks	ESPN, BeIN Sports USA
Superstations that broadcast sports	TBS, WGN
Regional cable sports	MSG Network, Comcast Sports Net Chicago, FOX Sports Net Pittsburgh
Sports specialty channels	NFL Network, MLB Network, NHL Network, NBATV, Golf Channel, Tennis Channel, Fox Soccer Channel
College sports networks	Big Ten Network, BYUtv, Pac-12 Network, Longhorn Network
Satellite TV	NFL Sunday Ticket (by DirectTV; subscriptions give viewers access to NFL games)

1.3 hours of sports highlights in this same time span.[20] As such, broadcast and cable networks can expect to earn billions of dollars per year from the traditional television model; ESPN and its various associated networks earn parent company Disney over $10 billion through providers, subscriptions and advertising.[21]

Regional sports cable networks and direct satellite broadcasts are growing rapidly, and they broadcast countless thousands of hours of sport each year. Perhaps the most remarkable trend is the sport organizations that are becoming their own media companies—such as the NFL (NFL Network reached about 57 million households in 2022), NBA (NBATV), MLB (MLB Network), NHL (NHL Network), the Big Ten Network, and the Longhorn Network—thus bypassing the traditional TV and cable networks. The Longhorn Network, which premiered in the fall of 2011, broadcasts round-the-clock coverage of University of Texas sports and was the first TV sports channel devoted to a single university. It has created considerable controversy, especially over its potential to give the University of Texas an unfair recruiting advantage over other universities.[22]

The Super Bowl has dominated network TV ratings during the past two decades, ranking as the top TV program nine of the past twenty years. Super Bowl telecasts usually attract 40 to 45 percent of the households watching TV. The 2017 Super Bowl between the New England Patriots and the Atlanta Falcons became the most-watched American television program in history, drawing a total audience of 172 million viewers.[23]

But the Super Bowl is not the only mega TV sport. The International Olympic Committee reported that some 3.6 billion people—or around half of the world's total population of 7 billion—tuned in to the 2016 Rio Summer Olympics for at least some of its days of TV coverage.[24] In the years when the World Cup is played, the month-long tournament draws a total worldwide audience of up to 33 billion viewers.

Pay-for-view television has been a growing reality throughout the United States since the mid-1990s, and it has expanded from its early years to cover nearly every type of sport. Some TV analysts believe PPV will become the norm for broadcasting major sporting events.

NFL Sunday Ticket, available on satellite or cable, cost between $300 and $400 depending on plan type in the 2021 season; subscribers get every out-of-market, non–nationally televised NFL game. As we noted previously, professional baseball, basketball, ice hockey, and intercollegiate athletics have similar PPV networks.

All-sports news channels are a unique innovation in sports television. ESPNews began this form of twenty-four-hour sports coverage in the fall of 1996. They do not carry live sports events. Instead, they telecast only sports news.

ECONOMIC ASPECTS OF TELEVISED SPORTS

Money is the fuel propelling the TV sports machine, and sport and television are mutual beneficiaries in one of the most lucrative business associations. In return for the rights to telecast sports events, professional and collegiate sports receive free publicity as well as broadcast rights fees. At the same time, television companies profit from the use of their products (the telecasts) by sport consumers. This relationship was keenly disrupted as a result of the COVID-19 pandemic, with the loss of live sport and accompanying declines in ad revenue. During this time stakeholders in the TV sports world scrambled to create and provide original sport content to consumers.[25]

The system typically works in the following manner: Television networks pay money for the "broadcast rights" to televise a professional (or college) league's (e.g., NFL) games. The networks hope to get that money back, plus a profit, by selling advertising time to corporations, like General Motors, for the games. For example, approximately 93.2 percent of Southwest Airlines Co. total ad spending is devoted to sports. Administrators of the sports leagues take the money received from the television network and distribute it according to the sports leagues' policies.

In essence, then, the television industry is basically a broker, bringing together the sellers (sports leagues), the buyers (advertisers), and the consumers (fans). The relationship between media and sport is one of planned, calculated business rationality.

The extent to which the fees for telecasting rights have escalated can be seen in Table 12.3. Sports rights

TABLE 12.3 TELEVISION NETWORK RIGHTS FEES TO OLYMPIC GAMES

Summer Olympic Games	Television rights fees (in U.S. dollars)
1960	394,000
1972	7,500,000
1984	225,000,000
1996	456,000,000
2008	894,000,000
2012	1,180,000,000
2016	1,226,000,000
2020	1,418,000,000
Winter Olympic Games	**Television rights fees (in U.S. dollars)**
1960	50,000
1972	15,500,000
1984	243,000,000
1996	545,000,000
2010	820,000,000
2014	775,000,000
2018	963,000,000

- CBS, Fox, NBC, and ESPN provide the NFL with a total of about $5 billion to $6 billion annually from contracts that run through 2021–2022. About 65 percent of all NFL team revenues comes from the sale of television rights.
- ESPN secured the rights to broadcast MLB games until the end of 2028 for the price of $550 million per year. TBS will also broadcast games at an estimated cost of $535 million annually. The MLB shares a percentage of its revenues with its thirty teams. It is estimated that each MLB club will earn $100 million per year, from national and regional broadcast deals.
- The NBA has a nine-year TV contract (2024–2025) with ESPN and Turner Sports for $24 billion. This deal represents a 180 percent increase in the amount of money over the previous TV rights contract.
- In 2010, the NCAA signed a fourteen-year television, Internet, and wireless rights agreement with CBS Sports and Turner Broadcasting to present the Division I Men's Basketball Championship beginning in 2011 through 2024 for more than $10.8 billion.
- MLB has struck a deal with Apple TV+ who will broadcast Friday night games in a deal that is worth $85 million per year to the league.
- In 2021, Amazon agreed to pay a reported $10 billion over 10 years to show NFL games on Thursday nights, exclusively for Amazon Prime subscribers.
- U.S. broadcaster NBC paid $4.38 billion for the four Olympic Games from 2014 until 2020. In 2014 the International Olympic Committee announced it had agreed to a $7.75 billion deal with NBCUniversal for broadcast rights to all media platforms covering six Olympics, from 2012 to 2032.

have grown to surpass half of all TV programming. With an estimated value between $40 billion and $60 billion, ESPN, the worldwide leader in sports media, is some twenty times larger than the New York Times Company, or nearly five times larger than News Corporation. The economics of television are changing because of these escalating broadcast rights fees, and the reign of the television networks as the exclusive carrier of the Olympics ended after the 1988 Summer Games in Seoul. Cable television has gotten a larger and larger piece of the Olympic pie. Satellite is also making its mark in the industry.

Professional sports are able to operate the way they do primarily through the television contracts they have been able to negotiate. Realizing the popularity of broadcast sports, the sports industry has successfully negotiated large contracts with media organizations for the rights to broadcast events. This in turn helps make commercial sports profitable. Following are a few examples of recent contracts:

It can be seen that the networks, the superstations, the cable sports stations, and local TV stations have bankrolled commercialized team sports with a veritable bonanza of dollars. Contracts like these have made the commercial sports industry very profitable, resulting in expanded franchises, higher salaries, and all-around plush lifestyles for many in the industry. Indeed, so many pro sports organizations have built their budgets around TV income that if television ever did withdraw its money, the entire pro sports structure in its present form would collapse. Sports executives often remark, "There is no way we could survive without television" or "If sports lost television revenues, we'd all be out of business."

One might ask, "Why is television so eager to spend such lavish sums for the rights to telecast sporting events?" It is simple. Corporations spend lavishly on advertising during sports events to create a demand for their products. Broadcast sporting events are immensely popular and attract large audiences; many people are interested in the beauty and drama of sports events and find them more exciting and suspenseful than most other broadcast programming. Audiences of broadcast commercials become consumers of the products, bringing profits to the advertisers. So sports are a natural setting for corporate advertising.

The escalating rates of advertising time can be seen from the following examples of recent Super Bowl rates for a thirty-second commercial (see Table 12.4). This type of commercial advertising at Super Bowl LVI in 2022 cost an unprecedented fee of $6.5 million dollars.[26]

TELEVISION'S INFLUENCE ON SPORT

Each medium has made an impact on sport in its own way. Newspapers of the late nineteenth and early twentieth centuries contributed to the rise of professional and collegiate sports by creating an interest in these activities. Magazines and books helped create and sustain the hero worship of the athlete in succeeding generations. Radio brought live sports action into the home for the first time. It was television, however, that had the most profound impact. Several interpreters of the impact of television on sport have argued that TV has produced more revolutionary and irrevocable changes in sport than anything since modern sport began in the mid-nineteenth century. Of course, sports social media is expanding in scope and will become an important aspect of sports going forward.

INCREASES IN SPORT REVENUE

Before the advent of television, professional sport was only a skeleton of what it has become, and the professional franchises that did exist were struggling

TABLE 12.4   SUPER BOWL RATES FOR A THIRTY-SECOND COMMERCIAL

Year	Advertising rate (in U.S. dollars)
1970	78,200
1985	525,000
1996	1,200,000
2002	1,900,000
2005	2,400,000
2008	2,700,000
2010	2,800,000
2012	3,500,000
2015	4,500,000
2017	5,000,000
2020	5,500,000
2022	6,500,000

financially. There were only sixteen MLB teams in the 1950s, and no new teams had come into the leagues in more than fifty years; now there are thirty teams. This expansion, and baseball's prosperity, has been a result of television. Similar patterns can be seen in professional football, basketball, and hockey. All of these sports entered the 1950s as struggling enterprises with fewer than ten franchises each, and neither the owners nor the players were making much money. These sports now have thirty or more franchises each, and all have expansion plans. Television contributes a substantial portion of every league's revenues. Professional golf, tennis, soccer, and other professional sports either did not exist or were inconsequential prior to the infusion of large sums of television money.

Professional sports owners have not been the only beneficiaries of this windfall. Television money has increased athletes' incomes as well. Pro athletes' salaries have tripled or even quadrupled; television money has largely made it possible for them to command their enormous salaries and endorsements. Table 12.5 lists the highest-earning athletes in 2021, according to Forbes.

These spectacular incomes of contemporary professional athletes have a high correlation with the increases in broadcast television rights. Television

TABLE 12.5 TEN HIGHEST-PAID ATHLETES IN THE WORLD, 2021

Name	Sport	Earnings (in U.S. dollars)
Conor McGregor	Mixed Martial Arts	180 million
Lionel Messi	Soccer	130 million
Cristiano Ronaldo	Soccer	120 million
Dak Prescott	Football	107.5 million
LeBron James	Basketball	96.5 million
Neymar	Soccer	95 million
Roger Federer	Tennis	90 million
Lewis Hamilton	Auto Racing	82 million
Tom Brady	Football	76 million
Kevin Durant	Basketball	75 million

Source: Brett Knight and Justin Birnbaum, "2021, Highest-Paid Athletes," *Forbes*, https://www.forbes.com/athletes/. Accessed June 14, 2022.

supports sports. TV networks move in with their money and support sports in a style that would have been unbelievable just a generation ago.

The extent to which sports has been influenced by its increasingly economic dependence on the mass media is illustrated by the number of professional sports teams that are owned wholly or partly by Rupert Murdoch. The media mogul has arguably the largest global media sports empire, and he once called sports the "cornerstone of our worldwide efforts."

TELEVISION DRIVES SHIFTS IN POPULARITY OF SPORTS

Television's dominating role is demonstrated most clearly in the changing popularity of the various sports in the United States. Telecasts have greatly increased the popularity of U.S. sports. Football and baseball with their series of crises, tennis and golf with their evolving drama, basketball and soccer with their fast and skillful actions, and boxing and Mixed Martial Arts with their violence in a confined space are all ideal sports for television. Natural breaks in the action permit viewers to contemplate the next moves; more important, they provide the opportunity for periodic commercial breaks without seriously disturbing the flow of the sporting event.

If television viewing is the criterion of national pastime status, football has replaced baseball as America's national pastime. There is little doubt that football is ideally suited for television, with its fast, strategic, and violent action confined to a rather restricted area, its periods of inaction between plays, and its rigidly controlled time orientation. Festive football fans' pregame "tailgate" parties contribute to the popularity of football and indirectly add to TV media coverage of the sport. Indeed, while some television broadcasts of sports have recently dipped due to other competing streaming services and mobile platforms, NFL football viewership has remained quite robust.

PROFESSIONAL SPORTS FRANCHISE LOCATIONS AND THE MEDIA

Not only has television influenced the popularity and the fortunes of entire sports, but also it has more selectively come to play a direct role in decisions about the number and locations of professional franchises. The promise of lucrative television contracts explains why the number of professional football, basketball, baseball, and hockey franchises has more than doubled in the past three decades. Moreover, when the NFL, NBA, MLB, MLS, and NHL have awarded new franchises, the size of the potential television market in a region has been a major consideration.

Prior to television, professional sports franchises were considered permanent fixtures in a city, but the practice of jumping from city to city has become common. There have been seven moves of NFL teams since 1983—three in the past few years: the Rams from St. Louis to Los Angeles and the Chargers from San Diego to Los Angeles; the Oakland Raiders moved to Las Vegas in 2020—and more than a dozen city changes for NBA teams, the most recent being the New Jersey Nets who moved to Brooklyn in 2012. A major factor for moving in almost every case has been the promise of additional television revenues. Given the economic structure of professional sports, it is not surprising that professional leagues and their franchise owners gravitate toward television money.[27]

Although television revenues have been responsible for the health and expansion of some professional sports enterprises, the lack of network television contracts has been responsible for the demise of others. In the early 1980s the U.S. Football League failed to secure network sponsorship and folded. Professional track died for similar reasons, and professional volleyball and several women's professional sports have had an off-and-on existence for lack of television contracts. The NFL European League was created by the NFL in 1991 primarily to provide American football to European audiences to capitalize on the popularity of televised American football. However, in the summer of 2007, it was shut down by the NFL because of significant financial losses.

TELEVISION: THE FINANCIAL FOUNDATION FOR BIG-TIME INTERCOLLEGIATE SPORT

At the same time that television was stimulating the expansion and financial status of the openly professional sports, it was also furthering the professionalization of a self-proclaimed amateur sport enterprise, intercollegiate sport, which has been a professional enterprise for many years. When collegiate football became one of the most popular viewer events on early TV, the NCAA, the regulatory organization of intercollegiate athletics, quickly stepped in to regulate television coverage of collegiate football games. Under that system of regulation, the NCAA always limited the number of football games that could be televised each week and the number of times a particular team could appear on television each season. Nevertheless, a few of the football "powers" were seen frequently, whereas most collegiate football teams never appeared on television. Teams that were televised received large payments per appearance, so the television package increased the gap between the haves and the have-nots in college football.[28]

A challenge to the NCAA's right to negotiate TV contracts on behalf of all of its member institutions was settled by a U.S. Supreme Court decision in which the court invalidated the NCAA's exclusive college football TV contract. The effect was to free individual colleges and conferences to negotiate their own television contracts with the networks, cable companies, and local stations. College football broadcasts on national cable and syndication channels have skyrocketed since that decision.

A book with the lengthy title *The Fifty-Year Seduction: How Television Manipulated College Football, from the Birth of the Modern NCAA to the Creation of the BCS* explains how television helped shape college football and how it became the common denominator in the sport's rise as a big business. In summary, the author declares, "Over the last half-century, televised college football has manufactured money, greed, dependence, and envy; altered the recruiting process, eventually forcing the colleges to compete with the irresistible force of National Football League riches; . . . fomented the realignment of conferences; and seized control of the postseason bowl games, including the formation of the lucrative and controversial Bowl Championship Series."[29]

The Supreme Court decision regarding college football did not affect the NCAA's control over its men's basketball tournament. The growth of the NCAA men's basketball tournament provides a vivid demonstration of television's influence on collegiate sports. Television money is the financial foundation for college sports. NCAA basketball TV revenue provides around 75 to 80 percent of the NCAA's total revenue. The more teams in the NCAA basketball tournament, the greater the television revenue and the greater the amount of money paid to the NCAA. Therefore, the NCAA continued to increase the number of teams participating in the tournament until it became a sixty-eight-team tournament.

In 1990 CBS signed a seven-year, $1 billion (yes, billion) contract with the NCAA for the rights to televise the men's basketball tournament. In December 1994 that contract was replaced with a new seven-year *$1.725 billion* deal. As we noted previously, in 2010 the NCAA negotiated a *$10.8 billion* fourteen-year television rights fee with CBS and Turner Sports to televise the Division I men's basketball tournament. In 2016, this agreement was extended at a cost of over $1 billion per year for 8 more years that were added to the initial contract.[30] In late 2011, the NCAA signed a $500 million television rights contract with ESPN, giving the network broadcasting control of 24 NCAA championships featuring a range of sports until the end of the 2023-2024 season.

Television money is the financial foundation for college sports. NCAA basketball TV revenue provides the majority of the NCAA's total revenue. (Photo: ZUMA Press, Inc./Alamy Stock Photo)

What is the financial impact of these television contracts on intercollegiate sports? As we explained in Chapter 10, the majority of universities with big-time intercollegiate sports programs run a deficit in their annual budgets; the deficits would be huge were it not for television money, and for those that do not run a deficit it is largely because of the television money they receive. With a view toward receiving television money and public exposure, universities throughout the country throw enormous human and financial resources into their football and basketball programs while they have been dropping other sports from their offerings. Some universities have dropped as many as six sports in

the past decade; we noted this, too, in Chapter 10. Universities have frequently blamed the abolishment of sports on Title IX, which requires gender equity in the expenditures of resources. But in most cases the dropping of sports has been precipitated by the desire to pour more money into football and men's basketball in the hopes of attracting more media money to the athletic program.[31]

TELEVISION TAPS HIGH SCHOOL SPORTS

The television industry has reached down to tap a different source of revenue: high school sports. In the fall of 1989, SportsChannel America, a cable network, signed a multiyear agreement with the NFHS, the administrative organization for high school sports. At the time the negotiations were under way, an executive for SportsChannel said, "We think high school sports are going to be the TV sport of the 90s." Although this prediction was a little too optimistic, televised high school sports, especially football and basketball, has become a regular feature of local television stations throughout the United States during the first two decades of the twenty-first century.

Several state high school activity associations now cover regular-season games. Television coverage of state championships and tournaments has become an annual event in many states. In fact, there have been several proposals in recent years for national championships in high school sports. This trend is exactly what many educators have feared. Can pressures for national high school championships be far behind if television becomes the financial support for high school sports? The answer is no. Educational leaders fear that if that happens, educational priorities will be sacrificed in the interests of keeping the television industry happy. As a University of Georgia sport sociologist remarked, "When you look at what the mission of scholastic sports is, you're getting away from the emphasis on the student body." Christine Brennan, *USA Today* sportswriter, agrees. She says, "We're almost prostituting ourselves putting high school games on TV."

ESPN has been in the business of televising high school football and basketball games since 2005. ESPN networks select the nationally top-ranked teams and televise about twenty football and fifteen basketball games as part of the GEICO ESPN High School Showcases. ESPN's coverage of high school football culminates with an annual All-America High School Football Game on ESPN. In an interview with the *Miami Herald*, one of the coauthors of this book warned that ESPN's incursion into "high school sport is moving in the wrong direction, away from its place in education and toward the big-time college model."[32]

Television has even become a factor in the recruitment of high school athletes. Many high school athletes are choosing to attend a university because of the TV coverage that university gets. The football games of some universities are carried on national TV much more frequently than those of others. In the case of big-time collegiate basketball, some high school athletes are selecting eastern universities because the viewing audiences of the games are much larger than in midwestern or western states because of the time the games are played. Football and basketball athletes believe that greater television exposure helps their chances of being drafted by the pros.

MODIFYING SPORTS TO ACCOMMODATE TV

To enhance spectator appeal and to accommodate programming needs, the television industry has increasingly manipulated the structure and the processes of televised sports. Because TV networks charge corporations advertising fees based on the anticipated number of viewers—the more viewers, the larger the advertising fee—the networks want the sports events to which they have bought broadcast rights to attract huge audiences. In their pursuit of viewers, media networks have been able to persuade pro sport leagues and franchise owners (who want larger broadcast rights fees) to modify rules and schedules in the hopes of attracting larger numbers of viewers. Because broadcasting rights fees are based on anticipated audience size, pro sport owners and leagues have been willing to make these changes to the game. Thus, to enhance viewer appeal and accommodate programming needs, both the media sports industry and the commercial sports industry have manipulated the structures and processes of sport. Here are some examples:

- In NFL football, rule changes (such as moving the sideline hash marks and the kickoff spot, reducing defensive backs' contact with receivers, and liberalizing offensive holding) have been adopted to open up the games and make them more attractive to television viewers. To permit more commercials, time outs are called at the discretion of television officials, and the automatic two-minute warning near game's end is merely a time out to show another set of commercials.
- To enhance spectator and viewer interest, NBA basketball led in the adoption of the shot clock, the

slam dunk, and the three-point shot. The NBA has acceded to a more physical, rougher style of play because television decision-makers believe that fans prefer this style and are more likely to watch games of this kind.

- In televised golf, match play (where the golfers compete hole by hole and the golfer who wins the most holes is the winner) has largely been replaced by medal play (the golfer with the lowest score over the entire course wins). The skins game—another variation of professional golf, where large sums of money ride on the outcome of each hole—has become a popular form of televised professional golf. These new forms of golf competition are more compatible with television coverage.

- In professional tennis, to accommodate television scheduling, tennis executives established the tie-breaker system for sets tied at six games all; tie-breakers tend to play out quickly, making it easier to complete matches within a designated time period.

- The MLB introduced the designated hitter and lowered the strike zone, and there is strong suspicion that the baseball itself has been modified to make it livelier. These changes have been motivated by an interest in increasing what spectators like to see: more extra-base hits and home runs. Time-honored afternoon World Series and All-Star games were switched to evenings to serve the interests of television.

- The sudden-death tiebreaking rule in professional football, ice hockey, and soccer and the extended playoff system in all of the pro sports leagues are additional examples of modifying rules to increase TV viewer interest and make the sporting events more profitable for both TV networks and professional sports.

- In 2012 the head of NBC Sports asked the Association of Boxing Commissions to increase the time between rounds an additional seven seconds to allow a full minute for commercials and, in addition, according to NBC, make the sport more broadcast friendly.

- For recent Winter and Summer Olympic Games, the International Olympic Committee agreed to reschedule championship events so they take place during the United States' prime time to accommodate television networks. Much of the Olympic Games TV coverage is broadcast after the events are completed, but frequently the events are presented to television viewers without informing them of this fact, leading them to believe they are seeing events live.

Most of the changes identified here, and others, are tied directly to television's interest in enhancing the action for television viewers and keeping them in their chairs to watch the commercials. After all, this is the means by which the television industry makes its profits. As the television industry's investment in sports continues to grow, so does TV's resolution to get the most for its investment by orchestrating the sporting events for maximum viewer appeal.

TELEVISION'S OWN SPORTS

As we have noted, sports have been an important part of television programming since the early years of network TV. Because sports are so popular with television viewers, television executives sought ways to broadcast other events involving sport-like characteristics—such as competition requiring physical strength, endurance, agility, tenacity, speed, and skill. This resulted in TV networks creating made-for-television sports events.

Made-for-television sports, with names like "Challenge of the Sexes" and "Battle of the Network Stars," began with outstanding elite athletes or TV actors and actresses competing in physically competitive events contrived by TV executives. The idea of these programs was promoted as a way to find out who the "best" athletes were and which sports had the best athletes (or at least the best athletes among TV personalities). Winners of these events were awarded titles like "World's Best Athlete." The point was to exploit the celebrity status of athletes and TV stars, whose status as celebrities had been constructed by the media, to attract viewers to the contrived sports program—and to the commercials shown on the program. In fact, however, the TV networks' motive was economic. Competitions of this sort were often called "trash sports."

Most of the original made-for-television sports events have disappeared. But with the popularity of almost any kind of competitive event and with the all-sports TV channels needing to fill numerous hours of programming time, various made-for-television and alternative sporting events now appear. Professional fighting leagues and even eating contests are examples of emerging competitions that are now broadcast on a regular basis.

Although some of these can be considered legitimate sports, few have a large number of participating athletes or a large spectator following. However, when they are telecast, nearly all aspects of the events are aimed at making the events appealing to viewers and thus to corporate advertisers and sponsors.

One lifestyle/action sport event that has a large following is ESPN's X Games (originally called eXtreme Games) which fits into this genre of TV sports. Some of the X Games activities, such as skateboarding, in-line skating, freestyle biking, and snowboarding, were originally popular among teenagers who were looking for alternatives to the traditional individual and team sports. In 1995 ESPN created the X Games as a made-for-TV alternative multisport festival. The X Games appeal to a large, young, TV-watching audience because many of them are involved in these action activities.

ESPN's marketing director said the network aims to "reach anybody between 12 and 24 who is interested" in these types of sports. Currently, these games are divided into two seasons: the Winter X Games, held in January or February, and X Games, usually held in August. X Games Asia debuted in 1998 and has been held annually in an Asian country.

Because the X Games were created by and are owned by ESPN, the network does not have to pay broadcast rights fees to air them. Thus, the network keeps all revenue from advertisers. Reruns and qualifying events fill many hours on the ESPN broadcast schedule. Advertising revenues pour in to ESPN from all of these.

There is widespread criticism of the X Games among lifestyle/action sports enthusiasts, claiming that ESPN's X Games have turned informal, alternative physical activities into mainstream sports with the codification of rules, equipment, categories of participants, and so forth. There is also the complaint that these annual events are fundamentally an advertising medium, targeting specific age, gender, and racial groups. Indeed, the X Games seem to illustrate social analysts' claim that capitalism—in this case in the form of television networks—is so enterprising that it will find a way to turn everything into a marketable commodity.

In the spring of 2001, the World Wrestling Federation and NBC co-created a made-for-television football league called the XFL. With teams nicknamed the Enforcers, the Hitmen, and the Maniacs, the XFL was hyped as a violent, trash-talking, sexualized form of football. XFL games started with TV ratings well above expectations, but interest declined drastically, and the league was canceled after the first season.

One of the newest contributions to the merging of sports to create a fanatical TV audience is UFC, a combat sport combining the striking techniques of boxing and kickboxing with floor techniques of jiu jitsu and wrestling. The action takes place in an octagon cage. As with the X Games, many of the young men attracted to combat sports disliked the mainstream combat sports and experimented with alternatives, one of which became UFC. It quickly became popular with the eighteen- to thirty-four-year-old male demographic.

Once TV executives saw how popular UFC was becoming, TV contracts followed. By 2010 PPV and Spike UFC programs often had higher television ratings than the NBA and baseball playoff games in the eighteen- to-thirty-four-year-old audience. UFC events had bigger PPV numbers than any pro wrestling event or boxing event. UFC's president, Dana White, recently commented that "Our goal is to open the sport everywhere." Since 2010, UFC has hosted fighting events in nineteen different nations with the intention to hold twenty events outside the United States per year.[33]

TELEVISED SPORT AS A SOCIALLY MEDIATED EVENT

Television has not only revised the way sport is played and the way it is watched; it has also redefined the social meaning of sport in many ways.

Contemporary sport has become part of media culture, meaning that its form and content have been altered to suit the interests of the media. A common assumption among the public is that a broadcast sport event is an objective mirror of the reality of the contest and that TV's framing, camera angles, use of scan and zoom, and sportscaster commentary are neutral conduits for presenting "the facts" of the event. In reality, however, a broadcast game is an entertainment spectacle sold in the marketplace, a tool for attracting and keeping listeners and viewers so the media can broadcast the commercials they have sold to advertisers. Even so-called "reality" shows, such as Nike's Elite Youth program, which follows young aspiring basketball players, are filmed, edited, and presented in ways that benefit the show's main corporate sponsor, the production team, and the host channel.

Superficially, sportscasters simply keep listeners and viewers apprised of essential information as the contest unfolds. But they do much more: they mediate the event and thus create the listeners' and viewers' experiences of the event through their intervention. Because of sportscasters' mediation, a sporting event becomes a collage of happenings—and thus "reality" is socially constructed by the sportscasters, who decide what to reveal to listeners and viewers and how. What they reveal and what they conceal become, in effect, the "event," and the way listeners and viewers experience it becomes their reference point for its very existence—but it is a mediated version of reality.

In a televised sports event, cameras, camera angles, producers' choices of focus, and sportscasters' interpretations—all of which are the invisible apparatus of a televised presentation—stand between the viewers and the event. Viewers do not see the entire event; instead, they see only those parts that are sifted and filtered through the broadcasting process. This is different from attending the event itself. Spectators in a stadium or arena perceive the event as is (at least, what can be seen and heard of it from the seats). But broadcast listeners and viewers experience an event that is socially constructed by a team of broadcast professional gatekeepers and dramatic embellishers.

The public has many options regarding what to listen to and watch, so a variety of techniques are used to attract listeners and viewers. Some of the most important decisions media executives must make are about selection, such as decisions about which sports events to broadcast and which not to broadcast, as well as decisions to accentuate certain aspects of the sporting event for listeners and viewers and not others. Thus, televised sports are the result of a carefully crafted selection process that takes into account listener and viewer interests, attitudes, and beliefs about sports.

Two examples of broadcast selection can illustrate the selection and exclusion in media sports coverage. First, coverage of male sporting events dominates broadcast sports and helps reinforce cultural attitudes about gender specificity in sport and gender appropriateness of sports. Second, team sports have dominated sports broadcasts. Indeed, male team sports are TV's "authorized sports"; in many ways, the media have advanced the popularity of male team sports at the expense of other forms of sport. Thus, social values are conveyed through particular choices made by the media's selective coverage.[34]

The selection process is at work within a particular sporting event. Production executives foreground particular aspects of the event for the viewers. In baseball, home runs are highlighted over "routine" singles; in football the quarterback gets the focus, rather than any of the ten other positions; in multiple events, such as track and field, some events get more attention than others—for example, sprinting gets more coverage than most other events.

Beyond mere selecting, viewers are provided with descriptions of what has been selected through narrative themes and interpretations of preferred meaning about the action or the event itself. Televised sporting events do not merely consist of pictures; they also involve commentary on the pictures—a commentary that shapes what viewers are seeing and believing.

This selective highlighting is not "natural." It is based on media assumptions about what is good television and what keeps viewers watching. Such decisions involve an active process of representation; what viewers see, then, is not the actual event but a mediated event—in other words, a media event. For example, this often occurs with global mega events such as the soccer World Cup and the Olympic Games, where leading media organizations are keen to prioritize particular values, identities, and experiences.

Once particular sports events are chosen for broadcasting, the next task is to "hook" listeners and viewers to the broadcasts. This begins with pregame programs that are mostly a contrived mix of interviews, network promos, and hoopla (e.g., theme building). The main purpose of these programs is to frame and contextualize the game by artificially building dramatic tension and solidifying allegiances, thus convincing listeners and viewers to stay tuned to the event, while preparing them for how they should hear, see, and understand it. The rhetoric concentrates listeners' and viewers' attention on the overall importance of this particular contest, individual athletes' (and coaches') personalities, "match-ups," statistics, records, and team styles of play.

The selecting, screening, and filtering of sports events that are carried out by television through images and verbal commentary result in the presentation of a whole new game, a game created from an entertainment perspective, because in essence entertainment is what televised sport is all about. In consequence, we wonder whether the basis for interest in sport involves not only appreciation of the beauty, style, skill, and technical accomplishments of the performers but also major concern for titillating excitement and productive action, usually meaning scoring and winning.

The overarching value in media sport is winning. Broadcast sports tend to be single-minded odes to winning, so much so that almost any action in the pursuit of victory is considered justified; indeed, sportscasters frequently admiringly declare that an athlete will do "whatever it takes to win." No sacrifice is too great in the interest of winning; athletes who surmount injury, endure pain, and continue to play are valorized.

During one NFL football game, the camera zoomed in on the heavily taped right arm of a defensive lineman. One of the sportscasters then explained that the player had incurred a compound fracture of one of his fingers—meaning the bone was sticking out of the skin. The player had gone to the bench, shoved the bone back in, taped up the finger, and returned to the game. The sportscaster then said, in a thoroughly admiring manner, "It just goes to show how badly these guys want to win." As another example, during another NFL game, one of the sportscasters applauded a quarterback by saying, "Here's a guy that probably had to take a painkiller shot in his lower back so he could play tonight." Because the definitions, values, and practices of media sport commentary are privileged, they become the "common-sense" constructions about sport that grow out of the production of broadcast sport.

The intrinsic, process-oriented participation motive to engage in sport has been redefined by media sport, as it has increasingly become the national definer of meaning in sport and how to "do" sport. Media sport valorizes the national obsession with winning above all else. Television executives, camera personnel, sportscasters, and even the vast majority of viewers are generally not attuned to the aesthetic nuances of a well-executed play; instead, the overriding ethos is to promote a "win at all costs" ideal.

THE IMPACT OF SPORT ON THE MASS MEDIA

INCREASED SPORT IN THE MEDIA

The relationship between the mass media and sport is one of financial interdependence. As noted in an earlier section of this chapter, the sports section helps sell newspapers; indeed, in many of these, sports occupy a special, separate section. Media managers like to say they publish what the public wants, and it is obvious that newspaper editors believe that the public wants vast amounts of sports news and that sports information will sell more and more subscriptions.

Sport has also invaded other sections of newspapers. Not too many years ago a sports story or photo on the front page of papers like the *New York Times* would have been unheard of. Now it is a regular occurrence. *USA Today*, the self-proclaimed "Nation's Newspaper," regularly features stories about sports in its "Newsline" section and often has a special section about sports leagues (e.g., the NFL) and about major sporting events (e.g., the Masters, the Indy 500). Editorial cartoonists routinely use sport themes to illustrate political, economic, and social issues.

Over the past fifty years, there were many peaks and valleys, as TV networks competed against each other for sports events, struggled with advertisers for revenue, and sought viewers for televised sports events. During that time, viewers became increasingly addicted to watching sports of all kinds on TV. Even the prime-time evening slots were invaded by Monday and Thursday Night Football, all-star games, the World Series, and the Super Bowl. The enormous popularity of all kinds of sports programs led to the creation of entire television networks, such as ESPN. But ESPN has moved well beyond simply televising sports events. Table 12.6 illustrates how ESPN communicates with its fans through numerous distribution channels.

SPORT'S PRIVILEGED TREATMENT BY THE MEDIA

The mass media are fiercely independent (or claim to be), and reporters staunchly defend their right to freedom of the press. But commercial sport receives an enormous amount of free publicity via the media. Media coverage of sports itself tends to promote sports—the leagues, teams, athletes, and coaches—but typical sports coverage is blatant boosterism designed to hype interest in the athletes and teams. Stories are withheld or distorted, and sports news is edited to ensure a favorable image of the home team.

Newspaper sport sections are basically advertising sections for commercial sports. Radio and television segments dealing with sports news are essentially advertising for commercial sports. Indeed, many

TABLE 12.6 A PARTIAL LIST OF ESPN'S PIPELINE OF SPORTS MEDIA

Television	ESPN, ESPN2, ESPN3, ESPNEWS, ESPN Classic, ESPN Deportes, ESPNU, ESPN Plus
Radio	ESPN Radio
Magazine	*ESPN the Magazine*
Mobile phone	ESPN Mobile
Restaurant	ESPN Zone

sports news announcers act like cheerleaders for the local professional sports teams, often referring to them as "our team." No other privately owned, profit-making industry—which is what the commercial sport industry is—receives as much free publicity for its product. The reciprocal business aspects of this are clear: the more interest generated in commercial sports, the greater the profits for the mass media.

The motives of the media are clear as well: the media ethos is rooted in profit maximization, and it is driven by the competition to be number one to reap the power and prestige that accompanies this. The more interest generated in local sports, the more people will buy local newspapers, listen to radio, and watch local television to follow the teams. The result is greater profits for the local mass media.

SPORTS CONSUMERS AND THE MASS MEDIA

The home has become the major site of leisure in postindustrial society. The main force for this has been the mass production of cheap home entertainment systems in the form of radio, television, audio and video equipment, and the computer.

Televised sports have produced a dramatic shift in the mode of the fans' consumption of sport. It has become a key source of sports spectating for the sports consumer, and television provides this at a relatively low cost to the fan (even assuming the price of the television set and the advertising costs that are passed on to the public). The opportunity to see sports events on television has also had the effect of creating fans among segments of the population that have traditionally had little interest in sport, especially women and the elderly. According to the National Cable and Telecommunications Association, there are more channels devoted to sports programming than news, music, and weather combined.

The specific factors that contribute to viewers' enjoyment in watching televised sports events are not well understood at present, but research into this topic has led to some tentative answers. Mass-communications researchers have found that viewers' enjoyment is related to broadcast commentary, the presence of a crowd, athletes' skills, and the viewers' disposition toward the players and the teams in competition.

Sport and television are mutual beneficiaries in a lucrative business association. Sport spectators consume sport to a greater extent through television than through personal attendance at sports events. (Photo: John Minchillo/AP Images for NFL Players)

The enjoyment of televised sports closely corresponds to the perception of roughness, enthusiasm, and even violence, and the perceptions of all of these aspects of play are strongly influenced by the commentary of the telecasters. The larger the crowd and the more enthusiastic its responses to play on the field, the more television viewers enjoy a game. Seeing teams battle down to the wire enhances suspense and increases the viewers' enjoyment. Finally, the highest level of fan enjoyment results when a well-liked team defeats an intensely disliked team.[35]

THE INTERNET: AN ESSENTIAL FORM OF MASS COMMUNICATIONS FOR SPORTS

A dominant mode of communication about sports is obviously the Internet. It is a quantum leap beyond earlier forms of mass communication because it makes possible the inexpensive transmission of messages and images throughout the world in seconds. Consequently, the Internet has profoundly altered many people's relationship to work and leisure, transforming both business and private life. By 2021, there were nearly 300 million internet users in the U.S. which reflects 90 percent of the American population.[36]

Sport is a central part of the Internet; indeed, it has become one of its most important thematic areas. The implications for the Internet as a source of sports information of all kinds for sports consumers are seemingly limitless. It has the potential to someday surpass all other forms of mass communication as a source of sport information and entertainment. Literally millions of websites currently provide sports information to consumers. In August 2021, a Google search using the keywords *sports AND websites* produced over 1 billion results. In the history of the Internet, sports sites have consistently ranked among the leaders in terms of traffic and commercial activity.

Once the technology was developed to make the Internet respect geographical borders, sports organizations began offering their TV rights holders the option to show sports events video on their websites. Online live sports coverage hit the big time in 2007 when TBS, for mlb.com, produced live online coverage of first-round MLB playoff games and the National League Championship series. During the 2016 Rio Summer Olympics, a variety of mobile apps kept spectators at the games abreast of the action. TorchTracker used GPS tracking about the location of the Olympic Torch. NBCUniversal streamed some 4,000 hours of Rio Olympics coverage and partnered with Facebook, Twitter, YouTube, and Google to continue its coverage across a number of social media platforms. Several broadcasters, including NBC, BBC, and the European Broadcasting Union, posted thousands of hours of free live-video coverage of events on the Internet. See Figure 12.1.[37]

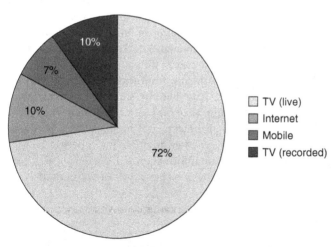

FIGURE 12.1 How People Watched the 2016 Rio Olympics Source: Compiled with data from "Faster, Higher, Smarter: Viewers Are Watching These Olympics Very Differently," CNBC, 17 August, 2016. https://www.cnbc.com/2016/08/17/rio-olympics-2016-faster-higher-smarter-viewers-are-watching-these-olympics-very-differently.html.

ESPN has created various synergistic platforms to provide round-the-clock live sports coverage and replays of global sports events to sports fans from a broad selection of global sports events each year.

INTEGRATION OF THE INTERNET, TELEVISION, COMPUTERS, AND VIDEO GAMES

Video games are one of the byproducts of the integration of television, the Internet, and computer technologies, which were introduced commercially in the early 1970s. The global video game industry, like other byproducts of these technologies, has had rapid and sustained growth. With 2.5 billion people playing worldwide, this became a $90 billion industry in 2020; around 456 million people play Esports games such as *Madden NFL*, *FIFA*, and *NBA2K*—rivaling the motion picture industry as the most profitable entertainment medium in the world.[38]

It has been reported that there are over 226 million video game players in the U.S. and that 38 percent of game players are between the ages of 18 and 34; it is considered the number one entertainment activity for Generation Z consumers.[39]

Over the past fifty years, nearly 100,000 video games have been released, and virtually every sport played in the world has had its own video game. Like the auto industry, the sports video game industry brings out a new version annually to prime the pump for profits. The processing power of the new generation of video game equipment—Microsoft's Xbox, Sony's PlayStation, and Nintendo Switch—has brought the real world, like real-time weather conditions, into game play. Since *John Madden Football* (renamed *Madden NFL* in 1994) was first released in 1989, more than 130 million copies of the sports video game have been sold. By 2022, the franchise generated over $7 billion in revenue.[40] Then, there is the *FIFA* soccer video game franchise which is a global phenomenon and stands as the highest selling sports game of all time (over 282 million copies sold as of 2022).[41] *FIFA Soccer 11* sold 2.6 million copies during its release week in 2010, which was once the biggest opening ever for a sports video game—undoubtedly stimulated by the popularity of the World Cup in South Africa that year. The 2018 *FIFA* video game has sold over 26 million copies since its release, and is the best-selling game in the series.

In 2006, Nintendo introduced the Wii, a wireless motion-sensitive remote, transforming people of all ages into video gamers. By 2014, 82.54 million copies of the game had been sold worldwide. The seventh major home video game console developed by Nintendo, Nintendo Switch, was introduced in March 2017.

Like Nintendo, many of the video games have undergone numerous editions, and that is not a topic that would be appropriate to pursue in this book. But video game creators continue to innovate and market their products in a changing society. Traditional gaming (e.g. Video game consoles including portable consoles and PC) is on the decline while mobile gaming (i.e. smartphones and tablets), are becoming more popular due to the shift in society toward using mobile devices. Mobile games became the largest selling subgroup in the global video game industry for the first time in 2018, and mobile gaming was expected to generate revenues of $94.5 billion in 2022.[42]

As with other forms of entertainment, especially television, sociological questions have arisen about the effects of video game playing on the habits, behaviors, and social development of players. For example, how does playing sports video games affect the play habits of children and youth who play these games? Do the games influence attitudes and behaviors toward values, such as sportsmanship, nonviolence, and morality? Does prolonged sports video game playing affect physical fitness, weight management, and social interaction with peers of participants? There is little research at this time that provides answers to these questions and many others as well, but undoubtedly this will be a rich area for psychological and sociological scholarship in the coming years.[43] Another growing debate pertains to how these video games and their "gaming" cultures provide particular ideologies about gender and other dimensions of human activity. Scholars and even employees of game-making companies have been grappling with these social issues recently.

SOCIAL MEDIA: FACEBOOK, INSTAGRAM, YOUTUBE, AND TWITTER

As we noted in an earlier section of this chapter, the most recent manifestation of the integration of computer and Internet technologies is found in the various social media networks. In 2021, YouTube (81 percent of American adults) and Facebook (69 percent of American adults) were the mostly heavily used social media platforms. For many users, social media is part of their daily routine, according to the Pew Research Center, with seven-in-ten Facebook users—and around six-in-ten Instagram and Snapchat users—visiting these sites at least once a day.[44]

Sport organizations throughout the world are employing direct communications with customers—mostly fans—through social media networks, especially Facebook and Twitter. These popular communications technologies have helped professional sports teams to quickly and inexpensively respond to customers and to tailor services for fans. Facebook and Twitter are fostering sport fan services through online communities to exchange comments, ideas, and questions. Through their respective services they can offer massive bulletin boards for consumers to weigh in on major issues about athletes and teams.

Twitter is rapidly becoming a staple in businesses customer service, and that includes sport organizations. In the first quarter of 2022, Twitter had more than 229 million monetizable daily users in the world, and it generated over $5 billion in revenue in the previous year.[45] Athletes, from the high school level to professionals, have become some of the most avid users of Twitter. They use Twitter to promote their own sport accomplishments and to share their personal views and ideas. They are finding it a perfect tool to quickly give out information to fans, during all types of events whether it be live games or player drafts.

MEDIA SPORT: GENDER, RACE, AND DISABILITIES ISSUES

REPRODUCTION OF HEGEMONIC MASCULINITY IN MEDIA SPORT

Linkages between sport and masculinity are longstanding. The British slogan "The Battle of Waterloo was won on the fields of Eton" suggests that participation in sport formed the manly qualities of a military leader. Parents urge their sons to play sports because "sports make men out of boys." Ideals of masculinity are constructed through competitive sport.

Communications scholars who have analyzed how male athletes and the male body are portrayed in the media make clear that media sport is a prominent site for sustaining and displaying traditional Western cultural ideals of masculinity. Verbal and visual media representations of the male athletic body are interpreted as a key source in cultivating, legitimating, and reinforcing the dominant definitions of masculinity as well as general masculine dominance. Although this is accomplished to some extent in all media sports, the sports that are especially physically violent—such as rugby, American football, ice hockey, mixed martial arts, and boxing—present the most frequent and most vivid examples of hegemonic masculinity.

Sports scholars have noted that football has come to occupy the place it holds in American culture in part because it provides a public platform for celebrating a traditional masculine ideal. NFL and NCAA football telecasts are exemplars for reproducing traditional images of masculinity that highlight three aspects of the male body—as instrument, weapon, and object of gaze—in their telecasts.[46]

Masculinity propagated throughout media sport has serious consequences for both women and men: it not only marginalizes, subordinates, and symbolically annihilates women but also marginalizes nontraditional images of masculinity for men, especially non-White and nonheterosexual images.

MEDIA SPORT AND GENDER INEQUITIES

Chapter 7 is devoted to a comprehensive examination of gender in sport. The focus here is on the specific topic of gender and media sport. Prior to the women's movement in the 1970s, sport was considered an exclusively male domain, and women in media sport were not deemed worthy of coverage. So sportswomen were rarely seen in either print or broadcast media. With widespread women's sport participation, media sport coverage began, but

women's achievements were denigrated, and female athletes were framed in terms of women's traditional private roles, such as girlfriends, wives, or mothers; they were objectified in ways similar to soft-core pornography; and their sports records were often compared with men's to deliberately belittle women's achievements.

Considerable progress has been made during the past decade in how media sport represents females, but women's sports have not achieved parity with men's sports in any of the media forms. Studies of the contents of newspapers and magazines in the United States, as well as several other Western countries, have consistently found that stories and photos of women's sports constituted a minority of the coverage; stories and photos of men's sports dominated the print media. Furthermore, much of the coverage still reveals a conventional and restricted view of female sport participation, often framing female athletes in terms of sexual appeal, homosexuality, and sports achievements that do not measure up to those of males.

A study that sampled data about gender and televised sport over a twenty-year period focused on three local network affiliates in Los Angeles and, in the evening, on ESPN's *SportsCenter*. The first-time data for this study were collected in 1989, and the researchers have repeated data collection every five years since then. By 1999 their beliefs were supported inasmuch as media coverage increased to 8.7 percent of all sports coverage. But in 2004 it fell back to 6.3 percent, and the data collected in 2009 surprisingly revealed that the coverage on the evening news programs had almost evaporated—down to 1.6 percent, the lowest amount ever. ESPN was down, too, with only 1.4 percent of its *SportsCenter* program. The researchers admitted that they were stunned by the drop-off.[47]

One of the most promising trends toward increasing women's sports coverage is the emergence of magazines and websites devoted exclusively (or almost exclusively) to women's sport and fitness. *Fitness Magazine* is highly acclaimed for its variety of articles. Other print and Internet outlets provide comprehensive coverage of women's sport activities, focusing on individual female athletes, women's teams, and women's sport organizations; they also examine issues and problems in women's sports.

Until 1996, no women's professional team sport league had ever secured a major national TV network contract. No doubt there were several reasons for this, but certainly a major one was that advertisers were not convinced that women would watch women's sport. Advertisers buy sports programming to reach a targeted audience, so they did not buy women's sports events.

This pattern was broken in the fall of 1996 when the new American Basketball League secured a national cable network contract; in 1997, when the WNBA began play, a national network television contract was in place. The American Basketball League went out of business, but the WNBA network coverage remained in place, and several WNBA teams negotiated local TV contracts with regional sports networks. Currently, ESPN has a broadcast rights contract with the WNBA through the 2022 season that reportedly is worth $12 million a year. Network radio and TV contracts for other women's sports organizations are gradually increasing. CBS will show three regular season games and the championship match for the NWSL (National Women's Soccer League) for three years beginning in 2020, while its CBSSN affiliate will show eleven regular season games and three playoff matches. Then, in a trend that is occurring with many major television broadcasters, eighty-two regular-season matches will also be hosted on the Paramount+ subscription streaming service.[48]

In the past thirty years there has been a significant social transformation in opportunities for

Lacrosse is one of the most recent sports to gain widespread popularity among female athletes—from youth through intercollegiate levels. Until recent years lacrosse was considered too rough and physically demanding for females. Like other sports that were once considered for men only, the skills and efforts displayed by female lacrosse players show that the myth that females are not capable of or willing to engage in strenuous sports is false. (Photo: Cal Sport Media/Alamy Stock Photo)

females to be involved in sports. Accompanying this trend, significant strides have been made to include females in media sport coverage. Although female athletes have historically occupied a limited space within the televised sport world, perhaps some change is coming due to the rising popularity of women's sports: it was found that female athletes received the majority of coverage (55.75 percent) within the seventeen nights of NBC's 2020 Tokyo Summer Olympic prime-time broadcast.[49]

MEDIA SPORT AND RACIAL AND ETHNIC INEQUITIES

In Chapters 2 and 6 we discussed the historical and contemporary struggles of racial and ethnic minority Americans for involvement in sport; here we focus specifically on ethnic and racial issues in *media* sport.

African Americans were largely segregated from commercial sports in the United States until about fifty years ago. Over the past five decades most barriers to African American participation in organized sports have been swept away. Consequently, African American male athletes have played an increasingly prominent role in U.S. sports; indeed, they dominate some of them in terms of percentage of players at the elite levels.

The recent history of outstanding African American and minority male athletes playing on the same teams with, and competing against, White male athletes has made it essential for the media to recognize and report their performances and achievements. Still, several studies over the past twenty years have documented underrepresentation of African American and minority male athlete coverage by both print and electronic media.

African American sportswomen have suffered more from the lack of coverage in media sport than African American males. One example will suffice to illustrate this point: there was a thirty-year gap between the first and second *Sports Illustrated* cover featuring an African American female athlete. Over a thirty-five-year period, African American female athletes appeared on only 5 of 1,835 *Sports Illustrated* covers.

Wherever athletes of color have had a presence in sport, subtle or overt racial stereotyping has historically occurred in all media forms. The most blatant examples are the frequent attributions of Black athletes' achievements to their "natural" abilities to run fast and jump high and their "instincts" to react fast; at the same time, White athletes' achievements are typically attributed to their "intelligence" and superior "thinking ability." Historical stereotypes of Black athletes are coded into characterizations of this kind.[50]

We can still see examples of racial and ethnic stereotyping in global high-profile events such as the European club soccer championships, known as the "Champions League"; CBS broadcast commentator Jim Beglin commented in May 2021 during a match that "It's that Latino temperament" when an Argentine player was given a red card; he subsequently apologized via Twitter, saying that "I wrongly used a racial stereotype."[51] Another recent incident occurred when a Detroit Tigers baseball analyst, former player Jack Morris, mocked English-speaking Asians when talking about Japanese star player Shohei Ohtani.[52]

Male African American athletes, in particular, have also been stereotyped in media sport commentaries as innately violent, thuggish, sexually uncontrolled, selfish, and arrogant. The social transgressions of high-profile Black athletes and media accounts of professional Black athletes as out-of-wedlock fathers and as drug addicts often are highlighted in print and broadcast news. Assuming the articles that accompany the photos are true, they are legitimate news stories, but the impression that the articles and photos make is unmistakable. Clearly, they reinforce stereotypical prejudiced representations of African American males, although, overall, the percentage of Black athletes involved in such actions is small.

The U.S. government's reservation system has been a major structural barrier to sport opportunities for Native American youth. Typically, the sports facilities at reservation schools are inadequate for Native Americans to develop sports skills and experience sports competition against a variety of skilled athletes. The media have generally portrayed stereotypical representations of the few Native American athletes who have achieved elite-level status using nicknames like "the Chief," "Redskin," and "Wahoo" in media stories about them. Native Americans' images as team mascots are approvingly portrayed in the media as TV cameras pan the spectators in arenas and stadiums when fans do the "tomahawk chop" and show close-up camera shots of costumed "Indians" dancing around venues after touchdowns and three-point baskets.[53]

Asian American and Latino American athletes have been either neglected in the media or, when covered, given stereotyped representations and nicknames. Media portrayals, rather than personal experiences, often become the primary source of information that shapes Whites' perceptions of other groups. Unfortunately, the depictions in media sports help institutionalize the social and information gap between people of color and Whites.

MEDIA SPORT AND DISABILITIES INEQUITIES

Many scholars who have researched the media coverage of athletes with disabilities have found common trends based on ablest notions of "normal" bodies. As one researcher notes, "People with disabilities have historically been excluded from the sport–media complex because of their failure to meet the hegemonically prescribed ideals of physicality. Thus, noncoverage of athletes with disabilities is the norm for North American media."

For example, two researchers from the University of Calgary analyzed how the *New York Times* covered the Olympics and Paralympics from 1955 to 2012 and found that the amount of coverage for Paralympians is much less than that for Olympians. In the time period of 2008–2012, the number of articles on Olympic athletes was 2,091 and on Paralympic athletes 246.[54] More recently, during the 2020 Tokyo Summer Paralympic Games, NBC Universal aired 1,200 hours of coverage including primetime broadcasts for the first time in history. Two hundred of these hours were shown on NBC, NBCSN, and the Olympic Channel, while streaming coverage was provided for more than 1,000 hours on other associated digital streaming platforms.[55] While this seems like a significant amount of television coverage, it is still dwarfed by the overall coverage given to the 2020 Summer Olympic Games, which was 7,000 hours across NBC's various media outlets.[56]

SPORTS JOURNALISM AND THE MASS MEDIA

Sports journalism, including sportscasting, is a peculiar occupation. On the one hand, a certain amount of prestige and power are associated with the occupation. Sports journalists' names are seen and heard by the public daily, they control access to the sports information that the public wants, and their stories and commentaries can influence the destinies of franchises and athletes. On the other hand, in a book titled *Sports Journalism: Context and Issues*, the author (a sportswriter) claims, "In the hierarchy of professional journalism, [sports journalism] has been traditionally viewed disparagingly as the 'toy department,' a bastion of easy living, sloppy journalism and 'soft' news." Another sportswriter remarked, "Sports writing is categorized alongside beer-tasting and aphrodisiac-evaluation. People say 'More of a hobby than a job, isn't it?' "[57]

Ostensibly, sports journalists are expected to report information about the results of sports events; provide inside information on particular players, teams, and sports organizations; and give opinions that help the public interpret sports news. Although accuracy and objectivity in reporting are valued norms in journalism, the image of the sports journalist is one of obsequious appeasement. More than one critic of sportswriters has observed that their work all too often reflects jock worship, press-agentry, and awe rather than solid, in-depth reporting.[58]

Several practices of sports journalists contribute to their disparagement as objective reporters. Some sportswriters, through their columns and reports about the local teams, convey the impression that *they* are extensions of the teams; they are frequently called "housemen" or "housewomen" because their stories often read like publicity on behalf of the local team or teams. In return, the local teams are expected to treat these reporters favorably in providing access to coaches and players and obtaining exclusive stories about the team or teams. This practice has declined because of the criticism within the journalism occupation itself, but it is easy to see how such an approach can create a cozy interdependence between journalists and sports teams. At the same time, the advent of many new sport blogs, websites, and other platforms of sports coverage indicates that more diverse and even critical views are being expressed by emerging journalists.

TV sports news reporters often share time with weather forecasters and with anchors reporting on local, national, and international events. Sports news is often relegated to a few minutes that are filled mostly with reporting scores and hyping upcoming events. In cities where pro teams reside or big-time collegiate sports (or both) are nearby, the TV sports reporters are frequently outright cheerleaders for these local teams, referring to them as "our team." In some cases they virtually become public relations agents for them.

In general, investigative journalism in sports occurs less frequently compared to straightforward sports news reporting. The major reason for the lack of investigative sports reporting is that media corporations, such as CBS, NBC, and ABC are sponsoring sports events and generating profits, so critical reporting of teams, leagues, and key participants can create conflicts and problems. Media corporations have major business relationships with sports organizations that are worth billions of dollars, so journalists working for, say, CBS Sports cannot readily critique the morals of the sports organizations that CBS does business with. There are a few emerging examples in the investigative genre, however, such as ESPN's "Outside the Lines" series, which has covered topics such as sexual abuse, football injuries, and steroid use in youth baseball.

However, because of the friendly business relations between the media industry and sports, broadcast news does not generally operate in a serious journalistic manner; its concern is more with promoting the teams and leagues in which it has invested than with functioning as professional journalism.

SPORTSCASTERS: NARRATORS OF MEDIATED SPORT

Because radio and TV sportscasters "tutor" listeners and viewers in what they should hear, see, and believe about the sports events being broadcast, they are extremely important in such broadcasts. Consequently, they are carefully selected for their ability to command credibility because they play a big role in attracting and holding listeners' and viewers' attention.

The usual selections are former professional and elite amateur athletes and coaches with high name recognition. The rise of celebrity sportscasters can be directly attributed to television. As sporting celebrities and "certified experts," these former athletes and coaches have immediate recognition and credibility with the listeners and viewers, and audiences of sporting event broadcasts will accept their interpretations and opinions as objective and true.

Employing former athletes and coaches to describe the technical skills, strategy, and tactics used during a broadcast sports event may seem reasonable enough, but it is important to realize that they also act to articulate moral values and to comment prescriptively on social relationships. Former sport stars are uniquely qualified for this task because they are survivors—even models—of the competitive sport meritocracy. Their attitudes and values are largely congruent with commercialized sports perspectives because they are fully integrated into the dominant values and beliefs of that system.

Preventing viewer boredom is one of the main concerns of broadcast producers, so one basic job of sportscasters is to keep listeners and viewers tuned in to the broadcast. To do this, they provide a commentary that heightens the drama of the event, using methods such as the following:

- Constructing themes, such as "these teams hate each other" or "this is a grudge game." The message in both cases: the audience can expect a hard-fought contest with lots of fierce action.
- Highlighting "matchups" between players on opposite teams. This sets up a kind of one-on-one competition on which the audience can focus. Similarly, elaborate discussions of "keys to winning" are calculated to get viewers absorbed in the contest.
- Framing the game as a crucial game for both teams (even if they are both hopelessly out of championship contention); heightening the significance of the game enhances audience interest (or so it is believed).
- Other sportscaster techniques include personal interest stories, recitation of statistics and records, anticipation of what to expect, dramatic embellishments of the action, and second-guessing.

All of these narratives are designed to keep audiences tuned in to the broadcast.

Another important job of sportscasters is selling the sport organization, league, and network for which they are broadcasting. Game commentary is frequently commercial hype for those organizations. For example, sportscasters tend to effusively praise the athletes, teams, and leagues throughout the broadcasts. Another favorite "sales" practice of sportscasters is creating attention-attracting monikers to develop team name recognition and get fans to identify with teams or athletes; for instance, the Dallas Cowboys of the NFL have become known as "America's Team."

Sportscasters who broadcast high-profile live events on radio or television typically have no background in journalism. They are usually selected by radio and television executives for their ability to narrate sports events as much as for their knowledge of the game. Many are former athletes and coaches who are articulate in explaining the intricacies of the game or are charismatic.

They must satisfy not only the media corporation that employs them but also the league commissioners and team owners whose games are being broadcast. The latter routinely screen the announcers and instruct the media executives as to how the announcers can improve their performances, letting it be known that all comments should cast the league, teams, and players in a favorable light. Consequently, objective reporting takes a backseat to the creation and maintenance of a favorable image of both sport and the media. A sportswriter for the *New York Times* once noted that "televised sport is not journalism; it is entertainment, shaped to keep people in front of the beer advertisements as long as possible." And other media analysts have suggested that a more appropriate portrayal of sportscasters would be sport public relations agents, whose main function is to elevate the banal.

In studies of the impact of commentary on audience perception and appreciation, researchers have exposed subjects to two segments of prerecorded, televised games that have been pretested for perception of roughness. Viewers were exposed to one of two presentation modes: with or without sportscasters'

commentary. The results showed that the viewers' perceptions of the play were dramatically influenced by the nature of the accompanying commentary. Thus, through the commentary by sportscasters, viewers can be influenced to "see" fierce competition and roughness where it really does not exist. The researchers concluded that viewers seem to become "caught up" in the commentary and the sportscasters' interpretation of the game, and they allow themselves to be persuaded by the narration of "drama" in the event. There is, then, overwhelming evidence that sports telecasts can be presented and manipulated to create different levels of enjoyment for viewers.[59]

It is one thing for television networks to employ up to three sportscasters to cover a game; it is quite another to believe that these persons are giving viewers an accurate or inside view of the game. They are, in fact, doing just the opposite. They report actions where they do not exist; they protect owners, coaches, and athletes from serious scrutiny; and they constantly hype the sport and its participants. All of these actions are predicated on obtaining high ratings for the network. The bottom line is that both professional sport and television are big businesses, each dependent on the fiscal health of the other. By reporting an exciting game, the sportscasters promote both sport and television.

What a person sees and reads about sports via the mass media has been deliberately filtered to show the best side of sports. Although a certain amount of criticism may be reported, sports journalists in the main are supportive of the system. Few report anything that might cause discomfort. By omission and commission, complicity and docility, the media reports seldom stray from the promotion of sport except for an occasional exposé.

The reason for sports journalists' cooperation with the sports establishment may be more fundamental than selling newspapers or obtaining high radio and TV ratings. Those few sports journalists who do not report sport in the traditional way often incur the outrage of committed sports fans. They are often targets of hate letters and ugly phone calls in the middle of the night. In one way, this is understandable because it is almost heretical to attack sport. To attack sport is to impugn the American value system. To challenge the sanctity of sport is to criticize what for many people is their main anchor for understanding how the real world works.[60]

MINORITY SPORT JOURNALISTS AND BROADCASTERS

Sportswriting and broadcasting have been largely White male professions in the United States, closely mirroring the hierarchical racial division of labor so evident in the broader mass communications occupational structure. Some examples follow.

In 2016, according to the American Society of Newspaper Editors, there were about 33,000 full-time daily newspaper journalists at 1,734 newspapers in the United States. Of the 33,000 employees, about 17 percent were minorities; women comprised 38 percent of daily newspaper employees.[61] Recently, the *New York Times* reported in 2020 that it its leadership staff was about 77 percent White, while the *Associated Press* revealed that its news management staff was about 81 percent White.[62]

Many fans have formed the impression that African Americans represent a substantial portion of sports journalism because they see African American professional athletes and coaches so often in sports. The reality is something quite different in sports journalism. According to the *Associated Press Sports Editors Racial and Gender Report Card* published by the Institute for Diversity and Ethics in Sport, the vast majority of people holding key positions on the major newspapers and media websites in the United States are White and male. The findings for 2021 indicate that 79.2 percent of the sports editors were white and 83.3 percent were men, 72.0 percent of the assistant sports editors were white and 75.8 percent were men, and 77.1 percent of the columnists were white and 82.2 percent were men. Moreover, it was found in this report that 77.1 percent of the reporters were white and 85.6 percent were men, 77.0 percent of the copy editors/designers were white and 75.3 percent were men, and 72.4 percent of web specialists were white and 78.1 percent were men.[63]

Then, in the realm of television, the overall news work force is predominantly White, with only 26.6 percent of this workforce being people of color. Meanwhile, radio broadcasting is also overwhelmingly comprised

of Whites at 84.6 percent, while Whites remain 92.9 percent of directors in this industry. This trend is mirrored in television and radio news coverage of professional sports. For instance, the *Guardian* newspaper found that in 2019, of the 251 broadcasters who did play-by-play and analyzed games or worked as sideline reports for the NFL's TV and radio partners, only 49 (or less than one-fifth) were African-American. The NBA does fare better compared to the NFL and is making progress in terms of its broadcasting diversity.[64]

Taken together, the figures remain concerning when one considers the fact that in the world of sports, especially at professional and collegiate levels, a disproportionate number of professional athletes are people of color. Of course, diversity is not just about numbers; it is also about making journalism and broadcasting better. Diverse staffs can lead to better journalism and broadcasting. Rather than being token members of broadcasting teams, they must be allowed to speak openly rather than simply maintain the status quo to keep their jobs. More diversity can also provide much-needed subjective insight into the experiences that people of color have had in the sport domain.

Many barriers have fallen by the wayside as people of color have gained increasing respect for their sports reporting and broadcasting skills, but one fact is clear: there are still few minority sportswriters and sportscasters in this profession. The percentages of those working in sports journalism and broadcasting are a poor reflection of the proportion of Black and minority athletes playing sports in the United States. The subordination of minorities in media sports continues, and each new breakthrough requires concerted struggle against the persistent, White-dominated division of labor in media sport.

WOMEN SPORT JOURNALISTS AND BROADCASTERS

Women who have wished to have careers in journalism and broadcasting have had an arduous struggle. Media organizations currently do not provide a level playing field for women. Women make up more than 50 percent of the adult population, but it has been found by the Institute for Diversity and Ethics in Sport that women made up only about 18 percent of the total staffs of Associated Press Sports Editors

(APSE) member newspapers and websites. In 2021, the percentage of APSE women serving as sports editors was 16.7 and the percentage of women columnists was about 17.8. Then, only 14.4 percent of reporters were women. Overall, just 19.3 percent of all SPSE staffs were women in 2021. Not a pretty picture for the principle of gender equity in media organizations (although conditions are better in radio and television broadcasting). As a result, Richard Lapchick and his colleagues at the Institute for Diversity and Ethics in Sport gave the APSE newspapers and websites a grade of F for gender hiring practices in the key positions covered.[65]

Despite the indignities and the discrimination that female sportswriters and sportscasters have experienced and the relatively few women working in the field, some gains have been made. Women now hold important positions in both print and broadcast media sports in the United States. They have acquired access to press boxes, locker rooms, and other facilities important to their work. A few sportscasters and reporters can be found working across several major sports, and individuals such as Robin Roberts have even moved from the realm of covering sports into prestigious mainstream network positions.

Notwithstanding the increased number of women in sports journalism and broadcasting, Lapchick's report conveys a sobering account of the barriers that still exist. At a time when White males hold the overwhelming majority of the APSE positions, whereas women of all races and ethnicities hold only a few such positions, it is clear that there are substantial obstructions to gender equity for women in sports journalism.

SUMMARY

A symbiotic relationship exists between sport and the mass media; each is a commercial industry whose success has been greatly influenced by the other. The print media contributed to the rise of sport during the nineteenth century. At the same time, the interest in sports information assisted in the growth of newspapers, magazines, and books. The electronic media—radio and television—have been instrumental in the promotion of big-time intercollegiate sports and professional sports. Indeed, without these media, collegiate and professional sports could not function as they currently do.

The dominating role that the mass media play in the economic aspects of sport has a number of effects. Televised sport has produced a dramatic shift in the mode of fans' consumption of sport; the popularity of several sports has been greatly influenced by television; and television has furthered the professionalization of amateur sport enterprises, such as intercollegiate athletics and the Summer and Winter Olympic Games. Television has also greatly manipulated the structures, meanings, and processes of sports.

Televised sports programs are some of the most popular on TV. The three major commercial networks no longer are the only major sports events providers. Beginning with ESPN as the first all-sports, all-the-time network and continuing with regional sports networks, single-sport networks, satellite networks, and so on, countless hours of live sports are a significant feature of contemporary entertainment and news. Internet sports have also become a huge player in the mediated sports industry. Then, given the rapid increase in mobile technology platforms within our society, there are now more opportunities to consume sports than ever before.

Media sport is a site where verbal and visual representations of the male athletic body are interpreted in ways that reinforce the dominant definitions of masculinity as well as general masculine dominance. The sports that are especially physically violent—such as rugby, Mixed Martial Arts, American football, ice hockey, and boxing—present the most frequent and most vivid images of hegemonic masculinity.

Sports journalists are typically employees of professional teams or of television networks, and their jobs are essentially promotional. They do not merely report the events; instead, their accentuated accounts of the events are intended to make these events seem important and interesting. Their role, rather than to provide information, is to translate unfolding games into mass and dramatic entertainment aimed at high ratings. In doing so, they promote the media and the sports in which they are employed. The status quo remains and potentially controversial topics or events are generally given short shrift or ignored completely.

Discrimination, both gender and racial, has been present in the ways in which the mass media report sports and in the hiring practices of media corporations. While there are a few high-profile women and ethnic and racial minorities working in the field, the vast majority of key positions such as sports editor are held by White males. This occurs despite the fact that major sports themselves are highly represented on the athlete side by women and minority groups. Thus, while women and members of ethnic and racial minority groups have gradually gained respect for their sports reporting and broadcasting skills, there are still few of these sportswriters and sportscasters in the sports journalism profession. Diversifying this profession would arguably serve to provide fresh and much-needed insights into the landscape of major competitive sports in the United States.

Learn more with this chapter's digital tools, including web resources, video links, and chapter self-assessment quizzes at www.oup.com/he/sage-eitzen-beal-atencio-12e.

NOTES

1. Derek Thompson, "The Most Valuable Network," *The Atlantic Monthly*, September 2013, 23.

2. Matthew Nicholson, Anthony Kerr, and Meryn Sherwood, *Sport and the Media: Managing the Nexus*, 2nd ed. (New York: Routledge, 2015).

3. Christian Fuchs, *Social Media: A Critical Introduction*, 2nd ed. (Thousand Oaks, CA: Sage, 2017); see also Stanley J. Baran and Dennis K. Davis, *Mass Communication Theory: Foundations, Ferment, and Future*, 7th ed. (Belmont, CA: Wadsworth, 2014).

4. Bernie Sanders, "Corporate Media Threaten Our Democracy," *In These Times*, February 2017, 28–31.

5. Sanders, "Corporate Media."

6. Yuliya Talmazan, "In Belarus, Unlike Most Places, Soccer Plays on Despite Virus," *ABC News*, April 20, 2020, https://www.nbcnews.com/news/world/belarus-unlike-most-places-soccer-plays-despite-virus-n1187701; and Peter Pae and Sohee Kim, "Without Fans or High-Fives, Baseball Plays On in Korea," *Bloomberg Businessweek*, May 30, 2020; https://www.bloomberg.com/news/articles/2020-05-30/baseball-on-espn-korea-s-major-league-plays-through-covid-19.

7. Phil Andrews, *Sports Journalism: A Practical Introduction*, 2nd ed. (Thousand Oaks, CA: Sage, 2013); see also Scott Reinardy and Wayne Wanta, *The Essentials of Sports Reporting and Writing* (New York: Routledge, 2009).

8. Scott McDonald," 'Sports Illustrated' Scaling Back to Publishing Just Once a Month in 2020," *Newsweek*, November 11, 2019, https://www.newsweek.com/sports-illustrated-scaling-back-publishing-just-once-month-2020-1471644.

9. Keith J. Kelly, "Sports Illustrated to Become Monthly Magazine in 2020," *New York Post*, November 13, 2019, https://nypost.com/2019/11/13/sports-illustrated-to-become-monthly-magazine-in-2020/.

10. http://www.rab.com/public/matteroffact/mar2017/MatterofFact-SportsRadio.html#:~:text=There%20are%20780%20AM%2FFM%20sports%20stations%20in%20the%20U.S. Accessed June 10, 2022

11. Staff, "Page 2's Top 20 Sports Movies of All-Time," ESPN Page 2, http://www.espn.com/page2/movies/s/top20/fulllist.html.

12. Leichtman Research Group, "46% of Adults Watch Video via a Connected TV Device Daily," Leichtman Research Group, June 3, 2022, https://www.leichtmanresearch.com/46-of-adults-watch-video-via-a-connected-tv-device-daily/.

13. Cotton Delo, "U.S. Adults Now Spending More Time on Digital Devices Than Watching TV," *Advertising Age*, August 1, 2013, https://adage.com/article/digital/americans-spend-time-digital-devices-tv/243414; see also "TV and Media," *Ericsson Consumer Lab TV and Media Study*, 2013, https://www.ericsson.com/investors/financial-reports; see also Brett Hutchins and David Rowe, *Sport beyond Television: The Internet, Digital Media and the Rise of Networked Media Sport* (New York: Routledge, 2013).

14. "About Three-in-ten U.S. Adults Say They Are 'Almost Constantly' Online," Pew Research Center, March 26, 2021, https://www.pewresearch.org/

fact-tank/2021/03/26/about-three-in-ten-u-s-adults-say-they-are-almost-constantly-online/.

15. Audrey Schomer, "U.S. Time Spent With Media 2021," eMarketer, May 27, 2021, https://www.insiderintelligence.com/content/us-time-spent-with-media-2021.

16. Christian Fuchs, *Social Media: A Critical Introduction*, 2nd ed. (Thousand Oaks, CA: Sage, 2017); see also Andrew Billings and Lawrence Wenner, eds., *Sport, Media, and Mega-Events* (New York: Routledge, 2017).

17. Jimmy Sanderson, *It's a Whole New Ballgame: How Social Media Is Changing Sports* (New York: Hampton Press, 2011), 3.

18. Sanderson, *It's a Whole New Ballgame*, 24.

19. "First Television of Baseball Scene," *New York Times*, May 18, 1939, 29.

20. "How Much Sports Content Are Americans Watching?," Wegryn Enterprises, July 28, 2022, https://wegrynenterprises.com/2022/03/24/report-1-in-4-americans-watch-5-hours-of-sports-weekly/.

21. Alex Sherman, "Disney's Shift to Streaming Puts ESPN in Awkward Position of CLinging to the Past," CNBC, October 10, 2021, https://www.cnbc.com/2021/10/10/disney-shift-to-streaming-puts-espn-in-position-of-clinging-to-past.html.

22. Dennis Deninger, *Sports on Television: The How and Why behind What You See* (New York: Routledge, 2012); see also Alexander Wolff, "The Revolution Will Not Be Televised," *Sports Illustrated*, December 12, 2016, 111–120.

23. Brent Axe, "Super Bowl 2017: Patriots' Comeback Win Most-Viewed Show in Television History," Syracuse, February 6, 2017, http://www.syracuse.com/superbowl/index.ssf/2017/02/super_bowl_2017_patriots_comeback_win_most-viewed_show_in_television_history.html.

24. Scott Roxborough, "Rio Olympics Worldwide Audience to Top 3.5 Billion, IOC Estimates," *The Hollywood Reporter*, August 18, 2016, https://www.hollywoodreporter.com/news/rio-olympics-worldwide-audience-top-920526.

25. Megan Graham, "Media Companies Expect a Tough Quarter for TV Advertising, with No Live Sports and Spending Delayed," *CNBC*, May 8, 2020, https://www.cnbc.com/2020/05/08/tv-advertising-bracing-for-tough-quarter-amid-coronavirus-pandemic.html.

26. Kristen Conti, "How Much Super Bowl Commercials Cost in 2022, and Through the Years," NBC Los Angeles, February 12, 2022, https://www.nbclosangeles.com/news/sports/super-bowl-2022/a-look-at-super-bowl-commercial-costs-through-the-years/2822339/.

27. Ken Belson and Victor Mather, "Die Is Cast: Owners O.K Raiders' Move to Las Vegas," *The New York Times*, March 28, 2017, B8; see also Brad R Humphreys, *Economics of Professional Sports* (Morgantown, WV: BRH Publishing, 2013).

28. Randy R Grant, *The Economics of Intercollegiate Sports*, 2nd ed. (Hackensack, NJ: World Scientific, 2015); see also John S. Watterson, *College Football: History, Spectacle, Controversy* (Baltimore: Johns Hopkins University Press, 2000).

29. Keith Dunnavant, *The Fifty-Year Seduction: How Television Manipulated College Football, from the Birth of the Modern NCAA to the Creation of the BCS* (New York: St. Martin's Press, 2004), xvi; see also Andy Staples, "How Television Changed College Football—and How It Will Again," *Sports Illustrated*, August 6, 2012, https://www.si.com/college-football/2012/08/06/tv-college-football#.

30. "Turner, CBS and the NCAA Reach Long-term Multimedia Rights Extension for D1 Men's Basketball," NCAAcom, April 12, 2016, https://www.ncaa.com/news/basketball-men/article/2016-04-12/turner-cbs-and-ncaa-reach-long-term-multimedia-rights.

31. Mark Yost, *Varsity Green: A behind the Scenes Look at Culture and Corruption in College Athletics* (Stanford, CA: Stanford University Press, 2010).

32. Quoted in Jim Halley, "Prep TV Has Pros and Cons," *USA Today*, August 22, 2013, 1C–2C; quoted in Christine Brennan, "Prep Football Best as Local Fare," *USA Today*, August 22, 2013, 3C; quoted in Fred Grimm, "Exploiting Sports Prodigies Now Is ESPN," *Miami Herald*, October 1, 2009, B1.

33. ESPN Creative Studio, "Inside the UFC's Plans to Expand Its Global Stronghold," ESPN, n.d., https://www.espn.com/espn/feature/story/_/id/31027599/inside-ufc-plans-expand-global-stronghold. Accessed June 14, 2022.

34. Michael A Messner, Michele Dunbar, and Darnell Hunt, "The Televised Sports Manhood Formula," in *Sport in Contemporary Society: An Anthology*, 9th

ed., ed. D. Stanley Eitzen (Boulder, CO: Paradigm, 2012), 59–72; see also Cheryl Cooky, Michael A. Messner, and Robin H. Hextrum, "Women Play Sport, but Not on TV: A Longitudinal Study of Televised News Media," *Communication & Sport* 1, no. 3 (2013): 203–230.

35. Brad Shultz, Philip H. Caskey, and Craig Esherick, *Media Relations in Sport*, 4th ed. (Morgantown, WV: Fit Publishing, 2013).

36. Simon Kemp, "Digital 2021: The United States of America," Datareportal, February 9, 2021, https://datareportal.com/reports/digital-2021-united-states-of-america#:~:text=%20357%20sag22711_ch12_325-358%20357%2007/07/22%2005:18%20PM%20Notes%20There%20were%20298.8%20million%20internet,at%2090.0%25%20in%20January%202021.

37. Matt Hanson and Jamie Carter, "How to Watch the Rio 2016 Olympic Games," *Techrad*, August 20, 2016; see also Jon Swartz and Matt Krantz, "For Marketers, This Olympics Is a Social Media Event," *USA Today*, July 27, 2012, 1C–2C.

38. Teodora Dobrilova, "How Much Is the Gaming Industry Worth in 2021? [+25 Powerful Stats]," *Techjury*, August 5, 2021, https://techjury.net/blog/gaming-industry-worth/#gref.

39. Todd Spangler, "Number of U.S. Video Gamers Hits 227 Million, and Most Say They've Played More During COVID, ESA Study," *Variety*, July 13, 2021, https://variety.com/2021/gaming/news/number-video-game-players-2021-esa-study-covid-1235016079/.

40. Kellen Browning, "How John Madden Became the 'Larger-Than-Life' Face of a Gaming Empire," *New York Times*, December, 29, 2021, https://www.nytimes.com/2021/12/29/sports/football/john-madden-nfl-video-game.html.

41. J.J. Pryor, "The 15 Highest Selling Sports Video Games of All Time," Medium, September 22, 2020, https://medium.com/illumination/the-15-highest-selling-sports-video-games-of-all-time-7ff44c1ab81.

42. Xiaowei Cai, Javier Cebollada, Monica Cortinas, "From Traditional Gaming to Mobile Gaming: Video Game Players' Switching Behavior," Entertainment Computing 40 (2022), https://doi.org/10.1016/j.entcom.2021.100445.

43. Garry Crawford and Victoria K. Gosling, "More Than a Game: Sports-Themed Video Games and Player Narratives," *Sociology of Sport Journal* 26, no. 1 (2009): 50–66; see also Paul J. C. Adachi and Teena Willoughby, "From the Couch to the Sports Field: The Longitudinal Associations between Sports Video Game Play, Self-Esteem, and Involvement in Sports," *Psychology of Popular Media Culture* 4, no. 4 (2015): 329–341; Craig A. Anderson, Akiko Shibuya, Nobuko Ihori, Edward L. Swing, Brad J. Bushman, Akira Sakamoto, Hannah R. Rothstein, and Muniba Saleem, "Violent Video Game Effects on Aggression, Empathy, and Prosocial Behavior in Eastern and Western Countries: A Meta-Analytic Review," *Psychological Bulletin*, 136, no. 2 (2010): 151–173.

44. "Social Media Fact Sheet," Pew Research Center, April 7, 2021, https://www.pewresearch.org/internet/fact-sheet/social-media/.

45. S. Dixon, "The Number of Monetizable Daily Active Twitter Users (mDAU) Worldwide from 1st Quarter 2017 to 1st Quarter 2022," Statista, Inc., May 17, 2022, https://www.statista.com/statistics/970920/monetizable-daily-active-twitter-users-worldwide/.

46. Kristi A. Allain, "'Real Fast and Tough': The Construction of Canadian Hockey Masculinity," *Sociology of Sport Journal* 25, no. 4 (2008): 462–481; and Michael A. Messner and Raewyn Connell, *Out of Play: Critical Essays on Gender and Sport* (Albany: State University of New York Press, 2007).

47. Michael A. Messner and Cheryl Cooky, *Gender in Televised Sports: News and Highlight Shows, 1989–2009*, Center for Feminist Research, University of Southern California, June 2010; see also Cheryl Cooky, Michael A. Messner, and Robin H. Hextrum, "Women Play Sports, but Not on TV: A Longitudinal Study of Televised News Media," *Communication & Sport* 1, no. 3 (2013): 203–230.

48. Sandra Herrera, "2021 NWSL TV Schedule: CBS to Air Championship, Paramount+ to Exclusively Stream 82 Matches," *CBS*, May 26, 2021, https://www.cbssports.com/soccer/news/2021-nwsl-tv-schedule-cbs-to-air-championship-paramount-to-exclusively-stream-82-matches/.

49. Women Dominate NBC Tokyo Olympic Primetime Coverage by Record Margin," *FiveRingTV*, August 9, 2021, https://fiveringtv.com/2021/08/09/women-dominate-nbc-tokyo-olympic-primetime-coverage-by-record-margin/.

50. Dana D. Brooks and Ronald C. Althouse, *Racism in College Athletics*, 3rd ed. (Morgantown, WV: Fitness Information Technology, 2013); see also David J. Leonard and C. Richard King, eds., *Commodified and Criminalized: New Racism and African Americans in Contemporary Sports*, reprint ed. (Lanham, MD: Rowman & Littlefield, 2012).

51. "Announcer Jim Beglin Sorry for Comment About PSG's Angel Di Maria," ESPN, August 9, 2021, https://www.espn.com/soccer/paris-saint-germain—frapsg/story/4377657/announcer-jim-beglin-sorry-for-comment-about-psgs-angel-di-maria

52. Madeline Coleman, "Tigers Broadcaster Jack Morris Apologizes for Racist Remark during Shohei Ohtani's At-Bat," *Sports Illustrated*, August 18, 2021, https://www.si.com/mlb/2021/08/18/shohei-ohtani-tigers-broadcaster-jack-morris-apologizes-racist-remark.

53. C. Richard King, ed. *The Native American Mascot Controversy: A Handbook* (Lanham, MD: Roman & Littlefield, 2015); see also Jennifer Guiliano, *Indian Spectacle: College Mascots and the Anxiety of Modern America* (New Brunswick, NJ: Rutgers University Press, 2015).

54. Jeremy Tynedal and Gregor Wolbring, "Paralympics and Its Athletes through the Lens of the *New York Times*," *Sports* 1, no. 1 (2013): 13–36.

55. "NBC Universal to Air Record Paralympic Coverage from Tokyo, Including Primetime," *NBC Sports*, February 24, 2021, https://olympics.nbcsports.com/2021/02/24/nbc-tokyo-paralympics-coverage/.

56. Scooby Axson, "What to Know About NBC's Coverage of the Tokyo Olympics," *USA Today*, July 20, 2021, https://www.usatoday.com/story/sports/olympics/2021/07/20/nbcs-2021-tokyo-olympics-coverage-includes-peacock/7791213002/.

57. These two quotes are from Raymond Boyle, *Sports Journalism: Context and Issues* (Thousand Oaks, CA: Sage, 2006), 1; see also Andrew Baker, *Where Am I and Who's Winning? Travelling the World of Sport* (London: Yellow Jersey Press, 2004), ix.

58. Kathryn T. Stofer, *Sports Journalism: An Introduction to Reporting and Writing* (Lanham, MD: Rowman & Littlefield, 2009).

59. Arthur A. Raney and Anthony J. Depalma, "The Effect of Viewing Varying Levels and Contexts of Violent Sports Programming on Enjoyment, Mood, and Perceived Violence," *Mass Communication and Society* 9, no. 3 (2006): 321–338; see also Linda K. Fuller, *Sportscasters/Sportscasting: Principles and Practices* (New York: Routledge, 2008).

60. Several excellent articles about sports fans can be found in Adam C. Earnheardt, Paul Haridakis, and Barbara Hugenberg, eds., *Sports Fans, Identity, and Socialization: Exploring the Fandemonium*, reprint ed. (Lanham, MD: Lexington Books, 2013); see also Eric Simons, *The Secret Lives of Sports Fans* (New York: Overlook, 2013).

61. "ASNE Releases 2016 Diversity Survey Results," News Leader Association, July 28, 2022, https://members.newsleaders.org/blog_home.asp?Display=2153.

62. David Bauder, "Efforts to Track Diversity in Journalism are Lagging," AP News, October 14, 2021, https://apnews.com/article/business-race-and-ethnicity-journalism-arts-and-entertainment-885ce3486382d7c3080519c50407aa18; see also "A Call to Action," *New York Times*, accessed July 28, 2022, https://www.nytco.com/company/diversity-%20and-inclusion/a-call-to-action/.

63. Richard Lapchick, "The 2018 Associated Press Sports Editors Racial and Gender Report Card," Institute for Diversity and Ethics in Sport, May 2, 2018, https://43530132-36e9-4f52-811a-182c7a91933b.filesusr.com/ugd/7d86e5_9dca4bc2067241cdba67aa2f1b09fd1b.pdf.

64. Andrew Lawrence, "The NFL is 70% Black, So Why is its TV Coverage So White?," *The Guardian*, January 31, 2019, https://www.theguardian.com/sport/2019/jan/31/nfl-tv-coverage-racial-demographics-super-bowl.

65. Richard Lapchick, "The 2021 Sports Media Racial and Gender Report Card: Associate Press Sports Editors (APSE)," Institute for Diversity and Ethics in Sport, July 28, 2022, https://www.tidesport.org/_files/ugd/138a69_e1e67c118b784f4cabao0a4536699300.pdf.

CHAPTER 13

SPORT AND POLITICS

Sport and politics are inextricably linked. [Many] argue that there is no place for
politics in sport because of the detrimental effects it can cause. Practicing sport
in an apolitical environment is not only impossible but in many ways also
undesirable.

—ISABELLE BOULERT, *Edinburgh University*[1]

A giant American flag is displayed as the U.S. Olympic Team marches into Japan's National Stadium during the
2020 Tokyo Summer Olympic Games. This patriotic pageantry is frequently employed at sports events,
symbolically uniting citizens in a common bond of patriotism. (Photo: Patrick Smith/Getty Images)

Astatement often heard in discussions among friends about issues and problems in sport is "Keep politics out of sport," or the reverse, "Keep sport out of politics." Such comments are usually followed by expressions of agreement with the speaker. But these assertions do not correspond at all with reality. A more realistic point of view is that sports and politics have long been bedfellows. "The truth of the matter is that sports do not exist in a vacuum, as purely an escape from life."[2]

Indeed, examples of the ties between sport and politics are plentiful. A few are described here:

- A 2019 tweet that gave support to pro-democracy protesters in Hong Kong by a former Houston Rockets general manager angered the Chinese government, whose state-run television network CCTV subsequently stopped showing NBA games. As a result, the NBA quickly distanced itself from Morey's comments while numerous U.S. politicians began to weigh in on this issue via Twitter. The NBA eventually lost hundreds of millions of dollars, and Morey himself conceded that he had made "the second-most powerful government on Earth mad."[3]
- Russian and Belarusian tennis players were banned from the 2022 Wimbledon grand slam tournament because of their governments' involvements in the war in Ukraine. Tournament organizers stated that this ban was in accordance with United Kingdom government directives. It was also stated that these players' participation at Wimbledon could be used as potential propaganda for the Russian government. [4]
- At the 1972 Munich Summer Olympic Games, Palestinian terrorists attacked Israeli athletes, killing 11 of them. The terrorists demanded the release and safe passage to Egypt of 234 Palestinians and non-Arabs jailed in Israel.
- The United States (and other nations) boycotted the 1980 Summer Olympic Games in Moscow; the Soviet Union (and other nations) subsequently boycotted the 1984 Los Angeles Summer Olympics.
- The lead-up to the 2016 Summer Olympics in Rio, Brazil, was marked by political controversies, including the instability of the country's federal government, health and safety concerns surrounding

the Zika virus, and a doping scandal involving Russian athletes, all of which affected the participation of its athletes in the Games.

Each of these examples illustrates the intermingling of sport and politics at the international level, but sport–political connections are present at all levels of sport and politics, from the local to the state (or province) to the national. Here are some examples:

- A decision by the city council of a town to build (or not to build) a public golf course is a political decision.
- A decision by a city metropolitan district to seek public funds to build a baseball field for the Colorado Rockies MLB team was a political decision.
- A decision to pay a large percentage of the cost to build the University of Phoenix, a multipurpose stadium in Phoenix, Arizona, as a home venue for the NFL's Arizona Cardinals was a political decision by several levels of the state's government.
- In 1990 President George H. W. Bush signed the Americans with Disabilities Act—a political decision—which turned out to include protecting the rights of athletes with physical or mental disabilities. As a result, the U.S. Olympic Committee provides sport training and competition for athletes with physical disabilities, and U.S. athletes participate in the Paralympics.
- The practice of U.S. presidents inviting championship sports teams to the White House is an example of a national-level connection between sports and politics.

POLITICS AS A SOCIAL INSTITUTION

Before exploring the sport and politics connections in depth, we believe it is necessary to develop some basic understandings about the social institution of politics.

There is no single agreed-on definition of *politics*, but the word brings forth considerations about government, politicians, and public policies. The network of administrative and bureaucratic agencies that make up municipal, state, provincial, and national government is the core political entity. Beyond that, there is an organized power structure comprising a great variety of organizations, including hundreds of elected officeholders, appointed officials, the military, the legal system, and the many public bureaucracies and agencies involved in public policymaking, opinion shaping, and ideology formation.

The feminist movement popularized the slogan "The personal is political" to rebut critics who accused women of "playing politics" when they sought equal treatment and opportunity in the economic, political, religious, educational, social, and sporting sectors of their lives. Since then, other oppressed groups have adopted this slogan.

In connection with politics, power is a central theme for sociologists because it is present in all social organizations. Max Weber, one of the most prominent pioneer sociologists, defined *power* as the ability to get others to do one's will even in the face of opposition. Power is present in personal relationships, in groups, in formal organizations, and in nation-states. It can be exercised by force and threats of force, meaning actual or threatened use of coercion or violence to impose one's will on others. Power can also be exercised by authority, which is a form of power that is recognized or legitimated by those over whom it is employed. Influence is a third form of exercising power, and it can be exercised through a power holder's persuasion or extraordinary personal qualities (*charisma*).[5]

Sociologists tend to study how power is distributed—who has power and who does not and why, who benefits by the power arrangements and who does not, and how power is distributed and changed. The struggle for power and authority can involve entire nations, large organizations, small groups, and even persons in intimate association.

SOCIAL THEORIES AND POLITICS

Functionalists view the political social institution as a system of people occupying specific positions because they are necessary for the orderly accomplishment of the group's, organization's, or nation's objectives. Where it involves the government, the use

of power and authority is seen as necessary and beneficial to all because it reflects the laws and customs of citizens—a government of, by, and for the people—and ensures order, stability, and justice. The will of the majority is believed to prevail, there is equality before the law, and decisions are made to maximize the common good.

The conflict/cultural perspective emphasizes that power often becomes concentrated in an economically elite group of people who are motivated largely by their own self-interests. For example, corporate media networks encourage public audiences to think of themselves as a market; they then create dramatic events to sell to advertisers who buy what they believe will be attractive products in the marketplace.

Conflict/cultural theorists view government as habitually existing for the benefit of the ruling, or dominant, class. "The power elite" is what social theorist C. Wright Mills labeled the leaders of the military, corporate, and political elements of society, and he argued that their power is exercised to serve their interests rather than the common good. Furthermore, he maintained that the ordinary citizen is a relatively powerless subject of manipulation by those entities. Several other scholars have advanced the same theme in the years since Mills first articulated it.[6]

INTERTWINING OF POLITICS AND SPORTS

In this section we focus on how politics is manifested in the world of sports. Our main contention is that sport and politics are closely intertwined.[7]

Governmental intervention into sports has never been a central feature of legislation and policymaking, but government involvement has played a role in the games and sports of citizens in a variety of ways. For instance, government actions to control or prohibit domestic sporting practices have a lengthy history in the United States. In the American colonies, religious influences resulted in laws prohibiting boxing, wrestling, and cockfighting because they were violent and play and games in general because they were often performed on the Sabbath. In the early twentieth century, U.S. President Theodore Roosevelt threatened to abolish intercollegiate football unless changes were made to reduce the brutality of the game.

More recently, the MLB has been one of the premier major sports leagues in taking action and putting an end to the use of performance-enhancing drugs. However, federal investigations of the MLB's drug-testing program also became involved with congressional hearings on the use of steroids and other drugs in baseball.[8]

Another example of the sports and politics connection is the allegiance that people have to a particular sports team or organization (e.g., "their" high school, university, company, community, nation), such that they become committed representatives of that sport organization. Many of the rituals accompanying sporting events (such as slogans, chants, music, wearing of special clothing, and so forth) are aimed at symbolically representing or affirming fidelity to a team or sponsoring organization, pitted against opposing teams. Such events are primarily affairs for spectators, who are drawn to them not so much by the spectacle or the rituals or by an appreciation of the skills involved but because they identify themselves with their team.

Yet another illustration of the close relationship between sport and politics is found in the process of organization itself. As sport has become increasingly organized, numerous teams, leagues, players' associations, and ruling bodies have been created. These groups acquire certain powers that by their very nature are distributed unequally. Thus, power struggles have developed between players and owners (e.g., threats of strikes by the players or lockouts by the owners), within organizations (e.g., the NCAA and university athletic departments moving too slowly on gender equity), between leagues, and between various sanctioning bodies.

As we noted previously, the essence of politics is power. In sports, various organizations have power over teams, coaches, and athletes. Television networks, for example, have enormous power over sport. They have insisted on changes in sports, such as converting golf from match play to medal play and interrupting the continuous sports of basketball and hockey with mandatory time outs to broadcast commercial advertising. The Disney Corporation owns or has a controlling stake in ABC Sports and ESPN and

through these entities has exerted tremendous power over schedules, moving times and dates to accommodate TV programming schedules rather than the fans or the teams involved.

Behind the scenes, power brokers for television networks have sometimes determined the opponents in football bowl games and invitational basketball tournaments. Other corporations, most notably those selling beer, soda, cars, cable television, and athletic apparel, have enormous power over sport. Some of these corporations own teams, such as Red Bull, which controls numerous teams in sports including ice hockey, soccer, Formula 1, and surfing. The linkage between sport and politics is obvious when the impact of the government on sports is considered. Several illustrations at the federal level make this point:

- Legislation has been passed exempting professional sports from antitrust laws.
- Tax laws give special concessions to owners of professional teams (see Chapter 11).
- Congress crafts legislation that exempts college sports and their benefactors from taxes. (See Box 13.1 for more information on this subject.)
- For the 2002 Winter Olympics in Salt Lake City, the federal government contributed an estimated $1.5 billion in taxpayers' dollars for road and sport venue construction, the laying of fiber-optic cable, and security.
- Los Angeles's bid committee has estimated it will cost $5.3 billion to stage the 2028 Summer Olympic Games and has projected it can cover all expenses through revenues such as sponsorships and ticket sales.
- The President's Council on Sports, Fitness & Nutrition advises the president through the Secretary of Health and Human Services about physical activity, fitness, and sports; it also recommends programs to promote regular physical activity for the health of all Americans.
- The U.S. Congress chartered the U.S. Olympic Committee to govern American participation in the Olympic movement.

The close relationship between sport and politics was on display when the United States boycotted the 1980 Olympics and the Soviet Union boycotted the 1984 Olympics in retaliation. The apartheid policies of South

3.0

BOX 13.1 *THINKING ABOUT SPORT:* GOVERN-MENT DECISIONS AID BIG-TIME COLLEGE SPORTS

Congress has passed legislation that subsidizes big-time college sports programs through a variety of tax breaks. For example:

- Boosters are allowed to claim 80 percent of the money they spend on the premiums (fees) they pay to obtain season tickets. These are considered (by Congress) charitable contributions. Thus, thanks to Congress, fans get to deduct their mandatory payments, just as if they were writing a check to the Salvation Army or the local food bank.
- Corporations underwrite bowl games and pay millions for the right to connect their corporate names to the bowls (Allstate Bowl, Cheez-It Bowl) and to display their names and logos throughout the stadiums. Congress ruled that this is not advertising, but philanthropy, thus exempting the bowl committees from taxation on the income money received from the corporations.
- Athletic departments benefit from taxpayer-subsidized loans to construct stadiums and arenas. Much of the multibillion-dollar building boom in college sports is underwritten with bonds that, because of the colleges' charitable status, are tax exempt. This helps the purchasers of the bonds to escape taxes and saves the schools millions of dollars because the bonds pay interest several points below market level.
- College sports are exempt from the unrelated business income tax, a tax levy on the commercial activities of nonprofit organizations. This means, in effect, that the colleges pay no taxes on the income they receive from individual contributors, booster clubs, television networks, bowl and tournament payouts, corporate gifts, and ticket sales (including the sale of luxury suites).

These subsidies to college sports amount to millions of dollars each year. Congress justifies these subsidies on the grounds that college sport is a vital part of the broader social fabric.

Sources: Patrick Hruby, "How the NCAA Scams Taxpayers for Welfare Money," *Vice Sports*, March 31, 2015, https://sports.vice.com/en_us/article/how-the-ncaa-scams-taxpayers-for-welfare-money; Joe Nocera, "Go Ahead, Republicans, Tax College Sports," *Bloomberg View*, November 14, 2017. https://www.bloomberg.com/view/articles/2017-11-14/go-ahead-republicans-tax-college-sports/.

Africa resulted in that nation being barred from many international sports competitions, including the Olympic Games. These actions clearly demonstrate that sport has been used as a tool of foreign policy, inasmuch as the refusal by one country to compete in sports against another is a way of applying political pressure on that country.

Within the United States and other Western nations, local and regional governments may encourage sports organizations through various forms of funding. These levels of government are generous in subsidizing local teams owned by private entrepreneurs (as we described in detail in Chapter 11). This type of support can extend to resourcing for major sporting events. For instance, a review of federal, provincial, and municipal reports suggests that government expenditures for the 2010 Vancouver Winter Olympic Games totaled over $6.4 billion. This is the amount of resources the government allocated to the Vancouver Olympics and includes expenditures on government Games-related planning and public support for various functions. It also includes the cost of major infrastructure projects required or advanced for the Games.[9]

The institutional character of sport is a final source of the strong relationship between sport and politics. Sport, like other social institutions, is conservative; consequently, it has served as a preserver and a legitimator of the existing order on many occasions. The patriotic pageants that accompany sporting events reinforce the political system. Moreover, sport perpetuates many myths, one of which is that anyone with talent, regardless of race or social station, has an equal chance to succeed.

We have seen that the very nature of sport makes politics endemic to it. The remainder of this chapter will demonstrate this relationship further by examining the various political uses of sport and the politics of various international sports events, including the Olympic Games.

THE POLITICAL USES OF SPORT

SPORT AS A VEHICLE FOR PROPAGANDA

Success in international competition frequently serves as a means by which a nation's ruling elite unites its citizens and attempts to impress the

TABLE 13.1 GOVERNMENT EXPENDITURES FOR THE 2010 WINTER OLYMPIC GAMES

Event related	Expenditures (nominal millions of $)
British Columbia	954
Canada	1,336
Municipal	589
Crown and/or government authorities	22
Total event related	2,902
Major related infrastructure	
Sea to Sky	600
Canada Line	2,051
Convention Centre	883
Total related infrastructure	3,534
Overall total	6,436

Source: Marvin Shaffer, "Looking Back on the Vancouver–Whistler Winter Games," Policy Note, February 6, 2014, http://www.policynote.ca/looking-back-on-the-vancouver-whistler-winter-games/.

citizens of other countries. Nations have increasingly forged direct propaganda links between sport triumphs and the viability of their political–economic systems. A classic example of this was Adolf Hitler's use of the 1936 Olympic Games to strengthen his control over the German people and to introduce Nazi culture to the entire world. According to Christopher Hilton in his book *Hitler's Olympics*, the activities planned for these Games were a shrewdly propagandistic and brilliantly conceived charade that reinforced and mobilized the hysterical patriotism of the German masses.[10] The success of the German athletes at those Olympics—they won eighty-nine medals, twenty-three more than U.S. athletes, and more than four times as many as any other country—was touted as "proof" of German superiority.

Before the reunification of the two Germanys and the demise of the Soviet Union, the Communist nations used successes in international sports, especially the Olympic Games, as evidence of the superiority of the Communist political–economic system. Even though Russia—once the major Communist nation—is no longer Communist, it continues to use sport as a national vehicle for promoting its global standing among nations. Dozens of

Russian athletes at the 2014 Winter Olympics in Sochi, Russia, were part of a government-run doping program planned and carried out for years to ensure Russian dominance in international sporting events. More recently, Sochi was stripped of the bobsleigh and skeleton world championships in the wake of reports of more than 1,000 Russian athletes being implicated in a Russian-sponsored doping program.[11] Of the few Communist nations that currently remain, perhaps Cuba and China take sport the most seriously. Fidel Castro, president of Cuba from 1976 to 2008, decreed that sport is a right of the people. Most of his policies toward sports remain, even after his death. No admission is ever charged to a sporting event. The most promising athletes are given the best coaching and training. Cuba devotes 3 percent of its national budget to its sports ministry, which encourages and trains elite athletes. In the Pan-American

America's Jesse Owens, second from right, salutes during the presentation of his gold medal for the long jump at what is often called the Nazi Olympic Games in Berlin, Germany, in 1936. Adolf Hitler used those Games to strengthen his control over the German people. (Photo: AP Photo/File)

TABLE 13.2 RIO OLYMPICS, 2016: MEDAL STANDINGS PER COUNTRY BY POPULATION (TOP 20 AND THE UNITED STATES)

Rank by population	Actual rank by medals won	Country	Population (millions)	Actual total medals
1	69	Grenada	0.1	1
2	51	Bahamas	0.4	2
3	16	Jamaica	2.7	11
4	54	New Zealand	4.6	18
5	17	Croatia	4.2	10
6	28	Denmark	5.7	15
7	45	Slovenia	2.1	4
8	48	Bahrain	1.4	2
9	12	Hungary	9.8	15
10	54	Fiji	0.9	1
11	38	Georgia	3.7	7
12	42	Armenia	3	4
13	39	Azerbaijan	9.7	18
14	11	Netherlands	16.9	19
15	10	Australia	23.8	29
16	32	Serbia	7.1	8
17	2	Great Britain	65.1	67
18	29	Sweden	9.8	11
19	18	Cuba	11.4	11
20	37	Slovakia	5.4	4
39	1	United States of America	321.4	121

Source: Bill Mitchell, "Bill Mitchell's Alternative Olympic Games Medal Tally—2016," August 20, 2016, http://www.billmitchell.org/sport/medal_tally_2016.html.

Games, Cuba tends to win about fifteen times more medals than the United States on a per capita basis, and Fidel Castro steadfastly proclaimed to the Americas that this was proof of the superiority of the Cuban people and the Cuban system. (See Table 13.2 for an analysis of how the nations ranked in the 2016 Rio Summer Olympics, *taking population into account*.) For example, according to Table 13.2, Grenada could be said to have won the Rio Summer Olympics, if the size of its population is taken into account in ranking

countries for the medals they won. Using those criteria, the United States took thirty-ninth place.

Currently, China is using the Soviet model to develop sports talent and to enhance the stature of the Chinese political and social system worldwide. There are about 3,000 sports schools in China, training almost half a million children, with those at the highest levels subsidized by the state. United States Olympic officials estimated that China spent from $400 to $500 million to train athletes in the four years leading up to the 2008 Olympic Games.[12]

National efforts to use sport for political purposes are not limited to Communist countries. International sports victories are just as important to nations such as the United States. Here, too, sport can be an effective propaganda tool only if it is associated with victorious performances.

After the 1972 Olympics, when the United States fared worse than was expected (especially in track and basketball), it was becoming obvious that the elite sports programs the Soviet Union and other Communist governments had developed were enabling their Olympic teams to be successful both for their athletes and as an instrument of propaganda on behalf of promoting their nationalistic interests. Consequently, many American editorial writers and politicians advocated plans whereby U.S. athletes would be subsidized and would receive the best coaching and facilities to regain international athletic supremacy for propaganda purposes. This did not happen, and the cry arose again after the 1976 Summer Olympics. As a result, Congress appropriated funds for the U.S. Olympic Committee (USOC) and for the establishment of permanent training sites for the Winter and Summer Games.

By 1990 the IOC had loosened the eligibility rules for participation, and athletes participating in the Olympic Games did not have to be amateurs—professional athletes could compete in the Olympics. The 1992 "Dream Team" of U.S. basketball players was a prominent example of this rule change; this team of mostly NBA all-stars easily swept aside the competition to win the gold medal in Barcelona. Currently, Olympic-level athletes in the United States receive money from a variety of sources and, most significantly, from the USOC and the sports' national governing bodies. The U.S. government uses athletes to promote international goodwill and to enhance the American image abroad. The State Department, for example, has historically sponsored tours of athletes to foreign countries for these purposes.

Sport as an instrument of propaganda is not limited to the industrialized nations of the world. The developing countries use sport even more for this purpose, with almost 90 percent having a cabinet-level post related to sport. The probable reason for such keen interest is that sport provides a relatively cheap political tool to accomplish national objectives of prestige abroad and unity at home.[13]

SPORT AND NATIONALISM

When athletes and teams of one country compete against those of another, nationalistic sentiments arise. Identification with the athletes and teams representing one's country tends to unite citizens regardless of social class, race, and regional differences. Citizens take pride in "their" athletes' accomplishments, viewing them as collective achievements. For example, even war-ravaged Iraq, with its ethnic and sectarian divides, was united briefly in 2008 when Iraqi athletes were permitted to participate in the 2008 Beijing Olympics. In 2012 the National Olympic Committee of Iraq sent a total of eight athletes to the Games, five men and three women, to compete in seven different sports.

Six Afghan athletes were selected for the 2012 London Games, competing in four different sporting events. In both countries spontaneous celebrations occurred, with people dancing in the streets and waving their national flags (see Box 13.2 concerning South Africa). The Rio Olympics featured a Refugee Olympic Team of athletes that came from no nation in particular. The R.O.T., as the International Olympic Committee abbreviated it, included ten athletes, across four sports, from four countries in the Middle East and Africa.[14]

The Olympic Games and other international games tend to promote an "us-versus-them" feeling among athletes, coaches, politicians, the press, and fans. The Olympic Games, in this sense, represent a political contest, a symbolic world war, in which nations win or lose. This interpretation is commonly held; that is why citizens of each nation involved unite behind their flag and their athletes.

Many people will watch the Olympic Games for one reason: there is a competitor or team who, they feel, is representing them. That athlete or team is *their* athlete or team—running, jumping, throwing, or boxing—for their country. For a few minutes at least, their own evaluation of themselves will be bound up with the performance. The athlete or team will be the embodiment of their nation's strength or weakness.

BOX 13.2 *THINKING ABOUT SPORT:* SPORT UNIFIES WHITES AND BLACKS IN SOUTH AFRICA

South Africa was barred for a time from the Olympic Games and other international competitions, most notably the World Cup of the favorite sport of Whites—rugby. With the fall of apartheid and the election of Nelson Mandela, the sports world accepted South Africa, so much so that it was allowed to host the 1995 World Cup in rugby.

President Mandela used the rugby World Cup as an opportunity to bring change in South Africa. He visited the training camp of South Africa's team—the Springboks. While there he put on a Springbok cap.

This was no casual gesture. The nickname *Springbok* is controversial in South Africa, strongly associated with the apartheid White regimes of the past.

Then Mandela pointedly told the rugby players, "The whole nation is behind you."

The Springboks (White except for one Black player) took that message to heart. The day before their game against Australia, the players requested a tour of Robben Island, off Cape Town, where Mandela had been imprisoned for eighteen years. They visited his former cell and afterward vowed to dedicate their efforts in the World Cup to their president.

Before one of the matches Mandela gave a speech in front of a primarily Black audience. He said, "This cap does honor to our boys. I ask you to stand by them tomorrow because they are our kind."

The Springboks won the World Cup, defeating the world's two rugby powers, Australia and New Zealand, in the process. For the first time in South Africa's troubled history, Whites and Blacks found themselves unified by a sport.

That was 1995. Now fast forward to 2006. Whereas the Springboks had only one Black player in 1995, eleven years later they had six Black or colored players in the starting fifteen. For the first time in the history of South African cricket, the national team was captained by a non-White player in 2006, and five of its squad of thirteen were Black or colored. Clearly, there has been progress, but Whites, who are but 9 percent of the population, remain the majority on the field.

Successive South African governments have encouraged racial quotas in the selection of its national teams—for rugby it was 50 percent of the squad by 2019. The imposition of quotas in elite sports is unique, but these are seen as a necessary step to reverse historic apartheid policies of racial division and systemic disadvantage. The point is that the national teams in rugby are multiracial, and in this country obsessed by sport, the constitution of players on its national rugby teams is an important symbol of progress toward racial integration and national unity.

Sources: Siga Mnyanda, "Imposing Racial Quotas Is a Vital Step forward for South African Sport," *The Guardian*, April 29, 2016, https://www.theguardian.com/world/2016/apr/29/south-africa-racial-quotas-sport-rugby-springboks-cricket; John Carlin, *Invictus: Nelson Mandela and the Game That Made a Nation* (New York: Penguin Press, 2009).

A victory will be victory for them; a defeat will be defeat for them.

This last point requires emphasis. Evidence from the Olympic Games and other international competitions shows that for many nations and their citizens, victory is an index of that nation's superiority (in its military might, its political–economic system, and its culture). Clearly, the outcomes of international sports contests are often interpreted politically, a topic we will return to later in this chapter.

The integral interrelationship of sport and nationalism is easily seen in the blatantly militaristic pageantry that often surrounds sporting events. The playing of the national anthem, the presentation of the colors, the jet aircraft flyovers, and the band forming a flag or a liberty bell are all political acts supportive of the existing political system.

This patriotic pageantry was especially evident at sports events following the terrorist attacks of September 11, 2001. This crisis momentarily brought people together, uniting them in a common cause and a common bond of patriotism. Whereas before the terrorist tragedies sports events began with the traditional singing of the national anthem, after September 11 sports events began with a moment of silent tribute to the fallen, a patriotic display of huge flags and other symbols, cannons firing, presentation of the colors, crowd chants of "U-S-A, U-S-A," and the sports crowds singing the national anthem with enthusiasm. Sport sociologist Samantha King noted that "it becomes increasingly hard within U.S. national culture to discern where the war ends and the games begin."[15]

Sports commentator Dave Zirin reflected on the politically themed pageantry that accompanies contemporary sporting events, saying the response to the assassination of Osama bin Laden resulted in spontaneous eruptions of patriotic zeal with fans of both teams joining in chants of "U-S-A, U-S-A." This was followed by organized patriotic celebrations at stadiums through-out the country, such as military appreciation nights; displays of football field–sized flags, and military fly-overs. Zirin, in the aftermath of September 11, argues that sports have been "co-opted, exploited, scarred, and turned inside out by the aftermath of 9/11 and the hunt for Osama bin Laden. Some have wondered if now that bin Laden is dead, life will go back to normal."[16] But the patriotic and symbolic celebrations can have the impor-tant political consequence of helping to "glue" citizens back together after a national tragedy.

The irony is that nationalistic displays typically are not interpreted as political because they are per-ceived as merely reinforcing nonpolitical patriotic feelings. But what would happen if during the previ-ous Iraq or Afghanistan Wars, a college band formed

a peace symbol at halftime? Such a display of what many would view as antiwar spirit would likely have been interpreted as blatantly political. But is not a halftime show in support of the government's poli-cies just as "political"?

Athletes who do not show proper respect for the flag or for the national anthem are subject to stiff pen-alties. Perhaps the most world-renowned example of this was when U.S. Olympic track athletes Tommie Smith and John Carlos raised gloved, clenched fists, and bowed their heads during the national anthem at the 1968 Olympics as a symbol of support for the anti-racism movement in the United States. The USOC banned them from further Olympic competition.

In 2003 the captain of the women's basketball team at Manhattanville College in Purchase, New

The gold medal winners of the Rio Olympics women's 4 × 100-meter relay; they set a world record–winning time. It has become common for winning track-and-field athletes to be given a flag of their home country to parade around the track with and then stand in front of TV camera operators, sometimes for several minutes, with their flags held in various postures. (Photo: AP Photo/Lee Jin-man)

York, turned her back on the U.S. flag during the pre-game playing of the national anthem to protest the U.S. invasion of Iraq. This action sparked outrage, with calls for the dismissal of the player, threats by several colleges not to play Manhattanville unless the offending player was dismissed, and debates about the issue throughout the sports and political worlds. Occasionally there are questions raised about the commonplace patriotic rituals at sports events on the grounds that they do not occur at most other public events (e.g., plays, lectures, concerts, and movies). However, the support for these patriotic rituals is so strong that whenever team leaders decide not to play the national anthem at a sports event, there is typically a public outcry.

SPORT AS AN OPIATE OF THE MASSES

We have shown that sport success can unite a nation through pride. This pride in and devotion to a nation's success transcends the social classes and has been said to serve as an "opiate of the masses" (a phrase used by Karl Marx about organized religion). In the present context, this means that sport conceals and obscures significant realities of contemporary life, thus distracting peoples' attention from the harshness of social or economic life that many of them daily endure, as well as leading them to disregard entrenched social inequalities and injustices all around them.

In 1994, for example, when Haiti was on the verge of a severe crisis, the embattled military ruler, Raoul Cedras, paid for the broadcasting rights to the World Cup soccer matches. The spirits of the Haitians were raised when their adopted team, Brazil, won the World Cup. Rather than massing in the streets to demonstrate against a political regime that oppressed them, citizens danced in the streets because their favorite team had won. Moreover, the matches were played on the government-owned television station, so the rulers used halftime to inflame anti-American feelings by showing footage of the U.S. invasion of Panama in 1989, focusing on the bombing of residential areas. Thus, sport served as a safety valve for releasing tensions that might otherwise be directed toward challenging the existing social order.

Sport can also act as an opiate by perpetuating the belief that persons from the lowest classes can be upwardly mobile through success in sports. Chapter 5 dealt with this topic in more detail; for this chapter, it is enough to say that for every professional team sport athlete who came up from poverty, tens of thousands failed in their quest to become professional athletes. The point, however, is that most people in the United States believe that sport is inherently good since it seemingly serves as a mobility escalator. Poor American youths who might otherwise invest their energies in improving their education work instead on a jump shot or catching a football. Thus, for many the potential for social mobility is impeded by sport.[17]

THE EXPLOITATION OF SPORT BY POLITICIANS

The reciprocity of politics and sports is made transparent when athletes become politicians. An athlete can use his or her athletic fame as a springboard to getting elected or appointed to office. Some examples of professional athletes who served in Congress during the past twenty years include the following: Heath Shuler served in the House of Representatives from 2007 to 2013; he played quarterback for the NFL Washington Redskins, the New Orleans Saints, and the Oakland Raiders. Steve Largent also served in the House from 1995 to 2003; he was a Hall of Fame wide receiver for the Seattle Seahawks. J. C. Watts, another football player, was a member of the House, serving from 1995 to 2003; he played professional football in Canada. Jon Runyan was a member of the House from 2010 to 2015; Runyan was an NFL offensive tackle who spent most of his career with the Philadelphia Eagles. Distance runner Jim Ryun served in the House from 1996 to 2007; although not technically a professional athlete, Ryun was an Olympic distance runner. He is the last American to hold the world record in the mile run.

Politicians find it beneficial to get the approval and active campaign support of sports stars. Athletes, because they are well known and admired, can secure votes either for themselves or for candidates whom they support. Moreover, politicians find it useful to identify with teams and to attend sports events. For example, on that special evening in 1995 when Cal Ripken Jr. broke Lou Gehrig's record of 2,130 consecutive games played, President Clinton was in attendance and was highly visible as he congratulated Ripken publicly and spent time in the television booth during the broadcast. Presidents Ronald Reagan, George H. W. Bush, Bill Clinton, George W. Bush, Barack Obama, and Donald Trump have sought to publicly interact with athletes and sports teams. Routinely, champions from colleges, the professionals, and the Olympics are invited to the White House, although in some cases these invitations are declined because of political conflicts. Presidents, governors, members of Congress, mayors, and other political officials are hoping to be identified with these popular sports and their sports stars.

Furthermore, politicians capitalize on the popularity of athletes by using them to support the system. In the United States, for example, athletes are often sent overseas to maintain the morale of service personnel. Athletes appear in advertisements that urge the viewer or reader to join the military or Reserve Officers' Training Corps, to vote, and to avoid drugs. Athletes are also asked to give patriotic speeches on holidays and other occasions.

Use of athletes for the maintenance of the ruling regime is common in other countries as well. Athletes may be asked to visit factories and villages to hold demonstrations and make political speeches. These activities spread the conventional political philosophy of the dominant class in those countries, helping to unify the general population and bolstering the morale of middle- and low-income workers to maintain their patriotic feelings toward existing societal conditions.

SPORT AS A VEHICLE OF CHANGE IN SOCIETY

A recurring theme of this book is that sport reflects the dynamics of the larger society. It is not surprising, therefore, that when social and political turmoil has occurred in the United States it has affected the sports world as well. To illustrate our point, we use several examples from the past.

Sport and sporting events were used by activists and reformers to attack racism, a major societal issue of the latter twentieth century. Racism was attacked in a number of ways. Most dramatic was the proposed boycott of the 1968 Olympics by African American athletes. Harry Edwards, an African American sociologist and former athlete, was a leader of this boycott. His rationale for the protest was that the roots of the revolt, called the Project on Human Rights, sprung "from the same seed that produced the sit-ins, freedom riders, and street protests, all based on the resentment found in the racism rampant in American society—including sports."[18] A number of boycotts and protests involving racist practices have occurred over the past half century, but we will focus on four examples to show another avenue for sport challenging the existing social order. In these cases it was the power structure of sport that was doing the confronting.

1. The first example of efforts by a sport organization to use its power to confront racism was a political decision made by the NFL in the 1990s. The NFL had awarded the 1993 Super Bowl to Tempe, Arizona, the home of the Arizona Cardinals, but because the Arizona legislature refused to have an official, statewide holiday to celebrate the birthday of Martin Luther King Jr., the NFL decided to take the 1993 Super Bowl away from Arizona and hold it in Pasadena, California. In effect, the league was saying to the citizens of Arizona, "If you want to play the game of bigotry, we'll take our millions of dollars in tourist trade and scores of hours of television time someplace else."[19] This strategy worked, and Arizona endorsed the King holiday, after which the league awarded Phoenix the 1996 Super Bowl.

2. Turning to the twenty-first century, we find an example of a sports organization using its power to bring social change. Shortly after the beginning of the new millennium, the NCAA executive committee agreed not to schedule championship events in South Carolina until at least 2004 because the Confederate flag was being displayed on the statehouse grounds. This boycott of South Carolina began in January 2000 with actions by the National Association for the Advancement of Colored People, followed by individual university

teams canceling games and matches in South Carolina. Several prominent individuals in sport expressed support of the boycott, including Lou Holtz, then head football coach at the University of South Carolina.[20]

3. As a follow-up to its position against racist symbolism in South Carolina, the NCAA ruled in 2005 that any school with a nickname or logo considered racially or ethnically "hostile" or "abusive" would be prohibited from using it in postseason events. This meant that mascots would not be allowed to perform at NCAA-sponsored tournament events and band members and cheerleaders would be barred from using Native Americans as symbols on their uniforms. In short, the NCAA made a political decision—that it would not permit the use of Native American symbols by athletic teams at their championship events because they often are demeaning caricatures of native peoples.

4. The WNBA devoted their entire 2020 season to raising awareness about social justice issues. As part of this, the league dedicated the 2020 season to Breonna Taylor, an African American medical worker who was killed by the police during a botched drug raid. The league created a social justice council led by players to address societal and political concerns about race-based inequities, voting rights, LGBTQ+ advocacy, and gun control, as well as other key issues.

All of these examples describe sport organizations challenging existing social practices, but

Colin Kaepernick explained the reasons for his actions. "I am not going to stand up to show pride in a flag for a country that oppresses black people and people of color," Kaepernick told NFL Media in an exclusive interview after the game. "To me, this is bigger than football and it would be selfish on my part to look the other way. There are bodies in the street and people getting paid leave and getting away with murder." (Photo: Michael Zagaris/Getty Images)

individuals are often the driving force behind social change. For example, in August 2016, San Francisco 49ers quarterback Colin Kaepernick sat down during the playing of the national anthem. His protest followed several high-profile fatal police shootings of Black men that summer. According to Kaepernick, his action was to call attention to police brutality and injustice in Black America. He elaborated, "When there's significant change and I feel like [the American] flag represents what it's supposed to represent, this country is representing people the way that it's supposed to, I'll stand."[21]

Kaepernick's act of protest spread not only across the NFL, but also to college and high school sporting events. Athletes stood with their hands resting over their hearts; several athletes of color either sat down or took a knee and raised a clenched fist in protest of police violence and racial inequities; many others have subsequently joined the protests to show solidarity with their teammates, who risk public backlash and are being ostracized for peacefully exercising their freedom of speech.[22]

Kaepernick is not the only athlete-activist objecting to the social violence in twenty-first-century America. Professional athletes and college athletes representing various other sports have used their celebrity status not only to publicly protest but also to try to find solutions to rampant police violence, racial injustice, and economic inequality.

Sports activism received mixed reactions. In Kaepernick's case, refusing to stand during the national anthem, many athletes, coaches, sport administrators, and fans expressed disapproval of his actions, although most acknowledged he had a constitutional right to do what he was doing. Most criticism came via social media, but some took more direct actions and even publicly burned his 49ers jersey.

Despite the support or criticism of recent sports activism, one thing seems evident: these protests and social actions are increasing and will continue to spark conversations and reactions for both sides.[23]

Internationalization of Social Activism and Sport

At the international level, there has been a campaign against the use of sweatshop labor to produce sporting goods in developing nations. United Students against Sweatshops organized anti–sweat shop campaigns on hundreds of campuses, mandating that the clothes bearing their collegiate logos be manufactured under fair and ethical conditions. This effort, most notably against Nike's exploitation of Third World workers, has been student led in the United States. As a consequence of activists pressing Nike and other companies, in 2005 Nike revealed the location of its factories in the Third World and admitted to widespread problems in its Asian factories.

Nike is not the only company that has followed this global economy model. However, because it has had the largest share of the sports footwear market and the accompanying profits, it can most easily afford to lead a change in corporate directions.[24]

These examples of sport serving as a vehicle of social change are interesting for three reasons:

1. The power structure of sports has typically been reluctant to take the lead in social causes, so the actions we have described are typically anomalies in the face of conservative institutions. Yet, these actions seem to be increasing and thus signal an emerging trend that must be grappled with in the sports world.

2. Sports have political potential, ironically, either way: (a) positively, because the powerful sport organizations hold the potential to "blackmail" recalcitrants into line, and (b) negatively, because of a backlash from the public that resents blatant politics—specifically, anti–status quo politics by sports organizations.

3. Each example of social change shows once again how sports and politics are intertwined.

The worldwide popularity of sport and the importance attached to it by fans and politicians alike make sport an ideal platform for political protest. However, the use of sport for protest can have limited capacity to instigate meaningful change because of the powerful institutional structures of sport, which serve to preserve and legitimize the status quo.

GLOBALIZATION AND SPORT

Sports have historically had a narrow geographical base. In this sense, sports were local. We have tended to identify with the local high school, college, or professional team. But this identification with the local is breaking down. Concurrent with trends and events in business, music, the other arts, education, politics, travel, and so forth, college and professional teams have become more global. They now often have foreign players, some of whom do not speak English well and are unfamiliar with American cultural habits and customs.[25]

Of course, international exchange is not a recent phenomenon. For thousands of years, people have traveled, traded, and migrated across political boundaries exchanging food, artifacts, and knowledge. But the current global perspective accentuates greater connectedness among the world's people. It is a process whereby goods, information, people, money, communication, sport, and various other forms of culture move across national boundaries and throughout the globe.

For example, for several centuries British colonists brought their sports (soccer, rugby, cricket) to their colonies, where they flourished. Golf began in Scotland and has become a sport played prominently in the United States and elsewhere. The Olympic movement spread around the globe during the twentieth century. Although the popularity of baseball began in the United States, it is now extremely popular in Latin America, the Caribbean countries, Japan, and South Korea. So, too, with basketball, which has spread especially to China, the Philippines, Australia, and western and central Europe.

Still, the frequency of international competition, the migration of athletes and coaches, and the proliferation of global sport organizations are rather recent. Some sports—golf and tennis, for example—are already global sports with athletes competing regularly in tournaments worldwide. The LPGA, primarily a U.S. organization, has been dominated in recent years by South Koreans and Mexicans. And the U.S. Open in tennis—both men's and women's—is routinely won by foreign players—mostly Europeans. (We examined this issue of the global migration of athletes in Chapters 6 and 7). Indeed, there is a large presence of U.S. influence around the world as sports events are televised globally and U.S. sports leagues seek global expansion.

It is the World Cup, however, that is the most widely viewed and followed sporting event in the world, outdoing even the Olympic Games. The sport played at the World Cup is soccer (known as football throughout the world, except in the United States and Australia), which is universally acknowledged to be the "the world's sport" because it is the most-played sport around the world; it is not sectioned off or dominated by one particular country. According to soccer's international governing body, there are 265 million players actively involved in soccer around the world, as well as 3.5 billion people who consider themselves to be fans of this sport.

The globalization of sport has political consequences. The process blurs national allegiances. Friendships through sport extend across political boundaries. However, nationalism may be exacerbated or diminished by global processes. People in one society may readily adopt new sports forms from other societies, or they may reject them as cultural imperialism. Similarly, transnational sports organizations may decide to exclude certain nations from participation because of their political actions, as we will see in the next section.[26]

THE POLITICAL OLYMPIC GAMES

The motto of the Olympic Games is "Citius, Altius, Fortius" (Faster, Higher, Stronger). It implies that athletes should strive for ever-better performances. Moreover, the goal of the Olympic movement is to "contribute to building a peaceful and better world by educating youth through sport practiced in accordance with Olympism and its values."[27] Since the revival of the Olympics in 1896, however, there has been an ascendance of political considerations in addition to athletes' sporting accomplishments. This section addresses the political side of the Olympics and offers suggestions for reducing the corrosive effects of politics on the Olympic movement and its ideals.

POLITICAL PROBLEMS AND THE OLYMPIC MOVEMENT

Politics surrounding the Olympics are manifested in five major ways:

1. Through excessive nationalism within nations concerning the performance of their athletes in the Olympics;

2. Through use of the Olympics as a site for political demonstrations and violence by political dissidents in the host country;
3. Through decisions by ruling bodies to deny participation by certain nations;
4. Through decisions by nations to boycott the Games for political reasons; and
5. Through the political organization of the Olympics.

Excessive Nationalism within Nations

Nationalism in the Olympics that goes beyond its appropriate boundaries is expressed in several ways. Foremost, there is the use of athletics to promote political goals. As we described in an earlier section, Adolf Hitler turned the 1936 Games in Berlin into a propaganda show to legitimate Nazi Germany. Similarly, nations tend to use their showing in international athletic events as an indicator of the superiority of their political–economic systems. This was especially true during the Cold War era from 1952 to 1988, when the United States and the Soviet Union were the two powers contending against each other for world supremacy. Some nations have been blatant in their efforts to demonstrate their superiority, offering large prizes to their athletes to win medals.

A second manifestation of excessive nationalism is that in the zeal to win, some national Olympic committees have ignored the use of performance-enhancing drugs for their athletes. In his book, *Spitting in the Soup: Inside the Dirty Games of Doping in Sports*, Mike Johnson convincingly shows that doping is as old as organized sports and that Olympic coaches and trainers have always enlisted chemistry both to push the boundaries of human performance and to promote the superiority of their nation-state. In each of the Olympics Games over the past thirty years, some athletes have been forced to forfeit medals because they have failed drug tests. Many Russian athletes at the 2014 Winter Olympics in Sochi, including at least fifteen medal winners, were part of a state-run doping program carried out for years to ensure Russian dominance at the Olympic Games.[28]

A third indication of national chauvinism has to do with the reporting of international events. Members of the media in reporting the Olympics may let their politics distort their analyses. Television coverage of the Olympics conveys a distorted, nationalized, and commercialized portrayal of the Games. The TV networks that buy the broadcast rights to Olympic events subcontract with TV outlets worldwide, which then add their own narratives to the broadcasts to appeal to audiences in their countries. Thus, the Olympics Games become filtered through individual nations, producing widely varying interpretations of the Games.[29]

Use of the Olympics by Political Dissidents in the Host Country

At virtually every recent Olympics there have been political demonstrations, threats, and violence by disaffected groups. The host country has usually responded with extra security and police violence. A bomb was exploded at the Atlanta Olympics in 1996 by a domestic terrorist who objected to the legalization of abortion. During the Sydney Olympics in 2000, there were peaceful demonstrations by Aborigines against the discrimination they face in Australia. The Athens Olympics in 2004 was confronted by demonstrators against the Iraq War who marched on the U.S. embassy, protesting a visit of U.S. Secretary of State Colin Powell. The Tokyo Olympics held in 2021 were marked by protests against these games as many Japanese people had concerns about the spread of COVID-19.

Anticipating Chinese protestors and demonstrators at the 2008 Beijing Olympics, organizers of the Games took preemptive action and incarcerated many activists, thereby crushing potential political dissidents. During the 2016 Summer Olympics, chaotic scenes marred the arrival of the Olympic torch in Rio de Janeiro, as protesters damaged the Olympic torch before its arrival for the opening ceremony. Hundreds of protesters angry at the high cost of hosting the Games protested, and riot police used tear gas and pepper spray to disperse the crowd.[30]

Use of the Olympics for Political Purposes by Organizations outside the Host Nation

We will not repeat what we have already said in this chapter about Tommie Smith and John Carlos's clenched-fist protest on the medal stand at the 1968

Mexico City Olympic Games, except that it was related to a boycott campaign organized in the United States as a way to reveal to the world the indignities and discrimination suffered by African Americans. The call to boycott failed (although a few athletes did boycott), but the mood of many African American athletes who participated in the Olympics was sullen and resentful.

Four years later, at the Munich Olympics, a group of Palestinian terrorists stormed the living quarters of the Israeli team, capturing them. Their goal was to negotiate a trade whereby the Israeli athletes would be freed if Israel would release 234 Palestinians held in Israeli jails. German commandos tried to free the captive athletes, but a terrorist unpinned a grenade, killing 11 Israeli athletes and 5 kidnappers.[31]

With the terrorist attacks on the World Trade Center in New York City and the Pentagon in Washington, D.C., on September 11, 2001, the world was on heightened alert for future attacks, whether by planes, bombs, germs, or computers. Although these attacks were not intended to affect the Olympic Games in any way, they did. For example, at the 2004 Athens Olympics, Greece spent an unprecedented 1 billion euros (US$1.33 billion) for the security of the first post–September 11 Summer Games.

Preceding the Beijing Olympics, various groups protested China's alleged complicity with mass killings in Sudan (because the Sudanese sell the Chinese 400,000 barrels of oil a day and China owns 40 percent of Sudan's largest oil company), calling those Games the "Genocide Olympics." Film director Steven Spielberg publicly withdrew from his appointment as artistic advisor to the opening ceremony of the Beijing Olympics, saying that his commitment to overcoming intolerance, bigotry, and the suffering they cause was incompatible with China's support for the Sudanese government. As a lead-up to the 2008 Beijing Olympics, Tibetan activists carried out a four-year campaign to spoil China's hosting of the event. At the same time, a demonstration was staged in Beijing, aiming to focus attention, in the protestors' words, on Tibetan political prisoners and stating that the Tibetan people live without human rights under Chinese rule.

More than two dozen groups staged protests against the 2012 London and 2016 Rio Olympics to highlight various issues they had about the Games. Protesters employed diverse methods in both Olympic cities prior to the Games, during the Games, and even after the Games were over.[32]

Political Decisions by National and International Olympic Committees

The international and national Olympic ruling bodies make a number of decisions based on politics. The choice of Olympic sites is made by the members of the IOC. This decision is crucial to the potential host nations and cities because of the possible economic benefits, the legitimacy of that nation's government, and the potential of being the center of world attention. This site-selection decision historically has been based on either bribery or politics (or both).

Let's consider bribery first. Andrew Jennings, an investigative journalist, has cited numerous scandals involving the IOC, including the use of bribery to buy votes for Olympic site selection.[33] His argument was validated by the scandals associated with the awarding of the 2002 Winter Olympics to Salt Lake City. The USOC spent $60,000 on favors for foreign sports officials who, in return, supported Salt Lake City's bid. Another $1.2 million was spent by the Salt Lake City Organizing Committee on scholarships, shopping sprees, cash payments, free housing, jobs, and other gifts to those who would make the decision—IOC members and their family members. Similar bribes were made by the organizers of the Nagano Winter Olympics in 1998 and the Atlanta organizers for the 1996 Summer Games. Even well before the 2020 Tokyo Summer Olympics, bribes were reported to have been made by the organizers of those Olympic Games.[34]

In 2001 the IOC selected Beijing for the 2008 Olympics in a highly charged political atmosphere. Opponents argued that China was in violation of human rights. Others argued that giving China the Olympics might promote a greater opening up of the country, promote ties with Taiwan, and ease tensions with the United States and its allies. Friends of China argued that awarding the Games to China would be a sign of that country's emergence as a major power, one befitting its population of 1.4 billion.

Although they do not officially vote in these decisions on Olympic sites, some unofficial players have power, such as corporations that sometimes pay millions of dollars for designation as an official sponsor. If a number of them threatened to withdraw their support, the IOC would likely give in to their demands. Likewise, when NBC paid the IOC $3.5 billion for the rights to televise the Olympics from 2000 to 2008, the network became a major player in the decision-making.

In addition to site selection, the IOC has made a number of other blatantly political decisions. The following are a few examples from the past thirty years of decisions made for political reasons by Olympic ruling bodies.[35]

- 1991: The IOC agreed to let South Africa participate in the 1992 Olympics provided that it met certain conditions regarding the dismantling of apartheid.
- 2000: North and South Korea marched as one nation in the opening ceremonies under a single white flag with a blue depiction of an undivided peninsula, although they competed as separate nations.
- 2008–2016: Research by the Centre on Housing Rights and Evictions on Olympic Games from 1992 through 2016 shows that the host nations displaced thousands.[36] (See Box 13.3 for examples.)

Political Decisions by Individual Nations Regarding the Olympics

International incidents that have nothing to do with the Olympic Games have sometimes caused nations to withdraw their teams from Olympic competition. Some examples follow:

- 1980: Some fifty-four nations, including the United States, West Germany, Canada, and Japan, boycotted the Games because of the Soviet Union's invasion of Afghanistan.
- 1984: Fourteen nations, most notably the Soviet Union, East Germany, Cuba, Bulgaria, and Poland, boycotted the Games because they were held in the United States.
- 1988: Cuba boycotted the Summer Games because North Korea was not allowed to cohost the Games

with South Korea North Korea joined in the boycott.
- 2008: There was talk of a boycott to the Beijing Olympic Games because of China's treatment of the Tibetan people and other human rights abuses, although no major protest eventuated.
- 2016: The International Bobsleigh and Skeleton Federation, facing a potential boycott by athletes upset over the Russian doping scandal, moved the 2017 bobsled and skeleton world championships out of Russia[37]

Political Organization of the Olympics

In addition to the corruptions of the Olympic ideals that have been outlined, the ways that the Games are organized are political. Nations select which athletes will perform (i.e., no athlete can perform without national sponsorship). The IOC provides ceremonies where athletes march behind their country's flag. After each event, the winner's national anthem is played and the flags of the three medal winners are raised at the awards ceremony. The IOC also considers political criteria in the selection of the site of the Olympics and in the choice of judges.

To be fair in this appraisal, the Olympic Games do attempt to promote the idea of oneness with the use of the Olympic hymn and the Olympic flag (five interlaced rings representing the five continents) and the meeting of athletes from all over the world at the Olympic Games in a spirit of fair competition. However, nationalism does not merely intrude, it dominates.[38]

PROPOSALS FOR REFORMING THE OLYMPIC GAMES

Is there a way to organize the Olympics to accomplish the aim of neutralizing the crippling political problems that work to negate the Olympic ideals? Many scholars, journalists, and other people from various walks of life have suggested ways to improve the Olympic Games. Even members of the IOC, international sport federations, and national Olympic committees have proposed ways of advancing the mission of the Olympics. In this section of the chapter we identify and describe a series of reforms that

BOX 13.3 *THINKING ABOUT SPORT:* THE OLYM-PIC GAMES AND THE DISPLACEMENT OF PEOPLE

The Switzerland-based Centre on Housing Rights and Evictions examined each Olympic Games from 1988 to the buildup for the Beijing Games in 2008 and concluded that the host countries, collectively, had displaced more than 2 million people, mostly minorities such as the homeless and the poor. Consider these examples:

- As a result of policies enforced at the 1988 Olympics in Seoul, South Korea, 720,000 people were evicted from their homes to provide space for various venues, street vendors were banned to "clean up" the city for visitors, and homeless people and beggars were rounded up and housed in a prison camp.
- The Barcelona Games in 1992 saw Romany communities evicted and dispersed. The streets were "cleansed" by dispersing beggars, prostitutes, and street sellers. Between 1986 and 1992, housing prices rose by 240 percent as the Olympic districts were gentrified and public housing was demolished.
- In preparation for the 1996 Olympics in Atlanta, large housing projects (whose residents mostly were African Americans) were demolished and replaced with middle-class homes. Around 30,000 families were evicted, and 9,000 homeless people were arrested and locked up until the Games were over.
- Because the 2000 Games in Sydney were built on surplus government land, no one was directly displaced, but as a result of the city's gentrification, housing prices more than doubled from 1996 to 2003 and rents soared by 40 percent, forcing people to move. In the year before the Olympics, there was a 400 percent increase in tenant evictions.

- In Beijing, a year before the Games were to begin, 1.25 million people had already been displaced and another 250,000 were due to be evicted.
- In London, more than two years before the 2012 Summer Olympic Games were due to be staged, more than 1,000 people faced the threat of displacement from their homes, and housing prices were escalating. Over the course of the negotiations for an area near the Olympic Stadium site, businesses employing nearly 15,000 workers in total were also reportedly forced to move.
- In the 2016 Rio Summer Olympics, according to estimates from local activists and human rights groups, somewhere between 70,000 and 90,000, mostly poor people, were forcefully evicted and relocated.
- In South Korea, a small village known as Sukam was leveled to make way for a luxury resort, parking lots, and a helicopter pad to build an Olympic-quality slope and amenities on Mount Gariwang for the 2018 Winter Olympic Games. All residents were displaced to a small village named Woo Myeon Joo that was created for the displaced South Koreans.

So, although the Olympic Games enhance the prestige of the host city and nation and many businesses and individuals benefit economically, some pay a huge price for the Games. Not surprisingly, the costs and burdens are borne by those least able to bear them—the powerless.

Sources: Centre on Housing Rights and Evictions, "Fair Play for Housing Rights: Mega-Events, Olympic Games and Housing Rights," 2007, https://www.ruig-gian.org/ressources/Report%20Fair%20Play%20FINAL%20FINAL%20070531.pdf; Travis Waldron and Edgar Maciel, "The Olympics Are Always a Disaster for Poor People," *The Huffington Post*, August 17, 2016, http://www.huffingtonpost.com/entry/olympics-poor-rio-atlanta_us_57aa27a2e4b0db3be07bde67. Aamar Madhani, "Olympic Venue Displaces Korean Village," *USA Today*, February 19, 2018, 6D.

have been proposed to achieve the goals of the Olympic Charter. Our objective is to encourage readers to consider them, analyze them, and then construct their own set of proposals for reforming the Olympic Games.

1. *Establish two permanent sites for the Games.* Each permanent site must be neutral; otherwise, the Games will continue to be subject to the influence of power politics. The choices often mentioned in connection with proposals like this are Greece for the Summer Olympics and Switzerland for the

Winter Games. Greece is a natural choice because the ancient Olympian Games were held there every four years for more than 1,000 years, ending in 393 CE. Even better, each of the permanent sites should be in a free zone—land ceded to the IOC and therefore land that no nation claims, just as the United Nations is located in a free zone in New York City.

2. *An alternative to two permanent sites is to use multiple sites for each Olympic Games.* For example, track and field might be held in one nation, boxing in

another, and so on. A format like that would enable poorer nations to be hosts and to benefit economically. It would also enable spectators watching on television to view and appreciate a variety of geographic and cultural landscapes instead of being restricted to the narrow focus on one city and nation that currently exists.

3. *Athletes must represent only themselves.* Athletes, in actuality and symbolically, should not represent a country, nor should any nation-state be represented by uniforms, flags, national anthems, or political leaders. When an athlete is awarded his or her medal for winning an event, only the Olympic hymn should be played. Athletes should also be randomly assigned to housing and eating arrangements at the Games to reduce national identification and to maximize cross-national interaction.

4. *Revise the opening ceremonies so that athletes enter the arena with other athletes in their events.* This would de-emphasize the nation in which athletes are citizens and emphasize the sports events of the Olympic Games, and it would promote fellowship among the athletes.

5. *Make all athletes (amateur and professional) eligible for competition.* The nation-state should not be involved in the selection process because this encourages nationalistic feelings. To ensure that the best athletes of the world are able to compete, a minimum standard for each event should be set by an Olympic governing board. Athletes meeting this standard would compete at a regional event where another and higher standard of excellence would be set for athletes to qualify for the Olympics. Those athletes qualifying for the regional competition and the Olympics would have all expenses for travel and per diem paid by the IOC.

6. *Subsidize the cost of the Olympics from revenues generated from spectators' admissions to the regionals, from admissions to the Games, and from television.* Establishing permanent sites would significantly reduce the cost of the Olympics. Revenues from admissions and television (the IOC receives one-third of television revenues) should cover the costs after the Games are established. During the building of the permanent sites, however, the IOC may need a subsidy or loan from the United Nations.

7. *All media coverage and broadcasts should be controlled by the IOC.* Television revenues present a particularly thorny problem because the revenue potential is great and this lends itself to threats of overcommercialization, the intrusion of corporations into the decision-making arena, and jingoism by chauvinistic television commentators. To reduce these potential dangers, all media coverage should be reported by a firm strictly controlled by the IOC. Media coverage of the Olympics should be provided to each country at a cost determined by the existing number of media outlets in that country. No single country would have any control over what would be shown or the commentary emanating from the Games.

8. *Establish an Olympic committee and a secretary general to prepare for and oversee each Olympic Games.* The composition of this committee would be crucial. Currently the members of the IOC are taken from national committees, with an important criterion being the maintenance of a political balance between opposing factions. The concept of a ruling body is essential, but the committee should be reorganized to reduce political considerations. This is a baffling problem because the selection will inevitably involve politics. One possibility would be to incorporate the selection procedures used in the United Nations to select its secretary general. These procedures have worked, despite national differences.

Although these ideas are speculative in nature, they are worthy of consideration and revision. Perhaps they can even inspire the development of new ideas; now is a propitious time to alter the structure, practices, and scope of the Olympics given significant concerns that are being raised by athletes, scholars, cultural commentators, and people in host communities like never before. The Olympic movement is an important piece of our societal fabric. That is why it must be radically altered from its present form if its lofty goals are to be realized.

SUMMARY

Two themes have dominated this chapter: sport is political in character, and sport, like all institutions, is conservative. This basic conservatism in sport has two important implications for society. First, the athletic programs of the schools to which most persons are exposed support and reinforce a view of the world and of society that perpetuates the status quo. In the United States this is accomplished through the promotion of national values and the support of the political–economic system.

A second implication, given the institutional character of sport, is that efforts to change sport will rarely come from those who control sport. Moreover, any attack on sport will be defined as an attack on society itself. Thus, change in sport will often be slow and congruent with challenges to dominant power structures and ideologies found elsewhere in our broader society.

Learn more with this chapter's digital tools, including web resources, video links, and chapter self-assessment quizzes at www.oup.com/he/sage-eitzen-beal-atencio-12e.

NOTES

1. Isabelle Boulert, "Relationship between Sport and Politics Seems Undeniable," *The Student*, October 21, 2014, http://www.studentnewspaper.org/relationship-between-sport-and-politics-seems-undeniable/.
2. Ben Gartland, "Sports and Politics Do Mix, As They Should," *The DePaulia*, September 11, 2016, http://depauliaonline.com/2016/09/11/sports-politics-mix/.
3. Jackie MacMullan, Dec3mber 3, 2020. ESPN, Philadelphia 76ers' Daryl Morey was worried Hong Kong tweet might end NBA career, https://www.espn.com/nba/story/_/id/30587457/philadelphia-76ers-daryl-morey-was-worried-hong-kong-tweet-end-nba-career, accessed July 18, 2021
4. George Ramsay, CNN, April 26, 2022, "Wimbledon 2022: Organizers feared Russian participation would fuel a 'propaganda machine.'" https://www.cnn.com/2022/04/26/tennis/wimbledon-russia-belarus-tennis-spt-intl/index.html, accessed June 8, 2022
5. Max Weber, *Economy and Society*, trans. Guenther Roth and G. Wittick (New York: Bedminster Press, 1968; first published in 1922); see also Betty Dobratz, Lisa Waldner, and Timothy L. Buzzell, *Power, Politics, and Society: An Introduction to Political Sociology* (Boston: Pearson, 2011).
6. C. Wright Mills, *The Power Elite* (New York: Oxford University Press, 2000; first published in 1956); see also G. William Domhoff, *Who Rules America? The Triumph of the Corporate Rich*, 7th ed. (New York: McGraw–Hill, 2013).
7. Good discussions of this topic can be found in the following books: Dave Zirin, *Game Over: How Politics Has Turned the Sports World Upside Down* (New York: New Press, 2013); see also Dave Zirin, *A People's History of Sports in the United States: 250 Years of Politics, Protest, People, and Play* (New York: New Press, 2009); George H. Sage, *Globalizing Sport: How Organizations, Corporations, Media, and Politics Are Changing Sport* (Boulder, CO: Paradigm, 2010); Alan Bairner, *Sport and Politics* (New York: Routledge, 2011).
8. Anthony F. Iliakostas, "Separation of Sport and State: The Federal Government's Involvement in Major League Baseball's Drug Testing Program," *3 Pace Intellectual Property, Sports & Entertainment Law Forum* 40, no. 1 (2013): 40–59.
9. Marvin Shaffer, "Looking Back on the Vancouver–Whistler Winter Games," Policy Note, February 6, 2014, http://www.policynote.ca/looking-back-on-the-vancouver-whistler-winter-games/.
10. John R. Webb, *Hitler's Olympics—The Facts* (London: Black House, 2013); see also Christopher Hilton, *Hitler's Olympics: The 1936 Berlin Olympic Games* (Charleston, SC: History Press, 2008).
11. Press Association, "Sochi Stripped of February's Bobsleigh and Skeleton World Championships," *The Guardian*, December 13, 2016, https://www.theguardian.com/sport/2016/dec/13/sochi-stripped-bobsleigh-skeleton-world-championships-2017; see also Rebecca R Ruiz and Michael Schwirtz, "An Insider in Sochi Tells How Russia Beat Doping Tests," *The New York Times*, May 13, 2016, A1.
12. Debi Edward, "Inside China's Grueling Sports Schools Where They Spend 10 Hours a Day Training to Be the Next Olympians," ITV News, August 3,

2016, http://www.itv.com/news/2016-08-03/inside-chinas-sports-schools-where-the-next-generation-of-olympians-are-made/.

13. Sage, *Globalizing Sport*, esp. ch. 6.

14. Alex Kirshner, "Meet the Refugee Olympic Team, Bringing Athletes from War-Torn Countries to Rio," SBNation, August 5, 2016, http://www.sbnation.com/2016/8/5/12387508/refugee-olympic-team-athletes-roster-rio-2016.

15. Samantha King, "Offensive Lines: Sport–State Synergy in an Era of Perpetual War," *Cultural Studies— Critical Methodologies* 8 (November 2008): 538.

16. Quoted in D. Stanley Eitzen, *Fair and Foul: Beyond the Myths and Paradoxes of Sport*, 5th ed. (Lanham, MD: Rowman & Littlefield, 2012), 23; John Sayle Watterson, *The Games Presidents Play: Sports and the Presidency* (Baltimore: Johns Hopkins University Press, 2009).

17. "Estimated Probability of Competing in College Athletics," National Collegiate Athletic Association, last updated March 10, 2017, http://www.ncaa.org/about/resources/research/estimated-probability-competing-college-athletics.

18. Harry Edwards, *The Revolt of the Black Athlete* (Champaign: University of Illinois Press, 2017).

19. Cindy Boren, "Why the NFL Moved the Super Bowl from Arizona in 1990," *The Washington Post*, February 26, 2014, https://www.washingtonpost.com/news/early-lead/wp/2014/02/26/why-the-nfl-moved-the-super-bowl-from-arizona-in-1990/?utm_term=.3d1bd4358233.

20. Josh Voorhees, "The Reason March Madness Steers Clear of South Carolina and Mississippi," *Slate*, March 20, 2014, http://www.slate.com/blogs/the_slatest/2014/03/20/ncaa_confederate_flag_ban_the_reason_march_madness_never_reaches_south_carolina.html/.

21. Aaron Morrison, "Colin Kaepernick's National Anthem Protest Will Go on Until 'Significant Change' Is Made," Identities.Mic, August 29, 2016, https://mic.com/articles/152905/colin-kaepernick-s-national-anthem-protest-will-go-on-until-significant-change-is-made#.ht5gHScSJ.

22. Jarrett Bell, "Kaepernick Earns Place in History," *USA Today*, May 18, 2017, 3C; Lorenzo Reyes, "Kaepernick Supporters Show Solidarity," *USA Today*,

May 25, 2017, 6C; Charles P. Pierce, "Civil Unrest," *Sports Illustrated*, September 18, 2017, 16–17.

23. Dave Zirin, "The Season for Dissent," *The Progressive*, November 2016, 44–45; Greg Bishop, "And Now What?" *Sports Illustrated*, December 19, 2016, 65–72; Lottie Joiner, "Colin Kaepernick, the Integrated NFL and When Protest Works," *Time*, September 16, 2016, http://time.com/4497357/social-activism-kaepernick-nfl/.

24. *Nike Sweatshops: Behind the Swoosh*, uploaded July 28, 2011, http://www.youtube.com/watch?v=M5uYCWVfuPQ-550k/; see also George H. Sage, *Globalizing Sport: How Organizations, Corporations, Media, and Politics Are Changing Sports* (Boulder, CO: Paradigm, 2010), 100–139.

25. Sage, *Globalizing Sport*; see also Sam Riches, "Basketball and Globalization," *The New Yorker*, October 7, 2013, http://www.newyorker.com/business/currency/basketball-and-globalization.

26. Sage, *Globalizing Sport*; see also Udo Merkel, "Sport and Physical Culture in North Korea: Resisting, Recognizing and Relishing Globalization," *Sociology of Sport Journal* 29, no. 4 (2012): 506–525; Gabriela Kruschewsky, "Wake Up, America: Here's Why Soccer Is the World's Best Sport," *The Huffington Post*, May 14, 2014, http://www.huffingtonpost.com/2014/05/14/soccer-worlds-best-sport_n_5248061.html/.

27. International Olympic Committee, *Olympic Charter* (September 2015), 15, https://stillmed.olympic.org/Documents/olympic_charter_en.pdf.

28. Thomas M. Hunt, *Drug Games: The International Olympic Committee and the Politics of Doping, 1960– 2008* (Austin: University of Texas Press, 2011); see also Mike Johnson, *Spitting in the Soup: Inside the Dirty Games of Doping in Sports* (Brooklyn, NY: Velo Press 2016); Rebecca R. Ruiz and Michael Schwirtz, "Russian Insider Says State-Run Doping Fueled Olympic Gold," *The New York Times*, May 13, 2016, A1.

29. Stephen Battaglio, "NBC's Olympic Ratings Drop while Online Viewing Surges: 'There Is a Cultural Shift,' " *Los Angeles Times*, August 16, 2016; see also Sage, *Globalizing Sport*, ch. 5.

30. Travis Waldron, "Nobody Asked Rio's Poor About the Olympics. So They Yelled Louder," *The Huffington Post*, October 6, 2016, http://www.huffingtonpost.

com/entry/rio-favelas-olympics-protest-legacy_ us_57e572d2e4b0e28b2b53cfc8; "Protest Mars Olympic Torch Rio Arrival Ahead of Ceremony," BBC News, August 4, 2016, http://www.bbc.com/news/ world-latin-america-36971906.

31. For an excellent account of the Palestinian terrorist attack at the 1972 Olympic Games, see Simon Reeve, *One Day in September: The Full Story of the 1972 Munich Olympics Massacre and the Israeli Revenge Operation "Wrath of God"* (New York: Arcade Books, 2011); see also David Clay Large, *Munich 1972: Tragedy, Terror, and Triumph at the Olympic Games* (Lanham, MD: Rowman & Littlefield, 2012).

32. "London 2012: Olympic Protests Planned against 'Corporate Dominance,' " *The Guardian*, July 15, 2012, http://www.theguardian.com/info/about-guardian-us/; Juliana Barbassa, "Brazil Is in Crisis ahead of 2016 Olympics in Rio," CNBC, August 17, 2015, http://www.cnbc.com/2015/08/17/brazil-is-in-crisis-ahead-of-2016-olympics-in-rio-commentary.html; Frances Martel, "Protesters Storm Brazil: Enjoy the Olympics, We Are Paying a High Price for It!" Breitbart, August 1, 2016, http://www.breitbart.com/sports/2016/08/01/thousands-brazilians-protest/.

33. Andrew Jennings, *The Lord of the Rings: Power, Money and Drugs in the Modern Olympics* (Transparency Books, 2012).

34. Stephen Wenn, Robert Barney, and Scott Martyn, *Tarnished Rings: The International Olympic Committee and the Salt Lake City Bid Scandal* (Syracuse, NY: Syracuse University Press, 2011); Matt Bonesteel, "The Return of Olympic Bidding Scandals: 2016, 2020 Games under Investigation," *The Washington Post*, March 1, 2016, https://www.washingtonpost.

com/news/early-lead/wp/2016/03/01/the-return-of-olympic-bidding-scandals-2016-2020-games-under-investigation/?utm_term=.b4edc84580fd.

35. For a sample of the sources dealing with the political aspects of the Olympics, see Ian Bremmer, "These 5 Facts Explain the Politics of the Olympic Games," *Time*, August 18, 2016, http://time.com/4456943/2016-olympics-rio-games-politics/; see also Sage, *Globalizing Sport*; David Goldblatt, *The Games: A Global History of the Olympics* (New York: Macmillan, 2016); Dick Pound, *Inside the Olympics: A Behind-the-Scenes Look at the Politics, Scandals and the Glory of the Games* (New York: Wiley & Sons, 2006).

36. Megan Corrarino, " 'Law Exclusion Zones': Mega-Events as Sites of Procedural and Substantive Human Rights Violations," *Yale Human Rights and Development Journal* 17, no. 1 (2014): 180; see also Daniela Fichino, Glaucia Marinhoe, and Mario Campagnani, *Guide for Journalists and Media Professionals: Human Rights Violations in the Olympic City* (Rio de Janeiro, Brazil: Justica Global, 2016), https://www.boell.de/sites/default/files/2016-08-human-rights-violations-olympic-city.pdf.

37. Rebecca R. Ruiz, "Boycott Looming, Sled Event Is Moved," *The New York Times*, December 14, 2016, B9; see also Press Association, "Sochi Stripped of February's Bobsleigh and Skeleton World Championships," *The Guardian*, December 13, 2016, https://www.theguardian.com/sport/2016/dec/13/sochi-stripped-bobsleigh-skeleton-world-championships-2017.

38. David Goldblatt, *The Games: A Global History of the Olympics*; see also Jules Boykoff, *Power Games: A Political History of the Olympics* (Brooklyn, NY: Verso, 2016).

CHAPTER 14

SPORT AND RELIGION

Sports are clearly attracting strong adherents as religion is shedding them. This raises the question: Are Americans shifting their spiritual allegiances away from praying places and toward playing places?

— CHRIS BENEKE AND ARTHUR REMILLARD[1]

People involved in sports—as participants or as spectators—employ numerous religious rituals as standard practice. It has become a common practice for athletes to publicly display their religious beliefs through prayers before and after games. (Photo: Cal Sport Media/Alamy Stock Photo)

On the one hand, there may seem to be little in common between sport and religion; going to religious services, singing hymns, studying scripture, and worshiping God all seem quite unrelated to the activities that we associate with sport. On the other hand, like religion, contemporary sport symbolically evokes fervent commitment from millions of people. Sports fans worship their favorite athletes much as followers of various religions worship their special deities. Also, sports fans, like religious groups, consider themselves part of a community. Finally, the rituals and ceremonies common to religion are paralleled by rituals and ceremonies in sport. One former NFL player summed up the connections between sport and religion by declaring that they go together "like peanut butter and jelly."

Religion is a major part of people's lives, and religious practices of some kind are present in every society. There are followers of a broad variety of religions in the United States, but the emphasis in this chapter will be on Christian linkages to sport. There are several reasons for this focus. First, those who self-identify as Christians are the overwhelming majority; indeed, about 71 percent of U.S. citizens identify themselves as Christians. About 6 percent self-identify with other religions, leaving about 23 percent who self-identify with no religion (see Table 14.1). Second, the historical tradition of the United States is closely tied to the colonizers who brought and promoted Christianity as the primary religion. Finally, as we pointed out in Chapter 2, the rise of sport in the United States was closely linked to Christian leaders and organizations; therefore, Christian attitudes, values, and practices have been a dominating force in American sport.[2] Although Christianity is the most common religion in the United States, in a globalizing world it is important not to lose sight of the significance of religions to a variety of cultures and to acknowledge that the U.S. Constitution guarantees the freedom of religion. From a sociological perspective, it is important to reflect on how our cultural norms and values, including religious ones, impact our perceptions of appropriate worship (See Box 14.1).

As sport and religion have become increasingly intertwined, each has made inroads into the traditional activities and prerogatives of the other. For example, for Christians of previous generations, Sunday was the day reserved for church and worship, but with the increase in opportunities for recreational pursuits—both for participants and for spectators—and the virtual explosion of televised or mediated sports, worship *on* weekends has been replaced by worship *of* weekends. As a result, sport has captured Sunday, and churches have had to revise their schedules to oblige. At most Roman Catholic churches, convenient Saturday late-afternoon and evening services are now featured in addition to traditional Sunday masses, and other denominations frequently schedule services to accommodate the viewing of professional sports events.

In many respects churches have had to share Sundays with sports, and the concept that the Sabbath should be reserved for worship now seems merely a quaint idea from the past. Clerics from several religious denominations have noted that God is competing more and more with Sunday sports—and losing.

At the same time that sport appears to be usurping religion's traditional time for worship and services, many churches and religious leaders are attempting to weld a link between the two activities by sponsoring sports events under religious auspices and by proselytizing athletes to religion and then using them as missionaries to spread the Word and to recruit new members. Thus, contemporary religion often uses sport for the promotion of its causes. Sport uses religion as well, and in more ways than just seizing the traditional day of worship. People involved in sports—as participants or as spectators—employ numerous activities with religious connotations in connection with the contests. Ceremonies, rituals, taboos, fetishes, and so forth—all originating in religious practice—are standard observances in the world of sport.

TABLE 14.1 MOST COMMON RELIGIOUS AFFILIATIONS IN THE UNITED STATES

Religious group	Adult population (percent)
Christian	71
Jewish	2
Muslim	1
Unaffiliated to any particular religion	23

Source: Adapted from https://www.pewforum.org/religious-landscape-study/.

BOX 14.1 *THINKING ABOUT SPORT*: RELIGION, SPORT, GENDER, AND EQUITY

In the United States, Christianity is the largest religion and it has influenced our cultural practices, impacting what we consider normal or "good" ways of being a religious person. This is evidenced by how people respond to a Christian athlete who thanks God for their success as opposed to a Muslim athlete who thanks Allah. Tim Tebow (a devout Christian and former NFL quarterback) prayed after games and scoring touchdowns without incident, but when Husain Abdullah (a devout Muslim and NFL safety) prayed after scoring a touchdown he was penalized fifteen yards for unsportsmanlike conduct. Many people recognized the double standard and, ultimately, the NFL acknowledged that the ruling was wrong.

Because Christianity dominates our cultural view, we often are unfamiliar with other religions. According to the Pew Research, Christianity is the largest global religion (approximately 31 percent of the world population) and Islam is the second largest (approximately 25 percent of the world population). Islam originated in the Middle East and North Africa. Currently, the majority of Muslims live in the Asia-Pacific region. Additionally, it is the fastest growing religion in the world. Nonetheless, many Americans are not familiar with Islam or have skewed understandings because of geopolitical issues around terrorism (especially after September 11, 2001, and the U.S. wars in Afghanistan and Iraq). Currently, about 1 percent of the U.S. population identifies as Muslim (about 3.5 million people). There is a growing awareness that Muslims face discrimination in the United States. According to Pew Foundation research, most American adults (82 percent) say Muslims are subject to at least some discrimination in the United States today, including a majority (56 percent) who say Muslims are discriminated against a lot. And nearly half of Muslim Americans have said they have experienced recent discrimination.

Governing bodies of sport that are centered in world regions that are predominantly Christian (i.e., Europe and North America) have created rules that have not taken into account Islamic traditions of women's clothing that covers the head and body. The international soccer association (FIFA), the international basketball association (FIBA), the international weightlifting association, and the international boxing association have recently changed their rules to allow hijabs to be worn. Of course, this change came from external activism. For example, U.S. women's basketball player Bilqis Abdul-Qaadir was the first NCAA Division I basketball player to wear a hijab. She wanted to play professional basketball, but encountered restrictions that FIBA had on headgear that effectively banned the hijab. Her activism played a prominent role in changing that rule. In turn, she created an organization called Muslim Girls Hoop Too.

Other well-known Muslim American athletes include the following:

Muhammad Ali, Amaiya Zafar (boxing)
Kareem Abdul-Jabbar, Hakeem Olajuwon, Shaquille O'Neal (basketball)
Muhammad Wilkerson, Aqib Talib (American football)
Ibtihaj Muhammad (Olympic fencer)
Dalilha Muhammad (track and field)

Primary source: Pew Research Center, https://www.pewresearch.org/topic/religion/religions/islam/muslim-americans/

In this chapter we examine the multidimensional relationship between religion and sport.

THE RELATIONSHIP BETWEEN RELIGION AND SOCIETY

Religion is the belief that supernatural forces influence human lives. There are many definitions of religion, but one by a founder of the discipline of sociology, French sociologist Émile Durkheim, has perhaps been cited most. Durkheim said that "religion is a unified system of beliefs and practices relative to sacred things, that is to say, things set apart and forbidden—beliefs and practices which unite into one single moral community called a Church, all those who adhere to them."[3]

As a social institution, religion is a system that functions to maintain and transmit beliefs about forces considered supernatural and sacred. It provides codified guides for moral conduct and prescribes symbolic practices deemed to be in harmony with beliefs about the supernatural. The world religions, including Christianity, Hinduism, Buddhism, Confucianism, Judaism, and Islam, are cores of elaborate cultural systems that have dominated world societies for centuries. For all practical purposes we may assume that religious behavior among human beings is universal in that ethnologists and anthropologists have not yet discovered a human group without traces of the behavior we call "religious."[4]

PERSONAL AND SOCIAL ROLES OF RELIGION

Religions exist because they perform important roles at several levels of human life, including personal, interpersonal, institutional, and societal. At the personal level, religious experiences meet psychic needs by providing individuals with emotional support in this uncertain world. The unpredictable and sometimes dangerous world produces personal fears and general anxiety that revering the powers of nature or seeking cooperation through religious faith and ritual may alleviate. Fears of death, too, are made bearable by beliefs in a supernatural realm into which a believer passes. If one can believe in a God-giving scheme of things, the universal quest for ultimate meaning is validated, and human strivings and sufferings seem to make some sense.

At the interpersonal level, religion contributes to human social bonding. It unites a community of believers by bringing them together to enact various ceremonies and rituals, and it provides them with shared values and beliefs that bind them together. The need to proclaim human abilities and to achieve a sense of transcendence is met and indeed fostered by many religions through ceremonies and rituals that celebrate humans and their activities.

At the social institutional level, one of the paramount functions of religion is the promotion of social integration. This idea has been a tenet of the functionalist theorists since it was advanced by Durkheim more than a century ago. The central point here is that religion advances a bonding of both the members of a society and the social obligations that help unite them because it organizes individuals' experiences in terms of ultimate meanings that include but also transcend the individual. When many people share this ordering principle, they can deal with each other in meaningful ways and can transcend themselves and their individual egoisms, sometimes even to the point of self-sacrifice.

Religious ceremonies and rituals also promote integration because they serve to reaffirm some of the basic customs and values of society. Here, the societal customs, folkways, and observances are symbolically elevated to the realm of the sacred. In expressing common beliefs about the supernatural, engaging in collective worship activities, and recounting the lore and myths of the past, the community is brought closer together and linked with its heritage.

Another functionalist view about the social integrative role of religion is that it tends to legitimize the secular social structures within a society. There is

a strong tendency for religious ideology to become united with the norms and values of secular structures, producing, as a consequence, religious support for the values and institutions of society. From its earliest existence, religion has provided rationales that serve the needs and actions of a society's leaders. It has legitimized as "God-given" such disparate ideologies as absolute monarchies and egalitarian democracies.

At the institutional level, too, religion serves as a vehicle for social control; that is, religious tenets constrain the behavior of the community of believers to keep them in line with the norms, values, and beliefs of society. In all the major religions, morals and religion are intertwined, and schemes of otherworldly rewards or punishments for behavior, such as those found in Christianity, become powerful forces for morality. The fear of hellfire and damnation has been a powerful deterrent and control in Christian societies. The virtues of honesty, conformity to sexual codes, and all the details of acceptable, moral behavior in a society become merged with religious beliefs and practices.

Advocates of a conflict/cultural perspective of religion are especially troubled by the notion of religion serving as a mechanism of social control. They recognize functionalist analysts' claim that religion meets the need that many people have for emotional support in dealing with the unknown, the unpredictable, the ultimate questions about life and death, and the inclinations of people to create gods and believe in supernatural phenomena. But conflict/culturists contend that religion for social control has been primarily a tool of the rich and powerful that has been particularly harmful to poor and oppressed people. Furthermore, they argue that religion has been a means of legitimating the interests of the dominant class, justifying existing social injustices and inequalities, and, like a narcotic, lulling people into ready acceptance of the status quo—into a "false consciousness." An extreme position on this notion is a frequently paraphrased statement of Karl Marx's, who argued, "Religion is the sigh of the oppressed creature, the heart of a heartless world, and the soul of soulless conditions. It is the opium of the people." Indeed, historically religion has often reinforced existing social structures and promoted socially in-equitable conditions.[5]

HISTORICAL AFFILIATION BETWEEN RELIGION AND SPORT

ANCIENT GREECE: CREATORS OF ORGANIZED SPORTS EVENTS

Scholars who have studied the origins of sport claim that it began as a religious rite. The ancient Greeks, who worshiped beauty, entwined religious obser-vance with their athletic demonstrations in such a way that to define where one left off and the other began is difficult. The strong anthropomorphic (hu-manlike) conceptions of gods held by the Greeks led to their belief that the gods took pleasure in the same things that mortals enjoyed, such as music, drama, and displays of physical excellence. The gymnasia lo-cated in every city-state for all male adults (females were not allowed in the Greek gymnasia) provided facilities and places for sports training as well as for the discussion of intellectual topics. Furthermore, fa-cilities for religious worship, an altar and a chapel, were located in the center of each gymnasium.

The Olympic Games, the most important athletic meetings of the Greeks, were part of religious festi-vals. They were sacred contests, staged in a sacred lo-cation and as a sacred festival; they were a religious act in honor of Zeus, king of the gods. Athletes who took part in the Olympics did so to please Zeus and the prizes they won came from him. Other Pan-Hel-lenic games were equally religious in nature. Victori-ous athletes presented their gifts of thanks on the altar of the god or gods whom they thought to be re-sponsible for their victory. The end of the ancient Olympic Games was a result of the religious convic-tion of Theodosius, the Roman emperor of 392–395 AD. He was a Christian and decreed the end of the Games as part of his suppression of paganism in favor of Christianity.[6]

THE EARLY CHRISTIAN CHURCH AND ROMAN SPORT SPECTACLES

In Western societies, religious support for sport found no counterpart to that of the Greeks until the beginning of the twentieth century. The Christian religion was dominated by the Roman Catholic Church until the Reformation in the sixteenth cen-tury. Since then, Roman Catholicism has shared reli-gious power with Protestant groups. At first Christians opposed Roman sport spectacles such as chariot racing and gladiatorial combat because of their pa-ganism and brutality, but later Christians opposed sport because they came to regard the body as an in-strument of sin.

The early Christians did not view sports as evil per se because the Apostle Paul wrote approvingly of the benefits of physical activity. He said, for example, "Do you not know that those who run in a race, all indeed run, but one receives the prize? So run as to obtain it" (1 Cor. 9:24). In another verse, Paul re-minded Timothy of the importance of adhering to the rules: "One who enters a contest is not crowned unless he has competed according to the rules" (2 Tim. 2:5).

The paganism prominent in the Roman sports events, however, was abhorrent to the Christians. Moreover, early Christianity gradually built a foun-dation based on asceticism, which is a belief that evil exists in the body and that therefore the body should be subordinate to the pure spirit. As a result, church dogma and education sought to subordinate all de-sires and demands of the body to exalt the spiritual life. A twelfth-century Catholic abbot, Saint Bernard, argued, "Always in a robust and active body the mind lies soft and more lukewarm; and, on the other hand, the spirit flourishes more strongly and more actively in an infirm and weakly body." Nothing could have been more damning for the promotion of active rec-reation and sport.[7]

PRE-COLUMBIAN SOCIETIES: SPORT IN THE AMERICAS

The Mayans and Aztecs are examples of pre-Colum-bian societies that included physical activities as part of their religious rituals and ceremonies. The pur-pose of many games of these societies was rooted in a desire to gain victory over foes seen and unseen, to influence the forces of nature, and to promote fertil-ity among crops and cattle. The Zuni Indians of New Mexico played games that they believed would bring rain and thus enable their crops to grow. One Inuit tribe, at the end of the harvest season, played a cup-and-ball game to "catch the sun" and thus delay its departure. In his monumental work on the Native Americans of the Plains, Stewart Culin wrote, "In general, games appear to be played ceremonially, as pleasing to the gods, with the objective of securing fertility, causing rain, giving and prolonging life, expelling demons, or curing sickness."[8]

REFORMATION AND PROTESTANTISM IN THE AMERICAN COLONIES

The Reformation of the early sixteenth century signaled the end of the viselike grip that Roman Catholicism had on the minds and habits of the people of Europe and England. But Protestantism had within it the seeds of a new asceticism and, in its Puritan form, became a greater enemy to sport than Roman Catholicism had been.

Puritans were among the earliest English immigrants to America, and they had considerable influence on the social life in the colonies. Perhaps no Christian group exercised a greater opposition to sport than the Puritans. As a means of realizing amusement and unrestrained impulses, sport was suspect for the Puritan; one historian asserted that "Puritans' opposition to sport was grounded on at least seven propositions: sport was frivolous and wasted time; sport did not refresh the body as good recreation should, but tired people instead; much sporting activity was designed deliberately to inflict pain or injury; sporting contests usually led to gambling; more sport took place on Sunday than on any other day, so sport encouraged people to defile the Sabbath; sport was noisy and disrupted others, sometimes entire communities; and many sports had either pagan or 'Popish' origins."[9] The renowned nineteenth-century English historian Thomas B. Macaulay claimed that the Puritans opposed bearbaiting (tying a bear to a stake and urging dogs to attack it) not so much because it was painful for the bear but because it gave pleasure to the spectators.

The Puritans of New England were not the only colonists who had compunctions about sports. Most of the colonies passed laws against play and sport on the Sabbath. Like the Puritans, the most prominent objection to sport by religious leaders in the other colonies was that participation would divert attention from spiritual matters. The practical matter was that survival in the New World required hard work from everyone; thus, time spent in play and games was typically considered time wasted. The tavern was the center for gambling and table sports, dancing had obvious sexual overtones, and field sports often involved gambling and cruelty to animals.[10]

RELIGIOUS OBJECTIONS TO SPORT DECLINED IN THE NINETEENTH CENTURY

Church opposition to leisure pursuits was firmly maintained in the first few decades of the nineteenth century, and each effort to liberalize attitudes toward leisure pursuits was met with a new attack on sport as "sinful." Sports were still widely regarded by the powerful Protestant religious groups as snares of the devil himself. However, in the 1830s social problems became prominent concerns of U.S. social reformers, many of whom were clergy and intellectual leaders. There were crusades against slavery, intemperance, and poor industrial working conditions; widespread support for the emancipation of women, for public education, and for industrial reform; and indeed, scrutiny of every facet of American life.

Social conditions had begun to change rapidly under the aegis of industrialization. The physical health of the population became a major issue leading a number of reformers to propose that people would be happier, more productive, and healthier if they engaged in vigorous sports activities. Surprisingly, some of the leading advocates were clerics who began to soften their attitude toward play and sport. Although the development of a more liberal attitude by church leaders toward sport began to appear by the mid-nineteenth century, not all church authorities subscribed to the trend. A staid Congregationalist magazine, the *New Englander*, vigorously attacked sport: "Let our readers, one and all, remember that we were sent into this world, not for sport and amusement, but for labor; not to enjoy and please ourselves, but to serve and glorify God, and be useful to our fellow men. That is the great object and end in life. In pursuing this end, God has indeed permitted us all needful diversion and recreation. . . . But the great end of life after all is work. . . . It is a true saying . . .

'We come into this world, not for sports.' We were sent here for a higher and nobler object."[11]

Although some church leaders fought the encroaching sport and leisure mania throughout the late nineteenth century, many gradually began to reconcile play and religion in response to pressure from medical, educational, and political leaders for games and sport. Increasingly, churches broadened their commitment to play and sport endeavors as a means of drawing people together. Between 1880 and 1920, American Protestants witnessed the flourishing in the pulpits and seminaries of a form of religiosity known, both admiringly and scornfully, as *muscular Christianity*.[12] (see Chapter 2) The church's prejudice against pleasure through play had broken down almost completely by the beginning of the twentieth century.

RELIGION AND SPORT CONCILIATION

Churches were confronted with ever-increasing changes in the twentieth century; economic pressures, political movements, and social conditions were the chief forces responsible for the drastically changed relationship between religion and sport. Increased industrialization turned the population into a nation of urban dwellers, and higher wages were responsible for an unprecedented affluence. The gospel of work (the Protestant work ethic) became less credible, and increased leisure enhanced the popularity of a new professional sports industry. The sport historian William J. Baker elaborates on these trends, writing, "In the 1920s and 1930s religious links to sport in the United States grew clearer and broader. Protestants and Catholics continued to stake claims on the American soul, frequently endorsing sport for sectarian purposes. At the same time other, smaller groups came to the marriage of religion and sport."[13]

The story of changes in the attitudes of religionists in the later twentieth and early twenty-first centuries was largely one of increasing accommodation. Much of both Catholic and Protestant America came to view sport as a positive force and even as a useful means of promoting God's work. Sports and leisure activities became an increasingly conspicuous part of the recreation programs of thousands of churches

and many church colleges, a trend that one sociologist called the "basketballization" of churches. One sports study scholar elaborated, suggesting that sport has "captured the imagination of modern evangelical churches. No forward-looking church will overlook the value of sport as an adjunct to its social programs, and no architect will overlook the opportunity to include at least one gymnasium in first drafts for a new church."[14] Times have changed, and the conciliation between sport and organized religion has approached finality.

SPORT AS RELIGION

Sport has taken on so many of the characteristics of religion that some have argued that sport has emerged as a new religion, supplementing, and in some cases even supplanting, traditional religious expressions. Almost two decades ago, a professor in the religious studies program at Pennsylvania State University made a claim that startled both clergy and laypeople—that "sport is a religion." He asserted, "For me, it is not just a parallel that is emerging between sport and religion, but rather *a complete identity. Sport is religion* for many Americans, and this is no product of simply facile reasoning or wishful thinking. It is reasonable to consider sport the newest and fastest growing religion, far outdistancing whatever is in second place."[15]

And there are still other sport sites where religion is alleged to reside. Eric Bain-Selbo, a professor of philosophy and religion at Western Kentucky University, claims that "there is a compelling case to conclude that college football in the South is a form and expression of religious life. . . . I believe that sport is replacing religion. . . . Expressing one's religiosity predominantly in the context of one's college football team in the South is really no different from being a Methodist or Baptist."[16]

Preceding all of the previous declarations was that of Avery Brundage, an American who for twenty years (1952–1972) was president of the IOC. Brundage claimed that the Olympic movement itself was a religion: "The Olympic Movement is a Twentieth Century religion, a religion with universal appeal which incorporates all the basic values of other religions, a modern, exciting, virile, dynamic religion. . . . It is a religion for which Pierre de Coubertin was the prophet, for Coubertin has kindled a torch that will enlighten the world."[17]

SIMILARITIES BETWEEN SPORT AND RELIGION

There is no doubt that organized sport has taken on the trappings of religion. A few examples will illustrate this point:

- Every religion has its god or gods (or saints or high priests) who are venerated by its members. Likewise, sports fans have gods (superstar athletes) they worship.
- Christianity has its saints, and other religions have religious models they admire and worship. Sports fans also have their saints—those who have passed to the great beyond (such as Jim Thorpe, Knute Rockne, Ted Williams, and Babe Didrikson Zaharias).
- Religion has priests and clergy. The high priests of contemporary sport are the professional, collegiate, and national amateur team coaches who not only direct the destinies of their athletes but also control the emotions of large masses of sports fans.
- Religion has scribes who record the word of God. Sport also has its scribes, the sport journalists and sportscasters who disseminate the "word" of sports deeds and glories.
- Religion has its churches, synagogues, mosques, and temples. Sport has its houses of worship, such as Fenway Park and Soldier Field.
- Religion has its congregations. Sport has its masses of highly vocal "true believers."
- Religion has its proverbs that express the "true" word of God. Numerous proverbs fill the world of sport: "Nice guys finish last," "When the going gets tough, the tough get going," "*Lose* is a four-letter word," and so forth. In sports, these proverbs are frequently written on posters and hung in locker rooms for athletes to memorize.
- Religious shrines are commonplace wherever religion is found. They preserve sacred symbols and memorabilia that followers can admire and honor. The achievements of athletes and teams are celebrated in numerous shrines, called halls of fame, built to commemorate and glorify sporting figures.

Halls of fame have been established for virtually every sport played in North America, and some sports have several halls of fame devoted to them.
- Religions demand fidelity from their followers in the form of faithfulness to obligations, duties, and observances. Symbols of fidelity abound in sport. The athletes are expected to give total commitment to the cause, including abstinence from smoking, alcohol, and in some cases even sex.
- Religions require devotion to specific beliefs, traditions, and practices. Devout followers of sports witness and invoke traditional and hallowed chants and show their devotion to the team by adding "spirit" to its cause. In cheering for the Green Bay Packers, New York Yankees, or Los Angeles Lakers, devoted fans can experience feelings of belonging to a "congregation." It is not unusual for these sports pilgrims to travel hundreds of miles, sometimes braving terrible weather conditions, to witness a sports event, thus displaying their devotion to their team.
- Religions sponsor a variety of holidays and festivals that function to promote communal involvement, thus nurturing a sense of belonging to the religious community. The Super Bowl functions as a major sporting festival for American culture, seeming to unite the entire nation with its pageantry and sporting extravaganza.

Two popular—one can even say iconic—motion pictures involving sports, *Field of Dreams* and *Bull Durham*, used numerous religious themes and symbols suggesting baseball as religion. They do not claim that baseball is a religion in a traditional theological way, but they do suggest a symbiosis (an intimate association or close union) between the two. *Bull Durham* reveals how baseball exemplifies the qualities of an institutional religion. The movie opens with gospel music in the background and the female lead, Annie (Susan Sarandon), delivering this prologue: "I believe in the church of baseball. I've tried all the major religions and most of the minor ones. . . . I gave Jesus a chance, but it just didn't work out between us. The Lord laid too much guilt on me. . . . There's no guilt in baseball, and it's never boring. . . . The only church that truly feeds the soul, day in and day out, is the church of baseball."

Field of Dreams makes clear its baseball-as-religion point of view. In the basic plot, a supernatural voice of revelation tells a young farmer and baseball fanatic (Kevin Costner) to plow up part of his cornfield and build a baseball field. The farmer does this, and soon baseball players from the past are playing on the baseball diamond, like saints from a land beyond the first rows of the cornfield. After the farmer has made a pilgrimage and faced his need for forgiveness, he is miraculously reconciled with his long-dead baseball-player father. At the end of the movie, the farmer's baseball field is a shrine that draws flocks of people seeking "the truth." The movie has many religious themes and symbols: life after death, a seeker who hears a voice and must go on a spiritual quest, an inner healing, becoming a child to enter the kingdom, and losing your life to gain it.

CRITICAL VIEWS ABOUT SPORT AS RELIGION

Despite the many seeming parallels between sport and religion, sport does not fulfill what are considered by many the key functions of "churchly" religion. For example, the question of why humans are created and continue to wrestle with their purpose here on earth and life hereafter is not addressed by sports. In this connection, several social scientists have noted that regardless of the eminence of those who contend that sports are a form of religion in this age of the Super Bowl and World Cup, sports and play are not even a natural religion. Instead, they are an entirely different category of human experience, one that is significant in itself. Some scholars contend that the appropriation of traditional religion by advocates of sport as religion borders on heresy.

Other critics of sport as religion also emphasize that many activities that humans become deeply committed to can be referred to as a religion, when speaking metaphorically, but if we include in religion all meaningful or spiritual activities, we then wind up including practically all activities into which humans pour their will, emotions, and energy. Although sport does have some religious-like symbols, rituals, legends, sacred spaces and time, and heroes, it is organized and played by humans for humans without supernatural sanction. So for James A. Mathisen, American sport is what he calls a folk religion. He says, "Sports looks like a religion, but it is not one. It is sort of like civil religion, but not quite. The best conceptual response amid this uncertainty is to interpret American sport as a contemporary folk religion." By this he means there "is a combination of shared moral principles and behavioral customs . . . a common set of ideas, rituals, and symbols . . . an overarching sense of unity." Joseph Price disagrees with Mathisen's comment about sport and civil religion. But for Price it is baseball, not sport in general, that is a civil religion. Price argues, "For true believers . . . the word of baseball is the gospel of an American civil religion that finds safety and wholeness—completion and salvation—where the game begins and where it ends: at home."[18] For religious historian Craig A. Forney, a holy trinity of football, baseball, and basketball forms a civil religion in American sports. He claims that "football, baseball, and basketball are yearly rituals of civil religion in the United States."[19] Religion from these perspectives is not the universalistic posture of the world's institutional religions.

RELIGION USES SPORT

CHURCHES

From a position of strong opposition to recreation and sport activities, most religions have made a complete reversal within the past century and now heartily support these activities as effective tools to promote "the Lord's work." Social service is a major purpose of the religious leaders who provide play and recreation under the auspices of their churches. Church-sponsored recreation and sport programs offer services to members and sometimes the entire community that are often unavailable in acceptable forms anywhere else. Church playgrounds and recreation centers in urban areas have facilities, equipment, and instruction that municipal governments often cannot provide. The Young Men's Christian Association, the Young Women's Christian Association, the Catholic Youth Organization, Jewish Community Centers, and other church-related organizations perform a variety of social services for old and young alike, one of which is the sponsorship of sports leagues.

Promoting sport to strengthen and increase fellowship in their congregations has been beneficial to the churches as well as to their members. In a time of increasing secularization, such as that witnessed by the United States in the past fifty years, it is understandable that churches would seek to promote activities that solidify and integrate church membership.

RELIGIOUS LEADERS EMBRACE SPORT

Not content merely to provide recreational and sports opportunities under the sponsorship of the church, some religious leaders outwardly avow the association between religion and sport in their preaching and use of sport as a metaphor for the social enterprise of the church. The now-deceased Jerry Falwell, founder of Liberty University and one of the self-styled leaders of fundamental Protestantism in the United States, told an audience, "[Jesus] wants you to be a victor for God's glory. A champion is not an individual star but one of a team who knows how to function with others." Several of the most popular contemporary evangelists enthusiastically support the virtues of sports competition and the sanctity of Christian coaches and athletes. They have made sport a basic metaphor in their ministries. For them, the source of Christianity, the Bible, legitimates sport involvement, and they often claim that the Bible says leisure and lying around are morally dangerous for us. Sports keep us busy.

CHURCH COLLEGES AND UNIVERSITIES

Intercollegiate sports programs were originally organized and administered by the students for their own recreation and amusement. By the early years of the twentieth century, however, the programs gradually changed form and character, and one of the new features that emerged was the use of collegiate sports teams to publicize the school and to bind alumni to their alma mater.

Church-supported colleges and universities began to use their athletic teams to attract students, funds, and public attention to impoverished (and sometimes academically inferior) institutions. The classic but by no means only example is Notre Dame; many other Roman Catholic colleges and universities also have used football and basketball for publicity.

Basketball, especially, has become a popular sport for Catholic colleges; indeed, Catholic university teams have played in the NCAA basketball championship games numerous times.

Protestant institutions have followed the same pattern of using their athletic teams to advertise; Brigham Young University (BYU), Texas Christian University, and Southern Methodist University (SMU) are among the most visible. Of these, BYU has become a renowned athletic powerhouse. It meshes conservative religious tenets with big-time sports and produces some of the more prominent professional athletes in the United States. One BYU All-American football player said that he believed the athletes bring more attention to the Mormon church than anything else, and when he enrolled at BYU, the president of the university told him BYU was giving him a chance to be a missionary for the church by playing football for it.

Liberty University has aggressively embraced big-time athletics to publicize the school and use the school as a means of carrying out its mission of preaching the gospel of Christ to the world. Falwell, its founder, said he wanted to make Liberty University to born-again Christians what Notre Dame is to Catholics and BYU is to Mormons. To that end, he hired a former NFL coach to lead the football team. Although the Liberty University teams have not achieved the exalted status that Falwell aspired to, the university has gradually climbed to NCAA Division I status.

Ironically, it was a church college, SMU, that was hit with the most severe penalty ever meted out by the NCAA, the so-called death penalty—canceling SMU's entire football season schedule for one year. The NCAA took this drastic action after those connected with the SMU football program continually lied, cheated, and generally violated NCAA rules.

RELIGIOUS ORGANIZATIONS AND SPORTS

One of the most notable outgrowths of religion's use of sport has been the rise of nondenominational religious organizations composed of coaches and athletes. According to one estimate, some eighty organizations minister to the needs of athletes throughout the world; but it seems likely that there are many more than this, because there are more than twenty-five organizations of this type just in the United States. These organizations provide a variety of programs designed to serve current members and recruit new members to religion. Several major incorporated organizations offer everything from national conferences to services before games. The best known have been Fellowship of Christian Athletes (FCA), Sports Ambassadors, Athletes in Action (AIA), Pro Athletes Outreach, Motor Sports Ministries, Hockey Ministries International, and Baseball Chapel. The movement that these organizations represent has been labeled *Sportianity* or, more derisively, *Jocks for Jesus.*[20]

THE FELLOWSHIP OF CHRISTIAN ATHLETES

The prototypical organization for using sport as a tool for evangelism is the FCA, which was founded in 1954 with a focus on high school and college coaches and athletes and currently has about 600 paid employees and a membership of 1.2 million athletes. Its avowed purpose, which appears on most of its publications and on the title page of each issue of the official magazine of the FCA, *Sharing the Victory,* is "to present to athletes and coaches, and all whom they influence, the challenge and adventure of receiving Jesus Christ as Savior and Lord, serving him in their relationship and in the fellowship of the Church." The FCA attempts to combat juvenile delinquency, elevate the moral and spiritual standards of sports in a secular culture, challenge athletes to stand up and be counted for or against God, and appeal to sports enthusiasts and youth through hero worship.

The FCA uses older athletes and coaches to recruit younger ones to Christianity. It has a mailing list of more than 55,000 persons, a field staff of 1,000 nationwide, and 350 local offices across the country. Its most important activity is the sponsorship of annual, week-long summer camps attended by more than 13,000 participants, where coaches and athletes mix religious and inspirational sessions with sport instruction and competition.

Another important facet of the FCA's work in junior high schools, high schools, and college campuses is for athletes to get together to talk about their faith, engage in Bible study, and pray. They also take part in projects such as becoming "big brothers" for

delinquent or needy children, visiting nursing homes, and serving as playground instructors.

There are now some 8,000 high school and college huddles in the United States, the bulk of which are found in the South, Southwest, and Midwest. Most of the members of the FCA are White, middle-class males; however, female athletes are admitted to the FCA, and their membership in the organization is growing. In addition to these activities, the FCA sponsors state and regional retreats and provides various informational materials such as films, records, and tapes.[21]

RELIGION AND PROFESSIONAL SPORTS ORGANIZATIONS

Organizations that focus on specific athletic groups supplement the work of the FCA. The NFL and major baseball leagues sponsor chapels and Bible studies for their athletes. Baseball Chapel, an evangelical Christian ministry, provides Sunday services to teams throughout the major and minor leagues.

Professional sport organizations have sponsored religious events. Several NBA teams have sponsored a God and Country Night for their fans, a mixing of basketball, church, and state that attempts to recognize the role faith and patriotism play in the lives of management, players, and fans associated with the NBA. Third Coast Sports Foundation is a nonprofit ministry organization focused on promoting and organizing "Faith Nights" that seek to provide churches with opportunities for outreach and church-wide fellowship through sports and music. They represent a brand of Christianity that, far from being inclusive, excludes any but the most conservative of Protestant perspectives.

Faith Nights began in minor league baseball parks in 2002; by 2006 more than seventy Faith Nights were scheduled for minor league teams across the United States. Faith Days and Faith Nights began in MLB ballparks in 2006, and in 2007 they were held in ten MLB cities. They have migrated from the Deep South to northern stadiums from Spokane, Washington, to Bridgewater, New Jersey. The popularity of Faith & Family Nights has declined, but in 2022, for example, the San Diego Padres hosted their annual Faith & Family Night when they played the Minnesota Twins. The event featured a postgame appearance and speech from select players and executives and a postgame concert by Phil Wickham. Today, there are still some events taking place with major and minor professional teams. A *Communication Currents* writer once noted, "I have concluded that these events use the language of typical ballpark promotions yet restrict the range of identities and voices that may participate in the 'church of baseball.'"[22]

Although these organizations and events have attracted the participation of many professional team franchises, athletes, coaches, and fans, not everyone is an advocate of this practice, claiming that it signals the Christianization of pro sports. Some believe that making religion part of the spectacle of public sporting events risks trivializing God and alienating nonbelieving teammates and fans. As one *USA Today* writer noted, "It is undoubtedly true that baseball, like the National Football League and National Basketball Association, has allowed itself to become a prime proselytizing vehicle for the evangelical sports ministries. No similar privilege is enjoyed by other religious movements." He continues, "Major league sports do not exist for the chief purpose of promoting Christianity."[23]

SPORT AND RELIGION PUBLICATIONS

Several of the religious organizations identified in this chapter publish magazines or newsletters; however, one publication with a focus on sport and religion but with no affiliation with any specific religious organization is *Sports Spectrum*. *Sports Spectrum* is not an institutionalized evangelical organization but, instead, a Christianized version of *Sports Illustrated*. According to its mission statement, it "seeks to highlight Christian athletes of all sports and levels to help motivate, encourage and inspire people in their faith through the exciting and challenging world of sports." Each issue covers a wide variety of sports, interviews with top athletes, and articles about top Christian athletes. Its website home page claims that "*Sports Spectrum* magazine gives you all the sports stuff you need with the values you want. . . . It is indeed the No. 1 Christian magazine for sports."[24]

MISSIONARY WORK OF CHURCHES AND SPORT

Religious leaders have increasingly used sport as a drawing card for attracting new members and retaining their followers. An often-used slogan of the clergy nicely sums up their view: "Many a one who comes to play remains to pray." Getting persons into church recreation and sports programs is often viewed as a first step into the church and into religious life. Playgrounds and recreation centers in or near churches, and the supervision of these facilities by clergy or laypersons with a strong religious commitment, provide a convenient setting for converting the non-church-going participant. A great deal of informal but successful missionary work is done in these settings. Famous sports figures make effective missionaries because of their prominence and prestige, and virtually every religious group has used coaches and athletes as evangelists to recruit new members.

RELIGIOUS EVANGELIZING BY ATHLETES AND COACHES

Of all the purposes or consequences, or both, of religion's association with sport, certainly one of the most important is the use of athletes, coaches, and the sports environment to recruit new members to the church. Evangelical athletes who have made a personal commitment to religion accept the responsibility of witnessing their faith to others. As a result, the practice of athletes and coaches serving as lay evangelists is so widespread that it has been called a modern crusade.

One of the best known of the sport missionary groups is AIA, a ministry of Campus Crusade for Christ, made up mostly of former collegiate athletes. Its mission is to build "spiritual movements everywhere through the platform of sport. . . . AIA staff reach athletic influencers for Christ and train them to talk about the Lord one-on-one, with the media, and in other public forums to help fulfill the great commission."[25] As part of each appearance of an AIA team, the AIA athletes make brief evangelical speeches and testimonials to the crowds and distribute free religious materials. Because athletes are among the most visible and prestigious persons in the United States, they may be used for missionary work in spreading their religion not only to their teammates but also to anyone with whom they come in contact. One sports scholar noted that many sports fans who would not think of attending church to hear the sermons of a member of the clergy will patiently sit and listen to an AIA athlete's inarticulate testimonial to "God, guts, and glory."

THE PROMISE KEEPERS: PATRIARCHY, GENDER, AND SEXUALITY

In 1990 Bill McCartney, then the University of Colorado football coach and a dedicated evangelical Christian, started the Promise Keepers as a fundamentalist Christian movement whose main goal is to evangelize men. It became one of the country's fastest-growing religious movements. By 1996 more than a dozen conferences were held nationwide, with between 20,000 and 75,000 in attendance at each. However, through the first decade of the twenty-first century the organization's leadership and attendance at Promise Keeper events fluctuated, and many claimed the Promise Keepers had lost its status for men. Yet, in 2022 numerous organizations were still listed as ministry partners, including Athletes in Action and Sports Spectrum ("Where Sport and Faith Connect"), while their 2021 conference was broadcast over 2 days from AT&T Stadium in Arlington, Texas and shown around the world at hundreds of church sites. This organization is therefore at the forefront of calling men to have a godly impact in their families, workplaces, churches, and communities.[26]

The central philosophical message of the Promise Keepers is that God commanded that men be dominant, the head of the family, and reclaim their leadership in the family and in the community, thus becoming better men of God. The traditional patriarchal gender role, with men as the family leader, is said to be dictated by God.

A focal theme of this male-only movement has been that current social problems, especially what Promise Keepers consider the moral depravity and confusion over appropriate female and male social roles in our society, are caused by a lack of appropriate male leadership. The result, they claim, has been a feminization of the American male that has produced a nation of sissified men who abdicate their role as spiritually pure leaders, thus requiring women to fill the vacuum. The Promise Keepers' solution is the promotion of a traditional masculinity, with men taking the leadership roles and women accommodating to

supporting roles. Perhaps to make the organization more palatable to greater numbers, in 2009, for the first time in its history, its single-mindedness was broadened to invite women, the poor, and Jewish believers to one of its events. In line with traditional masculine–feminine role definitions, the Promise Keepers share the position of religious fundamentalist Protestants and the Catholic Church that homosexuality violates God's creative design for males and females. McCartney publicly denounced homosexuality as "an abomination of almighty God."

For women and men who have been struggling against traditional patriarchy and gender-specific social roles in contemporary society, groups like the Promise Keepers seem to be a threat to the progress that has been made in recent decades. A number of women's organizations have been highly critical of the Promise Keepers, complaining that the organization preaches a subservient role for wives and, more broadly, assigns second-class citizenship to all females, a condition that women have lived with for generations. Gay and lesbian groups have expressed dismay at what they feel is a classic example of old-fashioned homophobic rhetoric.[27]

The connections of the Promise Keepers to sport have been described in this way: "Although this group does not engage in sport or directly promote sport as an important part of its movement, it has used sport symbolically to communicate the ideologies of the organization. Sport venues become religious settings, sport rituals are converted into religious ones, sport heroes are revered as saints and moral exemplars, and sport metaphors are means for communicating key truths and desirable character traits."[28] The Promise Keepers and sports intersect in a common vision of traditional male dominance and leadership. Sports culture has long been the site of male domination and the main source for defining appropriate masculine attitudes, values, and behaviors.

SPORTIANITY CONFRONTING SOCIAL ISSUES

There is little inclination on the part of religious leaders and the various organizations that make up Sportianity to confront the pressing social issues of sport or of the larger society. Virtually all of the leaders in the Sportianity movement are reluctant to take a stand on moral issues within sports. In reviewing the numerous publications circulated by the organizations involved in Sportianity, one thing stands out glaringly, namely, that there is little in the way of thoughtful critique of the culture of sport or little direct effort being channeled into improving the morality of sports.

There is no noticeable social reform movement on the part of Sportianity. Tom Krattenmaker, author of *Onward Christian Athletes*, contends that "many evangelical athletes who publicly thank Jesus for victory have nothing to say about other issues such as the pervasive use of steroids in sports or racial discrimination against aspiring minority coaches. It's an incomplete Christianity that's brought to bear on sports. They are blind and silent on the larger moral issues that vex the sports sector."[29]

The various religious organizations and their members have not taken forceful or prominent stands or been at the forefront against racism, sexism, cheating, violence, the evils of collegiate athletic recruiting, or any of the other well-known unethical practices, excesses, and abuses in the world of sport, with the exception of exhortations about refraining from drugs. Instead, the pervasive theme is "stick with the positive; don't deal with the problems in sports." The impression is, "Don't stir the waters. Just publicize the good story about the good ole boy who does good things."

In the final analysis, then, sports morality does not appear to have been improved by the Sportianity movement. Instead, Sportianity seems willing to accept sport as is and seems more devoted to recruiting new members and publicizing the achievements of athletes and coaches who publicly avow their religion than to dealing with sports as a social practice with many of the same problems of the larger society that need attention and resolution.

VALUE ORIENTATIONS OF RELIGION AND SPORT

Value orientations underlying competitive sports in the United States may appear only remotely connected with religion, but most values that are central to sports are more or less secularized versions of the core values of Protestantism, which has been a dominant religious belief system throughout U.S. history.

THE PROTESTANT ETHIC AND SPORTS

The classic treatise of the Protestant ethic and its relationship to other spheres of social life is sociologist Max Weber's *The Protestant Ethic and the Spirit of Capitalism*, originally published near the beginning of the twentieth century.[30] The essence of Weber's thesis is that there is a parallel relationship between the Calvinist doctrine of Protestantism as a theological belief system and the growth of capitalism as a mode of economic organization. Weber suggested the relationship between Protestantism and capitalism was one of mutual influence; he used the term *elective affinity* (one of his translators used the word *correlation* in place of *elective affinity*).

The relationship exists in this way: For John Calvin, God could foresee and therefore know the future; thus, the future was predestined. In a world whose future was foreordained, the fate of every person was preestablished. Each person was, then, saved or doomed from birth by a kind of divine decree; nothing the individual did could change what God had done. Although each person's fate was sealed, the individual was plagued by "salvation anxiety" and craved some visible sign of his or her fate; and since Calvin taught that those elected by God acted in a godly manner, the elected could exhibit their salvation by glorifying God, especially by their work in this world.

According to Weber, "the only way of living acceptably to God . . . was through the fulfillment of obligations imposed upon the individual by . . . his calling." Thus, the best available sign of being among the chosen was to do one's job, to follow one's profession, to succeed in one's chosen career. According to Weber, "In practice this means that God helps those who help themselves." Work per se was exalted; indeed, it was sacred. The clearest manifestation of being chosen by God was success in one's work. Whoever enjoyed grace could not fail since success at work was visible evidence of election. Thus, successful persons could think of themselves, and be thought of by others, as righteous persons. The upshot was that this produced an extreme drive toward individual achievement, resulting in what Weber called "ascetic Protestantism," a life of strict discipline and hard work as the best means of glorifying God.[31]

Although the Protestant ethic gave divine sanction to the drive to excel and encouraged success in business, industry, and science, it condemned the material enjoyment of success. The chosen person merely used success to document salvation. Persons who used success for personal gratification and luxury merely showed that they were doomed by God. To avoid the accumulation of vast personal wealth, Calvinism promoted the reinvestment of profits to produce more goods, which created more profits and, in turn, represented more capital for investment ad infinitum, the essence of entrepreneurial capitalism.

Weber's study of the relationship between religious beliefs and capitalism investigated the religious principles that provided a rationale for the ideology of capitalism and for the authority of the capitalist. The spirit of capitalism, according to Weber, consisted of several principles, each of which was compatible with Protestant principles. Collectively, they constituted a clear, elective affinity (correlation) between Calvinist Protestantism and the spirit of capitalism. Weber made it clear that he was not suggesting that one social process was a causal agent for the other. In his final paragraph, he said, "It is . . . not my aim to substitute for a one-sided materialistic an equally one-sided spiritualistic causal interpretation of culture and history."[32]

What does this have to do with sport? It is rather obvious that Weber's notion about the relationship between the Protestant ethic and the spirit of capitalism can be applied to the "spirit" of sport. In a book-length essay titled *The Protestant Ethic and the Spirit of Sport: How Calvinism and Capitalism Shaped America's Games*, Steven Overman undertook to examine the forms, values, meanings, and spirit of American sport within the context of secular Protestantism. He argues that American sport reveals the legacy of Protestantism. He goes on to say, "My basic premise is that the Protestant ethic became the dominant social and cultural force that influenced American values and shaped the nation's institutions—including sport." In American sport, Overman contends, the

Protestant ethic has instilled a spirit, an *ethos*, providing it with a distinct character, meaning, and guiding beliefs.[33]

Anyone familiar with twenty-first-century sports and the Protestant ethic cannot overlook the unmistakable link between them (a correspondence also exists between capitalistic ideology and modern sports, but that will not be examined here). The emergence of sport as a pervasive feature of American life undoubtedly owes its development to various social forces, one of which may be Protestant Christianity, the value orientations of which form the basis of the fundamental doctrine of the American sport ideology. This ideology suggests that persons involved with sports, especially coaches and athletes, adhere to a particular kind of orthodoxy, the overriding orientation of which is individual achievement through competition. The phrase *ideology of sport* is a generic designation for all ideas espoused by or for those who participate in and exercise authority in sports as they seek to explain and justify their beliefs.

If we place the values inherent in the Protestant ethic and the ideology of sport side by side, it immediately becomes apparent that the two are congruent; that is, they share a significant equivalence. Without attempting to claim a causal link between the two belief systems, it does seem possible to suggest an elective affinity between them. Success, self-discipline, and hard work, the original tenets of the Protestant ethic, are the most highly valued qualities in sport.

Success

The Protestant emphasis on successful, individual achievement is in keeping with the values of contemporary sport. The characteristics of the good Christian are also those needed by the successful athlete. The social climate of organized sport is competitive, with an overriding sense of wins and losses. The notion that achievement separates the chosen from the doomed is seen in the winning-is-everything ideology in sports. Winners are the good people; personal worth is equated with winning. The loser is obviously not one of God's chosen people; failure in one's occupation stamps the Protestant-ethic believer as doomed to hell.

The Protestant ethic re-created in sport is captured by this assertion: Christians play their games for fun, but more important than fun is the responsibility to play them well and, of course, to win. Self-described "Christian athletes" have told researchers studying values in sports that to be successful in sports you must be downright mean sometimes, and sometimes you have to beat your opponent up to do well. Researchers report that most of the Christian athletes they study do not seem to have a conflict between their Christian faith and the values of their sporting behaviors.

The importance of winning is legitimized by implying that Christ himself would do whatever it takes to win. One MLB player who was a member of Baseball Chapel told a postgame interviewer that if Jesus Christ was sliding into second base, he would knock the second baseman into left field to break up a double play.

Religious groups that use athletes to evangelize and persuade potential converts to religion recognize the importance of selecting athletes who are winners. They know quite well that evangelical appeals by chronic losers or bench sitters are not likely to be effective. AIA teams play throughout the world, and AIA athletes often comment, "We have to win. That's what the world looks at. The world won't listen to our message if we are losers." This is true. Winning is critical to evangelical work. To the similar values of Protestantism and sports can be added American societal values. Christian athletes from the United States who represent their countries in international sports events recurrently note, "It's important for us to win, not because God wants winners, but because our country does."

Although the quest, even the obsession, for victory in sport is congruent with the Calvinistic view as it is manifested in the Protestant ethic, the theology of Christianity contains a worldview that places the unmitigated quest for winning in question. To the question "What would Jesus do?" on the baseball field, Frank Deford, a Hall of Fame member of the National Association of Sportscasters and Sportswriters before his death, described the sports ideal of a legendary Hall of Fame MLB pitcher in this way: "Young Christian men didn't have to be wimps. They won games, but they won them only in Jesus' image, playing by the rules."[34]

Self-Discipline

The notion that dedication, self-discipline, and sports participation may be an occupational calling is central to the ideology of Sportianity. God is glorified best, so the thinking goes, when athletes give totally of themselves in striving for success and victory. This is manifested in the traditional Christian asceticism that emphasizes sacrifice, control, and self-discipline as relevant means to salvation.

Christian athletes frequently describe their self-discipline and commitment in terms of not wanting to disappoint Jesus by giving anything less than a total effort with the talents they have been given by God. The greatest self-discipline challenge for the Christian athlete is to maintain the desire to win without compromising his or her faith, to maintain competitive enthusiasm with just the right amount of spiritual grace, to create the requisite competitive disposition without diminishing their Christian witness. The eternal quest of Christian athletes seems to be to attain spiritual control over their competitive attitudes while being careful not to be overly controlled and thus ineffective as a competitor.

Hard Work

Just as the businessperson is responsible to God to develop his or her talents to the fullest, according to the Protestant ethic, so it is that if God has granted one athletic abilities, then one is obligated to use those abilities to glorify and honor God; anything less than total dedication to the task is insufficient. A major league pitcher echoed this sentiment, saying that he had a responsibility for the talent he had been given and that on the days when he did not give his best, God should be upset with him.

Firmly embedded in the American sport culture is a belief that hard work, training, and unremitting dedication by athletes and coaches not only will lead to success but also are ways of using God-given abilities to glorify God, an important Protestant requirement. Sport culture is replete with slogans touting the necessity for hard work: "Workers are winners," "The harder you work, the luckier you get," "Winning is 99 percent perspiration and 1 percent inspiration." A favorite exhortation of coaches during practices is "Work, work, work!" And the highest praise a coach can give an athlete is to say that she or he "has a good work ethic."

Success can be considered the justly deserved reward of a person's purposeful, self-denying, hard work. Giving less than 100 percent is regarded by some Christian athletes as a direct violation of God's law. A testimonial often expressed by these athletes is, "I have been blessed with a lot of ability. My motivation for working hard is to use tools that God gave me for His glory."

PROTESTANTISM AND CONTEMPORARY SPORT

Any belief system that can help provide athletes and coaches with a rationale for their deep commitment to sports provides a means of expressing the essence of their striving, and Protestant theology does just that. In short, it is a belief system to which athletes and coaches can hold an elective affinity. Whether they actually do hold such an elective affinity remains a matter of speculation. Moreover, we hasten to add that Protestantism certainly is not responsible for the creation of the sport culture, but it does provide religious reinforcement for it.

Perhaps it is not coincidental that the belief systems of fundamentalist Protestantism and modern sports are so congruent. The two institutions use similar means to respond to their members' needs. Each tries to enforce and maintain, through a strict code of behavior and ritual, a strict belief system that is typically adopted and internalized by most involved. Each performs cohesive, integrative, and social control functions for its members, giving them meaningful ways to organize their world. Both religion and sport, because of the sacredness nurtured by these systems, resist social change and, in this way, support traditional values and practices.

SPORT USES RELIGION

Religious observances and competitive sports constantly impinge on each other, and religious practices of various kinds are found wherever one finds sports. Religion can be viewed from one point of view as an

important means of coping with situations of stress. There are several categories of stress situations. One of these comprises situations in which largely uncontrolled and unpredictable forces may imperil the vital personal and social concerns of an individual or group. Sports competition falls into this category of stress because competition involves a great deal of uncertainty about a typically important outcome—winning and losing a sports event.

Coaches and athletes have great respect for the technical knowledge, skills, tactics, and strategy required for successful sports performance, but they are also aware of their limitations. As a supplement to the practical techniques, sports participants often employ religious practices. Coaches and athletes do not believe that these practices make up for their lack of technical knowledge, failure to acquire necessary skills, or employment of inappropriate strategy. However, religious practices help them adjust to stress by providing opportunities for them to dramatize their anxieties, thus reinforcing their self-confidence.

Religion invokes a sense of "doing something about it" in uncertain undertakings where practical knowledge and techniques alone cannot guarantee success. One of the most noted twentieth-century anthropologists, Bronislaw Malinowski, concluded from his research that when the outcome of vital social activities is greatly uncertain, magico-religious or other comparable techniques are inevitably used as a means of allaying tension and promoting adjustment.[35]

THE USE OF PRAYER AND DIVINE INTERVENTION

Prayer is perhaps the most frequently employed use of religion by coaches and athletes; prayer for protection in competition, prayer for good performance, and prayer for victory are three examples. Sometimes the act of prayer is observed in gestures, such as a Roman Catholic basketball player crossing himself or herself before shooting a free throw, or an athlete pointing an index finger skyward, or a football team praying in the huddle before or after a game. Several researchers who have studied so-called born-again Christian athletes concur that most of them use prayer to influence God to help their team win or to help them perform well.

Little is known about the actual extent to which individual athletes use prayer in conjunction with their participation, but it seems probable that if some athletes are seen praying, others are doing so without outward, observable signs. Coaches often arrange to have religious services on the Sabbath or on game days. At present, almost every professional MLB and football team—more than fifty of them—hold Sunday chapel services, at home and away, and Sunday services are also held in sports as varied as NASCAR racing and golf. One of the claims for these religious services and prayers is that it strengthens a group's sense of its own identity, provides unity, and accentuates its "we" feeling.

There are probably other reasons why coaches sanction locker room prayers. Observers who suspect that locker room prayers are about coaches' only concession to religion imply that one coach does it because the other coaches are doing it, and "you can't let them get the edge." Others have suggested that it may be only a sweaty-palmed response to the anxieties and uncertainties of competition, a way to seek help in those gut-wrenching moments before a big game. In *The Prince of Tides* (also made into a movie), author Pat Conroy relates the events in one high school locker room before a football game. Although the book is a novel and the locker room is therefore fictitious, the situation as Conroy relates it seems very close to the reality many athletes have experienced in real-life locker rooms.

The coach began to speak:

"Tonight I'm gonna learn and the town's gonna learn who my hitters are. All you've proved so far is that you know how to put on pads and get dates to the sock hop after the game, but until I see you in action, I won't know if you're hitters or not. Real hitters. Now a real hitter is a headhunter who puts his head in the chest of his opponent and ain't happy if his opponent is still breathing after the play. A real hitter doesn't know what fear is except when he sees it in the eyes of a ball carrier he's about to split in half. A real hitter loves pain, loves the screaming and the sweating and the brawling and the hatred of life down in the trenches. He likes to be at the spot where the blood

flows and the teeth get kicked out. That's what this sport's all about, men. It's war, pure and simple. Now tonight, you go out there and kick butt all over that field. If something moves, hit it. If something breathes, hit it. . . .

"Now do I have me some hitters?" he screamed, veins throbbing along his temple.

"Yes, sir," we screamed back. . . .

"Do I have me some goddamn headhunters?"

"Yes, sir."

"Am I going to see blood?"

"Yes, sir."

"Am I going to see their guts hanging off your helmets?"

"Yes, sir."

"Am I going to hear their bones breaking all over the field?"

"Yes, sir," we happy hitters cried aloud. "Let us pray," he said.

He led the team in the recitation of the Lord's Prayer.[36]

This seems to epitomize what many coaches have been accused of—treating religion as group bonding that has little, if anything, to do with genuine heartfelt religious faith.

Although there is little empirical work on the use of prayer by athletes and coaches, a review of the research on this topic concluded, "This review has identified that athletes utilized religious prayer in sport for three main reasons: coping with uncertainties and the concomitant anxiety, putting life and sport into perspective, and providing meaning to sports participation and competition" (also see Figure 14.1).[37]

A survey by the Public Religion Research Institute in 2017 found that nearly three of ten Americans believe God plays a role in outcomes of sports events, so it is not surprising that many athletes who pray believe that the use of prayer might affect the outcome of the game. So they ask God for a victory. One professional athlete asserted, "The question was posed to us, 'Does [God] control wins and losses?'

Yes, He does." Another described the prayer he uses: "I ask for victories: 'God, I want to win so I have an even bigger platform for you.'" A college football player acknowledged that he and his teammates prayed that an opposing placekicker would miss a field goal that, if made, would have defeated his team. After the field goal was missed, the player said, "God came through and answered all our prayers on the sidelines and out there on the field."[38]

Many athletes, coaches, and sport managers strongly believe that God intervenes on their behalf. After an Auburn University football win over Clemson, the coach declared, "It's a God thing," and after a national championship victory over the University of Oregon, he told a national TV audience, "God was with us."[39]

Perhaps the most public sign that athletes believe that God is aiding their performance is the seemingly ever-present index finger pointed to the sky, thanking God. Baseball players point to the heavens as they cross home plate after hitting a home run; NFL players drop to a knee and pray in the end zone after scoring a touchdown. In postgame interviews college and professional athletes often thank Jesus for their success.

These expressions have become commonplace at sports venues, even after run-of-the-mill performances. A few athletes who use them claim they are not religious signs, but rather that they use the displays to pay tribute to a relative or friend. Most, however, admit they are a "thank you" to God.

Some religious leaders, athletes, coaches, and even fans renounce asking God for a victory, claiming it is crass and greedy. Furthermore, for many of them the idea that God intervenes in sports—that God roots for one team, but not the other—is offensive, even absurd and blasphemous. As one cleric recently put it, "Watching athletes pointing to the heavens to acknowledge their savior after scoring a touchdown, you'd think God actually cared about which team won. While I hope God's presence can be felt in all places, including football stadiums, I find it offensive to reduce the almighty to a football mascot in the sky."[40] Even executives within the AIA are critical. As one of them said, "What's become so distasteful is this idea that God is only on the side of the

One of the most frequent public signs that athletes believe that God is aiding their performance is their pointing the index finger or clasped hands to the sky, thanking God for a notable achievement—a home run, a touchdown, a made basket in basketball. (Photo: Winslow Townson/USA Today Sports)

winner. Winning players say they've been blessed, that God was in the details when it worked out in their favor. It's become almost a cliché among winners to go there. [But] to be credible you have to go there in both cases—winning *and* losing."[41]

Tom Krattenmaker moves beyond the actions of individual athletes and coaches into a more sociological perspective. He contends, "The athletes' gestures and shout-outs to God are fruits of a campaign by well-organized, well-financed evangelical sports ministries committed to leveraging sports to reach and change the broader American culture." In another publication Krattenmaker asks, "Should we be pleased that the civic resource known as 'our

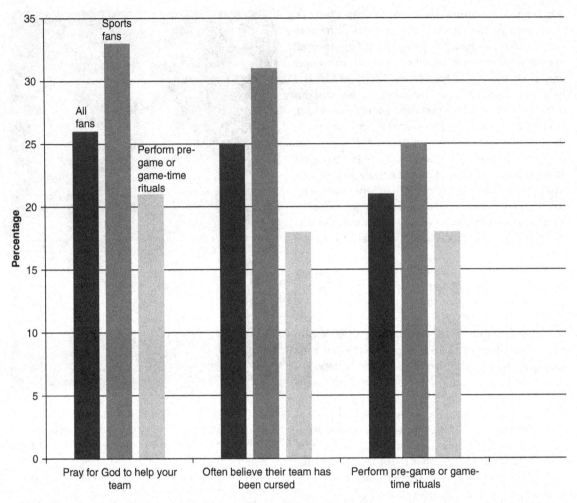

Note: The same fan categories of respondents apply in the middle and right sets of bars as shown for left set of bars.

FIGURE 14.1 American Fans Believe That Supernatural Forces Function in Sports. Source: Adapted from Public Religion Research Institute, Religion & Politics Tracking Survey, January 2014.

team'—a resource supported by the diverse whole through our ticket-buying, game-watching, and tax-paying—is being leveraged by a one-truth evangelical campaign that has little appreciation for the beliefs of the rest of us?"[42]

Freedom of religious expression is guaranteed to citizens of the United States. But fewer than 40 percent of the people regularly attend religious services. Moreover, millions of Americans do not subscribe to any institutionalized religion. In the United States, the Constitution requires the separation of religion and state.

In this context, there is growing debate and tension with regard to the use of prayers in the locker room before games, in the huddles before and after games, and as public ceremonies before sports events. This is especially the case when these activities are part of public school events. Controversy thus surrounds how some clergy, athletes, and coaches utilize prayer as a part of public school and university sporting events. This type of controversy regarding the proper interpretation of church–state relations in public educational institutions has a long history in the United States. On the one side, Christian individuals and organizations have promoted prayer and other religious activities in the schools; on the other side have been individuals and groups who have claimed that the First Amendment to the Constitution specifically prohibits religious practices of any kind under the jurisdiction of the public schools. Since 1962 the U.S. Supreme Court has handed down several rulings on prayer in the schools, but lawsuits continue to arise against schools that practice religious observances of various kinds. The most recent United States Supreme Court case is discussed in Box 14.2).

Religious services in connection with sporting events are still held at church-sponsored high schools and colleges, as well as at professional sporting events; indeed, to have an important sports event started by a religious invocation is not unusual. Some invocations are brief and to the point, but others are used by clergy to conduct a religious service or to metaphorically dramatize the relationship between sports and religion.

THE USE OF MAGIC

The reader may be surprised, even shocked, that a section on magic is included in this chapter, because many people see no relationship between magical practices and religion. In practice, however, religion and magic, as defined by anthropologists, are closely intertwined. Although magic and religion are alike in assuming the existence of supernatural powers, a significant difference exists between the ends that they seek. Religion is oriented to the otherworldly, toward a supreme supernatural god, and religion typically centers on such overarching issues as salvation and the meaning of life and death; this is not true of magic. The practitioner of magic seeks ends that are in the everyday world of events; magic is oriented toward immediate, practical goals.

There are other ways in which religion and magic differ. Religious worshipers possess an attitude of awe and reverence toward the sacred ends they pursue, but the users of magic are in business for practical and arbitrarily chosen ends. The latter are manipulators of the supernatural for their own

private advantage rather than worshippers of it; the attitude of magic users is likely to be utilitarian. In this respect, Bronislaw Malinowski noted that magic has an end in pursuit of which the magical ritual is performed. The religious ritual has no purpose; that is, the ritual is not a means to an end but an end in itself. Malinowski said, "While in the magical act the underlying idea and aim is always clear, straightforward and definite, in religious ceremony there is no purpose directed toward a subsequent event."[43] Furthermore, the content of magic and religion differs. On the one hand, the content of magic has no unified inclusive theory but instead tends to be atomistic, somewhat like a book of recipes. Religion, on the other hand, tends to encompass the whole of life; it often provides a comprehensive theory of both the supernatural and human society.

The Malinowski Thesis

According to Malinowski, magic flourishes in situations of uncertainty and threat; it is most commonly invoked in situations of high anxiety about accomplishing desired ends. The origin of most magical rites can be traced to fears experienced individually or collectively. These rites are associated with human helplessness in the face of danger and unpredictability, which give rise to superstitious beliefs and overt practices to ward off impending danger or failure and to bring good luck. Malinowski reported, "We find magic wherever the elements of chance and accident, and the emotional play between hope and fear have a wide and extensive range. We do not find magic wherever the pursuit is certain, reliable, and well under control of rational methods."[44]

Malinowski's thesis about the conditions under which magic appears is applicable to the world of sport. Athletes and coaches are engaged in an activity of uncertain outcome in which they have a great deal of emotional investment. Even dedicated conditioning and practice and the acquisition of high-level skills do not guarantee victory because opponents are often evenly matched and player injury and other dangers are often present. Thus, "getting the breaks" or "lucking out" may be the determining factor in the outcome of a contest. Having a weakly hit baseball fall in for a base hit, a

BOX 14.2 *THINKING ABOUT SPORT:* PRE OR POST GAME PRAYER AT PUBLIC SCHOOL SPORTS EVENTS: CONSTITUTIONAL OR UNCONSTITUTIONAL?

The fusing of sport and religion is readily observable at sporting events: the index finger pointed to the sky after a good performance, a team huddling together to pray just before or immediately after a game, and religious objects worn around the neck are tangible religious symbols that have become a common feature of the sports landscape. Many athletes admit to silently saying a brief prayer just before shooting a free throw, stepping into the batter's box, while crouching in the starting blocks, and so forth. These are all acts of individual conscience and do not require anyone's attention or participation. They also meet the First Amendment freedom of speech guarantee.

The U.S. Constitution invokes *religion* only once, stating, "No religious test shall ever be required as a qualification to any office or public trust under the United States" (Article VI, C). The First Amendment to the Constitution states, "Congress shall make no law respecting an establishment of religion, or prohibiting the free exercise thereof." It is clear that the founders of the Constitution wished to establish a separation of church and state, and once the United States was established, many of them spoke out and wrote adamantly opposing any state–church integration. Indeed, Thomas Jefferson referred to the First Amendment as creating a "wall of separation" between church and state.

Efforts to merge state and religion have been persistent throughout the history of the United States. However, when these efforts have confronted the U.S. judicial system, the courts have overwhelmingly sided with the separation-of-church-and-state doctrine.

Individual acts of religious prayer and ritual, such as those mentioned previously, have been interpreted by the courts as protected by the "free exercise" clause in the First Amendment because the state has no role in their practice. However, when prayers or religious rituals are conducted under the auspices of a federal, state, or municipal governmental entity during a public event, the courts have interpreted these as falling within the "establishment clause" of the First Amendment," meaning the state is favoring a religion and therefore it is illegal. As we will discuss with the two cases highlighted below, the Supreme Court has had to weigh both the "free exercise" and the "establishment" clauses when deciding cases about religious expression in public spaces.

From the beginning of public education in the early nineteenth century to the present, some Christian church leaders and their congregations have attempted to use the power of government, through the schools, as an instrument for promoting one favored view of religion—Christianity. Holding official prayers in the classrooms, posting the Ten Commandments in classrooms, distributing Bibles to students, and promoting attendance at specific churches during classes are a few of the techniques used.

With the rise of modern sports organizations during the twentieth century, two pregame rituals gradually became widespread: playing/singing the national anthem and prayers being given by a clergy or a designee. The former is a patriotic observance, whereas the latter is clearly a religious ceremony. When a public prayer is conducted at a sporting event under the jurisdiction of either a private organization (as in the case of a professional sports event) or a religious organization, the courts have judged the prayer to be legal, since government agencies are not involved.

However, when a pregame prayer is conducted at a sporting event sponsored by a government agency, such as a public high school or college, it clearly raises an issue about violating the establishment clause of the First Amendment. We provide a compelling case to situate the historical trajectory of the Supreme Court's rulings with regard to weighing the "establishment" and "free exercise" clauses. The first case we provide, shows how the Supreme Court gave more credence to the establishment clause.

In 1999 a lawsuit was filed against the Galveston, Texas, Santa Fe Independent School District for permitting "student-selected, student-given" prayers to be read over the public address system at football games. Such prayers are a long-standing tradition in Texas and in some other states as well. Nevertheless, the U.S. Court of Appeals for the Fifth Circuit declared the Santa Fe School District practice to be unconstitutional, saying that football games are "hardly the type of event that can be appropriately solemnized with prayer."

Then-governor of Texas George W. Bush instructed the Texas attorney general to file an appeal, and thirteen Texas members of Congress introduced a resolution in the U.S. House of Representatives to negate the Circuit Court of Appeals decision. Congress passed a nonbinding resolution—which has no legal status in law—that encouraged Christian prayer before public school athletic games. Within two weeks of the congressional resolution, the U.S. Supreme Court announced that it would hear arguments on this case during 2000.

Consistent with several previous court decisions in similar cases, on June 19, 2000, by a vote of six to three, the U.S. Supreme Court declared that the practice of Santa Fe School District school administrators of allowing students to conduct formal prayers before school games was unconstitutional. The court's rulings clearly drew on the establishment clause and found the following:

- Including prayers before a sports event when school administrators were involved was a state-sponsored religious activity and was therefore unconstitutional;
- Formal prayers unconstitutionally coerced attendees into participating in a religious activity;
- The state may not endorse overtly religious messages, even if the majority of the people favor it;

(continued)

(continued)

- A prayer truly initiated by an individual student is protected free speech. For example, a player can spontaneously call for a group prayer huddle. A person in the stands can assemble an informal group prayer; and
- An individual, truly voluntary prayer by a student is protected speech, both before, during, and after school.

A second case demonstrates a different interpretation of the religious expression in public school setting, one which favored the "free exercise" clause. In 2022, the U.S. Supreme Court ruled on the *Kennedy v Bremerton School District* case. First, we will provide the facts of the case and then subsequently discuss the Supreme Court's assessment.

This particular case addressed the behavior of an assistant public high school football coach, Mr. Kennedy, who started prayer rituals in 2008 and for over 8 years led prayers after games, on the 50-yard line of the football field. His students (and sometime other team's players and the members of the public) would also join him in prayer. The school district consequently asked him to express his religion in an alternative place that would not invoke any assumption that the school district was sanctioning his religion. However, Mr. Kennedy continued to conduct his 50-yard audible prayers, so the school district put him on administrative leave. Instead, of seeking reappointment, Mr. Kennedy filed a lawsuit claiming that his First Amendment rights were violated. Mr. Kennedy's claims were rejected in both district court and the 9th US circuit Court of Appeals; both of these courts said that he was a public employee and his prayer was government speech not protected by the First Amendment.

Then, on June 27, 2022, with a 6-3 decision, the Supreme Court found that the Washington State School district violated Mr. Kennedy's First Amendment rights. The majority of justices placed more significance on the free exercise clause than on the establishment clause. Justice Neil Gorsuch wrote the majority opinion in which he noted, "Respect for religious expressions is indispensable to life in a free and diverse Republic – whether those expression take place in a sanctuary or on a field, and where they manifest through spoken word of a bowed head." He also referred to Mr. Kennedy's actions as private, noting that Kennedy "offered his prayers while his students were otherwise occupied."

Writing the dissenting opinion was justice Sonia Sotomayor who was concerned about the facts that were used to justify the majority decision. In particular, this opinion challenged how Mr. Kennedy's prayers were framed as personal and not publicly broadcasted. Sotomayor provided counter evidence that showed the public nature of the 50-yard line prayers. Additionally, the 1971 case Lemon v Kurtzman created a metric (the Lemon Test) to evaluate whether actions are in line with the establishment clause; the majority ruling in Mr. Kennedy's case did not take this into account. Sotomayor bemoaned the weakening of the establishment clause in her dissent, arguing that "(the decision) elevates one individual's interest in personal religious exercise over society's interest in protecting the separation between church and state, eroding the protections for religious liberty for all." In addition, Sotomayor expressed concern about the coercion of students. Would students feel pressure to go along with the coach's prayer in order to be considered part of the team to get playing time? This was an established concern in previous cases of this nature and indeed this most recent decision upended over 50 years of precedent. Going forward, we anticipate that there will be more intense debates about the nature and scope of religious practice within publicly funded sport venues. Will all religions be treated equally in their constitutional claims to expression in public spheres? Will the courts address the potential of religious coercion of youth in public school and sporting environments?

Sources: The text of the Supreme Court's decision in *Santa Fe Independent School District v. Doe* can be found at http://supct.law.cornell.edu/supct/html/99-62.ZS.html/.

Supreme Court of the United States, June 27,2022, KENNEDY v. BREMERTON SCHOOL DISTRICT; No. 21-418 https://www.supremecourt.gov/opinions/21pdf/21-418_i425.pdf

Ariane de Vogue, Tierney Sneed and Devan Cole, CNN, "Supreme Court further erodes separation between church and state in case of praying football coach," https://www.abc12.com/news/national/supreme-court-further-erodes-separation-between-church-and-state-in-case-of-praying-football-coach/article_1d11d523-9fe0-5301-9fc5-69c19c496d86.html, accessed June 30, 2022

Adam Liptak, NY Times, "*Supreme Court Sides With Coach Over Prayers at the 50-Yard Line,*" June 27, 2022 NY Times https://www.nytimes.com/2022/06/27/us/politics/supreme-court-coach-prayers.html; accessed June 30, 2022

Amy Howe, June 27, 2022, "Justices side with high school football coach who prayed on the field with students" https://www.scotusblog.com/2022/06/justices-side-with-high-school-football-coach-who-prayed-on-the-field-with-students/ accessed June 30,2022

Ian Millhiser, "The Supreme Court hands the religious right a big victory by lying about the facts of a case: Kennedy v. Bremerton School District is a big victory for the religious right, but only because Gorsuch misrepresents the facts of the case" June 27, 2022, https://www.vox.com/2022/6/27/23184848/supreme-court-kennedy-bremerton-school-football-coach-prayer-neil-gorsuch accessed June 30,2022

deflected hockey puck go in the net, or a redirected football pass caught by an unintended receiver are examples of luck or getting the breaks in sports. Although the cliché "the best team always wins" is part of the folk wisdom of sport, athletes and coaches know that this is not always so and indeed believe that factors leading to a win or a loss are somewhat out of their control.

According to Malinowski's theory, athletes and coaches may use magic to bring them luck and to ensure that they get the breaks, thus supplying themselves with beliefs that serve to bridge uncertainty and threat in their pursuit of victories. The magic enables them to carry out their actions with a sense of assurance and confidence and to maintain poise and mental integrity in the face of opponents.

MAGIC AND ITS USES IN SPORTS

It is difficult to assess just how extensive the uses of magic are in sport. Newspaper and magazine stories leave little doubt, however, that magical beliefs and practices play a prominent role in the lives of athletes and coaches. One form of magical belief is superstition, which is a belief that one's fate is in the hands of mysterious external powers, governed by forces over which one has no control. Sports studies scholars who have scrutinized the superstitions of athletes claim that many athletes turn to superstitions for the same reasons that others turn to religion—they provide a mental confidence, a feeling of assurance, that often makes the difference between success and failure at the highest levels of athletic competition.

In a book-length treatment of magic in sports, Andrew Podnieks describes the fascinating and fun world of hockey superstitions: their origins, their quirks, and the mythology around them. In the process, he illustrates that athletes and coaches employ almost anything imaginable that might ensure getting the breaks, and this often involves some form of superstitious behavior.[45]

Sport superstitions are similar for athletes who compete in teams and for those who compete in individual sports, but team athletes indicate greater use of superstitions related to equipment and its use, to the order of entering the sports arena, and to dressing-room rituals than do individual-sport athletes. Pregame superstitions of basketball players center on warm-up rituals; game superstitions are directed toward free-throw shooting, team cheers, and gum chewing. Endorsement of superstitions increases with involvement in sport; in other words, the higher the competitive level and the greater the involvement in a sport, the greater the prevalence of superstition.

The gender of the athlete is less important than the level of involvement. Superstitions are related to the uncertainty and importance of the outcome, as Malinowski indicated.

Beyond superstitions, other forms of magic such as rituals, taboos, fetishes, and witchcraft can also become commingled in a sport. Applying the Malinowski thesis to baseball, anthropologist George Gmelch, a former professional ball player, published what has now become one of the classic studies of athletes and their uses of magical practices. Gmelch hypothesized that in baseball magical practices would be associated more with hitting and pitching than with fielding; the first two involve a high degree of chance and unpredictability, whereas the average fielding success rate is about 97 percent, reflecting almost complete control over the outcome. From his observations as a participant in professional baseball, Gmelch reported that there was indeed a greater incidence and variety of rituals, taboos, and use of fetishes related to hitting and pitching than in fielding. He concluded—in support of Malinowski's hypothesis about the relationship between magic and uncertainty—that baseball players associate magic with hitting and pitching, but not with fielding. Indeed, despite the wide assortment of magic associated with both hitting and pitching, Gmelch never observed any directly related to fielding.[46]

To illustrate how magical practices are used in sports, we devote a section to each of these forms of magic practice: ritual, taboo, fetishism, and witchcraft.

Ritual

Rituals are standardized routines that impart the sense that cause-and-effect relationships are within an individual's power to control, and sports are infused with ritualistic practices. An almost infinite variety of rituals are practiced in sport because all athletes are free to ritualize any activity they consider important for successful performance. Whether they are a psychological placebo, a desire to control fate, or merely a way of sustaining a winning method, rituals have been a long-standing staple in sports.

Typically, rituals arise from successful performances. Unable to attribute an exceptional performance to skill alone but hoping to repeat it in future contests, athletes and coaches single out something they did before the performance as being responsible for their success. That "something" might be a certain food they had eaten before the game, a new pair of socks or sneakers they had put on, or a specific sequence of behaviors preceding the contest. For example:

- Serena Williams will not change her socks at tournaments she is winning.
- Brian Urlacher, who spent his entire thirteen-year career as a linebacker with the Chicago Bears, ate exactly two chocolate chip cookies prior to every game. Not one, not three, two.

In addition to individual rituals, there are a number of team rituals. In basketball the ritual of stacking hands is frequently employed just before the team takes the floor at the beginning of the game and after time outs. The most universal hockey ritual occurs just before the start of a game when players skate in front of their goal and tap the goalie on the pads for good luck. In a story of the rituals of a girls' high school field hockey team, the reporter revealed that before every game the girls would kneel before the coach; he then blessed them with a charitable helping of "hockey dust" (which was an exclusive blend of ninety-nine-cent sparkle and precious good luck).

Taboo

A taboo is a strong social norm prohibiting certain actions that are punishable by the group or by magical consequences. There are numerous institutional taboos in each sport and, of course, many personal taboos. Athletes and coaches believe breaking a taboo will lead to undesirable outcomes or bad luck. Two of the strongest taboos in baseball prohibit crossing the handles of bats and mentioning that the pitcher has a no-hitter in progress. Crossing bats is believed to bring bad luck and mentioning a no-hitter to the pitcher is believed to break his spell on the batters, ending his chances to complete a no-hit game.

During a winning streak, athletes and coaches in many sports will insist on wearing some or all of the same clothing—uniform, socks, jock, bra, shoes, sweatshirt, warm-up, etc.—that they were wearing when the winning streak started. Washing apparel during a winning streak is one of the most common taboos. Some athletes develop taboos about not stepping on portions of the playing surface, such as the chalk foul lines (just as children avoid stepping on sidewalk cracks). One of the common game taboos in baseball and softball is to avoid stepping on the foul line when sprinting onto or off the field. Next time you watch a game in one of these sports, notice how often players jump over the lines as they run to and from the dugout.

Fetishism

Fetishes are revered objects believed to have "supernatural" power to attain the desired ends for the person who possesses or uses them. Fetishes are standard equipment for coaches and athletes. They include a bewildering assortment of objects: rabbits' feet, pictures of heroes or loved ones, pins, coins, remnants of old equipment, certain numbered uniforms, and so forth. Typically, these objects obtain their power through association with successful performances. For example, if the athlete or coach happens to be wearing or using the object during a victory, the individual attributes the good fortune to the object; it then becomes a fetish embodied with supernatural power.

Particular items of athletic apparel and equipment commonly are turned into fetishes, and athletes and coaches believe that not wearing that apparel or not using certain equipment will result in poor performance and cause a loss. Uniform numbers also frequently become fetishes for athletes. For some professional athletes, the uniform number attains fetish significance to the point that if they are traded they seek assurances that they will be assigned that number by the new team.

Almost everyone who has been around sports has a story of an athlete, coach, or team that had apparel or equipment fetishes of some kind and went to bizarre extremes to make sure nothing interfered with the use of those items.

Youth sports players gather to stack hands before a game, one of the oldest rituals in several sports. (Photo: © iStock/kali9)

Witchcraft

Magical practices that are intended to bring misfortune on others are known as black magic, witchcraft, or sorcery. In sport, those who employ this form of magic believe that supernatural powers are being harnessed to harm or bring misfortune on opponents. In Africa witchcraft dominates some sports. Medicine men who claim that they can make the ball disappear or that they can cast a spell on opposing players are especially active in soccer. It is estimated that about 95 percent of Kenyan soccer teams hire witch doctors to help them win, and matches have been marred by witchcraft-inspired riots.

In the United States we laugh when reading about African soccer teams traveling with witch doctors, and we are amused by such practices of witchcraft as players painting their bodies with pig fat to ward off evil spirits, reasoning that sports teams in the United States are much too sophisticated to travel with witch doctors or to wear pig fat. American teams, instead, often travel with Catholic priests and Protestant ministers and wear medals around their necks! We may not recognize that some of the social antics of our athletes and coaches aimed at calling for the intervention of the supernatural on their behalf can be viewed as acts of sorcery.

SUMMARY

In this chapter we have examined the reciprocal relationship between sport and religion. Although sport and religion may appear to have little in common, we have attempted to demonstrate that contemporary sport and contemporary religion are related in a variety of ways. Religions perform several important functions: at the individual level, they provide individuals with emotional support; at the interpersonal level, they provide a form of human bonding; at the institutional level they serve as a vehicle for social control; and at the societal level they promote social integration. For many centuries Christian church dogma was antithetical to play and sport activities, but over the past century, with the enormous growth of organized sport, churches and religious leaders have welded a link between these two institutions by sponsoring sports events under religious auspices and by proselytizing athletes to religion and then using them as missionaries to convert new members.

Although contemporary religion uses sport for the promotion of its causes, sport uses religion as well. Numerous activities with a religious connotation—ceremonies, rituals, and so forth—are employed in connection with sports contests.

The most common use of religion by athletes, coaches, and fans is prayer. One of the persisting social problems is the use of public prayer ceremonies before sporting events and the practice of some coaches of conducting prayers with their athletes in locker rooms and in sporting venues before a sporting event. Such practices give rise to many personal objections and legal controversies. The practice of magic—through rituals, taboos, fetishism, and witchcraft—is widespread in sport. Such behaviors are most common in sporting situations where there is uncertainty, threat, and high anxiety about accomplishing desired ends.

Learn more with this chapter's digital tools, including web resources, video links, and chapter self-assessment quizzes at www.oup.com/he/sage-eitzen-beal-atencio-12e.

NOTES

1. Chris Beneke and Arthur Remillard, "Is Religion Losing Ground to Sports?" *The Washington Post*, January 13, 2014, https://www.washingtonpost.com/opinions/is-religion-losing-ground-to-sports/2014/01/31/6faa4d64-82bd-11e3-9dd4-e7278db80d86_story.html?utm_term=.b3342d6fafb8.
2. For a good source of detailed information about religious affiliation, see the Pew Forum on Religion & Public Life, *U.S. Religious Landscape Study* (Washington, D.C.: Pew Research Center, 2017), http://www.pewforum.org/about-the-religious-landscape-study/; for a superb comprehensive examination of religion and its relationship with sports, see Shirl L Hoffman, *Good Game: Christianity and the Culture of Sports* (Waco, TX: Baylor University Press, 2010).
3. Émile Durkheim, *The Elementary Forms of Religious Life*, trans. Carol Cosman (New York: Oxford University Press, 2001), 62.
4. For a good explanation of religion as a social institution, see Keith A Roberts and David A Yamane, *Religion in Sociological Perspective*, 6th ed. (Thousand Oaks, CA: Sage, 2016); see also Peter Clarke, ed., *The Oxford Handbook of the Sociology of Religion* (New York: Oxford University Press, 2011).
5. Lois Tyson, *Critical Theory Today: A User-Friendly Guide*, 3rd ed. (New York: Routledge, 2014); and Paul D'Amato, *The Meaning of Marxism*, 2nd ed. (Chicago: Haymarket Books, 2014).
6. Nigel Spivey, *The Ancient Olympics* (New York: Oxford University Press, 2012); see also Henry G. Brinton, "Olympics' Religious Roots," *USA Today*, July 30, 2010, 7A.
7. Scott Kretchmar, Mark Dyreson, Matthew P. Llewellyn, and John Gleaves, *History and Philosophy of Sport and Physical Activity* (Champaign, IL: Human Kinetics, 2017).
8. Stewart Culin, *Games of the North American Indian* (Washington, D.C.: U.S. Government Printing Office, 1907), 34; see also Joseph Oxendine, *American Indian Sports Heritage* (Champaign, IL: Human Kinetics, 1998); and Thomas Vennum, *American Indian Lacrosse: Little Brother of War*, reprint ed. (Baltimore: Johns Hopkins University Press, 2007).
9. Bruce C. Daniels, *Puritans at Play: Leisure and Recreation in Colonial New England* (New York: Palgrave, 2005), 166.
10. Bruce C. Daniels, "Sober Mirth and Pleasant Poisons: Puritan Ambivalence toward Leisure and Recreation in Colonial New England," in *Sport in America: From Colonial Leisure to Celebrity Figures and Globalization*, Vol. 2, ed. David K Wiggins (Champaign: IL: Human Kinetics, 2010), 5–21.

11. Quoted in "Amusements," *New Englander* 9 (1851): 358; see also Clifford Putney, *Muscular Christianity: Manhood and Sports in Protestant America, 1880–1920* (Cambridge, MA: Harvard University Press, 2003); Tony Ladd and James A Mathisen, *Muscular Christianity: Evangelical Protestants and the Development of American Sports* (Grand Rapids, MI: Baker Books, 1999), 22–68.

12. Putney, *Muscular Christianity*, 1; see also John Macaloon, ed., *Muscular Christianity and the Colonial and Post-Colonial World* (New York: Routledge, 2013); Bruce Kidd, "Muscular Christianity and the Value-Centered Sport: The Legacy of Tom Brown in Canada," *Sport in Society* 13, no. 5 (2013): 901–910.

13. Jeffrey Scholes and Raphael Sassower, *Religion and Sports in American Culture* (New York: Routledge, 2014); see also Nick J. Watson and Andrew Parker, eds., *Sports and Christianity: Historical and Contemporary Perspectives* (New York: Routledge, 2013).

14. Shirl Hoffman, "The Decline of Civility and the Rise of Religion in American Sport," *Quest* 51 (February 1999): 80.

15. Tom Faulkner, "A Puckish Reflection on Religion in Canada," in *From Season to Season: Sports as American Religion*, ed. Joseph L Price (Macon, GA: Mercer University Press, 2004), 185, 200.

16. Eric Bain-Selbo, *Game Day and God: Football, Faith, and Politics in the American South* (Macon, GA: Mercer University Press, 2009), 213, 235.

17. *The Speeches of Avery Brundage* (Lausanne, Switzerland: Comité International Olympique, 1968), 80.

18. James A Mathisen, "American Sport as Folk Religion: Examining a Test of Its Strength," in *From Season to Season: Sports as American Religion*, ed. Joseph L Price (Macon, GA: Mercer University Press, 2004), 142; and Joseph L Price, *Rounding the Bases: Baseball and Religion in America* (Macon, GA: Mercer University Press, 2006), 175.

19. Craig A Forney, *The Holy Trinity of American Sports: Civil Religion in Football, Baseball, and Basketball* (Macon, GA: Mercer University Press, 2010), 189; see also Jeffrey Scholes and Raphael Sassower, *Religion and Sports in American Culture* (New York: Routledge, 2014).

20. Tom Krattenmaker, *Onward Christian Athletes* (Lanham, MD: Rowman & Littlefield, 2010).

21. Official site for the Fellowship of Christian Athletes, http://www.fca.org/; see also Krattenmaker, *Onward Christian Athletes*, 51–67; see also Mark Oppenheimer, "In the Fields of the Lord," *Sports Illustrated*, February 4, 2013, 38–43.

22. Michael L Butterworth, "Saved at Home: Christian Branding and Faith Nights in the 'Church of Baseball,'" *Quarterly Journal of Speech*, 97:3 (2011): 309-333, DOI: 10.1080/00335630.2011.585170

23. Garth Woolsey, "Christian Theme Riding High on a Pigskin," ThirdCoastSports, October 7, 2010, http://www.faithnights.com/content.asp?CID=89573/.

24. Home page, *Sports Spectrum Magazine*, http://www.sportsspectrum.com/daily/.

25. Home page, "About Athletes in Action," *Athletes in Action Online*, http://www.athletesinaction.org/.

26. Promise keepers. https://promisekeepers.org/promise-keepers/about-us/ministry-partners/ accessed June 10, 2022

27. Promise Keepers, http://www.youtube.com/user/PromiseKeepers/; see also John P. Bartkowski, *The Promise Keepers: Servants, Soldiers, and Godly Men* (Piscataway, NJ: Rutgers University Press, 2004); the following book shifts the focus away from males to females: Annie Blazer, *Playing for God: Evangelical Women and the Unintended Consequences of Sports Ministry* (New York: New York University Press, 2015).

28. George D. Randels Jr. and Becky Beal, "What Makes a Man? Religion, Sport and Negotiating Masculine Identity in the Promise Keepers," in *With God on Their Side: Sport in the Service of Religion*, ed. Tara Magdalinski and Timothy J. L Chandler (New York: Routledge, 2002), 160.

29. Quoted in John Blake, "When Did God Become a Sports Fan?" CNN, May 25, 2010, http://articles.cnn.com/2010-05-25/living/God.sports_1_god-athletes-faith?_s=PM:LIVING/; see also Krattenmaker, *Onward Christian Athletes*.

30. Max Weber, *The Protestant Ethic and the Spirit of Capitalism*, 2nd ed., trans. Talcott Parsons (Los Angeles: Roxbury, 1998). This essay, probably the most famous work on the sociology of religion, has aroused a great deal of controversy among sociologists and historians.

31. Weber, *The Protestant Ethic*, 80, 115

32. Weber, 183.

33. Steven J. Overman, *The Protestant Ethic and the Spirit of Sport: How Calvinism and Capitalism Shaped America's Games* (Macon, GA: Mercer University Press, 2011), 4.

34. Frank Deford, *The Old Ball Game* (New York: Atlantic Monthly Press, 2005), 36.

35. Bronislaw Malinowski, *Magic, Science, and Religion and Other Essays* (Long Grove, IL: Waveland Press, 1992).

36. Pat Conroy, *The Prince of Tides* (New York: Bantam, 2002), 394–395.

37. Nick J. Watson and Daniel R. Czech, "The Use of Prayer in Sport: Implications for Sport Psychology Consulting," *Athletic Insight* 7, no. 4 (December 2005): 29.

38. Daniel Cox and Robert P. Jones, "One-Quarter Say God Will Determine the Super Bowl's Winner—but Nearly Half Say God Rewards Devout Athletes," Public Religion Institute, January 30, 2017, https://www.prri.org/research/poll-super-bowl-women-sports-god-athletes-marijuana/.

39. Greg Garrison, "Championship Coach Tackles God on the Gridiron," *Huffington Post*, May 9, 2011, http://www.huffingtonpost.com/2011/07/06/coach-gene-chizik_n_891382.html/; see also Chad Gibbs, *God & Football: Faith and Fanaticism in the SEC* (Grand Rapids, MI: Zondervan, 2010).

40. Quoted in Michael Medved, "War on Religious Gestures," *USA Today*, July 9, 2012, 11A

41. Quoted in Krattenmaker, *Onward Christian Athletes*, 81.

42. Krattenmaker, *Onward Christian Athletes*, 6; Tom Krattenmaker, "And I'd Like to Thank God Almighty," *USA Today*, October 12, 2009, 11A

43. Malinowski, *Magic, Science, and Religion*, 12–30.

44. Malinowski, *Magic, Science, and Religion*, 116.

45. Andrew Podnieks, *Hockey Superstitions: From Playoff Beards to Crossed Sticks and Lucky Socks* (Toronto: McClelland & Stewart, 2010); see also Lysann Damisch, Barbara Stoberock, and Thomas Mussweiler, "Keep Your Fingers Crossed! How Superstition Improves Performance," *Psychological Science* 21, no. 7 (2010): 1014–1020; Barry Wilner and Ken Rappoport, *Crazyball: Sports Scandals, Superstitions, and Sick Plays* (Lanham: MD: Taylor, 2014).

46. George Gmelch, *Inside Pitch: Life in Professional Baseball* (Lincoln: University of Nebraska Press, 2006), 133–143.

5

SPORT, FUTURE TRENDS, AND SUSTAINABILITY

CHAPTER 15

FUTURE TRENDS

The Sustainability of Sport
in the United States

Sports, which in the past were essential in forging a tribal and then a national identity, are now forging a planetary identity.

—MICHIO KAKU[1]

Many Americans yearn for high-risk, high-adventure, extreme sports. These sports are rapidly becoming one of the most popular new categories of sports. BASE—an acronym for four categories of objects from which one can jump: building, antenna, span (the word used for a bridge), and earth (the word used for a cliff)—is an example of an approach to sports that coincides with a larger sensation-seeking cultural shift toward high-risk experiences. (Photo: © Vitalii Nesterchuk/123RF)

415

"We live in a changing society" is an often-heard cliché It is realistic to depict contemporary social life as dynamic and progressive. One only has to consider recent events to understand that our lives are subject to instant change; we only need to look as far as the COVID-19 pandemic and its profound impacts on daily life to see how rapidly changes in society can occur. Indeed, many would legitimately contend that the pace of living is fast, with growth and change as the only constants, marked by an accelerating rate of technological change. These ideas are buttressed by an apparent obsession with the future and what it may hold.

In the economic realm, business leaders look for predictions about population trends and shifts in consumer preferences. Meanwhile, young adults seek information about occupational trends in hopes that the career for which they prepare will be a gateway to opportunity, even as we are all constantly reminded that "most of tomorrow's jobs have yet to be created."

Meanwhile, groups of social forecasters, societal scientists who are actively involved in forecasting societal activity, have also been busy with futuristic studies under the auspices of private foundations and government agencies. Two well-known groups include the International Institute of Forecasters and the Trends Research Institute. There is also the World Future Society, a thriving organization with members in more than eighty countries who are interested in how social and technological developments are shaping the future. Finally, the publication of at least five periodicals on futurism (e.g., *The Futurist*) indicates that people like to speculate about what the remaining decades of the twenty-first century will be like.

Change in the United States is therefore a ubiquitous fact. Today's social, economic, technological, and physical environments are vastly different from those of only a generation ago, to say nothing of those of three or four generations ago. Our institutions and values are undergoing rapid shifts at an unprecedented rate and scale. Therefore, we conclude this volume with a chapter that examines the trends and the future of sport in the United States because, as we have frequently argued, sport reflects society, and as the society changes, sport will also undoubtedly undergo transformation.

In this chapter, we will highlight how a culture's context impacts the direction and rate of change. Similar to the chapter on history, we will focus on key drivers of change and, although we introduce these drivers separately, we acknowledge how those factors are interdependent and in flux. We will examine social factors such as demographic trends, economic shifts, the patterns of work and leisure, and technology. Taken together, these factors will profoundly impact how sport is produced and consumed at all levels. As noted throughout this book, we have used social science research to understand how current social arrangements benefit some groups while leaving others disadvantaged.

The future of sports in our world has also been a popular topic. Numerous news features, blogs, and organizations continue to speculate about the future iterations of sport.[2] Given the heightened interest in our sporting future, we will therefore unpack some upcoming trends in the following sections.

Future sport will be integrally associated with broader sustainability issues. One organization, the Aspen Institute, recently outlined several key facets of sustainability that could impact the future of sports. This organization suggests that our public health, as well as social justice and equity concerns, will need to be addressed.[3] We will concomitantly describe and evaluate new sporting trends in terms of sustainability. We specifically focus on the intersectionality of economic security, social inclusion/justice, and environmental/ecological quality so as to guarantee the welfare of both the present and the future generations.

Furthermore, the Aspen Institute has identified technology as an obvious yet critical element that will drive future sport. Whether it be the creation of the urethane wheel in skateboarding or the emergence of wearable technologies for athletes, new technologies play a vital role in sports. Yet, it has been suggested from a sustainability perspective that we need to critically consider what our *preferred* sporting future will be like alongside technological innovation.[4] This means reflecting upon how technological innovation in sport, and the various new relationships that are created, impacts upon "human and ecological well being, social and economic development, and cultural identity."[5]

Taking the above ideas into consideration, we frame this concluding chapter with an opening question: How will the lens of sustainability influence future sporting engagements? To anchor this discussion, we first outline key social factors and patterns that will profoundly shape the ways in which people participate in future sports.

KEY SOCIAL FACTORS THAT DRIVE SOCIAL CHANGE

THE ECONOMY, TECHNOLOGY, AND LABOR: THE INFORMATION SOCIETY

A sociological imagination allows us to examine how societal norms, values, and institutions influence the organization of our daily lives. With respect to sport and physical activity patterns, a sociological perspective allows us to "take a step back" and assess what is influencing the patterns of sport participation and spectatorship. For the vast majority of adults, involvement in sport is related to their work. Whether they are participating in sport themselves or watching others perform, the extent to which they can do either depends on the nonwork time (so-called free or leisure time) available to them. In brief, the less time they must work, the more free time they have available for sporting activities; thus, trends in the work life of people will be instrumental in trends that take place in sport.

Our work lives are shaped by the dominant forms of economies and labor policies. In the United States, the economic systems are complex mixtures of capitalism and socialism. Throughout the world during the twentieth century there was steady movement away from laissez-faire (virtually unregulated) capitalism and toward managerial capitalism, with the adoption of many socialistic features, which has caused some observers to predict that capitalism will end in the United States. This view is not shared by most futurists, however. Capitalism has been entrenched to the point that there has been no fundamental challenge to the capitalist economic model in the United States. Given the enormous influence of the corporate rich and the tendency for most Americans to accept the present economic structure as

proper, capitalism will undoubtedly remain dominant in the United States.

In fact, neoliberalism is another policy trend in the United States whose ethos counters the social welfare model. Since the 1980s, this social and political philosophy asserts that public domains such as education, recreation, and health are best served by free market competition and limited government intervention. This disinvestment has negatively impacted life opportunities for the most disadvantaged and can be observed in the growing disparity between the very wealthy and most of the rest of the population. A 2020 report from the Pew Research Center shows that income inequality in the United States is the highest of all the G7 nations (which also includes Germany, France, Canada, the United Kingdom, Italy, and Japan), according to data from the Organisation for Economic Co-operation and Development.[6]

The future economy, barring nuclear holocaust, unforeseen energy problems, or other catastrophic events, will probably continue to go through its cycles of prosperity and recession. The terrorist attacks on September 11, 2001, were a severe shock to the social climate and economic systems of the United States. This was followed by the great recession of 2008 that negatively affected a majority of Americans. An economic recovery followed, but that was upended by the COVID-19 pandemic of 2020. Everyone has heard "The world will never be the same" repeated over and over. But despite these events and the security measures that we all live with in their aftermath, our lives do go on. According to economic forecasters, the United States will face increasing international economic competition and will be challenged to find better ways to accommodate the emerging global economy rather than trying to dominate international economic competitors. It is also a trend that large transnational corporations have come to dominate economies around the world. Indeed, economically they exceed the size of many nation-states.

Fundamental to the U.S. economic systems is the role of industrialization and technology because this has changed not only the way that goods are produced but also the conditions under which they are produced. As the industrial revolution evolved, factories brought workers into sweatshops to toil, literally, from sunrise to sunset. Later, as steel and other large industries grew, workers were attracted to the plants by the prospect of steady work and a livable wage. Hours were long, but until the emergence of labor unions, workers could do little about that if they wished to remain employed. However, in the early twentieth century, a gradual reduction in the average workweek began for nonagricultural workers, from about sixty-five hours to just over forty hours.

Economic trends over the past century have been underpinned by technological innovations, to the point that the technology sector increasingly dominates the economy. The previous state of the art in production and services is being quickly replaced by new high-tech developments. The twenty-first-century society is expected to become increasingly more of a "learning society." In part, this will be a function of the "information explosion"; thus, information (its acquisition and use) will become extremely important. A major problem will be the lack of an adequate supply of educated persons with professional and technical competence; therefore, futurists expect education, especially college and graduate education, to be acquired by a much greater proportion of the population than at present.[7] Combined, these forces form the most salient feature of life in the United States, and their effects are manifested in the contours of labor and leisure.

AN INFORMATION SOCIETY

The ways in which the economy is being transformed and the occupational system reworked by new technology confirm that the United States has entered an "information-based" society, or an information-producing service economy, rather than a goods-producing manufacturing economy. One only has to look at contemporary communication and technology companies such as Microsoft to see how their ability to create and leverage proprietary information generates billions of dollars in profits (see Figure 15.1).

While the United States is clearly an information-driven society, this does not mean that manufacturing is not happening. Cars are built, running shoes are made, and clothing is produced. However, while "Made in America" still resonates with consumers, the trend is that goods are more and more being manufactured in other countries (especially in countries where labor has few legal protections). Often, corporate centers are located in the United States, while the production of goods is commonly outsourced to other countries. For example, Nike headquarters are in Beaverton, Oregon, where they design and test

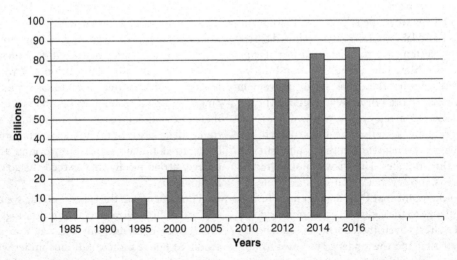

FIGURE 15.1 Microsoft Annual Revenue. Source: Microsoft Annual Reports, 2016.

their products, develop their advertising campaigns, and create content for their social media, whereas the factories they subcontract to produce their goods are located in other countries. Importantly, economies are globally interconnected, especially with the trend of countries and regions focusing on different steps in supply chain and production: from extracting natural resources, to manufacturing, to marketing, to transportation. This interconnectedness was clearly demonstrated during the COVID-19 pandemic as global supply chains were disrupted because certain world regions were on lockdown and could not deliver their contributions to production.

With every new iteration of the economy and job markets, there is an impact on labor. As jobs in technology grow, "traditional" jobs could be reduced. For example, the tech sectors are using robotics and computer-integrated manufacturing, which, in turn, reduces the need for human labor in factories. Humans in factories are now overseeing the machines that make the products as opposed to humans making the products with their own hands. Agriculture has increasingly turned to the use of automated processes based on both ground sensor and satellite data trends; this information guides tractors now in terms of how and where to seed, and perhaps these machines will eventually become completely self-driven.

Futurists predict that computers and other technological innovations will change the nature of work and the balance between jobs and personal lives. In the next ten years, four of five people will be doing jobs differently from the way they have been done in the past thirty years. Computer networking and social media will be one reason for this trend. We will, in essence, become an electronically connected society, as these technologies enable work to be done anywhere, at any time, at any distance from the office or factory. This trend was heightened during the COVID-19 pandemic as many in the technology and information sector worked from home and will continue to do so for the next few years. But the pandemic also clearly made visible the economic discrepancy in the United States. Millions of people were referred to as "front-line" or "essential" workers: those in the agricultural, medical, and service industries. They did

not have the same flexibility to do their work from home. They either lost their jobs or had to risk their well-being to provide basic necessities (food, medicine, building maintenance) for other people. People who were hit the hardest economically were women of color (often overrepresented in essential work), whereas the wealth of U.S. billionaires increased significantly during the pandemic.[8]

Technological developments that have brought about, on an ever-increasing scale, giant organizations have spawned a depersonalization of social relationships and the eclipse of personalized community. Several social analysts during the past decade amassed impressive data on the decline of social capital and civic engagement in American society. They claim that Americans have lost much of the social glue that once held this society together, that we have become a nation of strangers to one another, lacking mutual social bonds. This view has been crystallized in the title of Robert Putnam's well-known book, *Bowling Alone.*[9] Then, the COVID-19 pandemic further alienated people from one another, whether in work, school, or sporting environments, as a result of lockdown and distancing measures. Scholars are already trying to decipher the impacts of this social isolation on human well-being and social life. As our economy and labor patterns change, our leisure time and options are impacted. Importantly, there is not a uniform effect. As noted previously, different groups of people will benefit more than others in different iterations of the economy.

Information Society and Flextime: Hopes and Realities of Increased Leisure

The trend toward a shorter workweek, which started in the early twentieth century, began to reverse itself in the past two decades. To a great extent, the prediction of a "leisure society" was based on a misperception of the amount of leisure time that would be made available by technological advances. Americans are frequently characterized as working more hours compared to other industrialized nations.

In addition, the average commuting time for American workers is twenty-six minutes. The consequence of longer commutes is that workers are spending as much as an additional working week traveling to and from work every year. In studies carried out at the Families and Work Institute in New York, 44 percent of the respondents said they were overworked often or very often, and many wished they could reduce their work hours. Researchers report that one-third of the U.S. workforce can be viewed as being chronically overworked.[10]

Many private and public organizations have experimented with four-day and flextime workweek schedules. The number of firms using flexible work hours has more than doubled in the past twenty years. These flexible arrangements take different forms, such as satellite work centers, customized work schedules, staggered shifts, and telecommuting with personal computers to the place of work. With the COVID-19 pandemic, many organizations were forced to develop flexible work schedules. In particular, there has been a recent shift toward "remote" work during this time, meaning that workers have been able to stay home while attending to their employment duties. It will be interesting to see how long this trend of telecommuting will continue and how it will impact upon our daily lives.

Taken together, these work schemes have been hailed as important steps toward creating a leisure society. However, in all four-day and flextime schemes tried so far, the workweek remains near forty hours, so this trend has little to do with a reduction in working time; it is merely a rescheduling of the workload. It fails to even touch on the more important issue—the public's desire to reduce the overall length of the workweek.

Although the hours of the workweek remain about the same under the various nontraditional plans, several potential benefits accrue with respect to leisure time. The extralong weekends make travel and other extended leisure activities possible, and commuting time may be reduced, some of which might be used for leisure activities. However, the extra time afforded by the four-day workweek may be a mixed blessing. For example, many people use the time working at a second job because continuing inflation tends to require more money to maintain the current living standard. Increases in free time, then,

are often used primarily as an opportunity to perform extra work of some kind. It appears that the emergence of a true leisure society will require a re-envisioning of our major social structures and labor systems. This will also necessitate the rise of a fundamentally different valuation of what actually constitutes work and leisure.

Ignoring for the moment that the greater amount of free time that technology was supposed to have provided has not materialized, how can we account for participation rates in leisure activities and expenditure on leisure pursuits being at an all-time high? Explanations for the leisure pursuits of Americans tend to converge on the idea that people are just cramming more activities into each twenty-four hours. The commonly heard "24/7" is not just an expression; it is a cultural institution that is changing the way people live. The main argument is that the nation's business day is now twenty-four hours long because many businesses stay open all night, while smartphones and other electronic devices enable business communication and transactions to be conducted literally 24/7.

The traditional schedule of being awake during the day and asleep at night has become obsolete; millions of people are awake at any given time throughout the twenty-four-hour day. Those who are awake do not just shop at supermarkets and department stores. They engage in around-the-clock leisure activities, including sports. Many golf ranges, gyms, batting cages, tennis courts, swimming pools, and so forth are now open around the clock. This trend is perhaps best crystallized by the popularity of a fitness center chain that remains open to customers all day and night. Televised sports can be found on cable, satellite, and phone apps at every hour of the day. Sports enthusiasts and consumers therefore have a plethora of choices 24/7 to fulfill their sporting interests.

The tendency to do several things simultaneously and to do many things in a short period of time—including using the ever-present digital devices—has been called *time deepening*. It has also been called "the more, the more"—meaning that under the pressure of expanding interests and motivations, the more people do, the more they wish to do, and vice versa. The consequence is that many people suffer from "leisure-time stress." Despite feeling free during their free time, many people fear they may be losing out in leisure and hurry from one activity to another, leaving little time to stop and think. Moreover, consumer obsession about leisure time, and intensive participation within a mainstream culture where one is constantly trying to maximize body conditioning and presentation, may detract from the essence of leisure.

Along with, or in addition to, four-day or flex-time workweeks, corporate wellness programs are now common. A 2019 study from the Centers for Disease Control found that over half of U.S. workplaces offer some type of wellness program, often including sport or physical activities.[11] Company wellness program advocates claim they are a strategic way to reduce smoking, obesity, diabetes, and hypertension. It remains to be seen, however, whether these types of programs inspire a passion for healthy leisure activity or whether they simply reinforce managerial values such as individualized efficiency and competitiveness.[12]

TECHNOLOGY

Computers, smartphones, and other technological devices are central objects in our current data-driven world, and going forward, new generations of these devices will continue to structure our increasingly information-based society, including sport. As noted in the chapters on history (Chapter 2) and social values (Chapter 3), technology has always had a major impact on sport. The world of sports has made tremendous use of technology, and much in current sport is the product of technological innovation. This has impacted how we practice sport, how sport organizations train their athletes, how sport organizations sell products, and how fans participate in sport.

The fascination with enhanced sports performances and the obsession with winning have meant that technological innovations have been eagerly sought and employed in sports. Coaches and athletes already receive instant information about their own

teams and their opponents, as we will describe. Coaches at all levels have used computer technologies for several years for the selection and performance monitoring of athletes, as well as an aid in scouting opponents; the use of such "tech toys" will proliferate as "start-ups," major corporations, and universities are all significantly investing in this domain.

In football, for example, college and professional teams often use computers to understand opponents' strategies and tendencies, thus helping coaches and athletes make decisions during the game. Each play that is called is informed by computer-generated data. For example, National Football League coaches use tablet technology called the Sideline Viewing System that is sponsored by Microsoft on the sidelines.[13]

In soccer, coaches have access to data created through various technological platforms that assist with tactical decision-making. Technology influences whether it is best to cross the ball from the wings for a header or to pass to the center of the field for a shot. Furthermore, most pro baseball teams now use Track-Man, a 3D Doppler radar system that captures twenty-seven different measurements when it comes to every pitching and batting performance.[14]

Specialists in these technologies are thus being increasingly employed to collect and generate data through various platforms to provide coaches with information that is used for training and competition purposes. In many cases, athletes wear technological devices that track performance information that is fed back to coaches' tablet screens in real time to determine whether individual and team benchmarks have been met. Drones are also being used to provide coaches with real-time information about players' performances. Then, performance data about other teams is collected and analyzed by specialists to inform players and coaching staff members about future opponents and their outputs and tactics.

A more controversial technological innovation used in soccer has been VAR, the video review system used in matches when refereeing calls seemingly need a second opinion. However, there have been criticisms of this technology that go beyond whether accurate calls are being made on the field or not. One line of critique involves questioning the move toward replacing human judgment (which includes referees making human errors) by technological machinery. Perhaps with the expansion of VAR technology, referees will eventually be replaced completely by cameras. VAR also represents yet another method of technological surveillance and control of people's activities, which we are already seeing at unprecedented levels in everyday life.[15]

We can see from the VAR example that thoughtful people within and outside the sports world are raising important social questions about heightened technological integration in sport. Just because science and technology make it possible for athletes and teams to set new speed, distance, and weight records, should they? Are the higher risks to the life and limb of athletes worth using whatever is scientifically and technologically possible? Many times people simply accept the idea that if it can be done, it should be done; the question of *whether* something should be done is seldom asked. There are compelling social and psychological reasons why that question, and others like it, will be increasingly asked, and with good reason. For example, there is no doubt that one of the consequences of employing the latest technological innovations is that various injuries and illnesses are increasing for athletes. Humans are being increasingly pushed to their physical limits, and beyond, through the incorporation of new technologies of the body. For example, the virtual epidemic of concussions in sports is raising serious questions in several sports, from the youth to the elite levels.

There is another dimension to questioning the unqualified acceptance of scientific and technical developments in the interest of enhanced performances and sporting victories. The scientific–technical ethos gives priority to the product—the outcome—but the aspect of sport that has always been its prevailing essence is its process: its fun, its spontaneity, its creativeness, its expressiveness. Does the use of technology and its data products eliminate the fluidity and spontaneity of sporting experiences? Perhaps scientizing and technocizing sport subverts what has always been sport's most endearing features. And it

can even be questioned whether this trend is effective when it comes to facilitating human games of play. For instance, during just one event, the 2014 World Cup in Brazil, the English national soccer team took a seventy-two-member entourage of scientific and technological specialists with them, including a sport psychologist, nutritionist, and turf specialist, while sport scientists utilized industrial fans, heat chambers, and individually customized recovery drinks based on the players' unique sweat patterns. Yet, despite this major investment in sport science and technology, the English team was sent home early after getting knocked out at the group stage for the first time since 1958.[16]

It is therefore likely that over the next twenty years a major debate will center on the social–ethical questions that have been raised here about the scientific–technical directions of sport. These questions are applicable to our broader society's participation in technology. Although most Americans would not wish to give up many of the products of technological creations—computers, smartphones, air conditioning, automobiles, and so forth—there are, nevertheless, many people who find our increasingly technocratic–bureaucratic society dehumanizing. There has been increasing hostility to the widespread forms of technological innovation brought forth by transnational corporate organizations. A wide range of spontaneous, activist, and democratic actions have tried to recapture some sense of control over daily lives.

DEMOGRAPHIC SHIFTS: DIVERSE AND AGING POPULATIONS AND LOCATION

One of the divisions of sociological study is called demography; it focuses on population size, characteristics, trends of groups, neighborhoods, communities, patterns of migration, and analyses of change. In describing the assumptions of the sociological perspective in Chapter 1, we noted that humans are naturally social beings who are greatly affected by their social and natural environments, but they are also capable of changing those social and natural formations within their lives. We have emphasized at various places in this volume that changes in population characteristics have played an important role in the rise of modern sport forms, the popularity and demise of some sports, and who plays and does not play sports. We now turn to trends in the U.S. populations and the potential impact they may have on sport. Trends in population growth, composition, and location are sociologically significant because they impact the social lives of people, including their lives as participants and consumers of sports.

One of the most significant trends in the United States is the changing nature of the population—total numbers, composition, and location. Futurists are quite interested in population trends. In the United States, the population grew by nearly 23 million between 2010 and 2020, with a total population of approximately 331,500,000 people. As populations grow and diversify, sports will continue to expand as well.

POPULATION COMPOSITION

Population composition is a driver for social change because different groups of people have different sporting and recreation preferences. This, in turn, impacts the markets for both recreational and professional sports. The history of the United States is founded on colonialism, forced immigration (slave trade), and waves of immigration from many other countries. Importantly, the nationalities of those who have come to the United States have changed with the political and economic winds. As different populations move to the United States, they bring cultural practices, including sport, with them. Concomitantly, markets arise for these different types of sport. Corporations are very aware of their target audiences and develop goods and services to develop businesses. Alongside different cultural practices, the sheer number of people also influences the provision of recreational and sporting opportunities. Finally, a significant trend in the United States is our aging population, which affects both spectator markets and sporting opportunities.

During most of the twentieth century the United States had a young population because the birth rate remained high for an increasing number of people of childbearing age. This condition is now changing rapidly because the long-term trends for birthrates and death rates are expected to decline. Thus, the proportion of young people will diminish, and the proportion of older people will increase, markedly affecting population composition. The median age in the United States will rise dramatically, from thirty-seven in 2010 to about forty in 2040. The U.S. Census Bureau projects that the over-sixty-five population will more than double between 2010 and 2050, when one in five Americans will be over sixty-five years old (see Figure 15.2).

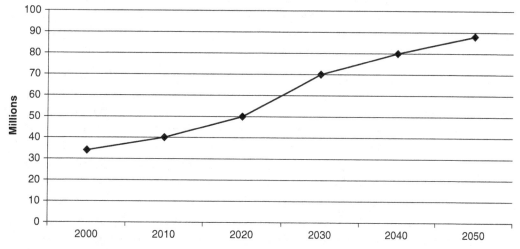

FIGURE 15.2 Projections of U.S. Seniors Sixty-Five and Older. *Source:* Jennifer M. Ortman, Victoria A Velkoff, and Howard Hogan, *An Aging Nation: The Older Population in the United States* (Washington, D.C.: U. S. Census Bureau, May 2014).

A larger proportion of the population is now over forty years old, a fact that is manifested in sport in a number of ways, including increasing opportunities for older adults to participate in recreational and professional sport. Some of the biggest sports stories of the past few years have been about older athletes: Tom Brady continues to play in the NFL into his forties, Serena Williams and Roger Federer still dominate tennis, and Susan Bird is still playing in the WNBA, all at forty years of age or older. The senior tours of the Professional Golfers' Association of America and the Professional Tennis Association illustrate quite well that older athletes can perform at high levels and that sports fans will pay to see them compete in their sport.

There is little doubt that people are remaining physically active later in their lives, and more and more sports programs are being created to allow the aging population to participate. According to a recent survey, nearly 60 percent of baby boomers (born between 1945 and 1964) said they were involved in fitness activities, and nearly 40 percent were participating in outdoor activities, followed by involvement in individual sports at 23 percent.[17]

The Masters Sports Tournaments and Senior Olympics have become major forces in organizing competitive sports for senior men and women. For instance, the recent 2017 World Masters Games held in Auckland, New Zealand, attracted 28,578 global competitors. These are only the most visible programs. Retirement communities are typically built to encourage the sport interests of their citizens. Many community recreation departments have expanded their programs to include senior leagues in several sports; indeed, in some communities these leagues are the fastest growing. Many informal senior groups have sprung up to participate in everything from bocce to skateboarding. In all likelihood, participant sports will be a major growth industry wherever large groups of older persons settle.

Another population trend is the increasing ethnic and racial diversity within the United States. There are many reasons people seek to come to the United States. For example, high tech jobs draw an international workforce to the United States. Political oppression or economic hardship continues to be an incentive for millions of people to migrate, legally or illegally. Recent data from the United Nations Refugee Agency show the global flow of refugees has increased. In 2020, one in ninety-five people worldwide were forcibly displaced from their home countries. The United States has been struggling to develop a clear policy on immigration for millions of asylum seekers and refugees, many of whom are children.

With regard to the growing diversity in the United States, the Hispanic population grew from 14.6 million in 1980 to 62 million in 2020, more than 100 percent in forty years. Hispanics became the largest ethnic minority in 2003, surpassing African Americans. Even more remarkably, although the United States as a whole grew 19.8 percent, growth in the Asian American population from 1980 to 2010 was 200 percent, mostly because of immigration. In 2020 Asian Americans were 6 percent of the total U.S. population, at 24 million.[18] It is projected that the U.S. population will continue to become more diverse in the coming decades and that, by 2050, 54 percent of the population will be ethnic minorities. This rapidly changing ethnic and racial complexion in the United States will alter everything in society, from politics and education to industry, values, and sports and leisure activities.

The rising popularity of soccer is a result, in part, of these demographic trends. The men's World Cup held in the United States in 1994 served as a strong stimulus to the growing popularity of soccer, which began to take a stronger foothold in suburban communities. Furthermore, the increase in immigrant populations from Mexico, Central and South America, and Asian countries, where soccer is extremely popular, helped create a subculture of support for the creation of the original ten-team MLS in 1996. Today, professional soccer has more devoted fans than ever before in the United States. The MLS has planned to increase to thirty teams by the 2023 season, while the second division United Soccer Leagues Championship now has thirty-one clubs spread across the various markets. The upcoming 2026 men's World Cup will be hosted by North American cities, mostly based in the United States, and this will continue to increase the popularity of this diverse sport.

The changing demographic composition of the U.S. population has provided greater opportunity for ethnic and racial minority groups in sports. It is one of the most salient trends at present and, if futurists' predictions are correct, will continue in the coming years. One of the main reasons to expect that minorities will secure increasing access and opportunities is, as we described previously, that their percentage of the population is increasing dramatically. There is no question that organized sports, from youth programs to the professional level, have made great strides toward equalizing opportunities in the past decade, but the goal has not yet been achieved.

In Chapters 6 and 7, we demonstrated that overt discrimination against ethnic minorities and females, such as denying them access to sports, has been gradually eliminated, but that inequalities and injustices continue in subtler forms. Major concerns remain and these have been highlighted in the recent Black Lives Matter protests enacted by many athletes of color and their supporters.

In general, minorities are underrepresented in many of the most popular high school, college, and professional sports, but each year new inroads are being made into more sports. Minorities are participating in new individual and team sports, taking their rightful place among teammates, and in a few cases, they are obtaining coaching and management positions in prominent sports programs. The future for racial, ethnic, and gender diversity in American sports appears to be promising, yet there is still much work to be done to have an equitable and inclusive sports scene.

With the increase in diversity and the number of people, professional sport leagues are growing to meet consumer demands. Despite a brief downturn recently caused by the COVID-19 pandemic, professional sport has been one of the most financially successful and growing industries during the past thirty years. Professional men's and women's golf and tennis have extended their tour seasons, and both tennis and golf now have seniors' tours. In addition, a number of other professional sports (such as NASCAR, Esports, Mixed Martial Arts, cycling,

The Ultimate Fighting Championship (UFC) is an American Mixed Martial Arts organization. It was founded in the United States. The UFC produces worldwide events that showcase eleven weight divisions. By 2021, the UFC had held over 573 events in 28 countries, and it has grown into a multibillion-dollar enterprise. (Photo: Josh Hedges/ Getty Images)

distance running, rugby, and lacrosse) are gaining followers in live attendance and television/media coverage. Consumer-spectator interest thus appears to have no limit. New franchises in the major sports—NBA, NFL, MLB, MLS, and NHL—will continue to spring up all over the United States to be greeted by large crowds.

Moreover, Title IX and the expansion of high school and college sports for females, in conjunction with trends in population characteristics, have created opportunities for women's professional sports to grow over the past fifty years. Perhaps the most notable examples of this growth are the professional basketball league (WNBA), which has twelve teams, and the professional soccer league (NWSL), which has twelve teams as of the 2022 season.

The future trajectory therefore seems clear: professional sports for men and women will remain a prominent industry in the foreseeable future. The current popularity of traditional and emerging sports in the United States reflects rising interest among increasingly diverse members of our society.

LOCATIONS

Demographic and economic shifts in society greatly influence how people can participate and spectate sport. In this regard, a major trend is the increased growth and diversification of urban areas, which has an impact upon American sport. More people are living in urban areas and these areas are highly socially diverse. About 85 percent of Americans are living in cities and their surrounding suburbs. These urban areas also tend to be economic engines for our nation, because they are home to the majority of financial and transportation hubs, technological innovation, scientific centers and companies, and various information and creative industries. However, during the recent COVID-19 pandemic, we have seen some urbanites either relocate or consider moving to less dense and more affordable rural areas.[19] States with significant rural regions are showing some of the highest population in-growth in the United States, including Vermont, South Dakota, South Carolina, Idaho, and West Virginia.[20] It will be interesting to see if this trend continues over the next few years; if so, researchers will want to study how rural growth and revitalization will impact American sports.

Currently, the social and economic diversity in urban regions fosters various types of sporting activities. For example, in the San Francisco Bay Area there are regular opportunities to be involved in sports such as roller skating, rugby, basketball, skateboarding, surfing, sailing, cricket, mountain biking, trail running, badminton, and figure skating. These activities occur both with organized structuring and in more drop-in, informal ways. Fans are also able to support several professional and semiprofessional teams in football, basketball, soccer, ice hockey, and baseball. Major sporting events have also been regularly hosted in this urban region, including the America's Cup yacht racing competition, the men's Copa America and World Cup soccer tournaments, the Rugby World Cup Sevens, and the X Games action sports event, to name just a few in recent yers.

In smaller city markets, sport is regularly used to develop and sustain community identity and generate business. For example, minor league baseball has over one hundred teams in these types of communities, usually with more intimate stadiums based in downtown locations. In Biloxi, Mississippi, the stadium is located on the Gulf Coast and the team is called the Shuckers, which represents the local food economy of oysters (shucking is how one opens the shell of an oyster). Another league that invests in smaller markets is the Women's Flat Track Roller Derby Association. This organization has hundreds of teams in the United States, in both large urban areas and smaller markets. For instance, Asheville, North Carolina, a mid-sized city of nearly 100,000 people, is home to the roller derby team called the Blue Ridge Rollergirls.

Moreover, many smaller cities are catering to the family and tourist demographics by constructing massive multisport facilities, often to jumpstart their postindustrial economies. A $42 million sportsplex in Spokane, Washington, for example, will feature a 180,000-square-foot facility consisting of a 200-meter six-lane pool, a championship-level running track, sixteen volleyball courts, ten basketball courts convertible to twenty-one wrestling mats, and an NHL-sized ice sheet.[21] It is expected that this complex will attract approximately 20,000 visitors and generate $19–$33 million in tourism spending each year.[22]

Perhaps the grandest of these facilities is the Spooky Nook sports complex in Hamilton, Ohio, which will cost $144 million and become the largest indoor sports complex in the United States, at 1.3 million square feet. Replacing an old paper mill, this sports site will be 700,000 square feet with two turf fields, ten hardwood courts, and a baseball facility, along with concessions and convention space.[23]

FUTURE TRENDS AND SPORTS

PROFESSIONAL SPORTS

The professional sports industry in the United States has grown at an unprecedented rate in the past twenty years. It is now a sprawling, multibillion-dollar-a-year industry that is clearly big business, in which making a profit is paramount. Professional sport franchise owners once generally had a deep emotional commitment to the sport and believed that the administrative and financial operations were merely necessary adjuncts to owning a team.

Current owners in the major sports are increasingly corporate conglomerates of one kind or another, and they think primarily of maximizing profit through rational business procedures. Providing sports entertainment for loyal hometown fans is only a secondary consideration. The most visible example of this is found in the numerous threats by ownership to move franchises if demands for new stadiums, better lease deals, and so forth are not met. They are not idle threats, as can be seen in the number of major franchise moves.[24]

As indicated in an earlier section in this chapter, the trend appears to be toward an expansion of professional sports in the foreseeable future. One way professional sports might expand is by becoming more international. The major American team sports are played worldwide, and with air travel becoming more convenient and faster, there seems little reason not to expand into other continents. The NBA has played several preseason and regular season games in foreign locales such as Japan, China, Mexico, and England, while the NFL once explored the possibility of creating a new franchise in London. Soccer is already a sport played worldwide, and perhaps American soccer teams will someday be incorporated into South American, European, and/or Asian soccer leagues. Already, the Seattle Sounders of MLS have qualified for the FIFA Club World Cup tournament which involves the top teams from leagues around the globe.

Fan support for professional sports depends on adequate disposable income. Within the past decade, serious economic downturns have occurred in the United States. Should a prolonged economic recession occur, people will have less disposable income, and this could adversely affect professional sports. Moreover, as noted earlier, if ticket prices outstrip the cost of living, professional sports may price themselves out of the market. However, new forms of technology may allow fans to have less expensive ways to watch their favorite teams. Thus, an economic divide in types of spectatorship may increase, with those who have disposable income watching in person, while the vast majority of others may spectate virtually.

Technology will be evident in playing arenas and other professional sporting facilities of the future. Domed and retractable-roof stadiums are now commonplace, and groundskeeping teams can flexibly install either artificial or natural grass playing surfaces in one venue. And rather than being fixed

physical edifices, future stadiums may move toward a more modular design where facility operators can flexibly add amenities such as concessions, team stores, scoreboards, and bleachers, depending on event type and need. One prototype design offers six unique "phases of building" to accommodate different types of sports based on a central operational core of a 3,000-seat stand with the playing surface.[25]

Future stadiums will also be internally equipped with spectacular accoutrements to enhance the spectating experience. "Connective" technologies are making the spectating experience more personalized, immersive, and efficient, thus reshaping fans' habits and sports consumption. Mobile phone apps will connect spectators with every aspect of the event. In terms of safety, through a mobile application, stadium visitors can anonymously report safety concerns, suspicious activity, and unattended packages directly to the stadium's security officials and seek medical assistance. Fans will also able to interact with security officials through two-way communications and send photos, videos, and audio to provide specific details, to essentially be the eyes and ears for security. Apps are already being used to find available parking, enter the stadium with mobile tickets, order in-seat food and beverage delivery, order merchandise through express pickup, and watch instant replays.[26]

Fans may also be able to view the game in more tactical ways to satisfy their "inner" coach or general manager. New York's Madison Square Garden recently outfitted four sections of club seating and all luxury suites with interactive seats. Through a complex system of computers and touch-screen monitors, those seating areas can access live, isolated camera angles, multiperspective replays with slow motion, sports highlights and statistics, and stored video and outside network feeds. Data feeds will help fans obtain key player and team performance analytics in real time. Undoubtedly, entire venues will be wired like this in the future, where seats will be equipped with earphones so that spectators can listen to press-box scouts giving advice to the bench, conversations at the pitching mounds, quarterbacks' calls in the huddle, and even locker room pep talks.

Architects and developers of future professional sports venues see these structures as more than purveyors of sporting events. They believe that in sync with the globalized economy, these sites can become entities of high consumption and spending akin to shopping malls and food courts. Live sporting events themselves may become, at best, an entertaining point of entry into a realm of brand marketing and high consumption. Although at first one might find this statement merely cynical, it is clearly the case that numerous types of business establishments (not just food and beverage ones) are already based in current sports venues.

ESPORTS AND VIDEO GAMES

- Intriguingly, in the new sporting world, or Sport 2.0, as one scholar deems it, there is a blurring of physical movement with the digital realm.[27] Thus, while those involved in physically grueling events such as Ironman triathlons would surely consider themselves sporting individuals, competitive sports video gamers would likewise contend that their virtual skills and strategizing are characteristic of sporting activity. Video games, which provide simulations of various kinds, including sporting ones, are extremely popular with a broad spectrum of age groups, both in the United States and around the world. Sony's PlayStation, Nintendo's Switch, and Microsoft's Xbox games all pose daunting intellectual challenges requiring detailed strategy, role-playing, and simulations. In 2021, more than 277 million people in the United States said that they played video games; 67 percent of American adults (aged 18+) are players while 76% of all those under 18 play video games. Fifty-one percent of video game players reported that they played more than seven hours per week.[28]

T. L. Taylor's volume *Raising the Stakes: E-Sports and the Professionalization of Computer Gaming* explains that the rise of Esports "is not simply a story about the transformation of digital play into sport, but the production of that activity as a new form of industry." The director of Esports at Riot Games (an American video game developer, publisher, and Esports tournament organizer) claims, "There's a generation of sports fans growing with eSports as their primary sport of choice. They're not dipping in and watching

Video game playing has become a popular activity in American society and around the globe. This activity attracts avid participants of all ages including some that are Esports competitors. (Photo: Olivia Castro)

basketball, hockey or football. This is a generation that really focused in on this as their sport."[29]

Non-sport-oriented games are major platforms where players regularly compete. About one-fourth of the products sold by computer game companies are simulated sports games. Some of the most popular sport video games are exhilarating simulations of professional and college football, soccer and basketball games, but racing games are also popular, as are action sports video games. The best of the sport video games are called *simulations* because of their capability to re-create the strategic requirements and sensuous experiences of the real sports. Entertainment Arts' *Madden NFL*, *FIFA* Soccer, *NBA 2K21*, *MLB The Show*, and *Tony Hawk's Pro Skater* series are among the most popular on the market. Players of these simulation games say that your muscles tighten, your pulse quickens, and you feel you are actually in the game. With the increase in technological sophistication over the past decade, the best sports video games feature outstanding graphics and put players squarely in the middle of the action. In football video games, players have play-calling options that mirror actual coaches' playbooks, making for a seamlessly realistic experience. Incredibly photorealistic graphics make the virtual sports games mesmerizing. Incredible as all of these technical innovations are, engineers and intellectual technologists promise that new and amazing breakthroughs will continue. Even more realistic simulation sports games will be developed in the future, with the incorporation of augmented reality and virtual reality technologies that allow game players to incorporate digitally generated sports scenarios within real-life situations or to replace them altogether. The goal in this industry is true-to-life experience.

Competitive video and computer game play is not new, but the emergence of funded collegiate and professional Esports competitors is a major element in the world of digital gaming. Rising stars are quickly snapped up by professional teams.

A recent NBC news story highlighted the fact that in 2018–19 school year, around 200 colleges in the U.S. offered a total of $16 million in Esports scholarships, which is three times the amount from 2015. Beyond that, the story also projected that Esports would be a $1.5 billion industry by 2020.[30] Indeed, there are now teams, leagues, sponsors, well-paid players, play-by-play broadcasts, and an active fan base representing all segments of society. There are regular tournaments, such as the World Cyber Games Grand Finals, which competitors and fans consider the equivalent of the Olympics. Major sports ownership groups such as Kroenke Sports & Entertainment (owners of the Premier League's Arsenal F.C., the NBA's Denver Nuggets, the NHL's Colorado Avalanche, and the Colorado Rapids of MLS) have recently invested heavily in this domain.[31] Moreover, celebrities and traditional sports athletes themselves are becoming involved in sponsoring gamers and their teams.[32]

Brand marketing of "cool" styles is integrally related to sport, and indeed certain sport projects have gained currency in our current consumer culture and information-based society.[33] It is therefore not just about competitiveness per se, and we can observe that video gaming has also expanded to become a major lifestyle element. The FaZe Clan (which includes LeBron James's son) video game and lifestyle brand is an example of this trend. Supported by several NBA and NFL star players, this coalition of professional gamers competes in sport games such as *FIFA* and *Rocket League* as well as nonsport games such as *Call of Duty* and *Counter-Strike*. According to a feature story about the FaZe Clan in *Sports Illustrated*, this group of gamers provide "community, entertainment, personality and endless hours of digital and social media content. . . . The universe they created now includes more than 90 esports pros and content creators from around the globe, along with a growing cohort of athletes and musicians who play video games but also post YouTube videos and create Twitch streams."[34]

However, while groups such as the FaZe Clan may reflect racial and ethnic diversity in the realm of Esports, it has been questioned whether this trend applies to everyday gaming activity. Also, women and girls as well as gamers who identify as LGBTQ+ are less likely to feel that they belong in these activities and are consequently more likely to quit gaming.[35]

Moreover, a number of social scientists have been warning that video gaming can lead to video addiction and the privatization of leisure; this form of sporting entertainment therefore has the danger of bringing about a collapse of a civic ethic—the sense of belonging—within society.[36] A countering view, however, is that these platforms provide increased opportunities for people to create social networks, both locally and globally, during times of prolonged social isolation such as the COVID-19 lockdowns.

THE FUTURE OF MEDIATED SPORT: TELEVISION AND THE INTERNET

Before television rescued the professional sports industry, professional sports owners were beset with decreasing attendance and the prospect of failure. The importance of broadcast and streaming markets has been a prominent factor in the growth and expansion of all professional sports. In 2021, approximately 57.5 million viewers in the United States watched digital live sports content at least one time per month.[37] Watching sports is not confined to TV viewing; 94 percent of fans watched sports on TV, but 71 percent also watched sports online, and 49 percent watched on mobile devices.[38]

Professional sport leagues and television corporations enjoy a reciprocal relationship in terms of how they seek mutual success in order to generate significant revenue. Professional sports seek to maintain their entertainment status and continue to expand, which also relies on their promotion through television. Huge sums of money will continue to be paid by television corporations to obtain the rights to televise major sport leagues. The NFL, NBA, and MLB each have contracts that exceed $1 billion with various television corporations.

Looking ahead, sports leagues and teams will continue to develop internal television platforms directly targeted at their fans. Sports leagues are becoming their own media companies and are interacting directly with their consumers without the assistance of traditional media outlets. For example, despite the NFL's lucrative television rights deals that it makes with major networks, the NFL has built its own television channel, the NFL Network, which broadcasts games throughout the season. It also showcases league legends through its popular NFL Films documentaries. Furthermore, NBATV, the Baseball Network, and other team-only channels are revolutionizing sports television and transforming the sports rights infrastructure. This trend has filtered down to the collegiate sporting landscape, where major universities and conferences now have channels that show their own respective games and produce original content.

Mediated sports spectating at first meant people sitting in their living rooms listening to accounts of the events on their radios. Today many people sit in their home entertainment centers and watch sports events on their high-definition, flat-screen TVs. But that is changing too. Anticipated technological advances with computer enhancement in the next decade or two will enable TV viewers to interact with the coverage and the game and to customize the content of the broadcast sports coverage they receive.

Viewers will have control over what aspects of events they will watch. They will be able to direct camera angles and request regular and slow-motion replays of viewer-defined action. They will be able to call up certain cameras to focus on a single player, coach, or part of the field or court, and they will be able to ask for statistics and personal background on the players and coaches. Sports TV networks will also proliferate. The prospect of the thousand-channel universe has excited many sports fans. It seems likely that all of the most popular sports will have their own networks, so viewers will be able to watch their favorite sport 24/7.

The Internet is one of the most sophisticated and useful innovations in modern technology. With the complete integration of Internet technology with various home and portable technological devices, it is possible for sport fans to use phones, computers, the Internet, and television interchangeably. Sport fans not only have incredible choices of sporting events at their command but also have virtually unlimited control over what they will watch and how they will view the events. With the wide availability of Internet connectivity, there is a proliferation of sport games and events that are being shown on various devices for relatively low cost. Simultaneously, the costs to attend live sports events are escalating, which means that future attendance at sports facilities is likely to dwindle. Furthermore, with the increasingly diverse demographics of the United States, Internet-based sports feeds and "streams" allow for fans of sports to easily follow international events and their favorite teams abroad.

At the same time as technology has expanded the scope and nature of mediated sport in the United States, social scientists are concerned about the effects a computer-based, Internet-connected lifestyle will have on social relations. Although television tended to turn social life indoors and to socially isolate entertainment, it did bring families together to watch the programs, especially sports, and sports bars became a popular social site for watching sports events. By contrast, as ownership of computers, cellphones, and tablet devices becomes universal and as free or low-cost live online coverage of sports events is now mainstream, mediated sports may become more individualistic rather than being a social activity.

ADVENTURE AND ACTION/LIFESTYLE SPORTS

At the same time that contexts such as professional major sports and Esports are expanding at an incredible pace, another trend is moving forward with momentum of its own. Adventure and lifestyle sports are often done outdoors, with limited oversight and boundaries, and sometimes with few or no codified rules. There are a variety of what have been called "non-traditional" or "alternative" physical activities (which are commonly placed under the general category of action or lifestyle sports). Some of the various forms identified here tend to emphasize cooperation rather than competition, the struggle rather than the triumph; the main point of many of them is to play, to enjoy, and to exist. We discuss two trends: activities where being in nature is the key feature and other forms of activity often called action and lifestyle sports.

Sports Immersed in Outdoor/Nature Spaces

Early-twenty-first-century society confronts us with a congested urban lifestyle. Houses are jammed more tightly against each other, apartments are stacked story on story, offices and factories are made up of steel and concrete, and our jobs are forcing us to work among multitudes of our fellow human beings. Thus, many Americans yearn for the outdoors, to be away from the crowds of humanity. The mountains, oceans, lakes, rivers, and sky all beckon.

Outdoor activities such as hiking, rock climbing, kayaking, scuba diving, canoeing, sailing, waterskiing, skydiving, snowboarding, and so forth are important life activities for many people. Attendance at national parks, recreational facilities, and local parks has skyrocketed. In the past decade the number of Americans participating in outdoor adventure activities has grown dramatically: Cross-country skiers have increased from just a few thousand in 1980 to more than several million now. The number of hikers has also greatly increased in this time, and national park usage in 2021 is reflected in the following robust statistics that demonstrate a rebound after COVID-19 closures: 297,115,406 recreation visits, 1,356,657,749 recreation visitor hours, and 2,745,455 overnight stays (recreation and non-recreation).[39] The number of mountaineers has been doubling about every five years. The trend is clear: the public mindset is moving toward outdoor physical activities as an alternative to traditional organized sports. Further, although statistics have shown that most people who utilize outdoor recreation spaces in national forests and parks are White, people from diverse backgrounds are making inroads into outdoor activities such as hiking and mountain biking.[40]

There is already an astonishing variety of adventure sports, including adventure racing (biking, running, climbing, hiking, and canoeing over courses of 80 miles or more), long-distance cycling (the Race across America is 2,983 miles), and extreme trail hiking—the Pacific Crest Trail is 2,655 miles long, the Continental Divide Trail is 2,600 miles long, and the Appalachian Trail is 2,168 miles long. The Primal Quest Adventure Race and others like it are five- to ten-day competitions of trekking, mountain biking, and whitewater rafting.

Then there are numerous types of adventurous bicycle riding activities, including various formats of road bicycle racing, gravel riding, trail and mountain biking, and triathlon. Bicycle racing on paved roads first became popular in the western European countries of France, Spain, Belgium, and Italy before it became popular in the United States. Some of Europe's earliest road bicycle races remain among the sport's biggest events. The Tour de France is probably the best known. The sport once spread throughout the United States, leading to dozens of "tour" road races being held annually. However, recent economic conditions have meant that professional racing has witnessed several road racing teams and major events being shut down as a result of sponsor withdrawal.[41] At the same time, "alternate" racing scenes with formats such as long-distance gravel racing and high-altitude mountain riding are becoming increasingly popular.[42]

In all of these outdoor activities, technology plays a vital role. According to outdoor studies scholars, "technology has been a game changer for adventure, in terms of facilitating access, enhancing skills and performances, and sharing information."[43] Cycling is a good example of technology that underpins adventure. Strava is widely used by cyclists to create body performance data and share route information, as well as for riders to challenge each other to be the

Gravel riding has become a fast-growing sport in the United States, with participants undertaking distance rides on unpaved roads often found in rural parts of the country. A 200-mile ride in Kansas known as Unbound Gravel is the most popular event (Photo: Courtesy of Linda Guerrette)

fastest. Interestingly, such data collection can also be used by urban planners to create better cycling routes. Electronic and wireless shifters, 3D printed bike components, and disc braking are technological upgrades already available to cyclists.[44] Emerging electronic bike technology also allows more opportunities for riders in terms of transport and allows older riders to keep up with younger ones.

Yet there are also questions about the key role that technology plays in adventure. Technology can give people a false sense of safety, as seen in recent catastrophes within high-altitude mountain climbing. Technology increases our environmental "footprint" as a result of greater access and travel, and it may also go against the core values of certain rugged adventure cultures.[45] Another critical idea pertains to how adventure activities can be relevant and inclusive to lower-income participants when technology and equipment costs become prohibitive. Indeed, commercial interest and profit-making in these adventure

activities is at an all-time high. Outdoor adventure, including its styles and values, is considered cool and will remain marketable. Corporations invested in adventure sports range from Red Bull to North Face; these corporations have turned massive profits in recent years. An outcome of the adventure running trend is the Ironman adventure competitions with corporate sponsors and prize money winners. On Ironmanlive.com at one point there was a sidebar titled "The Anatomy of an Ironman Product," followed by this statement: "The process of identifying, developing, manufacturing and selling an Ironman-Triathlon-branded product can be just as challenging as the long and obstacle-ridden path an athlete follows to become an Ironman. Just like every elite tri-athlete who crosses an Ironman finish line anywhere, these products can only bear the Ironman label if they can meet the Ironman standards. Simply put, Ironman-licensed products must deliver the benefits implied by the Ironman label."[46] This description makes clear that Ironman sports is not just an adventure activity, but also a significant branding identity and cultural marketing phenomenon.

Action/Lifestyle Sports

The demand for physical activities that emphasize co-operation and playfulness is increasing. The sporting goods industry has labeled them *action sports*, while others have deemed them *lifestyle sport* activities.[47] In-line skating, with 29 million skaters, is one of the largest contributors to the explosive growth in action sports in the United States. Other rapidly growing sports in this category are skateboarding, snowboarding, surfing and windsurfing, BMX, kayaking, and mountain biking. Skateboarding, for example, was considered the fastest growing sport in the United States soon after the turn of the millennium.[48] Once considered mainly a street-oriented activity for anti-establishment guys, skateboarding has over the past ten years become more inclusive for families as well as girls and women who wish to participate.[49] In terms of surfing, gender participation has expanded at all levels, from recreational endeavors to Olympic level. Then, it has also been found that numerous women have recently become leading participants in the "big wave" surfing scene.[50]

Importantly, the trend in action and lifestyle sport participation reaches across generations. Recent research highlights that adults over forty years of age are continuing or taking up sports such as surfing, windsurfing, skateboarding, and roller skating.[51] At the same time, some of these activities, such as skateboarding, are attracting more diverse participants than ever before.[52] For example, Brown Girls Surf, from the San Francisco Bay Area, attracts women of color to weekly surf events in Half Moon Bay.[53] Skateboarding has also become increasingly diversified, according to one major report commissioned by Tony Hawk's non-profit foundation. According to one researcher cited in *The New York Times*, "The reality in 2020 is the skateboarding community is really, really diverse, and not only are they diverse, for many skaters, that's a point of pride."[54]

Some view these forms of sport as a reaction not only against the technocorporate form of organization characteristic of American social institutions,

but also against the organized and corporate levels of sport described earlier in this chapter, where the outcome supersedes the process. This certainly may be why many participants of these action sports took them up and popularized them, yet these seemingly countercultural activities and lifestyles are increasingly being seized on by commercial interests as new markets for products and services. Unfortunately for those who seek physical activities that are not dominated by codified rules, professional event organizers, and corporate sponsorships or hyped by paid endorsers, it is highly likely that commercial involvement will continue to exist alongside attributes such as creative expression and carefree independence. For instance, the IOC made a decision to introduce surfing, skateboarding, and rock climbing at the 2020 Olympic Games, putting these formerly countercultural activities on the world's stage.[55] This decision was seemingly made to attract younger audiences, thus increasing participation and consumption.[56]

Indeed, many action and lifestyle sports that were once unorganized and antiestablishment have become more mainstream, commercial, and organized—with special training camps, elite coaches, and global competitions. This raises significant issues because typically the commercial sports industry seeks to organize sports activities on strict market principles—the pursuit of profits, rather than the satisfaction of personal and social needs. The creative play and pleasure elements of the activities are squeezed out as corporate profit motives increase. More than forty-five years ago social analyst Harry Braverman eloquently described this trend toward the commercialization of all sporting activities: "So enterprising is [capitalism] that even where the effort is made by one or another section of the population to find a way to nurture sports . . . through personal activity . . . these activities are rapidly incorporated into the market so far as is possible."[57] Another related concern pertains to the increased usage of corporate technology in lifestyle and action sports, with innovations such as GPS tracking, participant cameras, and drones being utilized, thus changing the nature of human and environmental relations originally found in these activities.[58]

Freestyle motocross is one form of dirt bike racing that is gaining tremendous popularity. Interestingly, the emerging popularity of such sports created a niche market for organized competitions such as the X Games and the Dew Tour. Yet, these activities are also being included in the most mainstream of sport competitions. The 2020 Tokyo Summer Olympics included skateboarding, surfing, and sports climbing for the first time. (Photo: Adam Duckworth/Alamy Stock Photo)

TRENDS IN SUSTAINABILITY: SOCIAL VALUES AND FUTURE SPORT

ORGANIZATIONAL TRENDS IN SPORT

In Chapter 3 we identified the dominant societal values in the United States. These mainstream values reflect beliefs in the importance of personal effort and accomplishment in defining one's status and worth, both economic and social, and one's orientation toward major social institutions. These values, like other aspects of American life, have been undergoing significant change as a result of the factors mentioned in the opening of this chapter: population trends, economic realities, and technological advancement. Diversity in our democratic context will lead to proliferating social and environmental values. In the

sporting future, numerous belief systems will be accompanied by various types of sporting lifestyles.

We will conclude this book by examining how changing social factors and values impact sport participation, with a particular focus on sustainability. Thus, we reflect on values that are necessary to ensure the viability and quality for both current and future sporting participants. These values are underpinned by a perspective that our social and natural worlds are interconnected. Indeed, as noted in the first chapter, a sustainability orientation is based on an assumption that we have a responsibility to others in society as well as to the natural world. We utilize theories reflecting a conflict/cultural perspective to understand how sport can move toward a more humane future amid social and environmental changes, particularly focusing on the values of democracy, inclusion, and equity.

Fundamental to democracy is the power that each person has to influence their own life and their communities. Voting is a prime example of this. With regard to formal politics, this translates to having a multiparty system where differing viewpoints are included and where debate is encouraged. In this sense, power does not mean that each person or political party gets to do what they want, but it does mean that different perspectives are heard and respected. Additionally, to develop democracies, it is essential that social and health resources are provided in an equitable manner. This would ensure that all people have the opportunity to grow and develop so they may be active members of their communities.[59]

During the past forty years the United States and much of the world have experienced tensions between the promise of democratic principles and the rise of neoliberal economics and authoritarian governments.[60] Neoliberal policies have challenged democratic practice especially in respect to ensuring that all people have an equitable chance to flourish. As noted in Chapter 5, there has been an increasing gap between the wealthy and the poor in the United States. This is underpinned by economic and social policies related to neo-liberalism that have created strong social class and racial inequalities.[61] In turn, many people have been protesting for more democratic policies. This trend is observed in social movements such as Occupy Wall Street in 2011 and Black Lives Matter throughout the past decade. This tension between economically and socially divided segments of society is also reflected in the sport domain. For example, owners of sport franchises generally seek the status quo in terms of maintaining their monopolistic economic practices, while conversely, some professional sports athletes have led efforts to unionize and to use their platform to address inequities and discrimination in sport. For example, some athletes have called for a change toward greater freedom and personal responsibility within the structure and functioning of sport, although they have been a minority; it is more often the case that the world of sports generates a fundamental acceptance of established norms and values. Yet, social movements led by a few high-profile athletes have gained appeal with people throughout the United States who have been disadvantaged by their ascribed statuses and are demanding to be considered full members of society. Overall, futurists expect that there will continue to be demands for more inclusion, more democracy, and greater participation in sport, as well as places of work and in government. All of these demands add up to a quest for more control over one's life and for the reduction of economic, political, and social inequalities that now restrict people from improving their quality of life.

At the same time, future generations will have to grapple with stewardship of the environment, given that many of our economic policies are intended to maximize profit at the expense of natural preservation. The quest for environmental sustainability is related to new ideas about humanity, and specifically our need to interact with natural resources and ecosystems in more harmonious ways, for the sake of future health and well-being.

Sustainability necessitates a shift in consciousness, a reorientation in personal goals and priorities and in the ways of perceiving and ordering the world outside the individual. A move toward sustainability in sport will lead to many changes in economic and political organization and the emergence of new and diverse sports activities and leisure patterns. Growing numbers of people and organizations are now re-envisioning sport policies, values, and social practices in accordance with sustainability principles, as we will describe.

Sport for Development and Peace Programs

One consequence of sustained neoliberal policies is the continued need for nongovernmental organizations and not-for-profit organizations to help meet the needs of those who remain underserved as a result of this economic model. Indeed, there has been an upsurge of these organizations addressing the void of public service left by governmental divestment. Under these conditions, local, regional, and international Sport for Development and Peace (SDP) groups will continue to flourish. These programs often ground their work in holistic human development principles (e.g., supporting the "whole person" through educational, cultural, health, and sporting program components). As such, these programs are considered vital to support those in need, especially during instances of economic insecurity, global war and terrorism, population displacement, climate change, and public health emergencies such as the COVID-19 pandemic. The future of sport will therefore be buttressed by many organizations that intentionally work for equitable access and democratic engagement, such as the prominent Skateistan and Soccer without Borders projects.

The organizational size and reach of these SDP groups vary tremendously. For example, Soccer without Borders was established in 2006 and has programs across the United States and in several foreign countries. Overall, Soccer without Borders participants come from sixty-eight countries and speak fifty-four languages, with participants and their families originating from some of the world's most challenging areas, including the Central African Republic, Somalia, Afghanistan, Congo, Eritrea, Honduras, El Salvador, Burma, Burundi, Iraq, Syria, and many others. The goal of Soccer Without Borders is therefore to aid refugees and immigrants in their transition from "newcomers" to established members in new communities.[62]

Soccer without Borders, a nonprofit organization, provides educational and sports programming in several American cities for recent immigrant youths. (Photo: Photo courtesy of Balazs Gardi)

Other programs, such as Harlem Lacrosse (New York) and Project Goal (Rhode Island), are more local in scope as they serve in-need members of American communities.[63]

Most of these SDP groups conduct their work in conjunction with both public and private entities and use partnership building to leverage their missions. These groups were given more prominence in the early 2000s when the United Nations established an office on Sport for Development and Peace. This office is now being run by the International Olympic Committee.[64] The United Nations views these programs as vital to support their 2030 Agenda for Sustainable Development, recognizing sport as an important element of sustainable development and peace-building efforts, through their focus on inclusion, tolerance, and respect.[65]

Sport for Development and Peace organizations are also considered crucial to achieve the United Nations' Millennium Development Goals, which were established at the 2000 UN Millennium Summit. The eight goals aim to eradicate or reduce poverty, hunger, child mortality, and disease and to promote education, maternal health, gender equality, environmental sustainability, and global partnerships.[66] However, the precise impacts of SDP projects will need to be continually evaluated in relation to program objectives, and program leaders need to remain vigilant so that they do not impose top-down values while ignoring participant voices.[67]

Youth and High School Sports

As noted in previous chapters, sport remains a popular pastime for many youths and the vast majority of U.S. youth sport is delivered through schools. The increasing reluctance of taxpayers to support education and the hesitancy of many state legislatures to raise taxes have forced many school systems to consider reducing extracurricular activities, including sports programs. If financial difficulties continue to plague high schools, modifications in the funding of the programs will probably occur. Indeed, one continuing trend is the *pay-for-play* or *participant fee* plans that require high school athletes to assume some of the costs of equipment and other expenses associated with their participation. This practice is likely to increase in scope given economic uncertainties that will continue to impact our education system. If so, this trend will reduce opportunities for high school youths from lower-income families to participate in sports.

As noted throughout this text, the economic inequities in the United States impact the types and amounts of sport opportunities available for different groups of people. Research by the Physical Activity Council in the United States has revealed that physical activity levels are directly correlated with family income. Those with the highest incomes are most active. The reverse is also true: those with the least amount of income are the least active.[68]

Looking at this issue through the lens of sustainability, it will be important to contemplate how youth and school sport organizations can work to increase participant access to quality programs. Crucially, there is a clear need to re-envision funding for youth and high school sports so that families and participants themselves are not required to pay. In this regard, one emerging trend is to use some of the proceeds from the newly legalized sports betting industry to fund community sports and recreation programs. This happened in New York, where a small percentage of gambling proceeds will go to youth sports programs.[69] Moreover, innovative community leadership that is committed to designing quality programs who serve society's diverse populations will be vital. In a recent book, B. David Ridpath proposed a variety of solutions for ensuring that more people can access sport and physical activity. At the youth level, Ridpath suggests moving away from relying on schools to provide sport opportunities and, instead, suggests more coordination and centralization among the providers of youth sport (schools, recreation programs, non-profit projects) so that resources are distributed and used more equitably and effectively for the population at large.[70]

Intercollegiate Sports

As we have noted at several places in this volume, professional sport is not limited to privately owned sport franchises. Big-time collegiate sports constitute a professional industry in every sense of the word.

They are every bit as dependent on economic considerations as other professional sports, and one can confidently predict that as television goes, with respect to buying rights to broadcast intercollegiate sports events, so will go the big-time collegiate programs.

Even with the bonanza of television money, intercollegiate athletic programs have had increasing financial problems. The major problem is money—or the lack of it. Growth in attendance has slowed as competition, from both professional sports and other sporting attractions, has increased. Meanwhile, increased costs have taken a brutal toll on the athletic budgets of many colleges. The epidemic of conference realignment, expanding playoff schedules in basketball and bowl games in football, and de-emphasizing or dropping so-called nonrevenue sports are all economic measures that have been adopted to add revenue or to reduce expenses in intercollegiate athletics.

All is still not well on America's university campuses. For example, many athletic departments at state-supported universities receive substantial support for their athletics programs from tax funds, and public opposition to this is growing. Legislatures are weighing the athletic appropriations against, for example, faculty salaries and state aid for disadvantaged students. Other educational considerations include more spending for community colleges and expansion of vocational education. Needs are also being considered in other fields, such as mental health, welfare, law enforcement, and the general administration of government.

What does the future hold for intercollegiate athletics? Finally, slowly, gradually, and reluctantly, major universities with big-time football and basketball programs are moving toward paying college athletes a salary for their hard work on behalf of the university. The charade that universities have advanced—that college sports are amateur athletics and therefore the athletes must not accept financial remuneration for playing—has become ludicrous. The NCAA has taken steps within the past few years to develop a system for direct payment to student-athletes at major universities. Even leaders in the NCAA have begun to acknowledge that athletes should be given some form of direct payment, but that does not mean they favor student-athletes becoming employees, and they oppose the unionization of student-athletes.

And as discussed in Chapter 10, new legislation has provided more revenue streams directly to college athletes, including their ability and right to profit from their name, likeness, and image (NIL). Other legislation has been proposed by members of the U.S. Congress to protect the rights of student-athletes. Senator Cory Booker, who was a football player and student at Stanford University, is championing one such bill. He stated, "The College Athletes Bill of Rights will set a new baseline standard to expand protections and opportunities for all college athletes by providing fair and equitable compensation, ensure comprehensive health and safety standards, and improve education outcomes for college athletes. College athletes deserve better, they deserve justice, and they deserve to share in what they help create."[71]

Meanwhile, sports club programs are growing on college campuses. These are student-oriented sports teams coached by older students or interested persons with an inherent passion for the sport (they typically receive no pay) and funded by the participants or by small sums from the institution's student activity funds. Some higher education administrators have even predicted that over the next twenty years most of the athletic teams on a college campus will be of the sports club type, with the university having only one or two sports of the high-visibility, commercial type.

The intramural sports program (called recreation sports on some campuses) has been the place where more student-athletes participate than anyplace else on a college campus. It is likely that this will continue as student enrollments increase and these students demand non-varsity sports opportunities with potential to satisfy their immediate and long-term needs. Consequently, campus leaders have had to devise new and different activities that capture the interest of today's generation of students. This includes creating equal sports opportunities that are accessible and meaningful for all students, including women and students with disabilities, and also provide greater use of facilities for open recreation.

Several colleges have experimented with the abolishment of all extrinsic rewards; no point systems or awards of any kind are employed. The importance of victory is de-emphasized by doing away with championships and limiting protests to on-the-spot, right-or-wrong, final decisions by activity supervisors. Any combination of undergraduate and graduate students and faculty are allowed to form teams. Indeed, one of the authors of this book participates in intramural sports alongside his students. Both women and men frequently participate together in these activities. Clearly, then, the social climate is favorable for continuing to create new forms of sports participation through non-varsity sport activities. The trend toward change and innovation to meet diverse student interests and backgrounds will likely endure.

Professional Teams and Leagues

As noted in Chapter 11, the United States allows professional sport leagues to act as monopolies, which provides unprecedented power for these leagues and their constituting teams. As long as the leagues and their teams are profitable, it would seem, the impetus for the current management to change their structures and policies will be marginal or, at best, nominal.

Yet, recent social events and movements have forced teams and leagues to change some of their practices. One primary example is the change of mascot imagery and names that either misrepresented Native Americans or were outright racist symbols. Although this trend has been practiced in educational settings for two decades, the professional sport world has been slower to change. In 2020, two professional teams changed their names and mascots. The NFL's Washington D.C. football team dropped the name Redskins and eventually became the Commanders. Additionally, the franchise will no longer allow fans to come to the games in costumes depicting Native Americans (headdress, eagle feathers, etc.). The Cleveland professional baseball team has also dropped their name, the Indians, and their former mascot, Chief Wahoo. The team is now called the Cleveland Guardians, which refers to an architectural feature of the city. Changes such as these signal a new era in terms of racial awareness, although they do not fundamentally represent power shifting. Indeed, we believe that the teams and leagues will accommodate these requests as long as it does not fundamentally change the power structure.

As described in Chapter 13, there has been growing pressure from athletes and fans for leagues to reconceptualize their missions and operating practices. In some cases, leagues and teams have enabled players and even fans to take leading roles in terms of creating policies. For example, MLS's Seattle Sounders held the first general manager vote in U.S. professional sports history on October 7, 2012. Season ticket holders voted on whether to retain or dismiss the team's general manager; this practice has continued to occur every four years. Throughout the team's history, season ticket members have voted on the name of the association (Alliance) and band name (Sound Wave).[72]

Athletes have also taken a lead in creating policies in their leagues. It is notable that leagues such as the WNBA are woman-led and have innovated the major sports scene in several ways. For example, WNBA players were instrumental in advocating for Black Lives Matter and LGBTQ inclusion. The athletes of the WNBA have been highly prominent advocates for racial justice in the sports world.[73]

Furthermore, some league organizations are radically changing the power structure of sport. One such experiment is the newly formed Athletes Unlimited league. It is organized so that athletes essentially serve in the general manager position: they are the ones to determine all policies. Currently, Athletes Unlimited has four sports (volleyball, softball, basketball, and lacrosse), all of which are women centered. It will be interesting to see whether this format will be successful.[74]

Aligned with the popularity and cultural relevance of sport, we believe individuals and groups will continue to foster innovation in how professional sport is organized and delivered. Some teams have missions and values that go beyond simply winning championships, because they are committed to community and environmental sustainability principles. One such example is the Oakland Roots Sports Club which plays in the U.S. second division of soccer. Teams such as the Oakland Roots Sports Club are explicitly designed to feature community building, social justice, and

environmental sustainability causes. The Roots' purpose is to use "the power of sport as a force for social good," especially in the context of the local Oakland community.[75] To this end, the club has installed the nation's first chief purpose officer in professional sports, Mike Geddes, to "ensure that the higher purpose of the organization is being met in the daily decision-making process of the business."[76] According to Geddes, "One of our principles is Oakland First, Always and everything that we do, we try to do it in service of making the city a better place . . . by thinking about what is it about a sports team which can support all these other areas that go towards making a safe, healthy, equitable city. So, supporting the arts, supporting culture, supporting community initiatives."[77] The Roots are therefore aligned with causes such as the Common Goal charity supported by soccer stars around the world, the Anti-Racist Project, which they helped create, and their own Justice Fund, a charitable fund that supports racial and gender causes. In addition to having a chief purpose officer, the Roots also employ a psychotherapist who serves as the team's athletes' mental health specialist. At the same time, the Roots are working toward becoming climate positive in their organizational practices, while simultaneously contributing to climate positivity initiatives in the Oakland community.

INCLUSION TRENDS IN SPORT
People with Disabilities

People with disabilities constitute nearly 20 percent of the U.S. population. Importantly, the conditions that are labeled a disability are broad, encompassing physical, psychological, and sensory impairments. Often people conceive of a disability as a condition that falls outside the statistical norm of human physical or mental functioning. This focus on biology is often called the *medical model* perspective, which directs attention to the rehabilitation of that person's biological capacity. In this way, the problem is individualized and the "cure" is medical. But using a sociological imagination, one can shift the focus solely from an individual's biology to an individual's context, where intervention happens through modifying social conditions. This is also the perspective of the World

Health Organization, which notes, "Disability arises from the interaction between people with a health condition and their environment. . . . These people (with disabilities) generally have poorer health, lower education achievements, fewer economic opportunities and higher rates of poverty. This is largely due to the barriers they face in their everyday lives, rather than their disability. Disability is not only a public health issue, but also a human rights and development issue." People with disabilities historically have been subject to systematic prejudice and injustice, and only in the past few decades have national laws and enlightened public attitudes reversed the practices that treated people with disabilities as outcasts.

The increased popularity of disability sport as showcased in the Paralympics is a promising trend. U.S. Paralympic athletes received equal pay compared to their able-bodied Olympians for the first time in 2021. Athletes with disabilities now have more access and opportunities not only to participate in sport, but also to become elite athletes competing for gold medals and large sums of money. The future for disabled athletes looks encouraging because widespread support is now in place for opportunities to increase. One of the most influential organizations in the United States is Move United. This group was formed by the recent merger of Disabled Sports USA and Adaptive Sports USA. The new organization focuses on youth and adults with disabilities, providing a wide variety of opportunities. It is also aligned with the U.S. Olympic and Paralympic Committee.

A world-renowned program for people with special needs is the Special Olympics, an international program of year-round sports training and athletic competition for developmentally disabled children and adults. The Special Olympics began in 1968 when Eunice Kennedy Shriver organized the First International Special Olympics Games at Soldier Field in Chicago. Since then, it has grown to include nearly 3.5 million athletes in 226 programs in 170 countries, providing year-round sports training and athletic competition for developmentally disabled children and adults. The mission is to provide a variety of Olympic-type sports for developmentally disabled individuals, thereby giving them opportunities to develop physical fitness, experience joy, and participate in a sharing of skills and friendship with their families and other Special Olympics athletes.

In the United States, there are Special Olympics chapters in all fifty states, the District of Columbia, Guam, the Virgin Islands, and American Samoa. About 25,000 communities in the United States have Special Olympics programs. There seems little doubt that these programs will continue to grow in the coming years and provide sporting opportunities to a broader spectrum of individuals with disabilities.[78]

We are optimistic about the increasing awareness and opportunities, but remain concerned because people with disabilities are overrepresented in lower socioeconomic classes and that has a major impact on accessibility, especially in neoliberal governments. So, as we applaud efforts to encourage elite athletes with disabilities, we believe that there is much work to do to create widespread opportunities for the majority of people with disabilities.

Older Adults

In an earlier section of this chapter, we noted that the over-sixty-five population will more than double between 2010 and 2050, when one in five Americans will be over sixty-five years old. The trend toward a greater proportion of the population being over fifty years of age has been under way for some time now, and older adults are remaining physically active. Statistics from the Physical Activity Council note that 60 percent of baby boomers (those born between 1946 and 1964) participated in fitness activities and 40 percent participated in outdoor activities in 2020.[79] Research on action/lifestyle sports indicates that older adults are taking up or continuing activities such as surfing, skateboarding, and mountain biking.[80]

The organizations that older adults choose to join for sports participation vary from local community recreation programs to the National Senior Games Association (NSGA). The NSGA is a nonprofit organization dedicated to motivating senior men and women to lead a healthy lifestyle through the senior games movement. The organization governs the Summer National Senior Games (Senior Olympics) and the Winter National Senior Games. About 250,000 senior athletes participate in these senior games competitions each year.

Tatyana McFadden is considered one of the world's best female wheelchair racers in history. She is a seven-time Paralympic champion and has won thirteen world championship titles in her category. (Photo: Matthew Stockman/Getty Images)

Participating athletes must be fifty years old or older and must qualify in an NSGA-sanctioned state senior game to compete. The Senior Olympics has grown to be one of the largest multisport athletic competitions in the world. Participation in the Summer National Senior Games has grown rapidly. In 2017, more than 12,000 athletes participated in this event. The Winter National Senior Games provide an opportunity for a new and different population of senior athletes to compete in a national sports event.[81]

Demographic trends that point to increasing life expectancy and a growing population of seniors who are healthy and active clearly indicate that sports of all kinds will grow in popularity and in participation among seniors. Indeed, sport planners claim that new sport organizations for seniors will proliferate in the coming years.

LGBTQ

The community of sexual and gender minorities, initialized as LGBTQ, comprises another group that has faced pervasive injustice. Historically, there has been little tolerance of diverse sexual orientations in the United States. Despite substantially improved attitudes over the past decade, gays, lesbians, bisexuals, and transgender persons still suffer various forms of social stigma and injustice. As we noted in Chapter 7, sport has been a bastion of homophobia; indeed, sport has been a cultural practice where homophobic attitudes have been socially constructed and reproduced.

As with other sectors of society, attitudes and values about human sexuality are gradually changing, and there is a greater acceptance of individuality in sexual orientation and gender expression. In sport as well, LGBTQs have been "coming out," acknowledging their sexual orientation. Although there is still a deep division in attitudes toward diversity in sexual orientation among Americans, the taboos that once prevailed in sport are diminishing.[82] LGBTQ athletes compete at all levels of sport, from novices to Olympic champions. And many of these athletes are now using their platform to address homophobia and transphobia, both within sport and in the larger society. In addition to competing with and against heterosexual athletes in sports at all age and proficiency levels, many LGBTQ individuals participate in privately sponsored and community-sponsored leagues and events.

The level of public acceptance in mainstream sports is on the rise. In the summer of 2021, Carl Nassib, a football player for the NFL's Las Vegas Raiders, came out as gay. He is the first openly gay NFL player to come out while still playing. On his Instagram he wrote, "I actually hope that, one day, videos like this [his coming out video] and the whole coming out process are just not necessary, but until then I'm going to do my best to cultivate a culture that's accepting and compassionate." His announcement was met with official support by the NFL and many other football players.[83]

This growing acceptance can also be illustrated through the number of openly LGBTQ athletes in the Summer 2021 Olympic Games in Tokyo, where 183 athletes were publicly out. In fact, thirty countries were represented by at least one openly LGBTQ athlete across thirty-four sports. This contrasts to 23 Olympians who were publicly out in the 2012 games and the 56 athletes in the 2016 games. Canadian swimmer Markus Thormeyer stated, "Being able to compete with the best in the world as my most authentic self at the biggest international multi-sport games shows how far we've come on inclusion in sport. I'm hoping that by competing at these Games I can show the LGBTQ community that we do belong and we can achieve anything we put our minds to."[84] Additionally, the first openly trans woman athlete, Laurel Hubbard, competed in Olympic weightlifting for New Zealand. The head of the New Zealand Olympic Committee reinforced their commitment to inclusion when she said,

As well as being among the world's best for her event, Laurel has met the IWF eligibility criteria including those based on IOC Consensus Statement guidelines for transgender athletes. We acknowledge that gender identity in sport is a highly sensitive and complex issue requiring a balance between human rights and fairness on the field of play. . . . As the New Zealand Team, we have a strong culture of manaaki (a Maori word for support and compassion) and inclusion and respect for all. We are committed to supporting all eligible New Zealand athletes and ensuring their mental and physical wellbeing, along with their high-performance needs, while preparing for and competing at the Olympic Games are met.[85]

The kinds of value changes that are taking place in the United States, and much of the world, with the adoption of new values in sport point clearly to a future where stereotyped and marginalized groups—people with disabilities, seniors, gays, lesbians, and others—are going to have more opportunities to play an integral role in sports of the future.

ENVIRONMENTAL SUSTAINABILITY IN FUTURE SPORTS

The United Nations has recently noted that global warming is placing our planet and its future generations at risk. In this context, sport is considered a key element that can be used to combat global warming, leading to enhancements in public health, social justice, and natural resource preservation as well as fostering other socio-economic contributions. Under this vision, participants in globalized sport can unite and provide climate leadership by promoting meaningful and transformative climate action. The United Nations recently created the Sports for Climate Action Initiative, whereby sports participants will pursue climate action in a consistent and mutually supportive fashion by learning from each other, disseminating best practices and lessons learned, developing new tools, and collaborating on areas of mutual interest.[86]

In one sense, it is argued that we must consider the environmental impact *of* sport. Sport stakeholders in the future must contemplate and plan for the environmental impacts of participation, in terms of reducing the impact of sporting members, events, and infrastructure on the natural environment.[87] In this vein, university athletic departments as well as professional sport teams are already seeking solutions to reduce their environmental impacts, and we believe that this trend will continue to accelerate. One sports trade organization, the Green Sports Alliance, is working to bring stakeholders from around the world (including teams, leagues, conferences, venues, corporate partners, governmental agencies, athletes, and fans) to promote environmentally sustainable practices. Key aspects of environmental sustainability that have been identified by the Green Sports Alliance include:

- Reducing the ecological impacts associated with food served at sports venues and events by promoting healthier, more sustainable food programs and foodservice practices that promote waste reduction and energy and water efficiency;
- Promoting purchasing policies that make use of ecologically preferable products, including paper, cleaning products, and serviceware;
- Encouraging a shift away from fossil fuel–dependent transportation by incorporating smarter travel strategies at sports venues and events, including public transit, bike racks, and pedestrian walkways;
- Advancing sustainable, high-performance design and operations of sports venues that promote environmental and human health for staff, athletes, and fans;
- Promoting zero-waste strategies through source reduction, recycling, composting, and food recovery; and
- Advancing water security by encouraging practices that reduce water pollution and promote water conservation.[88]

Some examples of these key environmental sustainability practices are consequently found in major professional team operations. For instance, the Indiana Pacers of the NBA will keep more than 76,000 pounds of plastic and steel out of Indiana landfills during seating renovation. Over 3,000 old seats will be converted into raw materials such as plastic and steel for manufacturing.[89] Moreover, the construction of entire arenas will continue to dovetail with environmental sustainability principles. In the United Kingdom, the fourth-tier Forest Green Rovers play in a home stadium that is powered by 100 percent green energy, and fully vegan food is served at matchday concession stands. Their new stadium, Eco Park, will aim to be carbon neutral and will be made entirely of wood, and it is already being labeled the greenest stadium ever built for soccer.[90]

A larger venue, the Climate Pledge Arena, is home to a new NHL franchise, the Seattle Kraken. This arena intends to be 100 percent powered by renewable electricity and will feature zero-waste compostable containers and reclaimed rainwater storage tanks. These tanks will be utilized for the Kraken's ice system. Most food in this venue will be locally sourced from regional farmers and producers. Game tickets will also serve as free public transit passes on the Seattle Monorail. The operators of the arena worked with Amazon.com, Inc., who own the naming rights, to create the venue's name. "Working with Amazon and naming it Climate Pledge Arena, instead of AWS or Amazon, shows that we mean business when we talk about sustainability," said Don Graham, senior vice president for event services and assistant general manager of the arena.[91]

It remains to be seen how the future involvement of multinational corporations such as Amazon.com, known for its mass and rapid shipping of products, aligns with environmental practices more broadly and extensively. Along these lines, while multinational sport and adventure corporations such as Adidas, Nike, and North Face will continue to market and sell products that are seemingly environmentally or "eco"-friendly, further scrutiny is required to understand how these corporations negatively impact the natural world through materials sourcing/extraction, manufacturing, transport, and product waste.

Several U.S. collegiate athletic departments have committed to climate change–limiting practices, which includes reducing facility usage and event travel, hosting zero-waste competitive events, and using solar energy in major facilities and other energy conservation measures such as LED lighting.[92] Sport participants at a more grass-roots level have taken action to promote environmental sustainability by creating charity organizations. For example, in the United Kingdom, Surfers against Sewage started in 1990 with a local community of surfers who were tired of surfing on their coast amid sewage[93]: "We began as a response by the surfing community to the dreadful state of our beaches. Those hardy souls who ventured into the water back then often found themselves swimming in raw sewage. There's tales of sanitary towels on heads and human poo sandwiched between bodies and boards. Completely unacceptable."

This group of surfers went on to establish a nationwide conservation and campaigning charity dedicated to taking action to protect British oceans, beaches, and wildlife. Through their Plastic Free Communities program, they work with over 50,000 volunteers each year to remove millions of pieces of plastic from hundreds of beaches.[94]

Another identified area of environmental sustainability pertains to the impact of environmental change *on* sport.[95] Under this view, cultural observers as well as sport leaders are re-envisioning sporting practices to better account for the impacts of climate change. The British Broadcasting Corporation has, for instance, recently dedicated a series of feature stories that imagine a new future for sport within the context of our changing environmental circumstances. For example, golf courses may have to adapt to the frequency of extreme hot and cold weather, and there may be a need to grow food on fertile land instead of using these prime land tracts for golf. Water shortages and conservation are already in place and will undoubtedly occur in the future, which means that golf will have to innovate to be less water intensive.[96] Winter sports will also have to take into account changing climatic conditions, with extreme snowfalls and, by contrast, lack of snow in competition locations becoming an increasingly frequent concern when hosting such events.[97] Major events typically held during summer months will also have to modify their formats and rules. For example, the soccer World Cup is usually held in the summer and this event may have to incorporate shorter time periods, increased rest breaks, larger squads, and more substitutions to account for increasing temperatures and heat waves.[98]

SUMMARY

This is an era of rapid change in the United States, and sport, like other societal institutions, is constantly evolving in both form and content. In this book, we have identified a number of salient social changes and speculated on how specific current and future trends may affect sport. A focus of this final chapter has been to outline how certain social actors and practices may challenge traditional norms and values in order to constitute a more sustainable version of sport. Indeed, we can observe that many broader societal structures and values have been called into question over the past decade, and since sport is a social practice, its traditions have also been challenged.

Value orientations have shifted in our society over the past decade. It is apparent that traditional sporting priorities and practices are being contested by an emerging set of standards emphasizing equality and pluralism within sport; these standards are premised on a renewed notion that democratic processes are essential to sport as well as other sectors of life. Athletes are demanding changes in sports at all levels; they are especially pressing for greater participation in the decisions that affect their athletic lives and for a greater responsiveness on the part of owners, coaches, and athletic administrators. Participants in sport have also pressed for more autonomy, for the freedom to be what they want to be and to choose how they will live. In previous eras, athletes tended to confront authorities infrequently; now the world of sport is indelibly marked by increased protest as athletes question and confront authoritarian leadership and institutions. This attitude is demonstrated by strikes in professional baseball, hockey, and football and the efforts to unionize and gain increased compensation by collegiate athletes. Perhaps the most visible example of sports activism over the past few years is that of Colin Kaepernick jarring America's consciousness by first sitting and then taking a knee during the national anthem. By his bold actions in fighting racism, he was using sports to lead the way, at great personal and professional cost. Kaepernick's activism has also inspired numerous other athletes, both in the U.S. and abroad, to protest and raise awareness about various social concerns.

Moreover, there has been acknowledgment that sport must take into account the deterioration of our natural world resulting from the neoliberal economic worldview that prioritizes profit making over environmental preservation. Crucially, several university athletics programs, professional teams, and nonprofit organizations are dedicating themselves to saving our natural world by raising awareness around ecological issues and concomitantly installing new missions and practices.

Sports at all levels, including youth/school, collegiate, and professional/elite, will be impacted by demographic shifts in the American population. Trends in population suggest that the rapid expansion of competitive sports is continuing in both larger and smaller markets across the United States. As the average age of the population increases, men and women will continue to stay active longer, even in competitive sport. Meanwhile, the proportion of ethnic and racial minorities in the population is increasing rapidly; the cultural traditions associated with these ethnic and racial minority groups will significantly influence the nature of sport involvement. Women, ethnic and racial minorities, and other oppressed and stereotyped groups will continue to strive for greater opportunities in all levels of sport.

Industrialization and technology reduced the average workweek until two decades ago, alongside a turn toward a more information-based economy. Yet other conditions have arisen since then to increase work time and nullify the leisure time of adults. Available leisure time in the future may be used to participate in sports involving both physical and digital interaction. We can already see that technological developments are leading to new, diversified modalities of sport participation. However, the rapid incorporation of new technologies in sports will continue to be questioned by those who wonder whether the human essence of sport is being lost. The spatial and temporal aspects of many popular "on-ground" sporting activities may soon change as a result of virtual reality and augmented reality technological advancements.

In closing, we hope the discussions throughout this book will stimulate critical thinking among the current generation about the place and meaning of sport under a vision of ecological and social sustainability. A sustainable sporting future is not a given. The values, practices, and outcomes of future sport will be shaped by diverse stakeholders and institutions that will be integrally linked in a global community. Quite simply, this means that the potential of sport to become a sustainable human endeavor remains in all of our hands.

Learn more with this chapter's digital tools, including web resources, video links, and chapter self-assessment quizzes at www.oup.com/he/sage-eitzen-beal-atencio-12e.

NOTES

1. *The Future of Sports* (Future Of, 2016), http://futureof.org/wp-content/uploads/The-Future-of-Sports-2016-Report.pdf.

2. Erik Brady, "What Could the World of Sports Look Like in 25 Years?" *USA Today*, January 26, 2016, https://www.usatoday.com/story/sports/2016/01/26/future-of-sports-athlete-stadium-broadcasting-e-sports-fans/79325114/; Jan Kees Mons, "10 Stunning Predictions About the Future of Sports in the Coming Decade," *Sport Tomorrow: Innovation and Future of Sports*, January 7, 2020, https://sporttomorrow.com/10-striking-predictions-about-future-of-sports/; Leo Sepkowitz, "The Future of Sports," *Bleacher Report*, July 2, 2020, https://bleacherreport.com/articles/2898327-the-future-of-sports; *The Future of Sports* (Future Of, 2015), http://www.gannett-cdn.com/usatoday/editorial/sports/The-Future-of-Sports-2015-Report.pdf.

3. Jon Solomon, "How COVID-19 in 2020 Could Impact the Future of Sports," The Aspen Institute, December 22, 2020, https://www.aspeninstitute.org/blog-posts/how-covid-19-in-2020-could-impact-the-future-of-sports/.

4. Brian Wilson and Brad Millington, eds., *Sport and the Environment: Politics and Preferred Futures* (Bingley, UK: Emerald, 2020).

5. "Our Mission," Centre for Sport and Sustainability, accessed August 20, 2021, https://css.ubc.ca/.

6. Katherine Schaeffer, "6 Facts About Economic Inequality in the U.S.," Pew Research Center, February 7, 2020, https://www.pewresearch.org/fact-tank/2020/02/07/6-facts-about-economic-inequality-in-the-u-s/.

7. Gary Marx, *Twenty-One Trends for the 21st Century: Out of the Trenches and Into the Future* (Bethesda, MD: Education Week Press, 2014).

8. Chuck Collins, "Updates: Billionaire Wealth, U.S. Job Losses and Pandemic Profiteers," Inequality, July 14, 2021, https://inequality.org/great-divide/updates-billionaire-pandemic/.

9. Robert Putnam, *Bowling Alone: The Collapse and Revival of American Community* (Simon & Schuster, 2001).

10. Lawrence Mishel, Josh Bivens, Elise Gould, and Heidi Shierholz, *The State of Working America*, 12th ed. (Ithaca, NY: ILR Press, 2012); see also Barbara Ehrenreich, *Nickel and Dimed: On (Not) Getting by in America* (New York: Holt Paperback, 2011).

11. Centers for Disease Control and Prevention, *CDC: Half of Workplaces Offer Health/Wellness Programs*, April 22, 2019, https://www.cdc.gov/media/releases/2019/p0422-workplaces-offer-wellness.html.

12. Joanne Kay and Suzanne Laberge, "The 'New' Corporate Habitus in Adventure Racing," *International Review for the Sociology of Sport* 37, no. 1 (March 2002): 17–36.

13. "Sideline of the Future," Technology, NFL, accessed August 20, 2021, https://operations.nfl.com/gameday/technology/sideline-of-the-future/.

14. Heather Marsten, "What Is TrackMan Data?" Trackman, accessed August 20, 2021, https://trackman.zendesk.com/hc/en-us/articles/115002776787-What-is-TrackMan-Data#:~:text=TrackMan%20Baseball%20is%20a%203D,have%20traditionally%20been%20qualitatively%20assessed.

15. Pierrick Desfontaine, "Carte Blanche to Tony Chapron," *Staps* 2021, no. 0 (pre-publication) (2021): 135–139.

16. Daniel Taylor, "World Cup 2014: England Got Everything Right—Except the Football," *The Guardian*, June 20, 2014, https://www.theguardian.com/football/blog/2014/jun/20/england-brazil-entourage-world-cup-2014.

17. Physical Activity Council, *2021 Physical Activity Council's Overview Report on U.S. Participation*, http://www.physicalactivitycouncil.com/.

18. U.S. Census Bureau, "2020 U.S. Population More Racially and Ethnically Diverse Than Measured in 2010," 2020, https://www.census.gov/library/visualizations/interactive/racial-and-ethnic-diversity-in-the-united-states-2010-and-2020-census.html.

19. Kaelyn Newman, "Survey: Amid the COVID-19 Pandemic, Urbanites Are Eyeing the Suburbs," *U.S. News*, May 6, 2020, https://www.usnews.com/news/cities/articles/2020-05-06/a-recent-survey-suggests-the-pandemic-has-urbanites-eyeing-the-suburbs.

20. Elliot Davis Jr., "Americans Moved South in 2021, Often Influenced by the Pandemic," *U.S. News*, January 3, 2022, https://www.usnews.com/news/best-states/articles/2022-01-03/americans-moved-south-in-2021-a-study-finds.

21. "A World-class Venue in the Heart of a Proven Sports Community," Spokane Sports, accessed August 21, 2021, https://www.spokanesports.org/podium.

22. Ian Smay, "New Spokane Sportsplex Will Host 2022 U.S. Indoor Track and Field Master's," KREM, December 12, 2019, https://www.krem.com/article/sports/sportsplex-groundbreaking/293-c2b8d6f1-8da1-4e86-a5fd-199d1f60a07c.

23. Matt Traub, "New Sports Venues to Watch in 2021," *SportsTravel*, February 18, 2021, https://www.sportstravelmagazine.com/new-sports-venues-to-watch-in-2021/.

24. Stefan Kzsenne, *The Economic Theory of Professional Team Sports: An Analytical Treatment*, 2nd ed. (Northampton, MA: Edward Elgar, 2015); Frank P. Jozsa Jr., *Football Fortunes: The Business, Organization and Strategy of the NFL* (Jefferson, NC: McFarland, 2010).

25. James Billington, "Modular Sports Complex Design Concept Wins International Award," *Stadia Magazine*, February 26, 2020, https://www.stadia-magazine.com/news/architecture-design/modular-sports-complex-design-concept-wins-international-award.html.

26. Ekaterina Glebova and Pierrick Desfontaine, "Sport et Technologies Numériques: Vers de Nouvelles Expériences Spectateur," in *Management du Sports 3.0*, ed. M. Desbordes and C. Hautbois (Economica, 2020), 245–270.

27. Andy Miah, *Sport 2.0: Transforming Sports for a Digital World* (Cambridge: MIT Press, 2017).

28. Mike Snider, "Two-thirds of Americans, 227 Million, Play Video Games," *USA Today*, July 13, 2021, https://www.usatoday.com/story/tech/gaming/2021/07/13/video-games-2021-covid-19-pandemic/7938713002/

29. T. L Taylor, *Raising the Stakes: E-Sports and the Professionalization of Computer Gaming* (Cambridge, MA: MIT Press, 2012), 180; see also Manny Anekal, "2017 Q2 Collegiate ESports Report: 40 Schools Giving $4M+ in Scholarships," *The Next Level: The Business of ESports*, May 31, 2017, http://tnl.media/esportsabout; Roland Li, *Good Luck Have Fun: The Rise of eSports*, reprint ed. (New York: Skyhorse, 2017); Martin Rogers, "Gamers Cashing in on Rise of eSports," *USA Today*, June 22, 2017, 1C, 6C.

30. Brian Seto McGrath, "High School Gamers are Scoring College Scholarships. But Can Esports Make Varsity?," NBC News, September, 20, 2019, https://www.nps.gov/aboutus/visitation-numbers.htm

31. Jacob Wolf, "Kroenke Sports & Entertainment Expands Esports Front Office," ESPN, October 17, 2019, https://www.espn.com/esports/story/_/id/27867097/kroenke-sports-entertainment-expands-esports-front-office.

32. Financialnewsmedia.com News Commentary, "Why Celebrities & Athletes Are Investing in Global eSports Market," *PR Newswire*, May 18, 2021, https://www.prnewswire.com/news-releases/why-celebrities--athletes-are-investing-in-global-esports-market-301293140.html.

33. Matthew Atencio and Becky Beal, "Beautiful Losers: The Symbolic Exhibition and Legitimization of Outsider Masculinity," *Sport in Society* 14, no. 1 (2011): 1–16.

34. Rohan Nadkarni, "Daily Cover: The Stream Team," SI, June 10, 2021, https://www.si.com/tech-media/2021/06/10/daily-cover-faze-clan-kyler-murray-bronny-james.

35. "Gaming for All: A Study of Toxicity and Plans for Inclusivity," *Evil Geniuses*, accessed August 21, 2021, https://assets.evilgeniuses.gg/dei/EG_YouGov_GamingForAll.pdf.

36. Jack Flanagan, "The Psychology of Video Game Addiction: What Turns a Hobby into a Sickness?" *The Week*, February 6, 2014, http://theweek.com/article/index/255964/the-psychology-of-video-game-addiction/.

37. "Number of Digital Live Sport Viewers in the United States from 2021 to 2025," Statista, Inc., https://www.statista.com/statistics/1127341/live-sport-viewership/. Accessed July 4, 2022.

38. "The Year in Sports Media Report: 2016," Nielsen, February 15, 2017, http://www.nielsen.com/us/en/insights/reports/2017/the-year-in-sports-media-report-2016.html.

39. "Visitation Numbers," National Park Service, https://www.nps.gov/aboutus/visitation-numbers.htm Accessed July 10, 2022.

40. Nicholas Collins as told to Taylor Dutch, "How Nicholas Collins Is Making Trail Running Diverse and Inclusive," *Runners World*, July 2, 2020, https://www.runnersworld.com/runners-stories/a32982283/nicholas-collins-trail-running-diversity/; Naomi Humphrey, "Breaking Down the Lack of Diversity in Outdoor Spaces," National Health Foundation, July 20, 2020, https://nationalhealthfoundation.org/breaking-down-lack-diversity-outdoor-spaces/; Brian Park, "Race & Accessibility in the Mountain Bike Community," Pinkbike, June 7, 2020, https://www.pinkbike.com/news/race-and-accessibility-in-the-mountain-bike-community.html.

41. Neal Rogers, "US Road Racing Is in a Downward Spiral—What Comes Next?" Cyclingtips, September 28, 2018, https://cyclingtips.com/2018/09/us-road-racing-is-in-a-downward-spiral-what-comes-next/.

42. "Mountains, Gravel, Long Distance: No Borders," Education First Pro Cycling, accessed August 21, 2021, https://www.efprocycling.com/alternativeracing/.

43. Simon Beames, C. J. Mackie, and Matthew Atencio, eds., *Adventure and Society* (London: Palgrave Macmillan, 2019).

44. James Bracey, "Disc Brakes: Everything You Need To Know," Cyclingweekly, July 28, 2016, https://www.cyclingweekly.com/news/product-news/everything-you-need-to-know-about-disc-brakes-202130.

45. Beames, Mackie, and Atencio, *Adventure and Society*, 2019.

46. Ironman Live, Sponsors and Licensees, http://www.ironman.com/#axzz3RV42xdpL Accessed August 1, 2022.

47. Belinda Wheaton, *Understanding Lifestyle Sports: Consumption, Identity, and Difference* (London: Routledge, 2004).

48. "Action Sports Facts and Figures," Active Marketing Group, February 6, 2018, https://vdocument.in/the-action-sports-market-active-network-2009actionsportspdfconnecting-with.html.

49. Matthew Atencio, Becky Beal, E. Missy Wright, and ZaNean McClain, *Moving Boarders: Skateboarding and the Changing Landscape of Urban Youth Sports* (Fayetteville: University of Arkansas Press, 2018).

50. Anne Schmitt and Anaïs Bohuon, "When Women Surf the World's Biggest Waves: Breaking Gender Barriers," *Sport in Society* (2021), https://doi.org/10.1080/17430437.2021.1897108.

51. Tyler Dupont and Becky Beal, *Lifestyle Sports and Identities: Subcultural Careers through the Life Course* (London: Routledge, 2021).

52. Atencio et al., *Moving Boarders*.

53. For more information, see Brown Girls Surf website at https://www.browngirlsurf.com/.

54. Jill Cowan, "How Skateboarding Can Help Fight Racism," *NY Times*, June 18, 2020, https://www.nytimes.com/2020/06/18/us/usc-skateboarding-study.html.

55. Ben McGrath, "Big Air: Are the X Games Aging Out? *The New Yorker*, July 21, 2014, https://search-proquest-com.unco.idm.oclc.org/docview/1552471741/fulltext/426B72A400164A76PQ/7?accountid=12832.

56. Belinda Wheaton and Holly Thorpe, *Action Sports and the Olympic Games: Past, Present, Future* (London: Routledge, 2022).

57. Harry Braverman, *Labor and Monopoly Capital* (New York: Monthly Review Press, 1974), 279.

58. Holly Thorpe, "Action Sports, Social Media, and New Technologies: Towards a Research Agenda," *Communication & Sport* 5, no. 5 (2017): 554–578.

59. Peter Donnelly and Jay Coakley, *The Role of Recreation in Promoting Social Inclusion* (Toronto: Laidlaw Foundation, 2002).

60. Berch Berberoglu, ed., *The Global Rise of Authoritarianism in the 21st Century: Crisis of Neoliberal Globalization and the Nationalist Response* (London: Routledge, 2020); see also Anne Applebaum, *Twilight of Democracy: The Seductive Lure of Authoritarianism* (New York: Doubleday, 2020).

61. For example, see Chuck Collins, "Updates: Billionaire Wealth, U.S. Job Losses and Pandemic Profiteers," Inequality, July 14, 2021, https://inequality.org/great-divide/updates-billionaire-pandemic/.

62. For more information, see https://www.soccer-withoutborders.org/.

63. For more information, see https://www.harlemlacrosse.org/ and also https://www.projectgoal.org/about-us.

64. "Sport for Development and Peace," United Nations Archives, https://archives.un.org/content/sport-development-and-peace. Accessed July 1, 2022.

65. "Recovering Better: Sport for Development and Peace," United Nations, COVID-19 Response, https://www.un.org/development/desa/dspd/wp-content/uploads/sites/22/2020/12/Final-SDP-recovering-better.pdf.

66. "Contribution of Sport to the Millennium Development Goals," United Nations, https://www.un.org/sport/sites/www.un.org.sport/files/ckfiles/files/Sport%20and%20the%20MDGs_FACTSHEET_February%202010.pdf; see also "What Is Sport for Development and Peace?," Right to Play, https://www.sportanddev.org/sites/default/files/downloads/what_is_sport_for_development_and_peace.pdf.

67. See Lindsay Blom, Lawrence Judge, Meredith Whitley, Lawrence Gerstein, Ashleigh Huffman, and Sara Hillyer, "Sport for Development and Peace: Experiences Conducting U.S. and International Programs," *Journal of Sport Psychology in Action* 6, no. 1 (2015): 1–16; also see Lyndsay Hayhurst, "The Power to Shape Policy: Charting Sport for

Development and Peace Policy Discourse," *International Journal of Sport Policy* 1, no. 2 (2009): 203–227.

68. Physical Activity Council, *2021 Physical Activity Council's Overview of Report on U.S. Participation* (Jupiter, FL: Sports Marketing Surveys, 2021), https://eb6d91a4-d249-47b8-a5cb-933f7971db54.filesusr.com/ugd/286de6_610088e5e73d497185ac181a240833a9.pdf.

69. Tom Farrey, "How to Bet on the Future of Youth Sports," *Aspen Institute*, June 28, 2021, https://www.aspeninstitute.org/blog-posts/how-to-bet-on-the-future-of-youth-sports/.

70. B. David Ridpath, *Alternative Models of Sports Development in America: Solutions to a Crisis in Education and Public Health* (Athens, OH: Ohio University Press, 2018).

71. "Senators Booker and Blumenthal Introduce College Athletes Bill of Rights," Cory Booker, December 17, 2020, https://www.booker.senate.gov/news/press/senators-booker-and-blumenthal-introduce-college-athletes-bill-of-rights.

72. "Sounders FC First Fan Vote for General Manager," *Sounders Football Club*, September 25, 2012, https://www.soundersfc.com/news/sounders-fc-first-fan-vote-general-manager.

73. For example, see "Future of Sports: Women Reimagining Pro Sports," Aspen Institute, April 16, 2021, https://www.aspeninstitute.org/videos/future-of-sports-women-reimagining-pro-sports/.

74. For more information, see https://auprosports.com/.

75. See Oakland Roots Soccer club website, https://www.oaklandrootssc.com/.

76. Nicholas Murray, "Geddes Charts Course for Purpose-Driven Roots," *USL*, November 19, 2020, https://www.uslchampionship.com/news_article/show/1133664.

77. Nicholas Murray, "With Purpose and Soul, Oakland Roots Is Representing," *USL*, September 16, 2020, https://www.uslchampionship.com/news_article/show/1123011.

78. For more information about the Special Olympics in the United States, see http://www.special-olympics.org/.

79. Physical Activity Council, *2021 Physical Activity Council's Overview Report.*

80. Dupont and Beal, *Lifestyle Sports and Identities.*

81. For more information about the National Senior Games Association, see http://www.nsga.com/.

82. In fact, a majority of Americans (across political differences) oppose antitransgender bills. See "New Poll Shows Americans Overwhelmingly Oppose Anti-transgender Laws," *NPR*, April 16, 2021, https://www.pbs.org/newshour/politics/new-poll-shows-americans-overwhelmingly-oppose-anti-transgender-laws.

83. See Tom Lutz, "'Proud of You': NFL Players Welcome Carl Nassib's Decision to Come Out," *The Guardian*, June 22, 2021, https://www.theguardian.com/sport/2021/jun/22/carl-nassib-nfl-comes-out-as-gay-players-reaction-jj-watt-julian-edelman.

84. As cited in Outsports, "At Least 183 Out LGBTQ Athletes Were at the Tokyo Summer Olympics, More Than Triple the Number in Rio," August 10, 2021, https://www.outsports.com/olympics/2021/7/12/22565574/tokyo-summer-olympics-lgbtq-gay-athletes-list.

85. As cited in "Tokyo Olympics: Laurel Hubbard to Become First Transgender Athlete to Compete at Games," *RNZ (Radio New Zealand)*, June 21, 2021, https://www.rnz.co.nz/news/sport/445187/tokyo-olympics-laurel-hubbard-to-become-first-transgender-athlete-to-compete-at-games.

86. "Sports for Climate Action Framework: Version 2.0," United Nations, https://unfccc.int/sites/default/files/resource/Sports_for_Climate_Action_Declaration_and_Framework.pdf; see also "United Nations Sport for Climate Action" at https://unfccc.int/climate-action/sectoral-engagement/sports-for-climate-action.

87. Brain McCullough, Madeleine Orr, and Timothy Kellison, "Sport Ecology: Conceptualizing an Emerging Subdiscipline within Sport Management," *Journal of Sport Management* 34, no. 6 (2020): 509–520.

88. See the Green Sport Alliance website at https://greensportsalliance.org/programs/.

89. Bankers Life Fieldhouse, "Sustainability Fuels Pacers Sports and Entertainment, RecycleForce Partnership," Green Sports Alliance, https://

greensportsalliance.org/sustainability-fuels-pacers-sports-entertainment-recycleforce-partnership/. Accessed July 7, 2021.

90. Michael Long and Matthew Campbell, "The Sports Industry and Sustainability Part One: Rights Holders Playing Their Part," *SportsPro*, June 15, 2020, https://www.sportspromedia.com/from-the-magazine/forest-green-juventus-formula-e-ocean-race-climate-change-sustainability.

91. Matt Traub, "Climate Pledge Arena Combines Sports with Sustainability," *Sports Travel Magazine*, February 18, 2021, https://www.sportstravelmagazine.com/climate-pledge-arena-combines-sports-with-sustainability/.

92. "USC Athletics Commits to Support United Nations Sports for Climate Action Initiative," University of Southern California, May 4, 2021, https://usctrojans.com/news/2021/5/4/usc-trojans-athletics-united-nations-sports-for-climate-change-action-initiative-mike-bohn.aspx.

93. See Surfer against Sewage website at https://www.sas.org.uk/about-us/.

94. See their website at https://www.royal.uk/surfers-against-sewage.

95. McCullough et al., "Sport Ecology."

96. "Sport 2050: How Climate Change Could Leave Golf with a Less Than Green Future," BBC, https://www.bbc.com/sport/56972370. Accessed July 19, 2021.

97. "Sport 2050: Snowless Snow Sport? How Climate Change Could Impact Winter Sports," BBC, https://www.bbc.com/sport/56972369. Accessed August 6, 2021.

98. "Sport 2050: 60-Minute Matches and Rolling Subs—a World Cup Like No Other?," BBC, https://www.bbc.com/sport/56972365. Accessed July 12, 2021.

INDEX

Boxes, figures, and tables are indicated by b, f, and t following the page number.